DICTIONARY OF
HOTELS, TOURISM AND
CATERING MANAGEMENT

Titles in the series

English Business Dictionary   ISBN 0-948549-00-9
American Business Dictionary   ISBN 0-948549-11-4
Dictionary of Accounting   ISBN 0-948549-27-0
Dictionary of Agriculture   ISBN 0-948549-13-0
Dictionary of Banking & Finance   ISBN 0-948549-12-2
Dictionary of Computing   ISBN 0-948549-44-0
Dictionary of Ecology and the Environment   ISBN 0-948549-32-7
Dictionary of Government and Politics   ISBN 0-948549-05-X
Dictionary of Hotels, Tourism, Catering   ISBN 0-948549-40-8
Dictionary of Information Technology   ISBN 0-948549-03-3
Dictionary of Law   ISBN 0-948549-33-5
Dictionary of Marketing   ISBN 0-948549-08-4
Dictionary of Medicine   ISBN 0-948549-36-X
Dictionary of Personnel Management   ISBN 0-948549-06-8
Dictionary of Printing and Publishing   ISBN 0-948549-09-2

(see back of this book for full title list and information request form)

DICTIONARY OF
HOTELS, TOURISM
AND
CATERING
MANAGEMENT

P.H.Collin

PETER COLLIN PUBLISHING

First published in Great Britain 1994
published by
Peter Collin Publishing Ltd
8 The Causeway, Teddington, Middlesex, TW11 0HE

British Library Cataloguing in Publication Data

A Catalogue record for this book is available from the British Library

ISBN 0-948549-40-8

Text computer typeset by Microgen Ltd, Welwyn Garden City, Herts
Printed in Finland by WSOY, Finland

Cover design by Gary Weston

PREFACE

This dictionary aims to provide the basic vocabulary of terms used in the hospitality industry; the fields covered include catering (restaurants and kitchens), hotels and guesthouses, travel, insurance, health and safety, together with terms relating to general business, such as accounts, personnel, etc.

The main words and phrases are defined in simple English and in some cases the definitions have been expanded by explanatory comments. We also give quotations from specialist magazines and other publications relating to the subjects.

The supplement at the back gives additional information in the form of tables. We are grateful to many people who have contributed to the work, in particular, Joseph Armstrong and Hazel and David Curties who read the text and provided many valuable comments.

Aa

Vitamin A *noun* retinol, vitamin which is soluble in fat and can be formed in the body, but which is mainly found in food, such as liver, vegetables, egg yolks and cod liver oil

> COMMENT: lack of Vitamin A affects the body's growth and resistance to disease and can cause night blindness

AA = AUTOMOBILE ASSOCIATION

AAA = AMERICAN AUTOMOBILE ASSOCIATION

abbey *noun* Christian religious establishment with living quarters, etc., grouped round a church

> COMMENT: in Great Britain, abbeys were abolished in the 16th century at the Reformation, but some abbey churches remain in use (such as Westminster Abbey); others became ruins (such as Fountains Abbey); others were converted into private houses (Lacock Abbey)

aboard *adverb* on a ship; *the passengers went aboard at 10 p.m.; when the ship docked, customs officers came aboard to inspect the cargo;* **all aboard!** = everyone come onto the ship, please

abonnement *French noun (meaning 'subscription')* used to apply to a European railpass

above the line *adjective* **(a)** *(companies)* income and expenditure before tax; *exceptional items are noted above the line in company accounts* **(b)** *(advertising)* advertising for which payment is made (such as an ad in a magazine or a stand at a trade fair) and for which a commission is paid to an advertising agency

aboyeur *French noun (meaning 'barker')* kitchen clerk, the person in the kitchen who shouts the order from the waiter to the chefs, and pins the waiter's written order on a hook relating to the particular table (called 'aboyeur' because he barks out the orders)

abroad *adverb* to or in another country; *the chairman is abroad on business; we are going abroad on holiday; she works abroad and only comes back here for her holidays; holidays abroad are becoming more expensive because of the falling exchange rate*

ABTA = ASSOCIATION OF BRITISH TRAVEL AGENTS *see also* BOND

accelerated freeze-drying (AFD) *noun* method of preserving food by heating for a short time, then freezing rapidly and drying in a vacuum

accept *verb* to take something which is being offered; *'all major credit cards accepted'; do you accept payment by cheque?*

access *noun* way of getting to a place; *the concert hall has access for wheelchairs;* **restricted access** = access (to a museum, for example) which is limited to small groups of people at certain times of the day only; **international access code** = number used to start making a telephone call to another country (from the UK, it is 010-; from most other countries it is 00-)

accident *noun* something unpleasant which happens by chance (such as the crash of a plane); **accident insurance** = insurance which will pay if an accident takes place; **the airline has a good accident record** = the airline has had few accidents, compared with other airlines; **to have an accident** = to crash *or* to hit something; *he had an accident as he was driving to the hotel; the group missed their flight, because their bus had an accident on the way to the airport; the accident happened on a mountain road*

accommodate *verb* to provide lodging for (someone); *the hostel can accommodate groups of up to fifty hikers*
◊ **accommodation** *noun* place to live; *visitors have difficulty in finding hotel accommodation during the summer; they are living in furnished accommodation; the hotel*

has accommodation for fifty guests; **accommodation address** = address used for receiving messages but which is not the real address of the company (NOTE: no plural in GB English, but US English also uses **accommodations**)

QUOTE the hall of residence accommodates 198 throughout the year with holiday visitors staying during vacation periods

Caterer & Hotelkeeper

QUOTE an airline ruling requires airlines to provide a free night's hotel accommodation for full fare passengers in transit

Business Traveller

QUOTE the airline providing roomy accommodations at below-average fares

Dun's Business Month

---

accompany *verb* to go with; *they travelled to Italy accompanied by their children; they sent a formal letter of complaint, accompanied by an invoice for damage; a white sauce is served to accompany the fish*

◊ **accompanied** *adjective* travelling with an adult passenger; **accompanied baggage** = baggage belonging to a passenger who is travelling in the same plane; **accompanied child** = child passenger travelling with an adult; *compare* UNACCOMPANIED (NOTE: accompanied **by** something)

◊ **accompaniment** *noun* small helping of food which is served with a dish (such as croutons with fish soup, grated parmesan cheese with minestrone, etc.)

accordance *noun* **in accordance with** = in agreement with *or* according to; *in accordance with your instructions we have deducted 10% to cover breakages and deposited the balance in your current account; I am submitting the claim for damages in accordance with the advice of our legal advisers*

◊ **according to** *preposition* as someone says or writes; *according to the leaflet, the tour should leave the central station at 10.30; the computer was installed according to the manufacturer's instructions*

◊ **accordingly** *adverb* in agreement with what has been decided; *we have received your letter and have altered the reservations accordingly*

account **1** *noun* (**a**) record of financial transactions over a period of time, such as money paid, received, borrowed or owed; *please send me your account or a detailed or an itemized account;* **expense account** =

money which a businessman is allowed by his company to spend on travelling and entertaining clients in connection with his business; *he charged his hotel bill to his expense account* (**b**) *(in a shop)* arrangement which a customer has to buy goods and pay for them at a later date (usually the end of the month); *to have an account or a charge account or a credit account with Harrods; put it on my account or charge it to my account; (of a customer)* **to open an account** = to ask a shop to supply goods which you will pay for at a later date; *(of a shop)* **to open an account** *or* **to close an account** = to start *or* to stop supplying a customer on credit; **to settle an account** = to pay all the money owed on an account; **to stop an account** = to stop supplying a customer until he has paid what he owes (**c**) **on account** = as part of the money owed; *he deposited £300 on account with the hotel* (**d**) customer who does a large amount of business with a firm and has an account; *he is one of our largest accounts; our salesmen call on their best accounts twice a month;* **account executive** = employee who looks after certain customers *or* who is the link between certain customers and his company (**e**) **the accounts of a business** *or* a **company's accounts** = detailed record of a company's financial affairs; **to keep the accounts** = to write each sum of money in the account book; *the accountant's job is to enter all the money received in the accounts;* **annual accounts** = accounts prepared at the end of a financial year; **management accounts** = financial information (sales, expenditure, credit, and profitability) prepared for a manager so that he can take decisions; **accounts department** = section of a company which deals with money paid, received, borrowed or owed; **accounts manager** = manager of an accounts department; **accounts payable** = money owed by a company; **accounts receivable** = money owed to a company (**f**) **bank account** *or* US **banking account** = arrangement to keep money in a bank; **current account** *or* **cheque account** *or* US **checking account** = account from which the customer can withdraw money when he wants by writing cheques; **deposit account** = account which pays interest but on which notice usually has to be given to withdraw money (**g**) notice; **to take account of inflation** *or* **to take inflation into account** = to assume that there will be a certain percentage inflation when making calculations **2** *verb* **to account for** = to explain and record a money transaction; *to account for a loss or a discrepancy; the cleaners have to account for all linen in* *guests' bedrooms; reps have to account for all their expenses to the sales manager*

◊ **profit and loss account (P&L account)** *noun* statement of company expenditure and income over a period of time, almost always one calendar year, showing whether the company has made a profit or loss (NOTE: the US equivalent is the **profit and loss statement** or **income statement**)

COMMENT: the balance sheet shows the state of a company's finances at a certain date; the profit and loss account shows the movements which have taken place since the end of the last accounting period, that is, since the last balance sheet

◊ **accountable** *adjective* (person) who is responsible for something (such as to record and then explain a money transaction); *the bar steward is accountable to the beverage manager* (NOTE: you are accountable **to** someone **for** something)

◊ **accountancy** *noun* work of an accountant; *he is studying accountancy or he is an accountancy student* (NOTE: US English uses **accounting** in this meaning)

◊ **accountant** *noun* (i) person who keeps a company's accounts; (ii) person who advises a company on its finances; (iii) person who examines accounts; *we send all our tax queries to our accountant; the books are kept by a freelance accountant; management accountant* = accountant who prepares financial information for managers so that they can take decisions

◊ **accounting** *noun* work of recording money paid, received, borrowed or owed; **accounting period** = period usually covered by a company's accounts (the balance sheet shows the state of the company's affairs at the end of the accounting period, while the profit and loss account shows the changes which have taken place since the end of the previous period); **current cost accounting** = method of accounting which notes the cost of replacing assets at current prices, rather than valuing assets at their original cost (NOTE: the word **accounting** is used in the USA to mean the subject as a course of study, where British English uses **accountancy**)

accredited *adjective* (agent) who is appointed by a company (such as a hotel chain or a tour operator) to act on its behalf

◊ **accreditation** *noun* appointment as an agent by a company

acetic acid *noun* acid which turns wine into vinegar, also used as a preservative in food such as pickles

◊ **Acetobacter** *noun* aerobic bacteria used in making vinegar

acid *noun* chemical compound containing hydrogen, which dissolves in water and forms hydrogen, or reacts with an alkali to form a salt and water, and turns litmus paper red; *hydrochloric acid is secreted in the stomach and forms part of the gastric juices*

◊ **acidity** *noun* level of acid in a solution; *the alkaline solution may help to reduce acidity*

COMMENT: acidity and alkalinity are measured according to the pH scale. pH7 is neutral; numbers above show alkalinity, while pH6 and below is acid

acknowledge *verb* to tell a sender that a letter *or* package *or* shipment has arrived; *he has still not acknowledged my letter of the 24th; we acknowledge receipt of your letter of June 14th; we acknowledge receipt of your booking form and deposit*

◊ **acknowledgement** *noun* act of acknowledging; *she sent an acknowledgement of receipt; they sent a letter of acknowledgement; I wrote to the hotel with a cheque two weeks ago but have not received any acknowledgement*

action *noun* (a) doing something; **action-packed holiday** = holiday where you do various activities (b) **out of action** = out of order, not working; *the extractor fan is out of action*

activity *noun* doing something *or* being active; **activity holiday** = planned holiday where you do certain things (such as painting, rock-climbing, etc.)

acute *adjective* (i) (disease) which comes on rapidly and can be dangerous; (ii) (pain) which is sharp and intense; *she had an acute attack of shingles; he felt acute chest pains*

ad *noun* = ADVERTISEMENT

adaptor *noun* something which holds a piece of equipment in a different way; **adaptor plug** = plug which allows a piece of equipment to be plugged into a different sized socket; *my hair-drier won't work here in France, because I haven't brought my adaptor plug*

COMMENT: adaptor plugs are necessary if you need to use electrical equipment in countries with different electrical systems (British hair-driers in France; American computers in Germany, etc.) because the type of plug is different. Where Britain uses mainly three-pin plugs, in Europe most plugs have two round pins. In the USA, plugs have two flat pins. To change voltage (as in the USA, where the voltage is 110V) a transformer will be necessary

add *verb* **(a)** to put figures together to make a total; *the waiter made a mistake when he added the wine twice* **(b)** to put things together to make a large group; *we are adding to the restaurant staff; by building the annexe, they have added thirty rooms to the hotel;* **this all adds to the company's costs** = this makes the company's costs higher; **added value** = amount added to the value of a product or service, being the difference between its cost and the amount received when it is sold (wages, taxes, etc., are deducted from the added value to give the retained profit); *see also* VALUE ADDED

◊ **add-on** *noun* extra optional item listed in the programme details of a conference or package tour, but for which an additional charge has to be paid

◊ **add up** *verb* to put several figures together to make a total; *to add up a column of figures; she made a mistake when adding up the bill;* **the figures do not add up** = the total given is not correct

◊ **add up to** *verb* to make a total of; *the total expenditure adds up to more than £1,000*

◊ **adding machine** *noun* machine which adds *or* which makes additions

◊ **addition** *noun* **(a)** thing or person added; *the management has stopped all additions to the hotel staff; the Spanish-speaking receptionist is the latest addition to the personnel* **(b) in addition to** = added to *or* as well as; *there are twelve registered letters to be sent in addition to this packet* **(c)** putting numbers together; *you don't need a calculator to do simple addition*

◊ **additional** *adjective* extra, which is added; *additional costs; additional charges; apart from the tours listed in the brochure, we have arranged two additional visits to local vineyards; additional duty will have to be paid*

additive *noun* chemical substance which is added, especially one which is added to food to improve its appearance, smell or taste, or to prevent it going bad; *the orange juice contains a number of additives; allergic reactions to additives are frequently found in workers in food processing factories*

COMMENT: colour additives are added to food to improve its appearance. Some are natural organic substances like saffron, carrot juice or caramel, but other colour additives are synthetic. Other substances are added to food to prevent decay or to keep the food in the right form: these can be emulsifiers, which bind different foods together as mixtures in sauces, for example, and stabilizers, which can keep a sauce semi-liquid and prevent it from separating into solids and liquids. The European Community allows certain additives to be added to food and these are given E numbers

address 1 *noun* details of number, street and town where an office is or a person lives; **accommodation address** = address used for receiving messages but which is not the real address of the company; **business address** = address of a business (as opposed to private address); *my business address and phone number are printed on the card;* **cable address** = specially short address for sending cables; **forwarding address** = address to which a person's mail can be sent on after he or she has left their current address; *they left the hotel and didn't leave a forwarding address;* **home address** *or* **private address** = address of a house or flat where someone lives; *please send the tickets to my home address;* **address list** = list of addresses; *we keep an address list of two thousand addresses in Europe* **2** *verb* to write the details of an address on an envelope, etc.; *she addressed the letter or the parcel to the hotel manager; please address your enquiries to the information officer; a letter addressed to the tourist information bureau*

◊ **addressee** *noun* person to whom a letter *or* package is addressed

adjoining *adjective* next to something *or* touching something; *there is an adjoining bathroom;* **adjoining rooms** = rooms which are next to each other; *they asked to be put in adjoining rooms; compare* CONNECTING ROOMS

administration *noun* organization *or* control *or* management of a company; **administration costs** *or* **the expenses of the administration** *or* **administration expenses** = costs of management, not including production, marketing or distribution costs
◊ **administrative** *adjective* referring to administration; *administrative details; administrative expenses; administrative staff*

admission *noun* **(a)** allowing someone to go in; *there is a £1 admission charge; admission is free on presentation of this card; free admission on Sundays* **(b)** person who has visited a museum; *we had 250 admissions last weekend* **(c)** saying that something really happened; *the tour company refunded his deposit, with an admission that the brochure was incorrect*

admit *verb* **(a)** to allow someone to go in; *children are not admitted to the bank; old age pensioners are admitted at half price* **(b)** to say that something is correct *or* to say that something really happened; *the tour operator admitted that the courier had made a mistake*
NOTE: **admitting - admitted**
◊ **admittance** *noun* allowing someone to go in; *no admittance except on business; admittance restricted to ticket holders only*

ad valorem *Latin phrase (meaning 'according to value')* showing that a tax is calculated according to the value of the goods taxed; *ad valorem duty; ad valorem tax*

> COMMENT: most taxes are 'ad valorem'; VAT is calculated as a percentage of the charge made, income tax is a percentage of income earned, etc.

advance 1 *noun* **(a)** money paid as part of a payment to be made later; *he paid $200 advance on account; can I have an advance of $50 against next month's salary?* **(b)** in **advance** = early *or* before something happens; *to benefit from the low fare price you have to pay in advance; the complete package is payable in advance; our prices are fixed in advance; if you want to be sure of a seat, you need to book in advance* **2** *adjective* early; *advance bookings are 50% higher this year; most tour companies insist on advance payment when a booking is made; you must give seven days' advance notice of changes in the itinerary;* **Advance Purchase Excursion (APEX)** = specially cheap air fare which must be booked a certain time before the flight (usually, three weeks), and which can only be changed or cancelled once it has been booked on payment of an extra charge; **advance reservation** = booking of a hotel room in advance (i.e., before the guest arrives at the hotel) **3** *verb* **(a)** to arrange for something to happen earlier; *the flight departure has been advanced to 9.30 a.m.* **(b)** to move a clock or watch to a later time; *when crossing from England to France, watches should be advanced by one hour; see also* PUT FORWARD

adventure *noun* new, exciting and dangerous experience; *adventure travel is becoming very popular;* **adventure holidays** = holidays where you do something exciting or dangerous

advertise *verb* to announce that something is for sale *or* that a job is vacant *or* that a service is offered; *to advertise a vacancy; to advertise for a secretary; to advertise a new product;* **advertised tour** *or* **advertised hotel** = tour *or* hotel which is detailed in a travel company's brochure
◊ **ad** *noun (informal)* = ADVERTISEMENT *we put an ad in the paper; she answered an ad in the paper; he found his job through an ad in the paper;* **classified ads** *or* **small ads** *or* **want ads** = advertisements listed in a newspaper under special headings (such as 'property to let', 'job vacancies'); *look in the small ads to see if there are any cottages to let in Wales;* **coupon ad** = advertisement with a form attached, which is to be cut out and returned to the advertiser with your name and address for further information; **display ad** = advertisement which is well designed to attract attention
◊ **advert** *noun* GB *(informal)* = ADVERTISEMENT *to put an advert in the paper; to answer an advert in the paper; classified adverts*
◊ **advertisement** *noun* notice which shows that something is for sale *or* that a service is offered *or* that someone wants something *or* that a job is vacant, etc.; *to put an advertisement in the paper; to answer an advertisement in the paper;* **classified**

advertisements = advertisements listed in a newspaper under special headings (such as 'property to let' or 'job vacancies'); **display advertisement** = advertisement which is well designed to attract attention

◊ **advertiser** *noun* person *or* company which advertises; *the catalogue gives a list of advertisers*

◊ **advertising** *noun* business of announcing that something is for sale *or* of trying to persuade customers to buy a product or service; **advertising gift** = something given free of charge to encourage a customer to spend more

aerogramme *noun* air letter, special sheet of thin blue paper which when folded can be sent by air mail without an envelope

aeroplane *noun* machine which flies in the air, carrying passengers or cargo

aerosol *noun* **(a)** tiny particles of liquid which stay suspended in the atmosphere (such as mist); **aerosol dispenser** = container *or* device from which liquid can be sprayed in tiny particles **(b)** can of liquid with a propellant gas under pressure, which is used to spray the liquid (such as an insecticide) in the form of tiny drops

COMMENT: commercial aerosols (that is, the metal containers) may use CFCs as propellants, but these are believed to be responsible for the destruction of ozone in the upper atmosphere and are gradually being replaced by less destructive agents

AFD = ACCELERATED FREEZE-DRYING

affiliated *adjective* connected with *or* owned by another company; *one of our affiliated hotels*

aflatoxin *noun* very toxic substance formed by a fungus *Aspergillus flavus,* which grows on seeds and nuts and affects stored grain

aft *adjective & adverb* towards the back part (of a ship or plane); *the game will be held on the aft recreation deck; the dining saloon is aft of the passenger lounge* (NOTE: the opposite is **forward**)

afternoon *noun* part of the day between midday and evening

◊ **afternoon tea** *noun* meal taken in the afternoon, usually between 4 and 5 o'clock; *see also* CREAM TEA, HIGH TEA, TEA

COMMENT: usually part of the full-board tariff in a hotel. Afternoon tea is usually served in the hotel lounge (if open to non-residents), or in the residents' lounge if it is served only to residents. It will normally consist of sandwiches (traditionally with the crusts removed), small cakes or slices of cake, pastries and various types of tea. Can also include the cream, scones and jam associated with cream teas

afters *noun GB (informal)* dessert course; *what do you want for afters? what's on the menu for afters?* (NOTE: very informal, used often by children, but also humorously by adults)

agency *noun* **(a)** office *or* job of representing another company in an area; *they signed an agency agreement or an agency contract;* **sole agency** = agreement to be the only person to represent a company *or* to sell a product in a certain area; *he has the sole agency for the tour company* **(b)** office *or* business which arranges things for other companies; **advertising agency** = office which plans *or* designs and manages advertising for companies; **furnished letting agency** = office which specializes in letting furnished rooms or flats; **travel agency** = office which arranges travel and travel accommodation for customers (NOTE: plural is **agencies**)

agent *noun* **(a)** person *or* company representing another person *or* another company in an area; *she is the local agent for the tour operator;* **sole agent** = person who has the sole agency for a company *or* a product in an area; *he is the sole agent for the airline;* **agent's commission** = money (often a percentage of sales) paid to an agent **(b)** person in charge of an agency; **commission agent** = agent who is paid by commission, not by fee; **forwarding agent** = person *or* company which arranges shipping and customs documents; **letting agent** = agent who is responsible for letting accommodation to visitors (the owners of the accommodation agree with the agent a fee or commission for this service); **travel agent** = person *or* company which arranges travel and hotel accommodation for customers; *the tour was arranged by our* *local travel agent; see your travel agent for details of our tours to Spain*

AGM = ANNUAL GENERAL MEETING

agree with *verb* **(a)** to say that you think the same way as someone; to be in favour of something; *most of the group agreed with the suggestion that the visit to the monastery should be cancelled* **(b)** not to agree with someone = to make someone ill; **rich food does not agree with me** = rich food makes me feel ill

◊ **agreement** *noun* **(a)** action of agreeing; **they are in agreement with our plan** = they agree with it **(b)** contract; **union agreement** = contract between management and trade union concerning employment, pay, conditions of work, etc.

aid *noun* **(a)** help; **medical aid** = (i) treatment of someone who is ill *or* injured, given by a doctor; (ii) medical supplies and experts sent to a country after a disaster; *see also* FIRST AID **(b)** machine *or* tool *or* drug which helps someone do something; *food processors are useful aids in preparing food*

ailment *noun* usually minor illness; *she suffers from a liver ailment; many people with skin ailments come to the spa*

air *noun* method of travelling (or sending goods) using aircraft; *we went by air, rather than by boat; over long distances, air travel is quicker than taking the train;* **air carrier** = company which sends cargo *or* passengers by air; **air fares** = different types of fares charged for travel on aircraft (Business fare, APEX fare, normal fare, group fare, etc.); **air forwarding** = arranging for goods to be shipped by air; **air congestion** = overcrowding of air routes, leading to delays in flight times; **air letter** = aerogramme, a special sheet of thin blue paper which when folded can be sent by air mail without an envelope; **air passenger** = passenger travelling in an aircraft (as opposed to a train passenger, coach passenger, etc.); **air ticket** = plane ticket, ticket to allow a passenger to travel by air

◊ **airbridge** *noun* covered walkway which connects an aircraft with the terminal building, so that passengers can walk onto or off the aircraft easily (it extends from the terminal to the forward door on the aircraft)

◊ **air cargo** *noun* goods sent by air

◊ **air-conditioned** *adjective* having the temperature controlled by an air-conditioner; *the restaurant is air-conditioned*

◊ **air-conditioner** *noun* machine which controls the temperature in a room; *how can we turn the air-conditioner off?*

◊ **air-conditioning** *noun* system of controlling the temperature in a room or office or train, etc.; *if you hire a car in Texas, make sure it has air-conditioning;* **to turn the air-conditioning on** = to start the cooling; **to turn the air-conditioning off** = to stop the cooling; **to turn the air-conditioning down** = to make a room warmer; **to turn the air-conditioning up** = to make a room cooler

◊ **aircraft** *noun* machine which flies in the air, carrying passengers or cargo; *the airline has a fleet of ten commercial aircraft; the company is one of the most important American aircraft manufacturers;* **to charter an aircraft** = to hire an aircraft for a special purpose (NOTE: no plural: **one aircraft, two aircraft**)

◊ **aircrew** *noun* people who fly an aircraft (i.e. the captain, copilot, navigator, etc.)

◊ **air-dry** *verb* to remove moisture from something by placing it in a current of air

◊ **airfield** *noun* field where small planes can land

◊ **air freight** *noun* **(a)** shipping of goods in an aircraft; *to send a shipment by air freight;* **air freight charges** *or* **rates** = money charged for sending goods by air **(b)** goods shipped in an aircraft

◊ **airfreight** *verb* to send goods by air; *to airfreight a consignment to Mexico; we airfreighted the shipment because our agent ran out of stock*

◊ **air hostess** *noun* woman who looks after passengers on a plane (NOTE: also called a **stewardess;** the term for a man who does this job is a **steward**)

◊ **airlift** *verb* to carry something or someone by air; *the climbers were airlifted to safety*

◊ **airline** *noun* company which carries passengers or cargo by air

◊ **airlink** *noun* link between two places, using planes or helicopters

◊ **air mail** *noun* way of sending letters *or* parcels by air; *to send a package by air mail; air-mail charges have risen by 15%;* **air-mail envelope** = very light envelope for sending air-mail letters; **air-mail sticker** = blue sticker with the words 'by air mail' which can be stuck to an envelope or packet to show it is being sent by air

◊ **air-mail** *verb* to send letters *or* parcels by air; *to air-mail a document to New York*

◊ **air miles** *plural noun* system of giving coupons for free air travel when purchasing goods or services (such as international flights, meals, etc.)

◊ **air miss** *noun* incident where two aircraft come very close to each other by accident when in the air, but without causing an accident

◊ **airpass** *noun* special ticket (paid for in advance) which allows unlimited travel by air in a country over a certain limited period of time (similar to a 'railpass' for train travel)

◊ **airplane** *noun (especially US)* aircraft, a machine which flies in the air, carrying passengers or cargo

◊ **airport** *noun* place where planes land and take off; *we leave from London Airport at 10.00; O'Hare Airport is the main airport for Chicago;* **airport bus** = bus which takes passengers to and from an airport; **airport hotel** = hotel which is very near to an airport, and so is convenient for passengers who need to leave early in the morning, or who arrive late at night, or who are in transit; *stranded passengers were put up at the airport hotel at the airline's expense;* **airport tax** = tax added to the price of an air ticket to cover the cost of running an airport; **airport terminal** = main building at an airport where passengers arrive and depart (NOTE: compare **air terminal**)

◊ **airsick** *adjective* ill because of the movement of an aircraft

◊ **airsickness** *noun* sickness caused by the movement of an aircraft

◊ **airside** *adjective* next to the part of an airport where aircraft stand; **airside lounge** = departure lounge near the boarding gate

QUOTE Business class passengers have the use of a small and quiet airside lounge. There's an adequate supply of orange juice, coffee and newspapers
Business Traveller

◊ **airstrip** *noun* small rough landing place for aircraft; *the plane landed on a jungle airstrip*

◊ **air terminal** *noun* building in a town where passengers meet to be taken by bus or train to an airport outside the town (NOTE: compare **airport terminal**)

◊ **airtight** *adjective* which does not allow air to get in; *the goods are packed in airtight containers*

◊ **air-traffic controller** *noun* person who organizes the movement of aircraft in the air

◊ **Air Travel Organisers' Licence (ATOL)** licence which has to be held by any company or person offering package holidays or charter flights and includes a bond to protect travellers if the company goes into liquidation

◊ **airworthiness** *noun* being able and safe to fly; **certificate of airworthiness** = document to show that an aircraft has passed an examination and is in a fit condition to fly; *compare* SEAWORTHINESS

aisle *noun (in a train, aircraft, cinema, etc.)* gap between rows of seats, where people may walk; *you're blocking the aisle and the stewardess can't get past with the drinks trolley;* **aisle seat** = seat in a train, plane, etc., next to an aisle (NOTE: the opposite is a **window seat)**

à la *French phrase (meaning 'in the style of')* à **la russe** = in the Russian style

à la carte *adverb & adjective* (meal) made of several dishes ordered separately from a menu; **à la carte menu** = menu with many different dishes at different prices, from which a guest can choose what to eat (the dishes are cooked specially to order, as opposed to the table d'hôte menu); *they chose from the à la carte menu*

à la mode *adverb US* served with ice cream; *apple pie à la mode*

alarm 1 *noun* device which gives a loud warning; **false alarm** = warning signal which is false; **fire alarm** = bell *or* siren which gives warning that a fire has started; **alarm (clock)** = clock which rings at a certain time **2** *verb* to warn (someone); to frighten (someone); *we don't want to alarm the guests*

Alaska baked Alaska *see* BAKE

alcohol (C$_2$H$_5$ OH) *noun* **(a)** colourless inflammable liquid, produced by the fermentation of sugars and used as an ingredient of organic chemicals, intoxicating drinks and medicines **(b)** drink made from fermented or distilled liquid; *the restaurant will not serve alcohol to anyone under the age of 18;* **duty-free alcohol** = alcoholic drink which can be bought in a duty-free shop; **low-alcohol beer** = beer containing very little alcohol; *I'm driving, so I'll have a low-alcohol lager*

◊ **alcohol-free** *adjective* containing no alcohol; *alcohol-free lager*

◊ **alcoholic** *adjective* containing alcohol; *alcoholic drinks are not allowed into certain countries*

◊ **alcoholism** *noun* excessive drinking of alcohol which becomes addictive

ale *noun* British-type beer, especially bitter beer, but not lager

alimentary canal *noun* tube in the body going from the mouth to the anus and including the throat, stomach, intestine, etc., through which food passes and is digested

◊ **alimentary system** *noun* arrangement of tubes and organs, including the alimentary canal, salivary glands, liver, etc., through which food passes and is digested

◊ **alimentation** *noun* feeding, taking in food

algae *plural noun* tiny plants living in water or in moist conditions, which contain chlorophyll and have no stems or roots or leaves; **blue-green algae** = Cyanophyta, algae found mainly in fresh water; **brown algae** = Phaeophyta *or* brown seaweed; **green algae** = Chlorophyta *or* green plants living in water; **red algae** = Rhodophyta *or* type of very small algae *or* phytoplankton, mainly found on the seabed and which cause the phenomenon called red tide

◊ **algaecide** *noun* substance used to kill algae

alien *noun* foreigner, a person who is not a citizen of the country; **resident alien** = alien who has a resident's permit; **undesirable alien** = foreigner who is not welcome in a country, and who can be expelled

alkali *noun* one of many substances which neutralize acids and form salts (NOTE: British English plural is **alkalis,** but US English is **alkalies)**

◊ **alkaline** *adjective* containing more alkali than acid

◊ **alkalinity** *noun* amount of alkali in something such as soil *or* water

COMMENT: alkalinity and acidity are measured according to the pH scale. pH7 is neutral, and pH8 and upwards are alkaline. One of the commonest alkalis is caustic soda, used to clear blocked drains

all *adjective & pronoun* everything *or* everyone; *all (of) the managers attended the meeting; all the guests asked to go on the tour; all the rooms are booked for the Christmas period; the customs officials asked him to open all his cases; all trains stop at Clapham Junction*

◊ **all-in** *adjective* including everything; **all-in price** *or* **rate** = price which covers all items in a purchase (goods, delivery, tax, insurance, etc.), or all items in a tour (travel, hotel accommodation, meals, etc.); *the hotel offers an all-in tariff of £150 a week*

◊ **all-inclusive** *adjective* = ALL-IN

allergen *noun* substance which produces hypersensitivity; **food allergen** = substance in food which produces an allergy

◊ **allergenic** *adjective* which produces an allergy; *the allergenic properties of fungal spores;* **allergenic agent** = substance which produces an allergy

◊ **allergic** *adjective* suffering from an allergy; *she is allergic to pollen; he showed an allergic reaction to strawberries;* **allergic agent** = substance which produces an allergic reaction; **allergic person** = person who has an allergy to something; **allergic reaction** = effect (such as a skin rash *or* sneezing) produced by a substance to which a person has an allergy

◊ **allergy** *noun* sensitivity to certain substances such as pollen *or* dust, which cause a physical reaction; *she has an allergy to household dust;* **food allergy** = reaction caused by sensitivity to certain foods (some of the commonest being strawberries, chocolate, milk, eggs, oranges)

COMMENT: allergens are usually proteins, and include foods, dust, animal hair, as well as pollen from flowers. Treatment of allergies depends on correctly identifying the allergen to which the patient is sensitive. This is done by patch tests, in which drops of different allergens are placed on scratches in the skin. Food allergens discovered in this way can be avoided, but it is hard to avoid other common allergens like dust and pollen, and these have to be treated by a course of desensitizing injections

allocate *verb* **(a)** to share out things among various people; *the party were allocated rooms in the hotel annexe* **(b)** to divide (a sum of money) in various ways and share it out; *we allocate 10% of revenue to publicity; $2,500 was allocated to furnishing the guests' lounge*

allot *verb* to allocate hotel rooms to a tour operator; *the group has been allotted 50 rooms in the hotel* (NOTE: **allotting - allotted**)

◊ **allotment** *noun* allocating hotel rooms to tour operators

allow *verb* (a) to say that someone can do something; *children are not allowed into the restaurant; you are allowed six litres of duty-free wine; the company allows all members of staff to take six days' holiday at Christmas* (b) to give; *we will allow you a student discount; the store allows 5% discount to members of staff* (c) to agree *or* to accept legally; *to allow a claim or an appeal*

◊ **allow for** *verb* (a) to give a discount for *or* to add an extra sum to cover something; *to allow for money paid in advance; to allow 10% for packing; gratuities are not allowed for* = gratuities are not included (b) to take something into account when calculating; **allow 14 days for delivery of the visa** = calculate that delivery of the visa will take at least 14 days

◊ **allowable** *adjective* legally accepted; **allowable expenses** = business expenses which can be claimed against tax

◊ **allowance** *noun* (a) money which is given for a special reason; *travel allowance or travelling allowance; foreign currency allowance;* **baggage allowance** = weight of baggage which an air passenger is allowed to take free when he travels; **entertainment allowance** = money which a manager is allowed by his company to spend on meals with visitors (b) **duty-free allowance** = amount of dutiable goods which a person can take into a country without paying tax; *he had several bottles more than the duty-free allowance and so was charged duty* (c) money removed in the form of a discount; *allowance for exchange loss*

◊ **allowed time** *noun* paid time which the management agrees a worker can spend on rest *or* cleaning *or* meals, not working

QUOTE most airlines give business class the same baggage allowance as first class

Business Traveller

almond *noun* sweet nut from the almond tree; *trout with almonds; an almond cake;* **almond paste** = paste made from ground almonds, sugar and egg, used to cover a cake before icing or to make individual little sweets

alongside *adverb & preposition* beside; *the ship berthed alongside the quay or came alongside the quay*

the Alps mountainous area of Switzerland, North Italy, including parts of Austria and France; *the number of visitors to the Alps is increasing each year; climbers in the Alps are warned of the danger of avalanches*

◊ **alpine** *adjective* referring to the Alps; *an alpine holiday resort*

QUOTE it appears that rugby and soccer are far, far more dangerous than Alpine downhill skiing

Sunday Times

alternative 1 *noun* thing which can be done instead of another; *what is the alternative to calling the trip off?;* **we have no alternative** = there is nothing else we can do **2** *adjective* other *or* which can take the place of something; *they were offered the choice of two alternative flights;* **to find someone alternative accommodation** = to find someone another hotel room

altitude *noun* height (measured above the level of the sea); **altitude sickness** = mountain sickness, a condition where a person suffers from oxygen deficiency from being at a high altitude (as on a mountain) where the level of oxygen in the air is low

a.m. *or US* **A.M.** *abbreviation* referring to the period between midnight and midday; in the morning; *the flight leaves at 9.20 a.m.; we will arrive at 10 a.m. local time; if you phone before 8 a.m. calls are charged at a cheaper rate*

ambassador, ambassadress *noun* person who represents his or her country in another country; *see also* CONSUL, EMBASSY

ambient *adjective* surrounding a person *or* an object; *deaths from ambient carbon monoxide poisoning are increasing;* **ambient noise** = general noise which surrounds you (such as traffic noise, waterfalls, etc.); **ambient quality standards** = levels of acceptable clean air which a national body tries to enforce; **ambient temperature** = temperature of the air in which you live or work

amenity *noun* facility for sports or entertainment; *the town offers amenities for children;* **amenity centre** = building housing various entertainment facilities, such as a cinema, sports hall, gymnasium, auditorium, swimming pool, etc.

> QUOTE rooms are stylish and uncluttered with every amenity, and service is generally good. Singles from DM310, doubles DM390
>
> *Business Traveller*

American *adjective* referring to the United States of America

◊ **American Express** *noun* company offering travel service, traveller's cheques, charge cards, and many other services worldwide; *his American Express travellers' cheques were stolen*

◊ **Americanos** *noun* cocktail of campari and vermouth

◊ **American plan** *noun US* hotel charge which includes all meals as well as the room charge; *compare* EUROPEAN PLAN

◊ **American service** *noun* **(a)** style of laying a table ready for guests (with cutlery, side plate, napkin, glasses, and sometimes coffee cup and saucer) **(b)** way of serving food to guests, where the portions of food are placed on plates in the kitchen ready for service at table; *compare* FRENCH SERVICE

Amex *noun (informal)* = AMERICAN EXPRESS *he paid by Amex or with his Amex card*

amino acid *noun* chemical compound which is broken down from proteins in the digestive system and then used by the body to form its own protein; *proteins are first broken down into amino acids;* essential amino acids = eight amino acids which are essential for growth, but which cannot be synthesized and so must be obtained from food or medicinal substances

> COMMENT: amino acids all contain carbon, hydrogen, nitrogen and oxygen, as well as other elements. Some amino acids are produced in the body itself, but others have to be absorbed from food. The eight essential amino acids are: isoleucine, leucine, lysine, methionine, phenylalanine, threonine, tryptophan and valine

amoeba *noun* form of animal life, made up of a single cell (NOTE: plural is **amoebae**. Note also the US spelling **ameba**)

◊ **amoebiasis** *noun* infection caused by amoeba, which can result in amoebic dysentery in the large intestine (intestinal amoebiasis) and can sometimes infect the lungs (pulmonary amoebiasis)

◊ **amoebic** *adjective* referring to an amoeba; **amoebic dysentery** = mainly tropical form of dysentery which is caused by *Entamoeba histolytica* which enters the body through contaminated water or unwashed food

◊ **amoebicide** *noun* substance which kills amoebae

ammonia (NH₃) *noun* gas with a strong smell, a compound of nitrogen and hydrogen, which is a normal product of organic metabolism and is used in compounds to make artificial fertilizers *or* in liquid form as a refrigerant

> COMMENT: ammonia is released into the atmosphere from animal dung. It has the effect of neutralizing acid rain but in combination with sulphur dioxide it forms ammonium sulphate which damages the green leaves of plants

amount 1 *noun* quantity of money; *amount paid; amount deducted; amount owing; amount written off; what is the amount outstanding?* **2** *verb* **to amount to** = to make a total of; *their debts amount to over £1m*

amp *noun* quantity of electricity flowing in a current; *a 3-amp plug*

amplifier *noun* machine which makes a sound louder

Amtrak *noun* national system of railways in the USA, which operates passenger services between main cities

amuse *verb* to give (someone) pleasure; **to amuse yourself** = to spend time happily; *on the final day of the tour there will be no organized visits, and members of the party will be left to amuse themselves in the town*

◊ **amusement** *noun* pleasure; **amusement arcade** = hall with slot machines for playing games, etc.; **amusement park** = open-air park with various types of entertainment, such as roundabouts, shooting galleries, etc.

analyse *or* **analyze** *verb* to examine in detail; *to analyse the accounts of a restaurant; to analyse the market potential for golfing holidays; when the food was analysed it was found to contain traces of bacteria*

◊ **analysis** *noun* detailed examination and report; *job analysis; market analysis; sales analysis; to carry out an analysis of the*

market potential; to write an analysis of the sales position; cost analysis = examination in advance of the costs of a new product; systems analysis = using a computer to suggest how a company can work more efficiently by analysing the way in which it works at present (NOTE: plural is **analyses**)
◊ **analyst** noun person who analyses; market analyst; systems analyst

anchor 1 noun heavy metal hook dropped to the bottom of the sea to hold a ship in one place; the ship was at anchor; to drop anchor = to let an anchor fall to the bottom of the sea to hold a ship steady **2** verb **(a)** (of a ship) to drop anchor **(b)** to hold (a ship) with an anchor
◊ **anchorage** noun place where ships can anchor safely

anchovy noun small fish with a strong, salty taste, used in dishes such as pizza, salade niçoise, etc.

ancillary adjective secondary; **ancillary services** = services such as cleaning, porterage, etc., in a hotel

Angostura see BITTERS

animator noun person employed to organise entertainments or other activities for guests in a hotel or holiday resort or for passengers on a ship

anise noun annual herb (Pimpinella anisum) which produces small aromatic fruit (called aniseed) used for flavouring
◊ **aniseed** noun seed of the anise plant

COMMENT: aniseed is much used in confectionery, especially in sweets. It is also the basis of several alcoholic drinks made in the Mediterranean area, such as pastis in France, ouzo in Greece, or raki in Turkey

annexe noun less important building attached to a main building; the party was put into the hotel annexe

announce verb to tell something to the public; the compere announced the results of the competition; the pilot announced that there was some turbulence ahead
◊ **announcement** noun telling something in public; announcement of the appointment of a new hotel manager; the chef made an announcement to the kitchen staff
◊ **announcer** noun = ABOYEUR

annual general meeting (AGM) noun annual meeting of all the shareholders of a company, when the company's financial situation is presented by and discussed with the directors, when the accounts for the past year are approved, when dividends are declared and auditors are appointed, etc. (NOTE: the US term is **annual meeting** or **annual stockholders' meeting**)

Annual Percentage Rate (APR) noun rate of interest (such as on a hire-purchase agreement) shown on an annual compound basis, including fees and charges

answer 1 noun reply, conversation or letter coming after someone has spoken or written; I am writing in answer to your letter of October 6th; my letter got no answer or there was no answer to my letter; I tried to phone his office but there was no answer **2** verb to speak or write after someone has spoken or written to you; **to answer a letter** = to write a letter in reply to a letter which you have received; **to answer the telephone** = to lift the telephone when it rings and listen to what the caller is saying
◊ **answering** noun **answering machine** = machine which answers the telephone automatically when someone is not in the office or not at home; **answering service** = office which answers the telephone and takes messages for someone or for a company

anteroom noun room next to and adjoining a larger room; the disco was held in the anteroom next to the bar

anthrax noun disease of cattle and sheep which can be transmitted to humans

COMMENT: caused by Bacillus anthracis, anthrax can be transmitted by touching infected skin, meat or other parts of an animal (including bone meal used as a fertilizer).

antibiotic 1 adjective which stops the spread of bacteria **2** noun drug (such as penicillin) which is developed from living substances and which stops the spread of microorganisms; he was given a course of antibiotics; antibiotics have no use against virus diseases

COMMENT: penicillin is one of the commonest antibiotics, together with streptomycin, tetracycline, erythromycin and many others. Although antibiotics are widely and successfully used, new forms of bacteria have developed which are resistant to them

anticaking additive *noun* additive added to food to prevent it becoming solid (in the EC, they are given E numbers E530 - 578)

antimalarial *adjective & noun* (drug) used to treat malaria

◊ **antioxidant** *noun* substance which prevents oxidation, used to prevent materials such as rubber from deteriorating; also added to processed food to prevent oil going bad (in the EC, antioxidant food additives have E numbers E300 - 321)

antiseptic 1 *adjective* which prevents germs spreading; *she gargled with an antiseptic mouthwash* **2** *noun* substance which prevents germs growing or spreading; *the nurse painted the wound with antiseptic*

◊ **antiserum** *noun* serum taken from an animal which has developed antibodies to bacteria and used to give temporary immunity to a disease (NOTE: plural is **antisera)**

◊ **antitoxin** *noun* antibody produced by the body to counteract a poison in the body

◊ **antivenene** *or* **antivenom (serum)** *noun* serum which is used to counteract the poison from snake *or* insect bites

AOC = APPELLATION D'ORIGINE CONTROLEE

AONB = AREA OF OUTSTANDING NATURAL BEAUTY

apartment *noun* set of rooms in a large building, as a separate living unit; **apartment block** = block of flats; **apartment hotel** = hotel which is formed of a series of furnished rooms or suites and where all normal hotel services are provided, although each suite will have its own kitchenette

apéritif *noun* alcoholic drink taken before a meal

COMMENT: the commonest apéritifs served in Britain are sherry, gin and tonic, whisky, or various martinis; outside Britain, port is drunk as an apéritif

APEX fare *noun* specially cheap fare which must be booked a certain time before the date of departure (usually, one to four weeks) and allows a stay of a certain length only (usually more than one week and less than six) (NOTE: short for **Advance Purchase Excursion)**

QUOTE a cheap APEX fare has been introduced for a car and up to five passengers who book 28 days in advance and return within five days
Business Traveller

apologize *verb* to say you are sorry; *we apologize for the delay in unloading baggage; she apologized for being late*

◊ **apology** *noun* saying you are sorry; *to write a letter of apology; I enclose a cheque for £10 with apologies for the delay in answering your letter; she was very annoyed and asked for an apology from the coach driver*

appellation d'origine contrôlée (AOC) *noun* French wine classification, indicating that the wine comes from a certain area and is of a certain quality; *compare* VDQS

appetite *noun* feeling that you want to eat; **good appetite** = interest in eating food; **poor appetite** = lack of interest in eating food

◊ **appetizer** *noun* (i) snack taken with drinks before a meal; (ii) hors d'oeuvres

◊ **appetizing** *adjective* (food) which looks or smells or tastes good (NOTE: the opposite is **unappetizing)**

apple *noun* common hard, edible fruit of the apple tree *(Malus domestica)* **apple charlotte** = hot dessert made of stewed apples cooked in a case of soft sponge cake; **apple crumble** = dessert made of cooked apples covered with a cake mixture of flour, fat and sugar; **apple sauce** = sauce made from cooked apples, served with meat, especially pork (NOTE: in American English, **apple sauce** can be eaten as a dessert, which in British English is called **stewed apples) cider apple** = apple used for making cider; **cooking apple** = sour apple which is used for cooking with sugar; **eating apple** = sweet apple which can be eaten raw; **stewed apples** *or* **apple purée** = apples which have been cooked until they are soft, served as a dessert

COMMENT: 6,000 apple varieties once grew in Britain, and all of them are recorded in the UK's National Apple Register. Of the recognized apple varieties the most important are Cox's Orange Pippin and Golden Delicious (dessert varieties) and Bramley's Seedling (cooking apple)

apply *verb* **(a)** to ask for something, usually in writing; *to apply for a visa* or *for a passport; to apply in writing; to apply in person;* **to apply for a job** = to write offering your services to an employer; *sixty people applied for jobs in the new restaurant* **(b)** to affect or to touch; *this clause applies only to travel in Africa*

◊ **applicant** *noun* person who applies for something; *visa applicants will have to wait at least two weeks*

◊ **application** *noun* asking for something, usually in writing; *an application for a visa* or *a visa application; an application for a job* or *a job application;* **application form** = form to be filled in when applying; *to fill in an application (form) for a new passport* or *a passport application (form);* **letter of application** = letter in which someone applies for something

approved *adjective* lowest grade in the English Tourist Board grading system

APR = ANNUAL PERCENTAGE RATE

après-ski *noun* (parties) which take place in the evening after a day's skiing

apricot *noun* small yellow fruit from a deciduous tree *(Prunus armeniaca),* similar to a small peach, but not as juicy; *you have a choice of marmalade or apricot jam for breakfast*

apron *noun* **(a)** piece of cloth worn over clothes to protect them when working; *the chef in the carvery wears a long white apron* **(b)** *(in an airport)* piece of tarmac on which planes can be parked for unloading, waiting, cleaning, etc.; **apron congestion** = situation where too many planes try to use the apron at an airport, resulting in slower turnround times

> QUOTE the chances are you'll be decanted from the plane onto a hot and sticky apron for the further stifling bus ride to the cramped terminal
>
> *Business Traveller*

aquatic *adjective* in water; **aquatic sports** = activities which take place on or in water, such as swimming, water polo, scuba diving, etc.

Arbroath smokies *noun* small whole haddock smoked to a brown colour (NOTE: called after the town of Arbroath in Scotland)

area *noun* **(a)** measurement of the space taken up by something (calculated by multiplying the length by the width); *the area of this restaurant is 3,400 square feet; we are looking for a shop with a sales area of about 100 square metres* **(b)** region of the world; *the tour will visit one of the most inaccessible desert areas in the world* **(c)** district or part of a town; *the office is in the commercial area of the town; their factory is in a very good area for getting to the motorways and airports* **(d)** part of a country, a division for commercial purposes; *his sales area is the North-West; he finds it difficult to cover all his area in a week*

◊ **area code** *noun* special telephone number which is given to a particular area; *the area code for central London is 071*

◊ **area manager** *noun* manager who is responsible for a part of the country

◊ **Area of Outstanding Natural Beauty (AONB)** region in England and Wales which is not a National Park but which is considered sufficiently attractive to be preserved from overdevelopment

arm *noun* **(a)** part of the body between hand and shoulder; **arm in arm** = with their arms linked **(b)** thing shaped like an arm; piece at the side of a chair to rest your arms on; *the buttons for the music channels are in the arm of your seat* **2** *verb* to equip with weapons

◊ **armband** *noun* piece of cloth worn round your arm; *the tour leader will be wearing a red armband*

◊ **armchair** *noun* chair with arms; *each bedroom is furnished with two armchairs and a TV*

◊ **armed** *adjective* equipped with weapons; *because of the dangerous situation, the party will travel with armed guards*

◊ **armrest** *noun* part of a seat which you put your arm on; *the ashtray and sound buttons are in the armrest; please put your armrests into horizontal position for landing*

aroma *noun* *(formal)* pleasant smell; *the aroma of freshly ground coffee*

◊ **aromatic** *adjective* (plant) which has a strong pleasant smell; **aromatic herbs** = herbs, such as rosemary or thyme, which are used to give a particular taste to food

arrange *verb* **(a)** to put in order; *the hotel is arranged as a series of small bungalows with a central restaurant and swimming pool; the restaurants are arranged in alphabetical order; arrange the invoices in order of their dates* **(b)** to organize; *we arranged to have the meeting in their offices; she arranged for a car to meet him at the airport; the courier will arrange transportation to the airport* (NOTE: you arrange **for** someone to do something; you arrange **for** something to be done; or you arrange **to** do something)

◊ **arrangement** *noun* way in which something is organized; *the secretary is making all the arrangements for her boss's visit to Spain; the group complained that the arrangements for the trip to the ruins were not clear*

arrive *verb* to come to a place; *the plane is due to arrive at 12.15; they arrived at the hotel in the middle of the night*

◊ **arrival** *noun* **(a)** action of coming to a place; *we announce the arrival of flight AB 987 from Tangiers;* **arrivals** = section of an airport where the passengers arrive; **arrivals hall** *or* **arrivals lounge** = hall *or* lounge where passengers can be met or can sit and wait; **arrival without notice** = coming to a hotel without having made an advance booking; **late arrival** = arrival of a plane *or* train after the scheduled time; *we apologise for the late arrival of the 14.25 Intercity express from Edinburgh* **(b)** person who has arrived; *the new arrivals were shown to the first-floor lounge;* **early arrival** = guest who arrives at a hotel earlier than expected; **late arrival** = guest who arrives at a hotel after the time when he was expected or after the date for which he had booked

arrowroot *noun* thickening agent, a white powder made from the ground root of a West Indian plant *Maranta arundinacea*

art *noun* painting, drawing, sculpture, music and dance; *when in Washington, you must not miss the Museum of Modern Art;* **art appreciation course** = course where students learn to recognise qualities in works of art; **art gallery** = museum of paintings, sculptures, etc.

artichoke *noun* **(a)** (globe) artichoke = green vegetable like the flower of a thistle **(b)** (Jerusalem) artichoke = root vegetable like a bumpy potato

COMMENT: globe artichokes are in fact a type of thistle; the flower heads are cut before the flowers open and are boiled;

the soft bottom parts of the outer leaves are eaten, often with vinaigrette, and then the prickly 'choke' in the centre has to be removed, and the base of the flower (called the 'heart') is cut up and eaten with vinaigrette. The 'heart' can also be served by itself as a salad. In a restaurant, the artichoke will be prepared in the kitchen before serving, so that the customer can eat it without too much difficulty. Jerusalem artichokes are quite different plants, but have a similar taste to globe artichokes. The roots are thick and oddly-shaped; they are peeled and boiled like potatoes, and eaten with butter or other sauces, or made into soup

asap = AS SOON AS POSSIBLE

ascariasis *noun* disease of the intestine and sometimes the lungs, caused by infestation with *Ascaris lumbricoides;* the disease is widespread in northern South America, parts of Africa and the Philippines

◊ **Ascaris lumbricoides** *noun* type of large roundworm which is a parasite in the human intestine

ascorbic acid *noun* Vitamin C, found in fresh fruit

ashore *adverb* on or onto the land (from a ship); *passengers can go ashore for a couple of hours to visit the town*

ashtray *noun* container for putting ash and unsmoked parts of cigarettes and cigars; *the table was covered with dirty plates and the ashtray was full; there was no ashtray, so he asked the waiter for one; in the smoking compartments, ashtrays are provided in the armrests of the seats*

asparagus *noun* cultivated plant of which you eat the new shoots as a vegetable

COMMENT: asparagus is a type of fern; the new shoots appear above the ground in late spring, and are cut off at ground level. They should be boiled, and then can be eaten hot with melted butter, or cold or warm with a vinaigrette dressing. Asparagus can also be made into soup. In England, asparagus can be eaten with the fingers, dipping the tip of the spear into the dressing, and nibbling them down to the point where they stop being tender. In other countries, asparagus is eaten with a knife and fork

aspergillosis *noun* infection of the lungs with *Aspergillus*, a type of fungus
◊ **Aspergillus** *see* AFLATOXIN

aspic *noun* **(a)** jelly made from the cooked juices of meat, poultry or fish **(b)** form of salad, with small pieces of cold meat, poultry, eggs or vegetables set in firm aspic jelly in a mould

asset *noun* anything which belongs to a company or person, and which has a value; **capital assets** *or* **fixed assets** = property or machinery which a company owns and uses in its business, but which the company does not buy or sell as part of its regular trade; **current assets** = assets used by a company in its ordinary work (such as materials, finished goods, cash, monies due) and which are held for a short time only; **intangible assets** = assets which have a value, but which cannot be seen (such as goodwill, a patent or a trademark); **liquid assets** = cash, or investments which can be quickly converted into cash; **personal assets** = moveable assets which belong to a person; **tangible assets** = assets which are visible (such as furniture, jewels or cash); **tangible (fixed) assets** = assets which have a value and actually exist (such as buildings, machines, fittings, etc.); **asset value** = value of a company calculated by adding together all its assets

assign *verb* **(a)** to give a place to someone; *he was assigned a room on the ground floor* **(b)** to give someone a job of work; *she was assigned the job of checking the sales figures*

assist *verb* to help; *the courier assisted the tourists at the customs check point;* **assisted passage** = journey for an immigrant to a foreign country which is partly paid for by the government of that country (to encourage immigration) (NOTE: you assist someone **in** doing something or **to do** something or **with** something)
◊ **assistance** *noun* help; *handicapped travellers may need assistance with their baggage;* **financial assistance** = help in the form of money
◊ **assistant** *noun* person who helps *or* a clerical employee; **shop assistant** = person who serves customers in a shop; **assistant manager** = person who helps a manager; **assistant waiter** = commis waiter, a waiter who helps a station waiter

assurance, assure, assurer *see* INSURE

ATB = AUTOMATIC TICKET AND BOARDING PASS

atmosphere *noun* general feeling (at a party, etc.); *the hotel has a very romantic atmosphere, set on the banks of a beautiful mountain lake*

ATOL = AIR TRAVEL ORGANISERS' LICENCE

attach *verb* to fasten *or* to link; *I am attaching a copy of my previous letter; please find attached a copy of my letter of June 24th; the tables are attached to the floor so they cannot move, even if the sea is rough; the bank attaches great importance to the deal*
◊ **attaché** *noun* junior diplomat who does special work in an embassy; **commercial attaché** = diplomat whose job is to promote the commercial interests of his country; **attaché case** = small case for carrying papers and documents

attend *verb* to be present at; *they organized the protest meeting in the kitchen, but only a few of the kitchen staff attended; chairman has asked all managers to attend the meeting*
◊ **attend to** *verb* to give careful thought to (something) and deal with it; *the managing director will attend to your complaint personally; we have brought in experts to attend to the problem of installing the new computer*
◊ **attendant** *noun* **(a)** person (in a museum) who guards the exhibits **(b)** person who is on duty to help customers; **lavatory attendant** = person who is on duty (in a public lavatory)

attention *noun* giving careful thought; *for the attention of the Managing Director; your orders will have our best attention*

attractive *adjective* interesting, which stimulates the senses or the mind; *there are some attractive bargains in weekend breaks; the attractive scenery round the lake makes the hotel very popular with older guests*

aubergine *noun* shiny purple-black fruit of the eggplant *(Solanum melongena),* used as a vegetable (NOTE: also called **eggplant**)

COMMENT: A native of tropical Asia, it is sometimes called by its Indian name 'brinjal'. Aubergines are used in Mediterranean cooking, especially stuffed with meat, or cooked with tomatoes in ratatouille and in moussaka

audience *noun* number of people who are exposed to a piece of advertising

audio-visual (AV) *adjective* referring to a method of teaching using tapes, records, films, etc.; *the hotel offers audio-visual equipment for hire*

audit 1 *noun* examination of the books and accounts of a company; *to carry out the annual audit;* **external audit** *or* **independent audit** = audit carried out by an independent auditor (who is not employed by the company); **internal audit** = audit carried out by a department inside the company; *he is the manager of the internal audit department* **2** *verb* to examine the books and accounts of a company; *to audit the accounts; the books have not yet been audited*

◊ **auditing** *noun* action of examining the books and accounts of a company

◊ **auditor** *noun* person who audits; *the AGM appoints the company's auditors;* **external auditor** = independent person who audits a company's accounts and who is not a member of the staff of the company; **internal auditor** = member of staff who audits a company's accounts; **auditors' report** = report written by a company's auditors after they have examined the accounts of the company (if they are satisfied, the report certifies that, in the opinion of the auditors, the accounts give a 'true and fair' view of the company's financial position)

COMMENT: auditors are appointed by the company's directors and voted by the AGM. In the USA, audited accounts are only required by corporations which are registered with the Stock Exchange Commission, but in the UK all limited companies must provide audited annual accounts

auditorium *noun* huge hall for meetings, concerts, etc. (NOTE: plural is **auditoriums** or **auditoria**)

au gratin *see* GRATIN

auto *noun* car; **auto insurance** = insurance covering a car, its driver and others

autopilot = AUTOMATIC PILOT

automatic *adjective* which works *or* takes place without any person making it happen; **automatic landing equipment** = computerized equipment in an aircraft which allows it to land in bad weather or when visibility is bad; **automatic pilot** = computerized equipment in an aircraft which allows it to fly without intervention from the captain; **automatic telling machine** *or US* **automatic teller machine (ATM)** = machine which gives out money when a special card is inserted and special instructions are given; **automatic ticket and boarding pass (ATB2)** = electronic ticket, which contains information about the passenger and the reservation on a magnetic strip

QUOTE using the new automatic ticket and boarding pass, travellers carrying hand baggage only will be allowed to check themselves in for a flight simply by swiping the card against a magnetic reader before boarding. Trials in Switzerland suggest the entire checking process for hand baggage carriers can be reduced to around 20 seconds
Business Travel
QUOTE airlines and airports have been working towards automated ticket and boarding passes - called ATB2s - for several years, to avoid the problem of airport overcrowding which could become worse as European deregulation stimulates more air travel. As a result, airlines are accelerating the installation of ATB2 technology
Times

autumn *noun* season of the year between the summer and winter; *the airline is offering autumn breaks of two- or three-night stays in the capital; fares tend to go down in the autumn and rise again at Christmas* (NOTE: US English uses **fall** in this meaning)

AV = AUDIO-VISUAL

available *adjective* which can be obtained *or* bought; *available in all branches; item no longer available; items available to order only; funds which are made available for investment in small businesses;* **available capital** = capital which is ready to be used

◊ **availability** *noun* being easily obtained; **offer subject to availability** = the offer is valid only if the goods or services are available

avalanche *noun* sliding of a heavy mass of snow down a mountainside; **avalanche season =** late spring, when increasing temperatures make the snow melt on high mountains, and cause avalanches

average 1 *noun* number calculated by adding together several figures and dividing by the number of figures added; *the average for the last three months or the last three months' average* **2** *adjective* middle (figure); *average sales per restaurant; the average occupancy rates for the last three months; the average increase in prices;* **average room rate =** figure calculated by dividing the total amount of room prices by the total number of rooms; **average achieved room rate =** average price received for room sales in a hotel (the total amount charged for all rooms, each night, divided by the number of rooms occupied)

avocado *noun* pear-shaped green fruit of a tree *(Persea americana)* which is native of South and Central America, although it is cultivated in Israel, Spain, the USA and elsewhere

COMMENT: the fruit has a high protein and fat content, making it very nutritious. It is normally served as an hors d'oeuvre. The fruit is cut in half and the stone removed. The hollow left by the stone can be filled with shrimps, etc., or the fruit can be served with vinaigrette which is poured into the hollow ('avocado vinaigrette')

avoid *verb* to try not to do something; *you must avoid travelling on Friday evenings; if you leave before 3 p.m. you will avoid the rush hour traffic; he should try to avoid fatty food* (NOTE: you avoid something or avoid **doing** something)

away *adverb* not here *or* somewhere else; *the managing director is away on business; my secretary is away sick*

azo dyes *plural noun* artificial colouring additives derived from coal tar, added to food to give it colour

COMMENT: many of the azo dyes (such as tartrazine) provoke allergic reactions; some are believed to be carcinogenic

Bb

Vitamin B complex *noun* group of vitamins which are soluble in water, including folic acid, pyridoxine, riboflavine and many others; **Vitamin B$_1$ =** thiamine, vitamin found in yeast, liver, cereals and pork; **Vitamin B$_2$ =** riboflavine, vitamin found in eggs, liver, green vegetables, milk and yeast; **Vitamin B$_6$ =** pyridoxine, vitamin found in meat, cereals and molasses; **Vitamin B$_{12}$ =** cyanocobalamin, vitamin found in liver and kidney, but not present in vegetables

COMMENT: lack of vitamins from the B complex can have different results: lack of thiamine causes beriberi; lack of riboflavine affects a child's growth; lack of pyridoxine causes convulsions and vomiting in babies; lack of vitamin B$_{12}$ causes anaemia

b. & b. = BED AND BREAKFAST

B hotel *or* **B tariff hotel =** 4-STAR HOTEL

QUOTE an increasing number of business travellers from the US and Europe are becoming budget conscious and are spending less on hotel accommodation and are staying in B tariff hotels. Such hotels usually have the same service and facilities as five-star hotels, except that the rooms may be slightly smaller and the decor may be different
South China Morning Post

baby *noun* very young child; **baby-listening service =** service provided by a hotel, with a small microphone to put over a baby's cot, so that the parents can hear if the baby cries when they are not in the room

◇ **baby-sit** *verb* to look after children while their parents are out

◇ **baby-sitter** *noun* person who baby-sits

◇ **baby-sitting service** *noun* service provided by a hotel, where a baby-sitter comes to the hotel room to look after a baby when the parents are out of the room

bacillus *noun* bacterium shaped like a rod; **Bacillus cereus** = microorganism found in cereals, such as rice (NOTE: plural is **bacilli**)

◇ **bacillary** *adjective* referring to bacillus; **bacillary dysentery** = dysentery caused by the bacillus *Shigella* in contaminated food

back 1 *noun* **(a)** opposite side to the front; *write your address on the back of the envelope; the conditions of sale are printed on the back of the invoice* **(b)** opposite part to the front; *we want two seats at the back of the plane; if you sit at the back of the bus, you may feel travel sick; they complained that they couldn't see the stage from the back of the stalls;* **back cabin** = section of seating in the back part of a plane (usually reserved for Economy class) **(c) back-of-the-house services** = services which are in the back part of a hotel, such as servicing the restaurants and bars, as opposed to front-of-the-house services; **back-of-the-house staff** = staff who work in the back of a hotel, such as kitchen staff, cleaners, etc., as opposed to front-of-the-house staff **(d) back-to-back arrangement** = arranging travel or hotel accommodation so that when one group arrives they occupy the same rooms as the previous group, who leave by the same plane **2** *adjective* referring to the past; **back pay** = salary which has not been paid; *I am owed £500 in back pay;* **back payment** = paying money which is owed; *the salesmen are claiming for back payment of unpaid commission;* **back payments** = payments which are due; **back rent** = rent owed; *the company owes £100,000 in back rent* **3** *verb* **(a)** to drive a car backwards; *he backed into the parking space; she backed into the car behind* **(b)** to **back a bill** = to sign a bill promising to pay it if the person it is addressed to is not able to do so

◇ **backdate** *verb* to put an earlier date on a cheque *or* an invoice; *backdate your invoice to April 1st; the pay increase is backdated to January 1st*

◇ **background** *noun* **(a)** past work *or* experience; *his background is in the fast-food business; the company is looking for someone with a background of success in the international hotel field; she has a travel industry background; what is his background or do you know anything about his background?* **(b)** past details; *he*

explained the background of the claim for compensation; I know the contractual situation as it stands now, but can you fill in the background details?*

◇ **backhander** *noun* (*informal*) bribe *or* money given to someone to get him to help you

◇ **backlog** *noun* work (such as orders *or* letters) which has piled up waiting to be done; *the airport is trying to cope with a backlog of flights held up by fog; my secretary can't cope with the backlog of paperwork*

◇ **back out** *verb* **(a)** to stop being part of a deal *or* an agreement; *the bank backed out of the contract; we had to cancel the project when our German partners backed out* **(b)** to drive a car backwards out of a place; *he backed out of the garage*

◇ **backpack** *noun* bag carried on a walker's back

◇ **backpacker** *noun* person who goes backpacking

◇ **backpacking** *noun* going for a long walk, carrying your clothes, food, tent, etc., in a backpack

◇ **back up** *verb* to support *or* to help; *he brought along a file of documents to back up his claim; the waiter said the manager had refused to back him up in his argument with the customer*

◇ **backup 1** *adjective* supporting *or* helping; *we offer a free backup service to customers; after a series of sales tours by representatives, the sales director sends backup letters to all the contacts;* **backup copy** = copy of a computer disk to be kept in case the original disk is damaged or lost **2** *noun* US delay in a flight caused by too much air traffic

bacon *noun* salt meat from the pig, which is sliced into thin strips and cooked before serving; **bacon and eggs** = fried bacon and fried eggs (served at breakfast)

COMMENT: there are various types of bacon: back bacon (which has more meat) and streaky bacon (which has more fat); bacon can be smoked (that is, cured in smoke) or unsmoked (also called 'green' in GB English). In the USA, bacon is sliced more thinly and cooked more than in the UK and is called 'crispy bacon'. Bacon is mainly eaten at breakfast, but it is often used in sandwiches (such as bacon, lettuce and tomato or BLT)

bacteria *plural noun* submicroscopic organisms which help in the decomposition of organic matter, some of which are permanently present in the intestines of animals and can break down food tissue; many of them can cause disease (NOTE: the singular is **bacterium**)

COMMENT: bacteria can be shaped like rods (bacilli), like balls (cocci) or have a spiral form (such as spirochaetes). Bacteria, especially bacilli and spirochaetes, can move and reproduce very rapidly

◊ **bacterial** *adjective* referring to bacteria *or* caused by bacteria; **bacterial contamination** = state of something (such as water *or* food) which has been contaminated by bacteria

◊ **bactericidal** *adjective* (substance) which destroys bacteria

◊ **bactericide** *noun* substance which destroys bacteria

◊ **bacteriology** *noun* scientific study of bacteria

◊ **bacteriophage** *noun* virus which affects bacteria

bag *noun* **(a)** light container made of paper, cloth, or plastic, used for carrying items; *he brought his lunch in a Harrods bag; we gave away 5,000 plastic bags at the exhibition;* **shopping bag** = bag used for carrying shopping **(b)** soft case for carrying clothes when travelling; *he left his bag in the cabin; the porter will carry your bags to the room;* **sponge bag** = small bag for carrying soap, flannel, toothbrush and other toilet articles **(c)** **sick bag** = strong paper bag provided in the pocket in front of each seat on planes or hovercraft, so that passengers suffering from airsickness can vomit without leaving their seats

baggage *noun* suitcases or bags for carrying clothes when travelling; **accompanied baggage** = baggage belonging to a passenger who is travelling in the same plane; **unaccompanied baggage** = baggage which is not accompanied by a passenger; **(free) baggage allowance** = weight of baggage which an air passenger is allowed to take free when he travels (usually 30kg for first class or business class passengers and 20kg for tourist class); **baggage check** = (i) examination of passengers' baggage for security reasons; (ii) receipt given to a passenger for baggage which has been checked in (it is usually stapled to the passenger's ticket counterfoil); **baggage**

check-in = place where air passengers have their bags and suitcases weighed and hand them over to be put on the aircraft; **baggage claim** = place in an airport where baggage comes off the plane onto a carousel to be claimed by the passengers; **baggage handler** = person who works at an airport, taking baggage off or putting it on planes; **baggage label** = label attached to a piece of baggage, with the owner's name and address on it; **baggage lift** = special lift for taking guests' baggage up to different floors of a hotel; **baggage lockers** = series of small cupboards in an airport, railway station, etc., where passengers can leave baggage locked away safely; **baggage rack** = device above the seats in a train for holding baggage; *US* **baggage room** = room at a railway station, coach station, ferry terminal or airport where suitcases, bags and parcels can be left (NOTE: GB English is **left luggage office**) **baggage stand** = special low bench for holding baggage in a hotel room; **baggage tag** = BAGGAGE LABEL; **baggage trolley** = trolley at an airport, railway station, ferry terminal, etc. on which passengers can put their baggage (NOTE: no plural; to show one suitcase, etc., you can say **a piece of baggage.** Note also that British English uses **luggage** more often than **baggage**)

COMMENT: certain items are not allowed onto aircraft, and should not be packed in baggage. These include ammunition, explosives, radioactive substances, flammable liquids, compressed gases. Battery-driven appliances (such as clocks) should be declared when checking in

baguette *see* BREAD

bain-marie *noun* pan holding hot water into which another vessel containing food to be cooked or heated is placed (NOTE: plural is **bains-marie**)

COMMENT: in a large kitchen, bains-marie are used to keep food hot: items of cooked food are placed in trays over hot water

baize *noun* soft felt cloth, usually green

COMMENT: baize is used to cover restaurant tables to prevent the tablecloth from slipping off, to cover card tables or billiard tables, and to cover the door leading from a kitchen into a dining room to prevent the door from banging

bake *verb* to cook in an oven; *to cook the dish, bake in a hot oven for 30 minutes; pizzas are baked in a pizza oven;* **to bake blind** = to cook a pastry case without a filling by covering it with paper and weighting it down with dried peas; **baked Alaska** = dessert made of ice cream covered with meringue, cooked in an oven for a short time to cook the meringue, eaten before the ice cream melts; **baked beans** = haricot beans, cooked in a tomato sauce (traditionally cooked in the oven with pieces of pork and molasses, and called 'Boston baked beans', but more generally available in cans); **baked potato** = potato cooked 'in its jacket', that is, is baked in an oven without being peeled, then served cut open, with butter or various fillings, such as cheese, chopped ham, baked beans, chilli, etc.

◊ **baker** *noun* person who makes bread

◊ **bakery** *or* **baker's shop** *noun* shop where bread is baked and sold

◊ **baking** *noun* cooking (in an oven); **baking apple** = sour apple which is used for cooking with sugar; **baking dish** = fireproof dish which can be put in the oven; **baking sheet** *or* **tray** = flat sheet of metal for baking biscuits, etc. on

baklava *noun* Turkish or Greek dessert, of thin pastry filled chopped nuts, covered with honey

balance sheet *noun* statement of the financial position of a company at a particular time, such as the end of the financial year or the end of a quarter, showing the company's assets and liabilities; *the company balance sheet for 1993 shows a substantial loss; the accountant has prepared the balance sheet for the first half-year*

COMMENT: the balance sheet shows the state of a company's finances at a certain date; the profit and loss account shows the movements which have taken place since the end of the previous accounting period. A balance sheet must balance, with the basic equation that assets (i.e. what the company owns, including money owed to the company) must equal liabilities (i.e. what the company owes to its creditors) plus capital (i.e. what it owes to its shareholders). A

balance sheet can be drawn up either in the horizontal form, with liabilities and capital on the left-hand side of the page (in the USA, it is the reverse) or in the vertical form, with assets at the top of the page, followed by liabilities, and capital at the bottom. Most are usually drawn up in the vertical format, as opposed to the more old-fashioned horizontal style

balcony *noun* **(a)** open floor area outside a room above the ground floor; *each room has a balcony overlooking the sea; breakfast is served on the balcony* **(b)** upstairs section of a theatre or cinema, with rows of seats above the stalls (NOTE: plural is **balconies)**

ball *noun* formal dance; **ball supper** = supper consisting of many light dishes, served as a continuous buffet during a ball

balloon *noun* large round object which is inflated; **hot-air balloon** = large passenger-carrying balloon inflated with hot air

◊ **ballooning** *noun* sport of racing large passenger-carrying balloons

ballroom *noun* large room for formal dances

bamboo shoots *plural noun* young shoots from the bamboo plant, used in Chinese and Malaysian cooking

banana *noun* long yellow fruit of a large tropical plant *(Musa sapientum)* and its varieties; **banana split** = dessert made of a banana cut lengthwise, with ice cream, cream and chocolate sauce, usually served in a long dish; *see also* PLANTAIN

band *noun* **(a)** group of people who play music; **dance band** = band which plays music for dances **(b)** **rubber band** = thin ring of rubber for attaching things together; *put a band round the filing cards to stop them falling on the floor*

bandage 1 *noun* piece of cloth which is wrapped around a wound or an injured limb; *the waitress put a bandage round his hand* **2** *verb* to wrap a piece of cloth around a wound or an injured limb; *she bandaged his leg; his arm is bandaged up*

banger *noun* GB *(informal)* sausage; **bangers and mash** = grilled sausages and mashed potatoes

bank 1 *noun* **(a)** edge of a river or canal **(b)** business which holds money for its clients, which lends money at interest, and trades generally in money; *he put all his earnings into his bank; I have had a letter from my bank telling me my account is overdrawn; payment was made by a cheque drawn on a Swiss bank* **(c)** the money held by the organizer in a gambling game **2** *verb* to deposit money into a bank or to have an account with a bank; *he banked the cheque as soon as he received it;* **where do you bank?** = where do you have a bank account?; *I bank at or with Barclays*

◊ **bank account** *noun* account which a customer has with a bank, where the customer can deposit and withdraw money; *to open a bank account; to close a bank account; how much money do you have in your bank account? she has £100 in her savings bank account; if you let the balance in your bank account fall below £100, you have to pay bank charges*

◊ **bank book** *noun* book, given by a bank, which shows money which you deposit or withdraw from your savings account

◊ **bank clerk** *noun* person who works in a bank, but not a manager

◊ **bank draft** *noun* order by one bank telling another bank (usually in another country) to pay money to someone

◊ **banker** *noun* person who is in an important position in a bank; **banker's bill** = order by one bank telling another bank (usually in another country) to pay money to someone; **banker's order** = instruction given by a customer asking a bank to make a regular payment; *he pays his subscription by banker's order; see also* STANDING ORDER

◊ **bank giro** *noun GB* method used by clearing banks to transfer money rapidly from one account to another; *you can pay the electricity bill by bank giro or by bank giro credit*

◊ **bank holiday** *noun* in the UK, a weekday which is a public holiday when the banks are closed

COMMENT: bank holidays in England and Wales are: New Year's Day, Good Friday, Easter Monday, the first Monday in May (May Day), the last Monday in May (Spring Bank Holiday), the last Monday in August (Summer Bank Holiday), Christmas Day and Boxing Day (December 26th). In Scotland, the first Monday in August and January 2nd is are also Bank Holidays, but Easter Monday and the last Monday in August

are not. In the USA, New Year's Day, 21st January (Martin Luther King Day), February 12th (Lincoln's Birthday), the third Monday in February (Washington's birthday), the last Monday in May (Memorial Day), July 4th (Independence Day), the first Monday in September (Labor Day), the second Monday in October (Columbus Day), 11th November (Veterans' Day), the fourth Thursday in November (Thanksgiving) and Christmas Day are public holidays nationally, although there are other local holidays

◊ **banking** *noun* the business of banks; *US* **banking account** = account which a customer has with a bank; **banking hours** = time when a bank is open for its customers; *you cannot get money out of the bank after banking hours;* **banking services** = services provided by a bank, such as withdrawal of money, cashing cheques, foreign currency exchange; *banking services are available in the departure lounge on the second floor*

◊ **bank manager** *noun* person in charge of a branch of a bank; *he asked his bank manager for a loan*

◊ **bank note** *or* **banknote** *noun* piece of printed paper money; *he pulled out a pile of used bank notes* (NOTE: US English is **bill**)

◊ **bank on** *verb* to count on, to be sure something will happen; *he is banking on getting a loan from his father to set up his restaurant; do not bank on having fine weather in November*

◊ **bank statement** *noun* written statement from a bank showing how much money is in an account and what transactions have been made

banquet *noun* large formal dinner for many people; **banquets manager** = person in a hotel who is responsible for organizing formal functions

◊ **banqueting** *noun* arranging or giving large formal dinners; **banqueting manager** = person in a hotel who is responsible for organizing formal functions; **banqueting room** = room in a hotel where banquets are organized; **banqueting suite** = series of rooms where banquets are organized (a room for people to meet and have drinks before dinner, then a separate dining room)

bar *noun* **(a)** (i) place where you can buy and drink alcohol; (ii) long counter in a pub from which drinks are served; *the group met in the bar of the hotel; the bar only opens at 6 p.m.; he was sitting at the bar;* **bar staff** =

people who work in a bar (in a hotel) or behind a bar (in a pub); **bar service** = (i) service in a bar; (ii) system where the customer orders, pays for and collects a drink or food from a bar; **bar trolley** = drinks trolley on an aircraft, with various drinks which are served by stewards or stewardesses; **cash bar** = bar where drinks have to be paid for in cash (at a function, drinks may be provided with the meal as part of the ticket price, but there may also be a cash bar for people who want different or additional drinks) **(b)** small shop, serving one special type of food; **coffee bar** = bar selling coffee, soft drinks and snacks; **oyster bar** = bar serving oysters, white wine, and usually other types of shellfish; **sandwich bar** = small shop where you can buy sandwiches to take away; **snack bar** = small simple restaurant where you can have a meal, usually sitting at a counter

◊ **bar code** *noun* system of lines printed on a product which can be read by a computer to give a reference number or price (NOTE: also called **universal product code (UPC)**)

COMMENT: bar codes are found on most goods and their packages; the width and position of the stripes can be recognized by a bar-code reader and give information about the goods, such as price, stock quantities, etc. Many packaged foods, even fresh foods, are bar-coded to allow quicker data capture in the supermarket

◊ **barmaid** *noun* woman who serves in a bar

◊ **barman** *noun* man who serves in a bar

◊ **barperson** *noun* man or woman who serves in a bar

◊ **bartender** *noun* person (usually a man) who serves in a bar

COMMENT: in the UK the terms 'barman' and 'barmaid' are not used in job advertisements to avoid sex discrimination

barbecue 1 *noun* **(a)** food cooked in the open air, over a charcoal fire; **barbecue sauce** = spicy sauce with tomato, chilli, garlic, used on barbecued meat **(b)** meal *or* party, where the food is cooked on a barbecue; *we held a barbecue for twenty guests* **(c)** metal holder for charcoal over which food is cooked in the open air **2** *verb* to cook food over a barbecue; *barbecued spare ribs; barbecued chicken*

barber *noun* person who cuts men's hair; **barber's** *or US* **barber shop** = shop where men have their hair cut

COMMENT: traditionally, a barber's shop has a red and white pole outside, as an advertisement

bard *verb* to put a strip of fat over meat to prevent it from drying out when cooking (rashers of bacon are often put over the breast of a pheasant when cooking)

bareboat charter *noun* system of chartering a ship where the owner provides only the ship, but not the crew, fuel or insurance

bargain 1 *noun* **(a)** agreement on the price of something; *to make a bargain;* **to drive a hard bargain** = to be a difficult negotiator; **to strike a hard bargain** = to agree a deal which is favourable to you; **it is a bad bargain** = it is not worth the price **(b)** thing which is cheaper than usual; *that car is a (real) bargain at £500;* **bargain hunter** = person who looks for cheap deals **2** *verb* to discuss a price for something; *you will have to bargain with the shopkeeper if you want a discount; they spent two hours bargaining about or over the price* (NOTE: you bargain **with** someone **over** *or* **about** *or* **for** something)

◊ **bargain basement** *noun* underground floor in a shop where goods are sold cheaply; *I'm selling this at a bargain-basement price* = I'm selling this very cheaply

◊ **bargain counter** *noun* counter in a shop where goods are sold cheaply

◊ **bargain offer** *noun* sale of a particular type of goods at a cheap price; *this week's bargain offer - 30% off all carpet prices*

◊ **bargain price** *noun* very cheap price; *these carpets are for sale at a bargain price*

◊ **bargain sale** *noun* sale of all goods in a store at cheap prices

barley *noun* common cereal crop (*Hordeum sativum*), grown in temperate areas; **pearl barley** = grains of barley used in cooking; **barley sugar** = sweet made of boiled sugar, originally flavoured with barley; **barley wine** = very strong beer

COMMENT: barley is grown in colder countries; it is used in the production of beer and whisky; it is also used to make Scotch broth

barometer *noun* instrument for measuring atmospheric pressure, and therefore for forecasting the weather
◊ **barometric** *adjective* referring to a barometer; **barometric pressure** = atmospheric pressure indicated by a barometer

barrel *noun* large round container for liquids; *beer served from the barrel; he bought twenty-five barrels of wine; to sell wine by the barrel*

barrier cream *noun* cream used to prevent damage to the skin from sun

basement *noun* section of a building which is underground; *the central heating boiler is in the basement; see also* BARGAIN BASEMENT

basil *noun* herb *(Ocimum basilicum)* with strongly scented leaves, used especially in Italian cuisine

basin *noun* large bowl; **pudding basin** = bowl used for cooking steamed puddings (such as steak and kidney pudding); *see also* WASH-BASIN, WASH-HAND BASIN

basket *noun* container made of thin pieces of wood *or* metal *or* plastic woven together; *a basket of apples;* **basket meal** = simple meal of fried chicken, sausage, scampi, etc., served in a basket with chips (called 'chicken-in-a-basket', etc.; often part of pub menus); **filing basket** = container kept on a desk for documents which have to be filed; **shopping basket** = basket used for carrying shopping; **wastepaper basket** = container into which paper or pieces of rubbish can be thrown; *see also* WINE BASKET

baste *verb* to spread juices over (meat which is cooking)

bath *noun* **1 (a)** washing the whole body; *he has a cold bath every evening; baths are 200 francs extra;* **mud bath** = therapeutic treatment where a person is covered in hot mud; **to have a bath** *or* **to take a bath** = to wash the whole body in a bath; *see also* BUBBLE BATH, JACUZZI **(b)** large container filled with water to wash the whole body in; *the chambermaid has not cleaned the bath* (NOTE: US English is **bathtub** *or* **tub) (c) public baths** = large (public) building with a swimming pool **2** *verb* to wash the whole body; *she baths twice a day in hot weather*

◊ **bath mat** *noun* small mat to step on as you get out of the bath
◊ **bath oil** *noun* scented oil to put in a bath
◊ **Bath Oliver** *noun* GB kind of round unsweetened biscuit, sometimes served with cheese
◊ **bathrobe** *noun* **(a)** loose coat of towelling worn before or after a bath **(b)** US man's dressing gown
◊ **bathroom** *noun* **(a)** separate room with a bath and hand basin (and usually a toilet); **room with private bathroom** = hotel room with its own bathroom attached; **bathroom fittings** = fittings in a bathroom (such as shower, wash basin, bidet, etc.); **bathroom linen** = towels, etc., which are provided in a bathroom; *guests complained that there was no fresh bathroom linen* **(b)** US toilet; *my daughter wants to go to the bathroom*
◊ **bath salts** *plural noun* scented crystals to put in a bath
◊ **bath towel** *noun* very large towel for drying yourself after a bath
◊ **bathtub** *noun especially* US large container filled with water to wash the whole body in (NOTE: British English uses the word **bath**)

bathe 1 *noun* swim (especially in the sea or in a river); *we went for a bathe before breakfast* **2** *verb* **(a)** to swim **(b)** to wash (a wound) carefully **(c)** US to have a bath
◊ **bather** *noun* person who is swimming; *the beach was crowded with bathers when the shark was sighted*
◊ **bathing** *noun* swimming (in the sea, river or a pool); **bathing cap** = rubber hat worn when swimming to prevent your hair getting wet; **bathing costume** = piece of clothing worn when swimming

batter *noun* thin liquid mixture of flour, eggs and milk, used for making pancakes, coating fish before frying, making toad-in-the-hole, etc.
◊ **battered** *adjective* covered with batter and cooked; *battered prawns*

battery *noun* series of small cages in which thousands of chickens are kept; **battery farming** = system of keeping thousands of chickens in a series of small cages; **battery hen** = chicken which spends its life confined in a small cage

COMMENT: a method of egg production which is very energy-efficient. It is criticized, however, because of the quality of the eggs, the possibility of disease and the polluting substances produced, and also on grounds of cruelty because of the stress caused to the birds. See also FREE-RANGE EGGS

bay *noun* **(a)** fragrant shrub whose leaves are used in cooking **(b)** large rounded inlet in a coast; *the Bay of Biscay; see also* DUBLIN BAY

BBQ = BARBECUE

beach *noun* area of sand by the edge of the sea; *they spent the afternoon on the beach; you can hire parasols on the beach; there are lifeguards on duty at the beach;* **beach chalet** = small wooden holiday home, near or on a beach; **beach hut** = small wooden building on a beach, where you can change, keep deckchairs, etc.; **beach towel** = large towel normally used on the beach; **beach umbrella** = large coloured umbrella to use on a beach

bean *noun* **French beans** *or* **green beans** *or* **string beans** = long thin green vegetable, eaten cooked; **baked beans** = haricot beans, cooked in a tomato sauce (traditionally cooked in the oven with pieces of pork and molasses, and called 'Boston baked beans', but more generally available in cans); **kidney beans** = type of bean with reddish seeds, shaped like kidneys

COMMENT: kidney beans must be cooked thoroughly, as undercooked beans can contain a toxin which causes nausea

beat *verb* **(a)** to win in a fight against someone; *they have beaten their rivals into second place in the package holiday market* **(b) to beat a ban** = to do something which is forbidden by doing it rapidly before the ban is enforced
NOTE: **beating - beat - has beaten**

Beaufort scale *noun* scale (from 0 to 12) used to refer to the strength of wind; *the meteorological office has issued a warning of force 12 winds*

COMMENT: the Beaufort scale was devised in the 18th century by a British admiral. The descriptions of the winds and their speeds in knots are: 0: calm (0 knots); 1: light air (2 knots); 2: light breeze (5 knots); 3: gentle breeze (9 knots); 4: moderate breeze (13 knots); 5: fresh breeze (19 knots); 6: strong breeze (24 knots); 7: near gale (30 knots); 8: gale (37 knots); 9: strong gale (44 knots); 10: storm (52 knots); 11: violent storm (60 knots); 12: hurricane (above 60 knots)

Beaujolais *noun* French red wine from Burgundy, a light wine, which can be drunk cool; **Beaujolais nouveau** = Beaujolais wine which has just been made, sold from November onwards of the year in which the grapes are picked

beauty *noun* state of being beautiful; **beauty parlour** *or* **beauty salon** *or* **beauty shop** = clinic specializing in women's appearance; **beauty spot** = famous beautiful place; *the Lake District has some of the most famous beauty spots in England*

bed *noun* piece of furniture on which you sleep; **single bed** = bed for one person; **double bed** = bed for two people; **twin beds** = two single beds in the same room; **bed, breakfast and evening meal** = tariff in hotels or guesthouses, covering the night's accommodation, breakfast and a meal taken in the evening
◊ **bed and breakfast (b. & b.)** *noun* **(a)** tariff in a hotel or guesthouse, covering a night's lodging and breakfast; *bed and breakfast: £32.00* **(b)** guesthouse or private house, offering accommodation and breakfast; *we got a list of b. & b.'s from the tourist office*
◊ **bedclothes** *noun plural* sheets, blankets, etc., on a bed
◊ **bedcover** *noun* cloth which covers a bed during the daytime
◊ **bedding** *noun* bedclothes (mattress, sheets, pillows, etc.); *bedding is provided at extra cost; visitors are requested to bring their own bedding*
◊ **bednight** *noun* one night's stay in a hotel (for administrative purposes)

QUOTE the group is offering regional corporate deals, based on a minimum number of bednights: for example, 100 bednights would trigger a discount of a minimum of 10%, while over 1,000 bednights could mean up to a 45% discount
Business Traveller

◊ **bedroom** *noun* room with a bed, in which someone sleeps; room for a traveller in a hotel; *a 42-bedroom hotel*
◊ **bedroomed** *adjective* with a certain number of bedrooms; *a 42-bedroomed hotel*
◊ **bedside** *noun* space at the side of a bed; **bedside lamp** = lamp next to a bed; **bedside table** = table next to a bed

◊ **bed-sitting room** or **bed-sitter** or **bed-sit** noun bedroom and living room combined

◊ **bedspread** noun decorative cloth to put over a bed

◊ **bedstead** noun solid frame of a bed

beef noun meat from a cow or a bull; **corned beef** = beef which has been salted and usually canned

◊ **beefburger** noun round, flat cake of minced beef, grilled or fried and usually served in a toasted bread roll

◊ **beefsteak** noun old name for a steak; **beefsteak tomato** = large fleshy variety of tomato suitable for stuffing

beer noun **(a)** alcoholic drink made from grain (barley, rice, etc.) and water; *she asked room service for a bottle of beer; he drank a glass of beer* **(b)** a glass of beer; *two beers, please; see also* DRAUGHT, REAL ALE

COMMENT: in Great Britain, the most popular beers are 'bitter' and 'lager'. 'Lager' is sold cold, but 'bitter' is served slightly cooler than room temperature. In Australia and the USA, all beers are served cold. Beer is either served from a bottle (or a can if you are buying it to drink away from the place where you bought it), but in pubs, can be served direct from the barrel. This is called 'draught beer'. In Great Britain, draught beer is sold in a glass mug (with a handle) or in a tall straight glass. Bottled beer is usually served in a goblet (i.e. a glass with a stem)

beet noun usually US = BEETROOT

beetle noun insect of the order Coleoptera, with hard covers on the wings; **black beetle** = cockroach, insect of the order Dictyoptera, a common household pest

beetroot noun GB vegetable with a dark red root, often eaten cooked as salad, or pickled with vinegar

COMMENT: in Russian cuisine, beetroot is the main ingredient of borshtch

behave verb to act

◊ **behaviour** US **behavior** noun conduct or way of acting; *guests complained about the behaviour of young men in the bar on Saturday night*

bell noun metal cup-shaped object which makes a ringing sound when hit; mechanism to make a ringing sound; **night bell** = bell outside a hotel, which you ring to wake up the porter during the night, after the front door has been locked

◊ **bellboy** US **bellhop** noun messenger boy employed in a hotel

◊ **bell captain** noun US person in charge of messengers in a hotel

◊ **bellman** noun US = BELLHOP

◊ **bellpush** noun button which rings a bell when pushed

below-the-line advertising noun advertising which is not paid for (such as work by staff manning an exhibition) and for which no commission is paid to the advertising agency

benzene noun simple aromatic hydrocarbon, produced from coal tar, and very carcinogenic; **benzene hexachloride (BHC) ($C_6H_6Cl_6$)** = white or yellow powder containing lindane, used as an insecticide as a dust or spray against pea and bean weevil, and as a seed dressing against wireworm

berry noun small fleshy seed-bearing fruit of a bush; there are usually many seeds in the same fruit, and the seeds are enclosed in a pulp (as in a tomato or gooseberry) (NOTE: plural is **berries**)

COMMENT: very many berries are used in cooking, or can be eaten raw. See also BLUEBERRY, RASPBERRY, STRAWBERRY

berth 1 noun **(a)** place in a harbour where a ship can tie up; *there are six ferry berths at Dover* **(b)** bed (on a ship or a train); **upper berth** = top bed; **lower berth** = bottom bed; **two-berth cabin** = cabin with two beds, usually one above the other **2** verb to tie up at a berth; *the ship will berth at Rotterdam on Wednesday*

best-before date noun date stamped on the label of a food product, which is the last date on which the product is guaranteed to be of good quality; *similar to* SELL-BY DATE, USE-BY DATE

best end noun cut of meat, especially lamb, taken from the neck and formed of a series of chops joined together; *see also* CROWN ROAST, GUARD OF HONOUR, RACK OF LAMB

better *adjective* very good compared with something else; *this year's results are better than last year's; we will shop around to see if we can get a better price*

beurre manié *French (meaning 'kneaded butter')* mixture of butter and flour, added at the last minute to soups or stews to make them thicken

beverage *noun* drink; **beverage manager** = person in charge of sales of drinks in a hotel; **beverage sales** = turnover from the sale of drinks

beware *verb* **beware of** = watch out for; *'beware of pickpockets!'*

BFL BUSINESS FACILITATED LEASE

bhaji *noun* Indian dish of chopped vegetables in a spicy batter, deep-fried; *onion bhaji*

BHC = BENZENE HEXACHLORIDE

bhindi *noun* okra, as used in Indian cooking; *see also* LADY'S FINGER

BHT = BUTYLATED HYDROXYTOLUENE

bicycle *noun* vehicle with two wheels, which you ride on and pedal with your feet; *bicycles can be hired by the hour or by the day;* bicycle path = special path for bicycles to ride on (either by the side of a road, or as part of the pavement) (NOTE: also called a **bike.** The person who rides a bicycle is a **cyclist.** Note also that to show the difference with a motorcycle, a bicycle is sometimes called a 'push bike')

bidet *noun* low wash-basin for washing the genitals

bike *noun (informal)* bicycle, a vehicle with two wheels, which you ride on and pedal with your feet; **mountain bike** = specially solid bicycle, with thick tyres, used for country cycling; **push bike** *see note at* BICYCLE
◊ **biker** *noun* person who rides a motorcycle
◊ **biking** *noun* going on a bicycle; *they went for a biking holiday in Holland*

bilberry *see* BLUEBERRY

Bilharzia *noun* Schistosoma, genus of fluke which enters the patient's bloodstream and causes bilharziasis

◊ **bilharziasis** *noun* schistosomiasis, tropical disease caused by flukes in the intestine or bladder (NOTE: although strictly speaking, **Bilharzia** is the name of the fluke, it is also generally used for the name of the disease)

COMMENT: the disease is found in certain parts of Africa, Brazil and China and can be caught from bathing in rivers and lakes. The larvae of the fluke enter the skin through the feet and lodge in the walls of the intestine or bladder. They are passed out of the body in stools or urine and return to water, where they lodge and develop in the water snail, the secondary host, before going back into humans. Patients suffer from fever and anaemia

bill 1 *noun* **(a)** written list of charges to be paid; *the receptionist printed out the bill; does the bill include VAT? the bill is made out to Smith Ltd; the caterer sent in his bill; he left the hotel without paying his bill;* **to foot the bill** = to pay the costs; *the airline will foot the bill for the hotel* **(b)** list of charges in a restaurant; *can I have the bill please? the bill comes to £20 including service; does the bill include service? the waiter has added 10% to the bill for service* **(c)** bill of fare = menu **(d)** *US* piece of printed paper money; *a five-dollar bill or a $5 bill* (NOTE: GB English is **note**) **2** *verb* to present a bill to someone so that it can be paid; *the tour operators billed him for the extra items*
◊ **bill of exchange** *noun* document signed by the person authorizing it, which tells another to pay money unconditionally to a named person on a certain date (usually used in payments in foreign currency)

COMMENT: a bill of exchange is a document raised by a seller and signed by a purchaser, stating that the purchaser accepts that he owes the seller money, and promises to pay it at a later date. The person raising the bill is the 'drawer', the person who accepts it is the 'drawee'. The seller can then sell the bill at a discount to raise cash. This is called a 'trade bill'. A bill can also be accepted (i.e. guaranteed) by a bank, and in this case it is called a 'bank bill'

billiards *noun* game involving hitting balls with a long rod on a smooth table covered with green cloth, the object being to hit a white ball so that it sends a ball of another colour into one of the 'pockets' at the edge of the table; **billiard ball** = small hard ball used in the game of billiards; **billiard table** = table on which billiards is played; *see also* POOL, SNOOKER

billion one thousand million (NOTE: in the US it has always meant one thousand million, but in GB it formerly meant one million million, and it is still sometimes used with this meaning. With figures it is usually written **bn: $5bn** say 'five billion dollars')

bin *noun* **(a)** large container; **dustbin** = large container for collecting rubbish (NOTE: US English is **garbage can**) **(b)** section in a warehouse, store or wine cellar; **bin card** = card saying what is stored in the bin (e.g. the type and date of wine)

binder *noun US* letter from an insurance company giving details of an insurance policy and confirming that the policy exists (NOTE: the GB English for this is **cover note**)

binding 1 *adjective* **(a) this contract is binding on both parties** = both parties have to do what the contract says **(b)** which sticks things together; **binding agent** = additive which makes prepared food remain in its proper form and not disintegrate **2** *noun* small belt for attaching boots to skis

biodegradable *adjective* (substance) which can be easily decomposed by organisms such as bacteria or by the effect of sunlight, the sea, etc.; **biodegradable packaging** = boxes, cartons, bottles, etc. which can be decomposed by organisms such as bacteria or by the effect of sunlight, the sea, etc.

◊ **biodegradability** *noun* degree to which a material, packaging, etc. can be decomposed by organisms such as bacteria or by the effect of sunlight, the sea, etc.

◊ **biodegradation** *noun* breaking down of a substance by bacteria

COMMENT: manufacturers are trying to produce more biodegradable products, as the effect of non-biodegradable substances (such as detergents) on the environment can be serious

QUOTE human sewage is a totally biodegradable product, and sea and sunlight will break it down through the natural process of oxidation
Environment Now

biotechnology *noun* use of technology to manipulate and combine different genetic materials to produce living organisms with particular characteristics; *a biotechnology company is developing a range of new pesticides based on naturally occurring toxins; artificial insemination of cattle was one of the first examples of biotechnology*

COMMENT: biotechnology offers great potential to increase farm production and food processing efficiency, to lower food costs, to enhance food quality and safety and to increase international competitiveness

biphenyl (C₆H₅C₆H₅) *noun* white or colourless crystalline substance used as a fungicide, in the production of dyes and as a preservative (E number E230) on the skins of citrus fruit

biscuit *noun* small hard cake, usually sweet; **cheese and biscuits** = cheese served with dry unsweetened biscuits; **water biscuit** = thin, hard, unsweetened biscuit made of flour and water, often served with cheese

bisque *noun* cream soup made with shellfish; *lobster bisque*

bitter 1 *adjective* not sweet; *this aperitif is very bitter; marmalade is made from bitter oranges* **2** *noun* British beer, made bitter by adding hops; *he asked for a half of bitter; two pints of bitter, please*

◊ **bitters** *noun* sharp-tasting liquid, added to gin and other drinks to make them bitter (also called **Angostura bitters**)

black 1 *adjective* of a very dark colour, the opposite of white; **black coffee** = coffee without milk or cream; **black pudding** = dark sausage made with blood (fried in slices and eaten for breakfast) **2** *verb* to forbid trading in certain goods or with certain suppliers; *three firms were blacked by the government; the union has blacked the hotel chain*

◊ **black beetle** *noun* cockroach, insect of the order Dictyoptera, a common kitchen pest

◊ **blackberry** *noun* small soft black berry, growing on plants with long spines, eaten in jams and pies (the wild berry is also called 'bramble')

◊ **blackboard** *noun* board on a wall which can be written on using white chalk (the opposite of a whiteboard)

◇ **black box** *noun* flight recorder, a device carried in an aircraft which records what happens during a flight, including conversations between pilots and the control tower

◇ **blackcurrant** *noun* cultivated small round black berry *(Ribes)*, eaten cooked in jams and pies, used also in making soft drinks and liqueurs; *blackcurrant yoghurt; a pot of blackcurrant jam; a glass of blackcurrant juice; see also* KIR

◇ **Black Forest** *noun* area of forest in south-west Germany; **Black Forest gâteau** = type of chocolate cake with cream and cherry filling

◇ **black list** *noun* list of goods *or* people *or* companies which have been blacked

◇ **blacklist** *verb* to put goods *or* people *or* a company on a black list; *his firm was blacklisted by the government*

◇ **black market** *noun* buying and selling goods in a way which is not allowed by law (as in a time of rationing); *there is a flourishing black market in secondhand jeans; you can buy gold coins on the black market;* **to pay black-market prices** = to pay high prices to get items which are not easily available

bladder worm *noun* cysticercus, the larva of a tapeworm found in pork, which is enclosed in a cyst, typical of *Taenia*

blade *noun* **(a)** sharp cutting part of a knife (in kitchen knives, the blade is sharpened by rubbing against a rod of rough metal, called a 'steel') **(b)** similar sharp metal strip forming an ice skate

blanch *verb* to cook (vegetables) for a short time in boiling water

> COMMENT: vegetables should be blanched before being frozen. They can also be blanched before frying. Nuts and vegetables can also be blanched to remove their skins

bland *adjective* (food) which is not spicy *or* not irritating *or* not acid; **bland diet** = diet in which contains mainly milk-based foods, boiled vegetables and white meat

blanket *noun* thick covering for a bed; *ask the reception for another blanket if you are cold; stewardesses bring round blankets and pillows on overnight flights*

blast freezing *or* **blast chilling** *noun* method of quick-freezing oddly-shaped food, by subjecting it to a blast of freezing air

blend 1 *noun* mixture (used especially of mixtures of different types of tea) **2** *verb* to mix together; *blend together the melted butter and sugar*

◇ **blender** *noun* kitchen device for mixing different food items together thoroughly

blind 1 *noun* **(a)** covering over a window; *the maid closed the blinds to keep out the sun;* **roller blind** = blind made of a roll of thick cloth, which can be let down to cover a window; **Venetian blind** = blind made of horizontal strips of plastic, wood, etc., which can be opened and shut or raised and lowered by pulling a string **(b) the blind** = people who cannot see **2** *adjective* not able to see

blizzard *noun* heavy snowstorm with strong winds

bloater *noun* dried whole salt herring

block 1 *noun* group of things together; *they booked a block of seats in the middle of the plane;* **block booking** = booking of a series of seats, hotel rooms, etc. at the same time **2** *verb* **to block a room** = to keep a room reserved for someone who has booked it, so as to prevent double-booking

Bloody Mary *noun* cocktail of vodka and tomato juice with ice and Worcester sauce, lemon juice, salt and pepper

bloom *noun* **(a)** powdery substance on the surface of a fruit such as grapes (in fact a form of yeast) **(b)** fine hairy covering on some fruit, such as peaches

blowfly *noun* name for a number of species of fly, such as *Lucila cuprina,* which deposit their eggs in flesh, especially meat

BLT bacon, lettuce and tomato (sandwich)

blueberry *noun* wild berry, found in North America and Europe, eaten raw with sugar and cream, or cooked in pies and jams; *a portion of blueberry pie and whipped cream; two blueberry muffins and coffee, please* (NOTE: also called **bilberry**)

bluebottle *noun* two-winged fly, with a shining blue body, whose maggots live in decomposing flesh

blue-green algae *noun* Cyanophyta, algae found mainly in fresh water

board 1 *noun* **(a)** meals (at a hotel); **board and lodging** *or* **room and board** = meals and a bed for the night; **full board** = special rate for guests staying in a hotel, who take all their meals in the hotel (usually in GB this will include breakfast, morning coffee, lunch, afternoon tea and dinner; also called 'en pension rate'); **half board** = special rate for guests staying at a hotel, who take breakfast and dinner at the hotel, but not lunch (also called 'demi-pension') **(b) to go on board** = to go onto a ship *or* plane *or* train **2** *verb* to go on to a ship *or* plane *or* train; *customs officials boarded the ship in the harbour; the party will board buses at the temple and proceed to the hotel for lunch*

◊ **boarding card** *or* **boarding pass** *noun* card given to passengers who have checked in for a flight to allow them to board the plane; card given to passengers going on board a ship

◊ **boarding house** *noun* small privately-run house where residents pay for accommodation and meals (similar to a guesthouse, but in a boarding house the guests stay longer)

board of directors *noun GB* group of directors elected by the shareholders to run a company; *the bank has two representatives on the board; he sits on the board as a representative of the bank; two directors were removed from the board at the AGM;* **she was asked to join the board** = she was asked to become a director; **board meeting** = meeting of the directors of a company

◊ **boardroom** *noun* room where the directors of a company meet

COMMENT: directors are elected by shareholders at the AGM, though they are usually chosen by the chairman or chief executive. A board will consist of a chairman (who may be non-executive), a chief executive or managing director, and a series of specialist directors in charge of various activities of the company (such as a finance director, production director or sales director). The company secretary will attend board meetings, but need not be a director. Apart from the executive directors, who are in fact employees of the company, there may be several non-executive directors, appointed either for their expertise and contacts, or as representatives of important shareholders such as banks

boast *verb* to possess something, and be proud of it; *the town boasts an 18-hole golf course*

boat *noun* ship; *cargo boat; passenger boat; we took the night boat to Belgium; boats for Greece leave every morning;* **rowing boat** *or US* **rowboat** = small boat, which can be made to go forward using oars; **sailing boat** *or US* **sailboat** = boat which uses mainly sails to travel

◊ **boating** *noun* going in small boats for pleasure, especially rowing or sailing; *a boating holiday on the Norfolk Broads*

body *noun* the main part of an aircraft

◊ **-bodied** *suffix* with a certain type of body; **narrow-bodied aircraft** = aircraft with a narrow body (less than 5 metres wide); **wide-bodied aircraft** = aircraft with a body wider than 5 metres (such as the Airbus or a Boeing 747)

boil *verb* **(a)** to heat water until it reaches 100°C; *you must boil the water or you must let the water boil before making tea; they recommend you to boil the tap water before drinking it* **(b)** to cook by putting in boiling water; *do you want boiled potatoes or chips with your steak?; the cabbage has been boiled too long; I want my eggs boiled for three minutes;* **hard-boiled egg** = egg which has cooked in boiling water until the yolk and white are set; **soft-boiled egg** = egg which has been cooked in boiling water for a short time so that the yolk is hot, but still liquid; **boiling chicken** *or* **boiling fowl** = chicken which is older and tougher and needs to be boiled to make it tender; **boiling pan** = large container used in a kitchen for boiling large quantities of food, and for making soup

◊ **boiler** *noun* piece of kitchen equipment, which heats water for making hot drinks (also providing steam)

bolster *noun* **(a)** long thick pillow, which is as wide as a double bed **(b)** thick round part of a knife, linking the blade to the handle

bond 1 *noun* paper showing that money has been deposited; **to post a bond** = to deposit money with an organization, as a form of surety; *the company was required to post a bond with the ABTA* **2** *verb* to deposit money with an organization as surety against potential future loss; *the travel centre was bonded through the Association of British Travel Agents*

bone 1 *noun* hard piece inside an animal's body; **off the bone** = (meat *or* fish) with the bones removed **2** *verb* to take the bones out of (a chicken, etc.) (NOTE: for fish, it is more usual to say 'to fillet')

book 1 *noun* **(a)** set of sheets of paper attached together; **account book** = book which records sales and purchases; **cash book** = record of cash; **order book** = record of orders; **purchase book** = records of purchases; **sales book** = records of sales; **book sales** = sales as recorded in the sales book; **book value** = value as recorded in the company's books **(b) bank book** = book given by a bank, which shows money which you deposit or withdraw from a savings account; **cheque book** = booklet of new cheques; **phone book** *or* **telephone book** = book which lists names of people and businesses in alphabetical order with their telephone numbers and addresses; *he looked up the number of the company in the phone book* **2** *verb* to order *or* to reserve something; *to book a room in a hotel or a table at a restaurant or a ticket on a plane; I booked a table for 7.45; he booked a ticket through to Cairo;* **to book someone into a hotel** *or* **onto a flight** = to order a room *or* a plane ticket for someone; *he was booked on the 09.00 flight to Zurich;* **the hotel** *or* **the flight is fully booked** *or* **is booked up** = all the rooms *or* seats are reserved; *the restaurant is booked up over the Christmas period;* **to book someone in** = to register someone when he arrives at a hotel; **to book someone out** = to deal with the paperwork when someone leaves a hotel, presenting the bill and getting it paid, etc.; *see also* DOUBLE-BOOK

◊ **booking** *noun* act of ordering a room *or* a seat *or* a table; *hotel bookings have fallen since the end of the tourist season;* **to make a booking** = to reserve a room *or* a seat *or* a table, etc.; *we tried to make a booking for the week beginning May 1st, but the hotel was full;* **booking charge** *or* **booking fee** = money paid to an agency for their services in addition to the cost of the ticket when you buy a ticket through them; **booking clerk** = person who sells tickets in a booking office; **booking form** = form to be filled in when making a booking; **booking office** = office where you can book seats at a theatre *or* tickets for the railway; **block booking** = booking of a series of seats, hotel rooms, etc. at the same time; **to confirm a booking** = to say that a booking is certain; **telephone booking** = booking (of a room in a hotel, a table in a restaurant, etc.) made by phone; *see also* DOUBLE-BOOKING

◊ **book-keeping** *noun* keeping of the financial records of a company *or* an organization

◊ **booklet** *noun* small book with a paper cover

◊ **bookstall** *noun* small open bookshop (as in a railway station)

◊ **book up** *verb* to fill all the rooms in a hotel, all the tables in a restaurant, all the seats in a theatre

booth *noun* **(a)** small place for one person to stand or sit; **telephone booth** = small cabin for a public telephone; **ticket booth** = small cabin out of doors where entrance tickets, theatre tickets, bus tickets, etc. are sold **(b)** *US* separate section of an exhibition or commercial fair where a company exhibits its products or services (NOTE: the GB English for this is **stand)**

boracic acid *or* **boric acid ($H_3 BO_3$)** *noun* soluble white powder used as a general disinfectant

◊ **borax** *noun* white powder used as a household cleaner and disinfectant

Bordeaux *noun* wine from the west of France (NOTE: there are both red and white Bordeaux wines; red Bordeaux wine is also called **claret)**

border *noun* frontier, the line between two independent countries; **border crossing** = place on the border between two countries where people can cross and where there are passport controls and customs posts

borshtch *noun* Russian soup, made with beetroot, other vegetables and small pieces of meat or sausage; it is eaten either cold or hot, with sour cream

botanical gardens *noun* gardens which are set up for scientific study and display of plants

Botrytis *noun* fungal disease affecting plants and fruit, especially grapes

bottle 1 *noun* container for liquids, with a narrow neck, made of glass or plastic; *a half-bottle of wine is included in the set menu; can I have a bottle of mineral water,* *please; she drank three bottles of Coca Cola; he bought his wife a bottle of perfume in the duty-free shop* **2** *verb* to keep in a bottle; to preserve (food) by heating it inside a glass jar with a suction cap; **bottled beer** = beer in a bottle, as opposed to beer in a can, or draught beer

> COMMENT: wine bottles have distinctive shapes. Burgundy, Beaujolais and Loire wines have bottles with tapered necks and wide bodies; Bordeaux wine bottles have shoulders and straight sides. German wine bottles have long tapering necks and taller, thinner bodies than French bottles

bottled water *noun* water sold in bottles (as opposed to tap water)
◊ **bottleneck** *noun* narrow road (where traffic often gets jammed)
◊ **bottle opener** *noun* device for opening bottles

botulism *noun* type of food poisoning caused by a toxin of *Clostridium botulinum* in badly canned or preserved food

> COMMENT: the symptoms include paralysis of the muscles, vomiting and hallucinations. Botulism is often fatal

bouillabaisse *noun* French fish soup, flavoured with olive oil and saffron

bouncer *noun* man at the door of a club, whose job it is to prevent non-members or other unwanted guests from entering

bound for *adjective* going towards; *a ship bound for India*

bouquet garni *French noun* bundle of herbs, used to flavour soups and stews (usually formed of thyme, parsley and bay leaves)

bourbon *noun US* corn whisky

boutique *noun* small specialized shop, especially for fashionable clothes; section of a department store selling fashionable clothes; *a jeans boutique; a ski boutique*

bovine *adjective* referring to cattle
◊ **bovine somatotropin (BST)** *noun* natural hormone found in cows, which has been produced artificially by genetic engineering; it is used to increase milk yields and is said to increase them by

between 12% and 20%. It is not licensed for use in the UK, but is being used in trials

> QUOTE the USA plans to approve the use of BST. The EC is uncertain and in making its decision will need to consider 1) milk surpluses; 2) that BST use will favour large-scale dairy operations over the small farmers; 3) possible consumer opposition; 4) US trade retaliation; 5) BST's effects on animal health
> *New Scientist*

◊ **bovine spongiform encephalopathy (BSE)** *noun* fatal disease of cattle, affecting the nervous system (NOTE: also called **mad cow disease)**

> QUOTE BSE first appeared on English dairy farms in 1987. By December, 1988, 1,677 cattle had been slaughtered after contracting the infection. BSE is a new addition to a group of animal viruses known for about 200 years. The similarity between BSE and scrapie suggests that scrapie has been transmitted from sheep to cattle. Processed sheep carcasses, offal and heads are commonly fed to cattle.
> *Guardian*

bowl *noun* container made of china, glass, plastic, wood, etc., for holding food or liquids; *there was a bowl of fruit in the room with the compliments of the management; she only had a bowl of muesli for breakfast*

box *noun* **(a)** cardboard *or* wood *or* plastic container; *the goods were sent in thin cardboard boxes; the watches are prepacked in plastic display boxes;* **box file** = file (for papers) made like a box **(b) box number** = reference number used when asking for mail to be sent to a post office or when asking for replies to an advertisement to be sent to the newspaper's offices; *please reply to Box No. 209; our address is: P.O. Box 74209, Edinburgh* **(c)** call box = outdoor telephone kiosk; **cash box** = metal box for keeping cash in; **letter box** *or* **mail box** = (i) place where incoming mail is put; (ii) public box into which mail is put to be collected and delivered; **box office** = office at a theatre or cinema where tickets can be bought **(d)** special section in a theatre, with chairs for two or three spectators

◊ **boxed** *adjective* put in a box *or* sold in a box; **boxed set** = set of items sold together in a box; *I bought him a boxed set of Beethoven's symphonies*

BR = BRITISH RAIL

brace *noun (of game birds)* a pair; **a brace of pheasant** = a male and female bird sold together

◊ **brace position** *noun* position for an emergency landing, where the passenger sits bent forward, with the hands behind the head

braise *verb* to cook (meat or vegetables) in a covered pot with very little liquid; *braised beef and onions*

bramble *noun* wild blackberry *(Rubus fruticosus)*, with edible black fruits; **bramble jelly** = jam made with blackberries

Bramley's seedling *noun* a common variety of cooking apple

bran *noun* outside covering of the wheat seed, removed when making white flour, but an important source of roughage and some vitamin B; *sprinkle a spoonful of bran onto the stew to increase the fibre content*

branch 1 *noun* local office of a bank or large business; local shop of a large chain of shops; *the bank or the store has branches in most towns in the south of the country; the insurance company has closed its branches in South America; he is the manager of our local branch of Tesco; we have decided to open a branch office in Chicago; the manager of our branch in Lagos or of our Lagos branch;* **branch manager** = person in charge of an office of a company **2** *verb* **to branch out** = to start a new, but usually related, type of business; *from selling train tickets, the company branched out into package holidays*

brandy *noun* **(a)** strong alcohol distilled from wine; **brandy sour** = cocktail of brandy, lemon juice and sugar **(b)** glass of this alcohol; *he ordered three brandies and a port* **(c) brandy snap** = thin, rolled biscuit, flavoured with ginger

COMMENT: Brandy is made in most wine-producing countries, such as Spain and Greece. Brandy from the Bordeaux region of France is called 'cognac'; that from south-west France is called 'armagnac'. Brandy made in Burgundy is called 'marc de bourgogne'. In Germany, brandy is called 'Brandwein'

brass *noun* **(a)** yellow metal made from copper and zinc **(b)** musical instruments made of brass; *a brass band* **(c)** *(in church)* memorial plate made of brass

◊ **brass rubbing** *noun* reproduction of a brass memorial plate by covering it with paper and rubbing the paper with dark wax

brasserie *French noun (meaning 'brewery')* used as a name for a continental-style cafe

brat pan *noun* cooking pan (for stewing, braising, poaching, etc.), which can be tilted to drain off liquid

brawn *noun* chopped meat mixed with jelly to form a loaf

brazil (nut) *noun* hard nut from a tropical tree *Bertholletia*

bread *noun* food made from flour, water, a little fat or oil, and usually a raising agent (either yeast or soda), then cooked in an oven; some breads are made without raising agents; **bread and butter** = slices of bread spread with butter; **bread sauce** = sauce made from white breadcrumbs, butter and milk, flavoured with onion, served hot as an accompaniment to roast chicken or turkey; **loaf of bread** = large single piece of bread, which is cut into slices before being eaten; **slice of bread** = thin piece cut from a loaf; **sliced bread** = loaf of bread which has already been sliced mechanically before it is sold; **brown bread** = bread made from less refined brown flour; **French bread** = bread in the form of a long thin stick (in France, called 'baguette'); **pitta bread** = flat white unleavened bread, served with Greek and Turkish food; **unleavened bread** = bread made without using a raising agent such as yeast (made in Mediterranean countries, and in India and Pakistan); **white bread** = bread made from refined white flour; **wholemeal bread** *or US* **wholewheat bread** = bread made from wholemeal flour

◊ **breadcrumbs** *plural noun* dried bread, crushed into powder, used to cover fish or meat before frying

◊ **breaded** *adjective* covered with breadcrumbs before cooking; *breaded escalope of veal*

◊ **breadfruit** *noun* starchy fruit of a tree *(Artocarpus communis)* grown in the Pacific Islands. The fruit is used as a vegetable

◊ **bread roll** *noun* small loaf of bread (offered to the guests by the commis waiter while they are studying the menu)

COMMENT: most British bread is white (made from refined flour), but brown bread, or wholemeal bread, is becoming more and more popular

break 1 *noun* short space of time, when you can rest; *she typed for two hours without a break;* **coffee break** *or* **tea break** = rest time during work when the workers can drink coffee or tea; **city break** = short holiday in a large city (usually a two- or three-day stay, over a weekend) at a specially low tariff; **weekend break** = short holiday (two or three nights) over a weekend at a specially low tariff **2** *verb* **(a)** to fail to carry out the duties of a contract; *the company has broken the contract or the agreement;* **to break an engagement to do something** = not to do what has been agreed **(b)** to stop doing something for a time; **to break one's journey** = to stop travelling and pass some time in one place before going on; *they broke their journey in Bombay, before flying on to Hong Kong*
NOTE: **breaking - broke - has broken**

◊ **breakages** *plural noun* broken items; *customers are expected to pay for breakages*

◊ **break down** *verb* **(a)** to stop working because of mechanical failure; *the baggage carousel has broken down; what do you do when your lift breaks down?; the visitors complained when the central air-conditioning system broke down* **(b)** to show all the items in a total list of costs *or* expenditure; *we broke the expenditure down into hotel, travel and entertainment costs; can you break down this invoice into travel costs and extras?*

◊ **breakdown** *noun* **(a)** stopping work because of mechanical failure; *we cannot communicate with our Nigerian office because of the breakdown of the telex lines; they are trying to repair a breakdown in the refrigerating system* **(b)** showing details item by item; *give me a breakdown of the travel costs*

break even *verb* to balance costs and receipts, but not make a profit; *last year the company only just broke even; we broke even in our first two months of trading*

◊ **breakeven point** *noun* point at which sales cover costs, but do not show a profit

breakfast (a) *noun* first meal of a day; **continental breakfast** = light breakfast of coffee, chocolate or tea, with rolls, croissants or bread; **(full) English breakfast** = meal of cereals, bacon, eggs, toast and marmalade, served with tea or coffee (often served as a buffet in motels and hotel chains); **breakfast room** = special room where breakfast is served **(b)** **wedding breakfast** = lunch served after a wedding (a full meal, which can take the form of a

buffet, at the end of which speeches are made and the wedding cake is cut)

COMMENT: a traditional 'full English breakfast' may include cereals, porridge, or stewed fruit (such as prunes), grilled fish (such as kippers), bacon and eggs, sausages, kidneys, fried or grilled tomatoes or mushrooms and fried bread, followed by toast and marmalade and tea or coffee

breast *noun* meat from the chest part of a bird or animal; *breast of chicken; do you want a wing or a slice of breast?*

breathe *verb* **to let the wine breathe** = to take the cork out of a bottle of red wine some time before it is to be drunk

brew 1 *noun* liquid which has been brewed **2** *verb* **(a)** to make beer **(b)** *(also, humorously)* to make tea

◊ **brewery** *noun* place where beer is made

bridge *noun* **(a)** construction to take a road or railway across a river or road or railway line **(b)** top part of a ship where a captain stands **(c)** type of card game for four people

bridlepath *or* **bridleway** *noun* track in the country which can be used by walkers or by people on horseback

briefcase *noun* flat case for carrying papers and documents; *he put all the files into his briefcase*

brigade *noun* group of people working together in a kitchen or restaurant

COMMENT: a kitchen brigade will be made up of the chef de cuisine, sous-chef, various specialized chefs and commis chefs. A restaurant brigade will be formed of the head waiter or maître d'hôtel, station waiters, wine waiters and assistant or commis waiters

bright *adjective* clear and sunny (weather); *the will be bright intervals during the afternoon*

brine *noun* solution of salt in water, used for preserving food

COMMENT: some meat, such as bacon, is cured by soaking in brine; some types of pickles are preserved by cooking in brine; some foodstuffs are preserved in brine in jars

brinjal *noun* Indian name for aubergine; *brinjal pickle*

brisket *noun* beef from the breast of an animal

brisling *noun* small sea fish, like a sardine

British Rail (BR) national system of railways in Great Britain

British Summer Time (BST) system of putting the clocks forward in Britain one hour in summer to provide extra daylight in the evening

British Tourist Authority (BTA) *noun* government organization which is responsible for promoting tourism in Great Britain as a whole (separate boards promote tourism in England, Scotland, Wales and Northern Ireland)

broadcast 1 *noun* radio or television programme; **outside broadcast** = radio or television programme recorded in the open air, not in a studio **2** *verb* to send out by radio or television; *they broadcast an urgent storm warning*

brochure *noun* publicity booklet; *we sent off for a brochure about holidays in Greece or about ferry services*

broil *verb especially US* to grill
◊ **broiler** *noun* **(a)** chicken which is young and tender and may be cooked by grilling **(b)** *US* pan *or* tray for grilling food on

broth *noun* light soup; **Scotch broth** = thick soup with barley, vegetables and lamb

brown 1 *adjective* coloured like the colour of wood or soil **2** *verb* to make brown; *brown the meat in hot fat*
◊ **brownie** *noun US* small chocolate cake
◊ **browns** *plural noun US* **hash browns** = boiled potatoes, diced or mashed and fried till crisp and brown

Brucella *noun* type of rod-shaped bacterium
◊ **brucellosis** *noun* disease which can be caught from cattle or goats or from drinking infected milk, spread by a species of the bacterium *Brucella*

COMMENT: symptoms include tiredness, arthritis, headache, sweating, irritability and swelling of the spleen

brunch *noun* meal served in the morning, between about 9.00 and 2.30, which is a combination of breakfast and lunch

COMMENT: brunch is especially popular on Sundays, when people tend to get up later than on other days of the week

Brussels sprouts *noun* small round green edible shoots from a type of cabbage (NOTE: also sometimes called simply **sprouts)**

COMMENT: Brussels sprouts are usually boiled or steamed and eaten served with butter

brut *French adjective (used only of champagne)* dry; *compare* SEC

BSE = BOVINE SPONGIFORM ENCEPHALOPATHY

BST = BOVINE SOMATOTROPIN, BRITISH SUMMER TIME

BTA = BRITISH TOURIST AUTHORITY

bubble and squeak *noun* traditional dish of leftover cabbage, potatoes, meat, etc., fried together to make a crisp cake

bubble bath *noun* (i) bath with liquid soap added to make a mass of foam; (ii) the liquid soap used to put in a bath; *each bathroom has a supply of soap, bottles of shampoo and bubble bath*

bucket *noun* round plastic or metal container with an open top and a handle; **ice bucket** *or* **wine bucket** = container of crushed ice and water in which a wine bottle is placed to keep cool
◊ **bucket shop** *noun (informal)* unbonded travel agent selling airline tickets at a discount

buck's fizz *noun* cold drink of champagne and fresh orange juice, typically served at breakfast

buckwheat *noun* grain crop *(Fagopyrum esculentum)* which is not a member of the grass family; it can be grown on the poorest of soils. When buckwheat is ground into flour, it is used to make pancakes

budget 1 *noun* **(a)** plan of expected spending and income (usually for one year); *to draw up a budget; we have agreed the budgets for next year;* **advertising budget** = money which it is planned to spend on advertising; **cash budget** = plan of cash income and expenditure; **overhead budget** = plan of probable overhead costs; **publicity budget** = money allowed for expected expenditure on publicity **(b) budget department** = department in a large store which sells cheaper goods; **budget fares** = fares which are cheaper than normal; **budget prices** = low prices; **budget travel** = cheap travel **2** *verb* to plan probable income and expenditure; *we are budgeting for £10,000 of sales next year*

buffet *noun* **(a)** meal where the food is laid out in dishes on a table, and each person helps himself; *the hotel serves a buffet breakfast;* **hot buffet** = buffet with hot dishes to choose from; **cold buffet** = buffet with cold dishes to choose from **(b)** snack bar in a railway station, airport, etc., serving food and drink

◊ **buffet car** *noun* railway coach which serves snacks and drinks which you may take back to your seat; *compare* RESTAURANT CAR

built-in *adjective* (cupboard, etc.) constructed as part of a building; *bedroom with built-in wardrobe*

bulb *noun* glass globe full of gas which produces light when an electric current passes through it; *there's a light bulb missing in the bedroom*

bulk *noun* large amount of goods; **in bulk** = in large amounts; **bulk buying** *or* **bulk purchase** = buying large amounts of goods at a lower price; **bulk discount** = discount given to a purchaser who buys in bulk

QUOTE by buying in bulk, companies can obtain hotel rooms at a fraction of the 'rack' rate, as well as airline tickets, often business class, below the quoted fare
Business Travel

bulkhead *noun* internal wall in a ship or aircraft

QUOTE frequent flyers are able to identify their favourite place in the aircraft: seats next to cabin bulkheads or alongside exit doors usually offer extra legroom
Business Travel

bulletin *noun* piece of information; report on a situation; *the ship's daily news bulletin;* **bulletin board** = board on which bulletins are pinned up

bumping *noun US* situation where someone takes the place of another (in a restaurant *or* in a plane)

bun *noun* small cake made of a bread-like dough, usually sweetened and flavoured; **currant bun** = bun with currants in it; **hot cross bun** = spiced bun, with a cross of sugar on top of it, eaten at Easter time, and especially on Good Friday

bunch *noun* **(a)** cluster of things tied together; *she bought a bunch of flowers in the market* **(b)** cluster of fruit on the same stem; *a bunch of bananas; a bunch of grapes* (NOTE: plural is **bunches**)

bungalow *noun* house with only a ground floor; *the hotel is made up of a main building, with restaurants and bars, and a series of individual bungalows set under the palm trees near the beach*

bunk *noun* bed fixed to a wall in a boat, train or aircraft; **bunk beds** = two beds, one on top of the other (in hotels, normally used for children)

bunting *noun* strings of little flags, used as decoration

bureau de change *French noun* office where money can be changed into the currency of another country (NOTE: plural is **bureaus** *or* **bureaux de change**)

burger *noun* round, flat cake of minced beef, grilled or fried and usually served in a toasted bread roll; *the children want burgers and fries for lunch;* **burger bar** = simple restaurant or stall serving burgers either to eat on the spot or to take away

Burgundy *noun* wine from the Burgundy district in France

burn *verb* to cook (food) too much, so that it becomes brown *or* black; *he's burnt the sausages; I don't like burnt toast*

NOTE: **burning - burnt** or **burned**

bus 1 *noun* **(a)** large motor vehicle for carrying passengers; *he goes to work by bus; she took the bus to go to her office;* **bus company** = company which runs the buses; **bus stop** = place where buses stop to pick up or drop passengers; *see also* REQUEST **(b)** = COACH; **airport bus** = bus which takes passengers to and from an airport; **tourist bus** = bus carrying tourists, visiting various places of interest **2** *verb US* to clear away dirty plates, cutlery, etc. from tables in a restaurant; *he spent the summer bussing tables in a downtown grill*
NOTE: **bussing - bussed**

◇ **busboy** or **busgirl** or **busser** *noun US* assistant waiter (the waiter who offers rolls, pours water, clear away dirty plates and cutlery, but does not take the order or serve the food)

business *noun* **(a)** work in buying or selling; **business call** = visit to talk to someone on business; **business centre** = (i) part of a town where the main banks, shops and offices are located; (ii) large facility offering business services to businessmen (especially at an airport, convention centre, railway station, etc., where businessmen may need to use the facilities when travelling); **business class** = type of airline travel which is less expensive than first class and more comfortable than tourist class (it has better and wider seats, special meals, more free drinks, more choice of newspapers and special airport lounges: the ticket code for Business class is C or J); **business district** = part of a town where the main banks, shops and offices are located, **business fare** = tariff for business class passengers; **business lunch** = meeting where people have lunch together to discuss business matters; **business services** = various services needed to conduct business (fax, answering service, secretarial services, etc.) offered to businessmen by a business centre, in a hotel, at an airport, etc.; **business travel** = travel for business purposes; *(compare* TRAVEL BUSINESS); **business traveller** = person who travels on business; **business trip** = journey to discuss business matters with clients; **on business** = on commercial work; *he had to go abroad on business; the chairman is in Holland on business* **(b)** commercial company; *he owns a small travel business; she runs a mail-order business from her home; he set up in business as a tour guide;* **business address** = details of number, street and town where a company

is located; **business card** = card showing a businessman's name and the name and address of the company he works for; **business correspondence** = letters concerned with a business; **business expenses** = money spent on running a business, not on stock or assets; **business facilitated lease (BFL)** = type of franchise, where a franchisee takes over an existing franchise on a short lease, buying the business with the cash which it generates; **business hours** = time (usually 9 a.m. to 5 p.m.) when a business is open **(c)** types of business taken as a group; **the travel business** = all companies and services dealing with travel and tourism (such as trains, buses, planes, travel agents, hotels, etc.); *he's been in the travel business for 15 years;* **the hotel business** = the business of running hotels

◇ **businessman** or **businesswoman** *noun* man or woman engaged in business; *she's a good businesswoman* = she is good at commercial deals (NOTE: plural is **businessmen, businesswomen**)

busy *adjective* occupied in doing something or in working; *he is busy preparing the annual accounts; the manager is busy at the moment, but he will be free in about fifteen minutes; the busiest time of year for stores is the week before Christmas; summer is the busy season for hotels;* **the line is busy** = the telephone line is being used

butcher *noun* person who prepares and sells uncooked meat; **butcher's (shop)** = shop where uncooked meat is prepared and sold

butter *noun* solid yellow fat made from cream

COMMENT: in a restaurant, butter is served either in a small individual dish or as separate pieces (sometimes wrapped in metal foil) which are kept cold in a bed of ice

◇ **buttered** *adjective* covered with butter; *hot buttered toast; buttered parsnips*

◇ **buttermilk** *noun* thin milk left after butter has been churned

◇ **butterscotch** *noun* sweet made from butter and sugar

button *noun* **(a)** small object stitched to clothes for attaching one part of clothing to another; *he asked room service if they could sew a button back on for him* **(b)** small round object which you press to make a machine work; *a push-button phone; when you get into the lift, press the button for the floor you need; he pressed the button to call the lift*

butylated hydroxytoluene (BHT) *noun* common antioxidant additive (E321) used in processed foods containing fat, probably carcinogenic

buyer *noun* person who buys; **a buyer's market** = market where products are sold cheaply because there are few buyers (NOTE: the opposite is a **seller's market**) **buyer's risk** = risk taken by a buyer when accepting goods or services without a guarantee; **impulse buyer** = person who buys something when he sees it, not because he was planning to buy it

bylaw *or* **byelaw** *or* **by-law** *or* **bye-law** *noun* rule *or* law made by a local authority *or* public body and not by central government; *the bylaws forbid playing ball in the public gardens; according to the local bylaws, noise must be limited in the town centre*

COMMENT: bylaws must be made by bodies which have been authorized by Parliament, before they can become legally effective

bypass 1 *noun* road which goes round a town **2** *verb* to go round (a town), avoiding the centre

Cc

C 1 *abbreviation for* Celsius **2** *chemical symbol for* carbon

Vitamin C *noun* ascorbic acid, vitamin which is soluble in water and is found in fresh fruit (especially oranges, lemons and blackcurrants), raw vegetables, liver and milk

COMMENT: lack of Vitamin C can cause anaemia and scurvy

CAA = CIVIL AVIATION AUTHORITY

cab *noun* **(a)** taxi, a car which takes people from one place to another for money; **black cab** = London taxi; *see also* MINICAB (NOTE: 'cab' is more used in the USA than in GB; also called **taxi** or **taxicab**) **(b)** separate compartment for a driver in a large vehicle, such as a truck
◊ **cab driver** *noun* person who drives a cab

cabaret *noun* entertainment given in a restaurant or club

cabbage *noun* green leafy vegetable *(Brassica oleracea)* with a round heart or head

COMMENT: green cabbage is usually eaten boiled; red cabbage may be eaten cooked or pickled in vinegar; white cabbage can be shredded to make

coleslaw; in Germany and Eastern France, it is pickled in brine to make 'sauerkraut'

cabin *noun* **(a)** separate room for a passenger on a ship; *she felt sick and went to lie down in her cabin; we asked for an outside cabin* **(b)** separate area for the pilot of a plane **(c)** separate area for passengers in a plane; *passengers are requested to remain seated until the cabin doors are open;* **cabin attendant** = person who looks after passengers on a plane; **cabin baggage** *or* **cabin luggage** = baggage which a passenger carries onto a plane; **cabin crew** *or* **cabin staff** = the stewards and stewardesses who look after the passengers on a plane; **cabin lights** = lights in the cabin of a plane; *cabin lights will be dimmed for takeoff*

QUOTE cabin layouts, as with cabin service, good timekeeping, and flight frequency, are important influences on frequent travellers' choice of carrier
Business Travel

cable 1 *noun* **(a)** strong wire, chain or rope; *the ship was attached to the quay by cables; the cable snapped and ten passengers died when their cable car fell to the floor of the valley* **(b)** telegram, a message sent by telegraph; *he sent a cable to his office asking for more money;* **cable address** = specially short address for sending cables **2** *verb* to send a message *or* money by telegraph; *he cabled his office to ask them to send more money; the office cabled him £1,000 to cover his expenses*

◊ **cable car** *noun* **(a)** vehicle which goes up a mountain, hanging on a wire cable **(b)** *US (in San Francisco)* type of tram which is pulled by a metal cable set in a channel in the road

◊ **cablegram** *noun* telegram *or* message sent by telegraph

◊ **cable television** *or* **cable TV** *noun* television system, where pictures are sent by cable

cadmium *noun* metallic element which is naturally present in soil and rock in association with zinc

| COMMENT: cadmium is used for making rods for nuclear reactors. It is also found in fish, and shellfish such as oysters

cafe *or* **café** *noun* small shop selling food and drink; **café set** = piece of restaurant equipment which heats water and makes steam, for preparing hot drinks; **transport café** = restaurant where truck-drivers eat

cafeteria *noun* (i) self-service restaurant; (ii) self-service restaurant in an office building or factory, used by the staff; **cafeteria manager** = person in charge of a cafeteria; **cafeteria service** = style of serving food, where the customer takes a tray and helps himself to cold food from a buffet (hot food is usually served on a plate by a server standing behind the buffet) and pays for it at a till as he leaves the buffet

cafetière *noun* coffee pot with a plunger, which is pressed down to trap the coffee grounds at the bottom

cake *noun* sweet food made from flour, sugar, eggs, milk and other ingredients, baked in an oven; *a slice of cherry cake; two pieces of chocolate cake, please;* **cup cakes** = little individual cakes baked in special paper cups; **cake knife** = thick wide knife used for cutting up cakes

◊ **cake shop** *noun* shop which sells mainly cakes and pastries, and sometimes serves tea as well

| COMMENT: a cake can be quite large, and is cut into individual slices (as for a wedding cake, Christmas cake, birthday cake, etc.; alternatively, small cakes can be made, each for one person

calamine (lotion) *noun* lotion, based on zinc oxide, which helps relieve skin irritation (such as that caused by sunburn)

calculate *verb* **(a)** to find the answer to a problem using numbers; *the bank clerk calculated the rate of exchange for the dollar* **(b)** to estimate; *I calculate that it will take us six hours to get to Madrid*

◊ **calculation** *noun* answer to a problem in mathematics; *according to my calculations, the hotel will cost us about £1,000;* **rough calculation** = approximate answer; *I made some rough calculations on the back of an envelope*

◊ **calculator** *noun* electronic machine which works out the answers to problems in mathematics; *my pocket calculator needs a new battery; he worked out the discount on his calculator*

calendar *noun* book *or* set of sheets of paper showing the days and months in a year, often illustrated with a series of pictures; **calendar month** = a whole month as on a calendar, from the 1st to the 30th or 31st; **calendar year** = whole year from the 1st January to 31st December

call 1 *noun* **(a)** conversation on the telephone; **local call** = call to a number on the same exchange; **trunk call** *or* **long-distance call** = call to a number in a different zone *or* area; **overseas call** *or* **international call** = call to another country; **person-to-person call** = call where you ask the operator to connect you with a named person; **reverse charge call** *or* **transferred charge call** *or* *US* **collect call** = call where the person receiving the call agrees to pay for it; **to make a call** = to dial and speak to someone on the telephone; **to take a call** = to answer the telephone; **to log calls** = to note all details of telephone calls made **(b)** **early morning call** = phone call or knock on the door to wake someone up in the morning; *he asked for a call at 6.15* **(c)** visit; **business call** = visit to talk to someone on business **2** *verb* **(a)** to telephone to someone; *I'll call you at your office tomorrow* **(b)** to phone someone to wake him up; *he asked to be called at 6.15* **(c)** to **call at a place** = to visit a place; *the cruise liner calls at Palermo on June 14th;* **to call for someone** = to come to find someone (at a hotel) and take them away; *I'll call for you at 8.30, so wait for me in the lobby;* **to call on**

someone = to visit; *our salesmen call on their best accounts twice a month*

◊ **call box** *noun* outdoor telephone kiosk

◊ **call girl** *noun* prostitute who can be called by telephone

calm *adjective (sea)* not rough; *the crossing was very calm, so no one was seasick*

calorie *noun* unit of measurement of heat *or* energy (especially that released by digesting food) (NOTE: the **joule** is now more usual; also written **cal** after figures: **2,500 cal)**

◊ **caloric** *adjective* referring to calories; **caloric energy** = amount of energy shown as a number of calories; **caloric requirement** = amount of energy (shown in calories) which an animal such as a human needs each day

◊ **calorific value** *noun* heat value of a substance *or* number of calories which a certain amount of a substance (such as a certain food) contains; *the tin of beans has a calorific value of 250 calories or has 250 calories*

COMMENT: one calorie is the amount of heat needed to raise the temperature of one gram of water by one degree Celsius. A Calorie or kilocalorie is the amount of heat needed to raise the temperature of a kilogram of water by one degree Celsius. The calorie is also used as a measurement of the energy content of food and to show the caloric requirement or amount of energy needed by an average person. The average adult in an office job requires about 3,000 calories per day, supplied by carbohydrates and fats to give energy and proteins to replace tissue. More strenuous physical work needs more calories. If a person eats more than the number of calories needed by his energy output or for his growth, the extra calories are stored in the body as fat

camcorder *noun* portable cine-camera which records video pictures and sound

camera *noun* machine for taking photographs

camp 1 *noun* place where people live in tents or cabins in the open; **camp bed** = folding bed; **camp fire** = fire round which campers sit at night; **holiday camp** = permanent facility where people spend holidays in cabins and enjoy organized entertainment and sport; *US* **summer camp** = camp organized for children or teenagers during the summer vacations **2** *verb* to live in a tent, as on holiday; *we camped on the beach for two nights; they spent two weeks camping in the Norwegian fiords*

◊ **camper** *noun* **(a)** person who goes camping **(b) camper (van)** = motor caravan which contains bunks, kitchen equipment, tables, etc., and in which people can drive around and park to stay overnight

◊ **campground** *noun US* = CAMPSITE

◊ **camping** *noun* going on holiday with a tent or caravan; *camping holidays are cheaper than staying in hotels;* **to go camping** = to visit a place and stay in a tent; *we are going camping in Norway;* **camping van** = CAMPER

◊ **campsite** *noun* area specially arranged for camping and caravans, with marked places for tents, central washing and toilet facilities

campaign *noun* planned method of working; **sales campaign** = planned work to achieve higher sales; **publicity campaign** *or* **advertising campaign** = planned period when publicity takes place; *they are working on a campaign to promote holidays in Scotland*

campus *noun* grounds occupied by a university (including student accommodation, refectories, sports facilities, etc.); **campus holidays** = holidays spent in student accommodation on a campus, during the vacation when the students aren't there

COMMENT: campus holidays are cheaper than hotel-based holidays, and often are centred round an intellectual or artistic activity (study of drama, watercolour painting) or a sporting activity (rock-climbing, canoeing) which can be organized using the campus facilities

Campylobacter *noun* bacteria found in chickens and dairy cattle: *Campylobacter jejuni,* is the main cause (along with Salmonella) of gastroenteritis

COMMENT: Campylobacter exists in meat, offal, eggs, unpasteurized milk and shellfish. It cannot survive temperatures of over 65°C, so is destroyed by cooking

can 1 *noun* metal container for food or drink, made of steel with a lining of tin *or* made entirely of aluminium; *a can of* *orange juice* **2** *verb* to preserve food by sealing it in special metal containers

◇ **canned** *adjective* in a metal box; *when the kitchen staff went on strike the hotel could only offer canned soup;* **canned music** = recorded music, as played in hotels, restaurants, shopping malls, supermarkets, etc.

◇ **can-opener** *noun* device for opening cans

canal *noun* artificial waterway; *you can take a boat trip round the canals of Amsterdam; holidays on canals are becoming very popular; you can go canal cruising right across France;* **canal boat** = long narrow boat made for going along British canals

canapé *noun* small cocktail snack

cancel *verb* **(a)** to stop something which has been agreed *or* planned; *to cancel an appointment or a meeting; he cancelled his booking at the last minute; there is no refund if you cancel less than three weeks before the date of departure; the flight was cancelled because the weather was too bad* **(b)** **to cancel a cheque** = to stop payment of a cheque which you have signed
NOTE: GB English: **cancelling - cancelled** but US English: **canceling - canceled**

◇ **cancellation** *noun* stopping something which has been agreed *or* planned; *cancellation of a booking or a sailing or a flight;* **cancellation charge** = charge which has to be paid by someone who cancels a booking; **cancellation clause** = clause in a contract which states the terms on which the contract may be cancelled; **cancellation rate** = number of people who cancel bookings, shown as a percentage of all bookings

candle *noun* stick of wax, with a piece of cotton in it, which can be lit and provides light; *a birthday cake with twenty-one candles*

◇ **candlelight** *noun* light from candles

◇ **candlelit** *adjective* lit only by candles; **candlelit supper** = evening meal lit by candles on the tables

candy *noun* US sweet food made of sugar, eaten as a snack (NOTE: GB English is **sweet)**

◇ **candyfloss** *noun* melted sugar spun to make a fluffy pink mass (often sold at fairgrounds and open-air entertainments)

cannelloni *plural noun* type of wide tube-shaped pasta, stuffed with a meat or spinach filling

cantaloupe *or* **cantaloup** *noun* variety of melon *(Cucumis melo)* with green or yellow rough skin and scented orange-yellow flesh

canteen *noun* **(a)** private self-service restaurant in an office block, factory, etc. **(b)** box containing knives, forks and spoons **(c)** portable flask for water

capacity *noun* amount which a container can hold; **seating capacity** = the number of seats (in a bus, cinema, etc.); **a capacity crowd** = a crowd of people which fills all the seats in a stadium

caper *noun* flowerbud of a Mediterranean bush *Capparis spinosa,* which is pickled and used in sauces (tartare sauce) or as a garnish for fish and meat

capital *noun* **(a)** main city of a country, a state, etc.; **capital break** = short holiday in a capital, such as Paris, Vienna, Rome **(b)** money, property and assets used in a business; *company with £10,000 capital or with a capital of £10,000;* **authorized capital** *or* **registered capital** *or* **nominal capital** = maximum capital which is permitted by a company's memorandum of association; **capital assets** = property or machinery which a company owns and uses in its business, but which the company does not buy or sell as part of its regular trade; **capital expenditure** *or* **investment** *or* **outlay** = money spent on fixed assets (such as property, machines, furniture); **capital gain** = money made by selling fixed assets or certain other types of property (if the asset is sold for less than its purchase price, the result is a capital loss); **capital gains tax (CGT)** = tax paid on capital gains; **capital loss** = loss made by selling assets (the opposite of a capital gain); **capital reserves** = part of share capital which can be distributed to the shareholders only when a company is wound up; **capital structure of a company** = way in which a company's capital is made up from various sources; **equity capital** = a company's capital which is owned by its ordinary shareholders (note that preference shares are not equity capital; if the company were wound up, none of the equity capital would be distributed to preference shareholders); **fixed capital** = capital in the form of fixed assets; **issued capital** = amount of capital issued as shares to the shareholders; **paid-**

up capital = amount of money paid for the issued share capital; **risk capital** *or* **venture capital** = capital for investment in the early stages of projects which may easily be lost; **working capital** = capital in the form of cash, stocks and debtors (less creditors) used by a company in its day-to-day operations

◊ **capitalize on** *verb* to take advantage of (something); *café owners capitalized on the good weather by putting tables and chairs out on the pavement*

QUOTE English seaside resorts must capitalize on their architectural heritage if they are to find a niche in the holiday market of the future

Caterer and Hotelkeeper

capon *noun* castrated edible cockerel (it grows and increases in weight more rapidly than a bird which has not been castrated)

cappuccino *noun* frothy Italian coffee, with milk and a sprinkling of powdered chocolate

capsicum *noun* group of plants (also called 'peppers') grown for their pod-like fruit, some of which are extremely pungent, such as the chilli pepper. Others, including the red and green or sweet peppers are less pungent and are used as vegetables

captain *noun* **(a)** person in charge of a ship *or* aircraft; **the captain's table** = table in the dining room of a cruise liner, where the captain sits, with the most important passengers **(b)** *US* a chief waiter who is in charge of a station, and takes the orders from customers (in GB, this is the 'station head waiter')

car *noun* **(a)** small motor vehicle for carrying people; **car ferry** = boat which carries vehicles and passengers from one place to another across water **(b)** *US* wagon on a railway; **observation car** = special wagon with a glass roof, so that passengers can see mountain scenery

◊ **car hire** *or* **car rental** *noun* business of lending cars to people for money

◊ **car hirer** *noun* (i) person who rents a car; (ii) company which owns cars and lends them to people for money

QUOTE the check-in counter at its Heathrow rental desk has full baggage facilities, so that car hirers handing in their keys can check in at the same time

Business Travel

◊ **car park** *noun* place where you can leave your car (NOTE: in US English, this is a **parking lot**) **short-term car park** = car park where you can leave your car for a period of hours; **long-term car park** = car park where you can leave for car for days or weeks

◊ **carsick** *adjective* ill because of the movement of a car

◊ **carsickness** *noun* sickness caused by the movement of a car

carafe *noun* glass jar, for serving wine or water; *wines by the carafe; can we have a carafe of ordinary water, please?;* half-carafe = a half-litre carafe; *he ordered a half-carafe of house wine;* **carafe wine** = cheapest wine sold in a restaurant or bar

COMMENT: carafes are used for serving ordinary table wine or house wine. Wine sold in carafes is cheaper than wine in bottles; carafe sizes are quarter-litre, half-litre or litre. The carafes are measured and approved by the licensing authorities

carambola *noun* yellow fruit of a tropical tree *(Averrhoa carambola)* found in Indonesia; the fruit are used in preserves and drinks

caramel *noun* **(a)** sweet made with sugar and butter **(b)** burnt sugar; **caramel custard** *or* **crème caramel** = dessert of egg custard topped with a thin sauce of browned sugar (usually served turned upside down onto the serving plate, though sometimes served in the bowl in which it is cooked)

◊ **caramelize** *verb* to heat sugar until it becomes brown

caravan *noun* **(a)** van with beds, table, washing facilities, etc., which can be towed by a car (NOTE: US English for this is **trailer**) **caravan park** *or* *US* **trailer park** = type of camp ground with permanently positioned caravans, which are rented to holidaymakers **(b)** group of vehicles or animals travelling together (especially across a desert)

◊ **caravanette** *noun* small camping van

◊ **caravanner** *noun* person who goes on holiday in a caravan

◊ **caravanning** *noun* going on holiday in a caravan

caraway *noun* seeds of a herb *(Carum carvi)* used as a flavouring in bread and cakes, etc.

carbohydrate *noun* organic compound which derives from sugar and which is the main ingredient of many types of food

COMMENT: carbohydrates are compounds of carbon, hydrogen and oxygen. They are found in particular in sugar and starch from plants, and provide the body with energy. Plants build up valuable organic substances from simple materials. The most important part of this process, which is called photosynthesis, is the production of carbohydrates such as sugars, starches and cellulose. They form the largest part of our food

carbon dioxide (CO₂) *noun* colourless gas produced when carbon is burnt with oxygen.
◊ **carbonated** *adjective* (liquid) which has had carbon dioxide put into it to make it fizzy; *a bottle of carbonated mineral water*

COMMENT: Carbon dioxide exists naturally in air and is produced by respiration and by burning or rotting organic matter. Carbon dioxide is used in solid form (called 'dry ice') as a means of keeping food cold. It is also used in fizzy drinks and has the E number 290.

carburettor *noun* device in a car for changing liquid petrol into vapour

carcinogen *noun* substance which produces cancer
◊ **carcinogenic** *adjective* which produces cancer

COMMENT: carcinogens are found in pesticides such as DDT, in asbestos, aromatic compounds such as benzene, and radioactive substances, etc.

card *noun* **(a)** small rectangle of stiff paper for writing on; *see also* POSTCARD **(b)** rectangle of stiff paper with a design on it used for playing games; **playing cards =** ordinary cards, marked in four designs (diamonds, hearts, clubs, spades); **card games =** games played with cards; **card table =** small table covered with green baize cloth, used for playing cards; **they were playing cards =** they were playing games of cards (for money) **(c) (visiting) card =** small piece of stiff paper with your name and address printed on it; **banker's card** *or* **cheque (guarantee) card =** plastic card from a bank which guarantees payment of a cheque up to a certain amount, even if there is no money in the account; **credit card =** plastic card which allows you to borrow money and to buy goods without paying for them immediately; **key card =** (i) card given to a guest on registration, which shows the number of his room and which he may need to show for identification purposes; (ii) electronic card given to a guest at registration, which acts as a key to his room; **phone card =** plastic card which you can buy at a post office, and insert into a special slot in a public telephone booth to make a phone call; **smart card =** plastic card with a built-in microprocessor; **card phone** = public telephone where you insert a phone card or credit card to make a call; **card reader =** electronic device which can read information on a magnetic card

COMMENT: there are two main types of magnetic key card: the 'dip' card, which is pushed down into a slot and then pulled out again when the door unlocks, and a 'swipe' card, which you run down a slot to unlock the door

QUOTE staff create key cards for guests using a card programming unit, linked to a point of sale system. The door lock updates itself with the guest identity code each time a new card authorized for that room is used.
Caterer & Hotelkeeper

career *noun* job which you are trained for, and which you expect to do all your life; *he made his career in the hotel trade; she's hoping to start her career in tourism;* **career prospects =** possibility of getting promoted in your work; **career woman** *or* **girl =** woman who is working in business and does not plan to stop working to look after the house or children

cargo *noun* goods carried (especially on a ship); **cargo boat** *or* **cargo ship =** ship which carries only goods (some also have accommodation for a few passengers)

carnet *noun* international document which allows dutiable goods to cross several European countries by road without paying duty until the goods reach their final destination

carnival *noun* festival often with dancing and eating in the open air

carousel *or US* **carrousel** *noun* device at an airport, where the baggage of arriving passengers is placed by baggage handlers on a turning platform so that the passengers can find it and take it away; *baggage from flight AC 123 is on carousel number 4*

carpet 1 *noun* woven or knotted covering for the floor **2** *verb* to cover with a carpet

◊ **carpeting** *noun* covering with a carpet; wide piece of carpet; *the carpeting for the entrance lobby needs to be renewed*

carriage *noun* **(a)** coach for passengers on a train; *he was sitting in a first-class carriage although he only had a second-class ticket* **(b)** act of transporting goods from one place to another; cost of transport of goods; *to pay for carriage; to allow 10% for carriage; carriage is 15% of the total cost;* **carriage forward** = deal where the customer will pay for the shipping when the goods arrive; **carriage free** = deal where the customer does not pay for the shipping; **carriage paid** = deal where the seller has paid for the shipping

◊ **carriageway** *noun* road for vehicles, especially one of the two sides of a motorway; *the westbound carriageway of the M4 is closed for repairs*

carrier *noun* **(a)** company which transports goods *or* passengers; *we only use reputable carriers; the tour always uses Spanish carriers;* **air carrier** = company which sends cargo *or* passengers by air; **common carrier** = firm which carries goods or passengers, and which anyone can use; **carrier's risk** = responsibility of a carrier to pay for damage or loss of goods being shipped **(b)** vehicle *or* ship which transports goods; **bulk carrier** = ship which carries large quantities of loose goods (such as corn) **(c)** person who carries bacteria of a disease in his body and who can transmit the disease to others without showing any sign of it himself **(d)** insect which carries disease which may infect humans

carrot *noun* bright orange root vegetable

COMMENT: eaten boiled, steamed or braised; also shredded cold as a salad

carry *verb (of vehicle)* (to be able) to contain a certain number of passengers; *the plane was carrying twenty passengers and five crew; a ship carrying pilgrims to the Middle East;* **carry on baggage** = baggage which a passenger carries onto a plane

◊ **carrycot** *noun* rectangular box with handles for carrying a baby in

carte *French noun* menu; **carte du jour** = 'menu of the day', list of special dishes prepared for the day and not listed in the printed menu; *see also* A LA CARTE, TAGESKARTE

carton *noun* **(a)** thick cardboard; *a folder made of carton* **(b)** box made of cardboard; *a carton of cigarettes*

carve *verb* to cut meat and poultry up at the table or in the kitchen for service to the table; **carving knife** = large sharp knife, used for carving

◊ **carver** *noun* **(a)** person who carves meat (often a special waiter in a restaurant, who carves a joint brought to the side of a table on a trolley) **(b)** chair with arms, placed at the head of a dinner table **(c)** = CARVING KNIFE

◊ **carvery** *noun* type of restaurant, where various hot roast meats are served at a buffet (the chef cuts slices of meat for the customer, who then helps himself to vegetables, sauces, etc., from the buffet)

case *noun* **(a)** suitcase *or* box with a handle for carrying clothes and personal belongings when travelling; *the customs made him open his case; she had a small case which she carried onto the plane* **(b)** cardboard or wooden box for packing and carrying goods; **a packing case** = large wooden box for carrying items which can be easily broken **(c)** **a case of wine** = cardboard or wooden box containing twelve bottles; **half-case** = cardboard or wooden box containing six bottles of wine; *he ordered ten cases of Beaujolais and twenty cases of Muscadet* **(d)** **display case** = table or counter with a glass top, used for showing items for sale **(e)** **pastry case** = piece of pastry used to line a dish and filled either before or after baking; *see also* BAKE, PASTRY

cash 1 *noun* **(a)** money in coins or notes; **hard cash** = money in notes and coins, as opposed to cheques or credit cards; **petty cash** = small amounts of money; **ready cash** = money which is immediately available for payment; **cash box** = metal box for keeping cash in; **cash card** = card used to obtain money from a cash dispenser; **cash desk** = place in a store where you pay for the goods bought; **cash dispenser** = machine which gives out money when a special card is inserted and instructions given; **cash payment** = payment in cash; **cash purchase** = purchase made in cash; **cash register** *or* **cash till** = machine which shows and adds the prices of items bought, with a drawer for keeping the cash received **(b)** using money in coins or notes; **'cash'** *or* **'pay cash'** = words written on a crossed cheque to show that it can be paid in cash if necessary; **to pay cash** = to pay the complete sum in cash; **to pay cash down** = to pay in cash immediately; **cash price** *or* **cash terms** = lower price *or* terms which apply if the customer pays cash; **settlement in cash** *or* **cash settlement** = paying a bill in cash; **cash sale** *or* **cash transaction** = transaction paid for in cash; **cash on delivery (COD)** = payment in cash when goods are delivered; **cash discount** *or* **discount for cash** = discount given for payment in cash **2** *verb* **to cash a cheque** = to exchange a cheque for cash; *where can I cash my traveller's cheques?*

◊ **cash flow** *noun* cash which comes into a company from sales (cash inflow) or the money which goes out in purchases or overhead expenditure (cash outflow); **cash flow forecast** = forecast of when cash will be received or paid out; **cash flow statement** = report which shows cash sales and purchases; **net cash flow** = difference between the money coming in and the money going out; **negative cash flow** = situation where more money is going out of a company than is coming in; **positive cash flow** = situation where more money is coming into a company than is going out; **the company is suffering from cash flow problems** = cash income is not coming in fast enough to pay the expenditure going out

◊ **cashier** *noun* **(a)** person who takes money from customers in a restaurant *or* hotel *or* shop; *please pay the cashier;* **cashier's record** = record of transactions kept by a cashier **(b)** person who deals with customers' money in a bank

◊ **cash up** *verb* to count the money taken in a shop, restaurant, etc., at the end of the day's business

cashew (nut) *noun* small sweetish nut with a curved shape, often eaten salted as a snack

casino *noun* building where people can gamble

COMMENT: in Britain, casinos are strictly regulated and only a certain number are allowed to operate; the person running a casino has to be licensed to do so. Casinos often exist in European spa towns

cassata *noun* Italian ice cream with dried fruit in it

casserole 1 *noun* **(a)** ovenproof covered dish **(b)** food cooked in a covered dish in the oven; *chicken casserole; casserole of lamb* **2** *verb* to cook in a casserole; *casseroled hare*

cassette *noun* magnetic tape in a plastic case which can fit directly into a playing or recording machine; **cassette player** = machine for playing cassettes; **cassette recorder** = machine which records sound on magnetic tape in a cassette; *cassette recorders are not allowed in the concert;* **video cassette** = videotape in a plastic case which can fit directly into a video cassette recorder

castle *noun* large fortified building; *the tour includes visits to Windsor Castle and Hampton Court Palace*

COMMENT: note that in Britain the word 'castle' usually is applied to medieval buildings, with towers, gatehouses, moats, etc. Windsor Castle is an example of this. In France, the word 'château', and in Germany, the word 'Schloss' can also be applied to buildings which in English would be called 'palaces', like the Château de Versailles.

casual *adjective* not permanent *or* not regular; **casual labour** *or* **casual staff** = workers hired for a short period; **casual work** = work for a short period; **casual worker** = worker hired for a short period; **on a casual basis** = not as a permanent member of staff; *we have taken on some* *students for the summer period on a casual basis*

catch *verb* to be in time to get on a bus, train, etc., before it leaves; *you'll have to run if you want to catch the 10.20 train; they stayed overnight in Dover and caught the 5.30 ferry to Calais* (NOTE: **catching - caught**)

category *noun* classification of things; *customers will stay in the Hotel Select or in another of the same category*

cater for *verb* to deal with *or* to provide for; *the store caters mainly for overseas customers*

◊ **caterer** *noun* person *or* company supplying food and drink, especially for parties; *the wedding reception has been organized by outside caterers*

◊ **catering** *noun* supply of food and drink for a party, etc.; **the catering industry** *or* **the catering trade** = food trade, especially supplying food ready to eat; **catering manager** = manager in charge of a catering service; **catering service** = service provided by a hotel or restaurant, offering to supply all the food and drink, etc., for a private party; **corporate catering** = catering for business guests, organized by a catering company for a large corporation

cathedral *noun* large church which is the seat of a bishop

catsup *noun US* tomato sauce, with special seasoning

cauliflower *noun* cabbage-like vegetable with a large white flower head which is eaten; **cauliflower cheese** = dish made of boiled cauliflower, covered with a cheese sauce and baked in the oven

cave *noun* large underground hole in rock or earth; **cave paintings** = paintings on walls of caves done by men who lived there millions of years ago

caveat emptor *Latin phrase (meaning 'let the buyer beware')* meaning that the buyer is himself responsible for checking that what he buys is in good order

cavern *noun* very large cave

caviar(e) *noun* the eggs of a sturgeon, an expensive delicacy

COMMENT: caviare is usually served in a small pot, on a bed of ice, with lemon; traditionally it is served as an hors d'oeuvre, with chilled vodka. Caviare is black, the eggs are very fine and from the Beluga sturgeon; there is a similar, but cheaper, form with larger red eggs

cayenne (pepper) *noun* very hot-tasting red powder made from ground seeds and pods of the *Capsicum*

celebrated *adjective* very famous; *many celebrated chefs have worked in this hotel*

celeriac *noun* vegetable with a thick root tasting like celery, often eaten grated as a salad or used to make a purée

celery *noun* white- or green-stemmed plant, eaten cooked as a vegetable, or more frequently raw as a salad; **a stick of celery** = a piece of the stem of the celery plant (often served raw with cheese)

cellar *noun* **(a)** underground room or rooms beneath a building; **beer cellar** = cellar where beer is kept or served; **wine cellar** = cellar where wine is kept or served **(b)** wine stored in a cellar; *the restaurant is well-known for its cellar;* **cellar book** = book which lists the details of the stock of wine kept in a cellar

◊ **cellarman** *noun* person who looks after beer barrels in a pub or hotel

COMMENT: a cellar should be kept at a steady temperature, to make sure that the wine or beer which is stored in it does not deteriorate. Wine should be stored at a temperature of about 10°C, and bitter beer at 13°C. Cellars are also converted to form bars or nightclubs

Celsius *adjective & noun* scale of temperature where the freezing and boiling points of water are 0° and 100° (NOTE: used in many countries, but not in the USA, where the Fahrenheit system is still preferred. Normally written as a **C** after the degree sign: **32°C** (say: 'thirty-two degrees Celsius'). Used to be called **centigrade)**

COMMENT: to convert Celsius temperatures to Fahrenheit, multiply by 1.8 and add 32. So 20°C is equal to 68°F. To convert Fahrenheit to Celsius, subtract 32 and divide by 1.8

cent (a) *noun* small coin, one hundredth of a dollar; *the stores are only a 25-cent bus ride away; they sell oranges at 10 cents each* (NOTE: **cent** is usually written **c** in prices: **25c,** but not when a dollar price is mentioned: **$1.25) (b)** *see* PER CENT

centigrade *noun* scale of temperature where the freezing and boiling points of water are 0°, and 100°; *see note at* CELSIUS

centimetre *or* US **centimeter** *noun* measure of length (= 0.39 inches, or one hundredth of a metre); *the paper is fifteen centimetres wide* (NOTE: usually written **cm** after figures: **260cm)**

centre *or* US **center** *noun* **(a)** middle part of something; *the waiter put the vase of flowers in the centre of the table; there is a dance floor in the centre of the room* **(b)** group of buildings for a special purpose; **conference centre** *or* **convention centre** = series of meeting rooms, with bedrooms, restaurants, etc., built specially for holding large meetings; **fitness centre** = special room or rooms (in a hotel or other building) with sauna, gymnasium, etc., where customers can go to take exercise; **shopping centre** = group of shops linked together with car parks and restaurants; **sports centre** = gymnasium, swimming pool, etc., combined in a group of connected buildings **(c) business centre** = (i) part of a town where the main banks, shops and offices are located; (ii) large facility offering business services to businessmen (especially at an airport, convention centre, railway station, etc., where businessmen may need to use the facilities when travelling) **(d)** important town; *industrial centre; manufacturing centre; the centre for the shoe industry* **(e)** group of items in an account; **cost centre** = group or machine whose costs can be itemized and to which fixed costs can be allocated; **profit centre** = person or department which is considered separately for the purposes of calculating a profit

◊ **central** *adjective* organized from a centre; **central air conditioning** = air-conditioning system in which cold air is pumped throughout a whole building; **central booking system** = computerized system where bookings can be made at any hotel in a group through a central office; **central heating** = heating system for a whole building from one single source; **central reservations bureau** = main office which organizes reservations for hotels, etc., in many different places; **central**

reservation system CENTRAL BOOKING SYSTEM; **central purchasing** = purchasing organized by one main office for all departments or branches

◊ **centralization** *noun* organization of everything from a central point

◊ **centralize** *verb* to organize from a central point; *all purchasing has been centralized in our main office; the hotel group benefits from a highly centralized organizational structure*

cereal *noun* **(a)** grain crop such as wheat, barley, maize, etc. **(b) (breakfast) cereal** = food made of seeds of corn, etc. which is usually eaten at breakfast; *he ate a bowl of cereal; put milk and sugar on your cereal*

COMMENT: buffet breakfasts may offer a variety of cereals in small individual packets

certificate *noun* official document which shows that something is true; **birth certificate** = document which shows when and where someone was born; **clearance certificate** = document showing that goods have been passed by customs; **certificate of airworthiness** = document to show that an aircraft has passed an examination and is in a fit condition to fly; **certificate of origin** = document showing where goods were made; **certificate of registration** = document showing that an item has been registered; **certificate of seaworthiness** = document to show that a ship has passed an examination and is in a fit condition to sail

chafing dish *noun* dish which keeps food hot at the table; **chafing lamp** = small lamp (burning alcohol) which is lit under a chafing dish

chain *noun* group of hotels, restaurants, etc. belonging to the same company; *a chain of hotels or a hotel chain; the chairman of a large restaurant chain; he runs a chain of pasta restaurants*

QUOTE the two small London catering chains are actively seeking to expand their operations in the capital
Caterer & Hotelkeeper

chairlift *noun* arrangement of simple seats attached to a moving cable, to allow skiers to be carried to the top of a mountain

chalet *noun* small holiday house, usually made of wood; *the company offers chalet holidays in Switzerland;* **beach chalet** =

small wooden holiday home, near or on a beach; **chalet maid** = girl or woman who does the cooking and cleaning for guests staying in a chalet in a ski resort

chambermaid noun girl or woman who cleans hotel rooms and changes the linen

chambré French adjective at room temperature

COMMENT: most red wines are best drunk at room temperature, around 20°C and should be brought up from the cellar well before serving, to allow them to warm to the temperature of the restaurant. Lighter red wines (such as Beaujolais nouveau, Gamay, Sancerre rouge) can be served cool

champagne noun sparkling French white wine (NOTE: also called **champers, bubbly** or **fizz**)

COMMENT: champagne comes from the part of north-eastern France, around the towns of Reims and Epernay. Many other countries produce sparkling white wine, and some of these are called 'champagne', although the use of name is disputed by the French champagne producers. Champagne is normally sweetish, but dry champagnes (called 'brut') are also popular. It should be served chilled, usually in tall narrow glasses called 'flutes'. It can also be served in a wide flat glass, called a 'champagne goblet'. It is served as an apéritif, and also at important functions, such as birthdays or weddings, where it is used to toast the bride and groom

chance sales plural noun (in a hotel) sales of food and drink to non-residents

change 1 noun **(a)** money in coins or small notes; **small change** = coins; **to give someone change for £10** = to give someone coins or notes in exchange for a ten-pound note; **change machine** = machine which gives small change for a larger coin or note **(b)** money given back by the seller, when the buyer can pay only with a larger note or coin than the amount asked; **he gave me the wrong change; you paid the £5.75 bill with a £10 note, so you should have £4.25 change; keep the change** = keep it as a tip (said to waiters, etc.) **(c)** getting off a train or aircraft or bus, etc., and getting onto another one; **getting from Richmond to**

Islington on the Underground involves three changes **2** verb **(a) to change a £10 note** = to give change in smaller notes or coins for a £10 note **(b)** to give one type of currency for another; **to change £1,000 into dollars; we want to change some traveller's cheques (c)** to get off a train or aircraft or bus, etc., and get onto another one; **we changed trains in Newport; you have to change twice during the journey;** 'all change' = instruction to all the passengers on a train to get off and get onto another one **(d)** to take off one set of clothes and put on another; **after the wedding reception, the bride and groom changed into their going-away clothes**

◊ **changeable** adjective which changes often or is likely to change soon; **the weather is changeable in July**

◊ **changing room** noun special small room at a swimming pool, golf course, sauna, etc., where you change from your normal clothes into sports clothes

channel noun **(a)** piece of water connecting two seas; **the English Channel** = sea between England and France; **Channel Tunnel** (or **Chunnel**) = tunnel for trains under the English Channel linking England and France; **cross-channel ferry** = ferry which takes passengers or vehicles between England and France **(b)** (at customs) **green channel** = exit from customs through which you pass if you are not importing goods which are liable to duty; **red channel** = exit from customs through which you pass if you are importing goods which are liable to duty; (in EC countries) **blue channel** = exit from customs through which you pass if you are arriving from another EC country and are not importing goods which are liable to duty

chapati noun flat unleavened Indian bread made from cereal flour and water

charcoal noun black fuel formed from wood which has been burnt slowly, used as fuel for barbecues and grills

◊ **charcoal-grilled** or **char-grilled** adjective grilled over hot charcoal; **a char-grilled steak**

charentais noun type of melon which is round with green striped skin and dark orange flesh

charge 1 noun **(a) to be in charge of** = to manage or to run; **he's in charge of the booking office; she's in charge of the children's crèche (b)** money which must be paid *or* price of a service; *to make no charge for cleaning; to make a small charge for rental; there is no charge for service or no charge is made for service;* admission charge *or* entry charge = price to be paid before going into an exhibition, etc.; **handling charge** = money to be paid for packing and invoicing *or* for dealing with something in general *or* for moving goods from one place to another; **inclusive charge** = charge which includes all costs; **scale of charges** = list showing various prices; **service charge** = amount added to a bill to cover the work involved in dealing with a customer *or* amount paid by tenants in a block of flats for general cleaning and maintenance; *a 10% service charge is added; does the bill include a service charge?;* a token charge is made for heating = a small charge is made which does not cover the real costs at all; **free of charge** = free *or* with no payment to be made **2** *verb* **(a)** to ask someone to pay for services later; **to charge a customer for packing** *or* **to charge the packing to the customer** *or* **to charge the customer with the packing** = the customer has to pay for packing; **to charge something to an account** = to ask for payment to be put on an account; *can I charge the restaurant bill to my room number? he asked for the hotel bill to be charged to the company account* **(b)** to ask for money to be paid; *to charge £5 for delivery; how much does he charge?;* he charges £6 an hour = he asks to be paid £6 for an hour's work

◊ **chargeable** *adjective* **repairs chargeable to the occupier** = repairs which are to be paid for by the occupier

◊ **charge account** *noun* arrangement which a customer has with a store or organization to buy goods or services and to pay for them at a later date, usually when the invoice is sent at the end of the month

◊ **charge card** *noun* credit card for which a fee is payable, but which does not allow the user to take out a loan (he has to pay off the total sum charged at the end of each month)

charlotte *noun* dessert made with fruit or cream in a thin biscuit or pastry case; **apple charlotte** = hot dessert made of stewed apples cooked in a case of soft sponge cake; **charlotte russe** = cold dessert of flavoured cream inside a case of thin sponge biscuits

chart *noun* **(a)** map of sea or river, showing the depth of water, rocks, sand banks, etc. **(b)** diagram showing information as a series of lines *or* blocks, etc.; **bar chart** = diagram where quantities and values are shown as thick columns of different heights *or* lengths; **flow chart** = diagram showing the arrangement of various work processes in a series; **organization chart** = diagram of people working in various departments, showing how a company *or* office is organized; **pie chart** = diagram where information is shown as a circle cut up into sections of different sizes; **sales chart** = diagram showing how sales vary from month to month

charter 1 *noun* hiring transport for a special purpose; **charter flight** = flight in an aircraft which has been hired for that purpose; **charter plane** = plane which has been chartered; **boat on charter to Mr Smith** = boat which Mr Smith has hired for a voyage **2** *verb* to hire for a special purpose; *to charter a plane or a boat or a bus*

◊ **chartered** *adjective* **chartered boat** *or* **bus** *or* **plane** = boat *or* bus *or* plane which has been hired for a special purpose

◊ **charterer** *noun* person who hires a boat, etc., for a special purpose

◊ **chartering** *noun* act of hiring for a special purpose

château *French noun (meaning 'castle')* **(a)** country house *or* manor house *or* castle in France; *a tour of the Châteaux of the Loire* **(b)** estate where wine is made, usually referring to the wine-producing estates of the Bordeaux region; **château-bottled** = (wine) which has been bottled on the estate where it was produced (NOTE: plural is **châteaux**)

COMMENT: the word château does not necessarily imply a top quality wine, as many appellation contrôlée wines are called after the château where they are made. The major Bordeaux wines are all called after châteaux: Château Latour, Château Lafite, Château Mouton Rothschild, Château Lynch-Bages, Château Beychevelle, etc.

chauffeur *noun* person who drives a car for someone; **chauffeur-driven car** = large car which is driven by a chauffeur

◊ **chauffeuse** *noun* woman who drives a car for someone

cheap *adjective & adverb* not costing a lot of money *or* not expensive; *are there any cheap hotels in London? they always stay in the cheapest hotel possible;* **cheap rate** = rate which is not expensive; *cheap-rate phone calls;* **to buy something cheap** = at a low price; **they work out cheaper by the box** = these items are cheaper per unit if you buy a box of them

check 1 *noun* **(a)** investigation *or* examination; *a routine check of the fire equipment;* **baggage check** = examination of passengers' baggage to make sure it contains nothing dangerous or illegal **(b)** *US (in restaurant)* bill **(c)** *US* = CHEQUE **(d)** *US* = TICK **2** *verb* **(a)** to examine *or* to investigate; *don't forget to check the bill to see if it is correct* **(b)** *(at an airport)* **checked baggage** = baggage which has been weighed at the check-in and passed to the airline to be put onto the aircraft

◊ **checkbook** *US* = CHEQUE BOOK

◊ **check in** *verb* **(a)** *(at a hotel)* to arrive at a hotel and write your name and address on a list; *he checked in at 12.15* **(b)** *(at an airport)* to give in your ticket to show you are ready to take the flight **(c) to check baggage in** = to pass your baggage to the airline to have it weighted and put it on the aircraft for you

◊ **check-in** *noun* **(a)** *(at a hotel)* action of arriving and registering; **check-in procedure** = formalities to be done when a guest checks in (allocating a room, taking the guest's name, asking the guest to sign the hotel register, etc.) **(b)** *(at an airport)* **check-in (desk)** = place where passengers give in their tickets for a flight; *the check-in is on the first floor;* **check-in counter** = counter where passengers check in; **check-in time** = time at which passengers should check in; **telephone check-in** = checking in by phoning the airline (usually only available to passengers with hand baggage)

◊ **checking** *noun* **(a)** examination *or* investigation; *the inspectors found some defects during their checking of the building* **(b)** *US* **checking account** = bank account on which you can write cheques

◊ **checklist** *noun* list of things which have to be checked (such as doors which have to be locked, items of linen which should be ready in the bathroom, etc.)

◊ **check out** *verb* *(at a hotel)* to leave and pay for a room; *we will check out before breakfast*

◊ **checkout** *noun* **(a)** *(in a supermarket)* place where you pay for the goods you have bought **(b)** *(in a hotel)* action of leaving and paying the bill; **checkout procedure =**

formalities to be done when a guest checks out (presenting the bill and making sure it is paid, taking the room key back, etc.); **checkout time** = time by which you have to leave your room; *checkout time is 12.00*

◊ **checkroom** *noun* *US* place where you leave your coat *or* luggage, etc.

cheers! *interjection (informal)* **(a)** thank you! **(b)** *(when drinking)* good health!

cheese *noun* solid food made from cow's milk curds; also made from goat's milk, and more rarely from ewe's milk; *he ordered a cheese omelette;* **a cheese** = a whole round cheese; **blue cheese** = type of cheese with blue fungus growth in it (such as Stilton, Roquefort, etc.); **blue-cheese dressing** = dressing for salad, made of mayonnaise or vinaigrette with blue cheese in it; **cream cheese** = soft smooth cheese which can be spread easily; **cheese and biscuits** = course in a meal, served after the main course, consisting of various types of cheese and dry or salt biscuits; **cheese knife** = knife with two points at the end of the blade, used for cutting and serving cheese

COMMENT: There are many varieties of both hard and soft cheese: the British Caerphilly, Cheddar, Cheshire and Gloucester are all hard cheeses; the French Brie and Camembert are soft. Goat's cheese is always soft. In a British-style menu, cheese is served at the end of the meal, after the dessert, while in French-style menus, the cheese is served before the dessert. A selection of cheeses will be placed on a cheeseboard, with a knife: the waiter will help each guest to a small piece of various cheeses as the guest asks for them. In Britain, cheese is served with water biscuits (or other dry crackers) and butter, and possibly celery; in France, cheese will be served with bread, but rarely with butter

◊ **cheeseboard** *noun* **(a)** flat piece of wood, on which cheese is served **(b)** selection of cheeses served on a cheeseboard

◊ **cheeseburger** *noun* hamburger with melted cheese on top

◊ **cheesecake** *noun* tart with a sweet pastry base and cooked cream cheese top, often covered with fruit

chef *noun* **(a)** person who is in charge of preparing food in a restaurant (also called **chef de cuisine** *or* **executive chef**) **chef's special** = special dish, sometimes one which the chef is famous for, which is listed separately on the menu; **chef de partie** = chef in charge of a particular section of a kitchen (such as vegetables or sauces); *see also* SOUS-CHEF; **chef de vin** = WINE WAITER; **chef entremétier** *or* **vegetable chef** = chef in charge of preparing vegetables and pasta; **chef garde-manger** *or* **larder chef** = chef in charge of cold dishes, salads and salad sauces, sandwiches, and who cuts meat and fish ready for cooking in the kitchen; **chef pâtissier** *or* **pastry chef** = chef who specializes in preparing pastries and sweet dishes; **chef poissonnier** *or* **fish chef** = chef in charge of preparing fish dishes; **chef potager** *or* **soup chef** = chef in charge of making soups; **chef restaurateur** = chef in charge of the à la carte menu; **chef rôtisseur** *or* **roast chef** = chef in charge of roast meats; **chef saucier** *or* **sauce chef** = chef in charge of preparing sauces; **chef tournant** = chef who is available to work in any of the sections of a kitchen, helping out when other chefs are ill or on holiday; **chef traiteur** = chef in charge of outside functions (buffets or meals which are prepared in the kitchen, but served in a different venue); **commis chef** = assistant chef to a chef de partie **(b)** name given to various specialized waiters; **chef d'étage** = floor waiter, a waiter responsible for room service in a series of hotel rooms on the same floor; **chef de rang** = station waiter, a waiter who serves a particular group of four or five tables in a restaurant (note that **chef** is used in many French phrases)

COMMENT: the executive chef organizes the running of the kitchen, selecting menus, tasting dishes, supervising the specialist chefs working under him. A sous-chef is the assistant to an executive chef: in a large kitchen you might have several sous-chefs. Each chef de partie will have one or more commis chefs working under him. Each will have a title corresponding to the section of the kitchen in which he works: commis pâtissier, commis garde-manger, etc.

cheque *noun* note to a bank asking them to pay money from your account to the account of the person whose name is written on the note; *he wrote out a cheque for £10 or a £10 cheque; you can pay by cash, cheque or credit card;* **crossed cheque** = cheque with two lines across it showing that it can only be deposited at a bank and not exchanged for cash; **open** *or* **uncrossed cheque** = cheque which can be cashed anywhere; **blank cheque** = cheque with the amount of money and the payee left blank, but signed by the drawer; *(informal)* **dud cheque** *or* **bouncing cheque** *or* **cheque which bounces** *or* *US* **rubber check** = cheque which cannot be cashed because the person writing it has not enough money in the account to pay it; **traveller's cheques** *or* *US* **traveler's checks** = cheques taken by a traveller, which can be cashed in a foreign country **(b) to cash a cheque** = to exchange a cheque for cash; **to endorse a cheque** = to sign a cheque on the back to show that you accept it; **to make out a cheque to someone** = to write someone's name on a cheque; *who shall I make the cheque out to?;* **to pay by cheque** = to pay by giving a cheque, and not by using cash or a credit card; **to pay a cheque into your account** = to deposit a cheque; **to sign a cheque** = to sign on the front of a cheque to show that you authorize the bank to pay the money from your account; **to stop a cheque** = to ask a bank not to pay a cheque you have written (NOTE: US spelling is **check**)

◊ **cheque book** *noun* booklet of new cheques (NOTE: US spelling is **checkbook**)

◊ **cheque card** *or* **cheque guarantee card** *noun* plastic card from a bank which guarantees payment of a cheque up to a certain amount, even if there is no money in the account

cherry *noun Prunus,* a tree with many small-stoned small summer fruit, usually dark red, but also light red or almost white, growing on a long stalks; **cherry pie** = pie filled with cherries; **cherry tomato** = variety of very small tomato

chervil *noun* herb *Anthriscus cerefolium,* used to flavour soups

chestnut *noun* bright red-brown nut; **sweet chestnut** = edible chestnut; *roast turkey and chestnut stuffing;* **chestnut purée** = purée made of cooked sweet chestnuts, usually with added sugar and vanilla

COMMENT: the sweet chestnut, *Castanea sativa,* is eaten in sauces with roast meat, is made into sweet purée or eaten hot roasted over charcoal in the street. There is another chestnut tree, which is common in Britain, the horse chestnut, *Aesculus hippocastanum,* which has similar brown nuts which are not edible

chez *French word (meaning 'at someone's home')* frequently used in the names of French restaurants, such as 'Chez Victor'

chianti *noun* dry red wine from Tuscany, Italy

chicken *noun* common farm bird which is eaten as food; *we had roast chicken for lunch; chicken soup; chicken salad; chicken sandwich;* **chicken Kiev** = boned piece of chicken, filled with garlic and butter, which is covered in breadcrumbs and deep-fried

COMMENT: chicken is the most widely used meat in Britain, and also one of the cheapest

chicory *noun* vegetable with a conical white head of crisp leaves, eaten raw as a salad or cooked and served with a sauce; the root of the plant is dried and ground to mix with coffee to make it bitter; *see also* ENDIVE

child *noun* young person (under 12 years old); **children's menu** = special menu for children (NOTE: children's menus usually contain fast food items, such as hamburgers or hot dogs) **children's play area** *or* **children's playground** = area outside a pub, hotel or restaurant, or in a town garden, or inside a ferry, where children can play; **child's portion** *or* **children's portion** = small portion for a child; **children's room** = room in a pub, usually away from the bar, where children can eat (NOTE: plural is **children**)

chill *verb* to make cold; *chilled orange juice;* **chilled food** = food which has been prepared, then made cold

COMMENT: low temperature retards the rate at which food spoils. Pre-cooked foods should be cooled rapidly down to - 3°C and eaten within five days of production. Certain high-risk chilled foods should be kept below 5°C; these foods include soft cheese and various pre-cooked products. Eggs in shells can be chilled for short-term storage (i.e. up to one month) at temperatures between - 10°C and -16°C. Bread goes stale quickly at chill temperatures. Potatoes, lettuces and strawberries must not be chilled at all.

chilli *or* *US* **chili** *noun* fruit of the *Capsicum,* a very hot-tasting pod with seeds in it; available fresh as green or red

chillis, dried or preserved in cans or bottles. The dried pods are ground to make Cayenne pepper; **chilli con carne =** Mexican dish of beans, minced beef and chilli sauce; **chilli sauce =** tomato sauce flavoured with chilli

chilly *adjective* quite cold; *you should pack a warm pullover, as even the summer evenings can be chilly in the mountains*

china *or* **chinaware** *noun* porcelain, cups, saucers, and other dishes made from fine white clay

QUOTE at his newly opened restaurant, he said the he chose white Italian bone china because 'plain food needed a plain backdrop'
Caterer & Hotelkeeper

Chinese gooseberry *see* KIWI FRUIT

Chinese restaurant syndrome *noun* allergic condition which gives people violent headaches after eating food flavoured with monosodium glutamate, often used in Chinese cooking to enhance flavour

chip *noun* **(a)** *GB* small stick-shaped piece of potato, fried in oil or fat; *she had a hamburger and a portion of chips; fried eggs and chips;* **fish and chips** = traditional British food, obtained from special shops, where portions of fish fried in batter are sold with chips; **fish-and-chip shop** = shop selling cooked fish and chips, and usually other food, such as pies (NOTE: in the USA, chips are called **French fries.** Note also that a fish-and-chip shop can also be called a **fish shop** or a **chip shop) (b)** *US* thin slice of potato, fried till crisp and eaten cold as a snack (NOTE: In GB English, this is called a **crisp) (c)** small piece of something; **chocolate chip** = small piece of hard chocolate, used in ice cream, biscuits or cakes; *chocolate chip biscuit; mint chocolate chip ice cream; chocolate chip cookies*

chit *noun* bill (for food or drink in a club)

chitterlings *plural noun* small intestines of pigs, used for food

chives *plural noun* onion-like herb *(Allium schoenoprasum)* of which the leaves are used as a garnish or in soups and salads; **cream cheese and chives** = common use of chives, chopped and mixed with cream cheese to form a spread

chlorine *noun* greenish gas used to disinfect swimming pools, sterilize drinking water, etc.

◊ **chlorinate** *verb* to disinfect or sterilize with chlorine

◊ **chlorination** *noun* disinfecting or sterilizing by adding chlorine; *chlorination tablets can be added to water to make it safe to drink*

◊ **chlorinator** *noun* apparatus for adding chlorine to water

COMMENT: chlorination is used to kill bacteria in drinking water, in swimming pools and sewage farms, and has many industrial applications such as sterilization in food processing

chlorophyll *noun* green pigment in plants

COMMENT: chlorophyll absorbs light energy from the sun and supplies plants with the energy to enable them to carry out photosynthesis. It is also used as a colouring (E140) in processed food

Chlorophyta *noun* genus of green algae, the largest class of algae

Chloroquine *noun* anti-malarial drug (taken in conjunction with Proguanil, especially in those areas where the malaria parasites are resistant to Chloroquine)

choc *noun (informal)* chocolate

◊ **choc-ice** *noun* hard block of ice-cream covered with chocolate

chocolate *noun* **(a)** popular sweet food made from the cocoa bean (the beans are roasted, and then mixed with oils and sugar); **milk chocolate** = sweet pale brown chocolate made with milk; **plain chocolate** = dark, bitter chocolate; **hot chocolate** = hot drink made of powdered chocolate; **chocolate biscuit** *or* **chocolate cake** *or* **chocolate ice cream** = biscuit *or* cake *or* ice cream flavoured with chocolate **(b)** small sweet made from chocolate; *a box of chocolates was left with the compliments of the management; the coffee is served with a small plate of chocolate mints*

COMMENT: good quality chocolate contains a minimum of about 34% cocoa solids

choke 1 *noun* **(a)** *(in a car engine)* valve which reduces the flow of air to the engine;

knob on the dashboard which activates this valve **(b)** central inedible part of a globe artichoke **2** *verb* **(a)** to block (a pipe, etc.) **(b)** to stop breathing because you have swallowed something; **to choke on something** = to take something into the windpipe instead of the gullet, so that the breathing is interrupted; *he choked on a piece of bread or a piece of bread made him choke*

cholera *noun* serious bacterial disease spread through food *or* water which has been infected by *Vibrio cholerae; a cholera epidemic broke out after the flood*

COMMENT: the infected person suffers diarrhoea, cramp in the intestines and dehydration. The disease may be fatal and vaccination is only effective for a relatively short period (no more than six months)

chop 1 *noun* piece of meat with a rib bone; *pork chop; lamb chop* **2** *verb* to cut into small pieces with an axe or sharp knife; **chopped livers** = Jewish dish, made of cooked chicken livers, chopped up into small pieces; **chopping board** = piece of thick wood, used in a kitchen to cut up food on

◊ **chopsticks** *plural noun* pair of small sticks used in the Far East to eat food or to stir food when cooking; *he said he didn't know how to use chopsticks and asked for a knife and fork instead*

chowder *noun US* fish soup; *clam chowder*

COMMENT: chowders are made from ordinary white fish or from shellfish such as lobsters or clams. The fish is cooked with vegetables and milk or cream is added to make a thick soup

Christian name *noun* first name *or* given name (as opposed to a surname or family name)

Christmas *noun* Christian festival on December 25th; **Christmas cake** = specially rich fruit cake, decorated with icing; **Christmas Day** = December 25th; **Christmas decorations** = coloured papers, bunting, holly, mistletoe, etc., used to decorate a restaurant or hotel for Christmas; **Christmas holidays** = holiday period from at least December 24th to after January 1st; **Christmas lunch** = special lunch menu with turkey and cranberry sauce, Christmas pudding, mince pies;

Christmas pudding = rich fruit pudding, cooked by steaming, served with brandy butter sauce

COMMENT: special food eaten at Christmas time includes Christmas pudding and mince pies (eaten at Christmas lunch or dinner), and Christmas cake, eaten at tea time. Typical decorations for Christmas include a Christmas tree with small lights, holly with red berries, and mistletoe

Chunnel *noun* the Channel Tunnel, a tunnel for trains under the English Channel, linking England and France

church *noun* large building for Christian religious ceremonies

cider *noun* alcoholic drink made from apple juice

COMMENT: cider is usually naturally fizzy; it can be sweet or dry. Strong traditional cider is known as 'scrumpy', especially in south-western England

cine-camera *noun* camera for taking moving pictures

cinema *noun* theatre where films are shown
◊ **cinemagoer** *noun* person who goes to the cinema

cinnamon *noun* spice made from the bark of a tropical tree

COMMENT: cinnamon is used to flavour sweet dishes, cakes and drinks

circle *noun* row of seats above the stalls in a theatre

circus *noun* (a) travelling show, often given under a large tent, with animals, clowns, acrobats, etc. (b) busy roundabout or road junction in a large town; *Oxford Circus; Piccadilly Circus*

citizen *noun* (a) inhabitant of a town (b) person with full rights as an inhabitant of a country; *he's a British citizen; she became an Irish citizen in 1991*

citrus fruit *noun* edible fruits of evergreen citrus trees, grown throughout the tropics and subtropics; the most important are oranges, lemons, grapefruit and limes; citrus fruit have thick skins, are very acidic and are an important source of Vitamin C
◊ **citric acid** *noun* acid found in fruit such as oranges, lemons and grapefruit

city *noun* (a) large town; *the largest cities in Europe are linked by hourly flights;* **city break** = short holiday in a large city (usually a two- or three-day stay, over a weekend) at a specially low tariff; **city centre** = centre of a city; *it's more convenient to stay in city-centre hotels, but they can be noisy;* **city hall** = building where the administration of a city is; **city terminal** = air terminal in the centre of a large town; **capital city** = main town in a country, where the government is located; *see also* INTER-CITY **(b) the City** = old centre of London, where banks and large companies have their main offices; the British financial centre

Civil Aviation Authority (CAA) *noun* British government agency which regulates the operation of civilian airlines

claim 1 *noun* **baggage claim** = place in an airport where baggage comes off the plane onto a carousel to be claimed by the passengers **2** *verb* to say that something belongs to you; *no one has claimed the umbrella left in the reception*

claret *noun* red wine from Bordeaux

class *noun* category *or* group into which things are classified according to quality or price; **first class** *or* **top class** = top quality *or* most expensive; *it's a first-class restaurant;* **economy class** *or* **tourist class** = cheapest category of seats on a plane; *I travel economy class because it is cheaper; tourist class travel is less comfortable than first class; he always travels first class because tourist class is too uncomfortable;* **high-class** = of very good quality; *a high-class coach service*
◊ **classy** *adjective (informal)* of good quality; *it's a really classy joint*

classify *verb* to put into classes *or* categories; **classified advertisements** = advertisements listed in a newspaper under special headings (such as 'property for sale' or 'jobs wanted'); **classified directory** = book which lists businesses grouped under various headings (such as computer shops *or* newsagents)
◊ **classification** *noun* way of putting into classes according to quality

COMMENT: the English Tourist Board uses the following classification symbols: for quality there are four grades: Approved, Commended, Highly Commended, De Luxe. For facilities offered by inns, bed and breakfast accommodation, boarding houses, etc. there are five grades, shown by one crown to five crowns. For facilities offered by self-catering accommodation there are five grades, shown by one key to five keys. These classifications refer to the facilities offered, not to the quality of the establishment

clean 1 *adjective* not dirty; *the maid forgot to put clean towels in the bathroom* **2** *verb* to remove dirt

◊ **cleaner** *noun* person or thing which removes dirt; **vacuum cleaner** = cleaning machine which sucks up dust; **(dry) cleaner's** = shop where clothes are taken to be cleaned with chemicals

◊ **cleaning** *noun* removing dirt; *the cleaning staff come on shift at 5.30*

clear *verb* to remove dirty plates, cutlery and glasses from (a table)

◊ **clearance** *noun* removing dirty plates, cutlery and glasses from a table

clerk *noun* person who works in an office; **booking clerk** = person who sells tickets in a booking office

client *noun* person with whom business is done *or* person who pays for a service

◊ **clientele** *noun* all the clients of a business; all the customers of a shop

cliff *noun* high rock face, usually by the sea; *the White Cliffs of Dover*

climate *noun* general state of the weather in a particular place; *the South Coast has a very mild climate; the climate in Central Europe is hot in the summer and cold and dry in the winter*

climb 1 *noun* act of going up; *it's a stiff climb to the top of the hill* **2** *verb* **(a)** to go up; *the road climbs up to 1,000m above sea level* **(b)** to climb mountains; *they went climbing in the Alps; we had a climbing holiday last Easter*

clingstone *see* PEACH

clip joint *noun* low-class club or bar, where guests are charged too much for their drinks, etc.

cloakroom *noun* **(a)** room where people can leave coats, hats, etc., when going into a restaurant, theatre, opera house, etc.; **cloakroom attendant** = person in charge of a cloakroom **(b)** *(informal)* public toilet (i.e. room with lavatories, washbasins, etc.)

◊ **cloaks** *noun (informal)* = TOILET

clock *noun* machine for telling the time; **alarm clock** = clock which rings a bell to wake you up; **bedside clock** = clock placed next to a bed; **clock radio** = radio and clock combined; **to work right round the clock** = to work all day long

◊ **clock golf** *noun* game like golf where you hit the ball into a central hole from points round a circle

◊ **clock in** *or* **clock on** *verb (of worker)* to record the time of arriving for work by putting a card into a special timing machine

◊ **clock out** *or* **clock off** *verb (of worker)* to record the time of leaving work by putting a card into a special timing machine

◊ **clocking in** *or* **clocking on** *noun* arriving for work and recording the time on a time-card

◊ **clocking out** *or* **clocking off** *noun* leaving work and recording the time on a time-card

close 1 *adjective* **close to** = very near *or* almost; *the hotel is close to the railway station* **2** *verb* **(a)** to stop doing business for the day; *the office closes at 5.30; we close early on Saturdays* **(b)** to close an account = (i) to stop supplying a customer on credit; (ii) to take all the money out of a bank account and ask the bank to remove it; **he closed his building society account** = he took all the money out and stopped using the account

◊ **closed** *adjective* shut *or* not open *or* not doing business; *most shops in Germany are closed on Saturday afternoons; all the banks are closed on the National Day;* **closed-circuit TV** = system where a TV picture is transmitted from a camera to receivers within a closed circuit, used for surveillance in factories, shops, banks, etc., and for showing pictures of events to people who are not able to attend the event themselves; *the conference was relayed to the lobby on closed-circuit TV; the shoplifters were filmed on closed-circuit TV cameras*

◇ **closing 1** *adjective* final *or* coming at the end; **closing date** = last date **2** *noun* shutting of a shop *or* being shut; **early closing day** = weekday (usually Wednesday or Thursday) when many shops close in the afternoon; **Sunday closing** = not opening a shop on Sundays; **closing time** = time when a shop or office stops work or when a pub stops selling alcohol

Clostridium *noun* type of bacterium

COMMENT: species of Clostridium include *Clostridium welchii* or *perfringens,* which is found in soil, and so is present on unwashed vegetables; also found in food which has been cooked, then cooled too slowly or chilled, and then reheated. Also *Clostridium botulinum,* which is very poisonous, and is found in home-made pickles or home-cured ham (it may cause death). *Clostridium tetani* causes tetanus

clotted cream *noun* thick solid cream made from milk which has been heated to boiling point (produced especially in the south-west of England)

cloud *noun* mass of vapour or smoke (in the air)
◇ **cloud-capped** *adjective* (mountain) topped with clouds
◇ **cloudy** *adjective* **(a)** covered with clouds; *a cloudy sky; the north coast is often cloudy* **(b)** not clear *or* not transparent; *my beer looks cloudy*

club *noun* **(a)** group of people who have the same interest; place where these people meet; *the members of the old people's club went to the seaside for the day; he has applied to join the sports club;* **club membership** = all the members of a club; **club subscription** = money paid to belong to a club **(b)** **club class** = specially comfortable class of seating on a plane, though not as luxurious as first class
◇ **club sandwich** *noun* sandwich made of three slices of bread, with a filling of meat, salad, fish, etc., between them

cm = CENTIMETRE

coach *noun* **(a)** (i) large comfortable bus, operated for long-distance travellers on a regular route; (ii) large comfortable bus, used by a group of tourists to travel long distances, not on a regular scheduled route, and often abroad; *they took a coach tour of southern Spain; the coach driver fell asleep while driving; coach travel is considerably cheaper than trains;* **tourist coach** = coach carrying tourists, visiting various places of interest; **coach party** = group of tourists, travelling by coach; **coach station** = central terminus from which coaches leave, and where coach journeys terminate (it has ticket office, waiting rooms, refreshments, telephones, etc.); **coach tour** = tour of various places, in a coach **(b)** wagon on a train; *passengers for Donniford should board the last two coaches of the train* **(c)** person who trains someone in a sport; *the hotel has a professional tennis coach available for lessons*

coast 1 *noun* land by the sea; **from coast to coast** = across an area of land from one sea to another **2** *verb* **(a)** to ride a vehicle without using the engine or the pedals **(b)** *(of a boat)* to sail along a coast
◇ **coastal** *adjective* referring to the coast; *coastal navigation*
◇ **coaster** *noun* **(a)** ship which sails from port to port along the coast **(b)** flat dish or small mat for standing a bottle or glass on
◇ **coastguard** *noun* person who guards a piece of coast (watching out for wrecks, smugglers, etc.)
◇ **coastline** *noun* edge of the coast

coat *noun* piece of outdoor clothing which covers the top part of the body
◇ **coat-hanger** *noun* piece of wood, wire or plastic on which you hang clothes in a wardrobe
◇ **coat-hook** *noun* hook (on a wall or door) for hanging clothes on

cob *noun* round loaf of bread

cockle *noun noun* small edible shellfish with a double shell

cockroach *noun* large brown or black beetle

COMMENT: two types of cockroach as common: the oriental cockroach, *Blatta orientalis,* and the German cockroach, *Blatta germanica.* Both live in dirty areas of buildings, such as badly cleaned kitchens. They can carry Salmonella and Staphylococcus

cocktail *noun* **(a)** mixture of alcoholic drinks, containing at least one spirit, usually served before a meal; **cocktail bar =** bar where cocktails are served; **cocktail**

lounge = smart lounge bar in a hotel; **cocktail snacks** = small items of food (olives, peanuts, etc.) served with drinks before a meal; **cocktail stick** = little piece of wood used to stick in food (such as small sausages) to make it easier to serve **(b)** mixture of food; **fruit cocktail** = mixture of fruit; **prawn cocktail** = starter consisting of shelled prawns in mayonnaise and tomato dressing, served in a glass

COMMENT: cocktails are mixes of various alcohols and juices, as opposed to long drinks (whisky and soda, gin and tonic), where the alcohol is diluted Most alcohols can be used as a basis for cocktails: the commonest are gin (gin and French, gin and Italian), vodka (screwdriver, Bloody Mary) and whisky (whisky sour, Manhattan)

cocoa *noun* **(a)** powder made from chocolate beans **(b)** drink made from this powder; *he had a mug of cocoa*

COMMENT: cocoa is obtained from beans which are the seeds of the *Theobroma cacao* tree and which are contained in a red or green fleshy fruit. The beans contain a fat (cocoa butter), which is removed in preparing cocoa for drinking. Cocoa beans are the raw material of chocolate, and extra fat and sugar are added in its preparation

coconut *noun* large nut from a tropical palm tree *(Cocos nucifera)* containing a white edible pulp; **coconut milk** = (i) liquid inside a coconut; (ii) white creamy liquid made from coconut pulp, used in Malaysian and Thai cooking; **coconut shy** = stall at a fair where you try to hit coconuts with a ball

cod *noun* large white sea fish, *Gadus morhua* **cod liver oil** = oil from the livers of cod, taken as a source of vitamins A and D (NOTE: plural is **cod**)

COD = CASH ON DELIVERY

code *noun* **(a)** system of signs *or* numbers *or* letters which mean something; **airline identification code** = letters which are given to all flights operated by an airline (such as BA for British Airways, LH for Lufthansa, AF for Air France, etc.); **airport code** = letters which are given to identify a particular airport (LHR for London Heathrow, CDG for Charles de Gaulle,

etc.); **area code** = special telephone number which is given to a particular area; *the area code for central London is 071;* **bar code** = system of lines printed on a product which can be read by a computer to give a reference number or price; **country code** = numbers which are used to make a telephone call to indicate a country (-33- for France, -44- for the UK, -1- for the USA and Canada, etc.); the number is dialled after the international access code and before the town code or subscriber's number; **date code** = signs or numbers which indicate a sell-by date; **international access code** = number used to start making a telephone call to another country (from the UK, it is 010-; from most other countries it is 00-); the number is followed by the country code; **machine-readable codes** = sets of signs or letters (such as bar codes *or* postcodes) which can be read by computers; **stock code** = numbers and letters which refer to an item of stock **(b)** set of rules; **code of practice** *or US* **code of ethics** = rules drawn up by an association which the members must follow when doing business

coffee *noun* **(a)** crushed beans of the coffee plant *(Coffea)*, used to make a hot drink **(b)** drink made from ground coffee beans or powder, mixed with hot water; **black coffee** = coffee without milk; **Irish coffee** = hot coffee with Irish whiskey, brown sugar and fresh cream; **morning coffee** = coffee served with biscuits as a mid-morning snack; **white coffee** = coffee with milk or cream; **Greek coffee** *or* **Turkish coffee** = finely ground coffee heated with sugar and water; **coffee cake** = cake made with coffee flavouring; **coffee ice cream** = ice cream flavoured with coffee

COMMENT: the two main varieties of coffee are Arabica and Robusta. The Arabica shrub, (Coffea arabica) was originally grown in the southern parts of the highlands of Ethiopia, and was later introduced into south-western Arabia. It represents 75% of the world's total coffee production. Arabica coffee beans are generally considered to produce a higher quality drink than those obtained from the Robusta coffee plant (Coffea canephora) which originated in West Africa. Robusta coffee has a stronger and more bitter taste than Arabica. The most important area for growing coffee is South America, especially Bolivia, Brazil and Colombia, though it is also grown in Kenya and Indonesia

◊ **coffee bar** *noun* small bar serving mainly coffee, non-alcoholic drinks and snacks

◊ **coffee cup** *noun* cup for coffee

COMMENT: coffee is served in large cups at breakfast (when it is usually taken with milk or cream) and in small cups after a meal. The small coffee cup is called a 'demi-tasse'

◊ **coffee lounge** *noun* restaurant which serves coffee and cakes

◊ **coffee machine** *noun* machine which provides coffee and other drinks when a coin is inserted

◊ **coffeemaker** *noun* small pot for making coffee, such as a percolator or espresso machine

◊ **coffee pot** *noun* pot in which coffee is made or served

◊ **coffee shop** *noun* less formal restaurant in a hotel, where light meals and snacks are served

◊ **coffee spoon** *noun* very small spoon, used with a small coffee cup

◊ **coffee table** *noun* low table (originally, a table on which coffee cups were put)

cognac *noun* brandy made in western France

coin *noun* piece of metal money; *he gave me two 10-franc coins in my change; I need some 10p coins for the telephone*

cola *noun* tree *(Cola acuminata)* which is indigenous to West Africa, but which is also grown in the West Indies and South America. The nut-like fruit contain caffeine, and can be chewed or used to make 'cola' drinks

cold *adjective* not hot; *the machines work badly in cold weather; the reception area was so cold that the staff started complaining; the coffee machine also sells cold drinks;* **cold room** *or* **cold store** = room where stores of food are kept cool, so as to prevent it going bad

coleslaw *noun* salad of shredded white cabbage mixed with mayonnaise

coley *noun* type of sea fish

coliform *adjective* (bacteria) which are similar to *Escherichia coli*

COMMENT: if *Escherichia coli* is found in water, it indicates that the water has been polluted by faeces, although it may not cause any illness

collect 1 *verb* **(a)** to make someone pay money which is owed; **to collect a debt** = to go and make someone pay a debt **(b)** to take someone or something away from a place; *a car will come to collect you from the hotel at 8.30* **2** *adverb & adjective US* (phone call) where the person receiving the call agrees to pay for it; *he made a collect call or he called his office collect*

college *noun* teaching establishment (for adults and adolescents); *he is taking a course at the catering college;* **college of further education** = college for study after secondary school

colour *or US* **color** *noun* shade or tint which an object has in light; **colour film** *or* **colour TV** = film or TV which is not black and white

◊ **colour coding** *noun* indicating different usages by colour

COMMENT: electric wires are colour coded as red (= live), blue (= neutral) and yellow-green (=earth). It has been suggested that kitchen knives should be colour-coded to identify knives used to cut raw meat, fish, vegetables, etc., so as to avoid possible contamination

◊ **colouring (matter)** *noun* substance which colours a processed food

COMMENT: colouring additives have E numbers 100 to 180. Some are natural pigments, such as riboflavine (E101), carrot juice (E160) or chlorophyll (E140) and are safe. Others, such as tartrazine (E102) and other azo dyes are suspected of being carcinogenic. Also suspect is caramel (E150), which is the most widely used colouring substance

come to *verb* to add up to; *the bill comes to £125*

comfort *noun* ease of living; *US* **comfort station** = public toilet

◊ **comfortable** *adjective* soft and relaxing; *there are more comfortable chairs in the lounge, if you find the dining room chairs too hard*

◊ **comfortably** *adverb* in a soft and relaxing way

commend *verb* to say that something *or* someone is good; **highly commended** *or* **commended** = second and third grades in the English Tourist Board's grading system for hotels, bed and breakfasts, and guesthouse accommodation

commercial 1 *adjective* referring to business; **commercial directory** = book which lists all the businesses and business people in a town; **commercial district** = part of a town where offices and shops are situated; **commercial hotel** = hotel which specializes in business travellers; **commercial traveller** = salesman who travels round an area visiting customers on behalf of his company **2** *noun* advertisement on TV or radio

commis *French noun* assistant (in a restaurant or kitchen); **commis chef** = assistant to a chef de partie; **commis saucier** = assistant to the chef saucier, helping him prepare sauces; **commis waiter** = assistant waiter, a waiter who helps a station waiter

commission *noun* money paid to a salesman *or* an agent, usually a percentage of the sales made; *she gets 10% commission on everything she sells*; **he charges 10% commission** = he asks for 10% of sales as his payment
◇ **commissionable** *adjective* (service *or* sale) on which commission will be paid to the agent

commissionaire *noun* man (usually in uniform) who stands at the entrance to a hotel *or* restaurant *or* club and welcomes guests

communicable disease *noun* disease which can be passed from one person to another *or* from an animal to a person

communicate *verb* to pass information to someone; *he finds it impossible to communicate with his staff; communicating with head office has been quicker since we installed the fax*
◇ **communication** *noun* (a) passing of information; *communication with the head office has been made easier by the fax;* **communication cord** = wire in a train carriage, which you pull to stop the train in an emergency; **to enter into communication with someone** = to start discussing something with someone, usually in writing; *we have entered into communication with the relevant government department* (b) **communications** = being able to contact people *or* to pass messages by telephone, radio, etc.; *after the flood all communications with the outside world were broken*

commute *verb* to travel to work in town every day; *he commutes 70 miles a day*
◇ **commuter** *noun* person who travels to work in town every day; **commuter belt** = area round a town where commuters live; **commuter flight** = flight between towns used regularly by commuters; **commuter train** = train for commuters

compactor *noun* machine which crushes waste into small packs which are relatively easy to dispose of

companion *noun* person travelling with a passenger

COMMENT: some airlines offer special promotional fares for a second person travelling with a full fare paying passenger

company *noun* business *or* group of people organized to buy, sell or provide a service; **company booking** *or* **company reservation** = booking on behalf of a company (usually at a discount to the normal rate); **company discount** = discount given to people working for a certain company

compartment *noun* section of a train carriage *or* of a plane, separated from other sections; *I had to go through the smoking compartment to get to the galley*

compensate *verb* to pay for damage done; *the airline refused to compensate him when his baggage was lost* (NOTE: you compensate someone **for** something)
◇ **compensation** *noun* **compensation for damage** = payment for damage done; **compensation for loss of property** = payment to someone whose property has been stolen or lost

complain *verb* to say that you are not satisfied; *he complained about the price of meals in the restaurant; she complained that no one spoke English in the hotel* (NOTE: you complain **to** someone **about** something or **that** something is no good)
◇ **complaint** *noun* grumble, statement that something is wrong; **complaints department** = section of a store *or* office which deals with complaints from customers

compliment 1 *noun* **compliments** = good wishes; *a box of chocolates with the compliments of the manager or with the manager's compliments; please accept these flowers with my compliments;* **compliments slip** = piece of paper with the name and address of the company printed on it, sent with documents, gifts, etc., instead of a letter **2** *verb* to praise; *the manager complimented the staff on their efficient service; I would like to compliment the chef on an excellent meal*

◊ **complimentary** *adjective* given free; **complimentary ticket** = free ticket, given as a present; *each guest receives a complimentary box of chocolates*

comply *verb* **to comply with** = to observe (a rule); to obey (an order)

comprehensive *adjective* which includes everything; **comprehensive insurance** = insurance policy which covers you against all risks which are likely to happen

comptroller *noun* person who controls the finances in a hotel

compulsory *adjective* which you are forced to do; *a compulsory injection against cholera*

computer *noun* electronic machine which calculates *or* stores information and processes it automatically; **computer bureau** = office which offers to do work on its computers for people who do not have their own computers with them; **computer department** = department in a company which manages the company's computers; **computer error** = mistake made by a computer; **computer listing** = printout of a list of items taken from data stored in a computer; **computer manager** = person in charge of a computer department; **computer program** = series of instructions given to a computer, to make it do a particular piece of work; **computer programmer** = person who writes computer programs; **computer reservation system (CRS)** = system by which flight bookings, rooms in hotels, etc. can be booked from the terminal in the travel agent's office or from an in-flight terminal system direct to a central booking computer

◊ **computerize** *verb* to change from a manual system to one using computers; *our booking system has been completely computerized*

◊ **computerized** *adjective* worked by computers; *a computerized reservation system*

◊ **computer-linked** *adjective* linked by computer; *all the hotels in the group use a computer-linked booking system*

QUOTE direct satellite links into ground-based computer reservations systems will let you book or change tickets and hotel rooms from your seat, thanks to today's ever more sophisticated computer reservations systems - known in the industry as CRS networks - which put travel agents and, increasingly, their customers directly on line to most of the available airline seats and business hotel rooms in the world

Business Travel

QUOTE independent hotels wishing to attract international business will be at a disadvantage if they are not linked to a global computerized booking system

Caterer & Hotelkeeper

concern 1 *noun* **(a)** business *or* company; **his business is a going concern** = the company is working (and making a profit); **sold as a going concern** = sold as an actively trading company **(b)** being worried about a problem; *the management showed no concern at all for the safety of the guests* **2** *verb* to deal with *or* to be connected with; *the waiters are not concerned with the cleaning of the restaurant; he filled in a questionnaire concerning computer utilization*

concession *noun* **(a)** right to be the only seller of a product in a place; *she runs a jewellery concession in the hotel lobby* **(b)** allowance; **tax concession** = allowing less tax to be paid

◊ **concessionaire** *noun* person who has the right to be the only seller of a product in a place

◊ **concessionary fare** *noun* reduced fare for certain types of passenger (such as employees or retired employees of the transport company)

concierge *French noun* **(a)** person who guards the door of a block of flats or offices, and decides who can come in **(b)** *(in a hotel)* member of staff who provides special services for guests, such as getting theatre or tour tickets for them

condiment *noun* spice which is put directly onto food by the eater

COMMENT: the commonest condiments are salt, pepper, mustard, vinegar, pickles, mayonnaise, and tomato sauce. In some restaurants, they are in pots on the table, and in self-service restaurants they may be provided in small sachets

condition *noun* **(a)** state; *snow conditions are good; the meterological office forecast poor weather conditions* **(b)** term of a contract; duties which have to be carried out as part of a contract; **conditions of employment** *or* **conditions of service** = terms of a contract of employment; **conditions of sale** = agreed ways in which a sale takes place (such as discounts *or* credit terms); **on condition that** = provided that; *they were granted the lease on condition that they paid the legal costs*

◊ **conditioning** *noun* making meat more tender by keeping it for some time at a low temperature; *see also* AIR-CONDITIONING

conductor *noun* person who takes money and gives out tickets on a bus or tram

cone *noun* round tube of biscuit, tapering to a point (used for serving ice cream) (NOTE: also called an **ice cream cornet**)

confectionery *noun* **(a)** shop selling sweets and chocolates **(b)** sweets and chocolates

conference *noun* **(a)** meeting of people to discuss problems; **to be in conference** = to be in a meeting; **conference phone** = telephone so arranged that several people can speak into it from around a table; **conference room** = room where small meetings can take place; **press conference** = meeting where newspaper and TV reporters are invited to hear news of a new product, a takeover bid, a court case, etc.; **sales conference** = meeting of sales managers, representatives, publicity staff, etc., to discuss results and future sales plans **(b)** meeting of an association *or* a society *or* a union; *the annual conference of the Electricians' Union; the conference of the Booksellers' Association; the conference agenda* or *the agenda of the conference was drawn up by the secretary; the conference will be held in the Manor Hotel;* **conference centre** = series of meeting rooms, with bedrooms, restaurants, etc., built specially for holding large meetings; **conference organizer** = person who organizes large meetings **(c)** informal agreement between airlines or shipping lines to restrict competition on certain routes

QUOTE two thirds of the UK's 100 or so universities take conference business in vacation time and 30 have year-round management centres

Caterer & Hotelkeeper

configure *verb* to plan the layout of seats in an aircraft

◊ **configuration** *noun* layout of the seats in an aircraft

QUOTE the economy class was configured 3-4-3 and both seat pitch and legroom were comfortable

Business Traveller

confirm *noun* to make definite *or* to make sure; *I am writing to confirm the booking made by telephone*

◊ **confirmation** *noun* making definite *or* making sure; **confirmation of a booking** = making a booking definite; **he received confirmation from the hotel that the deposit had been received** = he was told by letter or by phone that the hotel had definitely received the deposit

congestion *noun* blocking (of streets); *traffic congestion* or *congestion on the motorways; flights have been delayed because of congestion at London Airport*

congress *noun* meeting of a group of people

connect *verb* to link with *or* to join; *the hotel is connected to a major European hotel chain; the flight from New York connects with a flight to Athens* = the plane from New York arrives in time for passengers to catch the plane to Athens

◊ **connecting** *adjective* **(a)** **connecting rooms** = rooms which are next door to each other and have a door which connects them **(b)** **connecting flight** *or* **train** = plane *or* train which a passenger will be on time to catch and which will take him to his next destination; *check at the helicopter desk for connecting flights to the city centre; there are no connecting trains to Halifax after 10.00 p.m.*

◊ **connection** *noun* **(a)** link *or* something which joins; *the train to York has connections to Scarborough and Whitby; passengers with onward connections should check at the transit desk on arrival* **(b)** **in connection with** = referring to; *I want to* speak to the restaurant manager in connection with the service

◊ **connections** plural noun people you know; **he has connections in the theatre** = he has friends or knows people who work in the theatre

consolidate verb **(a)** to group goods together for shipping **(b)** to group bookings made in different travel agencies together

◊ **consolidation** noun grouping together of goods for shipping or of ticket bookings

◊ **consolidator** noun company which groups together bookings made by various agencies so as to get cheaper group fares on ordinary scheduled flights

QUOTE airline consolidators which sell scheduled airline tickets at greatly reduced prices are basically seen by many as the acceptable face of bucket shops
Sunday Times

consommé noun clear soup made from meat, poultry, fish or vegetables; *chicken consommé; beef consommé;* cold consommé = jelly-like soup, which is served cold

consortium noun group of companies (such as independent hotels) which work together (NOTE: plural is **consortia**)

consul noun representative of a country in another country, dealing with questions relating to nationals of his own country and issuing visas for foreigners who wish to enter his country; *the British Consul in Lisbon;* consul-general = main consul, who supervises several staff, or several consuls in different parts of the country

◊ **consulate** noun office of a consul; *the consulate is closed on Sundays; members of the consulate staff visited the accident victims in hospital; see also* AMBASSADOR, EMBASSY

COMMENT: consulates deal with administrative details, such as passports and visas, but also look after their own nationals when they are in trouble, as when they lose their money, get arrested, etc.

consume verb to use; to eat; *the guests consumed over 100 hamburgers*

◊ **consumables** plural noun things which are bought and used (such as fax paper, food and drink)

◊ **consumption** noun buying or using goods or services; *a car with low petrol consumption; the hotel has a heavy consumption of gas;* home consumption or domestic consumption = use of something in the home; not for human consumption = not to be eaten by people

contact 1 noun **(a)** person you know or person you can ask for help or advice; *he has many contacts in the city; who is your contact in the Ministry of Tourism?* **(b)** act of getting in touch with someone; **I have lost contact with them** = I do not communicate with them any longer; **he put me in contact with a good lawyer** = he introduced me to a good lawyer **2** verb to get in touch with someone or to communicate with someone; *he tried to contact his office by phone; can you contact the courier at the airport?*

contaminate verb to make something impure by touching it or by adding something to it; *supplies of drinking water were contaminated by refuse from the factories; a whole group of tourists fell ill after eating contaminated food*

◊ **contaminant** noun substance which contaminates

◊ **contamination** noun **(a)** making something impure by touching it or by adding something to it **(b)** state of something (such as water or food) which has been contaminated and so is harmful to living organisms; *the contamination resulted from drinking polluted water*

content noun proportion of a substance in something; *these foods have a high starch content; dried fruit has a higher sugar content than fresh fruit*

continent noun **(a)** one of the major land areas in the world (Africa, North America, South America, Asia, Australia, Europe) **(b)** *(in Britain)* the rest of Europe, as opposed to Britain itself which is an island

◊ **continental** adjective referring to the continent of Europe; **continental breakfast** = light breakfast of rolls, croissants, and coffee (as opposed to a 'full English breakfast'); *US* **continental plan** = hotel tariff including accommodation and a continental breakfast; *see also* INTERCONTINENTAL

contraband noun contraband (goods) = goods brought into a country illegally, without paying customs duty

contract *noun* **(a)** legal agreement between two parties; *to draw up a contract; to draft a contract; to sign a contract;* **the contract is binding on both parties** = both parties signing the contract must do what is agreed; **under contract** = bound by the terms of a contract; *the firm is under contract to deliver the goods by November;* **contract of employment** = contract between management and employee showing all conditions of work **(b) contract catering** *or* **contract cleaning** = providing food and drink *or* cleaning offices, public buildings, etc. under the terms of a contract; **contract caterer** *or* **contract cleaner** = company which provides food and drink *or* cleans offices, public buildings, etc. under the terms of a contract

control 1 *noun* restricting *or* checking something *or* making sure that something is kept in check; **control button** = on a TV, radio, etc., the button which switches it on, changes channel, increases volume, etc.; **under control** = kept in check; *expenses are kept under tight control; the police tried to keep the soccer fans under control;* **out of control** = not kept in check; *the fans have got out of control; planning authorities have allowed the hotel building boom to get out of control;* **air traffic control** = organization of the movement of aircraft in the air; **exchange control** = control by a government of the way in which its currency may be exchanged for foreign currencies; *the government had to impose exchange controls to stop the rush to buy dollars;* **price control** = legal measures to stop prices rising too fast **2** *verb* **(a)** to **control a business** = to direct a business; *the business is controlled by a company based in Luxembourg; the tour company is controlled by its majority shareholder which is a hotel group* **(b)** to make sure that something is kept in check *or* is not allowed to develop; *police tried to control the tourists;* **controlled atmosphere packaging** = packaging of foods in airtight containers in which the air has been treated by the addition of other gases (this allows a longer shelf-life); **controlled temperature storage** = keeping food at temperatures between -1°C and +4°C; *see also* REFRIGERATE

NOTE: **controlling - controlled**

◊ **controller** *noun* person who controls (especially the finances of a company); **air traffic controller** = person who organizes the movement of aircraft in the air

◊ **control tower** *noun* high building at an airport, which houses the radio operators

who direct planes on landing or takeoff (that is, the air traffic control)

convenience *noun* **(a) at your earliest convenience** = as soon as you find it possible; **convenience food** = food which is prepared by the shop before it is sold, so that it needs only heating to be made ready to eat; *US* **convenience store** = small store selling food or household goods, open until late at night, or even 24 hours a day **(b) public conveniences** = public toilets

◊ **convenient** *adjective* suitable *or* handy; *a bank draft is a convenient way of sending money abroad; is 9.30 a convenient time for the meeting?*

◊ **conveniently** *adverb* handily; *the hotel is conveniently situated next to the railway station*

convention *noun* **(a)** general meeting of an association or political party; **convention centre** = series of meeting rooms, with bedrooms, restaurants, etc., built specially for holding large meetings **(b)** formal agreement between several countries

conversion *noun* change; **conversion price** *or* **conversion rate** = rate at which a currency is changed into a foreign currency

◊ **convert** *verb* to change money of one country for money of another; *we converted our pounds into Swiss francs*

◊ **convertibility** *noun* ability to exchange one currency for another easily

◊ **convertible 1** *adjective* **convertible currency** = currency which can be exchanged for another easily **2** *noun* car with a roof which can be folded back or removed; *you can hire a small convertible for $100 a day*

cook 1 *noun* person who prepares food in a restaurant; *he worked as a cook in a pub during the summer* **2** *verb* to heat food, to prepare it for eating; *the meat is cooked for six hours in a clay oven;* **cook chill** *or* **cook freeze** = methods of preparing food for preserving, where the food is cooked to a certain temperature and then chilled or frozen

◊ **cookbook** *noun* = COOKERY BOOK

◊ **cooked** *adjective* food which has been heated to prepare it for eating; **cooked breakfast** = breakfast which includes bacon, eggs, sausages, etc. (as opposed to a continental breakfast)

◊ **cooker** *noun* device (run on gas *or* electricity *or* charcoal, etc.) for cooking food

◊ **cookery** *noun* style of cooking; *French provincial cookery;* **cookery book** = book of recipes, showing how dishes should be prepared; *the restaurant sells a cookery book, written by the chef*

◊ **cookie** *noun* US small hard sweet biscuit, made of flour, water, sugar and other flavourings; **chocolate chip cookie** = sweet biscuit made with little pieces of hard chocolate inside

◊ **cooking** *noun* **(a)** action of preparing food, usually by heating; *the cooking in this restaurant is first-class;* **cooking apple** = sour green apple which needs cooking; **cooking oil** = oil which is used in cooking **(b)** particular style of preparing food; *French provincial cooking; a wok is used for stir-fry cooking*

cool 1 *adjective* quite cold; *wines should be stored in a cool cellar; it gets cool in the evenings in September* **2** *noun* colder area which is pleasant; *after the heat of the square, it is nice to sit in the cool of the monastery garden*

◊ **cool bag** *or* **cool box** *noun* insulated container for keeping food and drink cool (as on a picnic) (NOTE: Australian English is **esky)**

copilot *noun* second pilot in an aircraft, who helps the captain

cordon bleu *adjective* top quality (cooking); *a cordon bleu chef*

core 1 *noun* central part of a fruit, such as an apple or pear **2** *verb* to remove the core from (an apple or pear)

◊ **corer** *noun* special knife for removing the core from a fruit

cork *noun* piece of soft bark from a cork oak tree, used to close a bottle

◊ **corkage** *or* US **cork charge** *noun* payment made by a customer to a restaurant, for permission to bring his own wine and have it opened by the wine waiter

◊ **corked** *adjective* **(a)** (bottle) with a cork in it **(b)** (wine) which tastes of vinegar, because of a dirty or faulty cork

◊ **corkscrew** *noun* device for taking corks out of bottles

◊ **corky** *adjective* = CORKED

corn *noun* maize, cereal which is used to make flour and of which the seeds are also eaten; **corn oil** = edible oil made from corn; **corn syrup** = sweet liquid, made from corn; **corn on the cob** = a piece of maize, with seeds on it, served hot, with butter and salt; **corn cob** = the woody stem of maize, to which the seeds are attached; *see also* POPCORN

◊ **cornflakes** *plural noun* breakfast cereal, made of flat crisp pieces of corn, eaten with milk and sugar

◊ **cornflour** *or* US **cornstarch** *noun* powdery flour made from maize, used to thicken sauces, etc.

corner *noun* place where two streets *or* two walls join; *the Post Office is on the corner of the High Street and London Road;* **corner seat** = seat in the corner (in a train, a seat near a window, as opposed to an aisle); **corner shop** = small, privately owned, general store in a town, often on a street corner; **corner table** = table in a corner of a restaurant (popular because it is more intimate)

cornet *see* CONE

corporate *adjective* referring to a whole company; **corporate catering** = catering for business guests, organized by a catering company for a large corporation; **corporate entertaining** = entertaining of business guests by a company; **corporate travel** = travel on business by executives of a large company, paid for and organized by the company

COMMENT: very large companies may employ the services of a single travel agency, and that agency may have an office in the company headquarters

corridor *noun* long, narrow passage; *the toilets are the second door on the left at the end of the corridor*

Corynebacterium *noun* genus of bacteria which includes the bacterium which causes diphtheria

cos *noun* type of lettuce with long stiff darker green leaves

cost 1 *noun* amount of money which has to be paid for something; *what is the cost of a first-class ticket to New York? travel costs are falling each year; we cannot afford the cost of two separate rooms;* **fixed costs** = business costs which do not rise with the quantity of the product made or the service provided (in a restaurant or hotel, these costs will include rent, maintenance of common areas, general cleaning, wages of

permanent staff, etc.); **labour costs** = cost of the workers employed to make a product or provide a service (not including materials or overheads); **operating costs** *or* **running costs** = cost of the day-to-day organization of a company; **variable costs** = production costs which increase with the quantity of the product made or service provided (in a restaurant or hotel, these are costs relating to the number of guests, i.e., raw materials for meals, guest bedroom cleaning and linen, wages for extra casual staff, etc.); **cost centre** = group or machine whose costs can be itemized and to which fixed costs can be allocated; **cost, insurance and freight** = estimate of a price, which includes the cost of the goods, the insurance and the transport charges; **low-cost travel** = cheap travel **2** *verb* to have a price; *how much does the camera cost? this cloth costs £10 a metre*
◇ **cost-benefit analysis** *noun* comparing the costs and benefits of different possible ways of using available resources
◇ **cost plus** *noun* system of calculating a price, by taking the cost of production of goods or services and adding a percentage to cover the supplier's overheads and margin; *we are charging for the work on a cost plus basis*

cot *noun* child's bed with sides; *see also* CARRYCOT

cottage *noun* **(a)** little house in the country; **cottage holidays** = holidays spent in a small cottage in the country **(b) cottage cheese** = mild white cheese formed into soft grains, made from skimmed milk, so with a very low fat content; **cottage pie** = minced meat cooked in a dish with a layer of mashed potatoes on top (NOTE: also called **shepherd's pie)**

couchette *noun* sleeping berth on a train, usually separated from others by a curtain or light partition

cough 1 *noun* reflex action, caused by irritation in the throat, when the glottis is opened and air is sent out of the lungs suddenly; *he gave a little cough to attract the waitress's attention; she has a bad cough and cannot make the speech* **2** *verb* to send air out of the lungs suddenly because the throat is irritated; *the smoke made him cough; he has a cold and keeps on coughing and sneezing*

counter *noun* **(a)** long flat surface in a shop for displaying and selling goods **(b)** similar long flat surface in a bar; *he sat at the*

counter to eat his breakfast; **counter service** = (i) cafeteria service; (ii) food service to people sitting at a counter **(c) ticket counter** = place where tickets are sold; **counter staff** = staff who work behind a counter

country *noun* **(a)** land which is separate and governs itself; *the insurance covers drivers driving in the countries of the Common Market; some African countries have tourist offices in London* **(b)** land which is not near a town; *road travel is difficult in country areas; the tour is mainly in the country, but with two nights in the town;* **up country** = in the interior of a country, usually away from large towns; **country club** = club in the country, usually offering special sports facilities such as golf, horse riding, etc.; **country house hotel** = hotel which is in a large house in the country; **country inn** *or* **country pub** = pub in the country
◇ **countryside** *noun* the country, the land (excluding towns and cities)

coupe *noun* **(a)** wide flat glass on a stem, used for serving ice cream and other sweets **(b)** ice cream or sorbet, served (sometimes with cream and sauces) in a wide flat dish with a stem

courgette *noun* fruit of the marrow at a very immature stage in its development, cut when between 10 and 20 cm long; it may be green or yellow in colour (NOTE: also called 'zucchini' in Italy and the USA)

courier *noun* **(a)** person *or* company taking messages, packages, etc. from one place to another by car, motorcycle, or aircraft **(b)** person who goes with a party of tourists to guide them on a package tour

course *noun* **(a)** one part of a meal; *a five-course meal* **(b)** series of lessons; *she attended a course for junior hotel managers; the hotel offers weekend courses in watercolour painting* **(c) golf course** = area of land specially designed for playing golf

COMMENT: a meal may have several courses: the first course (or starter), which can be soup or pâté or other savoury food; the main course, with meat or fish, served with vegetables; and the sweet course with puddings, pies, ice cream, etc. Sometimes a meal can have four courses, with a separate fish course as well as a meat course. More elaborate meals, such as banquets or gastronomic meals, can have five or more courses, with cheese being served as a separate course

court *noun* area where a game of tennis or squash, etc., is played; *the tennis courts are behind the hotel*

courteous *adjective* very polite; *I found the hotel staff particularly courteous*

◊ **courtesy** *noun* politeness; **by courtesy of** = with the kind permission of; *a box of chocolates by courtesy of the management;* **courtesy bus** *or* **car** *or* **coach** = bus *or* car *or* coach which transports guests from the airport to a hotel, a car park, etc. free of charge; **courtesy phone** = free telephone service, usually for calling rooms within a hotel or for a special service such as a central hotel reservation system or calling a taxi

courtyard *noun* square yard surrounded by buildings; *the hotel is built round a courtyard, with fountains and palm trees*

couscous *noun* North African dish of meat and vegetables stewed in a spicy sauce, served with steamed semolina

cover 1 *noun* **(a) under cover** = under a roof, not in the open air; *if it rains the buffet will be served under cover* **(b) insurance cover** = protection guaranteed by an insurance policy; *do you have cover against theft?;* **to ask for additional cover** = to ask the insurance company to increase the amount for which you are insured; **to operate without adequate cover** = without being protected by insurance; **full cover** = insurance against all risks; **cover note** = letter from an insurance company giving details of an insurance policy and confirming that the policy exists (NOTE: the US English for this is **binder) (c)** *(in restaurant)* place for a customer at a restaurant table, with the cutlery and glasses ready set out; *a dinner for sixty covers; he bought a fifty-cover restaurant;* **cover charge** = charge in addition to the charge for food **2** *verb* **(a) to cover a risk** = to insure against a risk; **to be fully covered** = to have insurance against all risks; *the insurance covers fire, theft and loss of work* **(b)** to have enough money to pay; to ask for security against a loan which you are making; **the damage was covered by the insurance** = the insurance company paid for the damage **(c)** to earn enough money to pay for costs, expenses etc.; *we do not make enough sales to cover the expense of running*

the shop; breakeven point is reached when sales cover all costs

crab *noun* **(a)** edible ten-footed crustacean with large pincers, which walks sideways; **dressed crab** = cooked crab, with the legs removed and the flesh broken up and put back into the shell **(b) crab apple** = bitter wild apple (used to make crab apple jelly)

cracker *noun* dry unsweetened biscuit

cradle *noun* wine basket, a type of basket with handles for holding a bottle of vintage red wine, so that the wine can be served without holding the bottle upright and the sediment is not disturbed

cramped *adjective* squeezed tightly; *on some aircraft, the seating in tourist class can be very cramped*

cranberry *noun* wild red berry, used to make a sharp sweet sauce; **cranberry sauce** = sharp sweet red sauce, eaten with meat, in particular turkey

crash 1 *noun* **(a)** accident to a car *or* bus *or* coach *or* plane *or* train; *the car was damaged in the crash; the plane crash killed all the passengers or all the passengers were killed in the plane crash* **(b)** financial collapse; *250 travellers lost all their money in the crash of the tour company* **2** *verb* **(a)** to hit something and be damaged; *the plane crashed into the mountain; the truck crashed into the post office* **(b)** to collapse financially; *the tour company crashed with debts of over £1 million; two groups of tourists were stranded when the travel group crashed*

crayfish *noun* kind of freshwater crustacean like a small lobster

cream 1 *noun* **(a)** rich fat part of milk; **clotted cream** = thick solid cream made from milk which has been heated to boiling point (produced especially in the south-west of England); **double cream** = thick cream with a high fat content; **single cream** = liquid cream, with a lower fat content; **whipped cream** = cream, beaten until it is stiff, flavoured with sugar and vanilla; **cream cake** = any cake or pastry filled with whipped cream; **cream horn** = cone of puff pastry filled with whipped cream; **cream tea** = afternoon tea, served with scones, thick cream and jam **(b) cream of asparagus** *or* **cream of mushroom soup** = asparagus *or* mushroom soup with milk or cream added **2** *verb* to mix ingredients together until they form a smooth mixture; **creamed potatoes** = potatoes which have been boiled, then mashed and beaten with butter and milk

crèche *noun* place where small children can be left by their parents, to be looked after by qualified staff; *the ship has a crèche for children over two years old*

credit *noun* **(a)** time given to a customer before he has to pay; *to give someone six months' credit; to sell on good credit terms;* **credit account** = account which a customer has with a shop which allows him to buy goods and pay for them later; *to open a credit account;* **credit agency** *or US* **credit bureau** = company which reports on the creditworthiness of customers to show whether they should be allowed credit; **credit facilities** = arrangement with a bank or supplier to have credit so as to buy goods; **credit freeze** *or* **credit squeeze** = period when lending by banks is restricted by the government; **credit limit** = fixed amount which is the most a customer can owe on credit; **he has exceeded his credit limit** = he has borrowed more money than he is allowed; **to open a line of credit** *or* **a credit line** = to make credit available to someone; **credit rating** = amount which a credit agency feels a customer should be allowed to borrow; **letter of credit** = letter from a bank, allowing someone credit and making him promise to repay at a later date; **irrevocable letter of credit** = letter of credit which cannot be cancelled; **on credit** = without paying immediately; *we buy everything on sixty days credit; the company exists on credit from its suppliers* **(b)** money received by a person *or* company and recorded in the accounts; **credit balance** = balance in an account showing that more money has been received than is owed by a person or company; *the account has a credit balance of £1,000;* **credit entry** = entry on the credit side of an account; **credit note** = note showing that money is owed to a customer; *the company sent the wrong order and so had to issue a credit note;* **account in credit** = account where more money has been received than is owed

◊ **credit card** *noun* plastic card which allows you to borrow money and to buy goods without paying for them immediately

crème brûlée *French noun* dessert of egg custard with a topping of caramelized sugar

◊ **crème caramel** *see* CARAMEL

cress *noun* plant used as a salad vegetable and garnish; *egg and cress sandwiches; see also* MUSTARD AND CRESS, WATERCRESS

crew *noun* group of people who work on a plane *or* ship, etc.; *the ship carries a crew of 250;* **cabin crew** = the stewards and stewardesses who deal with the passengers on a plane; **crew rest seat** = seat on an aircraft for the use of a member of the crew during a long flight; *see also* AIRCREW

crisp 1 *adjective* hard and thin, which can be broken into pieces; *these biscuits are not crisp any more, they have gone soft* **2** *noun* thin slice of potato, fried till crisp and eaten cold as a snack (NOTE: US English for this is **potato chip**)

◊ **crispy bacon** *noun* thin slices of bacon, fried or grilled until they are hard and crisp

criticize *verb* to make an unfavourable comment about someone *or* something; to say that something *or* someone is wrong *or* is working badly, etc.; *the manager criticized the receptionist for not being polite to the guests; the design of the new restaurant has been criticized*

◊ **criticism** *noun* unfavourable comment

crockery *noun* plates, cups and saucers, etc.

croissant *noun* rolled pastry, made in the shape of a crescent moon, often served at breakfast

◊ **croissanterie** *noun* snack bar serving hot croissants with various fillings

croquette *noun* small ball or cake of mashed potato, minced meat, vegetables or fish, covered with breadcrumbs and fried

cross *verb* to go across; *Concorde only takes three hours to cross the Atlantic; to get to the bank, you turn left and cross the street at the post office*

◊ **cross-** *prefix* across; *cross-harbour ferry services*

◊ **cross-channel** *adjective* across the English Channel; **cross-channel ferry** = ferry which carries passengers and vehicles between England and France; **cross-channel services** = ferry, hovercraft and hydrofoil services across the English Channel

◊ **cross-country** *adjective* across the country, not necessarily following paths; **cross-country skiing** = skiing for long distances following marked tracks across country, as opposed to downhill skiing (NOTE: also called **XC skiing**)

◊ **crossing** *noun* **(a)** act of going across water; *the crossing was rough because of the storm; we had a good crossing, and sat on the deck most of the time;* crossing the line *see* EQUATOR **(b)** pedestrian crossing *or* zebra crossing = place marked with white lines where pedestrians can cross a road

crouton *noun* small piece of fried or toasted bread, served with soup or as part of a salad

crowd *noun* mass of people; *crowds of people were queuing to get into the exhibition; if you travel early, you will avoid the crowds of Christmas shoppers*

◊ **crowded** *adjective* **(a)** with many people; *the Oxford Street shops are always crowded in the week before Christmas; the airport was crowded with holidaymakers* **(b)** busy; *we have a crowded itinerary*

> QUOTE recent snow shortages have meant that areas which have had good snow have become especially crowded
> *Sunday Times*

crown *noun* **(a)** gold and jewelled headdress for a king, queen, emperor, etc.; *the crown of St Wenceslas is in Prague cathedral* **(b)** *(rating system)* indicator of quality; *the hotel rates three crowns in the guide* **(c)** the monarchy; **the Crown Jewels =** jewels belonging to the British monarch, which are on display in the Tower of London

> COMMENT: the rating system used by the English Tourist Board for the facilities offered by hotels, bed and breakfasts and boarding houses runs from one crown to five crowns

crown cap *noun* metal bottle cap with a soft lining

◊ **crown roast** *noun* dish of lamb, formed of two pieces of best end of neck, tied together to form a shape like a crown

CRS = COMPUTER RESERVATION SYSTEM

cru *French noun (meaning 'growth')* used to refer to a classified or named vineyard, or an appellation contrôlée wine from that vineyard

cruet *noun* set of containers for salt, pepper, mustard, etc., sometimes placed on a tray or special stand

cruise 1 *noun* travel on a ship going from place to place; *they went on a winter cruise to the Caribbean; the cruise takes us round the Mediterranean;* cruise liner *or* cruise ship = ship which takes holidaymakers on cruises **2** *verb* **(a)** to sail from place to place for pleasure; *they spent May cruising in the Aegean; the ship cruised from island to island* **(b)** to go along at a regular speed; cruising altitude = normal height at which a plane is flying

◊ **cruiser** *noun* small motorboat, with cabins, which goes on rivers or lakes

crumb *noun* small piece of bread or cake; *after the meal, the waiters brushed the crumbs from the table; the table was covered with crumbs* (NOTE: to show different types of crumbs, you can say **breadcrumbs, cakecrumbs**, etc.)

◊ **crumb down** *verb* to remove crumbs from the tablecloth between courses

> COMMENT: crumbing down can be done with a special brush, but is often done by flicking or wiping the table with the service cloth

crumble *noun* dessert made of fruit covered with a cake mixture of flour, fat and sugar; **apple crumble =** dessert made of cooked apples covered with a crumble top

crust *noun* (i) hard, outer part of a loaf of bread or of a roll or of a slice of bread; (ii) pastry top of a pie; *a plate of cucumber sandwiches with the crusts cut off*

◊ **crusty loaf** *noun* loaf with a particularly hard crust

Crustacea *noun* class of animals (such as crabs *or* lobsters) which have hard shells which are shed periodically as the animals grow

◊ **crustacean** *noun* crab *or* lobster *or* shrimp, etc.

cryogenic freezing *noun* freezing to very low temperatures

crystallized fruit *noun* fruit which has been preserved by soaking in a strong sugar solution (used particularly in Middle Eastern countries)

cucumber *noun* long cylindrical green vegetable used in salads or for pickling, the fruit of a creeping plant *(Cucumis sativus)*

COMMENT: cucumber is usually sliced thinly, and can be used to make sandwiches. It is also used with mint and yogurt to make tsatsiki

cuisine *French noun (meaning 'kitchen')* style of cooking; *Chinese cuisine is very different from European;* **haute cuisine** = high class French cooking; **nouvelle cuisine** *or* **cuisine nouvelle** = type of French cooking which aims at less heavy traditional dishes and attractive presentation (and often served in very small portions)

culinary *adjective* referring to cooking

QUOTE the college wishes to appoint a chef/manager to lead its small catering team in providing a high quality service to students and staff. Good culinary skills and a financially aware approach to business are essential
Caterer & Hotelkeeper

cup *noun* container for drinking hot liquids, always with a saucer; *I would like a cup of tea, please; she drank two cups of coffee; tea is 50p a cup;* **coffee cup** = small cup for coffee; *see note at* COFFEE; **teacup** = large cup for tea

cupboard *noun* large piece of furniture with shelves and doors; alcove in a wall with shelves and doors

curdle *verb* to make food, especially milk products, go sour

curds *noun* solid food made from sour milk
◊ **curd cheese** *US* = COTTAGE CHEESE

cure *verb* to preserve fish or meat by salting or smoking; **cured ham** = ham which has been soaked in salt water and then smoked; **dry cure** = to preserve fish or meat in salt crystals as opposed to brine

COMMENT: meat is cured by keeping in brine or dry salt for some time; both salting and smoking have a dehydrating effect on the meat, preventing the reproduction and growth of microorganisms harmful to man

currant *noun* small dried black grape

currency *noun* money in coins and notes which is used in a particular country; **convertible currency** = currency which can easily be exchanged for another; **foreign currency** = money of another country; **foreign currency account** = bank account in the currency of another country (e.g. a dollar account); **hard currency** = currency of a country which has a strong economy and which can be changed into other currencies easily; *to pay for imports in hard currency;* **legal currency** = money which is legally used in a country; **soft currency** = currency of a country which has a weak economy and which is cheap to buy and difficult to exchange for other currencies; **currency note** = bank note (NOTE: currency has no plural when it refers to the money of one country: **he was arrested trying to take currency out of the country**)

QUOTE the strong dollar's inflationary impact on European economies, as national governments struggle to support their sinking currencies and push up interest rates
Duns Business Month
QUOTE today's wide daily variations in exchange rates show the instability of a system based on a single currency, namely the dollar
Economist
QUOTE the level of currency in circulation increased to N4.9 billion in the month of August
Business Times (Lagos)

current 1 *noun* flow of water or electricity **2** *adjective* referring to the present time; **current account** = account in a bank from which the customer can withdraw money when he wants by writing cheques; *to pay money into a current account;* **current assets** = assets used by a company in its ordinary work (such as materials, finished goods, cash, monies due) and which are held for a short time only; **current liabilities** = debts which a company has to pay within the next accounting period; **current price** = the price which is being charged now; **current rate of exchange** = today's rate of exchange

curriculum vitae *noun* summary of a person's career showing details of education and work experience; *candidates should send a letter of application with a curriculum vitae to the personnel officer* (NOTE: the plural is **curriculums vitae** *or* **curricula vitae.** Note also that the US English is **résumé**)

curry *noun* **(a)** curry **(powder)** *or* curry **paste** = hot spicy powder *or* paste, used to make Indian dishes **(b)** Indian food prepared with spices; *lamb curry; chicken curry*
◊ **curried** *adjective* served with a curry sauce; *curried prawns*

curtain 1 *noun* long piece of material hanging by hooks from a pole, covering a window or door **2** *verb* **to curtain off** = to separate with a curtain; *the end of the dining room is curtained off to form a private meeting room*

custard *noun* **(a) (egg) custard** = sweet sauce, made with eggs and milk, flavoured with vanilla, baked until set and eaten warm or cold; **caramel custard** = crème caramel, desert of egg custard topped with a thin sauce of browned sugar, turned upside down on the serving plate **(b)** *(in the UK)* sweet yellow sauce made with milk and powder of cornflour and vanilla
◊ **custard apple** *noun* fruit of the *Annona* genus, grown in the West Indies for its sweet pulpy fruit

custody *noun* keeping; *the jewels were in the custody of the manager, and he had placed them in the hotel safe; the hijacker was taken into police custody on landing*

custom *noun* **(a)** use of a restaurant *or* hotel *or* bar *or* shop by regular customers; **to lose someone's custom** = to do something which makes a regular customer go to another restaurant, shop, etc.; **custom-built** *or* **custom-made** = made specially for one customer; *he drives a custom-built Rolls Royce* **(b)** general habit; *it's an old Greek custom to smash plates at the end of a meal*
◊ **customer** *noun* person *or* company which buys goods or services; *the shop was full of customers; can you serve this customer first, please? he is a regular customer of ours;* **customer appeal** = what attracts customers to a product; **customer service department** = department which deals with customers and their complaints and orders

customs *plural noun* government department which organizes the collection of taxes on imports; office of this department at a port *or* airport *or* national border; **to go through customs** = to pass through the area of a port or airport where customs officials examine goods; **to take something through customs** = to carry something illegal through the customs area without declaring it; *he was stopped by customs; her car was searched by customs;* **customs barrier** = customs duty intended to prevent imports; **customs clearance** = document given by customs to a shipper to show that customs duty has been paid and the goods can be shipped; *to wait for customs clearance;* **customs declaration** = statement showing goods being imported on which duty will have to be paid; *to fill in a customs (declaration) form;* **customs duty** = tax paid on goods brought into or taken out of a country; **the crates had to go through a customs examination** = the crates had to be examined by customs officials; **customs formalities** = declaration of goods by the shipper and examination of them by the customs; **customs officers** *or* **customs officials** = people working for the customs; **customs tariff** = list of duties to be paid on imported or exported goods; **customs union** = agreement between several countries that goods can travel between them without paying duty, while goods from other countries have to pay special duties

cut 1 *noun* **cut of meat** = piece of meat cut (in a special way) from a larger piece; *US* **cold cuts** = plate of slices of cold cooked meat (such as ham, salami, etc.) **2** *verb* **(a)** to remove pieces *or* to put into pieces with a knife; *he cut off two slices of ham; she cut her hand opening the can;* **cutting board** = piece of thick wood, used in a kitchen to cut up food on **(b)** to make lower; *they have cut the prices of tours;* **to cut down on cigarettes** *or* **on expenses** = to reduce the amount of cigarettes you smoke *or* of money you spend; *compare* CHOP, DICE

cutlery *noun* knives, forks, spoons

cutlet *noun* flat cake of minced meat or fish, covered with breadcrumbs and fried; *a veal cutlet*

cut-price *adjective* sold at a cheaper price than usual; *cut-price goods; cut-price petrol;* **cut-price store** = store selling goods at cheaper prices

cyclamate *noun* sweetening substance (a salt of cyclamic acid) used instead of sugar, believed to be carcinogenic and banned in the USA as a food additive

cycle 1 *noun* **(a)** bicycle, a vehicle with two wheels, which is moved when the rider pushes on pedals; **cycle hire** = rental of a bicycle for a period (paid for at a certain rate per hour, per half-day, per day or per week); **cycle path** = special path for cyclists;

there are thousands of cycle paths in Holland **(b)** period of time when something leaves its original position and then returns to it; **beverage cycle** = cycle by which beverages pass from supplier to hotel or restaurant and then to the ultimate consumer; **economic cycle** *or* **trade cycle** *or* **business cycle** = period during which trade expands, then slows down and then expands again;

food cycle = cycle by which food passes from supplier to hotel or restaurant and then to the ultimate consumer; **wash cycle** = series of operations in a dishwasher, to wash dishes (ending with the 'drain cycle') **2** *verb* to ride on a bicycle; *to go on a cycling holiday*

◊ **cyclist** *noun* person who rides a bicycle

Dd

Vitamin D *noun* vitamin which is soluble in fat, and is found in butter, eggs and fish; it is also produced by the skin when exposed to sunlight

COMMENT: Vitamin D helps in the formation of bones, and lack of it causes rickets in children

daily *adjective* done every day; **a daily flight to Washington** = a flight which goes to Washington every day at the same time; **a daily newspaper** *or* **a daily** = newspaper which is produced every day; **daily room rate** = rate which is charged for a hotel room for one day (or night)

dairy produce *or* **dairy products** *noun* foods prepared from milk (including milk, cream, yoghurt, butter, cheese, etc.)

damage 1 *noun* **(a)** harm done to things; **fire damage** = damage caused by a fire; **storm damage** = damage caused by a storm; **to suffer damage** = to be harmed; **to cause damage** = to harm something; *the fire caused damage estimated at £100,000* **(b)** **damages** = money claimed as compensation for harm done; *to claim £1,000 in damages; to be liable for damages; to pay £25,000 in damages;* **to bring an action for damages against someone** = to take someone to court and claim damages **2** *verb* to harm; *the storm damaged the telephone lines; stock which has been damaged by water*

damson *noun* small purple plum; tree which bears this fruit

dance 1 *noun* evening entertainment where people dance to music; *there is a 21st*

birthday dance at the hotel this evening; **dance floor** = specially polished floor for dancing on **2** *verb* to move (in time to music); **restaurant licensed for music and dancing** = restaurant which has a special permit allowing music to be played for customers to dance to

dangerous *adjective* which can be harmful; *tourists are warned that it is dangerous to go out alone at night*

Danish *adjective* referring to Denmark; **Danish pastry** = sweet pastry cake with jam or fruit folded in it (NOTE: also called simply **Danish: an apple Danish**)

date 1 *noun* **(a)** number of day, month and year; *I have received your letter of yesterday's date; the dates of the exhibition have been changed;* **date of birth** = date on which someone was born; *please write your date and place of birth on the registration form;* **arrival date** *or* **date of arrival** = day on which a traveller or tour group arrives at a destination; **departure date** *or* **date of departure** = day on which a traveller or tour group leaves; **return date** = day on which a traveller or a tour returns; **date code** = signs or numbers which indicate a sell-by date; **date coding** = putting a sell-by date on a product **(b)** small sweet brown fruit of the date palm, a staple food of many people in the Middle East; **date palm** = a tall subtropical tree *(Phoenix dactylifera)* with very large frond leaves; its fruit are dates **2** *verb* to put a date on a document; *the cheque was dated March 24th; you forgot to date the cheque;* **to date a cheque forward** = to put a future date on a cheque

◊ **date line** *noun* line of longitude (in the Pacific Ocean) which indicates the change in date from east to west

dawn *noun* beginning of day, when the sun rises; *we set off for the pyramids at dawn, so you'll have to get up very early*

day *noun* **(a)** period of 24 hours; *there are thirty days in June; the first day of the month is a public holiday; a ten-day tour of Southern Spain;* three clear days = three whole working days; *you will get a refund only if you give ten clear days' notice of cancelling; allow four clear days for the cheque to be paid into the bank* **(b)** period from morning to night; **day rate** = tariff for using a hotel room during the day (for a meeting, etc.); **day tour** *or* **day excursion** *or* **day trip** = tour *or* excursion which leaves in the morning and returns the same evening; **day trippers** *or* **day visitors** = people who are on a day trip **(c)** work period from morning to night; **she took two days off** = she did not come to work for two days; **he works three days on, two days off** = he works for three days, then has two days' holiday; **to work an eight-hour day** = to spend eight hours at work each day; **day release** = arrangement where a company allows a worker to go to college to study for one or two days each week; *she is attending a day release course for hotel managers*

◊ **daylight** *noun* light of day; **daylight saving time (DST)** = system of putting the clocks forward one hour in summer to provide extra daylight in the evening

DCF = DISCOUNTED CASH FLOW

DDT = DICHLORODIPHENYLTRICHLOROETHANE; **DDT-resistant insect** = insect which has build up a resistance to DDT

COMMENT: DDT is a highly toxic insecticide which remains for a long time as a deposit in animal organisms. It gradually builds up in the food chain as smaller animals are eaten by larger ones. It is no longer recommended for use

dead *adjective* **(a)** not alive; *six people were dead as a result of the accident* **(b)** not working; **the line went dead** = the telephone line suddenly stopped working; **dead loss** = total loss; *the car was written off as a dead loss;* **dead season** = time of year when there are few tourists about

dear *adjective* **(a)** expensive *or* costing a lot of money; *clothes are very dear in the market, but carpets are cheap* **(b)** way of starting a letter; **Dear Sir** *or* **Dear Madam** = addressing a man or woman whom you do not know, or addressing a company; **Dear Sirs** = addressing a company; **Dear Mr Smith** *or* **Dear Mrs Smith** *or* **Dear Miss Smith** = addressing a man or woman whom you know; **Dear James** *or* **Dear Julia** = addressing a friend *or* a person you do business with

debit 1 *noun* money which a company owes, an entry in accounts which shows an increase in assets or expenses or a decrease in liabilities, revenue or capital (entered in the left-hand side of an account); *compare* CREDIT; **debit balance** = balance in an account, showing that the company owes more money than it has received; **debit card** = plastic card, similar to a credit card, but which debits the holder's account immediately through an EPOS system **2** *verb* **to debit an account** = to charge an account with a cost; *his account was debited with the sum of £25*

decaffeinated *adjective* from which the caffeine has been removed; *decaffeinated coffee; decaffeinated tea* (NOTE: decaffeinated coffee is also called simply **decaff**)

decant *verb* **(a)** to pour vintage wine from a bottle into another container, so as to remove the sediment **(b)** to put jam, marmalade, pickle, etc. from large jars into small serving dishes for each table

◊ **decanter** *noun* (i) open glass bottle into which wine is decanted, and from which the wine is served; (ii) glass bottle (with a glass stopper) in which whisky, sherry, etc., is stored for a time

deck *noun* **(a)** flat floor in a ship; **lower decks** = decks below the main deck; **main deck** = deck with the most important facilities, such as the restaurant, bars, etc.; **upper decks** = decks above the main deck; **deck quoits** = game played on the deck of a ship (players throw rings, trying to hook them over posts set in the deck) **(b)** floor on a bus; **lower deck** = ground level section of a double-decker bus; *let's sit on the top deck to get a good view;* **open deck** = top deck of a bus without a roof, to allow tourists to see and take photographs more easily; **top deck** *or* **upper deck** = upstairs part of a double-decker bus

◊ **deckchair** *noun* folding chair, made of canvas and wood, used to sit on out of doors

declaration *noun* official statement; **customs declaration** = statement showing goods being imported on which customs duty will have to be paid; *to fill in a customs declaration form;* **VAT declaration** = statement declaring VAT income to the VAT office

◊ **declare** *verb* to make an official statement; **to declare goods to customs** = to state that you are importing goods which are liable to customs duty; *the customs officials asked him if he had anything to declare; go through the green channel if you have nothing to declare*

decorate *verb* **(a)** to paint (a room *or* a building); to put new wallpaper in (a room) **(b)** to put up flags or lights (to celebrate an occasion); *the streets were decorated with bunting for the music festival* **(c)** to put coloured icing on a cake

◊ **decorations** *plural noun* flags, lights, etc., used to celebrate an occasion; *the restaurant staff came in early to put up Christmas decorations*

dedicated *adjective* set aside for a special purpose; **dedicated Business class lounge** = lounge set aside for Business class passengers only; **dedicated line** = telephone line used only for a particular purpose (such as a line linking computers in a CRS)

QUOTE the best conference hotels provide a dedicated member of staff for each conference to liaise with the organizer and ensure the event proceeds smoothly
Caterer & Hotelkeeper

deduct *verb* to remove money from a total; *the hotel deducted £3 from the room price; she deducted a sum to cover breakages; after deducting costs the gross margin is only 23%*

◊ **deductible** *adjective* which can be deducted; **tax-deductible** = which can be deducted from an income before tax is paid; **some travelling expenses are not tax-deductible** = tax has to be paid on those expenses

◊ **deduction** *noun* removing of money from a total *or* money removed from a total; *net salary is salary after deduction of tax and social security payments;* **tax deductions** = (i) money removed from a salary to pay tax; (ii) *US* business expenses which can be claimed against tax

deep-freeze *noun* refrigerator where food is kept at very low temperatures

◊ **deep-fried** *adjective* cooked in deep oil or fat

◊ **deep-fry** *verb* to cook food in a deep pan of boiling oil or fat

◊ **deep pan pizza** *noun* American-style pizza with a thicker base and more ingredients than usual

defreeze *verb* to thaw (frozen food)

defrost *verb* **(a)** to remove ice which has formed inside a refrigerator **(b)** to thaw (frozen food); *a large turkey will take 24 hours to defrost*

dehydrate *verb* **(a)** to remove water from (something) in order to preserve it; **dehydrated milk** = milk which has been dried and reduced to a powder **(b)** to lose water; *after two days without food or drink, he became dehydrated*

◊ **dehydration** *noun* **(a)** removing water from something in order to preserve it **(b)** loss of water; *the passengers were suffering from dehydration*

COMMENT: food can be dehydrated by drying in the sun (as in the case of dried fruit), or by passing through various industrial processes, such as freeze-drying. Water is more essential than food for a human being's survival. If someone drinks during the day less liquid than is passed out of the body in urine and sweat, he begins to dehydrate

delay 1 *noun* time when someone *or* something is later than planned; *there was a delay of thirty minutes before the flight left or the flight left after a thirty-minute delay; we are sorry for the delay in replying to your letter* **2** *verb* to be late; to make someone late; *he was delayed because his taxi had an accident; the company has delayed payment of all invoices*

Delhi belly *noun (humorous)* diarrhoea which affects people travelling in foreign countries as a result of eating unwashed fruit or drinking water which has not been boiled (NOTE: also called **gippy tummy, Montezuma's revenge, etc.)**

deli *noun (informal)* = DELICATESSEN

delicacy *noun* rare thing to eat

delicatessen *noun* shop selling cold meats and imported food products

delicious *adjective* very good to eat; *Italian ice cream is delicious; can I have another piece of that delicious cake?*

de luxe *adjective* very expensive; of very high quality; *the airline offers first-class passengers a bag of de luxe toiletries; a de luxe tour of India*

> COMMENT: 'de luxe' is the highest grade in the English Tourist Board grading system for accommodation

demand 1 *noun* (a) asking for payment; **payable on demand** = which must be paid when payment is asked for (b) need for goods or services at a certain price; *there was an active demand for interpreters during the trade fair;* **to meet a demand** *or* **to fill a demand** = to supply what is needed; *the factory had to increase production to meet the extra demand; the factory had to cut production when demand slackened; the office cleaning company cannot keep up with the demand for its services;* there is not much demand for this item = not many people want to buy it; **this book is in great demand** *or* **there is a great demand for this book** = many people want to buy it **2** *verb* to ask for something and expect to get it; *she demanded a refund; the suppliers are demanding immediate payment of their outstanding invoices*

demi-pension *see* HALF-BOARD

demi-tasse *noun* small coffee cup

denomination *noun* unit of money (on a coin, banknote or stamp); *coins of all denominations; small denomination notes; the bank refused to accept low denomination coins*

density *noun* number of people per unit of area; **occupation density** = number of people in a hotel *or* restaurant, shown as a ratio of the floor area

depart *verb* to leave; *the plane departs from Paris at 11.15*

◇ **department** *noun* (a) specialized section of a large company; *write to the complaints department about the service in the hotels on the tour;* **accounts department** = section in a company which deals with money paid or received, borrowed or owed (b) section of a large store selling one type of product; *you will find beds in the furniture department;* **budget department** = department in a large

store which sells cheaper goods (c) section of a government

◇ **department store** *noun* large shop with sections for different types of goods

departure *noun* (a) going away; *your departure time is 3 o'clock; the plane's departure was delayed by two hours; flight departures are delayed because of the strike of the air traffic controllers* (b) **departures** = part of an airport terminal which deals with passengers who are leaving; **departure lounge** = room in an airport where passengers wait to get on their planes after going through passport control and baggage check; **departure tax** = tax payable by passengers leaving a country

deplane *verb* to get off a plane; *the party will deplane at Delhi*

deposit *noun* money given in advance so that the thing which you want to buy will not be sold to someone else; *to pay a deposit on a room; you will need to pay 10% deposit to secure the booking*

depot *noun* centre for transportation; *buses leave the central bus depot every hour*

dept = DEPARTMENT

deregulate *verb* to remove government restrictions over an industry

◇ **deregulation** *noun* removal of official restrictions; *deregulation of US airlines resulted in fierce competition and price-cutting*

desiccated *adjective* dried; *desiccated coconut*

designated carrier *noun* airline which is licensed to operate a service between two countries

◇ **designator** *noun* two-letter code by which an airline is identified (BA for British Airways, LH for Lufthansa, etc.)

desk *noun* (a) writing table in an office, usually with drawers for stationery; *desk diary; desk drawer; desk light;* **desk pad** = pad of paper kept on a desk for writing notes; **desk research** = looking for information which has already been published (as in a directory) (b) **front desk** = reception desk at the entrance to a hotel or restaurant; **cash desk** *or* **pay desk** = place in a store where you pay for the goods bought; *please pay at the cash desk*

dessert *noun* sweet dish eaten at the end of a meal; *what do you want for dessert?; I have eaten so much, I don't want any dessert;* **dessert menu** = special separate menu for desserts in a restaurant; **dessert fork** *or* **dessert knife** = smaller fork and knife used to eat dessert; **dessert trolley** = sweet trolley, a trolley in a restaurant with dishes of the various desserts which are on offer; **dessert wine** = sweet wine (such as muscat) which is served with a dessert (NOTE: usually no plural; **desserts** means types of dessert)

◊ **dessertspoon** *noun* spoon for eating desserts (smaller than a soup spoon, but larger than a teaspoon)

COMMENT: on formal menus, a dessert is a course of fruit or nuts taken after the cheese and before coffee is served. On an ordinary menu, a dessert can take the form of a pudding, pastry, ice or fresh fruit

destination *noun* place to which something is sent *or* to which something is going; *the ship will take ten weeks to reach its destination;* **final destination** *or* **ultimate destination** = place reached at the end of a journey after stopping at several places en route

detect *verb* to notice something which could be difficult to see; *a smoke detector detects the presence of smoke*

◊ **detector** *noun* apparatus which notices something which is difficult to see; **fire detector** = apparatus which sense heat and notices if a fire breaks out and automatically sounds an alarm, sets off a sprinkler system, etc.; **smoke detector** = device which is sensitive to smoke, and sets off alarms or sprinklers when it senses smoke; *smoke detectors are fitted in all the rooms; all the men smoked cigars, and this set off the smoke detectors*

detergent *noun* cleaning substance which removes grease and bacteria from clothes, dishes, etc.

detour *noun* journey away from the usual or planned route; *we made a detour to visit the caves; we had to make a detour because of the road works*

detrain *verb* to get off a train

Deutschmark *noun* unit of money used in Germany (NOTE: also called a **mark;** when used with a figure, usually written **DM** before the figure: **DM250** (say 'two hundred and fifty Deutschmarks')

develop *verb* **(a)** to expand; *we are developing the harbour facilities to allow larger ferries to berth; the company is developing a chain of motorway self-service restaurants* **(b)** to produce and fix (a photograph) from film; *we can develop your film in an hour*

◊ **developed country** *noun* country which has an advanced manufacturing system

◊ **developer** *noun* **(a)** liquid for developing photographs **(b)** person who builds property

◊ **developing country** *or* **developing nation** *noun* country which is not fully industrialized

◊ **development** *noun* building of property; *unrestricted hotel development has ruined the coastline*

dextrose *noun* simple sugar found in fruit; also extracted from corn starch

dhal *or* **dal** *noun* Indian term for pulses, such as lentils and pigeon peas; also used for curries and soups prepared from these pulses

diabetes *noun* illness where the sugar content of the blood rises because of lack of insulin

◊ **diabetic** *adjective* referring to diabetes; **diabetic food** = food with a low sugar content which can be eaten by people suffering from diabetes

dial *verb* to call a telephone number on a telephone; *to dial a number; to dial the operator; dial 9 to get an outside line;* **to dial direct** = to contact a phone number yourself without asking the operator to do it for you; *you can dial New York direct from London* NOTE: GB English: **dialling - dialled,** but US English: **dialing - dialed**

◊ **dialling** *noun* act of calling a telephone number; **dialling code** = special series of numbers used to make a call to another town; **dialling tone** = noise made by a telephone to show that it is ready for you to dial a number; **international dialling code** = special series of numbers used to make a call to another country; **international direct dialling (IDD)** = calling telephone numbers in other countries yourself without asking the operator to do it for you

diarrhoea *or US* **diarrhea** *noun* condition where a patient frequently passes liquid faeces; *he had an attack of diarrhoea after going to the restaurant; she complained of mild diarrhoea;* **travellers' diarrhoea =** diarrhoea caused by eating unwashed vegetables or fruit, or drinking unboiled water, contracted by travellers

COMMENT: diarrhoea can have many causes: types of food or allergy to food; contaminated or poisoned food; infectious diseases, such as dysentery; sometimes worry or other emotions

diary *noun* book in which you can write notes or appointments for each day of the week; *desk diary;* **to keep a diary =** to write down what you have felt or done each day; *the children on the study tour have to keep a diary of the places they visit*

dichlorodiphenyltrichloroethane (DDT) *noun* highly toxic insecticide, no longer recommended for use

COMMENT: DDT is a highly toxic insecticide which remains for a long time as a deposit in animal organisms. It gradually builds up in the food chain as smaller animals are eaten by larger ones. It is no longer recommended for use

dice *verb* to cut food into small cubes; *diced potato*

diet 1 *noun* **(a)** amount and type of food eaten; *the normal western diet is too full of carbohydrates;* **balanced diet =** diet which contains the right quantities of basic nutrients; **low-calorie diet =** diet with few calories (which can help a person to lose weight); **salt-free diet =** diet which does not contain salt **(b)** eating only certain types of food, either to become thinner, to cure an illness or improve a condition; **to be on a diet =** to eat only certain types of food, especially in order to become thin or to deal with an illness; *two of the passengers are on diets* **2** *verb* to eat only certain food, in order to become thinner

◇ **dietary** *adjective* referring to a diet; **dietary fibre** *or* **roughage =** fibrous matter in food, which cannot be digested; **Dietary Reference Values (DRV) =** list published by the British government of nutrients that are essential for health

COMMENT: dietary fibre is found in cereals, nuts, fruit and some green vegetables. It is believed to be necessary to help digestion and avoid developing constipation, obesity, appendicitis and other digestive problems

◇ **dieter** *noun* person who is on a diet

◇ **dietetics** *noun* study of food and its nutritional value

◇ **dietician** *or* **dietitian** *noun* person who specializes in the study of diets

difference *noun* way in which two things are not the same; **to split the difference =** to share the payment of the difference between two prices

◇ **differential 1** *adjective* which shows a difference; **differential tariffs =** different tariffs for different classes of goods **2** *noun* **price differential =** difference in price between products in a range; **wage differentials =** differences in salary between workers in similar types of jobs

digest *verb* to break down food in the stomach and intestine and convert it into elements which can be absorbed by the body; **I cannot digest my dinner =** I am feeling unwell after my dinner

◇ **digestible** *adjective* which can be digested

◇ **digestif** *French noun (meaning 'digestive')* alcoholic drink such as brandy or liqueur, taken after a meal, to help the digestion

◇ **digestion** *noun* action of breaking down food in the stomach and intestine and converting it into elements which can be absorbed by the body

◇ **digestive** *adjective* which helps you to digest; **digestive biscuit =** sweet wholemeal biscuit

digit *noun* single number; *a seven-digit phone number*

◇ **digital** *adjective* **digital clock =** clock which shows the time as a series of figures (such as 12:05:23) rather than on a circular dial

dim *verb* to make a light less bright; *the captain dimmed the cabin lights before takeoff*

◇ **dimmer switch** *noun* light switch which makes a light less bright

dime *noun US* ten-cent coin

dim sum *noun* Southern Chinese style lunch, where many different small dishes are served

dine *verb* to have dinner, to eat an evening meal; **to dine out** = to have dinner away from home or in a restaurant outside the hotel where you are staying; **to dine in** = to have dinner in the restaurant of the hotel where you are staying

◊ **diner** *noun* (a) person who is eating an evening meal; *when the restaurant caught fire, the diners ran into the street* (b) dining car on a train (c) *US* small restaurant selling simple hot food (NOTE: originally, these were made from old dining cars from railway trains)

◊ **dining car** *noun* railway carriage where meals are served; *the dining car joins the train at Lyon*

◊ **dining room** *noun* room in a hotel where people eat

◊ **dining table** *noun* table on which meals are served and eaten

dinghy *noun* small boat

dinner *noun* evening meal; *dinner is served at 7.30; the restaurant is open for dinner or serves dinner from 7.30 to 11.30; half-board includes breakfast and dinner, but not lunch;* **dinner jacket** = formal jacket worn with a bow tie (both usually black); **dinner party** = (i) private dinner to which guests are invited; (ii) *(in a restaurant)* group of people having dinner together; **dinner plate** = wide flat plate for serving the main course on; **dinner service** = set of matching plates, bowls, etc. for serving a main meal; **dinner table** = table (where people eat)

◊ **dinner-dance** *noun* formal dinner followed by dancing to music played by a live band; *the company is having a Christmas dinner-dance at the Imperial Hotel*

dip *noun* (a) purée into which pieces of bread or biscuits can be dipped; *a bowl of avocado dip* (b) **dip card** = type of magnetic key card which is pushed down into a slot and then pulled out again when the door unlocks

direct 1 *verb* to tell *or* show someone how to go to a place **2** *adjective* straight *or* with no interference; **direct debit** = system where a customer allows a company to charge costs to his bank account automatically and where the amount charged can be increased or decreased with the agreement of the customer; **direct flight** = flight which goes from one place to another, without stopping; **direct mail** = selling a product by sending publicity material to possible buyers through the post; **direct-mail advertising** = advertising by sending leaflets to people through the post even though they have not asked for them; **direct service organization** = part of the permanent staff of a local authority, which runs a section of the authority's services, such as staff catering **3** *adverb* straight; with no stops; *the plane flies direct to Anchorage;* **to dial direct** = to contact a phone number yourself without asking the operator to do it for you; *you can dial New York direct from London if you want*

◊ **directions** *plural noun* instructions telling someone how to go somewhere; *he gave her directions to get to the Post Office*

◊ **director** *noun* person appointed by the shareholders to help run a company; **managing director** = director who is in charge of the whole company; **chairman and managing director** = managing director who is also chairman of the board of directors

directory *noun* list of people *or* businesses with information about their addresses and telephone numbers; **classified directory** = list of businesses grouped under various headings, such as bakers, boarding houses, Chinese restaurants, etc.; **commercial directory** *or* **trade directory** = book which lists all the businesses and business people in a town; **street directory** = (i) list of people living in a street; (ii) map of a town with all the streets listed in alphabetical order in an index; **telephone directory** = book which lists names of people and businesses in alphabetical order with their phone numbers and addresses; *to look up a number in the telephone directory; his number is in the London directory;* **directory enquiries** = telephone service which finds phone numbers which you do not know or cannot find; *call directory enquiries on 192*

disabled 1 *adjective* (person) with a physical handicap **2** *noun* **the disabled** = physically handicapped people; *the library has facilities for the disabled;* **disabled access** *or* **access for the disabled** = entrances with sloping ramps instead of steps, which are easier for people in wheelchairs to use; **disabled toilets** = public toilet with a larger room than usual to make it easier for people in wheelchairs to use

◊ **disability** *noun* physical handicap

disagree *verb* (a) to say that you do not think the same way as someone (b) cabbage

disagrees with me = cabbage makes me feel ill

discolour *verb* to change the colour of something; *fruit can be discoloured by the use of sprays*

◊ **discoloration** *noun* change of colour, especially a change of colour of fruit

discontinue *verb* not to continue to do something; *the service to the island has been discontinued*

discount 1 *noun* **(a)** percentage by which a full price is reduced to a buyer by the seller; *to give a discount on summer holidays booked before Christmas;* **basic discount** = normal discount without extra percentages; *we give 25% as a basic discount, but can add 5% for cash payment;* **quantity discount** = price reduction given to someone who buys a large amount of goods; **10% discount for quantity purchases** = you pay 10% less if you buy a large amount of goods; **10% discount for cash** *or* **10% cash discount** = you pay 10% less if you pay in cash; **staff discount** = discount given to people working in the company; **trade discount** = discount given to a customer in the same trade **(b) discount holiday** = package holiday where the price is reduced; **discount store** = shop which specializes in cheap goods bought at a high discount **2** *verb* to reduce prices to increase sales; *tour operators are discounting prices on package holidays*

◊ **discounted cash flow (DCF)** *noun* calculating the forecast return on capital investment by discounting future cash flows from the investment, usually at a rate equivalent to the company's minimum required rate of return

COMMENT: Discounting is necessary because it is generally accepted that money held today is worth more than money to be received in the future. The effect of discounting is to reduce future income or expenses to their 'present value'. Once discounted, future cash flows can be compared directly with the initial cost of a capital investment which is already stated in present value terms. If the present value of income is greater than the present value of costs the investment can be said to be worthwhile

QUOTE unofficially discounted fares are fares sold at a discount to the officially approved full or promotional rates. Discounting is now commonplace in most countries.

Business Traveller

discretionary *adjective* which can be done if someone wants; **discretionary income** = income which a person has left after spending on basic necessities (and which is therefore available for spending on leisure activities)

discrimination *noun* treating people in different ways because of class, religion, race, language, colour or sex; **sexual discrimination** *or* **sex discrimination** *or* **discrimination on grounds of sex** = treating men and women in different ways

disease *noun* serious illness (of animals, plants, humans, etc.)

diseconomies of scale *noun* situation where increased production actually increases unit cost

COMMENT: after having increased production using the existing workforce and machinery, giving economies of scale, the company finds that in order to increase production further it has to employ more workers and buy more machinery, leading to an increase in unit cost

disembark *verb* to get off a ship, hovercraft, plane, etc.; *the passengers disembarked at the ocean terminal*

◊ **disembarkation** *noun* getting off a ship, hovercraft, plane, etc.; **disembarkation card** = LANDING CARD

dish 1 *noun* **(a)** large plate (for serving food); **to wash the dishes** *or* **to do the dishes** = to wash plates, glasses, cutlery, etc. after a meal **(b)** part of a meal; (plate of) prepared food; *ratatouille is a Provençal dish of stewed vegetables* **2** *verb* he is **dishing up the food** = he is serving the meal

◊ **dishcloth** *noun* cloth for washing dishes

◊ **dishwasher** *noun* machine for washing dishes; **dishwasher-proof** = (china, etc.) which is not harmed by being washed in a dishwasher

◊ **dish-washing** *noun* washing-up, the washing of dirty plates, glasses, etc.

dismiss verb to dismiss an employee = to remove an employee from a job; *he was dismissed for being late*

◇ **dismissal** noun removal of an employee from a job; **dismissal procedure** = correct way of dismissing an employee, following the rules in the contract of employment; **constructive dismissal** = situation where an employee does not leave his job voluntarily but because of pressure from the management; **unfair dismissal** = removal of someone from a job by an employer who appears not to be acting in a reasonable way (i.e., as by dismissing someone who wants to join a union); **wrongful dismissal** = removal of someone from a job for a reason which does not justify dismissal and which is in breach of the contract of employment

COMMENT: an employee can complain of unfair dismissal to an industrial tribunal, or of wrongful dismissal to the County Court

dispense cellar noun cellar in which wine is kept for immediate serving; **dispense bar** = bar for serving drinks (other than bottles of wine) for guests in a restaurant

◇ **dispenser** noun machine which automatically provides something (an object or a drink or some food), often when money is put in; *automatic dispenser; towel dispenser;* **cash dispenser** = machine which gives out money when a special card is inserted and instructions given

QUOTE five-litre milk dispensers are made from stainless steel. A separate base takes an ice or freezer bag to keep the milk cool. Fruit juice dispensers have the same base, but there is a choice of four-, five- or six-litre cylinders

Caterer & Hotelkeeper

display noun show or exhibition; *the hotel lobby has a display of local crafts;* **display advertisement** = advertisement which is well designed to attract attention; **display case** = table or counter with a glass top, used for showing items for sale; **refrigerated display case** = cabinet with glass sides and top, cooled by a refrigerating plant underneath, used to keep prepared food dishes such as salads and desserts, fresh and cool

disposable adjective **(a)** which can be used and then thrown away; *disposable cups* **(b)** **disposable personal income** = income left after tax and national insurance have been deducted

dispute noun **industrial dispute** or **labour dispute** = argument between management and workers; **to adjudicate** or **to mediate in a dispute** = to try to settle a dispute between other parties

distil verb **(a)** to make strong alcohol by heating wine or other alcoholic liquid and condensing it **(b)** to make pure water by heating and collecting the vapour; **distilled water** = pure water

◇ **distillation** noun act of distilling water or alcohol

◇ **distiller** noun person who distils alcohol

◇ **distillery** noun factory for distilling alcohol

district noun section of a country or of a town; **the commercial district** or **the business district** = part of a town where offices and shops are located; *the hotel is well placed in the main business district of the town*

disturb verb to bother or worry (someone); to interrupt (someone); **'do not disturb'** = notice placed on a hotel room door, to ask the hotel staff not to come into the room

◇ **disturbance** noun noise

dive 1 noun **(a)** plunge downwards head first into water **(b)** (informal) disreputable bar **2** verb to plunge headfirst into water

◇ **diver** noun person who plunges headfirst into water or who swims underwater

◇ **diving** noun plunging headfirst into water or swimming under water as a sport; *to go diving in the Red Sea; diving holidays on the Barrier Reef;* **diving board** = plank at swimming pool from which people plunge into the water

diversion noun turning off a road to take another route to avoid road works, flooding, etc.; *all traffic has to take a diversion and rejoin the motorway 10km further on*

divert verb to send to another place or in another direction; *because of fog in London, flights have been diverted to Manchester; traffic has been diverted to avoid the town centre*

DJ DINNER JACKET, DISK JOCKEY

DM or **Dm** or **D-mark** = DEUTSCHMARK, MARK

dock 1 *noun* harbour *or* place where ships can load or unload; **the docks** = part of a town where the harbour is; *cars should arrive at the docks 45 minutes before sailing time;* **dry dock** = dock where the water is pumped out to allow repairs to be done to a ship **2** *verb* to go into dock; *the ship docked at 17.00*

◇ **docker** *noun* man who works in the docks

◇ **dockside** *noun* edge of a dock where ships load or unload; *customs officers were waiting at the dockside to board the ship*

◇ **dockyard** *noun* place where ships are built

doctor *noun* person who looks after people's health; **the hotel doctor** = the doctor who is on call to treat guests who become ill in the hotel; **ship's doctor** = doctor who travels on a ship and so is ready to treat passengers who become ill (NOTE: shortened in names to **Dr: Dr Thorne is the hotel doctor)**

document *noun* paper with writing on it; *customs will ask to see the relevant documents concerning the shipment*

◇ **documentation** *noun* all papers referring to something; *please send me the complete documentation concerning the sale*

dollar *noun* **(a)** unit of money used in the USA and other countries; *the US dollar rose 2%; fifty Canadian dollars; it costs six Australian dollars;* **five dollar bill** = banknote for five dollars **(b)** the currency used in the USA; **dollar area** = area of the world where the dollar is the main trading currency (NOTE: when used with a figure, usually written **$** before the figure: **$250**. The currencies used in different countries can be shown by the initial letter of the country: **Can$** (Canadian dollar) **Aus$** (Australian dollar), etc.)

domestic *adjective* referring to the home market *or* the market of the country where the business is situated; *domestic sales; domestic turnover;* **domestic flight** = flight inside a country; **domestic terminal** = airport terminal which has flights inside a country only; *passengers arriving on international flights transfer to the domestic terminal for onward flights to destinations inside the country;* **domestic tourist** = tourist who is visiting (either for pleasure or on business) the country where he lives

don *verb* to put on (clothes); *instructions for donning the life jacket are given on the card in the pocket in front of your seat*

doner kebab *noun* Turkish meat dish, where a large piece of meat is cooked on a spit in front of a grill, and slices are cut off and served with pitta bread and salad, usually as a takeaway

door *noun* barrier of wood, glass or metal, etc., which closes an entrance; **back door** = door at the rear of a building; **front door** = main door of a building; *the reception gave him a key to the front door or to the main door of the hotel*

◇ **doorkeeper** *noun* person who is on duty at a main door

◇ **doorkey** *noun* key to a door; *do not forget to give back your doorkey when you leave the hotel*

◇ **doorknob** *noun* handle for opening and shutting a door

◇ **doorman** *noun* man who is on duty at the door of a restaurant *or* hotel *or* club

dormobile *noun* trademark for a motor caravan

double *adjective* **(a)** twice as large *or* two times the size; **double saucepan** *or* **double boiler** = cooking utensil, made up of two saucepans, one of which fits on top of the other; the lower pan contains hot water and the top pan contains the food to be cooked; **double whisky** = portion of whisky, twice the amount of a normal measure **(b)** for two people; **double occupancy** = occupancy of a room by two people; **double room** = room for two people; **double bed** = large bed for two people; **double-bedded room** = room with two beds (usually two twin beds)

◇ **double-book** *verb* to let the same hotel room *or* plane seat, etc., to two people at the same time (sometimes by mistake); *we had to change our flight as we were double-booked*

◇ **double-booking** *noun* booking (sometimes by mistake) of two people into the same hotel room *or* the same seat on a plane at the same time

◇ **double-decker** *noun* **(a)** bus with two decks (like the London buses) **(b)** sandwich made of three slices of bread, with a filling of meat, salad, fish, etc., between them

◇ **double glazing** *noun* two panes of glass in windows, which insulate; *all the rooms in the hotel are double-glazed to reduce noise from the airport*

◇ **double-park** *verb* to park alongside a car which is already parked at the side of the street

◇ **double-parking** *noun* parking alongside a car which is already parked at the side of the street

dough *noun* uncooked mixture of water and flour for making bread, etc.

◇ **doughnut** *noun* small round or ring-shaped cake cooked by frying in oil

downgrade *verb* to reduce something to a less important level; *he was downgraded from first class to business class; her job was downgraded in the company reorganization*

QUOTE according to a recent poll of more than 400 leading companies, 49 per cent said they had downgraded the class of travel and hotel of their executives
Business Travel

downhill *adverb* towards the bottom (of a hill); **downhill skiing** = skiing fast down slopes (as opposed to cross-country skiing which is mainly walking)

◇ **down-market** *adjective* cheaper or appealing to a less wealthy section of the population

◇ **down payment** *noun* part of a total cost paid in advance

◇ **downpour** *noun* heavy fall of rain

◇ **downstairs 1** *adverb* towards or in the lower part of a building or vehicle; *all the guests ran downstairs when the alarm rang* **2** *adjective* in the lower part of a building or vehicle; *there is a downstairs bar for guests* **3** *noun* lower part of a building or vehicle

downtown *noun, adjective & adverb US* in the central business district of a town; *downtown will be very crowded at this time of day; his office is in downtown New York; a downtown hotel; they established a restaurant downtown*

drachma *noun* currency used in Greece (NOTE: usually written **Dr** before a figure: **Dr22bn**)

draft beer *see* DRAUGHT

drain *verb* to remove water from something; *boil the potatoes for ten minutes, drain and leave to cool;* **drain cycle** = last of a series of operations in a dishwasher, when the water is drained and the dishes left to dry

drapes *plural noun US* curtains

draught *noun* **(a)** current of cold air which blows in a room *or* train *or* bus, etc.; *he sat in a draught and caught a cold* **(b)** draught beer *or* **beer on draught** = beer which is served from a barrel, and not in a bottle or can **(c)** depth of water in which a ship can float; **shallow-draught vessel** = boat which can sail in shallow water

drawer *noun* sliding compartment in a desk or cupboard which you open by pulling on a handle; **chest of drawers** = piece of bedroom furniture made of several sliding compartments

drawing room *noun* sitting room; room for sitting and talking in, but not eating; *the guests' drawing room is on the right of the main entrance*

dregs *plural noun* cold remnants of a drink, left in a cup or glass

dress 1 *noun* **(a)** piece of woman's or girl's clothing, covering more or less the whole body **(b)** special clothes; **evening dress** = formal clothes worn to an evening banquet or reception (long dresses for women and dinner jacket and bow tie for men); **dress circle** = first balcony of seats above the stalls in a theatre; **dress coat** = man's formal long black coat **2** *verb* **(a)** to put on clothes, especially formal clothes; *we're expected to dress for dinner when we're sitting at the captain's table* **(b)** to prepare (a chicken) for cooking; **dressed crab** *or* **dressed lobster** = cooked crab *or* lobster, with the legs removed and the flesh broken up and put back into the shell

◇ **dressing** *noun* **(a)** putting on clothes; **dressing table** = bedroom table with mirrors **(b)** sauce (for salad); *a bottle of Italian dressing; would you like French dressing or Thousand Island dressing?;* **French dressing** = vinaigrette, salad dressing made with oil, vinegar, salt and other flavourings; *see also* SALAD, THOUSAND ISLAND

dried *adjective* (foodstuff) preserved by dehydration (which removes water and so slows down deterioration); *dried mushrooms; sun-dried tomatoes;* **dried fruit** = fruit that has been dehydrated to preserve it for later use (currants, sultanas and raisins are dried grapes); **dried milk** = milk powder produced by removing water from liquid milk; *see also* DRY

drier *noun* = DRYER

drill *noun* **boat drill** *or* **fire drill** = procedure to be carried out to help people to escape from a sinking boat *or* from a burning building

drink 1 *noun* **(a)** liquid which someone swallows; *would you like a drink?; drinks are served before the meal on transatlantic flights;* **drinks trolley** = trolley on an aircraft, with various drinks which are served by stewards or stewardesses **(b)** alcoholic drink; *drinks are being served on the terrace;* **soft drink** = drink which is not alcoholic (sold either ready prepared in a bottle or can, or in concentrated form which can be mixed with water); **he has a drink problem** = he suffers from alcoholism; **he was much the worse for drink** = he was drunk **2** *verb* to swallow liquid; *she was so thirsty she drank four glasses of lemonade; do you want something to drink with your meal?;* **she doesn't drink** = she never drinks alcohol; **let's drink to the success of the tour** = let us raise our glasses and wish it success

COMMENT: the word 'drink' is often used to refer to alcoholic drinks

◊ **drinkable** *adjective* which is quite nice to drink; *this wine is hardly drinkable*
◊ **drinking chocolate** *noun* sweet chocolate powder, used to make a hot drink
◊ **drinking water** *noun* water for drinking, as opposed to water for washing

drip *noun* small drop of liquid, falling from a tap, etc.; **drip tray** = tray placed under a tap to catch drips (as under a beer tap, for example)

drive 1 *noun* **(a)** ride in a motor vehicle **(b)** way in which a car is propelled or guided; **car with front-wheel drive** = car where the engine is connected directly to the front wheels; **car with left-hand drive** = car where the driver sits on the left-hand side **(c)** path leading to a house wide enough for a car to drive along it **2** *verb* to make a car *or* lorry, etc. go in a certain direction; *he was driving to work when he heard the news on the car radio; she drives a tour bus*
NOTE: **driving - drove - has driven**
◊ **drive along** *verb* to ride along a road in a motor vehicle
◊ **drive away** *verb* to go away in a motor vehicle
◊ **drive back** *verb* to go or come back in a motor vehicle

◊ **drive in** *verb* to go in by car; **drive-in cinema** *or* **restaurant** = cinema *or* restaurant where you can drive in in a car and watch a film or eat while still sitting in the car
◊ **drive on** *verb* to continue one's journey; *the policeman signalled us to drive on*
◊ **driver** *noun* person who drives; *you pay the driver as you get on the bus; don't talk to the driver when the bus is in motion;* **driver-only bus** = bus with only a driver, and no conductor to take the fares
◊ **driving licence** *or* *US* **driver's license** *noun* permit which allows you to drive; **international driving licence** = driving licence which allows you to drive legally in various countries provided you have a valid driving licence from your own country

drizzle 1 *noun* thin mist of rain **2** *verb* to rain in a thin mist
◊ **drizzly** *adjective* (weather) where it is raining in thin mist

drop *verb* to fall *or* to go to a lower level; *take a warm sweater, because at night the temperature can drop quite sharply;* **the wind dropped** = the wind stopped blowing hard

DRV = DIETARY REFERENCE VALUES

dry 1 *adjective* **(a)** not wet; **dry curing** = curing meat in salt, as opposed to brine **(b)** with no rain; **dry season** = period of the year when it does not rain much (as opposed to the rainy season) **(c)** not sweet (wine); *a dry white wine is served with fish; some German wines are quite dry; I prefer dry champagne to sweet champagne;* **dry martini** = cocktail of gin and French vermouth, served with an olive **(d)** (area) where alcohol is forbidden; *the whole state is dry* **2** *verb* to remove water from (something); *guests are asked not to hang clothes to dry on the balcony*
◊ **dry-clean** *verb* to clean (clothes) with chemicals
◊ **dry-cleaner's** *noun* shop where clothes are dry-cleaned
◊ **dry-cleaning** *noun* clothes which are ready to be sent for cleaning *or* which have been returned after cleaning
◊ **dryer** *noun* machine which dries, especially a machine to dry clothes; **hair dryer** = machine for drying wet hair
◊ **dry ice** *noun* carbon dioxide (CO_2) in solid form; it is extremely cold, with a temperature of -78°C, and is used for keeping food such as ice cream cold when being transported

◊ **drying** *noun* method of preserving food by removing moisture (either by leaving it in the sun, as for dried fruit, or by passing it through an industrial process)

DSO = DIRECT SERVICE ORGANIZATION

DST = DAYLIGHT SAVING TIME

Dublin Bay prawn *noun* large prawn, such as those served as scampi

duck *noun* (a) common water bird (b) meat of this bird used as food; **Peking duck** = duck cooked in the Chinese style, with a sweet brown glaze (eaten with pancakes and raw onions)

◊ **duckling** *noun* baby duck

COMMENT: roast duck is traditionally eaten with orange sauce

dude *noun* US visitor to a dude ranch; **dude ranch** = ranch which people visit as a tourist attraction and where they can stay and spend a holiday

due diligence *noun* requirement of the food safety legislation that food producers must take all reasonable care that the food they produce is safe, and is produced and packed in a way which prevents contamination

dumb waiter *noun* (a) sideboard in a restaurant, on which cutlery, condiments, etc., are kept ready for use (b) device for raising and lowering trays of food , dirty dishes, etc., between floors of a building

dumping *noun* getting rid of excess goods cheaply in an overseas market

dumpling *noun* small ball of paste (often with a filling) which is boiled or steamed; **apple dumplings** = pieces of apple cooked in dough; **suet dumplings** = small balls of flour, suet and water, flavoured with herbs

dune *noun* **sand dunes** = grass-covered sandy ridges by the seashore

durian *noun* tropical fruit from a tree *(Durio zibethinus)* native to Malaysia. The fruit has an extremely unpleasant smell, but is highly regarded as a dessert fruit in south-east Asia

durum wheat *noun* hard type of wheat *(Triticum durum)* grown in southern Europe and used to make pasta

COMMENT: the best pasta is made with 100% durum wheat and should be labelled to this effect

dusk *noun* twilight, the period in the evening just before it gets dark; *the gardens close at dusk*

dust 1 *noun* thin layer of dry dirt **2** *verb* (a) to remove dust from (something); *the chambermaid has not dusted the room* (b) to sprinkle sugar onto a cake

◊ **dustbin** *noun* large container for collecting rubbish

◊ **duster** *noun* cloth for removing dust; **feather duster** = brush made of feathers for removing dust

◊ **dustpan** *noun* small wide shovel for scooping up dirt

Dutch *adjective* referring to Holland; **Dutch treat** = party where each person pays his share; **to go Dutch** = to share the cost of a meal equally between everyone

dutiable *adjective* **dutiable goods** *or* **dutiable items** = goods on which a customs duty has to be paid

duty *noun* (a) work which a person has to do; *one of his duties is to see that the main doors are locked at night* (b) official work which you have to do in a job; *he's on duty from 9.00 to 6.00;* **duty manager** = manager who is on duty at the present time (c) tax which has to be paid; *to take the duty off alcohol; to put a duty on cigarettes;* **ad valorem duty** = duty calculated on the sales value of the goods; **customs duty** *or* **import duty** = tax on goods brought into a country; **excise duty** = tax on certain goods produced in a country (such as alcohol and petrol); **goods which are liable to duty** = goods on which customs or excise tax has to be paid; **duty-paid goods** = goods on which tax has been paid

◊ **duty-free** *adjective & adverb* sold with no duty to be paid; *he bought a duty-free watch at the airport or he bought the watch duty-free;* **duty-free shop** = shop at an airport *or* on a ship where goods can be bought without paying duty

◊ **duty of care** *noun* duty which every citizen has not to act negligently; **duty of care code** = list of guidelines which personnel must follow (as in the safe disposal of waste)

COMMENT: the duty of care code requires business which produce waste to ensure that it is carefully stored until it is disposed of, that it is disposed of by a registered waste disposal contractor and that a written record is kept each time the waste is removed

QUOTE Canadian and European negotiators agreed to a deal under which Canada could lower its import duties on $150 million worth of European goods

Globe and Mail (Toronto)

QUOTE the Department of Customs and Excise collected a total of N79m under the new advance duty payment scheme

Business Times (Lagos)

duvet *noun* large bag filled with feathers, used to cover a bed; **duvet cover** = decorative bag used to cover a duvet

dysentery *noun* infection and inflammation of the colon causing bleeding and diarrhoea

◊ **dysenteric** *adjective* referring to dysentery

COMMENT: dysentery occurs mainly in tropical countries. The symptoms include diarrhoea, discharge of blood and pain in the intestines. There are two main types of dysentery: bacillary dysentery, caused by the bacterium *Shigella* in contaminated food; and amoebic dysentery or amoebiasis, caused by a parasitic amoeba *Entamoeba histolytica* spread through contaminated drinking water

Ee

E number classification of additives to food according to the European Community

COMMENT: additives are classified as follows: colouring substances: E100 - E180; preservatives: E200 - E297; antioxidants: E300 - E321; emulsifiers and stabilizers: E322 -E495; acids and bases: E500 - E529; anti-caking additives: E530 - E578; flavour enhancers and sweeteners: E620 - E637

Vitamin E *noun* vitamin found in vegetables, vegetable oils, eggs and wholemeal bread

e. & o.e. = ERRORS AND OMISSIONS EXCEPTED

COMMENT: note written on an invoice to show that the seller is not responsible for any mistakes in the invoice

Form E111 *noun* form used in the EC, which entitles a resident of one EC country to free medical treatment in another EC country

early *adjective & adverb* **(a)** before the usual time; *let's have an early lunch; you should leave the hotel early to miss the rush-hour traffic;* **early arrival** = guest who arrives at a hotel earlier than expected *or* who is the first to arrive; **early bird special** = specially cheap meal if the meal is taken early in the morning *or* specially reduced fare for travel very early in the morning; **early (morning) call** = phone call or knock on the door to wake someone up in the morning; *he asked for an early call or he asked to be called early;* **early closing day** = weekday (usually Wednesday or Thursday) when many shops close in the afternoon; **at your earliest convenience** = as soon as you find it possible; **at an early date** = very soon **(b)** at the beginning of a period of time; *he took an early flight to Paris;* **we hope for an early resumption of services** = we hope services will start again soon

earphone *noun* part of a pair of headphones which fits over one ear

◊ **earplug** *noun* ball of wax, cotton, etc. which is pushed into the ear so that you cannot hear anything; *luckily we took earplugs with us, as the traffic outside our room was very noisy*

east 1 *noun* one of the points of the compass, the direction of the rising sun; the eastern part of a country; *the sun rises in the east; the pilgrims turned towards the east;* **the Far East** = countries to the east of India; **the Middle East** = countries to the east of Egypt and west of Pakistan **2** *adjective* referring to the east; **East Anglia** = eastern part of England to the north-east of London; **east wind** = wind which blows from the east **3** *adverb* towards the east; *drive east along the motorway for ten miles*

◊ **eastbound** *adjective* going towards the east; *the eastbound carriageway of the motorway is closed*

◊ **easterly 1** *adjective* **(a)** towards the east; **in an easterly direction** = towards the east **(b) easterly wind** = wind which blows from the east **2** *noun* wind which blows from the east

◊ **eastern** *adjective* referring to the east

◊ **easternmost** *adjective* furthest east

◊ **eastward** *adjective & adverb* towards the east

◊ **eastwards** *adverb* towards the east

Easter *noun* Christian festival (in March or April); **Easter Day** *or* **Easter Sunday** = Sunday celebrating Christ's rising from the dead; **Easter egg** = chocolate or sugar egg eaten at Easter

eat *verb* **(a)** to chew and swallow (food); **eating apple** = sweet apple which may be eaten raw (as opposed to a cooking apple) **(b)** to have a meal (especially dinner); *eat as much as you like for £5.95!;* **to eat in** = to have a meal in the restaurant of the hotel where you are staying; **to eat out** = to have dinner away from home or in a restaurant outside the hotel where you are staying

◊ **eatable** *adjective* which can be eaten

◊ **eatables** *plural noun* things to eat

◊ **eater** *noun* person who eats

◊ **eatery** *noun (informal)* place to eat

◊ **eating place** *noun* place (such as a restaurant, cafeteria, canteen, etc.) where you can eat

EC = EUROPEAN COMMUNITY *EC ministers met today in Brussels; the USA is increasing its trade with the EC;* **EC directive** = official order from the European Community offices

economy *noun* **(a)** saving (of money or resources); **economy car** = car which does not use much petrol; **economy class** = cheapest category of seat on a plane; *to travel economy class;* **economy pack** *or* **economy size** = packet of goods which works out cheaper to buy, normally because it contains more; **economies of scale** = providing a service more profitably because of the large size of the organization **(b)** financial state of a country *or* way in which a country makes and uses its money; **black economy** = work which is paid for in cash or goods, but not declared to the tax authorities

QUOTE let no one pretend that taking a long-haul Economy class flight is a pleasurable experience
Business Traveller

ecu *or* **ECU** *noun* = EUROPEAN CURRENCY UNIT

EEC = EUROPEAN ECONOMIC COMMUNITY *EEC ministers met today in Brussels; the USA is increasing its trade with the EEC*

eel *noun* long thin river fish

COMMENT: eels may be eaten as smoked (usually with horseradish sauce) or stewed in the traditional London fashion - 'jellied eels'

efficiency *noun* ability to work well *or* to produce the right result or the right work quickly

◊ **efficient** *adjective* able to work well *or* to produce the right result or the right work quickly

◊ **efficiently** *adverb* in an efficient way; *the waitresses served the 250 diners very efficiently*

EFT = ELECTRONIC FUNDS TRANSFER

e.g. for example *or* such as; *the contract is valid in some countries (e.g. France and Belgium) but not in others*

egg *noun* (i) hard-shelled ovum of a domestic hen; (ii) hard-shelled ovum of any bird; **hen's egg; duck's egg; quail eggs; fried egg** = egg which has been fried in hot fat; **hard-boiled egg** = (egg) which has been cooked in boiling water until the white and yolk are set; **poached egg** = egg which is taken out of its shell and cooked whole in hot water (usually eaten on toast, at breakfast); **scrambled eggs** = eggs which are beaten with salt and pepper and cooked in butter, often served on toast as part of an English breakfast; **soft-boiled egg** = (egg) which has been cooked in boiling water for a short time so that the yolk is hot but still liquid

◇ **eggcup** *noun* holder for a boiled egg

◇ **eggshell** *noun* shell around an egg

◇ **eggtimer** *noun* device for timing how long an egg is boiled

eggplant plant with shiny purple-black fruit *(Solanum melongena)*, used as a vegetable - a native of tropical Asia, it is also called 'aubergine'; its Indian name is 'brinjal'

COMMENT: eggplants are used in Mediterranean cooking, especially with tomatoes in ratatouille and moussaka

EHO = ENVIRONMENTAL HEALTH OFFICER

800 number *noun US* telephone number which the caller can use without paying for the call (used to reply to advertisements; the supplier pays for the call, not the caller)

elastic *adjective* which stretches and contracts, and is not rigid; **elastic demand** = demand which can expand or contract easily because of small changes in price

electricity *noun* current used to make light *or* heat *or* power; *the electricity was cut off this morning, so the air-conditioning could not work; our electricity bill has increased considerably this quarter; electricity costs are an important factor in our overheads*

◇ **electric** *adjective* worked by electricity; *the flat is equipped with an electric cooker*

◇ **electrical** *adjective* referring to electricity; *the engineers are trying to repair an electrical fault*

electronic *adjective* **electronic data processing (EDP)** = selecting and examining data stored in a computer to produce information; **electronic funds transfer (EFT)** = system for transferring money from one account to another electronically (as when using a smart card); **electronic point of sale (EPOS)** = system where sales are charged automatically to a customer's credit card or debit card and stock is controlled by the shop's computer

electroplated nickel silver (EPNS) *noun* cutlery which is made of ordinary metal, but covered with silver, giving the impression that it is made of solid silver

(used in high-class restaurants as being superior to stainless steel)

elevator *noun US* lift, a machine which carries people or goods from one floor to another in a building; *take the elevator to the 26th floor; compare* ESCALATOR, TRAVELATOR

elevenses *noun* snack served in the middle of the morning

embark *verb* to go on a ship, hovercraft, aircraft, etc.; *the passengers embarked at Southampton*

◇ **embarkation** *noun* going on to a ship or plane; **port of embarkation** = port at which you get onto a ship, etc.; **embarkation card** = card given to passengers getting onto a ship, etc.

embassy *noun* building where an ambassador has his office; *the British Embassy is holding a party for exhibitors at the trade fair*

emergency *noun* dangerous situation where decisions have to be taken quickly; **the government declared a state of emergency** = the government decided that the situation was so dangerous that the police or army had to run the country; **emergency exit** = special way out of a building, used if there is a fire or other emergency; **in case of emergency** *or* **in an emergency** = if a dangerous situation develops; *in an emergency, press the red button*

QUOTE the problem with emergency evacuation systems is that they do not adequately satisfy safety needs during emergencies. Many systems use emergency powered signs placed high on walls or above doors. These work well when you can see them, but smoke rises, decreasing visibility and increasing the risk of confusion
Hotel Security Worldwide

emigrate *verb* to leave a country to settle in another

◇ **emigration** *noun* leaving one country and settling in another

◇ **emigrant** *noun* person who leaves one country to settle in another

employ *verb* to give (someone) regular paid work; **to employ twenty staff** = to have twenty people working for you; **to employ**

twenty new staff = to give work to twenty new people

◊ **employee** *noun* worker, person employed by a company; *employees of the firm are eligible to join a profit-sharing scheme; relations between management and employees have improved; the company has decided to take on new employees;* employee conduct report = report on how a worker has performed over a certain period of time

emporium *noun* large shop (NOTE: plural is **emporia**)

emptor *see* CAVEAT

empty *adjective* with nothing inside; *the restaurant was half-empty; the ski resorts are empty because there is no snow*

◊ **empties** *plural noun* empty bottles *or* cases; **returned empties** = empty bottles *or* containers which are taken back to a shop *or* supplier, where any deposit paid will be given back

emulsify *verb* to mix (two liquids) so thoroughly that they will not separate

◊ **emulsifier** *or* **emulsifying agent** *noun* substance added to mixtures of food (such as water and oil) to hold them together (used in sauces, etc.), and also added to meat to increase the water content so that the meat is heavier. (In the EC, emulsifiers and stabilizers have E numbers E322 to E495); *see also* STABILIZER

enclose *verb* to put (something) inside an envelope with a letter; *to enclose a leaflet about the hotel; I am enclosing a copy of our current room rates; letter enclosing a cheque; please find the cheque enclosed herewith*

◊ **enclosure** *noun* document enclosed with a letter; *letter with enclosures* (NOTE: usually shortened to **encl.** when written at the end of a letter)

endemic *adjective* (any disease) which is very common in certain places; *yellow fever is endemic to parts of Central Africa*

endive *noun* **(a)** green salad plant similar to a lettuce, with curly bitter-tasting leaves **(b)** vegetable with a conical head of white crisp leaves packed firmly together, eaten raw in salads or cooked with a sauce; *see also* CHICORY

endotoxin *noun* poison from bacteria which pass into the body when contaminated food is eaten

engaged *adjective* busy (telephone line); *you cannot speak to the manager - his line is engaged;* engaged tone = sound made by a telephone when the line dialled is busy; *I tried to phone the complaints department but I just got the engaged tone*

English 1 *adjective* referring to England **2** *noun* language spoken in the UK, the USA and many other countries; *do you speak English? the hotel has an English-speaking manager*

◊ **English service** *noun* way of serving at a meal, where the waiter or waitress serves each guest from a large dish, serving from the guest's left (as opposed to 'French service')

◊ **English breakfast** *noun* meal of cereals, bacon, eggs, toast and marmalade, served with tea or coffee (often served as a buffet in motels and hotel chains)

COMMENT: a traditional 'full English breakfast' may include cereals, porridge, or stewed fruit (such as prunes), grilled fish (such as kippers), bacon and eggs, sausages, kidneys, fried or grilled tomatoes or mushrooms and fried bread, followed by toast and marmalade and tea or coffee

◊ **English Tourist Board (ETB)** organization which promotes tourism in England and promotes tourism to England from other parts of the UK

enhance *verb* to make (something) better *or* stronger

◊ **enhancement** *noun* something which makes a service better

◊ **enhancer** *noun* artificial substance which increases the flavour of food, or even the flavour of artificial flavouring that has been added to food (in the EC, flavour enhancers added to food have the E numbers E620 to 637)

en pension *adjective* en pension terms *or* rate = special price for guests staying in a hotel who take all their meals in the hotel (the same as 'full board'; normally in GB this will include breakfast, morning coffee, lunch, afternoon tea and dinner; there will probably be a reduced special menu for 'en pension' guests, which will not include special dishes found on the 'à la carte' menu

enplane *verb* to get onto an aircraft (NOTE: the opposite is **deplane)**

enquire = INQUIRE

◊ **enquiry** = INQUIRY

en route *adverb* on the way; *we stopped for lunch en route to the coast; the ship ran into a storm en route to the Far East*

en suite *adverb & adjective* **bedroom with bathroom en suite** *or* **with en suite bathroom** = bathroom which leads off a bedroom; *the hotel has 25 bedrooms, all en suite*

Entamoeba *noun* genus of amoeba which lives in the intestine; **Entamoeba coli** = harmless intestinal parasite; **Entamoeba histolytica** = intestinal amoeba which causes amoebic dysentery

enter *verb* **(a)** to go in; *the group entered France by road; several immigrants enter the country illegally every day* **(b)** to write (something) in a record; *to enter a name on a list* **(c)** **to enter into** = to begin; *to enter into relations with someone; to enter into negotiations with a foreign government; to enter into a partnership with a legal friend; to enter into an agreement or a contract; see also* ENTRANCE, ENTRY

◊ **entering** *noun* writing something in a record

enteritis *noun* inflammation of the mucous membrane of the intestine; **infective enteritis** = enteritis caused by bacteria

◊ **Enterobacteria** *noun* important family of bacteria, including Salmonella and Escherichia

◊ **enterotoxin** *noun* bacterial exotoxin which particularly affects the intestine

entertain *verb* to offer meals *or* hotel accommodation *or* theatre tickets, etc. to (business) visitors

◊ **entertainment** *noun* **(a)** offering meals, etc. to business visitors; **entertainment allowance** = money which a manager is allowed by his company to spend on meals with visitors; **entertainment expenses** = money spent on giving meals, theatre tickets, etc. to business visitors **(b)** games, films, etc. offered to amuse passengers; **in-flight entertainment** = films which are shown during a long flight; *(on a cruise ship)* **entertainment officer** = person who is responsible for organizing sports competitions, shows, dances, cabarets, etc. for the passengers

entitle *verb* to give the right to (someone); *the token entitles you to two free admissions to the museum; he is entitled to ten days' holiday a year*

QUOTE membership of the club, free to business travellers and conference delegates, entitles guests to 10% discounts on their room bill and the hotel's business centre facilities
Business Traveller

entrance *noun* way in *or* going in; *the taxi will drop you at the main entrance; the group will meet at the London Road entrance of the hotel;* **entrance (charge)** *or* **entrance fee** = money which you have to pay to go in; *entrance is £1.50 for adults and £1 for children*

entrée *noun* **(a)** dish of meat (such as vol-au-vent, fricassée) served after the fish course and before the main course in a formal meal **(b)** *(especially US)* main course of a meal

entremets *noun* sweet course, consisting of puddings, pastries, ices, etc.

entry *noun* **(a)** act of going in; place where you can go in; *to pass a customs entry point; entry of goods under bond;* **entry charge** = price to be paid before going into an exhibition, etc.; **entry visa** = visa allowing someone to go into a country; **multiple entry visa** = visa allowing someone to enter a country as often as he likes **(b)** written information in a ledger *or* register; **to make an entry in a ledger** = to write details of a deal; *the police looked at the entries in the hotel's register*

environmental *adjective* referring to the environment; **environmental annoyance** = nuisance caused by such environmental factors as traffic noise; **environmental quality standards** = amount of an effluent *or* pollutant which is accepted in a certain environment, such as the amount of trace elements in drinking water or the amount of additives in food

◊ **Environmental Health Officer (EHO)** *noun* official of a local authority who examines the environment and tests for air pollution *or* bad sanitation *or* noise pollution, etc.

COMMENT: in particular EHOs inspect the kitchens of hotels, restaurants, etc. to see if they are clean and free from pests

EPNS = ELECTROPLATED NICKEL SILVER

epos or **EPOS** = ELECTRONIC POINT OF SALE

equator noun imaginary line running round the surface of the earth, at an equal distance from the North and South Poles

COMMENT: crossing the equator (or 'crossing the line') is a the subject of elaborate rituals on ships. Passengers who are crossing the equator for the first time are shaved, thrown into the swimming pool, etc., and finally presented with a certificate from the captain

equip verb to provide with machinery; *the ship has a fully-equipped gymnasium; a holiday flat equipped with washing machine and dishwasher; all rooms in the hotel are equipped with hair-dryers and coffeemakers*
◊ **equipment** noun machinery and furniture required to make a factory or office work; *kitchen equipment; kitchen equipment supplier; kitchen equipment catalogue*

ergot noun fungus which grows on rye
◊ **ergotism** noun poisoning by eating rye which has been contaminated with ergot

COMMENT: the symptoms are muscle cramps and dry gangrene in the fingers and toes

escalator noun moving staircase, with metal stairs which move upwards or downwards; *compare* ELEVATOR, TRAVELATOR

escalope noun thin slice of meat, especially veal, pork, chicken or turkey; *see* WIENER SCHNITZEL

escape verb to get away from home or from an awkward or unpleasant situation; *escape with us to the tropical island of Barbados*
◊ **escapism** noun getting away from real life

Escherichia noun one of the Enterobacteria commonly found in faeces; **Escherichia coli** = Gram-negative bacillus associated with acute gastroenteritis and traveller's diarrhoea

escort 1 noun person who accompanies another; **escort agency** or **escort service** = office which provides men or women companions for people who are alone (mainly for going out in the evening) 2 verb to go with someone; *the courier escorted the group into the hotel*

escudo noun currency used in Portugal

esky noun (in Australia) insulated container for keeping food and drink cool (as on a picnic)

espresso noun (i) type of strong Italian coffee, made in a special machine, where steam or boiling water is forced through ground coffee under pressure; (ii) a cup of this coffee; *an espresso machine; two cups of espresso* or *two espressos, please*

establishment noun (a) commercial business; *he runs an important catering establishment* (b) number of people working in a company; **to be on the establishment** = to be a full-time employee; **kitchen with an establishment of fifteen** = kitchen with a budgeted staff of fifteen

estimate 1 noun (a) calculation of probable cost or size or time of something; **rough estimate** = approximate calculation (b) calculation of how much something is likely to cost in the future, given to a client so as to get him to make an order; *estimate of costs* or *of expenditure; before we can give the grant we must have an estimate of the total costs involved; to ask a builder for an estimate for building the annexe;* **to put in an estimate** = to state in writing the probable costs of carrying out a job; *three firms put in estimates for the job* 2 verb (a) to calculate the probable cost or size or time of something; *to estimate that it will cost £1m* or *to estimate costs at £1m; we estimate current sales at only 60% of last year's* (b) **to estimate for a job** = to state in writing the probable costs of carrying out a job; *three firms estimated for the refitting of the bar*
◊ **estimated** *adjective* calculated approximately; **estimated time of arrival (ETA)** = time when an aircraft or a coach or a group of tourists is expected to arrive; **estimated time of departure (ETD)** = time when an aircraft or a coach or a group of tourists is expected to leave

ETA = ESTIMATED TIME OF ARRIVAL

ETB = ENGLISH TOURIST BOARD

ETD = ESTIMATED TIME OF DEPARTURE

ethnic *adjective* referring to a particular race or country; **ethnic food** = food (such as Chinese, Indian, Caribbean food) from a particular country which is not European; **ethnic restaurant** = restaurant serving ethnic food

Euro- *prefix* referring to Europe or the European Community

◊ **Eurocheque** *noun* international European cheque which can be cashed in any European bank or used to pay a bill if the seller accepts it

◊ **Eurodollar** *noun* US dollar in a European bank, used for trade within Europe; *a Eurodollar loan; the Eurodollar market*

◊ **Europe** *noun* group of countries to the West of Asia and the North of Africa; *most of the countries of Western Europe are members of the Common Market; Canadian visitors to Europe have risen by 25%*

◊ **European** *adjective* referring to Europe; **the European Economic Community** = the Common Market; **European food** = food from a country in Europe (French, Spanish, Italian, Greek, etc.), as opposed to ethnic food

◊ **European Currency Unit (ECU)** *noun* monetary unit used within the EC

◊ **European plan** *noun US* hotel tariff which covers the room charges and service charges but no meals (the opposite is American plan)

evacuate *verb* to get people to leave (a dangerous building *or* an aircraft on fire, etc.); *the hotel guests were evacuated by the fire service*

◊ **evacuation** *noun* action of getting people out of a dangerous building *or* aircraft, etc.; **evacuation plan** = diagram pinned up in a hotel room, showing guests how to escape if there is a fire; **evacuation route** = way (clearly indicated by signs and diagrams) which people must follow to escape from a dangerous building

QUOTE evacuation of a building in darkness or smoke is always difficult and hazardous. Whether it is a fire, or a storm, an explosion or any major or minor emergency, nothing makes it more frightening than darkness
Hotel Security Worldwide

evening *noun* part of the day, between the afternoon and night; *they took an evening flight to Madrid; the evening meal is served from 7.30 to 10.30;* **evening dress** = formal clothes worn to an evening banquet or reception (long dresses for women and dinner jacket and bow tie for men)

exact *adjective* very correct; *the exact time is 10.27; the salesgirl asked me if I had the exact sum, since the shop had no change*

◊ **exactly** *adverb* very correctly; *the total cost was exactly £6,504; the train arrived at exactly 10.03*

examine *verb* to look at (someone *or* something) very carefully to see if it can be accepted; *the customs officials asked to examine the inside of the car*

◊ **examination** *noun* **(a)** looking at something very carefully to see if it can be accepted; **customs examination** = looking at goods *or* baggage by customs officials **(b)** test to see if someone has passed a course; *he passed his management examinations; she came first in the final examination for the course; he failed his proficiency examination and so had to leave his job*

exceed *verb* to go beyond (a limit); *he was exceeding the speed limit*

excess *noun* amount which is more than what is allowed; **excess baggage** = (i) baggage which is heavier than the weight allowed as free baggage for a certain category of ticket; (ii) extra payment at an airport for taking baggage which is heavier than the normal passenger's allowance; **excess fare** = extra fare to be paid (such as for travelling first-class with a second-class ticket *or* for travelling further than originally intended); **in excess of** = above *or* more than; *quantities in excess of twenty-five kilos are charged at a higher rate*

◊ **excessive** *adjective* too large; *excessive costs*

QUOTE most airlines give business class the same baggage allowance as first class, which can save large sums in excess baggage
Business Traveller

exchange 1 *noun* **(a)** giving of one thing for another; **part exchange** = giving an old product as part of the payment for a new one; *to take a car in part exchange* **(b)** **foreign exchange** = (i) exchanging the money of one country for that of another; (ii) money of another country; **rate of exchange** *or* **exchange rate** = price at which one currency is exchanged for another; *the* *current rate of exchange is 8.85 francs to the pound;* **exchange control** = control by a government of the way in which its currency may be exchanged for foreign currencies; *the government had to impose exchange controls to stop the rush to buy dollars;* **exchange premium** = extra cost above the normal rate for buying a foreign currency **(c) bill of exchange** = document which tells a bank to pay a person (usually used in foreign currency payments) **(d) telephone exchange** = central office where the telephones of a whole district are linked **2** *verb* **(a) to exchange one article for another** = to give one thing in place of something else; *he exchanged his ticket for a flight on Monday 22nd for a ticket on the same flight on the following Wednesday; if the trousers are too small you can take them back and exchange them for a larger pair; goods can be exchanged only on production of the sales slip* **(b)** to change money of one country for money of another; *to exchange francs for pounds*

◊ **exchangeable** *adjective* which can be exchanged

excise *noun* **(a) excise duty** = tax on certain goods produced in a country (such as alcohol and petrol); *to pay excise duty on wine* **(b) Customs and Excise** *or* **Excise Department** = government department which deals with taxes on imports, with taxes on products such as alcohol produced in the country, and also with Value Added Tax; *Excise officer*

◊ **exciseman** *noun* person who works in the Excise Department

exclude *verb* to shut out (something) from somewhere

◊ **excluding** *preposition* not including; *the total cost, excluding gratuities, is £1,520.00 per person for the 6-night trip*

◊ **exclusive** *adjective* which does not include something; **exclusive of tax** = not including tax

excursion *noun* short visit (often no longer than one day), returning to the place from which you left; **excursion fare** *or* **excursion rate** *or* **excursion ticket** = special cheap fare offered on certain journeys

executive 1 *adjective* who carries out plans and puts things into practice; **executive chef** = main chef in charge of a large restaurant, with many other chefs reporting to him; **executive committee** =

committee which runs the business, etc. **2** *noun* **(a)** important businessman who makes decisions; **executive class** = better and more expensive type of air travel, specially for businessmen; **executive suite** = special suite of rooms in a hotel for businessmen; **executive travel** = business travel by important businessmen

exempt 1 *adjective* not covered by a rule or law; not forced to obey a law; **exempt from tax** *or* **tax-exempt** = not required to pay tax; *as a non-profit-making organization we are exempt from tax* **2** *verb* to free something from having tax paid on it or someone from having to pay tax; *non-profit-making organizations are exempted from tax; food is exempted from sales tax*

◊ **exemption** *noun* freeing something from a contract *or* from having tax paid on it *or* freeing someone from having to pay tax; **exemption from tax** *or* **tax exemption** = not being required to pay tax; *as a non-profit-making organization you can claim tax exemption*

exhibit 1 *noun* **(a)** thing which is shown; *the buyers admired the exhibits on our stand* **(b)** collection of objects *or* goods shown; single section of an exhibition; *the British Trade Exhibit at the International Computer Fair* **2** *verb* **to exhibit at the Motor Show** = to display new models of cars *or* new products

◊ **exhibition** *noun* **(a)** show of works of art; *there is a Goya exhibition on at the Prado; have you visited the Turner exhibition at the Tate Gallery?* **(b)** show of goods so that buyers can look at them and decide what to buy; *the government has sponsored an exhibition of good design; we have a stand at the Ideal Home Exhibition;* **exhibition room** *or* **hall** = place where goods are shown so that buyers can look at them and decide what to buy; **exhibition stand** *or* US **fair booth** = separate section of an exhibition or a commercial fair where a company exhibits its products or services

◊ **exhibitor** *noun* person who shows a work of art *or* company which shows products at an exhibition

exit *noun* way out; *the customers all rushed towards the exits;* **emergency exit** *or* **fire exit** = special way out of a building, used if there is an emergency or a fire

expatriate *noun* person who lives and works in another country

expenditure *noun* amounts of money spent; **below-the-line expenditure** = exceptional payments which are separated from a company's normal accounts; **capital expenditure** = money spent on fixed assets (such as property, machines or furniture); **the company's current expenditure programme** = the company's spending according to the current plan; **heavy expenditure on equipment** = spending large sums of money on equipment (NOTE: no plural in British English, but US English often uses **expenditures)**

expenses *plural noun* money paid for doing something; **the salary offered is £10,000 plus expenses** = the company offers a salary of £10,000 and will repay any expenses incurred by the employee in the course of his work; **all expenses paid** = with all costs paid by the company; *the company sent him to San Francisco all expenses paid or he went on an all-expenses-paid trip to San Francisco;* **to cut down on expenses** = to reduce spending; **allowable expenses** = business expenses which can be claimed against tax; **business expenses** = money spent on running a business, not on stock or assets; **entertainment expenses** = money spent on giving meals, theatre tickets, etc., to business visitors; **fixed expenses** = money which is spent regularly (such as rent, electricity, telephone); **incidental expenses** = small amounts of money spent at various times, in addition to larger amounts; **legal expenses** = money spent on fees paid to lawyers; **overhead expenses** *or* **general expenses** *or* **running expenses** = money spent on the day-to-day cost of a business; **travelling expenses** = money spent on travelling and hotels for business purposes

◊ **expense account** *noun* money which a businessman is allowed by his company to spend on travelling and entertaining clients in connection with his business; *he charged his hotel bill to his expense account; I'll put this lunch on my expense account; expense-account lunches form a large part of our current sales*

◊ **expensive** *adjective* which costs a lot of money; *first-class air travel is becoming more and more expensive*

express 1 *adjective* rapid *or* very fast; *express letter; express delivery;* **express service** = very fast train *or* coach *or* delivery of parcels, etc. **2** *noun* very fast train *or* coach; *we're taking the 10.25 express to Edinburgh* **3** *verb* **(a)** to put into words or diagrams; *this chart shows visitors from*

Europe expressed as a percentage of the total number of tourists coming to the UK each year **(b)** to send very fast; *we expressed the order to the customer's warehouse*

◊ **expressly** *adverb* clearly in words; *the contract expressly forbids sales to the United States*

◊ **expressway** *noun* US very fast road for cars, with few entrances or exits (NOTE: GB English is **motorway)**

ext = EXTENSION

extender *noun* food additive which makes the food bigger or heavier (without adding to its food value); **meat extender** = any edible material or mixture added to meat preparations to increase their bulk

extension *noun* (in a hotel or office) individual telephone linked to the main switchboard; *can you get me extension 21? extension 21 is engaged; the restaurant manager is on extension 53*

external *adjective* outside a country; **external account** = account in a British bank of someone who is living in another country; **external phone** = phone directly linked to an outside line; **external trade** = trade with foreign countries

extinguish *verb* to put out (a fire); *please extinguish your cigarettes as the plane is preparing to land*

◊ **fire extinguisher** *noun* device full of foam, water, or chemicals, used for putting out fires

COMMENT: foam extinguishers cover a fire with a mixture of water, air and foam-producing chemicals; carbon dioxide extinguishers send out liquid carbon dioxide which turns to sold white 'snow' on contact with air and then turns back to gas again under the effect of heat: this has the effect of smothering the fire. Water-based extinguishers should not be used for fires in electrical equipment or involving burning oils

extra 1 *adjective* which is added *or* which is more than usual; *there is an extra charge for a single room; to charge 10% extra for postage; the staff are paid extra pay for working on Sundays; service is extra;* **extra bed** = additional bed brought into a room for a guest; *the hotel is very full but we can put an extra bed in the room if you want;* **extra charge** = additional charge on top of what is already paid; *there is no extra charge for heating* **2** *plural noun* **extras** = items which are not included in a price; *packing and postage are extras*

extractor *noun* machine which removes something; **juice extractor** = machine which squeezes the juice from fruit;

extractor fan = fan which sucks air out; *when you switch on the light in the bathroom, the extractor fan switches on*

extremely *adverb* very much; *it is extremely difficult to spend less than $50.00 a day on meals; the restaurant service is extremely efficient*

Ff

F FRANC

F&B = FOOD AND BEVERAGE

FAA *US* = FEDERAL AVIATION ADMINISTRATION

face 1 *noun* front part of the head **2** *verb* to turn towards; **the room faces east** = the room looks towards the east

◊ **facecloth** *or* **face flannel** *noun* small piece of towelling for washing the face or body

◊ **face towel** *noun* hand towel, a small towel for drying the hands and face

facility *noun* **(a)** **facilities** = means *or* method of doing something easily; *we offer facilities for payment* **(b)** **facilities** = equipment *or* buildings which make it easy to do something, *storage facilities; harbour facilities; transport facilities; the campsite has laundry facilities;* **there are no facilities for unloading** *or* **there are no unloading facilities** = there is no way in which cargo can be unloaded here; **the museum has facilities for the disabled** *or* **for the handicapped** = the museum has special ramps *or* special lifts, etc. to allow disabled or handicapped people to visit it **(c)** *US* single large building; *we have opened our new warehouse facility*

facsimile *noun* facsimile (copy) = exact copy of a document; *see also* FAX

faeces *plural noun* stools *or* bowel movements, solid waste matter passed from the bowels through the anus

◊ **faecal** *adjective* referring to faeces; **faecal matter** = solid waste matter from the bowels (NOTE: spelt **feces, fecal** especially in the USA)

Fahrenheit *noun* scale of temperatures where the freezing and boiling points of water are 32° and 212°; *compare* CELSIUS, CENTIGRADE (NOTE: used in the USA, but less common in the UK. Normally written as an **F** after the degree sign: **32°F** (say: 'thirty-two degrees Fahrenheit')

COMMENT: to convert Fahrenheit to Celsius, subtract 32 and divide by 1.8. To convert Celsius temperatures to Fahrenheit, multiply by 1.8 and add 32. So 68°F is equal to 20°C.

fair 1 *noun* **(a)** group of sideshows, amusements, food stalls, etc., set up in one place for a short time; **fun fair** = small permanent amusement park, place where people can ride on roundabouts, shoot at targets, etc. **(b)** **trade fair** = large exhibition and meeting for advertising and selling a certain type of product; *to organize or to run a trade fair; the fair is open from 9 a.m. to 5 p.m.; the computer fair runs from April 1st to 6th; there are two trade fairs running in London at the same time - the carpet manufacturers' and the computer dealers';* *US* **fair booth** = separate section of an exhibition or a commercial fair where a company exhibits its products or services (NOTE: British English equivalent is **stand**) **2** *adjective* **(a)** honest *or* correct; **fair deal** = arrangement where both parties are treated equally; *the group feel they did not get a fair deal from the holiday company;* **fair price** = good price for both buyer and seller **(b)** **fair copy** = document which is written or typed with no changes or mistakes

◊ **fairly** *adverb* quite *or* relatively; *the hotel is fairly close to the centre of town*

faites marcher *French phrase (meaning 'get (something) started')* used by waiters to ask the kitchen to get a dish ready

fall 1 *noun* **(a)** drop; *a fall in temperature* **(b)** *especially US* autumn; *you should go to New England for the fall; the fall colors are at their best in the first week of October* **(c)** falls = large waterfall; *Victoria Falls; Niagara Falls* **2** *verb* to drop down; *the temperature fell to -30°*

famed *adjective* well known

familiarize *verb* **to familiarize yourself with** = to get to know something well; *the booking clerks were sent on a course to familiarize themselves with the new computer system*
◊ **familiarization** *noun* getting to know something well; **familiarization trip** = visit organized by an airline, tourist resort, etc., so that journalists and tour operators can get to know the facilities offered

family *noun* group of people who are closely related, especially mother, father and their children; **family name** = surname, the name of a family (Smith, Jones, etc.) as opposed to first name or Christian name; **family pack** *or* **family size** = packet of goods which works out cheaper to buy, normally because it contains more; **family room** = room for a family, with main bed for the parents and a small bed or beds or bunk beds for children

famous *adjective* very well known; *the company owns a famous department store in the centre of London*

fan *noun* device which turns to move the air (used to change the air in a kitchen or bathroom, or make a room cooler); **ceiling fan** = fan attached to the ceiling; **extractor fan** = fan which sucks air out; *when you switch on the light in the bathroom, the extractor fan switches on*

fancy *adjective* **(a)** **fancy goods** = small attractive items **(b)** **fancy prices** = high prices; *I don't want to pay the fancy prices they ask in London shops*

fare *noun* **(a)** price to be paid for a journey, for a ticket to travel; *train fares have gone up by 5%; the government is asking the airlines to keep air fares down;* **business fare** = tariff for business-class passengers; **concessionary fare** = reduced fare for certain types of passenger (such as

employees or retired employees of the transport company); **full fare** = ticket for a journey by an adult paying the full price; **half fare** = half-price ticket for a child; **single fare** *or US* **one-way fare** = fare for one journey from one place to another; **return fare** *or US* **round-trip fare** = fare for a journey from one place to another and back again **(b)** passenger in a taxi; *he picked up a fare in Oxford Street and took him to Kensington* **(c)** *(especially in publicity)* food; *good country fare*

farinaceous *adjective* referring to flour *or* containing starch; **farinaceous foods** = foods (such as bread) which are made of flour and have a high starch content

farm *noun* land used for growing crops and keeping animals; *we went to spend the week on a farm in Devon;* **farm tourism** = holidays spent on farms
◊ **farmhouse** *noun* house where the farmer and his family live; **farmhouse holidays** = holidays in the country, living on a farm

fascia *noun* board over a shop on which the name of the shop is written

fast food *noun* cooked food which can be prepared, bought and eaten quickly, such as hamburgers, hot dogs, pizzas, etc.; *she decided to invest in a fast-food franchise;* **fast-food outlet** = snack bars or restaurants offering fast food (often part of a franchise operation)

fat 1 *adjective* **(a)** *(person)* big and round; overweight; *two fat men got out of the little white car; I'm getting too fat - I need to slim* **(b)** thick; *a fat file of complaints on the manager's desk* **(c)** containing a lot of fat; *fat bacon* **2** *noun* **(a)** type of food which supplies protein and Vitamins A and D, especially that part of meat which is white *or* solid substances (like lard *or* butter) produced from animals and used for cooking *or* liquid substances like oil; *he asked for a slice of lamb without too much fat; if you don't like the fat on the meat, cut it off; fry the eggs in some fat;* **cooking fat** = refined oil (either vegetable or animal) used in frying, roasting, baking, etc.
◊ **fattening** *adjective* (foods) which make you fat

◊ **fatty acid** *noun* acid (such as stearic acid) which is an important substance in the body; **essential fatty acid** = unsaturated fatty acid which is essential for growth but which cannot be synthesized by the body and has to be obtained from the food supply

COMMENT: fat is a necessary part of diet because of the vitamins and energy-giving calories which it contains. Fat in the diet comes from either animal fats or vegetable fats. Animal fats such as butter, fat meat or cream, are saturated fatty acids. It is believed that the intake of unsaturated and polyunsaturated fats (mainly vegetable fats and oils and fish oil) in the diet, rather than animal fats, helps keep down the level of cholesterol in the blood and so lessens the risk of atherosclerosis. A low-fat diet does not always help to reduce weight

fathom *noun* measure of depth of water (= 1.8 metres)

faucet *noun* US tap

fauna *noun* wild animals (of an area)

favourite *or* US **favorite** *adjective* which is liked best; *a favourite tourist spot; this brand of chocolate is a favourite with the children's market*

fax 1 *noun* (a) (i) system for sending the exact copy of a document via the telephone; (ii) document sent by this method; *we received a fax of the order this morning; can you confirm the booking by fax?* (b) fax (machine) = machine for sending or receiving faxes; **fax paper** = special paper which is used in fax machines **2** *verb* to send a message by fax; *the details of the offer were faxed to the brokers this morning; I've faxed the documents to our New York office*

COMMENT: banks will not accept fax messages as binding instructions (as for example, a faxed order for money to be transferred from one account to another). Most hotels, on the other hand, will accept confirmation of a booking by fax

feasibility *noun* ability to be done; **feasibility study** = study to see if something can be done

feast 1 *noun* (a) special religious day when a saint or special event is remembered (b) very large meal; **2** *verb* to eat a very large meal

feature 1 *noun* important aspect; *the gastronomic restaurant is a feature of the hotel; long fjords are a feature of the coastline of Norway* **2** *verb* to show as an important item; *the tour features a visit to the Valley of the Kings*

Federal Aviation Administration (FAA) *noun* US government agency which regulates the operation of civilian airlines

fee *noun* (a) money paid; **entrance fee** = money which you have to pay to go into an exhibition, etc. (b) money paid for work carried out by a professional person (such as an accountant *or* a doctor *or* a lawyer); *we charge a small fee for our services; director's fees; consultant's fee*

feed 1 *noun* meal, especially given to babies **2** *verb* (a) to give food to (someone); *the student cafeteria feeds two thousand people a day* (b) to pass aircraft from an international route into domestic services
NOTE: **feeds - fed**

◊ **feeder airline** *noun* airline which connects with a hub and so into services throughout the country

ferment *verb* to change by fermentation; *cider has to ferment for at least ten weeks before it is ready to drink*

◊ **fermentation** *noun* chemical change brought about in liquids usually leading to the production of alcohol

ferry *or* **ferryboat** *noun* boat which takes passengers or goods across water; *we are going to take the night ferry to Belgium;* **car ferry** = boat which carries vehicles and passengers from one place to another; **night ferry** = boat which travels during the night; **passenger ferry** = boat which carries only passengers

festival *noun* (a) religious celebration which comes at the same time each year; *the party will be in Hong Kong for the Lantern Festival* (b) artistic celebration, entertainment which is put on at regular intervals; *we saw some excellent plays at the Edinburgh Festival this year;* **arts festival** = performances, exhibitions and competitions in music, drama, painting and handicrafts, etc.; **beer festival** = (i) festival to celebrate the making of beer; (ii) exhibition for advertising, sampling and selling different types of beer; *the Munich Beer Festival;* **music festival** = series of concerts and recitals given over a short period of time

fête *noun* little local festival; *a village fête; the school summer fête*

FF = FRENCH FRANCS

fibre *or* *US* **fiber** *noun* **dietary fibre** = fibrous matter in food, which cannot be digested; **high-fibre diet** = diet which contains a lot of cereals, nuts, fruit and vegetables

> COMMENT: dietary fibre is found in cereals, nuts, fruit and some green vegetables. There are two types of fibre in food: insoluble fibre (in bread and cereals) which is not digested and soluble fibre (in vegetables and pulses). Foods with the highest proportion of fibre are bread, beans and dried apricots. Fibre is thought to be necessary to help digestion and avoid developing constipation, obesity and appendicitis

field *noun* **in the field** = outside the office *or* among the customers; *we have sixteen reps in the field;* **first in the field** = first company to bring out a product *or* to start a service; **field research** *or* **field work** = examination of the situation among possible customers (as opposed to desk research); *they did a lot of field work to find the right market for their new service*

fig *noun* juicy sweet fruit of a semi-tropical tree *(Ficus),* grown mainly in Mediterranean countries and eaten either as 'fresh figs' or 'dried figs'

fill 1 *verb* **(a)** to make something full; *the waiter filled his glass again* **(b)** **to fill a gap** = to provide a product *or* service which is needed, but which no one has provided before; *the new series of golfing holidays fills a gap in the market* **(c)** **to fill a post** *or* **a vacancy** = to find someone to do a job; *your application arrived too late - the post has already been filled*

◊ **fill in** *verb* to write the necessary information in the blank spaces in a form; *fill in your name and address in block capitals*

◊ **filling** *noun* food used to put into something, such as inside a sandwich, pie, cake, etc.

◊ **filling station** *noun* place where you can buy petrol; *he stopped at the filling station to*

get some petrol before going on to the motorway

◊ **fill out** *verb* to write the required information in the blank spaces in a form; *to get customs clearance you must fill out three forms*

◊ **fill up** *verb* **(a)** to make something completely full; *come on, fill the glasses up again!; he filled up the car with petrol; my appointments book is completely filled up* **(b)** to finish writing the necessary information on a form; *he filled up the form and sent it to the bank*

fillet 1 *noun* **(a)** piece of good-quality meat, with no bones; *fillet of beef; fillet of pork; fillet steak* **(b)** piece of fish from which the bones have been taken out; *a fillet of sole* **2** *verb* to take the bones out of (a fish); *ask the waiter to fillet the fish for you*

filter 1 *noun* **(a)** piece of cloth, plastic, paper or crystals through which water passes and which holds back solid particles such as dirt; *the filter in the swimming pool has become clogged; the inspector asked the restaurant to replace the filter on the air extractor* **(b)** piece of paper through which coffee passes in a coffee machine; **filter coffee** = coffee which is made by passing boiling water through coffee grounds, often in a paper cone **2** *verb* to pass (liquid) through a paper or cloth filter, or through crystals; *the water is filtered through a cloth before being used*

finance 1 *noun* **(a)** money used by a company, provided by the shareholders or by loans **(b)** **finances** = money *or* cash which is available; *the bad state of the company's finances* **2** *verb* to provide money to pay for (something); *the development of the marina was financed by the local council*

◊ **financial** *adjective* concerning money; **financial adviser** = person *or* company giving advice on financial matters for a fee; **financial assistance** = help in the form of money; **financial resources** = money which is available for investment; *a company with strong financial resources;* **financial year** = the twelve-month period for a firm's accounts

fine 1 *adjective* *(weather)* which is good; with no rain; *when the weather is fine, the view from the hotel is splendid; don't rely on having fine weather in the middle of November* **2** *noun* money paid because of something wrong which has been done; *he was asked to pay a $25,000 fine; we had to* *pay a $10 parking fine* **3** *verb* to punish (someone) by making him pay money; *to fine someone £2,500 for obtaining money by false pretences* **4** *adverb* very thin *or* very small; *chop the vegetables very fine*

◊ **finely** *adverb* very thin *or* (cut) into very small pieces; *finely chopped parsley*

finger *noun* **(a)** one of the five parts at the end of a hand, usually other than the thumb; **finger biscuit** = biscuit shaped like a finger; **finger bowl** = bowl of water (often with a slice of lemon in it) put beside a guest's plate, so that he can wash his hands after eating (especially used when serving shellfish); **finger buffet** = buffet where snacks are served which guests eat with their fingers (sandwiches, small pastries, etc.), as opposed to a 'fork luncheon'; **fish fingers** = pieces of white fish shaped into oblongs and coated with breadcrumbs and fried **(b)** covered walkway which connects an aircraft with the terminal building, so that passengers can walk onto or off the aircraft easily (it extends from the terminal to the forward door on the aircraft) (NOTE: also called **airbridge** or **jetway)**

fire 1 *noun* thing which is burning; *she lost all her belongings in the hotel fire;* **to catch fire** = to start to burn; **fire alarm** = bell or siren which gives warning that a fire has started; **fire damage** = damage caused by fire; *he claimed £250 for fire damage;* **fire-damaged goods** = goods which have been damaged in a fire; **fire detector** = special appliance which detects fire by sensing heat; **fire door** = special door to prevent fire going from one part of a building to another; **fire drill** = procedure to be carried out to help people to escape from a burning building; *we will be holding a fire drill this morning;* **fire escape** *or* **fire exit** = door *or* stairs which allow people to get out of a building which is on fire; **fire extinguisher** = device full of foam, water, chemicals, used for putting out fires; *see also* EXTINGUISHER; **fire hazard** *or* **fire risk** = situation *or* goods which could easily start a fire; *that room full of old furniture is a fire hazard;* **fire hose** = length of pipe ready to be attached to a water supply, used to put out fires; **fire insurance** = insurance against damage by fire; **fire notice** = notice pinned to a wall, telling guests what to do in case of fire; **fire precautions** = safety measures to protect a building and its occupants if a fire breaks out **2** *verb (informal)* **to fire someone** = to dismiss someone from a job; *the new proprietor fired half the hotel staff;* **to hire**

and fire = to engage new staff and dismiss existing staff very frequently

◊ **firebrat** *noun* small insect *(Thermobia domestica)* which lives in warm places, such as near boilers or hot-water pipes and feeds on food scraps, etc.

◊ **fireproof** *adjective* (material) which is treated so that it cannot burn; *all soft furniture is covered in fireproof fabric*

◊ **firetrap** *noun* place which could easily catch fire, in which people could be trapped because of inadequate fire safety equipment or because of its construction; *the hotel has no fire escape - it's a real firetrap*

QUOTE each room is equipped with a fire detector. The five floors, with 120 rooms each, are divided into 15 fireproof zones, individually ventilated, and equipped with a fire detector, a siren, a glass breaker and a fire door. Each floor has 5 fire hoses and an extinguisher every 10 metres. Finally, the hotel has 8 fire exits accessible from each floor
Hotel Security Worldwide

first *adjective* person *or* thing which is there at the beginning *or* earlier than others; **first name** = a person's Christian name or given name, as opposed to the surname or family name

◊ **first aid** *noun* help given rapidly to someone who is suddenly ill *or* hurt until full-scale medical treatment can be given; *she ran to the man who had been knocked down and gave him first aid until the ambulance arrived;* **first-aid hut** = small building containing a first-aid post; **first-aid kit** = box with bandages and dressings kept ready to be used in an emergency; **first-aid post** *or* **station** = tent or other small building in which first aid can be given to people at an exhibition, agricultural show, etc.

QUOTE how much first-aid equipment should be provided in a workplace depends on the number of people employed. For a small establishment a single first-aid box may be sufficient. It should be in the charge of a responsible person and should be properly stocked
Health and Safety in Kitchens (HSE)

◊ **first-class** *adjective & adverb* **(a)** top quality *or* most expensive; *the hotel has a first-class restaurant; we had a first-class meal last night* **(b)** most expensive and most comfortable type of travel *or* type of hotel; *to travel first-class; first-class travel provides the best service; a first-class ticket;*

to stay in first-class hotels; **first-class mail** = *GB* most expensive mail service, designed to be faster; *US* mail service for letters and postcards; *a first-class letter should get to Scotland in a day*

fish 1 *noun* cold-blooded animal with fins and scales, that lives in water; **fish chef** *or* **chef poissonnier** = chef in charge of preparing fish dishes; **fish fingers** *or US* **fish sticks** = pieces of white fish shaped into oblongs and coated with breadcrumbs and fried; **fish and chips** = traditional British food, obtained from special shops, where portions of fish fried in batter are sold with chips; **fish pie** = dish of various types of fish, cooked in a white sauce with a topping of potatoes (NOTE: no plural when referring to the food: **you should eat some fish every week**) **2** *verb* to catch fish (usually with a rod and line); *they offer salmon-fishing holidays in Scotland; he spent two weeks fishing in Florida*

> COMMENT: fish is high in protein, phosphorus, iodine and vitamins A and D. White fish has very little fat. Certain constituents of fish oil are thought to help prevent the accumulation of cholesterol on artery walls

◊ **fish-and-chip shop** *noun* shop selling fried fish and chips, and usually other food, such as pies

◊ **fishbone** *noun* bone in a fish

◊ **fishcake** *noun* round cake of fish and potato mixed together and fried

◊ **fisherman** *noun* man who catches fish, either as his job or for sport; **fisherman's pie** = dish of various types of fish, cooked in a white sauce with a topping of potatoes

◊ **fishing** *noun* catching fish; **deep-sea fishing** = catching fish out at sea, as opposed to fishing near the coast or in rivers or lakes; **fishing boat** = boat used for fishing; **fishing rod** = long thin piece of wood, etc. to which is attached the line and hook; **fishing tackle** = all the equipment used by a fisherman

◊ **fish knife** *noun* special wide knife, with a blunt blade, used when eating fish

◊ **fish shop** *noun* (i) shop selling uncooked fresh fish; (ii) shop selling fried fish and chips

◊ **fish slice** *noun* wide flat utensil used for turning fish and removing it from a frying pan

fit 1 *adjective* **(a)** suitable; *the meat was declared to be fit for human consumption* **(b)**

healthy; *he keeps fit by jogging every day* **2** *verb* **(a)** to be the right size for; *the chef's cap doesn't fit me* **(b)** **fitted carpet** = carpet cut to the exact size of the room and fixed to the floor; **fitted cupboard** = specially made cupboard which fit into a bedroom, bathroom, etc.

◊ **fittings** *plural noun* objects in a property which are sold with the property but are not permanently fixed and can be removed (such as carpets or shelves); **fixtures and fittings** *see* FIXTURES

fix *verb* **(a)** to arrange *or* to agree; *the date for the reception has been fixed for 10th October* **(b)** to mend; *the technicians are coming to fix the telephone switchboard; can you fix the flat tyre?*

◊ **fixed** *adjective* permanent *or* which cannot be removed; **fixed assets** = property or machinery which a company owns and uses in its business, but which the company does not buy or sell as part of its regular trade; **fixed costs** = business costs which do not rise with the quantity of the product made or the service provided (in a restaurant or hotel, these costs will include rent, maintenance of common areas, general cleaning, wages of permanent staff, etc.); **fixed-price agreement** = agreement where a company provides a service *or* a product at a price which stays the same for the whole period of the agreement; **fixed scale of charges** = rate of charging which cannot be altered

◊ **fixtures** *plural noun* objects in a property which are permanently attached to it (such as sinks and lavatories); **fixtures and fittings** = objects in a property which are sold with the property, both those which cannot be removed and those which can

◊ **fix up with** *verb* to arrange for (someone); *my secretary fixed me up with a car at the airport; can you fix me up with a room for tomorrow night?*

fizz *noun (informal)* champagne; **buck's fizz** = cold drink of champagne and fresh orange juice, typically served at breakfast

fizzy *adjective* (drink) with gas in it; *I don't like fizzy orange - do you have any squash?* (NOTE: the opposite is **still: still orange.** Drinks which should be fizzy but are not, are said to be **flat**)

fl = GUILDER

flag *noun* piece of cloth with a design on it which is the symbol of a country or company; *a ship flying a British flag;* **flag carrier** *or* **flag airline** = the main national airline of a country, seen as the representative of the country abroad; **ship sailing under a flag of convenience** = ship flying the flag of a country which may have no ships of its own, but allows ships of other countries to be registered in its ports

◊ **flagship** *noun* main or largest ship belonging to a shipping line; **flagship hotel** = main hotel belonging to a chain

flagellate *noun* type of parasitic protozoan which uses whip-like hairs to swim (such as Leishmania)

◊ **flagellum** *noun* tiny growth on a microorganism, shaped like a whip (NOTE: plural is **flagella)**

flaky pastry *noun* type of soft pastry which breaks into flakes easily when cooked

flambé 1 *adjective* (food) which has had brandy or other alcohol poured over it and set alight; **flambé lamp** = small lamp (heated by methylated spirits) used for cooking food at the customer's table **2** *verb* to pour brandy or other alcohol over food and set it alight; *pancakes flambéed in brandy*

flan *noun* open tart

flapjack *noun* flat cake made of oats, honey, nuts, etc.

flat 1 *adjective* **(a)** *(drink)* not fizzy when it ought to be; *this beer is flat; the champagne has gone flat* **(b)** fixed *or* not changing; **flat rate** = charge which always stays the same; *we pay a flat rate for bed and breakfast* **2** *noun* **(a)** set of rooms in a large building, as a separate living unit; *he has a flat in the centre of town; she is buying a flat close to her office;* **company flat** = flat owned by a company and used by members of staff from time to time; **service flat** = furnished flat which can be rented, together with the services of a cleaner, cook, etc.; **flat swap** = arrangement where two families exchange flats for a holiday (NOTE: US English is **apartment) (b)** flat dish with low straight sides (such as a ramekin)

◊ **flatware** *noun* **(a)** knives, forks, spoons, etc. **(b)** flat pieces of china, such as plates

Flavobacteria *plural noun* type of rod-shaped bacteria which live in soil and water

flavour *or* US **flavor 1** *noun* taste; *the dish has a distinctive Italian flavour;* **flavour enhancer** *see* ENHANCER; **2** *verb* to add spices and seasoning in cooking to add a flavour to (something)

◊ **flavoured** *adjective & suffix* which tastes of something; *a lemon-flavoured drink*

◊ **flavouring** *noun* substance added to food to give a particular taste; **flavouring agent** = substance added to give flavour

flea *noun* tiny insect which sucks blood and is a parasite on animals and humans

COMMENT: fleas can transmit disease, most especially bubonic plague which is transmitted by infected rat fleas

◊ **flea market** *noun* market, usually in the open air, selling cheap second-hand goods

fleece *verb* to charge (someone) too much; *the bars round the harbour are waiting to fleece the tourists*

fleet *noun* **(a)** group of ships belonging together **(b)** group of vehicles belonging to the same owner; *the airline's fleet of Boeing 747s; the hotel has a fleet of limousines to take guests to the airport*

flesh *noun* **(a)** soft part of the body covering the bones **(b)** soft part of a fruit

flexible *adjective* which can adapt easily

QUOTE the lack of reasonably priced yet flexible tickets is one of the biggest complaints among European business people
Business Traveller

flight *noun* **(a)** journey by an aircraft; *flight AC267 is leaving from Gate 46; he missed his flight; I always take the afternoon flight to Rome; if you hurry you will catch the six o'clock flight to Paris;* **flight attendant** = steward or air hostess, who looks after passengers during a flight; **flight crew** *or* **flight deck crew** = the captain, copilot, flight engineer and navigator, who are involved with the flying of an aircraft (as opposed to the 'cabin crew'); **flight deck** = section at the front of a large aircraft where the pilots sit; **flight engineer** = member of the flight deck crew who is responsible for the engines, hydraulics, electrical systems, etc. during flight (as opposed to a 'ground engineer'); **flight number** = number given to a specific flight (it consists of the airline designator code followed by three figures); **flight recorder** = black box, device carried in a plane which records what happens during a flight, including conversations between pilots and control tower **(b)** series of straight steps between floors in a building; *there are two flights of stairs up to the bedrooms*

flip chart *noun* way of showing information to a group of people, a set of large sheets of paper held on a support, each sheet can be turned over to show the next one

floor *noun* **(a)** part of the room which you walk on; **floor space** = area of floor in a building; *the hotel has 35,000 square metres of floor space on three floors* **(b)** all rooms on one level in a building; *he got into the lift and pushed the button for the fourth floor; the ladies' hair salon is on the first floor; her office is on the 26th floor; we were given a bedroom on the top floor or a top-floor bedroom, overlooking the sea;* **floor attendant** = chef d'étage, a waiter responsible for room service in a series of hotel rooms on the same floor; **floor maid** = maid who cleans rooms on one floor of a hotel; *US* **floor manager** = person in charge of the sales staff in a department store; **floor service** = service on one floor of a hotel (NOTE: the numbering of floors is different in GB and the USA. The floor at street level is the **ground floor** in GB, but the **first floor** in the USA. Each floor in the USA is one number higher than the same floor in GB.)
◊ **floor show** *noun* show (dancers, singers, comedians, striptease, etc.) in a club, bar, restaurant, etc.

flora *noun* wild plants (of an area)

floret *noun* little flower which is part of a flowerhead (such as a cauliflower)

florist *noun* person who sells flowers; **florist's (shop)** = shop which sells flowers

flotel *noun* floating hotel

flotilla *noun* group of small ships sailing together; *we went flotilla cruising in the Aegean*

flour *noun* grain crushed to powder, used for making bread, cakes, etc.; *wheat flour; rice flour*
◊ **floury** *adjective* like flour; *floury potatoes*

flourishing *adjective* doing good business; *she runs a flourishing tour company*

flow 1 *noun* movement of people, liquid, air, etc.; *the flow of tourists into the temple has worn away the steps* **2** *verb* to move along smoothly; *the river flows very fast here, and bathing is forbidden*
◊ **flow chart** *or* **flow diagram** *noun* diagram showing the arrangement of various work processes in a series

flower *noun* colourful part of a plant which produces the seed; *a bouquet of flowers and a basket of fruit is left in each suite with the compliments of the management; fresh flowers are put on the dining room tables every evening;* **flower garden** = garden with flowers growing in it (as opposed to a vegetable garden); **flower shop** = shop which sells flowers; **flower show** = exhibition of flowers

flush *verb* to flush the toilet = to pull or push a knob or handle to get rid of the waste in a toilet bowl; **flush toilet** = toilet where the waste matter is removed by a rush of water

flute *noun* tall narrow wine glass on a stem, used for serving champagne

fly 1 *noun* general term for a small insect with two wings, of the order *Diptera* which carries bacteria and other micro-organisms onto food (flies must be controlled, as they are very harmful to human health); *there are clouds of flies around the meat stalls in the market; flies can carry infection onto food; waiter, there's a fly in my soup!;* **flypaper** = special paper, treated with chemicals, which will kill flies which stick to its surface; **fly swat** *or* **fly whisk** = small fan, held in the hand, used to chase away and squash flies; *see also* HOUSEFLY **2** *verb* to move through the air in an aircraft; *the chairman is flying to Germany on business; the overseas sales manager flies about 100,000 miles a year visiting the agents; we fly to Athens, and then take a bus to the hotel*
◊ **fly-by-night** *adjective (informal)* company which is not reliable *or* which might disappear to avoid paying debts; *I want a reputable tour operator, not one of these fly-by-night outfits*
◊ **fly-drive** *noun & adjective* **fly-drive holiday** *or* **fly-drive package** = arrangement where the traveller flies to an airport and has a rented car waiting for him to pick up (the rent of the car being paid in advance as

part of the package price); *we have many fly-drive bargains still available*

fog *noun* thick mist through which it is difficult to see; *the airport was closed by fog; drivers are asked to drive slowly when there is fog on the motorway;* **fog lights** = very bright red lights at the rear of a car, which are lit when driving in fog

◊ **foggy** *adjective* misty

foil *noun* thin metal sheet; **(cooking) foil** = thin sheet of aluminium *or* tin used especially to wrap food in

fold away *verb* to bend something so that it takes less space; *(in a plane)* **fold-away table** = table attached to the back of the seat in front of the passenger, which can be folded away after use; **fold-away seats** = seats which can be folded up to take less room

folder *noun* cardboard envelope for holding papers

◊ **folding** *adjective* which can be folded; *they brought in some folding chairs as there were not enough chairs for all the guests*

fondue *noun* **cheese fondue** *or* **fondue bourguignonne** = dish of melted cheese, wine and kirsch, into which cubes of bread are dipped (the dish is found in Switzerland and Eastern France)

food *noun* things which are eaten; *he is very fond of Indian food; the food in the staff restaurant is excellent; this restaurant is famous for its food; do you like Chinese food? this food tastes funny;* **health food** = food with no additives *or* natural foods, such as cereals, yoghurt, dried fruit and nuts, which are good for your health; **food additive** = chemical substance added to food, especially one which is added to food to improve its appearance or to prevent it going bad; **food allergy** = reaction caused by sensitivity to certain foods (some of the commonest being strawberries, chocolate, milk, eggs, oranges); **food handler** = person who touches food, as part of his job; **food handling** = touching food as part of one's job; **food hygiene** = keeping clean, healthy conditions for handling storing and serving food

◊ **food and beverage (F&B)** *noun* food and drink as served in a hotel's restaurants, bars, and room service; **food and beverage facilities** = facilities for serving food and drink in a hotel; **food and beverage manager**

= person who is in charge of ordering, preparing and serving food and drink in the restaurants, bars, and in room service of a large hotel

QUOTE F&B is a headache for all hoteliers. Doing away with F&B removes high operating costs and focuses management attention on room management and room sales
Caterer and Hotelkeeper
QUOTE the successful candidate will have full F&B responsibility for the golf clubhouse, the fitness club, the brasserie and conference centre
Caterer & Hotelkeeper

◊ **food poisoning** *noun* illness caused by eating food which is contaminated; *the hospital had to deal with six cases of food poisoning; all the people at the party went down with food poisoning*

COMMENT: food poisoning can be caused by chemicals present in food (some chemicals are naturally present in plants, but others, such as insecticides, get into the food chain from overuse by farmers. Most cases of food poisoning are biological, caused either by eating poisonous food (such as toadstools) or food which is contaminated by bacteria

◊ **food processor** *noun* machine for chopping, cutting, slicing, mixing food, etc.

◊ **foodstuffs** *plural noun* things which can be used as food; **essential foodstuffs** = very important food, such as bread or rice

fool *noun* type of creamed fruit dessert, usually made with acid fruit such as gooseberries or rhubarb

foot 1 *noun* **(a)** part of the body at the end of the leg; **on foot** = walking; *we visited the main temples on foot; the rush-hour traffic is so bad that it is quicker to go to the museum on foot* **(b)** bottom part; *he signed his name at the foot of the invoice* **(c)** measurement of length (= 30cm); *the piece of cloth is two feet long; the hotel beds are less than 6 feet by three; a six-foot wide rug* (NOTE: the plural is **feet** for (a) and (c); there is no plural for (b). In measurements, **foot** is usually written **ft** or **'** after figures: **10ft; 10')** **2** *verb* **to foot the bill** = to pay the costs; *the airline will foot the bill for the hotel*

◊ **footbridge** *noun* small bridge for people to walk across, as over a stream or railway line

◊ **footpath** *noun* path for walkers; **long-distance footpath** = path laid out by an official organization, which goes for a very long way (over 100 miles)

forbid *verb* to tell someone not to do something *or* to say that something must not be done; *women are forbidden to go into the temple; the staff are forbidden to use the front entrance; swimming in the reservoir is forbidden*
NOTE: **forbidding - forbade - forbidden**

force 1 *noun* **(a)** strength; **to be in force** = to be operating *or* working; *the new schedules have been in force since January;* **to come into force** = to start to operate *or* work; *the new regulations will come into force on January 1st* **(b)** group of people; **labour force** *or* **workforce** = all the workers in a company *or* in an area; **sales force** = group of salesmen **2** *verb* to make someone do something; *competition has forced the tour company to lower its prices*

◊ **forcemeat** *noun* mixture of breadcrumbs, onions and flavouring, used to stuff meat and poultry

◊ **forcing bag** *noun* soft bag of fabric or plastic, to which various nozzles can be attached, used to pipe icing, pureed potato, etc. in a decorative way

fore and aft *adverb* to the front and to the back of an aircraft; *the toilets are located fore and aft*

forecast 1 *noun* description *or* calculation of what will probably happen in the future; **cash flow forecast** = forecast of when cash will be received or paid out; **sales forecast** = calculation of future sales; **weather forecast** = description of the weather about to come in the next few hours or days; **medium-range weather forecast** = forecast covering two to five days ahead; **long-range weather forecast** = forecast covering a period of more than five days ahead **2** *verb* to calculate *or* to say what will probably happen in the future; *they are forecasting rain for tomorrow; experts have forecast a steady rise in the number of tourists*
NOTE: **forecasting - forecast**

forecourt *noun* area in front of a building, into which vehicles can be driven; *there are taxi waiting in the station forecourt*

foresee *verb* to feel in advance that something will happen; *they foresee a big increase in tourism*
NOTE: **foresees - foresaw**

foreign *adjective* not belonging to one's own country; *foreign tourists are all over the town for the Easter break; we are increasing our trade with foreign countries;* **foreign currency** = money of another country; **foreign goods** = goods manufactured in other countries; **foreign money order** = money order in a foreign currency which is payable to someone living in a foreign country; **foreign trade** = trade with other countries

◊ **foreign exchange** *noun* (i) exchanging the money of one country for that of another; (ii) money of another country; **foreign exchange broker** *or* **dealer** = person who deals on the foreign exchange market; **foreign exchange dealing** = buying and selling foreign currencies; **foreign exchange market** = market where people buy and sell foreign currencies; **foreign exchange transfer** = sending of money from one country to another

◊ **foreigner** *noun* person from another country

forest *noun* large area covered with trees (a large area is a forest, a small area is a wood); *the whole river basin is covered with tropical forest; forest fires are widespread in the dry season and can sometimes be started by lightning;* **National Forest** = large area of forest owned and managed by the government for the nation; *see also* BLACK FOREST

◊ **forester** *or* **forest ranger** *noun* person in charge of the management and protection of a forest

◊ **forestry** *noun* management of forests, woodlands and plantations of trees; *UK* **Forestry Commission** = government agency responsible for the management of state-owned forests (the Forestry Commission seeks to attract tourists by making picnic areas, nature trails, etc. in its forests)

forex *or* **Forex** = FOREIGN EXCHANGE

QUOTE the amount of reserves sold by the authorities were not sufficient to move the $200 billion Forex market permanently

Duns Business Month

forge *verb* **(a)** to copy money or a signature, so as to trick someone; *he paid his bill with a forged £50 note; when paying with a stolen credit card, she forged the signature on the slip* **(b) forged knife** = best quality kitchen knife, made of a single piece of steel which forms the blade and centre of the handle

forget *verb* not to remember; *she forgot to tell the group that breakfast was at 7.30 sharp; don't forget we're leaving the hotel early tomorrow*
NOTE: **forgetting - forgot - forgotten**

fork 1 *noun* **(a)** piece of cutlery, with a handle at one end and sharp points at the other, used for picking food up; **cake fork** *or* **pastry fork** = small fork with two of the prongs joined together, used for eating cake or pastries with; **fish fork** = fork with flat prongs used with a fish knife for eating fish with; **fork buffet** *or* **fork luncheon** = lunch where food is eaten from a plate with a fork when standing up (as opposed to a 'finger buffet') **(b)** place where two roads split **2** *verb* **(a)** to turn off a road; *fork right at the next junction* **(b)** *(of a road)* to split into two parts

form *noun* official printed paper with blank spaces which have to be filled in with information; *you have to fill in form A20; customs declaration form;* a pad of order *forms;* **application form** = form which has to be filled in when applying; **claim form** = form which has to be filled in when making an insurance claim; **registration form** = form which has to be filled in when registering at a hotel, a conference, etc.; *see also* E111

formality *noun* something which has to be done to obey the law; **customs formalities** = declaration of goods by the shipper and examination of them by the customs

fortify *verb* to make strong; **a fortified town** = a town with thick walls round it to protect it; **fortified wine** = wine, such as port or sherry, which has extra alcohol added

fortnight *noun* two weeks; *I saw him a fortnight ago; we will be on holiday during the last fortnight of July* (NOTE: not used in American English)

forward 1 *adjective* **(a)** (i) in advance; (ii) to be paid at a later date; **forward bookings** = reservations made in advance; **forward buying** *or* **buying forward** = buying currency at today's price for delivery at a later date; **forward (exchange) rate** = rate for purchase of foreign currency at a fixed price for delivery at a later date; *what are the forward rates for the pound?* **(b)** towards the front part (of a ship or plane); *the forward section of an aircraft; the stewardess is in the forward galley; the passenger lounge is*

forward of the dining saloon (NOTE: the opposite is **aft**) **2** *adverb* **(a)** to date a cheque forward = to put a later date than the present one on a cheque; **carriage forward** *or* **freight forward** = deal where the customer will pay for the shipping when the goods arrive; **charges forward** = charges which will be paid by the customer when he takes delivery of the goods **(b)** to buy forward = to buy foreign currency before you need it, in order to be certain of the exchange rate; **to sell forward** = to sell foreign currency for delivery at a later date **(c)** balance brought forward *or* carried forward = balance which is entered in an account at the end of a period and is then taken to be the starting point of the next period **(d)** towards the front part (of a ship or plane); *please move forward to the passenger lounge* (NOTE: the opposite is **aft**) **3** *verb* to forward something to someone = to send something to someone; *we will forward the visa application to the consulate;* **please forward** *or* **to be forwarded** = words written on an envelope, asking the person receiving it to send it on to the person whose name is written on it

foster *verb* to encourage (an idea, etc.); *tourism fosters interest in other countries*

four *number* **the four O's** = simple way of summarizing the essentials of a marketing operation, which are objects, objectives, organization and operations; **the four P's** = simple way of summarizing the essentials of the marketing mix, which are product, price, promotion and place

fowl *noun* domestic birds kept for food or eggs (chickens, ducks, turkeys and geese); **wild fowl** = game birds which are shot for sport

foyer *noun* entrance lobby of a hotel *or* restaurant *or* theatre *or* cinema; *we'll meet in the foyer at 9 p.m.*

Fr = FRANC

franc *noun* currency used in France, Belgium, Switzerland and many other countries; *French francs or Belgian francs or Swiss francs; it costs twenty-five Swiss francs;* **franc account** = bank account in francs (NOTE: in English usually written **FF** before the figure: **FF2,500** (say: 'two thousand, five hundred francs'). Currencies of different countries can be shown by the initial letters of the countries: **FF** (French francs); **SwFr** (Swiss francs); **BFr** (Belgian francs)

franchise 1 *noun* licence to trade using a brand name and paying money for it; *he has bought a hot dog franchise;* **master franchise** = main franchise for an area, from which other outlets are sub-franchised **2** *verb* to sell licences for people to trade using a brand name and paying money for it; *his sandwich bar was so successful that he decided to franchise it; the family owns a franchised chain of restaurants*

◊ **franchisee** *noun* person who trades under a franchise

◊ **franchiser** *noun* person who licenses a franchise

◊ **franchising** *noun* act of selling a licence to trade as a franchise; *he runs his sandwich chain as a franchising operation*

◊ **franchisor** *noun* = FRANCHISER

QUOTE the company wants to franchise many of its restaurants away from the three big metropolitan areas of London, Birmingham and Manchester. Although it has some existing franchisees it also has regional headquarters which can easily manage local restaurants

Caterer & Hotelkeeper

frankfurter *noun* long thin sausage of spicy pork meat

COMMENT: frankfurters originally came from Frankfurt in Germany, but are now made all over the world. They are cooked in hot water, and are the sausages used in hot dogs

free *adjective & adverb* **(a)** not costing any money; *to be given a free ticket to the exhibition; the price includes free transport from the airport to the hotel; goods are delivered free to the customer's hotel; catalogue and price list sent free on request;* **admission free** = visitors (to the exhibition) do not have to pay; **carriage free** = deal where the customer does not pay for the shipping; **free gift** = present given by a shop or business to a customer who buys a certain amount of goods; *there is a free gift worth £25 to any customer buying a video recorder;* **free sample** = sample given free to advertise a product; **free trial** = testing of a machine with no payment involved; *to send a piece of equipment for two weeks' free trial;* **free of charge** = with no payment to be made **(b)** with no restrictions; **free currency** = currency which is allowed by the government to be bought and sold without restriction; *GB* **free house** = public house which does not belong to a brewery and so can serve any beer or spirits which the owner decides to serve; **free port** *or* **free trade zone** = port *or* area where there are no customs duties to be paid; **interest-free credit** *or* **loan** = credit *or* loan where no interest is paid by the borrower; **free of duty** *or* **duty-free** = with no duty to be paid; *to import wine free of duty or duty-free;* **free-range eggs** = eggs from hens that are allowed to run about in the open and eat more natural food (as opposed to battery hens); **free trade** = system where goods can go from one country to another without any restrictions; *the government adopted a free trade policy;* **free trade area** = group of countries between which no customs duties are paid; **free trader** = person who is in favour of free trade **(c)** not busy *or* not occupied; *are there any free tables in the restaurant? I shall be free in a few minutes; we always keep Friday afternoon free for a game of bridge*

QUOTE can free trade be reconciled with a strong dollar resulting from floating exchange rates?

Duns Business Month

QUOTE free traders hold that the strong dollar is the primary cause of the nation's trade problems

Duns Business Month

freedom *noun* being free to do something; **the freedoms of the air** = special internationally agreed rights given to air lines to allow them to fly without interference; **first freedom** = the right to overfly a country without landing at an airport in that country; **second freedom** = the right to land at an airport for refuelling or repairs; **third and fourth freedoms** = the right to land passengers or mail and the right to pick up passengers or mail; **fifth freedom** = the right to use a carrier of one country to take passengers between two other countries (for example, the right to use British Airways to fly from Bahrain to Karachi); **sixth freedom** = the right of a carrier of one country to carry passengers from another country, stopping in its own country, and then continuing to a third country (for example, the right of British Airways to take passengers from New York to Frankfurt, via London)

freephone *noun GB* system where one can telephone to reply to an advertisement *or* to place an order *or* to ask for information and the seller pays for the call; *the advertisement gives a freephone number for you to call*

COMMENT: British Telecom freephone numbers have the code 0800 and Mercury freephone numbers have the code 0500

◊ **freepost** *noun GB* system where one can write to an advertiser to place an order *or* to ask for information to be sent, and the seller pays the postage

◊ **freeway** *noun US* major expressway where no toll charge is made

freeze 1 *noun* **(a) deep-freeze** = refrigerator where food is kept at very low temperatures **(b) price freeze** *or* **a freeze on prices** = period when prices are not allowed to be increased **2** *verb* **(a)** to change the state of something from liquid to solid because of the cold **(b)** *(of weather)* to become very cold; *it was freezing when we reached the hotel* **(c)** to store (food) at below freezing point; *you can freeze fresh produce easily; strawberries cannot be frozen* **(d)** to keep prices *or* costs, etc., at their present level and not allow them to rise; *we have frozen our prices for two years*
NOTE: **freezing - froze - has frozen**

◊ **freeze-drying** *noun* method of preserving food by freezing rapidly and drying in a vacuum

◊ **freezer** *noun* deep-freeze, where food is kept at very low temperatures

◊ **freezing point** *noun* temperature at which a liquid becomes solid

freight 1 *noun* **(a)** cost of transporting goods by air, sea or land; *at an auction, the buyer pays the freight;* **freight charges** *or* **freight rates** = money charged for transporting goods; *freight charges have gone up sharply this year;* **freight costs** = money paid to transport goods; **freight forward** = deal where the customer will pay for the shipping when the goods arrive **(b) air freight** = shipping of goods in an aircraft; *to send a shipment by air freight;* **air freight charges** *or* **rates** = money charged for sending goods by air **(c)** goods which are transported; **to take on freight** = to load goods onto a ship, train or truck; *US* **freight car** = railway wagon for carrying goods; **freight depot** = central point where goods are collected before being shipped; **freight elevator** = strong lift for carrying goods; **freight plane** = aircraft which carries goods, not passengers; **freight train** = train used for carrying goods **2** *verb* **to freight goods** =

to send goods; *we freight goods to all parts of the USA*

◊ **freighter** *noun* aircraft or ship which carries goods

French 1 *adjective* referring to France; **French beans** = beans grown on low bushes and eaten when green in their pods; **French toast** = slice of bread, dipped in beaten egg and fried, usually served with syrup or sprinkled with sugar; **French window** = door with glass panels, usually opening on to a garden (NOTE: sometimes spelt with a small 'f', when referring to certain types of food) **2** *noun* language spoken in France, Belgium and other countries

COMMENT: because of the importance of French cooking (or 'cuisine'), French words and phrases are widely used in kitchens and menus

◊ **French dressing** *noun* vinaigrette, salad dressing made with oil, vinegar, salt and other flavourings

◊ **french fried potatoes** *or* **french fries** *noun* thin stick-shaped pieces of potato, fried in deep oil or fat (NOTE: also called **chips** in British English, but not in US English)

◊ **French service** *noun* **(a)** style of laying a table ready for guests (a plate, called the 'show plate' is in the centre of each setting, with a folded napkin on it, and cutlery and glasses beside it: the plate is not used for food, and may be removed, or other plates, such as a soup plate, may be put on it) **(b)** way of serving at a meal, where the waiter or waitress offers the guest a dish (from the left), and the guest helps himself from it (as opposed to 'English service')

frequent *adjective* happening often; doing something often; **frequent flyer** *or* **frequent traveller** *or* **frequent user** = person who travels often (with the same company), and so gets special treatment

◊ **frequently** *adverb* often; *we frequently get requests for information about camping facilities*

QUOTE cabin layouts, as with cabin service, good timekeeping, and flight frequency, are important influences on frequent travellers' choice of carrier
Business Travel

fresh *adjective & adverb* **(a)** (food) which has been made recently; fruit *or* vegetables *or* meat *or* fish which have been recently picked or killed or caught, not frozen; **fresh**

fruit salad = pieces of fresh fruit, mixed and served cold; **oven-fresh loaves** = bread which has just been baked **(b)** not used or not dirty; **fresh air** = open air; *they came out of the mine into the fresh air*

◊ **freshly** *adverb* recently; *freshly picked strawberries;* freshly squeezed orange juice = orange juice which has just been squeezed from the fruit, not taken from a can or carton

◊ **fresh water** *noun* water in rivers and lakes which contains almost no salt (as opposed to salt water in the sea)

◊ **freshwater** *adjective* (lake) containing fresh water; (animal) living in fresh water; *some freshwater fish such as pike can withstand levels of acidity*

fricassee 1 *noun* dish of pieces of meat cooked in a rich white sauce; *chicken fricassee* **2** *verb* to stew meat (usually chicken) with vegetables in a little water, which is then used to make a rich white sauce

fridge *noun* *(informal)* refrigerator, machine for keeping food cold

fried *see* FRY

fringe 1 *noun* edge; *hotels on the fringe of the desert* **2** *verb* **fringed with palm trees** or **palm-fringed** = with palm trees growing along the side

frisk *verb* to search (someone) by running the hands over his body; *when they frisked him at the airport, they found a knife hidden under his shirt*

fritter *noun* piece of fruit, meat or vegetable, dipped in a mixture of flour, egg and milk and fried; *apple fritters; banana fritters*

front 1 *noun* **(a)** part which faces forward; **in front of** = next to the part which faces forward; *I'll meet you in front of the hotel; the safety instructions are in the pocket in front of your seat* **(b)** road which runs beside the sea in a seaside town; *the hotel is on the front; see also* SEAFRONT **2** *adjective* most important or first; **front desk** = reception desk at the entrance to a hotel or restaurant; **front door** = main door of a building; **front hall** = (i) room or passage through which you enter a building; (ii) the people who work in the front part of a hotel; **front office** = main office of a hotel, with the reservations department and the reception desk; **front office manager** = manager in charge of the front office

◊ **front of house** *noun* part of a hotel which deals with customers direct, including departments such as reception, porters, room service, housekeeping, etc.; **front-of-house manager** = person in charge of the front part of a hotel (the entrance, reception, reservations, etc.); **front-of-the-house services** = services which are in the front of a hotel (such as reception, porters); **front-of-the-house staff** = staff, such as the receptionist, doorman, porters, who deal with customers direct; *compare* BACK-OF-HOUSE

frost *noun* **(a)** weather when the temperature is below the freezing point of water; **ten degrees of frost** = ten degrees below freezing point **(b)** white covering on the ground or trees, etc., when the temperature is below freezing

froze *see* FREEZE

frozen *adjective* **(a)** very cold **(b)** at a temperature below freezing point; *use frozen prawns if you can't get fresh ones;* **frozen food** = food stored at a temperature below freezing point; *see also* FREEZE

fruit *noun* part of a plant which contains the seeds and which is often eaten raw; **fruit salad** = pieces of fresh fruit mixed and served cold; **dried fruit** = fruit that has been dehydrated to preserve it for later use (currants, sultanas and raisins are dried grapes) (NOTE: no plural when referring to the food: **you should eat a lot of fruit**)

COMMENT: fruit contains fructose and is a good source of vitamin C and some dietary fibre. Dried fruit has a higher sugar content but less vitamin C than fresh fruit

◊ **fruitcake** *noun* cake with a lot of dried fruit in it

◊ **fruit juice** *noun* juice from fruit, often served as an appetizer or starter (the commonest fruit juices are: orange juice, apple juice, pineapple juice and grapefruit juice)

fry *verb* to cook in oil or fat in a shallow pan; **to deep-fry** = to cook food in a deep pan of boiling oil or fat

◊ **fries** *see* FRENCH FRIES

◊ **fryer** *noun* large device for frying quantities of food at the same time; **deep-fat fryer** = fryer for frying in deep fat

◊ **frying pan** *noun* shallow, open pan used for frying

ft = FOOT

fuel surcharge *noun* extra amount added to an air fare, to cover increased fuel costs which have come into effect since the air fare was calculated

full *adjective* **(a)** with as much inside it as possible; *the train was full of commuters; the hotel is full next week* **(b)** complete *or* including everything; **full board** = special rate for guests staying in a hotel, who take all their meals in the hotel (usually in GB this will include breakfast, morning coffee, lunch, afternoon tea and dinner; also called 'en pension rate'); *full-board rates are shown on the back of the leaflet;* **full costs** = all the costs of a service; **full cover** = insurance cover against all risks; **full fare** = ticket for a journey by an adult at full price; **full price** = price with no discount; *he bought a full-price ticket;* **full-service hotel** = hotel offering all services, such as restaurants, bars, room service, cleaning, valeting, etc. **(c) in full** = completely; *give your full name and address or your name and address in full; he accepted all our conditions in full; full refund or refund paid in full; he got a full refund when he complained about the service;* **full payment** *or* **payment in full** = paying all money owed

◊ **full English breakfast** *noun* breakfast of cereals, eggs, bacon, toast and marmalade, served with tea or coffee (as opposed to continental breakfast, often served as a buffet in motels and hotel chains)

COMMENT: a traditional 'full English breakfast' may include cereals, porridge, or stewed fruit (such as prunes), grilled fish (such as kippers), bacon and eggs, sausages, kidneys, fried or grilled tomatoes or mushrooms and fried bread, followed by toast and marmalade and tea or coffee

◊ **full-time** *adjective & adverb* working for the whole normal working day (i.e. about eight hours a day, five days a week); *she is in full-time work or she works full-time or she is in full-time employment; he is one of our full-time staff;* **full-time equivalent** = way of calculating the cost of part-time employment for accounting purposes, by converting the hours worked by part-timers to their equivalent on a full-time basis

◊ **full up** *adjective* (hotel) in which all the rooms are occupied

◊ **fully** *adverb* completely; *the hotel is fully booked for August;* **fully comprehensive insurance** = insurance policy which covers you against all risks which are likely to happen

function *noun* **(a)** gathering of people **(b)** party, usually when a group of people gathers for a meal; *a club function is being held in the main restaurant;* **function chart** = chart showing the function rooms in a hotel, with the functions which will be held in them over a period of time; **function diary** = list of dates of functions to be held in a hotel, with times, rooms booked, etc.; **function room** = special room for holding functions in

COMMENT: functions can range from a small lunch party to a large wedding; they are arranged and booked some weeks or months in advance

fund *verb* to provide money for (a special purpose)

furnish *verb* **(a)** to supply *or* to provide; *we can furnish all the equipment necessary for a hotel gym* **(b)** to put furniture in a room; *the hotel bedrooms are furnished with typical Spanish furniture; he furnished his office with second-hand chairs and desks; the hotel spent £10,000 on furnishing the residents' lounge;* **furnished accommodation** *or* **furnished flat** *or* **furnished house** *or* **furnished rooms** = flat *or* house, etc., which is let with furniture in it

furniture *noun* chairs, tables, beds, etc.; **bedroom furniture** = furniture found in a bedroom, such as beds, chests of drawers, etc. (NOTE: no plural: for one item say **'a piece of furniture'**)

futures *plural noun* trading in shares or commodities for delivery at a later date; **futures contract** = contract for the purchase of commodities for delivery at a date in the future

COMMENT: a futures contract is a contract to purchase; if an investor is bullish, he will buy a contract, but if he feels the market will go down, he will sell one

Gg

g = GRAM

galley *noun* kitchen on a boat *or* aircraft; *the stewardess will get you some water from the galley*

gallon *noun GB* unit of measurement of liquids (= 8 pints or 4.55 litres); *US* unit of measurement of liquids (= 3.79 litres); **the car does twenty-five miles per gallon** *or* **the car does twenty-five miles to the gallon** = the car uses one gallon of petrol in travelling twenty-five miles (NOTE: the British gallon is also called the **imperial gallon**; **gallon** is usually written **gal** after figures: **25gal)**

game *noun* **(a)** contest played according to rules and decided by skill, strength or luck; *they all wanted to watch a game of football* **(b)** animals which are hunted and killed for sport (and food); **big game** = large wild animals (such as elephants, tigers, etc.) which are hunted and killed for sport; **game reserve** = area of land where wild animals are kept to be hunted and killed for sport; **game warden** = person who protects big game for photographers or for hunters **(c)** food from animals (such as deer or pheasants) which have been hunted and killed; **game bird** = any bird which is hunted and killed for sport (and food); **game pâté** *or* **game pie** = pâté *or* pie made from hare, rabbit, pheasant, etc.; **game soup** = soup made from game

> COMMENT: common types of game are rabbit, hare and venison; the commonest game birds in the UK are pheasant, partridge and grouse

◊ **gamekeeper** *noun* person working on a private estate who protects wild birds and animals bred to be hunted

gamma rays *plural noun* rays which are shorter than X-rays, given off by radioactive substances and used in food irradiation

gammon *noun* smoked or cured ham, either whole or cut into slices; **gammon**

steak = thick slice of gammon; *grilled gammon steak with pineapple*

g & t = GIN AND TONIC

gangway (a) *(in a theatre, cinema, etc.)* passage between rows of seats **(b)** walkway for going on board a ship

◊ **gangplank** *noun* wooden walkway for going on board a ship

garage *noun* **(a)** place where cars can be serviced and repaired, and where petrol can be bought; *the next garage is 50 miles from here; you can hire cars from the garage near the railway station;* **garage attendant** = person who works in a garage, filling customers' cars with petrol, etc. (NOTE: a garage is also called **service station) (b)** building where one or several cars can be parked; *get a ticket from the hotel desk which allows you to park in the hotel garage; each of the apartments has its own garage;* **garage facilities** *or* **garage space** = space in a garage for parking cars; *the hotel has garage space for thirty cars*

◊ **garaging** *noun* space in a garage for parking cars; *the hotel has garaging for thirty cars; free garaging for exhibitors at the trade fair*

garbage *noun* refuse or rubbish; *US* **garbage can** = dustbin, a container for refuse

garden *noun* **(a)** piece of ground used for growing flowers, fruit, or vegetables; **herb garden** = garden where herbs are grown; **kitchen garden** = garden where vegetables and fruit are grown; *the hotel has its own kitchen garden;* **garden suite** = suite of rooms with doors leading to a garden; **garden view** = view over a garden **(b)** **gardens** = large area of garden; *the hotel is surrounded by flower gardens;* **botanical gardens** = gardens which are set up for scientific study and display of plants; **public gardens** = space in a town where plants are grown and the public is allowed to visit (usually free of charge)

COMMENT: most large cities are well provided with public gardens, which are usually open free of charge; botanical gardens may belong to a university, or an academy of science, and are also usually open to the public, though a charge may be levied

garlic *noun* plant whose bulb has a strong smell and taste, used as a flavouring; **garlic bread** = bread spread with a mixture of butter and crushed garlic, warmed in an oven

◊ **garlicky** *adjective* tasting or smelling of garlic

garnish 1 *noun* small piece of food used as a decoration; *fish served with a garnish of lemon slices and chopped chives* **2** *verb* to decorate (especially food); *slices of beef garnished with capers*

garoupa *see* GROUPER

gas *noun* **(a)** substance often produced from coal or found underground and used to cook or heat; *the flat is equipped with a gas cooker; the hotel is heated by gas; each gas appliance should be installed in a well-lit and draught-free position* **(b)** *US* = GASOLINE

◊ **gas station** *noun US* petrol station, a place where you can buy petrol

gasoline *noun US* petrol

gastric *adjective* referring to the stomach; **gastric acid** = hydrochloric acid secreted into the stomach by acid-forming cells; **gastric flu** = general term for any mild stomach disorder; **gastric juices** = mixture of hydrochloric acid, pepsin, intrinsic factor and mucus secreted by the cells of the lining membrane of the stomach to help the digestion of food; *the walls of the stomach secrete gastric juices*

gastroenteritis *noun* inflammation of the membrane lining the intestines and the stomach, caused by a viral infection and resulting in diarrhoea and vomiting

◊ **gastrointestinal tract** *noun* the digestive tract, comprising the stomach and intestine

gastronome *noun* expert on food and drink

◊ **gastronomic** *adjective* referring to food and drink of particularly high quality; *the restaurant offers a special gastronomic menu*

◊ **gastronomy** *noun* art of food and cooking

gate *noun* door leading to an aircraft at an airport; *flight AF270 is now boarding at Gate 23*

◊ **gateway** *noun* town which leads to an area; *Washington, gateway to the south*

GATT = GENERAL AGREEMENT ON TARIFFS AND TRADE

gavel *noun* small wooden hammer, used by an auctioneer to hit the table to show that a bid has been successful, or by a toastmaster to call the attention of guests to a speaker

gazpacho *noun* Spanish-style soup, made of tomatoes, onions, cucumber, garlic, oil and vinegar, served cold

geese *see* GOOSE

gelatin *noun* protein which is soluble in water, made from collagen

COMMENT: gelatin is used in foodstuffs to make liquids (such as desserts or meat jellies) set into a semi-solid

◊ **gelatinous** *adjective* like jelly

general *adjective* **(a)** including or affecting everything or nearly all of something; **general clean** = cleaning of all parts of a room; **general expenses** = all kinds of minor expenses *or* money spent on the day-to-day cost of a business; **general manager** = manager who is in charge of the administration of a whole establishment; *the general manager of a hotel* **(b) in general** = as a rule **(c)** *US* **General Delivery** = system where letters can be addressed to someone at a post office, where they can be collected (NOTE: the GB English for this is **Poste Restante**)

◊ **General Agreement on Tariffs and Trade (GATT)** *noun* international agreement to try to reduce restrictions in trade between countries

gentleman *noun* **(a)** *(polite way of referring to a man)* *could you show this gentleman to his table? well, gentlemen, shall we begin the meeting?* (NOTE: the plural is **gentlemen**) **(b)** 'gentlemen' = public toilet for men

◊ **gents** *noun (informal)* public toilet for men; *can you tell me where the gents or the gents' toilet is? the gents is down the corridor* *on the left* (NOTE: it is singular, and takes a singular verb)

German *adjective* referring to Germany; **German sausage** = frankfurter or other similar smooth meat sausage; **German wine** = wine from Germany

get back *verb* (a) to return to a place; *the coach leaves at 8.30 a.m., and we should get back to the hotel by 9 o'clock in the evening* (b) to receive something which you had before; *I got my money back after I had complained to the manager*

◊ **get off** *verb* to come down from (a vehicle); *she got off the bus at the post office; you have to get off the Underground at South Kensington*

◊ **get on** *verb* to board (a train, a bus, an aircraft) *or* to mount (a bicycle, etc.); *she got on at Charing Cross; he got on the plane at Frankfurt*

◊ **get ready** *verb* (a) to prepare oneself for something; *how long will it take you to get ready for the meeting? all guests must get ready to leave the hotel at 7.30 a.m.* (b) to get something prepared; *we need to get the bedrooms ready by 12.00; the courier is trying to get the tour notes ready before the party leaves*

◊ **get through** *verb* (a) to speak to someone on the phone; *I tried to get through to the complaints department* (b) to try to make someone understand; *I could not get through to her that I had to be at the airport by 2.15*

◊ **get up** *verb* (a) to get out of bed; *it is 9.30 and Mr Jones has still not got up: can you give him a call?* (b) to make someone get out of bed; *we must get all the party up by 7.30 if we are going to leave on time*

geyser *noun* hot spring, where water shoots up into the air at regular intervals

gherkin *noun* small vegetable of the cucumber family used for pickling

Giardia *noun* microscopic protozoan parasite in the intestine which causes giardiasis

◊ **giardiasis** *or* **lambliasis** *noun* disorder of the intestine caused by the parasite *Giardia lamblia,* usually with no symptoms, but in heavy infections the absorption of fat may be affected, causing diarrhoea

giblets *plural noun* liver, heart, etc., of poultry, removed before the bird is cooked

gift *noun* thing given to someone; **gift coupon** *or* **gift token** *or* **gift voucher** = card, bought in a store which is given as a present and which must be exchanged in that store for goods; *we gave her a gift token for her birthday;* **gift shop** = shop selling small items which are given as presents; **free gift** = present given by a shop or business to a customer who buys a certain amount of goods

◊ **gift-wrap** *verb* to wrap (a present) in attractive paper; *do you want this book gift-wrapped?*

◊ **gift-wrapping** *noun* (a) service in a store for wrapping presents for customers (b) attractive paper for wrapping presents

gill *noun* measure of liquids, equal to a quarter of a pint

gin *noun* (a) strong colourless alcohol, distilled from grain and flavoured with juniper; **gin and French** = gin and French vermouth; **gin and Italian (gin and it)** = gin and Italian vermouth; **gin and tonic (g. and t.)** = drink made from gin, ice, a slice of lemon and tonic water; **gin sling** = drink made from gin, ice, sweetened water and lemon or lime juice; **sloe gin** = gin flavoured with the juice of blackthorn berries; *see also* PINK GIN (b) glass of this alcohol; *two gin and tonics, please; he drank three gins before dinner*

COMMENT: gin is usually drunk with tonic water (making a 'g. & t.'), but also forms the basis of dry martinis. The word 'gin' is also used to refer to Dutch 'genever', which is drunk cold and neat

ginger *noun* (a) plant with a hot-tasting root used in cooking and medicine; **ginger ale** = fizzy ginger-flavoured drink (also called 'dry ginger'); **ginger beer** = fizzy ginger-flavoured alcoholic drink; **ginger biscuit** *or* **ginger nut** = hard sweet biscuit, flavoured with ginger (b) **dry ginger** = fizzy drink flavoured with ginger, often served mixed with whisky or brandy

◊ **gingerbread** *noun* cake made with treacle and flavoured with ginger

gippy tummy *noun (humorous)* diarrhoea which affects people travelling in foreign countries as a result of eating unwashed fruit or drinking water which has not been boiled (NOTE: also called **Delhi belly, Montezuma's revenge, etc.**)

GIT = GROUP INCLUSIVE TOUR

gîte *noun* house or cottage in France which can be rented for self-catering holidays

given name *noun especially US* first name *or* Christian name of a person, as opposed to the surname or family name

glacier *noun* river of ice which moves slowly down from a mountain

glass *noun* **(a)** vessel made of glass used especially for drinking; *each place setting should have two glasses;* sherry glass = small glass suitable for serving sherry in **(b)** contents of such a glass; *he drank six glasses of white wine; add a glass of red wine to the sauce* **(c)** substance made from sand and soda or potash, usually transparent, used for making windows, etc.; **glass-bottomed boat** = boat with a bottom made of glass, so that tourists can see into the water under the boat; **glass-breaker** = alarm panel, with a glass window, which you have to break to sound the alarm
◊ **glassful** *noun* amount contained in a glass
◊ **glassware** *noun* articles made of glass, especially drinking glasses used in a restaurant or hotel

COMMENT: there are various shapes of glasses used for different drinks: Champagne is served in tall tapering glasses (or 'flutes'), and also sometimes in wide flat glasses called 'coupes'. Bordeaux wines are served in taller narrower glasses than those for Burgundies, which are fatter. In Germany, wines are served in coloured glasses, usually pale yellow, with a green or orange stem. Draught beer is served in moulded glasses with handles, or in tall plain glasses without handles. Bottled beers are served in glasses on stems. Water can be served in ordinary wine glasses or in tumblers. Sherry glasses have short stems. Brandy glasses (or 'balloons') have wide bodies tapering to a narrower mouth

Glorious Twelfth August 12th; *see comment at* GROUSE

glucose *noun* dextrose, simple sugar found in some fruit, but also broken down from white sugar or carbohydrate and absorbed into the body or secreted by the kidneys

gm = GRAM

GMT = GREENWICH MEAN TIME

go *verb* to move; *he's going on a tour of the south of Spain;* to go on board = to move onto a ship *or* plane *or* train; *they went on board the boat at 10.00*
NOTE: **going - went - has gone**
◊ **go down** *verb* to descend *or* to go to a lower level; *after having a rest in her bedroom, she went down to the hotel bar; part of the tour is a visit to the coal mines, and you go down into the mine in a little lift*
◊ **going** *adjective* **(a)** active *or* busy; **to sell a business as a going concern** = to sell a business as an actively trading company; **it is a going concern** = the company is working (and making a profit) **(b)** the going price = the usual *or* current price or the price which is being charged now; *what is the going price for two weeks in a three-star hotel in Cyprus?;* the going rate = the usual *or* the current rate of payment; *we pay the going rate for waitresses; the going rent for snack bars is £10 per square metre*

goal *noun* aim, the thing you are trying to achieve

goat *noun* a hardy ruminant animal, usually with horns; **goat's cheese** = cheese made from the milk of a goat (NOTE: males are **bucks,** females are **does,** and the young are **kids)**

COMMENT: In Europe goats are important for milk production; goat's milk has a higher protein and butterfat content than cow's milk, and is used especially for making cheese. Elsewhere goats are reared for meat

goblet *noun* drinking glass with a stem (large goblets are used for serving bottled beer, small goblets are for wine)

golf *noun* game for two people, or two couples, where a small hard ball is struck with long-handled clubs into a series of holes (either 9 or 18), the object being to use as few strokes as possible
◊ **golf club** *noun* **(a)** wooden- or metal-headed stick for striking the golf ball **(b)** (i) group of people who play golf, and allow others to join them on payment of a fee; (ii) house where golfers meet
◊ **golf course** *noun* area of land specially designed for playing golf
◊ **golfer** *noun* person who plays golf

◊ **golfing** *noun* playing games of golf; *a golfing holiday; they organize golfing tours of France*

goods *plural noun* **(a)** items which can be moved and are for sale; **goods in bond** = imported goods held by the customs until duty is paid; **consumer goods** *or* **consumable goods** = goods bought and used by the general public and not by businesses; **household goods** = items which are used in the home; **luxury goods** = expensive items which are not basic necessities **(b) goods depot** = central warehouse where goods can be stored until they are moved; **goods lift** *or* *US* **goods elevator** = lift for transporting goods, rather than people; **goods train** = train used for carrying freight

goodwill *noun* good reputation of a business; *he paid £10,000 for the goodwill of the restaurant and £4,000 for the fittings*

COMMENT: goodwill can include the trading reputation, the patents, the trade names used, the value of a 'good site', etc., and is very difficult to establish accurately. It is an intangible asset, and so is not shown as an asset in a company's accounts, unless it figures as part of the purchase price paid when acquiring another company

goose *noun* **(a)** web-footed water bird, larger than a duck; *goose-liver pâté* (NOTE: plural is **geese) (b)** meat from this bird; *roast goose*

◊ **gooseberry** *noun* soft fruit, usually green or red in colour, from a small prickly bush; gooseberries are rarely eaten raw, but are usually cooked or preserved; *gooseberry fool; gooseberry jam*

goulash *noun* Hungarian stew flavoured with paprika

gourmand *noun* person who is fond of eating and eats and drinks too much (NOTE: compare **gourmet)**

gourmet *noun* person who knows a lot about and appreciates food and wine; *a gourmet meal; the restaurant offers a gourmet menu*

grade 1 *noun* category of something which is classified according to quality or size; **high-grade** = of very good quality; *high-grade petrol;* **low-grade** = not very important *or* not of very good quality; *a low-grade hotel; the car runs well on low-grade petrol;* **top-grade** = most important *or* of the best quality **2** *verb* to sort (something) into different categories, according to its quality or size; *eggs are graded into classes A,B, and C;* **grading system** = system of classifying hotels or restaurants into different levels of quality; **graded hotel** = good quality hotel

COMMENT: there are various systems of grading hotels and restaurants; the British Tourist Board gives hotels and other accommodation crowns for the type of facilities offered and keys for facilities offered by self-catering accommodation. Restaurants are graded for quality by stars by the Michelin organization. The French national system gives stars to hotels according to the facilities offered

gram *or* **gramme** *noun* measure of weight (= one thousandth of a kilo); *she bought 500g of butter; coffee is sold in 250g packs* (NOTE: usually written **g** or **gm** after figures: **25g)**

granadilla *noun Passiflora edulis,* the passion fruit, a climbing plant with purple juicy fruit. It is native to Brazil

granary *noun* place where threshed grain is stored (now often used as a trade name for bread or flour containing malted wheat grain)

grape *noun* fruit of the grapevine *(Vitis)* **dessert grapes** = grape which are eaten raw, and not used to make wine

◊ **grapevine** *noun* plant *(Vitis)* with long flexible stems on which grapes grow

COMMENT: grapes are grown in most areas of the world that have a Mediterranean climate, and even in temperate areas like southern England and central Germany. There are two main colours of grapes: black and white (actually they are very dark blue and pale green). Grapes are not usually cooked, but are eaten raw or in fruit salads. They are crushed to make grape juice and wine, and are also dried to produce currants, raisins and sultanas. In some parts of the world (such as Greece) bunches of very small currant grapes are sold as dessert grapes

grapefruit *noun* citrus fruit of an evergreen tree *(Citrus paradisi)* similar to the orange, but not as sweet. The fruit is lemon-yellow when ripe, about twice the size of an orange, and very juicy. The flesh is normally pale greenish-yellow, but can also be pink; *a glass of grapefruit juice;* **grapefruit segments** = sections of peeled grapefruit, served in a glass bowl as an hors d'oeuvre and at breakfast

COMMENT: grapefruit are usually served cut in half, with sugar; they are usually eaten at breakfast. They are also used to make marmalade

grate *verb* to shred into very small pieces, using a rough metal tool; *do you want grated cheese on your pasta? there was a salad of grated carrot and French dressing*

◊ **grater** *noun* tool with a rough metal surface, or with rough holes, used for grating food such as cheese; **nutmeg grater** = small device on which a nutmeg is rubbed, to produce fine nutmeg powder

gratin *noun* **(a)** food which has been topped with breadcrumbs, cream sauce or cheese, and is then browned under a grill or in an oven; *cauliflower gratin* (NOTE: strictly speaking, one should use the proper French term and say **cauliflower au gratin) (b)** low flat dish in which food can be browned under a grill

gratis *adverb* free *or* without paying anything; *we got into the exhibition gratis*

gratuity *noun* money given to someone who has helped you; *the staff are instructed not to accept gratuities* (NOTE: also called a **tip)**

gravlax *or* **gravadlax** *noun* Scandinavian dish of raw salmon pickled in salt, sugar and herbs, served sliced thinly with brown bread

gravy *noun* brown sauce, served with meat

COMMENT: in many British restaurants, gravy is prepared from dry powder, mixed with water and meat juices. Real gravy is made from the juices of the meat only

grease *noun* thick oil, used to make machines run smoothly

◊ **greasy** *adjective* oily (food); *I don't like the chips they serve here - they're too greasy;* **greasy spoon** = small cheap, and often dirty, cafe (NOTE: **greasy - greasier - greasiest)**

greedy *adjective* (person) who is always wanting to eat a lot of food (NOTE: **greedy - greedier - greediest)**

Greek *adjective* referring to Greece; **Greek coffee** = coffee heated with sugar and water (NOTE: also called **Turkish coffee)**

green *adjective* referring to a concern about the environment; **green space** = area of land which has not been built on, containing grass, plants and trees; **green holidays** *or US* **green vacations** = holidays spent in the countryside doing work which helps the environment

◊ **greenback** *noun US (informal)* dollar bill

◊ **Green Belt** *noun* area of agricultural land *or* woodland *or* parkland which surrounds an urban area

COMMENT: Green Belt land is protected and building is restricted and often prohibited completely. The aim of setting up a Green Belt is to prevent urban sprawl and reduce city pollution

◊ **green card** *noun* **(a)** special British insurance certificate to prove that a car is insured for travel abroad **(b)** work permit for a person going to live in the USA

◊ **greengage** *noun* bitter green plum, used for cooking, making pies, jam, etc.

◊ **greengrocer** *noun* person who sells fruit and vegetables

Greenwich Mean Time (GMT) *noun* local time on the 0° meridian where it passes through Greenwich, England; used to calculate international time zones

greeter *noun US* man whose job it is to receive guests as they enter a restaurant and show them to their tables (a woman who does this is called a 'hostess')

griddle *noun* flat metal sheet which is heated, and on which food can be cooked (used for short-order breakfasts, Japanese food, etc.)

◊ **griddlecake** *noun* cake cooked on a griddle

> QUOTE cooking breakfast to order on the griddle provides guests with a more direct service and helps avoid the unattractive accumulation of fried food which can easily occur on breakfast buffets at large hotels
>
> *Caterer & Hotelkeeper*

gridlock *noun* traffic jam, particularly at a busy road junction

◊ **gridlocked** *adjective (traffic)* which is jammed and unable to move

grill 1 *noun* **(a)** open metal surface with heat above or below, used to cook meat, fish and some vegetables; **charcoal grill** = burning charcoal over which a metal rack is placed on which food can be cooked **(b)** food which has been cooked on a grill; **mixed grill** = dish of various sorts of meat which have been grilled (usually including a chop, sausages, liver, bacon, together with mushrooms and onions) **(c)** restaurant, or part of a restaurant, which specializes in grilled food **2** *verb* to cook food on or under a grill; *grilled fish is drier and less greasy than fried fish; I'll have a grilled chop, please*

◊ **griller** *noun* kitchen device with an open metal rack with heat beneath, used to cook meat, fish and some vegetables

◊ **grillroom** *noun* restaurant which specializes in grilled food

grind *verb* to pass food through a machine which reduces it to powder or pulp; **ground coffee** = coffee beans which have been ground to small pieces, ready for making coffee; *US* **ground beef** = finely minced beef (used for making hamburgers) (NOTE: British English for this is **minced beef** *or* **mince**) NOTE: **grinding - ground - has ground**

◊ **grinder** *noun* machine for grinding food such as coffee or spices

grip *noun* holdall, a soft bag for carrying clothes, etc., when travelling

grits *plural noun US* ground maize, cooked in milk or water, then fried and eaten as a breakfast dish

grocer *noun* person who sells food in packets and tins, such as biscuits, sugar, tea, etc.

groom *verb* to look after *or* to make smart; *you groom ski slopes before a competition*

gross 1 *noun* twelve dozen (144); *he ordered four gross of paper towels* (NOTE: no plural in this meaning) **2** *adjective* **(a)** total *or* with no deductions; **gross earnings** = total earnings before tax and other deductions; **gross income** *or* **gross salary** = income *or* salary before tax is deducted; **gross margin** = percentage difference between the unit manufacturing cost and the received price; **gross profit** = profit calculated as sales income less the cost of the goods sold (i.e. without deducting any other expenses); **gross receipts** = total amount of money received before expenses are deducted; **gross turnover** = total turnover including discounts, VAT charged, etc. **(b)** **gross tonnage** = total amount of space in a ship; **gross weight** = weight of both the container and its contents **3** *adverb* with no deductions; *his salary is paid gross* **4** *verb* to make a gross profit; *the group grossed £25m in 1993*

grotto *noun* picturesque small cave *or* room decorated with shells to look like a cave

ground 1 *noun* soil *or* earth; **ground engineer** = person who maintains and repairs aircraft on the ground, as opposed to a flight engineer; **ground handling** = dealing with airline passengers on the ground, after they have arrived at an airport; **ground hostess** = woman who looks after passengers at the airport before they board the plane; **on the ground** = not in the air **2** *verb* **(a)** **to ground an aircraft** = to say that an aircraft must not fly, usually because of a mechanical failure; *after the crash, all planes were grounded until their engines were inspected* **(b)** *see also* GRIND

◊ **ground floor** *or* **main floor** *noun* floor (in a shop *or* office) which is level with the ground; *the men's department is on the ground floor; he has a ground-floor office* (NOTE: in the USA this is the **first floor**)

◊ **grounds** *plural noun* **(a)** gardens round a large house; *if the weather is fine, the concert will be held in the grounds of the house* **(b)** basic reasons; *does he have good grounds for complaint? there are no grounds on which we can be sued for negligence* **(c)** **coffee grounds** = crushed coffee beans left at the bottom of a cup or coffee jug after the coffee has been served

group 1 *noun* **(a)** several things or people together; *a group of Japanese tourists;* **group booking** = booking of seats *or* hotel rooms *or* restaurant places *or* theatre seats, etc., for a group of people together at the same time;

group inclusive tour (GIT) = tour for a group of people, where the price per person includes all travel, accommodation and meals; **group travel** = travelling in a group of people (as opposed to individual travel) **(b)** several companies linked together in the same organization; *the group owns hotels in several European cities; a major travel group;* **group results** = financial accounts of a group of companies taken together **2** *verb* **to group together** = to put several items together; *sales from six different agencies are grouped together under the heading 'European sales'*

grouper *noun* large tropical sea fish, used as food (NOTE: also called **garoupa** in Chinese cooking)

grouse 1 *noun* **(a)** small black game bird, found in the UK, especially in the north of England and in Scotland; **grouse moor** = land where grouse live (NOTE: no plural; two of the birds are called **a brace of grouse**) **(b)** complaint; *the manager is tired of listening to the guests' grouses* **2** *verb* to complain; *the group was grousing about the service in the hotel restaurant*

COMMENT: grouse are shot and eaten in season; the season starts on August 12th, also called the 'Glorious Twelfth', and ends on December 10th

grub *noun (informal)* food; **pub grub** = simple snacks which are typically available in most pubs (pies, sandwiches, salads, etc., the hot food usually being warmed in a microwave)

guarantee 1 *noun* legal document which promises that a machine will work properly *or* that an item is of good quality *or* that a service will be provided; *the tour company refused to give the guarantee that the group would be accommodated in the hotel mentioned in the brochure;* **certificate of guarantee** *or* **guarantee certificate; the guarantee lasts for two years; it is sold with a twelve-month guarantee; the car is still under guarantee** = is still covered by the maker's guarantee; **extended guarantee** = guarantee offered by a dealer on a product such as a dishwasher, which goes beyond the time specified in the manufacturer's guarantee (NOTE: also called **warranty**) **2** *verb* to give a promise that something will happen; *I guarantee that this will not happen again;* **the product is guaranteed for twelve months** = the manufacturer says that

the product will work well for twelve months, and will mend it free of charge if it breaks down; **guaranteed price** = price which the seller promises will not change; **guaranteed wage** = wage which a company promises will not fall below a certain figure

guard *noun* person *or* group of people, whose job it is to protect someone or something; *the tourist bus carries armed guards when going into the bandit country; the hotel grounds are patrolled by security guards;* **changing of the guard** = military ceremony, where one shift of soldiers is replaced by another on guard duty at a palace, etc. (a very popular attraction for tourists); *at 10.30, we're going to watch the changing of the guard*

guava *noun* orange-coloured tropical fruit with pink flesh, from a common tree *(Psidium guajava)*

guéridon *French noun* **(a)** side table, on which the waiter places dishes, and from which the guests are served **(b)** trolley (for bringing food to the table)

guest *noun* **(a)** person staying in a hotel or guesthouse; **guest bills** = bills made out to guests in a hotel, for room, restaurant and other services; **guest rooms** = bedrooms and suites in a hotel which are used only by guests (as opposed to 'public rooms') **(b)** person who is visiting another person; **paying guest** = (i) person who stays with a family in their home and pays a rent; (ii) person who stays at a boarding house and pays for room and board

◊ **guesthouse** *noun* **(a)** privately-owned house, which takes several guests, usually not more than ten **(b)** *(in the Far East)* small state-owned hotel for official guests, but where other visitors may be offered accommodation

COMMENT: guesthouses are similar to small hotels, but may not be licensed to serve alcohol, and may only offer bed and breakfast. Guesthouses are always family-owned and -run

guide 1 *noun* **(a)** person who shows tourists round a site or house; *our guide took us into the castle chapel; the guide to the museum spoke so rapidly that we couldn't understand what she was saying* **(b)** a guide book; *this is the best guide to the region; you can get a small guide to walks round the town at the tourist information office* **2** *verb* to show (tourists) round a site; **guided tour =** tour led by a guide; *we had a guided tour of the ruins*

◇ **guide book** *noun* book for tourists, explaining what there is to see in a place, where to stay, how to travel around, where to eat, etc.

guilder *noun* unit of money used in the Netherlands (NOTE: usually written **fl** after figures: **25fl)**

guinea fowl *noun* small black bird with white spots, raised for its meat which has a delicate flavour similar to that of game birds

gullet *noun* oesophagus, the tube down which food and drink passes from the mouth to the stomach; *she had a piece of bread stuck in her gullet*

gumbo *noun* **(a)** okra, a vegetable *(Hibiscus esculentus)* with a green pod used in soups **(b)** dish from the South of the USA, especially Louisiana; a type of thick soup or stew, made with meat or fish and okra

gymnasium *noun* hall for indoor athletics and exercises (NOTE: also called **gym** for short)

Hh

haddock *noun* common white sea fish; **smoked haddock =** common smoked fish, which is yellow in colour

> COMMENT: smoked haddock is smoked until yellow on the bone (called 'Finnan haddock') or as fillets. Small whole haddock smoked until they are brown are called 'Arbroath smokies'. Smoked haddock is used in various recipes including kedgeree, and omelette Arnold Bennett

haggis *noun* Scottish dish, made of sheep's stomach stuffed with a mixture of the sheep's heart, liver, etc., and oatmeal, boiled in water

haggle *verb* to discuss prices and terms and try to reduce them; *to buy anything in the local market you will have to learn to haggle; after two hours' haggling over the price we bought the carpet* (NOTE: you haggle **with** someone **over** something)

hail 1 *noun* small pieces of ice which fall like frozen rain **2** *verb* **(a)** to fall as frozen rain **(b)** to wave to (a taxi) to stop; *he whistled to hail a taxi*

hair *noun* **(a)** single long thread growing on the body of a human or animal; *waiter, there's a hair in my soup!* **(b)** mass of hairs growing on the head; *your hair is too long, you must get it cut*

◇ **hairbrush** *noun* special brush for keeping hair tidy

◇ **haircut** *noun* making hair shorter by cutting; *he went to the hairdresser's to get a haircut* (NOTE: used only about men; also a bit old-fashioned)

◇ **hairdresser** *noun* person who cuts or dyes or styles hair; **the hairdresser's =** shop where people can have their hair cut and dyed and styled

◇ **hairdressing** *noun* cutting or dyeing or styling hair; **hairdressing salon =** shop where people can have their hair cut, dyed and styled

◇ **hair drier** *or* **hair dryer** *noun* machine for drying wet hair; *each bathroom is equipped with a hair dryer*

◇ **hairnet** *noun* very fine cover put over the hair to keep it tidy; *kitchen staff with long hair must wear hairnets*

hake *noun* type of white sea fish

halal *adjective* (food) prepared according to Moslem law; **halal butcher =** butcher who prepares meat according to Moslem law

half board *noun* special rate for guests staying at a hotel, who take breakfast and dinner at the hotel, but not lunch (also called 'demi-pension')

◇ **half-day** *adjective* referring to the morning or afternoon; *a half-day tour of the island; a half-day excursion to the old town* *costs £10.00;* **half-day closing** = system by which a shop closes, usually at lunchtime and remains closed for the rest of that day

◇ **half-dollar** *noun US* fifty cents

◇ **half-fat milk** *adjective* milk from which some of the fat has been removed

◇ **half price** *noun & adjective* 50% of the usual price; *tour operators are offering tours at half price or half-price tours to people making last-minute bookings;* **to sell goods off at half price** = to sell goods at 50% of the usual price; **half-price sale** = sale of all goods at 50% of the usual price

halibut *noun* type of flat white sea fish

hall *noun* **(a)** large building for public meetings; **sports hall** = large building where indoor sports (such as basketball) are played; **town hall** = building in the centre of a town where the town council meets and where the town's administrative offices are **(b)** **(entrance) hall** *or* **front hall** = (i) room or passage through which you enter a building; (ii) the people who work in the front part of a hotel; **hall porter** = person who is on duty in the hall of a hotel, especially one who stands near the main door of a hotel and deals with arriving or departing guests and their baggage

ham *noun* **(a)** **a ham** = the thigh of a pig (i.e., its back leg) **(b)** meat from this part of the pig, usually cured in brine and sometimes dried in smoke; *a ham sandwich; a plate of salad with two slices of ham;* **ham and eggs** = fried ham with fried eggs

COMMENT: ham is cooked by boiling or roasting, and may be bought ready-cooked in a piece or in slices. Some types of smoked ham, such as prosciutto and Parma ham and sliced very thinly and eaten raw; Parma ham is sometimes served with melon as an hors-d'oeuvre

hamburger *noun* round, flat cake of minced beef, grilled or fried and usually served in a toasted bread roll; *the children want hamburgers and fries for lunch;* **hamburger bar** = simple restaurant serving hamburgers; **hamburger roll** = soft round bread roll suitable for serving a hamburger in

COMMENT: the hamburger is so called because it was originally minced beef steak cooked in the style of Hamburg, the town in Germany. It has nothing to

do with ham. It is also called simply a 'burger' or 'beefburger'

hamlet *noun* small village

hand *noun* **(a)** part of the body at the end of each arm; **to shake hands** = to hold someone's hand when meeting to show you are pleased to meet him or to show that an agreement has been reached; *the visitors shook hands and sat down at the table; the restaurant proprietor always shakes hands with regular customers;* **to shake hands on a deal** = to shake hands to show that a deal has been agreed **(b)** **by hand** = using the hands, not a machine; *these shoes are made by hand; the chef makes all his pasta by hand* **(c)** **in hand** = kept in reserve; **balance in hand** *or* **cash in hand** = cash held to pay small debts and running costs; *we have £10,000 in hand* (NOTE: US English is **on hand**) **(d)** **to hand** = here *or* present; *I have the invoice to hand* = I have the invoice in front of me **(e)** **to change hands** = to be sold to a new owner; *the hotel changed hands for £300,000*

◇ **hand dryer** *noun* machine for drying the hands: it switches itself on when hands are placed under it or when a button is pressed, and blows hot air onto the hands

◇ **hand baggage** *or* **hand luggage** *noun* small bags and cases which passengers can take with them into the cabin of a plane

◇ **handmade** *adjective* made by hand, not by a machine; *handmade pasta*

◇ **hand towel** *noun* small towel for drying the hands

handicap *noun* physical or mental disability

◇ **the handicapped** *plural noun* people with a disability; *the cinema has facilities for the handicapped; there is a toilet for the handicapped on the ground floor*

handle 1 *noun* part of an object which is held in the hand; *don't touch the pan - the handle is hot; the handle has come off my suitcase; push the knob in the door handle if you want to lock the door from the inside* **2** *verb* **(a)** to deal with something *or* to organize something; *the accounts department handles all the cash; we can handle up to 1,500 passengers per hour; they handle all our overseas visitors* **(b)** to sell *or* to trade in (a sort of service *or* product); *we do not handle tours for old-age pensioners; they will not handle tours to the Far East*

◊ **handler** *noun* **baggage handler** = person who works at an airport, taking baggage off or putting it on planes; **food handler** = person who touches food, as part of his job

◊ **handling** *noun* (i) moving something by hand; (ii) dealing with something; **baggage handling facilities** = arrangements *or* machines for moving passengers' baggage; **handling charge** = money to be paid for packing and invoicing *or* for dealing with something in general *or* for moving goods from one place to another; *the bank adds on a 5% handling charge for changing traveller's cheques;* **food handling** = touching food as part of one's job

> QUOTE shipping companies continue to bear the extra financial burden of cargo handling operations at the ports
> *Business Times (Lagos)*

handy *adjective* useful *or* convenient; *paper handkerchiefs are sold in handy-sized packs; this small case is handy for use when travelling*

happy hour *noun* time (usually in the very early evening) when a bar offers cheaper drinks, to encourage customers to come in early

harbour *or* US **harbor** *noun* port, place where ships come to load or unload; **fishing harbour** = harbour which is used by fishing boats; **yachting harbour** = harbour with special facilities (such as mooring buoys) for yachts; **harbour dues** = payment which a ship makes to the harbour authorities for the right to use the harbour; **harbour installations** *or* **harbour facilities** = buildings *or* equipment in a harbour

hard *adjective* not soft, firm to the touch; *we prefer to have a hard mattress;* **hard cheese** = cheese which has been pressed and so is hard

> COMMENT: many German, British, Dutch and Swiss chesses are hard. A very hard cheese is Parmesan, from Italy, which is only used grated in cooking, etc. sprinkled on pasta dishes

◊ **hard-boiled** *adjective* (egg) which has been cooked in boiling water until the white and yolk are set

◊ **hard currency** *noun* currency of a country which has a strong economy and which can be changed into other currencies easily

hare *noun* common field mammal, like a large rabbit; **jugged hare** = hare cooked slowly in a covered dish

hash *noun* dish prepared from chopped meat and vegetables; *US* **corned beef hash** = dish made of corned beef, onions and mashed potatoes, cooked in the oven; **hash browns** *see* BROWNS

hat *noun* covering for the head; **chef's hat** = tall white hat, traditionally worn by chefs; the hat indicates who is the main chef, and is also useful in keeping the hair out of sight; the Michelin restaurant guides use a chef's hat as a symbol of quality

hatch *noun* opening in the floor or wall with a little door; **service hatch** *or* **serving hatch** = small opening in a wall for passing food and crockery from a kitchen to a dining room

haute cuisine *see* CUISINE

have *verb* **(a)** to possess; *the holiday flat has no telephone; do you have a room for two people for one night? do you have a table for three, please?* **(b)** to take (a meal or a bath); *we had breakfast on the balcony* **(c)** **have a nice day!** = I hope the day passes pleasantly for you; **have a good trip!** = I hope your journey is pleasant

haze *noun* light mist

◊ **hazy** *adjective* misty

hazelnut *noun* small round nut with a smooth shiny shell

head *noun* **(a)** most important person; **head of department** *or* **department head** = person in charge of a department **(b)** most important *or* main; **head buyer** = main person in a shop responsible for buying goods which are to be sold; **head chef** = main chef in a restaurant; **head office** = main office building where the board of directors works and meets; **head porter** = porter in charge of all the other porters; **head waiter** = maître d'hôtel, the person in charge of a restaurant, who is responsible for all the service and himself takes orders from customers **(c)** person; **per head** = for each person; *each chef costs on average £25,000 per head per annum; the tickets for the dinner dance will cost £35.00 per head; we calculate the cost per head at £45.25*

◊ **headcheese** *noun* US = BRAWN

◇ **headrest** *noun* cushion to support your head (attached to a seat, as in a car or plane)

◇ **headwind** *noun* wind blowing straight towards a ship or aircraft

health *noun* **(a)** state of the body where there is no sickness; **your health!** *or* **good health!** = wish said when raising your glass and drinking from it; **to drink someone's health** = to wish someone good health, and celebrate it by raising your glass and drinking from it; **health club** = club for people who want to improve their health by taking exercise, dieting, etc.; **health diet** = diet for someone who wants to improve his health; **health farm** = clinic in the country where people go who want to improve their health and appearance by taking exercise, dieting, etc.; **health food** = food with no additives *or* natural foods, such as cereals, yoghurt, dried fruit and nuts, which are good for your health; **health resort** = resort town which has special facilities to improve the health of its visitors **(b) Health and Safety Executive (HSE)** = British government organization responsible for checking the conditions of work of workers, including farmworkers; **Health and Safety at Work Act** = Act of Parliament which rules how the health of workers should be protected by the companies they work for; **Environmental Health Officer (EHO)** *or* **Public Health Inspector** = official of a local authority who examines the environment and tests for air pollution *or* bad sanitation *or* noise pollution, etc.

◇ **healthy** *adjective* **(a)** having good health *or* not ill **(b)** giving good health; *a healthy climate; a healthy diet*

heat 1 *noun* great warmth; **heat exhaustion** = collapse due to overexertion in hot conditions; **heat wave** = sudden period of high temperature **2** *verb* to warm to a higher temperature; *the room was heated by a small gas fire*

◇ **heater** *noun* apparatus which warms; *there is an electric heater in the bedroom; Cyprus can be cool in the winter, so the flat has several portable electric heaters*

◇ **heating** *noun* means of making something warm; **central heating** = heating system for a whole building from one single source; *the central heating comes on at 6.30*

◇ **heat-sealing** *noun* method of closing plastic food containers; air is removed from a plastic bag with the food inside and the bag is then pressed by a hot plate which melts the plastic and seals the contents in the vacuum

helicopter *noun* aircraft with a large propeller on top which allows it to lift straight off the ground; *he took the helicopter from the airport to the centre of town; it is only a short helicopter flight from the centre of town to the factory site; club class travellers have a free helicopter connection to the city centre*

◇ **helipad** *noun* small area of tarmac for helicopters to land on or take off from; *visitors can land at the helipad next to the hotel*

◇ **heliport** *noun* airport used only by helicopters

help 1 *noun* thing which makes it easy to do something; *she finds the word-processor a great help in writing publicity material; the safari park was set up with financial help from the government; her assistant is not much help in the office - he cannot type or drive* **2** *verb* to make it easy for someone to do something *or* for something to be done; *the porter helped the visitors to get off the coach; the computer helps in the rapid processing of reservations or helps us to process reservations rapidly; the government helps exporting companies with easy credit;* **to help oneself** = to serve oneself; *at the buffet, you are asked to help yourself to food* (NOTE: you help someone *or* something **to do** something)

◇ **helping** *noun* portion of food served to one person; *he asked for another helping of chips; can I have a second helping of pudding, please? the helpings are very small, and seem even smaller because the plates are so large; children's helpings are not as large as those for adults*

hemisphere *noun* one of two parts into which the earth is divided

hepatitis *noun* inflammation of the liver; **infectious (virus) hepatitis** *or* **infective hepatitis** *or* **hepatitis A** = hepatitis transmitted by a carrier through food or drink; **serum hepatitis** *or* **hepatitis B** *or* **B viral hepatitis** = serious form of hepatitis transmitted by infected blood *or* unsterilized surgical instruments *or* shared needles *or* sexual intercourse

COMMENT: infectious hepatitis and serum hepatitis are caused by different viruses (called A and B), and having had one does not give immunity against an attack of the other. Hepatitis B is more serious than the A form, and can vary in severity from a mild gastrointestinal upset to severe liver failure and death

herb *noun* plant which can be used to give a certain taste to food *or* to give a certain scent

heritage *noun* the environment, including the countryside, historic buildings, etc. seen as something to be passed on in good condition to future generations; *the Highland Games is part of Scotland's cultural heritage;* **heritage attraction** *or* **heritage museum** *or* **heritage park** = tourist facility which is based on a country's historical or cultural background

herring *noun* common sea fish; **soused herring** = herring which has been pickled in vinegar and herbs

high *adjective* **(a)** tall; *the shelves are 30cm high; the door is not high enough to let us get the wardrobe into the bedroom; they are planning a 10-storey-high hotel next to the royal palace* **(b)** which goes far above other things; *a very high mountain overlooks the town* **(c)** large *or* not low; *high overhead costs increase the room price; high prices put customers off; they are budgeting for a high level of expenditure on renovation; high interest rates are killing small businesses* **(d)** (meat, especially game) which has been kept until it is beginning to rot and has a strong flavour
◊ **highball** *noun US* any long drink, such as whisky and soda
◊ **highchair** *noun* little chair on tall legs, so that a baby or small child can sit and eat at a normal table
◊ **high-class** *adjective* of very good quality; *a high-class hotel or coach service*
◊ **high-energy food** *noun* food such as fat or carbohydrate, containing a large number of calories, which give a lot of energy when they are broken down by the digestive system
◊ **high-grade** *see* GRADE
◊ **highland(s)** *noun* area of high hills or mountains; *the Scottish Highlands; the Cameron Highlands of Malaysia*
◊ **high season** *noun* period when there are lots of travellers, and when fares are higher (high-season tariffs usually apply to the period July to September); *rates in high season are 30% higher than in low season*
◊ **High Street** *noun* most important street in a British town, where the shops and banks are; *the pub in the High Street; the High Street shops; a High Street bookshop;* **the High Street banks** = main British banks which accept deposits from individual customers

high tea *noun* large meal taken in the late afternoon

COMMENT: 'high tea' is common in the North of England, the Midlands, Wales and Scotland. It is eaten around 5 o'clock in the afternoon and may consist of cold meat, hot or cold pies, salad, cakes, scones, and of course, tea

high temperature short time (HTST) method *noun* usual method of pasteurizing milk, where the milk is heated to 72°C for 15 seconds and then rapidly cooled

highway *noun* main road; **highway code** = official rules for people using public roads

hike 1 *noun* strenuous walk **2** *verb* to go for a strenuous walk
◊ **hiker** *noun* person who goes for strenuous walks
◊ **hiking** *noun* strenuous walking as a sport

hill *noun* higher area of land, lower than a mountain; *the Cheviot Hills are between England and Scotland; (in hot countries)* **hill station** = resort town in a hill area, where the weather is cooler in the summer than on the plain

hinterland *noun* area inland from a sea port *or* around a large town

hire 1 *noun* **(a)** paying money to rent a car *or* boat *or* piece of equipment for a period of time; **boat hire** *or* **cycle hire** *or* **car hire** = lending of boats, cycles, cars to people for money; **car hire firm** *or* **coach hire firm** = company which owns cars *or* coaches and lends them to people for money; **hire car** = car which is rented; *he was driving a hire car when the accident happened* **(b)** 'for hire' = sign on a taxi showing it is empty **2** *verb* **(a)** **to hire staff** = to engage new staff to work for you; **to hire and fire** = to engage new staff and dismiss existing staff frequently; *we have hired the best lawyers to represent us; they hired a small company to repaint the dining room* **(b)** **to hire a car** *or* **a bus** = to pay money to use a car *or* a bus for a period of time; *when their coach broke down, they hired a van to take them to the next hotel* **(c)**

to hire (out) cars or **coaches** = to own cars or coaches and lend them to customers who pay for their use

◊ **hired** adjective **hired car** = car which has been rented

hitch verb **to hitch (a lift)** = to ask a car driver or truck driver to take you as a passenger, usually by signalling with the thumb or by holding a sign with your destination written on it

◊ **hitch-hike** verb to travel by hitching lifts from drivers

◊ **hitch-hiker** noun person who travels by hitching lifts from drivers

COMMENT: in the UK, hitch-hikers are not allowed on motorways. Although it is a cheap way of travelling, it can be dangerous, and is not recommended

hock noun **(a)** any white wine from the Rhine valley in Germany **(b)** lower part of a leg of a pig, used for food

hold 1 noun bottom part of a ship or an aircraft, in which cargo is stored; **cargo hold** = part of the hold in which cargo is carried **2** verb **(a)** to own or to keep; *they ask for a 25% deposit and hold it against breakages caused by the visitor* **(b)** to contain; *the plane holds 250 passengers; in the rush hour, trains often carry more passengers than it is safe for them to hold; the carton holds twenty packets; each box holds 250 sheets of paper; a bag can hold twenty kilos of sugar* **(c)** to make something happen; *to hold a reception* or *a party; the computer show will be held in London next month; the wedding reception will be held in the Blue Room* **(d)** to keep; *we will hold the room for you until 8.00* **(e)** *(on telephone)* **hold the line please** = please wait; *the chairman is on the other line - will you hold?*
NOTE: **holding - held**

◊ **holdall** noun soft bag for carrying clothes, etc., when travelling

◊ **hold-up** noun delay; *long hold-ups are expected as the air-traffic controllers go on strike*

holiday noun **(a)** day on which no work is done because of national or religious law; **bank holiday** = weekday which is a public holiday when the banks are closed; *New Year's Day is a bank holiday;* **public holiday** = day when all workers rest and enjoy themselves instead of working; **statutory holiday** = holiday which is fixed by law; *the office is closed for the Christmas holiday; see*

also BANK HOLIDAY, PUBLIC HOLIDAY **(b)** period when a worker does not work, but rests, goes away and enjoys himself; *to take a holiday* or *to go on holiday; we always go on holiday in June* or *we always take our holidays in June; when is the manager taking his holidays? my head waiter is off on holiday tomorrow; he will be away on holiday for two weeks;* **the job carries five weeks' holiday** = one of the conditions of the job is that you have five weeks' holiday each year; **the summer holidays** = (i) period during the summer when children do not go to school, the longest holidays during the school year (in the UK about six weeks, but much longer in the USA); (ii) any holiday taken during the summer; **holiday camp** = permanent facility where people spend holidays in cabins and enjoy organized entertainment and sport; **holiday centre** = town or area which is popular for holidays; **holiday entitlement** = number of days' paid holiday which a worker has the right to take; **holiday home** = small house or flat, used by a family for their holidays; **holiday pay** = salary which is still paid during the holiday; **holiday period** = time when people take their holiday; *the restaurant will be closed for the holiday period;* **holiday resort** = place where people often go on holiday; **the holiday season** = time of year when most people take their holidays; *late winter is the main holiday season in the Alpine resorts; the holiday season on the North Italian coast lasts about three months* (NOTE: US English is **vacation**)

◊ **holidaymaker** noun person who is on holiday; *in August the town is full of holidaymakers*

hollandaise sauce noun sauce for meat, fish or vegetables, made of egg yolks, butter, lemon juice and sometimes vinegar

hollowware noun metal or china dishes from which food is served

home noun **(a)** place where a person lives; *please send the letter to my home address, not my office; US* **home fried potatoes** or **home fries** = potatoes which have been boiled, sliced and then fried **(b)** **home country** = country where a person lives

◊ **homeward** adjective going towards the home country; *homeward flight; homeward journey*

◊ **homewards** adverb towards the home country; *journey homewards*

hominy *noun US* ground maize which can be cooked in milk or water; **hominy grits** *see* GRITS

homogenize *verb* to mix various parts until they become a single whole; to treat milk so that the cream does not separate; *a litre of homogenized milk*

◇ **homogenization** *noun* treatment of milk so that the cream does not separate

honey *noun* sweet substance produced by bees; *yoghurt served with honey is a popular Greek dessert*

◇ **honeycomb** *noun* construction of wax cells in which bees store honey

◇ **honeydew (melon)** *noun* type of melon which has yellow skin and pale green flesh

honeymoon 1 *noun* holiday taken by man and wife immediately after their wedding; **honeymoon couple** = two people on their honeymoon; **honeymoon suite** = specially decorated suite of rooms for honeymoon couples **2** *verb* to go on a honeymoon

hop *noun* **(a)** short trip (especially in an aircraft) **(b)** bitter fruit used in making beer

COMMENT: hops are used to give the bitter flavour to British beer; they are not used in sweeter Continental beers

hors-d'oeuvre *noun* cold food served at the beginning of a meal (NOTE: a French word, meaning 'outside the main work'; in English, the plural 'hors-d'oeuvres' can be used but not in French)

COMMENT: hors-d'oeuvres can simply consist of pâté, prawns, radishes, etc. or can be more a complicated dish, such as a salad with scallops, or hard-boiled eggs with mayonnaise. Several items can be served together as 'mixed hors-d'oeuvres', and in some restaurants are brought to the table on an hors-d'oeuvre trolley

horse *noun* large animal with hooves, which is used for riding or pulling vehicles; *you can hire horses to go into the mountains*

◇ **horseback** *noun* **on horseback** = riding a horse

◇ **horse-drawn** *adjective* pulled by a horse; *you can go for rides in the woods in horse-drawn sleighs; holidays in Ireland in horse-drawn caravans*

◇ **horseradish** *noun* plant with a large root which is grated to make a sharp sauce

COMMENT: horseradish sauce is very sharp, similar to hot mustard. It is served with meat, particularly beef, and also with smoked fish, such as smoked eel. Jewish cuisine uses a type of red horseradish sauce flavoured with beetroot

◇ **horse-riding** *noun* riding horses for pleasure; *we often go horse-riding in the summer; the hotel offers horse-riding holidays in the mountains; see also* PONY-TREKKING

hospitality *noun* looking after guests well; *the town is famous for its old-fashioned American hospitality;* **hospitality industry** = all companies involved in providing services for guests (hotels, inns, restaurants and other recreational activities); **hospitality pad** = small portable electronic pad on which a waiter or waitress can key orders for food or drink (the orders are then relayed to the kitchen and bar, and are also logged to output the bill

host 1 *noun* **(a)** person who invites guests; *he was the host at the reunion; the waiter presented the bill to the guest, not to the host* **(b)** landlord of a hotel *or* inn, also sometimes of a restaurant; **'mine host'** = old-fashioned or humorous way of referring to the landlord of an inn **2** *verb* **to host a conference** *or* **a meeting** = to be the place where a conference is held; *Geneva is hosting the IATA conference this year; Barcelona hosted the Olympic games in 1992*

◇ **hostess** *noun* **(a)** woman who looks after passengers *or* clients; **air hostess** = woman who looks after passengers on a plane; **ground hostess** = woman who looks after passengers at an airport before they board the plane **(b)** *US* woman whose job it is to receive guests as they enter a restaurant and show them to their tables (a man who does this is called a 'greeter')

hostel *noun* **(a)** building providing rooms for students, etc. **(b) youth hostel** = building where young people may stay the night cheaply

hostelry *noun* inn
(NOTE: an 'old-fashioned' word, suggesting that the inn is very traditional)

hot *adjective* **(a)** very warm; *the guests complain that the rooms are too hot in the* *daytime and too cold at night; the drinks machine sells coffee, tea and hot soup; switch on the air-conditioner if you find the room too hot; travellers in hot countries are advised to take light clothes;* room with hot and cold running water = room with a washbasin, providing both hot and cold water from taps; hot chocolate = hot drink made of powdered chocolate (b) (food) which has a very strong and spicy taste; *this lime curry is particularly hot* (NOTE: the opposite is **mild**)

◊ hot dog *noun* snack made of a hot frankfurter sausage in a long bun; hot dog bun = long thin bread roll suitable for serving a sausage in

◊ hotplate *noun* piece of metal heated usually by electricity, used to cook food or to keep it hot

◊ hotpot *noun* meat stew with sliced potatoes on top cooked in the oven

COMMENT: 'Lancashire hotpot' is a stew of lamb chops, onions and carrots, cooked in the oven with sliced potatoes on top

◊ hot-water bottle *noun* container filled with hot water which is placed in a bed to warm it

hotel *noun* building where travellers can rent a room for a night, or eat in a restaurant, or drink in the bar, and non-residents can eat and drink also; *hotel bill; hotel expenses; hotel manager; hotel staff;* hotel accommodation = rooms available in hotels; *all hotel accommodation has been booked up for the exhibition;* hotel bus = special bus belonging to a hotel, which takes guests between the hotel and various destinations (often the airport or railway station); the hotel business *or* the hotel industry *or* the hotel trade = the business of running hotels; *he did not know anything about the hotel trade when he started his business;* hotel chain *or* chain of hotels = group of hotels belonging to the same company; hôtel garni = French term for a building with furnished rooms or apartments to let for periods of time, but usually with no restaurant (similar to an 'apartment hotel'); hotel group = large public company which owns a chain of hotels; hotel inspector = (i) person from an official body who visits hotels to check that they are observing health, hygiene and fire regulations; (ii) person who visits a hotel to assess what grade of hotel it is; hotel plate = heavy EPNS cutlery, still used in some hotel restaurants; hotel school = college

where students study hotel management; hotel tax = local government tax added to the basic rate for a hotel room; hotel transfer = transport from an airport or railway station to a hotel; apartment hotel = hotel which is formed of a series of furnished rooms or suites and where all normal hotel services are provided, although each suite will have its own kitchenette; first-class hotel *or* four-star hotel = good hotel, with comfortable rooms; luxury hotel *or* five-star hotel = very good hotel, with luxurious rooms and higher prices; tourist class hotel *or* two-star hotel = hotel which provides quite basic accommodation at cheaper prices (NOTE: although most people say **a hotel** [ə həʊˈtel] some people still use the older form **an hotel** [ænəʊˈtel])

◊ hotelier *or* hotelkeeper *noun* person who owns or manages a hotel

◊ hotelman *noun* person who owns or works in a hotel

QUOTE the hotel operator has called in the receiver after failing to come to terms with trading difficulties coupled with a fall in hotel property values
Caterer & Hotelkeeper
QUOTE hoteliers are emerging from the recession with a new energy and enthusiasm for their brands, marketing and customer service
Caterer & Hotelkeeper

hour *noun* (a) period of time lasting sixty minutes; to work a thirty-five hour week = to work seven hours a day each weekday; the restaurant staff work an eight-hour day = they work for eight hours a day, e.g. from 8.30 to 4.30, or from 16.00 to 24.00; happy hour = time (usually in the very early evening) when a bar offers cheaper drinks, to encourage customers to come in early (b) sixty minutes of work; *he earns £4 an hour; we pay waiters £6 an hour;* to pay by the hour = to pay people a fixed amount of money for each hour worked; *the chambermaids are paid by the hour; an hour's ski lesson costs $25.00* (c) banking hours = time when a bank is open for its customers; *you cannot get money out of a bank outside banking hours;* office hours = time when an office is open; *do not telephone during office hours;* outside hours *or* out of hours = when the office is not open; *he worked on the accounts out of hours*

house 1 *noun* (a) building in which people live; *we rented a house by the sea for the summer holidays;* house moth = small moth which sometimes lives in houses and whose larvae can destroy clothes and blankets, etc. kept in cupboards; **house swap** = arrangement where two families exchange houses for a holiday **(b)** company or business; **house journal** *or* **house magazine** *or* *US* **house organ** = magazine produced for the workers or shareholders in a company to give them news about the company **(c)** **public house** = licensed building selling beer, wines, spirits, and often food, to the public for consumption on the premises; **drinks are on the house** = drinks offered free by the landlord or innkeeper **(d)** referring to a restaurant, hotel, bar, club, etc.; **house doctor** = doctor who is on call to treat guests who become ill in a hotel; **house porter** = porter at the main entrance to a hotel or large restaurant; **house phone** *or* **house telephone** = telephone which links different rooms in a hotel, but is not connected to an outside line; *call room service on the house phone;* **house special** = special dish for which a restaurant is famous (or says it is famous); **house wine** = cheaper wine which a restaurant buys in bulk, often with its own label on it (house wine is usually better quality than carafe wine); *a bottle of the house red, please* **2** *verb* to provide accommodation for (someone *or* something); *the art gallery is housed in a former cinema; the group of students will be housed with Japanese families*

◊ **housecraft** *noun* skill at looking after a house or hotel

◊ **housefly** *noun* common fly *(Musca domestica)* living in houses, which carries bacteria and other micro-organisms onto food and can spread disease by laying its eggs in decaying meat and vegetables

◊ **housekeeper** *noun* person employed to look after the rooms in a hotel, in charge of the cleaning staff, and providing linen, etc.

◊ **housekeeping** *noun* looking after the rooms in a hotel; **housekeeping department** = department in a hotel which deals with looking after the rooms, especially cleaning and providing linen, etc.

> QUOTE housekeeping tends to be a department that is forgotten about. But it is very important, and gives employees a wonderful opportunity to contribute to a department that makes the most money for the hotel
> *Caterer & Hotelkeeper*

◊ **housemaid** *noun* woman *or* girl who looks after the cleaning of a hotel room

◊ **houseman** *noun* *US* man who does general jobs in a hotel

hovercraft *noun* vehicle which moves over water or land on a cushion of air

HSE = HEALTH AND SAFETY EXECUTIVE

HTST method = HIGH TEMPERATURE SHORT TIME METHOD

hub *noun* **(a)** centre of a wheel where it is connected to the axle **(b)** central airport, from which domestic flights (called 'spokes') connect to international flights

human relations *plural noun* relations between people, especially between managers and staff, or between staff and customers

◊ **human resources** *plural noun* workers which a company has available

humid *adjective* (air) which is damp *or* which contains moisture vapour; *the climate in the summer is hot and humid*

◊ **humidify** *noun* to make damp

◊ **humidifier** *noun* device for adding moisture to dry air (often used in centrally-heated buildings where the air remains very dry)

◊ **humidity** *noun* measurement of how much water vapour is contained in the air; **absolute humidity** = vapour concentration *or* mass of water vapour in a given quantity of air; **relative humidity** = ratio between the amount of water vapour in air and the amount which would be present if the air was saturated (shown as a percentage); **specific humidity** = ratio between the amount of water vapour in air and the total mass of the mixture of air and water vapour; **humidity control** = method of making the air humidity remain at a certain level, often by adding moisture to the air circulating in central heating systems

hurricane *noun* violent tropical storm with extremely strong winds, in the Caribbean or Eastern Pacific Ocean (NOTE: in the Far East called a **typhoon)**

huss *noun* small white sea fish

hydrocooling *noun* chilling of food, especially fruit and vegetables, by putting them in chilled water, which stops the process of ripening; *see also* REFRIGERATE

hydrofoil *noun* boat which skims fast over water on thin legs

hygiene *noun* (i) being clean and keeping healthy conditions; (ii) science of health; *the inspectors' report criticised the hygiene in the kitchen; food handlers have to maintain strict personal hygiene;* **environmental hygiene** = study of health and how it is affected by the environment; **personal hygiene** = keeping oneself clean and healthy, by washing the body, hands, hair, etc. often, and keeping one's clothes clean

◊ **hygienic** *adjective* (i) clean; (ii) which produces healthy conditions; *don't touch the food with dirty hands - it isn't hygienic*

◊ **hygienically** *adverb* in a hygienic way

hypermarket *noun* very large supermarket, usually on the outskirts of a large town

Ii

IAPA = INTERNATIONAL AIRLINE PASSENGERS ASSOCIATION

IATA = INTERNATIONAL AIR TRANSPORT ASSOCIATION

ice 1 *noun* **(a)** water which is frozen and has become solid; *can we have some ice for the drinks, please?;* **crushed ice** = ice which has been broken into very small pieces, used to cool dishes set out on a serving table; **dry ice** = carbon dioxide (CO_2) in solid form; it is extremely cold, with a temperature of -78°C, and is used for keeping food such as ice cream cold when being transported; **ice bucket** = container of crushed ice and water in which a wine bottle is placed to keep cool; **ice cube** = little block of ice, used to cool a drink **(b)** ice cream; *she ordered a strawberry ice;* **choc ice** = block of ice cream covered with chocolate **(c)** frozen water, as a surface for skating, etc.; **ice rink** = special area for ice skating, or for playing ice hockey, etc.; **ice skating** = skating on ice with skates fitted with blades (as opposed to roller skating) **2** *verb* **(a)** to add ice to (a drink); *she asked for a glass of iced water* **(b)** to put icing on a cake; *she ordered a dozen cup cakes to be iced with chocolate icing*

◊ **icebox** *noun* **(a)** part of a refrigerator for making or storing ice **(b)** box containing ice to keep food or drink cool **(c)** *US* refrigerator

◊ **ice cream** *noun* mixture of cream, eggs, sugar and flavouring *or* of milk, sugar, water and flavouring, frozen until quite hard; *she ordered a strawberry ice cream; what flavours of ice cream do you have?;* **soft ice cream** = ice cream mixed with air, dispensed from a machine

◊ **ice lolly** *noun* mixture of water and flavouring, frozen until solid with a stick in it (NOTE: US English is **popsicle**)

◊ **icing** *noun* covering of sugar and flavouring, spread over a cake or biscuits

◊ **icing sugar** *noun* fine powdered white sugar, mixed with water or egg white and flavouring, used to cover cakes or biscuits

ID card *noun* card which shows a photograph of the holder, with the name, date of birth and other details

IDD = INTERNATIONAL DIRECT DIALLING

ideal *adjective* perfect *or* very good for something; *the cottage is an ideal place for birdwatching; this is the ideal site for a new swimming pool*

◊ **Ideal Home Exhibition** *noun* annual exhibition in London showing new houses, new kitchens, new products for the home, etc.

identification *noun* **(a)** saying who someone is or who something belongs to **(b)** document which shows who someone is; *the manager asked him for identification*

◊ **identity** *noun* who someone is; **identity card** *or* **ID card** = card which shows a photograph of the holder, with the name, date of birth and other details; **identity document** = document, such as a passport, which shows who someone is; **proof of identity** = proof (in the form of a document, such as a driving licence) that a person is who he says he is; *the police asked her for proof of identity*

ill *adjective* sick, not well; **to be taken ill** = to become sick suddenly; *one of the guests was* *taken ill during the night and we had to call the doctor*

◊ **illness** *noun* sickness

illegal *adjective* not legal *or* against the law

◊ **illegally** *adverb* against the law; *he was accused of illegally importing arms into the country*

illicit *adjective* not legal *or* not permitted; *illicit sale of alcohol; trade in illicit alcohol*

immediate *adjective* happening at once; *he wrote an immediate letter of complaint; your order will receive immediate attention*

◊ **immediately** *adverb* at once; *as soon as he heard the news he immediately phoned his wife; can you phone immediately the chalet becomes vacant?*

immigrate *verb* to come into a country to settle

◊ **immigration** *noun* settling in a new country; **immigration control** = restriction placed by a country on the numbers of immigrants; **immigration office** = office dealing with immigrants

◊ **immigrant** *noun* person who comes to a country to settle

immunization *noun* giving a person protection against an infection, either by injecting an antiserum (passive immunization) or by giving the body the disease in such a small dose that the body does not develop the disease, but produces antibodies to counteract it; **immunization centre** = clinic where travellers can get immunization before travelling

◊ **immunize** *verb* to give someone protection against an infection (NOTE: you immunize someone **against** a disease)

QUOTE no particular immunization is required for travellers to the United States, Europe, Australia or New Zealand
British National Formulary

import 1 *noun* **(a) imports** = goods brought into a country from abroad for sale; *imports from Poland have risen to $1m a year;* **invisible imports** = services (such as banking, tourism) which are paid for in foreign currency; **visible imports** = real goods which are imported **(b) import ban** = forbidding imports; *the government has imposed an import ban on arms;* **import duty** = tax on goods brought into a country; **import levy** = tax on imports, especially in the EC, a tax on imports of farm produce

from outside the EC; **import licence** *or* **import permit** = official document which allows goods to be imported; **import quota** = fixed quantity of a particular type of goods which the government allows to be imported; *the government has imposed an import quota on cars;* **import surcharge** = extra duty charged on imported goods, to try to prevent them from being imported and to encourage local manufacture **2** *verb* to bring (goods) from abroad into a country for sale; *the company imports television sets from Japan; this car was imported from France; the union organized a boycott of imported cars*

QUOTE European manufacturers rely heavily on imported raw materials which are mostly priced in dollars
Duns Business Month

◊ **importation** *noun* bringing goods from abroad into a country for sale; *the importation of arms is forbidden*

◊ **importing 1** *adjective* which imports; *oil-importing countries; an importing company* **2** *noun* bringing goods from abroad into a country for sale; *the importing of arms into the country is illegal*

improve *verb* to make (something) better; to become better; *we are trying to improve our image with a series of TV commercials; the general manager has promised that the bus service will improve; they hope to improve the cash flow position by asking for payment in advance; we hope the cash flow will improve or we will have difficulty in paying the suppliers' bills;* **bar takings have improved sharply during the first quarter** = more money has been taken over the bar during the period

◊ **improved** *adjective* better; *improved service has resulted in another star in the hotel's grade*

◊ **improvement** *noun* **(a)** making or becoming better; *there has been no improvement in the train service; hotel bookings are showing a sharp improvement over last year* **(b)** thing which is better; *the new annexe is a great improvement over the old hotel*

in = INCH

inaugural flight *noun* first flight over a new route *or* first flight of a new aircraft, etc.

inbound *adjective* returning to the home country; *the inbound flights all leave on the hour; the copilot flew the inbound leg from*

Durban to London; **inbound tourism** = tourism by visitors to the home country (NOTE: the opposite is **outbound)**

incentive *noun* something which encourages someone to work better; **staff incentives** = pay and better conditions offered to workers to make them work better; **incentive bonus** *or* **incentive payment** = extra pay offered to a worker to make him work better; **incentive scheme** = plan to encourage better work by paying higher commissions or bonuses; *incentive schemes are boosting production;* **incentive travel** = travel scheme which gives cheap or free flights to someone who has earned them (such as to a salesman for increased sales); **incentive trip** = journey or holiday awarded to a worker to encourage him to work better

inch *noun* measurement of length (= 2.54cm) (NOTE: usually written **in** or **"** after figures: **2in** or **2")**

include *verb* to count (something) with other things; *the charge includes VAT; the total comes to £1,000 including service; the total is £140 not including insurance and handling charges; the room is £40 including breakfast; service is not included in the bill*

◊ **inclusive** *adjective* which counts something in with other things; *inclusive of tax; not inclusive of VAT;* **the conference runs from the 12th to the 16th inclusive** = it starts on the morning of the 12th and ends on the evening of the 16th; **inclusive charge** *or* **inclusive sum** = charge which includes all costs; **inclusive tour (IT)** = package holiday, where the price includes travel, hotel accommodation and meals and is cheaper than it would be if each items were bought separately

income *noun* money which you receive; **disposable income** = income left after tax and national insurance have been deducted; **income tax** = tax on income; **unearned income** = money received from interest or dividends

incoming *adjective* **incoming call** = phone call coming into a building from someone outside; **incoming mail** = mail which comes into an office; **incoming tour** = group of tourists who are arriving at their destination (taking the place of another group which is just leaving) (NOTE: the opposite is **outgoing)**

incorrect *adjective* wrong *or* not correct; *the details of the tour were incorrect and the publicity had to be changed*

◊ **incorrectly** *adverb* wrongly *or* not correctly; *the suitcase was incorrectly labelled*

increase 1 *noun* **(a)** growth *or* becoming larger; *increase in tax* or *tax increase; increase in price* or *price increase; profits showed a 10% increase* or *an increase of 10% on last year;* **increase in the cost of living** = rise in the annual cost of living **(b)** higher salary; *increase in pay* or *pay increase; increase in salary* or *salary increase; the government hopes to hold salary increases to 3%;* **cost-of-living increase** = increase in salary to allow it to keep up with higher cost of living **(c) on the increase** = growing larger *or* becoming more frequent; *overseas travel is on the increase; stealing from shops is on the increase* **2** *verb* **(a)** to grow bigger *or* higher; *the number of package holidays sold has increased by 20% over last year; profits have increased faster than the increase in the rate of inflation; exports to Africa have increased by more than 25%; the price of oil has increased twice in the past week;* **to increase in price** = to become more expensive; **to increase in size** *or* **in value** = to become larger *or* more valuable **(b)** to make higher; *room charges were increased on January 1st; the company have increased their fares by 10%*

incubation period *noun* time during which a virus *or* bacterium develops in the body after contamination *or* infection, before the appearance of the symptoms of the disease

indicator *noun* device or light which shows something, such as that a machine is on or that a vehicle is going to turn; **indicator board** *or* **indicator panel** = large device with letters or words on moving strips, used to show information about arrivals and departures at railway stations and airports

individual 1 *noun* one single person; *we aim to cater for the private individual as well as for groups* **2** *adjective* single *or* belonging to one person; *we sell individual portions of ice cream*

indoor *adjective* situated inside a building; *an indoor swimming pool*

◊ **indoors** *adverb* inside a building; *since it is raining, we will hold the reception indoors*

industry *noun* business of making something *or* of providing a service; **the travel industry** = all companies and services dealing with travel and tourism (such as trains, buses, planes, travel agents, hotels, etc.)

inexpensive *adjective* cheap *or* not expensive
◊ **inexpensively** *adverb* without spending much money; *you can still eat quite inexpensively in Greece*

infect *verb* to contaminate with disease-producing microorganisms *or* toxins; to transmit infection
◊ **infection** *noun* entry of microbes into the body, which then multiply in the body
◊ **infectious** *adjective* (disease) which is caused by microbes and can be transmitted to other persons by direct means; **infectious (virus) hepatitis** = hepatitis transmitted by a carrier through food or drink

infest *verb (of parasite, vermin)* to be present in large numbers
◊ **infestation** *noun* having large numbers of parasites or vermin; *the inspector reported cockroach infestation in the kitchens*

in-flight *adjective* during a flight; **in-flight catering** = food served during a flight; **in-flight entertainment** = film which passengers can watch or music which they can listen to during a long-distance flight

influx *noun* entry of a crowd of people; *an influx of tourists in summer*

inform *verb* to tell (someone) details of something; *please inform the group that the coach will leave the hotel at 10.30*
◊ **information** *noun* (a) details which explain something; *please send me information on or about holidays in the USA; have you any information on or about discounts for groups of more than 10 people? I enclose this leaflet for your information; to disclose a piece of information; to answer a request for information; for further information, please write to Department 27;* **flight information** = information about flight times; **tourist information** = details of places visitors might like to visit, how to get there, opening times, available accommodation, etc. (b) **information bureau** *or* **information office** = office which gives information to tourists *or* visitors; **information desk** = desk in a hotel *or* on a ship *or* at an exhibition, etc., where you can ask for information (NOTE: no plural; for one item say **a piece of information)**

COMMENT: tourist information offices are usually indicated by the international sign showing the letter 'i'

infusion *noun* drink made by pouring boiling water on a dry substance (such as a herb tea *or* a powdered drug)

ingredient *noun* item used in making a dish of food; *all the ingredients for the barbecue can be bought locally; the ingredients are listed on the packet*

inhabitant *noun* person who lives in a place; *the local inhabitants do not like noisy tourists in summer*

in-house *adverb & adjective* working inside a company's building; *the in-house staff; we do all our catering in-house;* **in-house training** = training given to staff at their place of work

inland *adjective & adverb* (a) referring to the interior of a country; **inland waterways** = rivers and canals (b) *GB* the **Inland Revenue** = British government department dealing with taxes (income tax, corporation tax, capital gains tax, inheritance tax, etc.) but not duties, such as VAT, which is collected by the Customs and Excise (NOTE: the US equivalent is the **Internal Revenue Service** *or* **IRS)**

inn *noun* building where alcoholic drinks are served, and which also has accommodation for visitors who wish to stay the night
◊ **innkeeper** *noun* person who runs an inn

inner *adjective* inside; **inner city** = central part of a large town; *inner city hotels are most convenient, but can be noisy; the capital has a inner ring road*

inoculate *verb* to introduce vaccine into a person's body in order to make the body create antibodies, so protecting the person against the disease; *the baby was inoculated against diphtheria* (NOTE: you inoculate someone **with** or **against** a disease)
◊ **inoculation** *noun* action of inoculating someone; injection to stop you catching a disease; *has the baby had a diphtheria inoculation?*

inquire *verb* to ask questions about something; *the chef inquired if anything was wrong; she inquired about APEX fares to Canada;* 'inquire within' = ask for more details inside the office *or* shop

◊ **inquire into** *verb* to investigate *or* to try to find out about (something); *we are inquiring into the background of the new hotel proprietor*

◊ **inquiry** *noun* official question; *I refer to your inquiry of May 25th; all inquiries should be addressed to this department;* **inquiries clerk** = person who answers inquiries; **inquiries desk** = desk in a hotel *or* train station *or* conference hall, etc., where an inquiries clerk sits to answer questions

insect *noun* small animal with six legs and a body in three parts, sometimes with wings; *insects were flying round the lamp; he was stung by an insect;* **insect bite** = sting caused by an insect which punctures the skin to suck blood, and in so doing introduces irritants

◊ **insecticide** *noun* substance which kills insects

COMMENT: most insect bites are simply irritating, but some patients can be extremely sensitive to certain types of insect (such as bee stings). Other insect bites can be more serious, as insects can carry the bacteria which produce typhus, sleeping sickness, malaria, filariasis, etc.

insipid *adjective* without much taste; *this sauce has no taste - it's really insipid*

inspect *verb* to examine in detail; *to inspect a kitchen or a toilet; to inspect the accounts of a hotel; to inspect a bedroom to see if it has been cleaned*

◊ **inspection** *noun* close examination of something; *to make an inspection or to carry out an inspection of a kitchen or a toilet; inspection of a room to see if it has been cleaned;* **to carry out a tour of inspection** = to visit various places *or* hotels *or* restaurants and examine them in detail; **VAT inspection** = visit by officials of the Customs and Excise Department to see if a company is correctly reporting its VAT

◊ **inspector** *noun* official who inspects; **health inspector** = official who inspects the kitchens of hotels, restaurants, etc. to see if they are clean; **inspector of taxes** *or* **tax inspector** = government official who examines tax returns and decides how much tax someone should pay; **inspector of weights and measures** = government official who inspects weighing machines and goods sold in shops to see if the quantities and weights are correct

◊ **inspectorate** *noun* all inspectors

instant coffee *noun* **(a)** soluble freeze-dried granules *or* powder used to make coffee; *the bedroom has a kettle with tea bags and sachets of instant coffee* **(b)** drink made from freeze-dried granules of coffee or from powder, over which boiling water is poured; *she made a cup of instant coffee*

instruct *verb* **(a)** to give an order to someone; **to instruct someone to do something** = to tell someone officially to do something; *he instructed the restaurant to replace its kitchen equipment* **(b)** to show someone how to do something; *the hotel fire officer will instruct you in how to evacuate the building if a fire breaks out*

◊ **instruction** *noun* order which tells how something is to be done; **to await instructions** = to wait for someone to tell you what to do; **in accordance with** *or* **according to instructions** = as the instructions show; **failing instructions to the contrary** = unless someone tells you to do the opposite

◊ **instructor** *noun* person who shows how something is to be done; **aerobics instructor** *or* **ski instructor** *or* **swimming instructor** = person who teaches people how to do aerobics *or* to ski *or* to swim

insulate *verb* to protect (something) against cold, heat or noise; *all the bedrooms are noise-insulated*

◊ **insulation** *noun* **(a)** protecting something against cold, heat or noise **(b)** material which protects against cold, heat or noise

insure *verb* to have a contract with a company where, if regular small payments are made, the company will pay compensation for loss, damage, injury or death; *to insure a building against fire; to insure someone's life; he was insured for £100,000; to insure baggage against loss; to insure against bad weather; to insure against loss of earnings;* **the life insured** = the person whose life is covered by a life assurance policy; **the sum insured** = the largest amount of money that an insurer will pay under an insurance policy

◊ **insurable** *adjective* which can be insured; *the hotel is a firetrap and isn't insurable*

◊ **insurance** *noun* **(a)** contract that in return for regular small payments, a company will pay compensation for loss, damage, injury or death; **to take out (an) insurance against fire** = to make a small regular payment, so that if a fire happens, compensation will be paid; **to take out (an) insurance on the building** = to make a small regular payment, so that if the building is damaged compensation will be paid; **the damage is covered by the insurance** = the insurance company will pay for the damage; **to pay the insurance on a car** = to pay premiums to insure a car **(b) accident insurance** = insurance which will pay if an accident takes place; **car insurance** *or* **motor insurance** = insuring a car, the driver and passengers in case of accident; **comprehensive insurance** = insurance policy which covers against all risks which are likely to happen; **contents insurance** = insurance policy which covers damage to or theft of items kept in a building; **fire insurance** = insurance against damage by fire; **life insurance** = insurance policy which pays a sum of money when someone dies; **medical insurance** = insurance which pays the cost of medical treatment, especially when travelling abroad; **third-party insurance** = insurance to cover damage to any person who is not one of the people named in the insurance contract; **travel insurance** = insurance which pays compensation if travel schedules are delayed, if the traveller becomes ill, if baggage is lost, if someone has an accident, etc. **(c) insurance agent** *or* **insurance broker** = person who arranges insurance for clients; **insurance claim** = asking an insurance company to pay compensation for loss, damage, injury or death; **insurance company** = company whose business is to receive payments and pay compensation for loss, damage, injury or death; **insurance contract** = agreement by an insurance company to insure; **insurance cover** = protection guaranteed by an insurance policy; **insurance policy** = document which shows the conditions of an insurance; **insurance premium** = regular small payment made by the insured person to the insurer

◊ **insurer** *noun* company which insures (NOTE: for life insurance, GB English prefers to use **assurance, assure, assurer**)

integration *noun* bringing several businesses together under a central control; **horizontal integration** = joining similar companies in the same type of business *or* taking over a company in the same line of business as yourself (as when a chain of restaurants takes over another restaurant); **vertical integration** = joining business together which deal with different stages in the production or sale of the same product (as when a restaurant chain takes over a wine importer)

intensive *adjective* **capital-intensive industry** = industry which needs a large amount of capital investment in plant to make it work; **labour-intensive industry** = industry which needs large numbers of workers *or* where labour costs are high in relation to turnover

inter- *prefix* between

interchange *noun* large road junction where motorways cross

intercity *adjective* between two cities; **the intercity rail services are good** = train services between cities are good

intercontinental *adjective* between two continents; **intercontinental flight** = flight between two continents

interest 1 *noun* **(a)** special attention; *the manager takes no interest in the guests;* **special interest holidays** = holidays arranged for people with particular hobbies, such as bird-watching, sketching, etc. **(b)** payment made by a borrower for the use of money, calculated as a percentage of the capital borrowed; **compound interest** = interest which is added to the capital and then earns interest itself; **fixed interest** = interest which is paid at a set rate; **high** *or* **low interest** = interest at a high or low percentage; **simple interest** = interest calculated on the capital only, and not added to it; **interest charges** = amount of interest paid; **interest rate** *or* **rate of interest** = percentage charge for borrowing money; **interest-free credit** *or* **loan** = credit or loan where no interest is paid by the borrower **(c)** part of the ownership of something, such as money invested in a company giving a financial share in it; **he has a controlling interest in the hotel** = he owns more than 50% of the shares and so can direct how the hotel is run; **majority interest** *or* **minority interest** = situation where someone owns a majority *or* a minority of shares in a company; *he has a majority interest in a supermarket chain;* **to acquire a substantial interest in the company** = to buy a large number of shares in a company **2** *verb* to attract someone's attention; *he tried to interest the guests in a game of tennis;* **interested in** = paying attention to; *the chef is not interested in Greek food*

interior *noun* inner part (of a building); **interior decorator** *or* **interior designer** = person who designs the inside of a building, including wall coverings, paint colours, furniture, fabrics, etc.

interline *adjective* between two airlines

internal *adjective* inside; **internal flight** = flight inside a country; *US* **Internal Revenue Service (IRS)** = government department which deals with tax

international *adjective* working between countries; **international access code** = number used to start making a telephone call to another country (from the UK, it is 010-; from most other countries it is 00-); the number is followed by the country code; **international call** = telephone call to another country; **international direct dialling (IDD)** = calling telephone numbers in other countries yourself without asking the operator to do it for you; **international law** = laws referring to the way countries deal with each other; **international hotel** = hotel which is part of a chain which has hotels in several countries, and which caters for guests of many different nationalities; **international operator** = telephone operator who deals with calls to other countries; **international tourist** = tourist who visits another country for at least one night's stay; **international travel** = travel between different countries

◊ **International Air Transport Association (IATA)** organization which regulates international air travel

◊ **International Date Line** *noun* line of longitude (in the Pacific Ocean) which indicates the change in date from east to west

interpret *verb* to translate what someone has said into another language; *the courier knows Greek, so he will interpret for us*

◊ **interpreter** *noun* person who translates what someone has said into another language; *the hotel porter will act as interpreter; we need an Italian interpreter*

interstate *adjective US* between two or more states in the USA; *interstate bus company*

interview 1 *noun* **(a)** talking to a person who is applying for a job; *we called six people for interview; I have an interview next week or I am going for an interview next week* **(b)** asking a person questions on radio or television or for a magazine or newspaper; *the manager gave an interview to the local paper* **2** *verb* to talk to (a person) applying for a job to see if he is suitable; *we interviewed ten candidates, but did not find anyone suitable*

inventory 1 *noun* **(a)** *especially US* stock, goods in a warehouse or shop; *to carry a high inventory; to aim to reduce inventory;* **inventory control** = system of checking that there is not too much stock in a warehouse, but just enough to meet requirements (NOTE: the word 'inventory' is used in the USA where British English uses the word 'stock'. So, the American 'inventory control' is 'stock control' in British English) **(b)** list of the contents of a house or hotel or restaurant for sale or for rent; *to draw up an inventory of fixtures; he checked the kitchen equipment against the inventory;* **to agree the inventory** = to agree that all the items on the inventory are there and in the stated condition (NOTE: plural is **inventories**) **2** *verb* to make a list of stock or contents

invest *verb* **(a)** to put money into shares or a business, hoping that it will produce interest and increase in value; *he invested all his money in a Chinese restaurant; she was advised to invest in a fast-food franchise;* **to invest abroad** = to put money into a business *or* shares in overseas countries **(b)** to spend money on something which you believe will be useful; *we invested in a new oven; the hotel has invested in a fleet of courtesy cars*

◊ **investment** *noun* **(a)** placing of money so that it will increase in value and produce interest; *they called for more government investment in new industries; investment in hotel property; to make investments in travel companies;* **investment income** = income (such as interest and dividends) from investments; **return on investment (ROI)** = interest or dividends shown as a percentage of the money invested **(b)** things bought with invested money; **long-term investment** *or* **short-term investment** = investment which is likely to increase in value over a long or short period; **safe investment** = investment which is not likely to fall in value; *he is trying to protect his investments* = he is trying to make sure that the money he has invested is not lost

◊ **investor** *noun* person who invests money; **the institutional investor** = organization (like a pension fund or insurance company) with large sums of money to invest; **the small investor** *or* **the private investor** = person with a small sum of money to invest

invisible 1 *adjective* **invisible earnings** = foreign currency earned by a country by providing services, not selling goods; **invisible imports** *or* **exports** *or* **invisible trade** = services which are paid for in foreign currency or earn foreign currency without actually selling a product (such as banking, insurance or tourism) **2** *plural noun* **invisibles** = invisible imports and exports

invoice 1 *noun* note asking for payment for goods or services supplied; *your invoice dated November 10th; they sent in their invoice six weeks late; to make out an invoice for £250; to settle or to pay an invoice;* **the total is payable within thirty days of invoice date** = the total sum has to be paid within thirty days of the date on the invoice; **VAT invoice** = invoice which shows VAT separately; **invoice price** = price as given on an invoice (including discount and VAT); **total invoice value** = total amount on an invoice, including transport, VAT, etc. **2** *verb* to send an invoice to (someone); *to invoice a customer;* **we invoiced you on November 10th** = we sent you the invoice on November 10th

iodine *noun* chemical element which is essential to the body, especially to the functioning of the thyroid gland; **tincture of iodine** = weak solution of iodine in alcohol, used as a disinfectant

Irish coffee *noun* hot coffee, served in a glass, with Irish whiskey added to it and whipped cream poured on top

iron 1 *noun* electric household instrument for smoothing the creases from clothes; **travelling iron** = small iron which you can carry with you when you travel **2** *verb* to press (cloth) with an iron

◊ **ironer** *noun* large machine for ironing sheets, pillowcases, etc.

◊ **ironing** *noun* **(a)** pressing clothes, sheets, etc. with an electric iron **(b)** clothes, sheets, etc. which need pressing

◊ **ironing board** *noun* high narrow table used for pressing clothes, sheets, etc. on

irradiation *noun* use of rays to kill bacteria in food

COMMENT: food is irradiated with gamma rays from isotopes which kill bacteria. It is not certain, however, that irradiated food is safe for humans to eat, as the effects of irradiation on food are not known. In some countries irradiation is only permitted as a treatment of certain foods

island *noun* piece of land entirely surrounded by water; *Greek island holidays; the Channel Islands are favourite holiday destinations;* **traffic island** = small raised piece of pavement in the centre of the road where pedestrians can safely stand; *see also* THOUSAND ISLAND DRESSING

IT = INCLUSIVE TOUR

item *noun* **(a)** thing; *do you have any items of jewellery in your luggage? valuable items should be left with the reception desk; she declared several items to the customs;* **cash items** = goods sold for cash **(b)** point on a list; *items 6 and 7 on the fire drill instructions do not apply*

◊ **itemize** *verb* to make a detailed list of things; **itemized account** = detailed record of money paid or owed; **itemized bill** = piece of paper giving details of each object or service and the price; **itemized invoice** = invoice which lists each item separately

itinerary *noun* list of places to be visited on one journey; *the members of the group were given a detailed tour itinerary by the courier; the itinerary takes us to six countries in ten days*

Jj

jab *noun (informal)* injection; *have you had your cholera jabs yet?*

jacket *noun* short coat which comes to the level of the waist or a little below the waist;

you have to wear a jacket and tie to enter the restaurant; **jacket potato** = potato cooked 'in its jacket', that is, baked in an oven without being peeled, then served cut open, with butter or various fillings, such as cheese, chopped ham, baked beans, chilli, etc.

jacuzzi *noun* type of bath with jets which circulate the water and keep it bubbling (often used as part of a health treatment, as the jets of water massage the body) (NOTE: also sometimes called **jacuzzi bath**)

jam 1 *noun* **(a)** sweet food made with fruit and sugar; *each table has little pots of jam and honey; help yourself at the buffet to individual packs of butter and jam* **(b)** blocking which prevents something moving; **traffic jam** = situation where there is so much traffic on the road that it moves only very slowly; *traffic jams are common in the rush hour* **2** *verb* to stop working *or* to be blocked; *the traffic lights failed and the traffic was jammed for miles; the switchboard was jammed with calls* NOTE: **jamming - jammed**

jar *noun* pot (usually glass) for keeping food in; *a jar of jam; there was a jar of marmalade on the breakfast table*

jaw *see* OPEN JAW

jeep *noun* trademark for a strongly built four-wheel drive vehicle used for travelling over rough ground

jell *verb (of liquid)* to become a jelly; *boil the jam until it jells*

◊ **jello** *noun US* type of sweet food made of gelatine, water and fruit flavouring, etc. (NOTE: GB English is **jelly**)

◊ **jelly** *noun* **(a)** semi-solid substance, especially a type of sweet food made of gelatine, water and fruit flavouring, etc. **(b)** type of preserve made of fruit juice boiled with sugar; *roast lamb served with mint jelly* **(c)** *US* sweet preserve, made with fruit and sugar (NOTE: GB English is **jam**)

◊ **jellied** *adjective* cooked or preserved in a jelly; *jellied eels*

◊ **jellybean** *noun US* sweet of coloured jelly, shaped like a bean

◊ **jelly roll** *noun US* Swiss roll

jet 1 *noun* jet-propelled aircraft; **executive jet** = small jet aircraft for use by a few passengers, usually important businessmen; **jumbo jet** = the Boeing 747, a very large jet aircraft; **jet foil** = hydrofoil, a boat which skims fast over water, propelled by gas turbine engines; **jet lag** = tiredness felt by travellers who fly by jet across time zones; **jet set** = wealthy people who frequently travel by jet; **jet-setter** = member of the jet set **2** *verb (informal)* to travel by jet

◊ **jet-propelled aircraft** *noun* aircraft with jet engines

◊ **jetway** *noun* covered walkway which connects an aircraft with the terminal building, so that passengers can walk onto or off the aircraft easily (it extends from the terminal to the forward door on the aircraft)

jetty *noun* small quay, a landing stage for smaller boats

jewel *noun* **(a)** precious stone **(b)** ornament to be worn, made from precious stones or precious metals, or of imitation stones

◊ **jewellery** *or US* **jewelry** *noun* ornaments to be worn, made from precious stones or precious metals, or of imitation stones

jitney *noun (in the Caribbean islands)* cheap bus

job *noun* **(a) job (of work)** = piece of work; **to do an excellent job (of work)** = to work extremely well; **to do odd jobs** = to do general work; *he does odd jobs for us around the hotel;* **odd-job-man** = man who does general work, such as repairs, in a building or on an estate **(b)** regular paid work; *he is looking for a job in the hotel industry; he lost his job when the tourist office closed; she got a job in a travel agency; to apply for a job with an airline;* **to look for a job** = to try to find work **(c) job analysis** = detailed examination and report on the duties of a job; **job application** *or* **application for a job** = asking for a job in writing; *you have to fill in a job application form;* **job classification** = describing jobs listed under various classes; **job description** = official document from the management which says in detail what a job involves; **job evaluation** = examining different jobs within an organization to see what skills and qualifications are needed to carry them out; **job satisfaction** = a worker's feeling that he is happy in his place of work and pleased with the work he does; **job security** = feeling which a worker has that he has a right to keep his job, or that he will stay in his job until he retires; **job sharing** = situation where a job is done by more than one person, each working part-time; **job specification** = very detailed description of what is involved in a job; **job title** = name given to a person doing certain work; *her job title is 'Chief Reservations Clerk'*

jog 1 *noun* rather slow run, especially taken for exercise; *he goes for a jog each morning* **2** *verb* **(a) to go jogging** *or* **to jog** = to run at an easy pace, especially for exercise; *he was jogging round the park; she goes jogging for half an hour every morning* **(c)** to shake or to push lightly; *when the turbulence started, my neighbour jogged my arm and made me spill my drink*

◊ **jogger** *noun* person who jogs for exercise

◊ **jogging** *noun* running at an easy pace for exercise; **jogging track** = track in the grounds of a hotel, health farm, etc. where guests can go jogging, without having to run on the street

join *verb* **(a)** to put things together; *the two bedrooms are joined together to make a suite* **(b) to join an association** *or* **a group** = to become a member of an association *or* a group; *two more people will join the group in Cairo*

joint 1 *noun* **(a)** piece of meat, especially one suitable for roasting; *a joint of beef; a bacon joint;* **a cut off the joint** = a slice cut from a piece of roast meat **(b)** *(informal)* low-class club or restaurant; *a hamburger joint;* **clip joint** = low-class club or bar, where guests are charged too much for their drinks, etc. **2** *adjective* **(a)** combined *or* with two or more organizations linked together; **joint discussions** = talks between management and workers before something is done; **joint management** = management done by two or more people; **joint venture** = very large business project where two or more companies join together, often forming a new joint company to manage the project **(b)** for two or more people; **joint account** = bank account for two people; **joint bill** = two bills added together and paid by one person; **joint ownership** = owning of a property by several people or companies

◊ **jointly** *adverb* together with one or more other people; *to own a property jointly; to manage a hotel jointly*

journey *noun* travelling from one place to another; *he planned his journey to visit all the capitals of Europe in two weeks*

jug *noun* container with a handle, used for pouring liquids; *a jug of milk; there is a jug of water by the bedside*

◊ **jugged hare** *noun* hare cooked slowly in a covered dish

juice *noun* liquid inside a fruit or vegetable; liquid inside meat or poultry; *she had a glass of orange juice for breakfast; I'd like a tomato juice with Worcester sauce; make gravy using the meat juices in the roasting pan;* **fruit juice** *or* **vegetable juice** = juice from fruit or vegetables, often served as an appetizer or starter (grapefruit juice, orange juice, tomato juice, carrot juice etc.); **juice extractor** = device for extracting juice from a fruit or vegetable

◊ **juicy** *adjective* full of juice; *a juicy orange; this grapefruit is not very juicy; slices of juicy roast chicken*

jumbo (jet) *noun* the Boeing 747, a very large jet aircraft

junior 1 *adjective* lower in rank; **junior clerk** = clerk, usually young, who has lower status than a senior clerk; **junior executive** *or* **junior manager** = young manager in a company **2** *noun (humorous)* the son of the family; *Harry Markovitz Junior;* **junior suite** = large hotel room divided into living room and bedroom areas

junk food *noun* bad commercially prepared food with little nutritional value and containing few fresh ingredients

junket *noun* expensive business trip, paid for by a company or by a government

jut *verb* **to jut out over something** = to stick out beyond something, usually horizontally; *the balcony juts out over the main street*

Kk

kaolin *noun* white powder, the natural form of aluminium silicate or china clay

COMMENT: kaolin is used internally in liquid form in mixtures with morphine and other substances to treat traveller's diarrhoea

karaoke *noun* entertainment, coming originally from Japan, where people sing to recorded music; **karaoke bar** = bar which has a karaoke machine; **karaoke machine** = machine which plays the music of well-known songs, and displays the words on a screen so that people can sing along; **karaoke night** = night at a pub or club, when people can use the karaoke machine

kebab *noun* dish of pieces of meat, fish or vegetables stuck on a skewer and cooked over a charcoal grill; *a lamb kebab; a pork kebab;* **doner kebab** = Turkish meat dish, where a large piece of meat is cooked on a spit in front of a grill, and slices are cut off and served with pitta bread and salad, usually as a takeaway; **shish kebab** = kebab made of lamb, with peppers, onions and tomatoes, cooked on a skewer over a charcoal grill

kedgeree *noun* spicy mixture of rice, fish, curry and eggs (traditionally eaten at breakfast)

keeper *noun* person who looks after something; **(zoo) keeper** = person who looks after animals in a zoo (each keeper has a special name: 'elephant keeper', 'lion keeper', etc.); **park keeper** = keeper who looks after a park (especially a town park)

keg *noun* small barrel, especially an aluminium barrel in which beer is stored with gas mixed in with it; **keg beer** = beer which is stored in a keg and served from a pressurized pump

kernel *noun* softer edible part inside a nut

ketchup *noun* tomato sauce, usually available in cafés, etc. in bottles or sachets; *hamburgers with ketchup; I know someone who likes ketchup on his omelettes*

kettle *noun* **(a)** metal or plastic container, with a lid and a spout, used for boiling water; *each bedroom has a kettle, tea bags and packets of instant coffee* **(b)** large container used in a kitchen for boiling soup, stew, etc.; **fish kettle** = long metal container for cooking a whole fish

key *noun* **(a)** piece of metal used to open a lock; **front door key** = key to a front door such as the main door of a hotel; **room key** = key to a room, such as a bedroom in a hotel; **key card** = (i) card given to a guest on registration, which shows the number of his room and which he may need to show for identification purposes; (ii) electronic card given to a guest at registration, which acts as a key to his room; *see also* CARD; **key rack** = board with hooks or a series of pigeonholes where room keys are put near the front desk of a hotel; **key money** = premium paid when taking over the keys of a flat or office which you are renting **(b)** part of a computer *or* typewriter which you press with your fingers; *there are sixty-four keys on the keyboard;* **control key** = key on a computer which works part of a program; **shift key** = key which makes a typewriter *or* computer move to capital letters or another function

kg = KILOGRAM

kidney *noun* **(a)** one of a pair of organs in animals that extract impurities from the blood **(b)** this organ used as food; *grilled kidneys with bacon;* **kidney bean** = type of bean with reddish seeds shaped like a kidney

COMMENT: lamb kidney, ox kidney and pig's kidneys are all used in cooking; they can be cooked in a red wine sauce, or used in kebabs. The best-known English dishes using kidneys are steak and kidney pie or pudding

Kiev *noun* chicken **Kiev** = boned chicken, filled with garlic and butter, which is coated in breadcrumbs and deep-fried

kilo *or* **kilogram** *or* **kilogramme (kg)** *noun* measure of weight (= one thousand grams); *she bought a kilo of tomatoes; you need two kilos of potatoes to serve six people* (NOTE: usually written **kg** after figures: **4kg)**

◊ **kilometre** *or* *US* **kilometer (km)** *noun* measure of length (= one thousand metres); **the car does fifteen kilometres to the litre** = the car uses a litre of petrol to travel fifteen kilometres (NOTE: usually written **km** after figures: **25km)**

king prawn *noun* type of very large prawn, the type which is served as scampi

king size bed *noun* double bed which is wider and longer than normal

kiosk *noun* small wooden shelter, for selling goods out of doors; *a newspaper kiosk;* **telephone kiosk** = shelter with a public telephone in it

kipper *noun* smoked herring, which has been opened up and is flat
◊ **kippered** *adjective* smoked (fish)

COMMENT: kippers are usually cooked by grilling and may be served for breakfast

kir *noun* drink of cold white wine, served with a dash of crème de cassis (blackcurrant liqueur); **kir royal** = similar drink made with sparkling white wine

kit *noun* clothes and personal equipment, usually packed for travelling; **first-aid kit** = box with bandages and dressings kept ready to be used in an emergency; **sewing kit** = small wallet with needle, thread, etc., which can be used for making repairs to clothing in an emergency (as for sewing on a button) (often supplied in a hotel room); **repair kit** = kit for repairing a machine, especially a kit for repairing a car; *there is a repair kit provided in the boot of each car*

kitchen *noun* room in which food is prepared before serving; *the inspector found cockroaches in the hotel kitchens;* **kitchen clerk** = aboyeur, the person in the kitchen who shouts the order from the waiter to the chefs, and pins the waiter's written order on a hook relating to the particular table (called 'aboyeur' because he barks out the orders); **kitchen hand** = person who does general work in a kitchen; **kitchen porter** = person who carries things about in a kitchen

COMMENT: the kitchen of a large restaurant will be organized in brigades: the chef (or chef de cuisine) is in charge of all sections of the kitchen; various sections (each under a chef de partie) include sauces, vegetables, pastries, etc. A clerk (the 'aboyeur') takes orders from the waiters and shouts them out to the various sections. Kitchen staff will also include assistants (or commis chefs), porters, plate washers (plongeurs), etc.

kitchenette *noun* small kitchen (in a corner of a living room); *each studio flat is equipped with a bathroom, kitchenette and balcony*

kite mark *noun GB* mark on goods to show that they meet official standards

kiwi fruit *noun* subtropical woody climbing plant *(Actinidia chinensis)* which bears brownish oval fruit with a green juicy flesh; the plant was developed in New Zealand, and is now grown in many subtropical regions including southern Europe; also called 'Chinese gooseberry'

Kleenex *noun* trademark for a paper handkerchief; *there is a box of Kleenex in the bathroom* (NOTE: there is a plural form **Kleenexes** which is used when referring to several handkerchiefs, but the word **Kleenex** can also be used as the plural form: **a box of Kleenex)**

km = KILOMETRE

knead *verb* to press and fold (dough) before it is cooked to make bread; *pizza dough must be kneaded for five minutes*

knife *noun* implement with a sharp blade, used for cutting and spreading; **bread knife** = (i) large knife with a serrated edge like a saw, used for cutting slices of bread from a loaf; (ii) small knife put on the bread plate, used for spreading butter on pieces of bread and cutting them; **fish knife** = knife with a blunt wide blade, ending in a point, used with a fish fork for eating fish; **steak knife** = very sharp knife, or knife with a serrated blade, used for eating meat, mainly steak (NOTE: plural is **knives)**

COMMENT: All chefs say that their knives (each one owns a set of several knives, which he takes with him from job to job) are the most important part of their equipment. The best knives are forged (i.e. the blade, bolster, and centre part of the handle are made from one piece of metal). A good knife needs to balance easily and so has to have a heavy handle: the tang is the central metal part of the handle, to which wooden or plastic grips are attached with rivets. The tang is the part which gives the weight to the handle

knot *noun* unit of measurement of speed of ships, aircraft, water currents or wind (equivalent to 1.85 km per hour); *the ship was travelling at 23 knots; wind speed of 60 knots*

knowledge *noun* what is known; *(informal)* **the Knowledge** = knowing the road map and street plan of London, which taxi drivers have to know by heart, and on which they are tested before getting their licence

knuckle *noun* joint on the leg of an animal (when used as food)

kosher *adjective* (food) prepared according to Jewish law; *there's a kosher restaurant on 21st Street*

krona *noun* currency used in Sweden and Iceland

krone *noun* currency used in Denmark and Norway

Ll

l = LITRE

label 1 *noun* **(a)** piece of paper *or* card attached to something to show its price, an address or instructions for use, etc; **gummed label** = label which you wet to make it stick on the item; **self-sticking label** *or* **sticky label** label which is ready to stick on an item; **tie-on label** = label with a piece of string attached so that it can be tied on to an item **(b) address label** = label with an address on it; **baggage label** *or* **luggage label** = label attached to a piece of baggage, with the owner's name and address on it; **price label** = label showing a price; **quality label** = label stating the quality of something; *see* OWN LABEL **2** *verb* to attach a label to (something); *all hand baggage must be labelled;* **incorrectly labelled parcel** = parcel with the wrong information on the label
NOTE: GB English: **labelling - labelled** but US English: **labeling - labeled**

COMMENT: government regulations cover the labelling of food; it should show not only the price and weight, but also where it comes from, the quality grade, the ingredients, listing the main ingredient first, and a sell-by date

labour *or* US **labor** *noun* **(a)** work, especially heavy work; **to charge for** materials and labour = to charge for both the materials used in a job and also the hours of work involved; **labour costs** *or* **labour charges** = cost of the workers employed to make a product or provide a service (not including materials or overheads); **labour is charged at £5 an hour** = each hour of work costs £5 **(b)** workers *or* the workforce; **casual labour** = workers who are hired for a short period; **local labour** = workers recruited near a business, not brought in from somewhere else; **organized labour** = workers who are members of trade unions; **skilled labour** = workers who have special knowledge or qualifications; **labour shortage** *or* **shortage of labour** = situation where there are not enough workers to fill jobs **(c) labour dispute** = argument between management and workers; **labour laws** *or* **labour legislation** = laws concerning the employment of workers; **labour relations** = relations between management and workers; *US* **labor union** = organization which represents workers who are its members in discussions with management about wages and conditions of work (NOTE: UK English is **trade union**)

◊ **Labour Day** American national holiday celebrated on the first Monday in September

◊ **labour-intensive industry** *noun* industry which needs large numbers of workers *or* where labour costs are high in relation to turnover

◇ **labour-saving** *adjective* which saves you doing hard work; *a labour-saving device*

ladle 1 *noun* spoon with a large bowl, used for serving soup **2** *verb* to serve with a ladle; *he ladled the soup into the plates*

lady *noun* **(a)** *(polite way of referring to a woman)* *could you show this lady to her table, please? there are two ladies waiting for you in reception* **(b)** *(informal)* 'ladies' (toilet) = public toilet for women; *can you tell me where the ladies or the ladies' toilet is? the ladies is down the corridor on the right* (NOTE: 'ladies' is singular and takes a singular verb)

◇ **lady's finger** *noun* okra, a vegetable *(Hibiscus esculentus)* with a green pod used in soups

COMMENT: also called 'bhindi' or 'gumbo'. Used in Caribbean and Indian cooking; also used in the south of the USA

lager *noun* German type of beer, which is pale yellow in colour, highly carbonated, and relatively sweet

COMMENT: lager is served cold, and usually from a pressurized metal keg. It is also available in bottles and cans

lagoon *noun* area of sea water almost completely surrounded by land, especially by a coral island

lake *noun* (large) inland stretch of fresh water; *the hotel stands on the shores of Lake Constance*

◇ **lakeside** *adjective* on the shores of a lake; *a lakeside villa*

lamb *noun* meat from a sheep, especially from a young sheep; *roast leg of lamb; lamb kebabs; lamb chops*

COMMENT: strictly speaking, meat from an older sheep is called 'mutton', but this term is rarely used. The commonest forms of lamb in British cooking are lamb chops or roast lamb; traditionally, lamb is served with mint sauce

lamp *noun* electric device which produces light; **bedside lamp** = lamp next to a bed; **standard lamp** = lamp in a room on a tall pole; **table lamp** = lamp on a table; *I had to call room service because the bedside lamp isn't working*

◇ **lampshade** *noun* (decorative) cover over a light

land *verb* **(a)** to put (goods *or* passengers) on to land after a voyage by sea *or* by air; *to land goods at a port; to land passengers at an airport* **(b)** to come down to earth after a flight; *the plane landed ten minutes late*

◇ **landing** *noun* **landing card** = (i) card given to passengers to fill in before passing through immigration and passport control; (ii) card given to passengers who have passed customs and can land from a ship; **landing charges** = payment made to a government for the right to put goods on land and for any customs duties payable on the goods; **landing fees** = payment made to an airport for landing there (airlines usually include the fee in the ticket price); **landing rights** = right of an airline to land its aircraft

◇ **landlady** *noun* **(a)** woman who owns a property which is let **(b)** woman who runs a public house or hotel

◇ **landlord** *noun* **(a)** person *or* company which owns a property which is let **(b)** man who runs a public house or hotel

◇ **landscape** *noun* scenery and appearance of the countryside; **landscape gardening** = making a garden more beautiful by making artificial lakes, hills, planting trees, etc.

◇ **landslide** *noun* slipping of large amounts of earth, etc. down a hillside; *after the rains, landslides buried several houses*

landau *noun* wide horse-drawn carriage with a top which can be lowered, often used for taking tourists on trips round old towns

lane *noun* **(a)** narrow road, often in the country **(b)** way for traffic, usually in a particular direction; **inside lane** *or* **slow lane** = track nearest the side of the road, used by slower-moving vehicles, or by vehicles planning to turn off the road; **middle lane** = track in the centre of a three-lane carriageway; **outside lane** *or* **fast lane** = track nearest the centre of a road, used by the fastest-moving vehicles; **four-lane motorway** = motorway with tracks for two rows of traffic in each direction; **bus lane** = part of a road where only buses may drive; **shipping lanes** = routes followed by ships

langlauf *German noun* cross-country skiing

langoustine *noun* very large prawn

language *noun* words spoken or written by people in a certain country; *the guidebook to the museum is written in three languages: English, German and Japanese*

laptop (computer) *noun* small computer which can be held on the knees when sitting

lard 1 *noun* rendered pig fat used in cooking **2** *verb* to cover (meat) with bacon, lard or other fat before cooking in the oven ◊ **lardy cake** *noun* type of bread, made with fat and covered with sticky sugar

larder *noun* room or cupboard for storing food; **larder chef** *or* **chef garde-manger** = chef in charge of cold dishes, salads and salad sauces, sandwiches, and who cuts meat and fish ready for cooking in the kitchen

larva *noun* stage (caterpillar *or* grub) in the development of an insect, after the egg has hatched but before the animal becomes adult (NOTE: plural is **larvae**) ◊ **larval** *adjective* referring to larvae; **larval stage** = early stage in the development of an insect after it has hatched from an egg

lasagne *or* **lasagna** *noun* flat sheets of pasta, arranged in layers in a dish, often with meat, sauce and cheese, and baked in the oven

last-minute *adjective* very very late; *tour operators are offering tours at half price or half-price tours to people making last-minute bookings*

late 1 *adjective* **(a)** after the time stated or agreed; **late arrival** = (i) arrival of a plane *or* train after the scheduled time; (ii) guest who arrives at a hotel after the time when he was expected or after the date for which he had booked; *we apologize for the late arrival of the plane from Amsterdam; most of the tour party arrived on time, but there were two late arrivals who were delayed in traffic;* **late booking** = booking after the final date allowed; **late cancellation** = cancellation of a booking made after the normal time limit **(b)** at the end of a period of time; **latest date for purchase of APEX tickets** = the last acceptable date for buying APEX tickets (usually, 21 days before the date of departure) **(c) the latest** = most recent; *he always drives the latest model of car; here are the latest figures for passengers carried; the latest snow reports are published each day in the papers* **2** *adverb* after the time stated or agreed; *the train arrived late, and we missed*

the connection to Paris; the plane was two hours late

◊ **latecomer** *noun* person who arrives after others *or* after the appointed time

◊ **late-night** *adjective* happening late at night; *he had a late-night meeting at the airport; there is a late-night bus which leaves at 23.45;* **late-night opening** = opening of a shop until late in the evening; **late-night shopping** = shopping in the late evening, with shops opening much later than usual (i.e. up to 10 p.m.)

latitude *noun* position on the earth's surface measured in degrees north *or* south of the equator

COMMENT: together with longitude, latitude is used to indicate an exact position on the earth's surface. Latitude is measured in degrees, minutes and seconds. The centre of London is latitude 51°30'N, longitude 0°5'W. The lines of latitude are numbered and some of them act as national boundaries: the 49th parallel marks most of the border between the USA and Canada

launch 1 *verb* **(a)** to put (a new boat) into the water for the first time **(b)** to put (a new product) on the market (usually spending money on advertising it); *they launched their new winter sports catalogue; the company is spending thousands of pounds to launch a new travel service* **2** *noun* act of putting a new product on the market; *the launch of the new caravan model has been put back three months; the company is geared up for the launch of the new package holiday; the management has decided on a September launch date* ◊ **launching** *noun* act of putting a new product on the market; **launching costs** = costs of publicity for a new product; **launching date** = date when a new product is officially shown to the public for the first time; **launching party** = party held to advertise the launching of a new product

laundry *noun* **(a)** room *or* building where clothes are washed; *the hotel's sheets and towels are sent to the laundry every day* (NOTE: plural in this meaning is **laundries**) **(b)** dirty clothes to be sent for washing; *please put any laundry into the bag provided and leave it at the desk on your hotel floor;* **laundry bag** = special bag in a hotel room, into which you can put dirty clothes to be taken to be washed; **laundry list** = printed form provided with a laundry bag, giving a list of items of clothing which you may want to have washed (the guest ticks the items, and puts the list in the laundry bag with the dirty clothes); **laundry service =** service in a hotel which takes away dirty clothing and returns it washed and ironed; **laundry staff =** staff who run the laundry service; *see also* DRY-CLEANING, VALET SERVICE

◊ **launder** *verb* to wash (clothes, sheets, etc.); *he asked to have two shirts laundered*

◊ **laund(e)rette** *US* **laundromat** *noun* shop with coin-operated washing machines for public use

◊ **laundress** *noun* woman who washes clothes, sheets, etc. for other people

lavatory *noun* **(a)** room with a toilet, usually with a flushing bowl for getting rid of waste matter from the body; *the lavatories are situated at the rear of the plane; there is a gentlemen's lavatory on the ground floor* **(b)** bowl with a seat and a flushing system, for getting rid of waste matter from the body

laver (bread) *noun* seaweed, used as food, in Wales (eaten at breakfast); *see also* SEAWEED

law *noun* **(a) laws =** rules by which a country is governed and the activities of people and organizations controlled; **labour laws =** laws concerning the employment of workers **(b) law =** all the laws of a country taken together; **civil law =** laws relating to arguments between individuals and the rights of individuals; **commercial law =** laws regarding business; **company law =** laws which refer to the way companies work; **contract law** *or* **the law of contract =** laws relating to private agreements; **international law =** laws referring to the way countries deal with each other; **maritime law** *or* **the law of the sea =** laws referring to ships, ports, etc.; **inside the law** *or* **within the law =** obeying the laws of a country; **against the law** *or* **outside the law =** not according to the laws of a country; *the company is operating outside the law;* **to break the law =** to do something which is not allowed by law; *he is breaking the law by selling goods on Sunday; you will be breaking the law if you try to take that computer out of the country without an export licence* **(c)** general rule; **law of diminishing returns =** general rule that as more factors of production (land, labour and capital) are added to the

existing factors, so the amount they produce is proportionately smaller

lay *verb* **to lay the table =** to get a table ready for guests (putting out cutlery, glasses, napkins, etc.); *the table was laid for six people, so when only five guests arrived the waiter removed one of the settings;* **laid-up table =** table which has been prepared ready for the guests

QUOTE the meal was served course by course on laid-up tables (the tray appears only for the hot entrée) and the bar service was more than generous
Business Traveller

layby *noun* place at the side of a road where vehicles can park

◊ **layover** *noun US* staying for a short time in a place on a long journey (NOTE: GB English is **stopover)**

lazy Susan *noun* revolving tray, placed in the centre of a dining table to hold condiments, extra dishes, hors d'oeuvres, etc.

lb = POUND

L/C = LETTER OF CREDIT

leaflet *noun* sheet of paper giving information about something *or* used to advertise something; *to mail leaflets or to hand out leaflets describing services; they carried out a leaflet mailing to 20,000 addresses*

lean 1 *adjective* **lean meat =** meat with very little fat; *animals are bred to produce lean meat; venison is a very lean form of meat* **2** *noun* meat with little fat

lease 1 *noun* written contract for letting or renting a building *or* a piece of land *or* a piece of equipment for a period against payment of a fee; **long lease =** lease which runs for fifty years or more; **short lease =** lease which runs for up to two or three years; *to take hotel premises on a long lease; we have a short lease on our current premises; to rent office space on a twenty-year lease;* **full repairing lease =** lease where the tenant has to pay for all repairs to the property; **the lease expires** *or* **runs out in 1999 =** the lease comes to an end in 1999; **on expiration of the lease =** when the lease comes to an end **2** *verb* **(a)** to let or rent a building *or* a piece of land *or* a piece of equipment for a period; *to lease offices to* *small firms; to lease equipment* (b) to use a building *or* a piece of land *or* a piece of equipment for a period and pay a fee; *to lease hotel premises from an insurance company; all our fax machines are leased; all the airline's aircraft are leased*

◊ **leasehold** *noun, adjective & adverb* holding property on a lease; *the company has some valuable leaseholds; leasehold property; to buy a property leasehold*

◊ **leaseholder** *noun* person who holds property on a lease

◊ **leasing** *noun* (a) letting or renting a building *or* a piece of land *or* a piece of equipment for a period; *an aircraft leasing company* (b) using a building *or* a piece of land *or* a piece of equipment for a period and paying a fee; *to run a copier under a leasing agreement*

leave 1 *noun* permission to be away from work; **six weeks' annual leave** = six weeks' holiday each year **2** *verb* to go away from; *he left his hotel early to go to the airport; the next plane leaves at 10.20*
NOTE: **leaving - left**

◊ **leave out** *verb* not to include; *she left out the date on the cheque; the brochure leaves out all details of travelling arrangements from the airport to the hotel*

lectern *noun* stand with a sloping surface on which you can put a book or papers, etc., from which you are going to read aloud in public; *the conference room is equipped with a lectern*

lecture *noun* talk, especially to students or any group of people, on a particular subject; **lecture tour** = tour with lectures on the places or buildings visited, paintings or other objects seen, etc.; *the museum has a programme of lecture tours on 20th-century art; the group went on a lecture tour of sites in Greece*

leek *noun* vegetable related to the onion, with white stem and long green leaves

lee *noun* sheltered side (of a hill, ship, etc.); *the house in the lee of the hill*

◊ **leeward** *adjective & adverb* on *or* to the sheltered side (of a ship) (i.e. not the side on which the wind is blowing); *compare* WINDWARD

left *adjective* opposite of right; *the flight destinations run down the left side of the page; they put the subtotals in the left*

column, and the final figure is at the bottom of the right-hand column; see also LEAVE (NOTE: on ships and aircraft, the left side is called the **port side**)

◊ **left-hand** *adjective* belonging to the left side; *the subtotals are in the left-hand column of the bill; he keeps the personnel files in the left-hand drawer of his desk*

◊ **left luggage office** *noun* room at a railway station, coach station, ferry terminal or airport where suitcases, bags and parcels can be left (NOTE: US English is **baggage room**)

◊ **leftovers** *plural noun* what is not used, especially food which has not been eaten

leg *noun* (a) part of the body with which you walk; **leg room** = amount of space available for the legs of a person sitting down (as between the rows of seats in a cinema or aircraft, or inside a car) (b) part of the body of an animal on which the animal walks; *a chicken leg;* **leg of lamb** = leg of a sheep, considered as food; *a slice of roast leg of lamb* (c) stage (of a journey); *the last leg of the trip goes from Paris to the final destination, Amsterdam*

◊ **legroom** *noun see* LEG ROOM

QUOTE virtually every airline's Boeing 747 will seat passengers ten abreast (3-4-3) with a tight 31-33 inches of legroom
Business Traveller

legionnaires' disease *noun* bacterial disease similar to pneumonia

COMMENT: the disease is thought to be transmitted in droplets of moisture in the air, and so the bacterium is found in central air-conditioning systems. It can be fatal to old or sick people, and so is especially dangerous if present in a hospital

Leishmania *noun* tropical parasite which is passed to humans by the bites of sandflies; hence people camping in the desert are potentially at risk

◊ **leishmaniasis** *noun* any of several diseases caused by the parasite *Leishmania*

leisure *noun* free time to do what you want; **at your leisure** = when there is an opportunity *or* without hurry; **leisure facilities** = facilities for enjoying oneself, such as a swimming pool, putting green, cinema, etc.; **leisure industry** = companies which provide goods and services used during people's leisure time (such as holidays, cinema, theatre, amusement parks, etc.); **leisure pursuits** = hobbies, things you do during your free time, for relaxation or enjoyment; **leisure customer** *or* **leisure traveller** = person who is going on holiday and is not travelling on business

◊ **leisurely** *adjective* without hurrying; *the group toured the museum at a leisurely pace; we enjoyed a leisurely lunch before going round the Prado*

QUOTE when hiring a car in Europe for three days or more, never overlook the so-called 'holiday rate' in the belief that it is intended for leisure customers only
Business Traveller

lemon *noun* yellow edible fruit of an evergreen citrus tree *(Citrus limon);* lemons have a very tart flavour and are used in flavouring and in making drinks; *a gin and tonic with a slice of lemon in it; she ordered a lemon sorbet;* **lemon curd** = preserve made with eggs and lemons, used to spread on bread; **lemon grass** = green lemon-flavoured herb, used especially in Thai cooking; **lemon squash** = drink made of concentrated lemon juice and water; **lemon tea** = black tea, served in a glass with a slice of lemon and sugar (without the lemon it is called 'Russian tea')

◊ **lemonade** *noun* **(a)** drink made from fresh lemon juice, sugar and water **(b)** ready-made fizzy drink, flavoured with lemon (also used to mix with beer to make shandy)

◊ **lemon-squeezer** *noun* device for pressing slices of lemon, to make the juice run out

length *noun* being long; **a stay of some length** = quite a long stay; **length of stay** = number of days a guest stays in a hotel

lentil *noun* small round dried yellow seed of *Lens esculenta,* used as food (especially in soups and stews)

let 1 *verb* to lend a house *or* an office *or* a farm to someone for a period against payment of a fee; **to let a cottage** = to allow someone to use a cottage for a period against payment of rent; **holiday flats to let** = furnished flats which are available to be leased by people on holiday (NOTE: **letting - let) 2** *noun* period of the lease of a property; *they took the house on a short let*

◊ **let-out clause** *noun* section in a contract which allows someone to avoid doing something in the contract; *he added a let-out clause to the effect that the payments would be revised if the exchange rate fell by more than 5%*

◊ **letting** *noun* **letting agency** = office which deals in property to let; **furnished lettings** = furnished property to let

letter *noun* **(a)** piece of writing sent from one person *or* company to another to ask for or to give information; **circular letter** = letter sent to many people; **covering letter** = letter sent with documents to say why they are being sent; **letter of acknowledgement** = letter which says that something has been received; **letter of application** = letter in which someone applies for a job; **letter of appointment** = letter in which someone is appointed to a job; **letter of complaint** = letter in which someone complains; **letter of reference** = letter in which a former employer recommends someone for a new job **(b) air letter** = special thin blue paper which when folded can be sent by air without an envelope; **registered letter** = letter which is noted by the post office before it is sent, so that compensation can be claimed if it is lost **(c) to acknowledge receipt by letter** = to write a letter to say that something has been received **(e)** written or printed sign (such as A, B, C, etc.); *write your name and address in block letters or in capital letters*

◊ **letter box** *noun* **(a)** public box into which mail is put to be collected and delivered **(b)** place where incoming mail is put

◊ **letterhead** *noun* name and address of a company printed at the top of a piece of notepaper

◊ **letter of credit (L/C)** *noun* document issued by a bank on behalf of a customer authorizing payment to a supplier when the conditions specified in the document are met (this is a common method of guaranteeing payment by overseas customers)

lettuce *noun* green salad plant

COMMENT: the commonest varieties of lettuce in Europe have relatively soft green leaves: round lettuces, or tall cos lettuces are the commonest in the UK. Lettuces are not always green: Italian varieties, such as 'lollo rosso', have red leaves. In the USA, 'iceberg' lettuces, with stiff crunchy leaves, are preferred

levy 1 *noun* money which is demanded and collected by the government; **import levy =** tax on imports, especially in the EC a tax on imports of farm produce from outside the EC; **levies on luxury items =** taxes on luxury items (NOTE: plural is **levies**) **2** *verb* to demand payment of (a tax *or* an extra payment) and to collect it; *the government has decided to levy a tax on imported cars; to levy a duty on the import of luxury items;* to levy members for a new club house = to ask members of the club to pay for the new building

QUOTE royalties have been levied at a rate of 12.5% of full production
Lloyd's List

library *noun* (a) place where books are stored (to be read or borrowed or consulted) (b) collection of books; *passengers can use the ship's library; the hotel has an excellent library of romantic novels*

licence *or* US **license** *noun* official document which allows someone to do something; *US* **license plate =** plate on a car, with its number (NOTE British English for this is **number plate) driving licence** *or* US **driver's license =** permit which allows you to drive; *applicants should hold a valid driving licence;* **export licence** *or* **import licence =** document which allows goods to be exported or imported; **liquor licence =** government document allowing someone to sell alcohol; *GB* **off-licence =** (i) licence to sell alcohol to be drunk away from the place where it is bought; (ii) shop which sells alcohol for drinking away from the shop

◊ **license 1** *noun* US = LICENCE **2** *verb* to give (someone) official permission to do something; *the store is licensed to sell beers, wines and spirits; the club is licensed for music;* **licensed hotel** *or* **licensed restaurant =** hotel *or* restaurant which has a licence to sell alcohol

◊ **licensee** *noun* person who has a licence, especially a licence to sell alcohol

◊ **licensing** *noun* which refers to licences; *a licensing agreement; licensing laws; GB* **licensing hours =** hours of the day when alcohol can be sold

COMMENT: in England and Scotland, pubs and bars can serve alcohol throughout the day, from 10.30 to 11 p.m., though not all are open as long as this; some only open for the full day on Fridays and Saturdays. Hotels can serve drinks to residents at any time. In the USA and Canada, local districts can vote to allow the sale of alcohol, and some vote to ban it altogether (these are said to be 'dry')

lichee = LITCHI

lie *verb* to be in a position; *the town lies at the end of the valley*

lifeboat *noun* boat used to rescue passengers from sinking ships
◊ **life belt** *or* **life buoy** *noun* ring which can float, used to throw to someone who has fallen into water
◊ **lifeguard** *noun* person who is on duty on a beach or at a swimming pool, and who rescues people who get into difficulty in the water
◊ **life jacket** *noun* (i) jacket with blocks of light material which allows it to float, provided for sailors and passengers on boats; (ii) jacket which can be inflated, provided by airlines for each passenger
◊ **life raft** *noun* construction which can float, carried by a ship, and used to carry passengers if the ship sinks

lift 1 *noun* (a) machine which takes people or goods from one floor to another in a building; *he took the lift to the 27th floor; the guests could not get to their rooms when the lift broke down;* **lift attendant** *or* **liftboy** *or* **liftman =** person (usually a young man) who operates a lift (NOTE: US English is **elevator**) *see also* CHAIRLIFT, SKI LIFT **(b) to give someone a lift =** to allow a pedestrian to ride in your car or lorry; *do you want a lift?; several people stopped to offer us lifts;* to **hitch a lift =** to ask a car driver or truck driver to take you as a passenger, usually by signalling with the thumb or by holding a sign with your destination written on it; *he hitched a lift with a long-distance truck* **2** *verb* (a) to go away; *the fog had lifted by lunchtime* (b) to take away *or* to remove; *the government has lifted the ban on imports from Japan;* to **lift trade barriers;** *the minister has lifted the embargo on the export of computers to East European countries*

light 1 *adjective* not heavy; *you need light clothing for tropical countries; he only has a light holdall with him* (NOTE: **light - lighter - lightest**) **2** *noun* (a) brightness, the opposite of darkness; **candlelight =** light given out by a candle; **moonlight =** light given out by the moon; **sunlight =** light given out by the sun; *see also* DAYLIGHT **(b)**

electric bulb which gives light; *a bedside light; there is an overhead light in the bathroom;* **night light** = weak electric light which gives a faint light and is used to light passages, stairs or a child's room at night; **strip light** = light made in the form of a tube; **(traffic) lights** = red, amber and green lights on a pole by a road, telling traffic when to stop or go; *turn left at the next set of lights*

◊ **lighthouse** *noun* tall building on a coast containing a light to guide ships

◊ **lighting-up time** *noun* time at which street lamps and car lights have to be switched on

◊ **light pen** *noun* pen with a tip which is sensitive to light, and which can 'read' lines or images and transfer them to a computer, used to read bar codes on products

◊ **lightship** *noun* ship which carries a large light to guide ships, acting as a floating lighthouse

lime *noun* **(a)** *Citrus aurantifolia,* a citrus fruit tree, with green fruit similar to, but smaller than, a lemon; **lime juice** = (i) juice of a lime; (ii) concentrated drink which tastes of lime; **gin and lime** = drink made with gin, lime juice and ice cubes **(b)** northern deciduous tree *(Tilia europea)* with smooth leaves and yellowish flowers; **lime tea** = drink made from the dried flowers of the lime tree

◊ **limeade** *noun* fizzy drink flavoured with lime

limo *noun (informal)* = LIMOUSINE; **stretch limo** = luxurious hire car, which is much longer than the normal models, used to carry important passengers

limousine *noun* large luxurious car; **limousine transfer to hotel** = transfer of passengers from an airport to their hotel in a limousine, provided free by the hotel or airline

line *noun* **(a)** long mark (on paper); *paper with thin blue lines; I prefer notepaper without any lines; he drew a thick line across the bottom of the column to show which figure was the total* **(b)** **airline** = company which carries passengers or cargo by air; *profits of major airlines have been affected by the rise in fuel prices;* **shipping line** = company which owns ships **(c)** **line of product** *or* **product line** = series of different products which form a group, all made by the same company; *we do not stock that line; computers are not one of our best-selling*

lines; *they produce an interesting line in garden tools* **(d)** row of letters *or* figures on a page; **bottom line** = last line in accounts, showing the net profit **(e)** **telephone line** = wire along which telephone messages travel; **the line is bad** = it is difficult to hear clearly what someone is saying; **a crossed line** = when two telephone conversations get mixed; **the line is engaged** = the person is already speaking on the phone; **the chairman is on the other line** = the chairman is speaking on his second telephone; **outside line** = line from an internal office telephone system to the main telephone exchange **(f)** *US* row of people, cars, etc. waiting one behind the other; **to stand in line** = to wait in a line with other people (NOTE: GB English is **queue**) **(g)** **(railway) line** = metal rails on which trains run; *please cross the line by the footbridge; a new line is being built between London and the Kent coast; the Waterloo line is closed for repairs*

◊ **lined** *adjective* **(a)** (paper) with lines on it; *a pad of A4 lined paper* **(b)** **lined with trees** *or* **tree-lined** = with trees along both sides; *the tree-lined avenues of Phnom Penh*

linen *noun* **(a)** cloth made from flax; *he was wearing a linen jacket* **(b)** (household) **linen** = sheets, pillowcases, tablecloths, etc.; **bed linen** = sheets, pillowcases, etc.; **room linen** = sheets, towels, etc., for use in a hotel bedroom; **table linen** = tablecloths, napkins, etc., for use on a table; **linen cupboard** = cupboard for keeping linen; **linen keeper** = person who is in charge of the linen in a hotel, and makes sure it is clean and ready for use when needed; **linen room** = room where clean linen is kept

liner *noun* **(a)** large passenger ship **(b)** dish on which another dish is placed containing food ready for serving

link 1 *noun* something which joins; **airlink** = link between two places, using planes or helicopters; **telephone link** = direct line from one telephone to another **2** *verb* to join *or* to attach to something else; *his salary is linked to the cost of living; to link bonus payments to productivity; all rooms are linked to the main switchboard*

linoleic acid *noun* one of the essential fatty acids which cannot be synthesized and has to be taken into the body from food (such as vegetable oil)

liqueur *noun* strong sweet alcohol, made from fruit or herbs; *raspberry liqueur;*

liqueur chocolate *or* **chocolate liqueur** = small chocolate containing a liqueur

COMMENT: liqueurs are served after a meal as a digestif. The most popular are Bénédictine, Chartreuse, Cointreau, Drambuie, Grand Marnier, Kirschwasser, Sambucca, Tia Maria

liquid 1 *noun* substance which flows easily like water, and which is neither a gas nor a solid **2** *adjective* **(a)** which is neither gas nor solid, and which flows easily; *in the desert you must take plenty of liquids to avoid dehydration* **(b)** **liquid assets** = cash, or bills which can easily be changed into cash

◊ **liquidity** *noun* having cash or assets which can be changed into cash; **liquidity crisis** = not having enough liquid assets

◊ **liquidize** *verb* to reduce fruit *or* vegetables, etc. to liquid

◊ **liquidizer** *noun* machine which liquidizes

liquor *noun* **(a)** alcohol; **liquor licence** = government document allowing someone to sell alcohol **(b)** liquid produced in cooking

lira *noun* currency used in Italy; *the book cost 2,700 lira or L2,700* (NOTE: usually written **L** when used with a figure: **L2,700)**

list 1 *noun* **(a)** several items written one after the other; *to add an item to a list; to cross an item off a list;* **address list** *or* **mailing list** = list of names and addresses of people and companies; **black list** = list of goods *or* people *or* companies which have been banned; **shopping list** = list of things which you need to buy **(b)** catalogue; **price list** = sheet giving prices of goods for sale **2** *verb* to write several items one after the other; *to list products by category; to list representatives by area; the guidebook lists twenty-five cheap hotels in the Bournemouth area*

◊ **listed building** *noun GB* building which is considered important because of its architecture or associations, and which cannot be demolished or altered without the consent of the local authority

Listeria *noun* bacteria found in some prepared foods and in domestic animals, which can cause infections such as meningitis

COMMENT: listeria can be present in ready-prepared meals which are reheated; it also occurs in cooked meats and ready-made salads. Listeria is killed by heating to at least 70°C

litchi *or* **lichee** *or* **lychee** *noun* subtropical fruit *(Litchi chinensis)* a native of China; it produces fruit with a hard red skin and a soft white juicy pulp surrounding a hard shiny brown seed

literature *noun* written information about something; *please send me literature about your tours to Italy*

litre *or US* **liter** *noun* measure of liquids; *the car does fifteen kilometres to the litre or fifteen kilometres per litre* = the car uses one litre of petrol to travel fifteen kilometres (NOTE: usually written **l** after figures: **25l**)

litter *noun* rubbish left on streets

◊ **litterbasket** *noun* special basket for rubbish

◊ **litterbin** *noun* special metal container for rubbish

live 1 *adjective* carrying an electric current; *do not touch the live wires* **2** *verb* to have your place of residence; *they live in the centre of Paris; where do you live?*

◊ **live in** *verb* to live in the building where you work; *most of the restaurant staff live in*

◊ **live-in** *adjective* (person) who lives in the building where he works; *we have six live-in staff;* **live-in doctor** = doctor who lives in a hotel and is employed by the hotel to treat guests who become ill

◊ **lively** *adjective* very active *or* very full of life; *it's the liveliest nightspot in town*

◊ **live off** *verb* to earn money from; *the whole population of the village lives off tourism*

◊ **living** *noun* means of subsistence; *he earns his living from selling postcards to tourists*

◊ **living room** *noun* room in a house for general use

liver *noun* (i) organ in the body which helps the digestion by producing bile; (ii) an animal's liver used as food; **calf's liver** *or* **lamb's liver** *or* **ox liver** *or* **pig's liver** = liver from a calf *or* a lamb *or* an ox *or* a pig; **chopped livers** = Jewish dish, made of cooked chicken livers, chopped up into small pieces; **liver pâté** = cooked paste made from livers of animals; *chicken-liver pâté*

COMMENT: the traditional English way of eating liver is fried with bacon and onions

load 1 *noun* goods which are transported; **load of a truck** *or* **of a container** = goods carried by a truck or container; **commercial load** = amount of goods *or* number of passengers which a bus *or* train *or* plane has to carry to make a profit; **maximum load** = largest weight of goods which a lorry *or* aircraft can carry; **load-carrying capacity** = amount of goods which a truck is capable of carrying; **load factor** = number of seats in a bus *or* a train *or* an aircraft which are occupied by passengers who have paid the full fare **2** *verb* **(a) to load a truck** *or* **a ship** = to put goods into a truck *or* a ship for transporting; *to load cargo onto a ship; a truck loaded with boxes; a ship loaded with iron;* **fully loaded ship** = ship which is full of cargo **(b)** *(of ship, aircraft)* to take on cargo; *the ferry will start loading in 15 minutes*
◊ **loading** *noun* **loading dock** = part of a harbour where ships can load or unload; **loading ramp** = raised platform which makes it easier to load goods onto a truck

loaf *noun* large single piece of bread, which is cut into slices before being eaten; **sliced loaf** = loaf of bread which has already been sliced mechanically before it is sold (NOTE: plural is **loaves)**

loan 1 *noun* money which has been lent; **bank loan** = money lent by a bank; **bridging loan** = short-term loan to help someone buy a new house when he has not yet sold his old one; **government loan** = money lent by the government; **short-term loan** *or* **long-term loan** = loans which have to be repaid within a few weeks or some years; **unsecured loan** = loan made with no security; **interest on a loan** = interest which the borrower has to pay on the money he has borrowed **2** *verb* to lend; *the furniture has been loaned by the museum*

lobby *noun* main entrance hall of a hotel, large restaurant, theatre, etc.

lobster *noun* shellfish with a long body, two large claws, and eight legs, used as food; **lobster bisque** = thick rich soup made with lobster; **lobster chowder** = milk soup made with lobster

COMMENT: lobster can be served cold (with mayonnaise, as 'lobster salad'), and in this case the customer is provided

with a pick and a pair of crackers to break the shell. Lobster is also served hot without its shell, for example as 'lobster Newburg' or cooked and served in its open shell as, for example, 'lobster Thermidor'

local 1 *adjective* referring to a particular area, especially one near a hotel *or* restaurant *or* office; **local authority** = elected section of government which runs a small area of the country, such as a town or county; **local call** = telephone call to a number in the same area as the person making the call; **local time** = time of day in a particular area; *it will be 1 a.m. local time when we land* **2** *noun* GB *(informal)* nearest pub to where someone lives; *he took us all to his local for lunch*
◊ **locally** *adverb* in the area near a hotel *or* restaurant *or* office; *we recruit all our restaurant staff locally*

QUOTE each cheque can be made out for the local equivalent of £100 rounded up to a convenient figure
Sunday Times
QUOTE EC regulations insist that customers can buy cars anywhere in the EC at the local pre-tax price
Financial Times

locate *verb* **to be located** = to be in a certain place; *the hotel is conveniently located near the motorway*
◊ **location** *noun* place where something is; *the hotel is in a very central location;* **the restaurant has moved to a new location** = the restaurant has moved to new premises

lock 1 *noun* **(a)** device for closing a door *or* box so that it can be opened only with a key; *the lock is broken on the safe; he left his room key in the lock; I have forgotten the combination of the lock on my briefcase; we changed the locks on the doors after a set of keys were stolen* **(b)** section of a canal or river with barriers which can be opened or closed to control the flow of water, so allowing boats to move up or down to different levels **2** *verb* to close (a door) with a key, so that it cannot be opened; *the manager forgot to lock the door of the reception office; the petty cash box was not locked*
◊ **locker** *noun* small cupboard for personal belongings which you can close with a key; *luggage lockers can be rented at the airport; you will need a 20p coin for the lockers at the swimming pool*

◇ **lock-up** *adjective* **lock-up shop** *or* **premises** = shop which has no living accommodation and which the proprietor locks at night when it is closed; **lock-up garage** = garage attached to a hotel, which is locked at night

lodge 1 *noun* **(a)** small house in the country used for parties of hunters, ramblers, etc. **(b)** type of motel, especially one where buildings are made of wood, and are (or appear to be) simple and rustic **2** *verb* to rent a room (in a boarding house) ◇ **lodger** *noun* person who rents a room ◇ **lodging** *noun* **(a)** accommodation **(b)** **lodgings** = rented rooms

loganberry *noun* soft red fruit, a cross between a blackberry and a raspberry

loggia *noun (in southern Europe)* covered gallery which is open on one side

logo *noun* symbol *or* design *or* group of letters used by a company as a distinctive mark on its products and in advertising; *the hotel group uses a small pine tree as its logo*

loin *noun* cut of meat, taken between the neck and the leg; *a loin of pork*

lollo rosso *see* LETTUCE

long *adjective* for a large period of time; *the hot season is very long;* **in the long term** = over a long period of time; **long drink** = (i) drink with a lot of liquid, such as a drink of spirits (gin, whisky, etc.) to which soda water, tonic water, fruit juice, etc. is added; (ii) drink of beer, cider, shandy, diluted fruit juice, etc. ◇ **long-distance** *adjective* **long-distance call** = telephone call to a number which is in a different zone or area; **long-distance flight** = flight to a destination which is a long way away; **long-distance (foot)path** = path laid out by an official organization, which goes for a very long way (over 100 miles); **long-distance skiing** = skiing for long distances following marked tracks across country; **long-distance ski trail** = marked path for skiers over a long distance ◇ **long-haul** *adjective* (flight) which is over a large distance, especially between continents ◇ **long-stay** *adjective* referring to a stay of weeks or months; **long-stay car park** = car park at an airport for travellers who will leave their cars there for a long time (several days or weeks); **long-stay guest** *or*

visitor = person who stays in a hotel for some weeks or months, rather than just a few days; *compare* SHORT-STAY ◇ **long-term** *adjective* for a long period of time; *a long-term project like building a new tunnel through the Alps*

longitude *noun* position on the earth's surface measured in degrees east *or* west

COMMENT: longitude is measured from Greenwich (a town in England, just east of London) and, together with latitude, is used to indicate an exact position on the earth's surface. Longitude is measured in degrees, minutes and seconds. The centre of London is latitude 51°30'N, longitude 0°5'W

loo *noun (informal)* toilet; *where's the loo? she's gone to the loo; he's in the loo* (NOTE: this is the term which is used most often in the UK)

loose *adjective* not packed or packaged together; **loose change** = money in coins; **loose tea** = tea which is not in teabags; **to sell loose sweets** *or* **to sell sweets loose** = to sell sweets in small quantities which are separately weighed, not in packets

lorry *noun GB* large vehicle used to transport goods; **lorry driver** = person who drives a lorry (NOTE: also called **truck**)

lose *verb* **(a)** not to have something any more; **to lose customers** = to have fewer customers; *their service is so slow that they have been losing customers* **(b)** to have less; **the pound has lost value** = the pound is worth less; **to lose weight** = to become thinner; *she spent a week at a health farm trying to lose weight* **(c)** to drop to a lower price; *the dollar lost two cents against the yen* **(d)** **to lose your way** = to get lost, to be unable to find the way to where you were going
NOTE: **losing - lost** ◇ **lost** *adjective* (something *or* someone) which cannot be found; **lost property** = personal belongings which have been lost by their owners; **lost property office** *or US* **lost and found office** = office which collects objects which people have left behind and keeps them until the owners claim them; **railway lost property office** = office which collects objects which people have left behind in trains and keeps them until their owners collect them; **to get lost** = to lose your way, to be unable to find the way to

where you were going; *they got lost in the fog and mountain rescue teams had to be sent out to find them*

loss *noun* having less money than before *or* not making a profit; **the company suffered a loss** = the company did not make a profit; **trading loss** = situation where the company's receipts are less than its expenditure; **at a loss** = making a loss *or* not making any profit; *the company is trading at a loss; he sold the shop at a loss;* **to cut one's losses** = to stop doing something which was losing money

lounge *noun* comfortable room in a hotel, cruise liner, etc.; **residents' lounge** = room in a hotel which is only open to residents of the hotel and their guests (often morning coffee and afternoon tea are served in this lounge); **departure lounge** = room in an airport where passengers wait to get on their planes after going through passport control and baggage check; **transit lounge** = room in an airport where passengers wait for connecting flights

◇ **lounge bar** *noun* bar in a pub or hotel which is more comfortable than the public bar, and where the drinks may be slightly more expensive

QUOTE British Airways is to open a £1.6 million lounge at Heathrow for arriving passengers. The lounge, which is claimed to be the first of its kind in the world, will enable passengers to freshen up after an overnight intercontinental flight with a shower while a valet irons their clothes
Times
QUOTE business passengers departing Heathrow Terminal 3 with hand luggage only, can avoid the queues and hurry straight through to the airline's new airside lounge to check in
Business Traveller

low *adjective* small *or* not high; *low overhead costs keep the room price low; we try to keep our wages bill low; by restricting the choice of dishes, the restaurant can keep its prices lower than those of the competition; the pound is at a very low rate of exchange against the dollar; our aim is to buy at the lowest price possible;* **low sales** = small amount of money produced by sales; **low volume of sales** = small number of items sold (NOTE: **low - lower - lowest**)

◇ **low-alcohol** *adjective* (drink) containing very little alcohol; *I'm driving, so I'll have a low-alcohol lager*

◇ **low-calorie** *adjective* (food or drink) containing very few calories *or* fewer calories than normal; *she's on a low-calorie diet*

◇ **low-cost** *adjective* cheap; *low-cost travel*

◇ **low-fat** *adjective* (food or drink) containing very little fat; *do you have any low-fat yoghurt?*

◇ **low-grade** *see* GRADE

◇ **low season** *noun* time of year (often during the winter) when there are fewer travellers, and so fares and room prices are cheaper; *tour operators urge more people to travel in the low season; air fares are cheaper in the low season*

luge *noun* sledge for downhill competition racing, on which two or more people lie on their backs, with their feet going first

luggage *noun* suitcases or bags for carrying clothes when travelling; **hand luggage** *or* **cabin luggage** = small bags and cases which passengers can take with them into the cabin of a plane or ship; **(free) luggage allowance** = weight of luggage which an air passenger is allowed to take free when he travels; **luggage claim** = place in an airport where luggage comes off the plane onto a carousel to be claimed by the passengers; **luggage lift** = special lift for taking guests' luggage up to different floors of a hotel; **luggage lockers** = series of small cupboards in an airport, railway station, etc., where passengers can leave luggage locked away safely; **luggage rack** = device above the seats in a train for holding luggage; **luggage stand** = special low bench for holding luggage in a hotel room; **luggage trolley** = trolley at an airport, railway station, ferry terminal, etc. on which passengers can put their luggage (NOTE: no plural; to show one suitcase, etc., you can say **a piece of luggage**. Note also that American English uses **baggage** more often than **luggage**)

lukewarm *adjective* slightly warm, not hot enough; *the bath water is only lukewarm; we sent back the coffee because it was lukewarm*

lunch *noun* meal eaten in the middle of the day; *the hours of work are from 9.30 to 5.30 with an hour off for lunch; the chairman is out at lunch; the restaurant serves 150 lunches a day; take your seats for the first sitting for lunch;* **business lunch** = meeting where people have lunch together to discuss business matters; **packed lunch** = cold food, such as sandwiches, fruit, etc., packed in a box or basket for eating when travelling; *the party took packed lunches went they set off on their walk in the mountains; we will ask the hotel to prepare packed lunches for us tomorrow*

◊ **luncheon** *noun (formal)* lunch; *luncheon is served in the small dining room from 12.30 to 2 p.m.;* **luncheon club** = group of people who meet regularly to eat lunch together and listen to someone make a speech after the meal; **luncheon meat** = tinned meat loaf containing mostly minced pork (NOTE: the word **luncheon** is usually used in formal menus)

◊ **luncheon voucher** *noun* ticket given by an employer to a worker in addition to his wages, which can be exchanged for food in a restaurant

◊ **lunch hour** *or* **lunchtime** *noun* time when people have lunch; *the office is closed during the lunch hour or at lunchtimes; a series of lunchtime concerts in the public gardens*

luscious *adjective* (fruit) which is sweet and juicy

luxury *noun* expensive thing which is not necessary but which is good to have; *luxury items or luxury goods; a black market in luxury articles;* **luxury hotel** = five-star hotel, a very good hotel, with luxurious rooms and higher prices; **luxury suite** = series of extremely comfortable rooms in a hotel, apartment block or on a ship

◊ **luxurious** *adjective* very comfortable; *the guest rooms have been refurnished with luxurious carpets and fittings*

lychee = LITCHI

Lyme disease *noun* viral disease transmitted by bites from deer ticks *(Borrelia burgdorferi).* It causes rashes, nervous pains, paralysis and, in extreme cases, death. The ticks are common in forests in the USA and Europe

lyophilize *verb* to freeze-dry (food), a method of preserving food by freezing it rapidly and drying in a vacuum

Mm

m = METRE, MILE, MILLION

macaroni *noun* short thick tubes of pasta, often served with a cheese sauce

macaroon *noun* small sweet almond biscuit

mackerel *noun* sea fish with dark flesh, eaten grilled or smoked; also used for canning

maggot *noun* soft-bodied, legless larva of a fly, such as a bluebottle, warble fly or frit fly

maid *noun* (i) girl or woman who helps in the house, especially doing cleaning and serving at meals; (ii) chambermaid *or* room maid, girl or woman who cleans rooms in a hotel; **maid service** = cleaning service for a rented house or flat, provided by a maid, paid for by the landlord of the property

maiden name *noun* surname of a woman before she married

◊ **maiden flight** *or* **maiden voyage** *noun* first flight by an aircraft *or* first voyage by a ship; *the 'Titanic' sank on her maiden voyage across the Atlantic in 1912*

mail 1 *noun* **(a)** system of sending letters and parcels from one place to another; *to put a letter in the mail; the cheque was lost in the mail; the invoice was put in the mail yesterday; mail to some of the islands in the Pacific can take six weeks;* **by mail** = using the postal services, not sending something by hand or by messenger; **air mail** = way of sending letters *or* parcels by air; *to send a package by air mail; air-mail charges have risen by 15%; to receive a sample by air mail;* **to send a package by surface mail** = to send a package by land or sea, not by air; **by sea mail** = sent by post abroad, using a ship; **we sent the order by first-class mail** = by the most expensive mail service, designed to be faster **(b)** letters sent or received; *has the mail arrived yet? your cheque arrived in* *yesterday's mail; my secretary opens my mail as soon as it arrives; the receipt was in this morning's mail;* incoming mail = mail which comes into an office; outgoing mail = mail which is sent out 2 *verb* to send something by post; *to mail a letter confirming the booking; we mailed our confirmation last Wednesday*

◊ mailbox *noun US* = LETTERBOX

main *adjective* most important; *main post office; main dining room; main lounge; main bar;* main door *or* main entrance = most important door *or* entrance to a hotel; main road *or* main thoroughfare = important road, used by a lot of traffic; *the hotel is noisy as it stands at the crossing of two main roads; US* Main Street = most important street in a town, where the shops and banks are (NOTE: in British English, this is **High Street**)

◊ main course *or* main dish *noun* largest and most important part of a meal (in a three-course meal, this would be the meat or fish dish)

maintain *verb* (a) to keep something going *or* working; *to maintain good relations with one's customers; to maintain contact with an couriers overseas by phone* (b) to keep something working at the same level; *the restaurant has maintained the same volume of business in spite of the recession*

◊ maintenance *noun* (a) keeping things going *or* working; *maintenance of contacts; maintenance of supplies* (b) keeping a machine in good working order; maintenance contract = contract by which a company keeps a piece of equipment in good working order; *we offer a full maintenance service;* maintenance staff = people employed to keep something in good working condition

maître d'hôtel *US* maître d' [metrə'diː] *noun* head waiter, the person in charge of a restaurant, who is responsible for all the service and takes orders himself from customers; maître d'hôtel de carré = station head waiter, a chief waiter who is in charge of a station, and takes the orders from customers (in the USA, this is the 'captain')

maize *noun* widely grown cereal crop *(Zea mays)* (NOTE: in US English called **corn**)

COMMENT: in Europe only a small proportion of the crop is sold for human consumption as 'corn on the cob'. Maize is the only grain crop which was introduced from the New World into the Old World, and it owes its name of Indian corn to the fact that it was cultivated by American Indians before the arrival of European settlers. It is the principal crop grown in the United States; in Mexico it is the principal food of the people, being coarsely ground into flour from which tortillas are made

make *verb* (a) to prepare; to do; to make the beds = to tidy the beds after they have been slept in (b) to make a call = to use the telephone; to make a deposit = to pay money as a deposit; to make a payment = to pay; to make a reservation = to book a room *or* seat *or* table, etc.

◊ make up *verb* to make up a room = to prepare a room in a hotel for the next guest, by cleaning it, putting clean sheets and pillowcases on the bed, putting fresh towels, shampoo, soap, etc. in the bathroom; to make up the beds = to put clean sheets, pillowcases, etc. on beds

◊ makeup *noun* room makeup = preparing a room in a hotel for the next guest, by cleaning it, putting clean sheets and pillowcases on the bed, putting fresh towels, shampoo, soap, etc. in the bathroom

malaria *noun* paludism, tropical disease caused by a parasite *Plasmodium* which enters the body after a bite from the female anopheles mosquito

COMMENT: malaria is a recurrent disease which produces regular periods of shivering, vomiting, sweating and headaches as the parasites develop in the body; the patient also develops anaemia. Malaria can be treated with Chloroquine, although some types of malaria are resistant to the drug. Such cases are treated with quinine. Prevention of malaria is not 100% certain, but travellers to Africa, the Middle East, India, the Far East and Central and South America should take a course of drugs before, during and after their trip

◊ malarious *adjective* (region) where malaria is endemic

mall *noun US* shopping mall = enclosed covered area for shopping, with shops, restaurants, banks and other facilities

malt *noun* (a) grain which has been prepared for making beer or whisky by being allowed to sprout and then dried; **malt (whisky)** = whisky made from barley which has been allowed to sprout and then dried **(b)** *US* = MALTED MILK

◊ **malted** *adjective* tasting of malt; **malted milk** = (i) dried milk powder, flavoured with malt; (ii) drink made by adding fresh milk to this powder

manage *verb* **(a)** to direct *or* to be in charge of; *she manages a restaurant; he manages one of our chain of hotels* **(b)** to manage **property** = to look after rented property for the owner **(c) to manage to** = to be able to do something; *did you manage to catch the train? she managed to confirm six flight bookings and take three phone calls all in two minutes*

◊ **management** *noun* **(a)** directing *or* running *or* being in charge of a business; *to study management; good management or efficient management; bad management or inefficient management; a management graduate or a graduate in management;* **line management** = organization of a business where each manager is responsible for doing what his superior tells him to do; **management committee** = committee which manages a club, block of flats, pension fund, etc.; **management consultant** = person who gives advice on how to manage a business; **management contract** = contract with a person or group of people to run a hotel, restaurant, etc., for a fee which is fixed in advance for a certain period of time; **management course** = training course for managers; **management by objectives** = way of managing a business by planning work for the managers and testing to see if it is completed correctly and on time; **management team** = group of managers working together; **management techniques** = ways of managing a business; **management trainee** = person being trained to be a manager; **management training** = training staff to be managers by making them study problems and work out ways of solving them **(b)** group of managers or directors; *the management has decided to give an overall pay increase;* **top management** = main directors of a company; **middle management** = department managers of a company who carry out the policy set by the directors and organize the work of a group of workers

◊ **manager** *noun* **(a)** head of a department in a company; *a department manager; personnel manager; production manager; sales manager; purchasing manager;* **area manager** = manager who is responsible for

the company's work (usually sales) in an area; *he is area manager for a brewing company;* **general manager** = manager who is in charge of the administration of a whole establishment **(b)** person in charge of a hotel *or* inn *or* branch *or* shop, etc.; *Mr Smith is the manager of our local pub; the manager of our New York hotel is in London for a series of meetings;* **branch manager** = person in charge of a branch of a company; **conference sales manager** = person in charge of organizing conferences held in a hotel; **reservations manager** = person in charge of the reservations department

◊ **manageress** *noun* woman in charge of a shop, department, etc.

◊ **managerial** *adjective* referring to managers; *managerial staff;* **to be appointed to a managerial position** = to be appointed a manager

mandatory meeting *noun* meeting which everyone has to attend

mango *noun* tropical tree *(Mangifera indica)* and the fruit it produces; the fruit is large, yellow or yellowish-green, with a soft orange pulp surrounding the very large flat seed; **mango chutney** *or* **mango pickle** = spicy chutney *or* pickle made from mangoes (NOTE: plural is **mangoes)**

mangosteen *noun* tree *(Garcinia mangostana)* which is native of Malaysia, but which is now cultivated in the West Indies; the fruit has a dark shiny rind and a soft sweet white flesh

Manhattan *noun* cocktail of rye whisky, Italian vermouth and angostura bitters

manifest *noun* list of goods, cargo, or passengers; **passenger manifest** = list of passengers on a ship or plane

manpower *noun* number of workers; **manpower planning** = planning to obtain the right number of workers in each job; **manpower requirements** = number of workers needed; **manpower shortage** *or* **shortage of manpower** = lack of workers

manufacturer's recommended price (MRP) *noun* price which a manufacturer suggests the product should be sold at on the retail market, though often reduced by the retailer; *'all portable computers - 20% off MRP'*

map *noun* diagram of a town or country as if seen from above; *the hotel has maps of the*

map 152 **market**

centre of the town; do you have any maps of the region? I'll draw you a map of the town, otherwise you can easily get lost; **physical map** = diagram showing mountains, rivers, etc.; **road map** = map showing the main roads in a country; **street map** *or* **town map** = diagram showing the streets of a town with their names

maraschino *noun* cherry preserved in liqueur, used to decorate a drink, etc.

Mardi Gras *noun* festival at the beginning of Lent (in English, 'Shrove Tuesday') celebrated in many Catholic countries with elaborate festivals

margarine *noun* mixture of animal or vegetable fat which is used instead of butter

marge *noun (informal)* = MARGARINE

margin *noun* difference between the money received when selling a product and the money paid for it; **gross margin** = percentage difference between the received price and the unit manufacturing cost or purchase price of goods for resale; **net margin** = percentage difference between received price and all costs, including overheads

◊ **marginal** *adjective* **marginal cost** = cost of making a single extra unit above the number already planned; **marginal costing** = costing a product on the basis of its variable costs only, excluding fixed costs; **marginal pricing** = basing the selling price of a product on its variable costs of production plus a margin, but excluding fixed costs

marina *noun* arrangement of a harbour with floating jetties where a large number of pleasure boats can be tied up

marinade 1 *noun* mixture of wine and herbs, etc., in which meat or fish is soaked before cooking **2** *verb* to soak (meat or fish) in a mixture of wine and herbs, etc.
◊ **marinate** *verb* = MARINADE

marital *adjective* referring to marriage; **marital status** = state of being married, single, divorced, widowed, etc.

marjoram *noun* herb *(Origanum)* used in Mediterranean cooking, especially pizzas

mark 1 *noun* **(a)** sign put on an item to show something; *GB* **kite mark** = mark on

goods to show that they meet official standards **(b)** currency used in Germany; *the price is twenty-five marks; the mark rose against the dollar* (NOTE: when used with a figure, usually written **DM** before the figure: **DM25.** Also called **Deutschmark, D-Mark**) **2** *verb* to put a sign on something; *to mark a product 'for export only'; article marked at £1.50; to mark the price on something*

◊ **mark down** *verb* to reduce the price of something; **to mark down a price** = to reduce the price of something; *the holiday package has been marked down to £224; we have marked all prices down by 30% for the sale*

◊ **mark-down** *noun* **(a)** reduction of the price of something **(b)** percentage amount by which a price is lowered; *we have used a 30% mark-down to fix the sale price*

◊ **mark up** *verb* to increase the price of something; **to mark a price up** = to increase a price; *these prices have been marked up by 10%*

◊ **mark-up** *noun* **(a)** increase in the price of something; *we put into effect a 10% mark-up of all prices in June* **(b)** amount added to the cost price to give the selling price; **we work to a 3.5 times mark-up** *or* **to a 350% mark-up** = we take the unit cost and multiply by 3.5 to give the selling price

market 1 *noun* **(a)** place (often in the open air) where farm produce is sold; *fish market; flower market; open-air market;* **antiques market** = series of shops or stalls under one roof where antiques are sold; **covered market** = market which is not in the open air, but with stalls or small shops in a special building; **flea market** = market, usually in the open air, selling cheap second-hand goods; **street market** = market held in a street, with stalls along both sides of the roadway; **market day** = day when a market is regularly held; *Tuesday is market day, so the streets are closed to traffic;* **market dues** = rent for a stall in a market **(b)** **the Common Market** = the European Economic Community; *the Common Market agricultural policy or the Common Market ministers* **(c)** possible sales of a certain type of product *or* demand for a certain type of product; *the market for fly-drive holidays has risen sharply; we have 20% of the British caravan market; there is no market for expensive package tours in November;* **a growth market** = area where sales are going to increase **(d)** **the black market** = buying and selling goods in a way which is not allowed by law (as in a time of rationing); *there is a flourishing black* which is not allowed by law (as in a time of rationing); *there is a flourishing black market in spare parts for cars;* **to pay black-market prices** = to pay high prices to get items which are not easily available **(e) market forces** = influences on the sales of a product; **market leader** = company with the largest market share; *we are the market leader in self-catering packages to Spain;* **market opportunities** = possibility of finding new sales in a market; **market penetration** *or* **market share** = percentage of a total market which the sales of a company cover; *we hope our new product range will increase our market share;* **market research** = examining the possible sales of a product before it is put on the market; **market survey** = general report on the state of a market; **market trends** = gradual changes taking place in a market **(f) up market** *or* **down market** = more expensive *or* less expensive; **to go up market** *or* **to go down market** = to make products which appeal to a wealthy section of the market *or* to a wider, less wealthy, section of the market **2** *verb* to sell (products); *this product is being marketed in all European countries*

◊ **marketing** *noun* techniques used in selling a product (such as packaging, advertising, etc.); **marketing department** = department in a company which specializes in ways of selling a product; **marketing manager** = person in charge of a marketing department; **marketing mix** = combination of elements that make up marketing, that is price, distribution and advertising

marmalade *noun* jam made of oranges, or other citrus fruit such as lemon or grapefruit; **Seville orange marmalade** = marmalade made with bitter oranges

> COMMENT: marmalade is eaten with toast at breakfast, and not at any other time of day

marquee *noun* very large tent, used for wedding receptions, prize-givings, etc.

marrow *noun* vegetable of the melon family, producing very large fruit

> COMMENT: usually marrows are picked when very small; at this stage they are called 'courgettes' or 'zucchini'

marsala *noun* sweet Italian wine

martini *noun* drink made of gin or vodka and dry or sweet vermouth; **dry martini** = cocktail of gin and French vermouth, served with an olive

marzipan *noun* paste made from ground almonds, sugar and egg, used to cover a fruit cake before icing or to make individual little sweets

mash 1 *noun (informal)* mashed potatoes; *a plate of sausage and mash or bangers and mash* **2** *verb* to crush food to a soft paste; **mashed potatoes** = potatoes which have been peeled, boiled and then crushed with butter and milk until they form a soft cream

mass *noun* **(a)** large group of people; **mass marketing** = marketing which aims at reaching large numbers of people; **mass media** = means of communicating information to the public (such as television, radio, newspapers); **mass tourism** = tourism involving large numbers of people **(b)** large number of things; *we have a mass of letters or masses of letters to write; they received a mass of inquiries or masses of inquiries after the TV commercials*

massage 1 *noun* rubbing of the body to relieve pain or to improve circulation, etc.; *she went to the sauna for a massage and a bath;* **massage parlour** = establishment where men are given massage (usually a cover for prostitution) **2** *verb* to rub (someone's body) to relieve pain or to improve circulation

◊ **masseur** *noun* man who massages

◊ **masseuse** *noun* woman who massages

master *adjective* controlling; **master bedroom** = main bedroom; **master key** = main key which opens all doors in a building; **master switch** = switch which controls all other switches

mat *noun* small piece of carpet or woven straw, etc. used as a floor covering; **bath mat** = small carpet to step on to as you get out of a bath; *see also* TABLE MAT

Maximum Permitted Mileage (MPM) *noun* distance calculated according to the IATA mileage allowance for a direct flight between two towns; a passenger paying full fare is allowed to stop over a certain number of times depending on the total mileage travelled, so on a flight from London to Istanbul, you might stop over in Paris and Frankfurt

Mayday *noun* SOS, the international signal to show that you are in distress; **the aircraft captain put out a Mayday =** he radioed a message to air traffic control to say the aircraft was in danger

mayonnaise *noun* sauce for cold dishes, made of oil, eggs and lemon juice or vinegar

COMMENT: mayonnaise is served with cold boiled eggs (oeufs mayonnaise), with cold lobster (lobster mayonnaise), and other cold dishes; it is also used as a base for other sauces, such as tartare sauce, Thousand Island dressing, etc.

mead *noun* alcoholic drink made from honey

meal *noun* **(a)** food eaten at a particular time of day; *full board includes three meals: breakfast, lunch and dinner; you can have your meals in your room at a small extra charge;* **meal service =** serving of meals on a plane; **meal time =** time when a meal is usually served; *meal times are shown on the noticeboard* **(b)** roughly ground flour; *see also* WHOLEMEAL

measure 1 *noun* **(a)** way of calculating size *or* quantity; **cubic measure =** volume in cubic feet or metres, calculated by multiplying height, width and length; **square measure =** area in square feet or metres, calculated by multiplying width and length **(b) made to measure =** made specially to fit; *he has his clothes made to measure* **(c) tape measure =** metal or plastic ribbon with centimetres or inches marked on it, used to measure how long something is **(d)** serving of alcohol or wine (when served by the glass); **short measure =** smaller amount than is legally allowed; **to give short measure =** to serve smaller quantities of alcohol than is allowed by law; *see also* WEIGHTS AND MEASURES **2** *verb* to find out the size *or* quantity of something; to be of a certain size *or* quantity; *to measure the size of a package; a package which measures 10cm by 25cm or a package measuring 10cm by 25cm;* **to be measured for a suit =** to have your measurements (arm length, chest, waist, etc.) taken by a tailor so that he can make you a suit

◊ **measurements** *plural noun* size (in inches, centimetres, etc.); *to take down a customer's measurements*

◊ **measuring tape** *noun* = TAPE MEASURE

meat *noun* food from an animal's body; **the meat course =** the main course in a meal, consisting of meat and vegetables; **meat extender =** any edible material or mixture added to meat preparations to increase their bulk; **meat loaf =** solid block of minced meat, vegetables, etc, cooked and usually served hot; **meat products =** pies, sausages, pâtés, etc., and other food made from meat

◊ **meatball** *noun* small ball of minced meat with flavourings; *meatballs in tomato sauce*

COMMENT: the names of different types of meat are different from the names of the animal from which it comes. Full-grown cows or bulls give 'beef'; calves give 'veal'; pigs give 'pork', or if salted, 'bacon' and 'ham'; sheep and lambs give 'lamb'; deer give 'venison'. Only the birds (chicken, duck, goose, and turkey), give meat with the same name). In menus, meat is often referred to by its French name: agneau (= lamb), boeuf (= beef), porc (= pork), jambon (= ham), etc.

media *noun* **the media** *or* **the mass media =** means of communicating information to the public (such as television, radio, newspapers); *the restaurant has attracted a lot of interest in the media or a lot of media interest;* **media coverage =** reports about something in the media; *we got good media coverage for the launch of the new tour guide* (NOTE: **media** is followed by a singular or plural verb)

medical *noun* referring to the study or treatment of illness; **medical certificate =** document signed by a doctor to show that a worker has been ill; **medical inspection =** examining a place of work to see if the conditions will not make the workers ill; **medical insurance =** insurance which pays the cost of medical treatment, especially when travelling abroad

medium-haul *adjective* (flight) which is longer than a short-haul flight, but not as long as an intercontinental flight

◊ **medium-term** *adjective* for a period of one or two years

meet *verb* **(a)** to come together with someone; *to meet a tour party at the airport; to meet an agent at his hotel; we're meeting our relatives at 2.00 at the main station* **(b)** to be satisfactory for; *to meet a customer's* *requirements;* **to meet the demand for a new service** = to provide a new service which has been asked for; **we will try to meet your price** = we will try to offer a price which is acceptable to you

◊ **meet with** *verb US* to come together with someone; **I hope to meet with him in New York** = I hope to meet him in New York

◊ **meeting** *noun* **(a)** coming together of a group of people; *management meeting; staff meeting;* **meeting point** = point at an airport or railway station where people can arrange to meet; **meetings room** = room where meetings can be held

Melba *noun* **(a) Melba toast** = toast made by toasting a slice of bread once, then slicing it in half and toasting it again quickly, so as to produce a sort of cracker **(b) Melba sauce** = raspberry sauce; **peach Melba** *or* **pear Melba** = dessert of sliced pears or peaches, with ice cream and raspberry sauce

COMMENT: named after the Australian opera singer, Dame Nellie Melba (1861-1931)

melon *noun* plant of the cucumber family *(Cucumis melo)* with a sweet fruit; the flesh of the fruit varies from green to orange or white; **water-melon** = plant of the genus *Citrullus vulgaris* with large green fruit with red flesh and black seeds; *see also* CANTALOUPE, CHARENTAIS, HONEYDEW, OGEN

COMMENT: melon may be served as a first course (sometimes with Parma ham), or as a dessert. The fruit can be cut into wedges or halves, with the seeds removed. The hole in a half melon can have port poured into it

member *noun* **(a)** person who belongs to a group *or* a society **(b)** organization which belongs to a group *or* a society; *the member countries of the EC; the member companies of ABTA*

men *plural noun* **men's toilet** *or especially US* **men's room** = public toilet for men (NOTE: also called **the gents)**

ménage *French noun (meaning 'housework')* the cleaning and preparing of a restaurant for guests

meningitis *noun* inflammation of the meninges, where the patient has violent headaches, fever, and stiff neck muscles, and can become delirious; **aseptic meningitis** = relatively mild viral form of meningitis

COMMENT: meningitis is a serious viral or bacterial disease which can cause brain damage and even death. The bacterial form can be treated with antibiotics

menu *noun* printed list of food available in a restaurant; *a breakfast menu; the menu changes every week; some special dishes are not on the menu, but are written on a special board; the dinner menu starts at £30 per person;* **menu card** = card placed on the table at a formal dinner, showing the dishes which will be served; **menu holder** = little metal or plastic holder for a menu on a table

COMMENT: the normal menu for a three-course meal (lunch or dinner) will consist of an hors d'oeuvre, starter or soup, followed by a main course of fish, meat or a vegetarian dish, then a dessert or cheese. More elaborate menus will have a fish or pasta course as well as a meat course, and a dessert as well as cheese. Note that in English menus, the dessert course comes before the cheese, while in French menus, the cheese comes before the dessert

merchandising *noun* organizing the display and promotion of goods for sale

meringue *noun* mixture of whipped egg white and caster sugar, dried slowly in the oven; **lemon meringue pie** = pastry filled with lemon-flavoured filling, topped with soft meringue

COMMENT: small individual meringues can be served with cream or fruit salad; meringue mixture can also be spread on top of a fruit pie before cooking

mess *noun* place where servicemen *or* policemen live and eat; **mess manager** = person in charge of catering, housekeeping, etc., in a mess

◊ **messing** *noun* arrangements for providing food, accommodation and leisure activities for servicemen

message *noun* piece of news which is sent to someone; *I will leave a message with the receptionist; can you give Mr Smith a* *message from his wife? he says he never received the message;* **message board** *or* **message rack** = special board or rack where messages are put

messenger *noun* person who brings a message; *he sent the package by special messenger or by motorcycle messenger*

meteorology *noun* science of studying the weather and the atmosphere

◇ **meteorological** *adjective* referring to meteorology *or* to the climate; **Meteorological Office** = central government office which analyses weather reports and forecasts the weather; **meteorological station** = research station which notes weather conditions

◇ **meteorologist** *noun* scientist who specializes in the study of the weather and the atmosphere

meter *noun* (a) device for counting how much of something has been used; **parking meter** = device into which you put money to pay for parking (b) *US* = METRE

method *noun* way of doing something; *what is the best method of payment? what method of payment do you prefer?;* **time and method study** = examining the way in which something is done to see if a cheaper or quicker way can be found

methylated spirits *or* **meths** *noun* alcohol, stained purple, used as fuel in small burners to keep food hot at table, or for cooking certain dishes at table

metre *or* *US* **meter** *noun* measure of length (= 3.4 feet) (NOTE: usually written **m** after figures: **the case is 2m wide by 3m long**)

◇ **metric** *adjective* using the metre as a basic measurement; **metric ton** *or* **metric tonne** = 1000 kilograms; **the metric system** = system of measuring, using metres, litres and grams

metro *noun* (a) *(in some countries)* underground railway system; *the Paris metro* (b) *US* metropolitan area, the area administered by a large town

◇ **metropolis** *noun* very large town

◇ **metropolitan** *adjective* referring to the whole of a large town; *metropolitan New York covers 200 square miles*

COMMENT: the Paris underground railway was called the 'métropolitain',

shortened to 'le métro' or 'the metro' in English, and this name is used in several other countries, including Newcastle in the UK and Brussels in Belgium. In Germany, underground railways are called 'U-Bahn'. The London underground railway is called the 'underground', or simply, the 'tube'. In North American, an underground railway is called a 'subway'

mezzanine *noun* floor between the ground floor and the first floor

mg = MILLIGRAM

mi = MILE

mice *see* MOUSE

microwave *or* **microwave oven 1** *noun* oven which heats by using very short-wave radiation; *put the pie in the microwave for two minutes to heat it up* **2** *verb (informal)* to heat (a dish) in a microwave; *the pie isn't very hot - can you microwave it a bit more?*

QUOTE among the 300 frequent travellers questioned, microwave ovens were cited as the single most important item in a hotel room

Caterer & Hotelkeeper

mid- *prefix* middle; **from mid-1992** = from the middle of 1992; *the hotel is closed until mid-July*

◇ **mid-month** *adjective* taking place in the middle of the month

◇ **midweek** *adjective & adverb* which happens in the middle of the week; *if you travel midweek, the fares are higher than if a Saturday night is included;* **midweek bargain break** = special holiday package in the middle of a week

mild 1 *noun* type of brown beer, which is less alcoholic and sweeter than 'bitter' **2** *adjective* (a) *(taste)* which is not sharp; *yoghurt-based sauces are milder;* (weather) which is not severe; *winters in the south of the country are usually milder than in the north*

mile *noun* measure of length (= 1.625 kilometres); **the car does twenty-five miles to the gallon** *or* **twenty-five miles per gallon** = the car uses one gallon of petrol to travel twenty-five miles (NOTE: usually written **m** after figures; miles per gallon is usually written **mpg** after figures: **the car does 25mpg)**

◊ **mileage** *noun* distance travelled in miles; **mileage allowance** = money paid per mile as expenses to someone who uses his own car for business travel; **unlimited mileage** = allowance with a hired car, where the driver is not charged for the number of miles covered

milk 1 *noun* white liquid produced by female mammals for feeding their young, especially the milk produced by cows; **milk bar** = bar which serves milk, other milk products such as ice cream, and non-alcoholic drinks; **milk chocolate** = pale brown chocolate made with milk; **milk products** = milk and other foodstuffs produced from it, which are sold for human consumption; the main milk products are liquid milk (homogenized, pasteurized, skimmed, sterilized or UHT), butter, cheese, cream, ice cream, condensed milk and milk powder; **milk shake** = milk mixed with flavouring and ice cream **2** *verb* to take the milk from (an animal)

millet *noun* grain used for food

milligram *or* **milligramme** *noun* one thousandth of a gram (NOTE: usually written **mg** after figures)

◊ **millilitre** *or* *US* **milliliter** *noun* one thousandth of a litre (NOTE: usually written **ml** after figures)

◊ **millimetre** *or* *US* **millimeter** *noun* one thousandth of a metre (NOTE: usually written **mm** after figures)

million *noun* number 1,000,000; *the company lost £10 million on the North American route; our turnover has risen to $13.4 million; the museum had over one million visitors in its first year* (NOTE: can be written **m** after figures: **$5m** (say 'five million dollars')

mince 1 *noun* meat (usually beef) which has been ground into very small pieces or into a paste; *she asked for a pound of mince* **2** *verb* to grind meat into very small pieces or into a paste; *a pound of minced beef or minced pork* (NOTE: US English for **minced beef** and **mince** is **ground beef)**

◊ **mincemeat** *noun* mixture of dried fruit, suet, nuts and spices, used to make pies at Christmas time

◊ **mince pie** *noun* small pie, filled with mincemeat, eaten at Christmas time, usually hot

mine host *see* HOST

mineral *noun* GB any sweet non-alcoholic drink of fizzy water and flavouring (NOTE: US English is **soda)**

◊ **mineral water** *noun* water which comes naturally from the ground and is sold in bottles

COMMENT: there are thousands of types of mineral water, each with different properties. From France, the commonest are Evian, Vichy, Perrier, Badoit, etc.; from Italy: San Pelligrino; from Belgium: Spa water, etc. British waters include Malvern, Ashbourne, Highland Spring

minestrone *noun* soup of Italian origin made of vegetables, beans, pasta and herbs, served with grated parmesan cheese

mini- *prefix* very small

◊ **minibar** *noun* small refrigerator in a hotel bedroom, with drinks in it (which are paid for on checking out of the hotel); **minibar key** = small key given to a guest with the room key, used to open a locked minibar

◊ **minibus** *noun* small bus, which carries approximately ten passengers (often used to take passengers from an airport to a hotel or vice versa)

◊ **minicab** *noun* small car, used as a taxi

◊ **minimarket** *noun* very small self-service store

mint *noun* common herb *(Mentha)* used in cooking as a flavouring, and to flavour commercially made sweets; **mint jelly** = jelly (made from apples) flavoured with mint, and served with lamb; *US* **mint julep** = alcoholic drink made from rye whiskey or brandy and sugar over crushed ice, garnished with leaves of mint; **mint sauce** = chopped mint mixed with vinegar and sugar, the traditional accompaniment in Britain to roast lamb

COMMENT: mint is widely used in British cooking to flavour vegetables, such as new potatoes or boiled peas. It is also used as a garnish for iced drinks. In Mediterranean cooking it is used in lamb dishes, such as keftedes.

mirror *noun* glass backed by metal which reflects an image; **bathroom mirror** = mirror in a bathroom; **full-length mirror** = mirror in which you can see a reflection of your whole body; **driving mirror** *or* **rear-view mirror** = mirror inside a car which enables the driver to see what is behind without turning his head

miscellaneous (charges) order *noun* voucher given by an airline which can be used to pay for meals or accommodation at the airline's expense

mise en place *French phrase (meaning 'putting in place')* (i) setting out chairs, tables, linen, etc., in a restaurant, ready for customers; (ii) preparing ovens, pans, etc., in a kitchen, ready to start cooking for the day; (iii) preparing the basic ingredients for sauces, chopping vegetables, etc. ready for cooking

Miss *noun* title given to a woman who is not married; *Miss Smith is our receptionist*

miss *verb* (a) not to catch (a bus, plane, train, etc.); *you will have to hurry if you don't want to miss the plane; he missed the bus and had to wait thirty minutes for the next one* (b) not to meet; *he missed the person he was supposed to meet by ten minutes* = he arrived ten minutes after the person left *or* he left ten minutes before the person arrived

mistake *noun* wrong action *or* wrong decision; **to make a mistake** = to do something wrong; *the shop made a mistake and sent the wrong items; there was a mistake in the address; she made a mistake in addressing the letter;* **by mistake** = in error *or* wrongly; *they sent the wrong items by mistake; she put my letter into an envelope for France by mistake*

misunderstanding *noun* lack of agreement *or* mistake; *there was a misunderstanding over my tickets*

mixed grill *see* GRILL

ml = MILLILITRE

mm = MILLIMETRE

mobile *adjective* which can move about; **mobile shop** = van fitted out like a small shop which travels round selling meat, fish, groceries or vegetables

◊ **mobile home** *noun* large caravan in which people can live permanently, which is permanently based in a special park (NOTE: US English is also **trailer**)

COMMENT: many 'mobile homes' are not mobile at all, but are firmly fixed in caravan parks

mode *noun* way of doing something; **mode of payment** = way in which payment is made (such as cash or cheque); *see also* A LA MODE

moderate *adjective* not very expensive; *the room rate is quite moderate in winter*

◊ **moderately priced** *adjective* (hotel *or* meal) which is not very expensive

molasses *noun US* thick dark-brown syrup produced when sugar is refined (NOTE: British English is **treacle**)

mollusc *noun* animal with a shell, such as an oyster or a snail

monastery *noun* group of buildings where monks live or lived

money *noun* (a) coins and notes used for buying and selling; **to earn money** = to have a salary; **to lose money** = to make a loss *or* not to make a profit; **the hotel has been losing money for months** = the hotel has been operating at a loss; **to get your money back** = to get a refund of money which you have paid out; **to make money** = to make a profit; **to put money down** = to pay cash, especially as a deposit; *he put £25 down and paid the rest in instalments;* **paper money** = money in notes, not coins; **ready money** = cash *or* money which is immediately available; **they are worth a lot of money** = they are valuable (b) **money order** = document which can be bought for sending money through the post; **foreign money order** *or* **international money order** *or* **overseas money order** = money order in a foreign currency which is payable to someone living in a foreign country

◊ **money belt** *noun* belt with a purse attached, which is worn round the waist to prevent theft

◊ **moneylender** *noun* person who lends money at interest

monkey nuts *plural noun* peanuts

monopoly *noun* situation where one person or company controls all the market in the supply of a product; *to have the monopoly of alcohol sales* or *to have the alcohol monopoly; the hotel is in a monopoly situation - it is the only hotel in town; the company has the absolute monopoly of imports of French wine*

monosodium glutamate (MSG) *noun* substance (E621) added to processed food to enhance the flavour, but causing a reaction in hypersensitive people; *see also* CHINESE RESTAURANT SYNDROME

monsoon *noun* **(a)** season of wind and rain in tropical countries **(b)** wind which blows in opposite directions according to the season, especially the wind blowing north from the Indian Ocean in the summer

Montezuma's revenge *noun (humorous)* diarrhoea which affects people travelling in foreign countries as a result of eating unwashed fruit or drinking water which has not been boiled (NOTE: also called **Delhi belly, gippy tummy, etc.)**

monument *noun* **(a)** stone or building or statue, etc., erected in memory of someone who is dead; **the Monument =** tall column put up in the City of London to commemorate the Great Fire of 1666 **(b)** building which is very old; **ancient monument =** very old building, especially one which belongs to the state and is open to visitors

moonlight *verb (informal)* to do a second job for cash (often in the evening) as well as a regular job
◊ **moonlighter** *noun* person who moonlights
◊ **moonlighting** *noun* doing a second job

morning *noun* period of the day from sunrise to 12.00 o'clock midday; *there are six flights to Frankfurt every morning; she took the morning train to Edinburgh;* **(early) morning call =** phone call or knock on the door to wake someone up in the morning; *he asked for an early morning call at 6.15;* **morning coffee =** coffee served with biscuits as a mid-morning snack; **morning dress** or **morning suit =** clothes for men consisting of a black tail coat, light grey waistcoat and striped black and grey trousers, worn by men at formal occasions such as weddings; **early morning tea =** tea brought to a guest's bedroom early in the morning, often with the day's newspaper and sometimes with letters

mosquito *noun* small flying insect which sucks blood; **mosquito net =** thin net spread over a bed to prevent mosquitoes biting at night; **mosquito repellant =** liquid which is sprayed or applied to the skin, to keep off mosquitoes (NOTE: plural is **mosquitoes)**

COMMENT: mosquitoes spread several tropical diseases, including malaria

motel *noun* hotel for car drivers, with special parking places near to the rooms

COMMENT: motels are found on main roads, and often on the outskirts of towns. They usually offer comfortable rooms, and sometimes have a small restaurant. Larger motels may have swimming pools and other facilities, but they are usually used for single-night stays

motion sickness *noun* sickness caused by the movement of a vehicle (car, aircrafts, etc.)

motor 1 *noun* car; **motor hotel =** hotel catering to travellers in cars (i.e., a motel); **motor insurance =** insuring a car, the driver and passengers in case of accident **2** *verb* to travel in a car (for pleasure); *we motored down to the coast*
◊ **motorcar** *noun* car
◊ **motor caravan** *noun* van with the back part made into a caravan, containing bunk beds, kitchen equipment, table, etc., in which people can drive around during the day and park to stay overnight
◊ **motor home** *noun* large very well-equipped motor caravan
◊ **motoring organization** *noun* organization which represents the interests of motorists, and provides services to motorists

COMMENT: motoring organizations provide breakdown services for their members, and many other services, such as insurance, travel information, etc. The main motoring organizations in the UK are the AA, the RAC, and the RSAC; in Germany, the ADAC; in the USA, the AAA

◊ **motor inn =** MOTEL
◊ **motorist** *noun* person who drives a car
◊ **motor lodge =** MOTEL
◊ **motorway** *noun* main road, with few entrances and exits, constructed for long-distance travel; **motorway service area**

(MSA) = facility next to a motorway, where drivers can buy petrol, shop, eat in a choice of restaurants, and in some cases, find hotel accommodation

COMMENT: called in various ways in different countries: in France: 'autoroute'; in Germany 'Autobahn'; in Italy: 'autostrada', etc. In the USA, the term 'motorway' is not used, and the roads are called 'thruway', 'expressway' or 'turnpike'

mould *or US* **mold 1** *noun* **(a)** hollow shape into which a liquid is poured, so that when the liquid becomes hard it takes that shape; **jelly mould** = shape for making jelly **(b)** greyish-green powdery fungus; *throw the bread away - it has got mould on it* **2** *verb* to shape (something)
◊ **mouldiness** *noun* being mouldy
◊ **mouldy** *adjective* covered with mould

mountain *noun* high land, much higher than the land surrounding it; *they spent August climbing in the mountains; a Swiss mountain resort;* **mountain bike** = specially solid bicycle, with thick tyres, used for country cycling; **mountain guide** = local person who leads groups of people climbing mountains; **mountain hut** = small wooden or stone shelter on a mountain; **mountain range** = series of mountains in a line; **mountain rescue service** *or* **team** = group of trained people who are on duty to help climbers and skiers who get into difficulties on mountains; **mountain stream** = little river in the mountains
◊ **mountain climber** *noun* person who climbs mountains for pleasure
◊ **mountain climbing** *noun* climbing mountains for pleasure
◊ **mountaineer** *noun* person who climbs mountains as a sport
◊ **mountaineering** *noun* sport of climbing mountains
◊ **mountainous** *adjective* (area) which has mountains

mouse *noun* small rodent *Mus musculus,* which lives in holes in walls, and eats refuse or fallen bits of food (the mouse is not as dangerous a pest as the rat) (NOTE: plural is **mice**)
◊ **mousetrap** *noun* device for catching and killing mice when they have become a pest

moussaka *noun* Greek dish, made of aubergines and minced meat in layers

mousse *noun* light food made of whipped eggs, cream and flavouring; *chocolate mousse; salmon mousse*

mouth-watering *adjective* (food) which looks and smells so delicious that it makes your mouth water; *a plate of mouth-watering cream cakes*

mpg = MILES PER GALLON

MPM = MAXIMUM PERMITTED MILEAGE

Mr *noun* title given to a man; *Mr Smith is the hotel manager*

Mrs *noun* title given to a married woman; *the guide is Mrs Smith*

Ms *noun* title given to a woman where it is not known if she is married, or where she does not wish to indicate if she is married or not; *Ms Smith is the courier*

MSA = MOTORWAY SERVICE AREA

MSG = MONOSODIUM GLUTAMATE

mud *noun* very wet earth; **mud bath** = therapeutic bath, where a person is covered in hot mud

muesli *noun* breakfast food of flakes of cereal, dried fruit, etc., eaten with milk

mulled wine *noun* red wine and brandy heated together with sugar and spices

mullet *noun* small sea fish; **red mullet** = small red sea-fish, used in Mediterranean cooking

mulligatawny *noun* hot soup made with curry

multigym *noun* apparatus on which you can do exercises and weight training; *the hotel has the very latest multigym in its fitness centre*
◊ **multinational** *noun* company which has branches or subsidiary companies in several countries; *the hotel chain has been bought by one of the big multinationals*

multiple 1 *adjective* many; **multiple entry visa** = visa allowing someone to enter a country as often as he likes; **multiple store** = one store in a chain of stores **2** *noun* company with stores in several different towns

multipot *noun* large tea or coffee urn, in which the liquid can be prepared in advance and then kept hot

museum *noun* building in which a collection of valuable or rare objects are put on show permanently; *we will visit the Victoria and Albert Museum this afternoon; the Natural History Museum has a special exhibition of dinosaurs*

mushroom *noun* little white plant, a fungus which grows wild in fields, but is usually grown commercially in mushroom farms; *bacon and grilled mushrooms for breakfast;* **button mushroom** = small white mushroom with a round cap; **open-cap mushroom** = large flatter type of mushroom

COMMENT: in the UK, mainly white mushrooms are used in cooking. In other parts of Europe, very many types of mushroom are eaten, and are either picked wild or bought in markets. You need to know which types of mushroom are good to eat, those which have an unpleasant taste, and those which are poisonous. In English, the word 'fungus' is used for all types of mushroom which are not the common white variety

mussel *noun* small mollusc with a dark blue shell, whose soft parts can be eaten

COMMENT: the usual way of eating mussels is as 'moules marinière', where the mussels are cooked quickly with onions, parsley and white wine

mustard *noun* very spicy yellow condiment, eaten with meat

COMMENT: English mustard is yellow and can be extremely strong. It is either sold as powder made from finely ground seeds of the mustard plant, which is then mixed with water to make a paste, or as ready-made paste in jars or tubes. In England, it is eaten mainly with beef, ham, pork pies, sausages, etc. French and German mustards are milder and there are very many different varieties of mustard with flavourings such as cider, garlic, herbs, etc.

◊ **mustard and cress** *noun* seedlings of white mustard and garden cress plants, usually sold growing in small plastic boxes, used in salads and as a garnish; *see also* CRESS

muster station *noun* place where passengers on a ship must gather in an emergency

mutton *noun* meat from a fully-grown sheep (NOTE: the word is not much used, as most meat from sheep is called **lamb** even when it comes from an older animal)

Nn

name *noun* word used to call a person *or* a thing; *what is the name in his passport? his first name is John, but I am not sure of his other names;* **brand name** = name of a particular make of product; **under the name of** = using a particular name; *they registered under the names of Mr and Mrs Smith*

napkin *noun* **(table) napkin** = square piece of cloth used to protect clothes and wipe your mouth at meal times; **paper napkin** = napkin made from paper (NOTE: also called a **serviette,** but some people think this is not correct English; **napkin** is the word used in hotels and restaurants)

COMMENT: napkins are usually placed on the table as part of the setting, either simply folded in the centre of the setting (on the show plate, if there is one) or folded into elaborate shapes, like fans, etc.

napperon *noun* small square tablecloth, placed over a larger tablecloth to keep it clean (NOTE: also called a **slip cloth**)

narrow *adjective* not wide

◊ **narrow-bodied** *adjective* (plane) with a narrow body (as opposed to a wide-bodied plane)

narrowboat *noun* especially long narrow boat, built for travelling on canals; *the company offers two-week narrowboat holidays*

national 1 *adjective* belonging to the people of a particular country; *(in the UK)* **National Nature Reserve** = nature reserve designated by the Nature Conservancy Council for the protection of plants and animals living in it; **national park** = large area of unspoilt land, owned and managed by the government for recreational use by the public; **National Trust** = organization in Britain which preserves historic buildings and parks and special areas of natural beauty **2** *noun* person of a particular country; *the passenger list included nationals of seven countries*

nationality *noun* **he is of British nationality** = he is a British citizen
◊ **nationwide** *adjective* all over a country; *we offer a nationwide delivery service; the new camping van is being launched with a nationwide sales campaign*

nature *noun* world of plants and animals; **Nature Conservancy Council (NCC)** *or* **English Nature** = official body in the UK, established in 1973, which takes responsibility for the conservation of fauna and flora. Since April 1991 the branch of the Council dealing with England has also been called English Nature; **nature reserve** = special area where the wildlife is protected (National Nature Reserves are designated by the English Nature); **nature trail** = path through countryside with signs to draw attention to important and interesting features, such as plants, birds or animals
◊ **naturism** *noun* nudism, belief in the physical and mental advantages of going about naked
◊ **naturist** *adjective & noun* nudist, person who believes in going about naked; **naturist beach** = beach where people are allowed to go about naked

nautical *adjective* referring to ships and the sea; **nautical mile** = unit of measurement of distance, used at sea and in the air (= 1.852 kilometres)

navigator *noun* **(a)** member of the flight deck crew, the person who calculates the distances and direction taken by the aircraft **(b)** person who deals with the maps, signs and timing for a car rally driver

NCC = NATURE CONSERVANCY COUNCIL

near miss *noun* incident where two vehicles come very close by accident and almost crash into each other

neat *adjective* (alcohol) with no water or any other liquid added; *a glass of neat whisky; I prefer my whisky neat* (NOTE: US English only uses **straight** in this meaning)

neck *noun* part of the body connecting the head to the shoulders; this part of an animal eaten as food; **best end of neck** = joint of lamb consisting of the ribs nearest the neck

nectarine *noun* fruit like a peach with a smooth skin

neighbourhood *or* US **neighborhood** *noun* **(a)** district and its people; *the hotel is pleasantly situated in a quiet neighbourhood* **(b) in the neighbourhood of** = near to (in space or amount); *there a three hotels in the neighbourhood of the conference centre; they spent in the neighbourhood of £12,000 on redecorating the restaurant*

nestle *verb* to be in a sheltered *or* comfortable position; *a chalet nestling in the bottom of a valley*

net *adjective* **(a)** price *or* weight *or* pay, etc. after all deductions have been made; **net margin** = net profit shown as a percentage of sales; **net price** = price which cannot be reduced by a discount; **net profit** = result where income from sales is more than all expenditure; **net receipts** = total money taken after deducting commission *or* tax *or* discounts, etc.; **net sales** = sales less damaged or returned items; **net weight** = weight of goods after deducting the weight of the packing material and container (NOTE: the spelling **nett** is sometimes used on containers) **(b) terms strictly net** = payment has to be the full price, with no discount allowed
◊ **network** *noun* **(a)** interconnecting system (of railways, etc.); *the Belgian railway network* **(b)** radio or TV system **(c)** interconnecting computer system; *you can book at any of our hotels throughout the country using our computer network*

news *noun* spoken or written information about events; **it's in the news** = it is of topical interest

◊ **newsagent** *noun* person who runs a shop selling newspapers

◊ **newsagent's** *noun* shop selling newspapers

◊ **newsletter** *noun* printed sheet giving news to members of a company, church or club, etc.

◊ **newspaper** *noun* daily or weekly paper containing news and information; *newspapers are available in the residents' lounge; he ordered a newspaper to be brought to his room with early morning tea; do you want a newspaper with your morning tea? he ordered a newspaper and a call at 6.45*

◊ **newsstand** *noun* small wooden kiosk on a pavement or at a railway station, selling newspapers and magazines

next *adjective* **(a)** *(in time)* coming after; *when's the next plane for Paris? the next train to London leaves in ten minutes' time* **(b)** *(in space)* adjoining; **the room next door to mine** = the room next to mine; *she's in the room next door to her parents; there was a lot of noise in the room next door or in the next-door room during the night*

NGO = NON-GOVERNMENTAL ORGANIZATION

niche *noun* special place in a market, occupied by one company (a 'niche company'); **niche market** = market for a very special product or service, which can be exploited by only a few suppliers; *holidays in the Antarctic are a niche market*

nickel *noun* US five-cent coin

night *noun* **(a)** period of time from evening to morning; **night bell** = bell outside a hotel, which you ring to wake up the porter during the night, after the front door has been locked; **night clerk** = person who is on duty at the reception desk during the night; **night duty** = period of work done at night; *he is on night duty three days a week;* **night flight** = flight which takes place during the night; **night light** = weak electric light which gives a faint light and is used to light passages, stairs or a child's room at night; **night manager** = person in charge of a hotel during the night; **night porter** = porter who is on duty at a hotel during the night (he answers calls from guest rooms as well as dealing with any late arrivals); **night safe** = safe with a special door in the outside wall of a bank, where money and documents can be deposited when the bank is closed; *see also* LATE-NIGHT, OVERNIGHT **(b)** an evening's entertainment; **first night** = the official opening performance of a play or entertainment; **karaoke night** *or* **quiz night** = night at a pub when karaoke is played *or* when a quiz is held; **night out** = evening spent outside the home; *they're planning to have a night out tomorrow;* **a night on the town** = an evening spent in restaurants, theatres, etc., in the town

◊ **nightclub** *noun* club only open at night

◊ **night life** *noun* entertainment which takes place in a town at night; *the beaches are fine, but the night life is very dull*

◊ **nightspot** *noun* entertainment place open at night (such as a nightclub); *it's the most expensive nightspot in town*

◊ **night-time** *noun* period of night; **night-time flight** = flight which takes place during the night

◊ **nightwatchman** *noun* man who guards a building at night

nil *noun* zero, nothing; **nil return** = report showing no sales *or* income *or* tax, etc.

nip *noun* single measure of alcohol; *Scotch: £1 per nip*

NITB = NORTHERN IRELAND TOURIST BOARD

no *adjective & adverb* showing the negative; **no admission** *or* **no admittance** = entrance not allowed; **no entry** = you cannot go in; **no parking** = do not leave your car here; **no smoking** = do not smoke here; **a 'no smoking' sign** = a sign to show that smoking is not allowed; *the captain has switched on the 'no smoking' sign;* **no vacancies** = the hotel, guesthouse, etc. is full

◊ **no-show** *noun* person who has booked a room in a hotel or a table in a restaurant or a seat on an aircraft and does not come; *seats were still available on the aircraft because there were several no-shows*

no-claims bonus *noun* reduction of premiums on an insurance policy because no claims have been made

noise *noun* loud (usually unpleasant) sound; *the noise of the street kept us awake at night*

◊ **noisy** *adjective* which makes *or* is affected by a lot of noise; *the best rooms are quiet, and overlook a garden: unfortunately, the hotel also has some rooms overlooking a* *noisy crossroads; she asked for her room to be changed, because it was too noisy*

non- *prefix* not; **non-alcoholic drink** = drink which does not contain alcohol; **non-food items** = items for sale (such as cigarettes, hotel rooms, etc.) which are not food; **non-refundable deposit** = deposit which will not be refunded under any circumstances

◊ **non-governmental organization (NGO)** *noun* organization (such as a pressure group *or* charity *or* voluntary agency) which is not funded by a government and which works on a local *or* national *or* international level

non-resident *adjective & noun* **(a)** (person) not staying in a hotel; *the hotel restaurant is open to non-residents* **(b)** (person) not living in a place; **a non-resident's entry visa** = visa allowing a person who is not a resident of a country to go into that country; *he has a non-resident account with a French bank; she was granted a non-resident visa*

non-stick *adjective* (pan) covered with a substance which prevents food from sticking when cooking

non-stop *adjective & adverb* without stopping; *a non-stop flight to Tokyo; to fly to Tokyo non-stop*

noodles *plural noun* flat strips of pasta; **egg noodles** = noodles made with flour, water and egg

COMMENT: noodles are widely used in oriental cooking, as well as in many western dishes

Nordic *adjective* referring to the people of Scandinavia; **Nordic skiing** = competitive cross-country skiing and ski-jumping

norm *noun* normal or standard pattern

north 1 *noun* **(a)** one of the points of the compass, the direction in which a compass needle points **(b)** the northern part of a country **2** *adjective* referring to the north; *the north coast of Scotland;* **north wind** = wind which blows from the north **3** *adverb* towards the north; *drive north along the motorway for ten miles*

◊ **northbound** *adjective* going towards the north; *the northbound carriageway of the motorway is closed*

◊ **north-east** *noun, adjective & adverb* direction half-way between east and north

◊ **north-easterly** *or* **north-eastern** *adjective* referring to the north-east; towards or from the north-east

◊ **northerly 1** *adjective* **(a)** towards the north; **in a northerly direction** = towards the north **(b)** (wind) which blows from the north

◊ **northern** *adjective* referring to the north; **Northern Ireland Tourist Board (NITB)** = organization which promotes tourism in Northern Ireland and promotes tourism to Northern Ireland from other parts of the UK

◊ **northerner** *noun* person who lives in or comes from the north

◊ **northernmost** *adjective* furthest north

◊ **northward** *adjective & adverb* towards the north

◊ **northwards** *adverb* towards the north

◊ **north-west** *noun, adjective & adverb* direction half-way between north and west

◊ **north-westerly** *or* **north-western** *adjective* referring to the north-west; towards or from the north-west

note *noun* **(a)** very short letter; very brief written or printed document **(b)** piece of printed paper money; *a £10 note* (NOTE: US English is **bill**)

◊ **notepaper** *noun* writing paper for letters; *there is some hotel notepaper in the drawer of the desk in the bedroom*

notice *noun* **(a)** advance information or warning about something; *you must give at least 24 hours' notice of cancellation;* **at short notice** = giving only a few hours' warning; *he found it difficult to get a hotel room at short notice;* **without notice** = without giving any warning; *the train times were changed without notice* **(b)** written information; *the courier pinned a notice on the hotel noticeboard*

◊ **noticeboard** *noun* flat piece of wood, etc. on a wall on which notices can be pinned

notify *verb* to inform someone officially; *the local doctor notified the Health Service of the case of cholera* (NOTE: you notify someone **of** something)

◊ **notifiable disease** *noun* serious infectious disease which in Great Britain has to be reported by a doctor to the Department of Health and Social Security so that steps can be taken to stop it spreading

COMMENT: the following are notifiable diseases: cholera, diphtheria, dysentery, encephalitis, food poisoning, jaundice, meningitis, ophthalmia neonatorum, paratyphoid, plague, poliomyelitis, relapsing fever, scarlet fever, smallpox, tuberculosis, typhoid and typhus

nought *noun* zero, nothing; **nought-per cent finance** = interest-free credit

nudist *adjective & noun* (person) believing in going about naked; **nudist beach** = beach where people are allowed to go about naked; **nudist colony** = club or camp for those who want to go about naked

◊ **nudism** *noun* belief in the physical and mental advantages of going about naked

number 1 *noun* **(a)** quantity of people *or* things; *the number of passengers carried has increased over the last year; the number of days of rain is very small; the number of tickets sold was disappointing* **(b)** a number of = some; *a number of the staff will be retiring this year; a number of guests fell ill after the banquet* **(c)** written figure; *account number; seat number; cheque number; invoice number; order number; page number; serial number; phone number or telephone number; ticket number; he was sitting in seat number 6A, but he had a ticket for 12B; cheques with the serial numbers 800 to 822 have been stolen;* box **number** = reference number used when asking for mail to be sent to a post office or when asking for replies to an advertisement to be sent to the newspaper's offices; *please reply to Box No. 209;* **flight number** = number given to identify a flight (NOTE: often written **No.** with figures) **2** *verb* to put a figure on something; *the seats are numbered from the front of the aircraft to the back; I refer to your invoice numbered 1234;* **numbered account** = bank account (usually in Switzerland) which is referred to only by a

number, the name of the person holding it being kept secret

◊ **numberplate** *noun* plate on the front and back of a vehicle, showing its registration number

COMMENT: flight numbers are identified with the airline code (in letters) followed by a series of figures

nursery *noun* room or building where babies or young children are looked after; *there is a children's nursery on 'C' Deck*

◊ **nursery slopes** *plural noun* snow-covered mountain slopes where people learn to ski

nut *noun* fruit with an edible centre inside a hard shell; **to crack nuts** = to open the shells to get at the edible centres

◊ **nutcracker(s)** *noun* device for cracking the shells of nuts

◊ **nutmeg** *noun* seed of a tropical tree, grated and used as a spice

◊ **nutshell** *noun* hard outer covering of a nut

◊ **nutty** *adjective* tasting of nuts; full of nuts

nutriment *noun* something which nourishes

◊ **nutrient** *adjective & noun* (food) which feeds or nourishes

◊ **nutrition** *noun* giving or receiving of nourishment

◊ **nutritionist** *noun* dietitian, person who specializes in the study of nutrition and advises on diets

◊ **nutritious** *adjective* nourishing, providing food which is necessary for growth

◊ **nutritive 1** *noun* food which is necessary for growth **2** *adjective* providing food or nourishment

Oo

0500 number *or* **0800 number** *noun* telephone numbers which the caller can use without paying for the call (used to reply to advertisements); the supplier pays for the call, not the caller

oatcake *noun* dry biscuit made of oatmeal (in England often served with cheese, in Scotland often eaten at breakfast)

◊ **oatmeal** *noun* coarse flour made from oats

◊ **oats** *plural noun* cereal food, grown in northern countries

COMMENT: oats are widely grown and used in Scotland, where the most common use for them is in making porridge and biscuits

obligatory *adjective* necessary according to the law or rules; *is the medical examination obligatory?*

occasional *adjective* which happens from time to time; *US* **occasional labor** = workers hired for a short period (NOTE: British English is **casual labour)**

occupancy *noun* living *or* working *or* staying in a property (such as a house, an office, a hotel room); **with immediate occupancy** = empty and available to be moved into straight away; **single occupancy** = one person in a room; **occupancy rate** *or* **room occupancy** = average number of guest rooms sold in a hotel over a period of time, shown as a percentage of the total number of rooms; *during the winter months the occupancy rate was down to 50%*
◊ **occupation** *noun* **occupation of a building** = living *or* working in a building
◊ **occupy** *verb* to live or work in a property (such as a house, an office, a hotel room); *all the rooms in the hotel are occupied; the company occupies three floors of an office block*

QUOTE while occupancy rates matched those of 1984 in July, August has been a much poorer month than it was the year before
Economist
QUOTE hotel occupancies in the high tariff B or four-star hotels recorded an average occupancy of 88.5 per cent for the first half of this year, compared with the previous year's 84 per cent
South China Morning Post

ocean *noun* large area of sea

COMMENT: the oceans are: the Atlantic, the Pacific, the Indian, the Antarctic (or Southern) and the Arctic

◊ **oceanarium** *noun* type of large saltwater aquarium where marine animals are kept

odd *adjective* **(a) odd numbers** = numbers (like 17 or 33) which cannot be divided by two; *odd-numbered buildings or buildings with odd numbers are on the south side of the street* **(b) a hundred-odd** = approximately one hundred; **keep the odd change** = keep the small change which is left over **(c)** one of a group; **an odd shoe** = one shoe of a pair; **we have a few odd boxes left** = we have a few boxes left out of the total shipment **(d) odd sizes** = strange sizes which are not usual
◊ **oddments** *plural noun* items left over

off 1 *adjective* **(a)** not on the menu any more; *liver is off today* **(b)** not good or rotten; *that fish smells a bit off; the milk has gone off; I'm afraid these prawns are off* **2** *preposition* a certain distance from *or* quite close to; *the spent their holiday on an island off the coast of Brittany; the restaurant is just off the High Street*
◊ **off-airport car rental firm** *noun* rental firm which is not based within an airport and so can offer cheaper rates

offal *noun* inside parts of an animal, such as liver, kidney or intestines, when used as food (NOTE: no plural. US English is **variety meats)**

offer 1 *noun* **(a)** statement that you are willing to pay a certain amount of money to buy something; **we are open to offers** = we are ready to discuss the price which we are asking; **cash offer** = being ready to pay in cash; **or near offer** *or* **or nearest offer** = or an offer of a price which is slightly less than the price asked; *the car is for sale at £2,000 or near offer* (NOTE: often shortened to **o.n.o.) (b)** statement that you are willing to sell something for a certain amount of money; **bargain offer** = sale of a particular type of goods at a cheap price; *this week's bargain offer - 30% off all holidays in the Middle East;* **introductory offer** = special price offered on a new product to attract customers; **special offer** = goods put on sale at a specially low price; *we have a range of luggage on special offer* **2** *verb* **(a)** to offer **someone a job** = to tell someone that he can have a job in your company; *he was offered a job as a receptionist* **(b)** to say that you are willing to pay a certain amount of money for something; *she offered £200 for the carpet* **(c)** to say that you are willing to sell something; *they are offering cheap weekend tours to European cities*

office *noun* **(a)** set of rooms where a company works *or* where business is done; **branch office** = less important office, usually in a different town or country from the main office; **head office** *or* **main office** = office building where the board of directors works and meets; *GB* **registered office** =

office address of a company which is officially registered with the Companies' Registrar **(b) office hours** = time when an office is open; *open during normal office hours; do not telephone during office hours; the manager can be reached at home out of office hours;* **office space** *or* **office accommodation** = space available for offices or occupied by offices; *we are looking for extra office space;* **for office use only** = something which must only be used in an office (words used on form to show a part which must only be filled in by the people in the office which issues the form) **(c)** room where someone works and does business; *come into my office; the manager's office is on the third floor* **(d) booking office** = office where you can book seats at a theatre *or* tickets for the railway; **box office** = office at a theatre *or* cinema where tickets can be bought; **general office** = main administrative office in a company; **information office** = office which gives information to tourists *or* visitors; **inquiry office** = office where someone can answer questions from members of the public; **ticket office** = office where tickets can be bought (either for travel or for theatres or other places of entertainment) **(e)** *GB* government department; **the Foreign Office** = ministry dealing with foreign affairs; *Foreign Office officials asked to see the prisoners*

official 1 *adjective* from *or* approved by a government department or organization; *he is travelling on official business; he left official documents in his car; she received an official letter of explanation;* **for official use only** = FOR OFFICE USE ONLY; **speaking in an official capacity** = speaking as a person with special knowledge or responsibilities (as opposed to an ordinary private person); **to go through official channels** = to deal with officials, especially when making a request; **the official exchange rate** = exchange rate which is imposed by the government; *the official exchange rate is ten to the dollar, but you can get twice that on the black market* **2** *noun* person working in a government department; *airport officials inspected the shipment; government officials stopped the import licence;* **customs official** = person working for the customs; **high official** = important person in a government department; **minor official** = person in a low position in a government department; *some minor official tried to stop my request for building permission;* **top official** = very important person in a

government department; *see also* UNOFFICIAL

◊ **officially** *adverb* according to what is said in public, but which may not, in fact, be true; *officially, you are not supposed to take money out of the country*

off-licence *noun* *GB* **(a)** shop which sells alcohol for drinking away from the shop (NOTE: the US equivalent is a **package store**) **(b)** licence to sell alcohol to be drunk away from the place where it is bought

off-peak *adjective* not during the busiest time; **during the off-peak period** = at the time when business is less busy; **off-peak tariff** *or* **rate** = lower charges used when the service is not busy

off-piste skiing *noun* skiing away from the marked tracks

off-season 1 *adjective* **off-season tariff** *or* **rate** = cheaper fares and room prices which are charged when there a fewer travellers **2** *noun* time of year (often during the winter) when there are fewer travellers, and so fares and room prices are cheaper; *tour operators urge more people to travel in the off-season; air fares are cheaper in the off-season*

offshore *adjective & adverb* on an island *or* in the sea near to the coast; *offshore floating casino;* **offshore wind** = wind which blows from the coast towards the sea

Ogen melon *noun* type of melon which has yellowish skin striped with green, and pale yellow flesh

oil 1 *noun* thick smooth-running liquid of various kinds (used in cooking); **olive oil** = oil made from olives **2** *verb* to put oil on; *oil the tin before putting the dough in*

> COMMENT: the commonest cooking oil is made from sunflower seeds; many others exist, such as olive oil, walnut oil, etc.

◊ **oiliness** *noun* being oily

◊ **oily** *adjective* like oil; covered with oil

okra *noun* vegetable *(Hibiscus esculentus)* with a green pod used in soups

> COMMENT: also called 'bhindi', 'gumbo' or 'lady's finger'. Used in Caribbean and Indian cooking; also used in the south of the USA

olive *noun* **(a)** Mediterranean tree *(Olea europaea)*, with small black or green fruit which produces oil and is used as food; **black olives** *or* **green olives** = ripe olives *or* unripe olives; **olive oil** = oil made from olives; **extra virgin olive oil** = olive oil produced from the first pressing (it has a low acidity) **(b) beef olives** = dish made from thin slices of beef, stuffed and rolled

omelette *noun* dish made of beaten eggs, cooked in a frying pan and folded over before serving; various fillings may be added

| COMMENT: the commonest forms of omelette are cheese omelette and ham omelette. A Spanish omelette is made with onion, tomato, peppers, potatoes, etc., and is not folded over, but served flat

on-airport car rental firm *noun* car rental firm with its base inside an airport complex, which is more convenient for travellers, although the rates may be higher

one-way *adjective* **one-way ticket** = ticket for one journey from one place to another; *US* **one-way fare** = fare for one journey from one place to another

◊ **one-way street** *noun* street where the traffic is allowed to go only in one direction; *the shop is in a one-way street, which makes it very difficult for parking*

onion *noun* strong-smelling vegetable with a round white bulb; *fried onion rings;* **French onion soup** = soup made with onions and stock, served with croutons; **spring onion** *or US* **green onion** *or* **scallion** = young onion eaten raw in salad

o.n.o. = OR NEAR OFFER

onshore *adjective* towards the coast; **onshore wind** = wind which blows from the sea towards the coast

on-site *adjective* on the premises; *the on-site courier is completely reliable*

on-the-rocks *see* ROCKS

open 1 *adjective* **(a)** at work *or* not closed; *most slopes are open on Sunday mornings; our offices are open from 9 to 6; they are open for business every day of the week* **(b) open cheque** = cheque which is not crossed and can be cashed anywhere; **open (date) ticket** = ticket which can be used on any date **(c) open sea** = area of sea away from land, with no islands or rocks; **open space** = area of land which has no buildings or trees on it; *the parks provide welcome open space in the centre of the city* **2** *verb* **(a)** to start a new business working; *she has opened a shop in the High Street; we have opened an office in London* **(b)** to start work *or* to be at work; *the information office opens at 9 a.m.; we open for business on Sundays;* **opening time** = time when a shop or office starts work **(c)** to make something begin officially; *the new hotel was opened by the Minister of Tourism; we are opening a new courier service to Japan*

◊ **open-air** *adjective* not in a building; *an open-air concert in Central Park*

◊ **open-jaw (arrangement)** *noun* **(a)** system where a passenger flies to one airport on the outward flight and returns from another airport **(b)** system where a passenger leaves from one airport on the outward trip and returns to another on the return trip

◊ **open up** *verb* **to open up a new air route** = to work to start flying a regular service on a route where such a service has not operated before

opera *noun* **(a)** dramatic performance with music, in which the words are partly or wholly sung; *we are going to see the new production of an opera by Britten* **(b)** company which performs operas; *the Covent Garden Opera plays in the Royal Opera House*

◊ **opera glasses** *plural noun* small binoculars for looking at performers on the stage

◊ **opera house** *noun* theatre in which opera is performed

operation *noun* **(a)** business organization and work; *the company's tour operations in West Africa; he is in charge of our hotel operations in Northern Europe* **(b)** **in operation** = working *or* being used; *the computerized booking system will be in operation by June; the new schedules came into operation on June 1st*

◊ **operational** *adjective* **(a)** referring to how something works; **operational costs** = costs of the day-to-day organization of a company; **operational planning** = planning how a business is to be run **(b) the system became operational on June 1st** = the system started working on June 1st

◊ **operative** *adjective* **to become operative** = to start working; *the new ticketing system has been operative since June 1st*

◊ **operator** *noun* **(a)** person who works a machine; *a keyboard operator* **(b)** person who works a telephone switchboard; *switchboard operator; to call the operator or to dial the operator; to place a call through or via the operator;* **operator-controlled call** = telephone call where the operator makes the connection, usually charged at a higher rate **(c) tour operator** = person *or* company which organizes tours

QUOTE the company gets valuable restaurant locations which will be converted to the family-style restaurant chain that it operates and franchises throughout most parts of the US
Fortune

QUOTE a number of block bookings by American tour operators have been cancelled
Economist

option *noun* **(a)** choice, alternative possibility; *the tour offers several options as half-day visits; when you hire a car, you have the option of a two-door or four-door model* **(b) option to purchase** *or* **to sell** = giving someone the possibility to buy or sell something within a period of time; **first option** = allowing someone to be the first to have the possibility of deciding something
◊ **optional** *adjective* which can be added if the customer wants; *the insurance cover is optional;* **optional extras** = items which can be added, such as a visit to a market when on a tour

orange 1 *noun* sweet citrus fruit *Citrus aurantium* with a reddish-yellow skin; *we saw orange trees growing in California; she asked for an orange sorbet; roast duck and orange sauce;* **caramel oranges** = slices of orange covered with a sauce of caramelized sugar; **Seville oranges** *or* **bitter oranges** = oranges which are not sweet, and are used to make marmalade; **orange marmalade** = marmalade made from oranges (usually bitter oranges)

COMMENT: its nutritional value is due mainly to its high vitamin C content; it is eaten as fresh fruit or used for juice and for making preserves. Blood oranges are coloured by the presence of anthocyanins; mandarin oranges such as satsumas and tangerines have loose peel. The Seville orange is a bitter orange, grown in Spain and used to make marmalade

◊ **orangeade** *noun* fizzy orange-flavoured drink

◊ **orangery** *noun* special house with large windows, in which orange and lemon trees can be grown in pots during the winter, and then put outside in a formal garden during the summer

order 1 *noun* **(a)** arrangement of records (filing cards, invoices, etc.); **alphabetical order** = arrangement by the letters of the alphabet (A, B, C, etc.); **chronological order** = arrangement by the order of the dates; **numerical order** = arrangement by numbers **(b)** working arrangement; **machine in full working order** = machine which is ready and able to work properly; **the telephone is out of order** = the telephone is not working; **is all the documentation in order?** = are all the documents valid and correct? **(c)** official request for goods to be supplied; *to give someone an order or to place an order with someone for twenty loaves of bread;* **to fill** *or* **to fulfil an order** = to supply items which have been ordered; **purchase order** = official order made out by a purchasing department for goods which a company wants to buy; **telephone orders** = orders received over the telephone; **terms: cash with order** = conditions of sale showing that payment has to be made in cash when the order is placed; **on order** = ordered but not delivered; *this item is out of stock, but is on order;* **items available to order only** = items which will be manufactured only if someone orders them **(d)** food or drink which a customer has asked for in a restaurant; *this is not my order; we only had twenty orders for the chef's special; (of a waiter)* **to take an order** = to write down the dishes and drinks which a guest orders; **last orders** = the final orders which a bar or restaurant will accept before closing time; *last orders: 10.30; see also* SHORT ORDER **2** *verb* **(a)** to ask for goods to be supplied; *the hotel has ordered a new set of dining room furniture* **(b)** to ask for food or drink in a restaurant; *he ordered a full English breakfast*

oregano *noun* common herb, used in Italian cooking, such as on pizzas

organic *adjective* (food) which has been cultivated naturally, without any chemical fertilizers *or* pesticides; **organic farming** = method of farming which does not involve using chemical fertilizers *or* pesticides

◊ **organically** *adverb* **organically grown** *or* **organically produced** = (food) grown *or* produced naturally, without any chemical fertilizers or pesticides

COMMENT: organic farming uses natural fertilizers and rotates the raising of animals with crop farming

organization *noun* **(a)** way of arranging something so that it works efficiently; **organization chart** = list of people working in various departments, showing how a company *or* an office is organized **(b)** group or institution which is arranged for efficient work; **a travel organization** = body representing companies in the travel business

◊ **organize** *verb* to arrange something so that it works efficiently; *to organize a tour of Egypt*

◊ **organizer** *noun* person who arranges things efficiently; **tour organizer** = company *or* person who arranges a tour

origin *noun* where something comes from; place where a traveller has started his journey; **certificate of origin** = document showing where goods were made; **country of origin** = country where a product is manufactured

ounce *noun* measure of weight (= 28 grams) (NOTE: usually written **oz** after figures: **14oz)**

outbound *adjective* going away from the home base; *the outbound flight departs at 09.15; the captain flew the outbound leg from London to Durban* (NOTE: the opposite is **inbound)**

outbreak *noun* series of cases of a disease which start suddenly; *tourists have been advised to drink only bottled water, as there is an outbreak of typhoid fever or a typhoid outbreak in the town*

outdoor *adjective* in the open air; *the hotel offers all sorts of outdoor activities;* **outdoor catering** = catering for large numbers of people in the open air (as at sporting events, shows, etc.)

◊ **outdoors** *adverb* (in or to) the open air; *the concert will be held outdoors if the weather is good*

outgoing *adjective* **outgoing call** = phone call going out of a building to someone outside; **outgoing mail** = mail which is sent out (NOTE: the opposite is **incoming)**

◊ **outside** *adverb & adjective* not in a company's office or building; **to send work to be done outside** = to send work to be done

in other offices; **outside caterer** = person *or* company who supplies food and drink to be consumed in a different place; **outside catering** = preparing food to be eaten in a different place (such as a wedding breakfast served in a marquee in the garden of the father of the bride); **outside line** = line from an internal office telephone system to the main telephone exchange; *you dial 9 to get an outside line* **2** *preposition* **outside office hours** *or* **outside restaurant hours** = when the office *or* restaurant is not open

◊ **outward** *adjective* going away from the home base; *on the outward voyage the ship will call in at the Canary Islands;* **outward mission** = visit by a group of businessmen to a foreign country

◊ **outward-bound** *adjective* (ship) which is going away from its home port

ouzo *noun* Greek alcoholic drink flavoured with aniseed

oven *noun* enclosed box which can be heated for cooking; *the kitchen has three large gas ovens; cook the vegetables in a microwave oven;* **tandoori oven** = traditional clay oven used in Indian restaurants to cook tandoori-style food

◊ **ovenproof** *adjective* (dish) which can be put into a hot oven without being damaged by the heat; *the potatoes are served in an ovenproof bowl*

◊ **ovenware** *noun* dishes which can be put in a hot oven without being damaged by the heat

over- *prefix* more than; **shop which caters for the over-60s** = shop which has goods which appeal to people who are more than sixty years old

◊ **overboard** *adverb* from a boat into the water; **man overboard!** = someone has fallen into the water!

◊ **overbook** *verb* to book more people than there are rooms or seats available; *the hotel or the flight was overbooked*

◊ **overbooking** *noun* booking of more people than there are rooms or seats available

◊ **overcapacity** *noun* having more seats *or* space than there are travellers or guests

◊ **overcast** *adjective* (sky) which is dull *or* cloudy

◊ **overcharge 1** *noun* charge which is higher than it should be; *to pay back an overcharge* **2** *verb* to ask too much money; *they overcharged us for meals; we asked for a refund because we had been overcharged*

◇ **overcrowded** *adjective* containing too many people; *we need to travel in the middle of the day to avoid the overcrowded commuter trains*

◇ **overdone** *adjective* (food) which has been cooked too long

◇ **overdue** *adjective* which has not been paid on time; **interest payments are three weeks overdue** = interest payments which should have been made three weeks ago

◇ **over easy** *adjective* US (egg) fried on both side; *compare* SUNNY SIDE UP

overfly *verb* to fly over a country

overhead 1 *adjective* **(a)** above one's head; **overhead reading light** = small light directly over a passenger's head in an aircraft **(b) overhead costs** *or* **expenses** = money spent on the day-to-day cost of a business; **overhead budget** = plan of probable overhead costs **2** *noun* **overheads** *or US* **overhead** = money spent on day-to-day cost of a business; *our sales revenue covers the cost of stocks but not the overheads*

overland *adverb & adjective* across land (as opposed to the sea); *they went down the river is small boats, and then went overland for a day to reach the safari station; an overland journey to China; they took the overland route to Egypt*

◇ **overlook** *verb* **(a)** to look out over; *we want a room which overlooks the gardens, not one overlooking the car park* **(b)** not to pay attention to; *in this instance we will overlook the delay*

◇ **overnight** *adjective & adverb* during all of a night; *an overnight stay in a hotel; they stay in the boat overnight, and make trips ashore at each port*

◇ **overrider** *or* **overriding commission** *noun* special extra commission which is paid on top of other commissions

◇ **overseas 1** *adjective* across the sea *or* to foreign countries; **an overseas call** = phone call to another country; **overseas markets** = markets in foreign countries; **overseas trade** = trade with foreign countries **2** *noun* foreign countries; *the profits from overseas are far higher than those of the home division*

◇ **overtake** *verb* to go faster than another vehicle on the road and pass it to get in front; *the road is too narrow to overtake; the coach overtook our car on the motorway*

◇ **overtime 1** *noun* overtime is paid at one and a half times the standard rate **2** *adjective*

working more than the normal working day; *overtime pay is calculated at one and a half times the standard rate; they worked overtime when the hotel was full*

own *verb* to have *or* to possess; *he owns 50% of the shares in the hotel chain;* **a state-owned airline** = airline which belongs to the state

◇ **owner** *noun* person who owns something; *a restaurant owner; she's the owner of the chain of hotels;* **owner-manager** = person who owns a hotel or restaurant and manages it; **owner-managed hotel** = hotel which is owned and managed by the same person; **owner-occupier** = person who owns and lives in a property; **goods sent at owner's risk** = situation where the owner has to insure the goods while they are being transported; **cars parked here at owner's risk** = if a car parked here is damaged or stolen, the owner will have to claim on his insurance

◇ **ownership** *noun* act of owning something; **common** *or* **collective ownership** = situation where a business is owned by the workers who work in it; **joint ownership** = owning of a property by several people or companies; **private ownership** = situation where a company is owned by private shareholders; **public ownership** *or* **state ownership** = situation where an industry is nationalized

oxtail *noun* tail of a cow or bull, used to stew or to make oxtail soup

oyster *noun* shellfish, with two rough, roundish shells; **oyster bar** = bar serving oysters, white wine, and usually other types of shellfish

COMMENT: oysters are usually served raw, opened, with the flat half of the shell removed; they are usually served with lemon, and slices of brown bread and butter. Traditionally, Guinness or dry champagne can be served with oysters, though nowadays a dry white wine is more usual. In restaurants oysters are served by the dozen or half-dozen. British oysters are only available between September and April, leading to the belief that they may only be eaten 'when there is an 'r' in the month'

oz = OUNCE

Pp

pack 1 *noun* **(a)** wrapping *or* container *or* box; **pack of items** = items put together in a container for selling; *pack of cigarettes; pack of biscuits; pack of envelopes;* **items sold in packs of 200** = sold in boxes containing 200 items; **blister pack** *or* **bubble pack** = type of packing where the item for sale is covered with a stiff plastic cover sealed to a card backing; **display pack** = specially attractive box for showing goods for sale; **dummy pack** = empty pack for display in a shop; **six-pack** = box containing six items (often bottles) **(b)** rucksack, a bag carried on the back **2** *verb* **(a)** to put things into a case for travelling; *did you remember to pack your winter underwear? he didn't pack his toothbrush; we're leaving tonight, and you haven't finished packing yet* **(b)** to put things into a container for selling *or* sending; *to pack goods into cartons; the biscuits are packed in plastic wrappers;* **packed lunch** = cold food, such as sandwiches, fruit, etc., packed in a bag, box or basket for eating when travelling; *the party took packed lunches when they set off on their walk in the mountains*

package 1 *noun* **(a)** goods packed and wrapped for sending by mail; *the Post Office does not accept bulky packages; the goods are to be sent in airtight packages* **(b)** **package deal** = deal where several items are agreed at the same time; **package holiday** *or* **package tour** = holiday *or* tour where the travel, the accommodation and sometimes meals are all included in the price and paid for in advance; *the travel company is arranging a package trip to the international computer exhibition;* *US* **package store** = shop which sells alcohol for drinking away from the shop (NOTE: the GB equivalent is an **off-licence**)

packet *noun* wrapping *or* container *or* box; *a packet of cigarettes; empty cigarette packets littered the floor*

pad *noun* keypad, a small terminal with keys, linked to a central computer, allowing orders to be keyed directly by a waiter or waitress

QUOTE pads are part of a network, so that in outlets with two or more pads, servers can move from pad to pad, and their orders move with them. Orders entered on any pad can be transmitted to kitchen or bar printers
Caterer & Hotelkeeper

paella *noun* Spanish dish of cooked rice with fish, shellfish and vegetables in it

page 1 *noun* young man who takes messages and carries luggage in a hotel **2** *verb* to call (someone) to the reception desk or to answer a telephone call in a hotel; *he is not in his room, so we will page him in the restaurant*
◇ **pageboy** *noun* young man who takes messages and carries luggage in a hotel
◇ **pager** *noun* small portable radio which makes a tone when it receives a message (NOTE: also called a **radiopager**)

COMMENT: pagers are used in many situations: to call members of staff to take incoming messages on an outside line, to call a doctor to an emergency, etc. Some pagers have small screens on which short written messages can be displayed

palace *noun* large ornate building, in which a king or nobleman lives; *the Palace of Versailles; Blenheim Palace; Buckingham Palace was opened to the public for the first time in 1993*

COMMENT: note that a 'palace' would often be called 'château' in French, and in German, 'Schloss'. See note at CASTLE

palm (tree) *noun* large tropical plant with branching fern-like leaves, producing fruits which give oil and other foodstuffs; **coconut palm** *or* **date palm** = palm which produces coconuts *or* dates; **palm oil** = edible oil produced from the seed or fruit of an oil palm; with only 5-12% polyunsaturated fatty acids, it is widely used in cooking fats and margarines

paludism *noun* malaria, a tropical disease caused by a parasite *Plasmodium* which enters the body after a bite from the female Anopheles mosquito

◊ **Paludrine** *noun* anti-malarial drug, taken together with Chloroquine

COMMENT: paludism is a recurrent disease which produces regular periods of shivering, vomiting, sweating and headaches as the parasites develop in the body; the patient also develops anaemia

pan *noun* metal container for cooking; **boiling pan** = large container used in a kitchen for boiling food, and making soup; *see also* FRYING PAN, SAUCEPAN

◊ **pan-fried** *adjective* cooked in shallow oil or fat in a frying pan; *pan-fried fillets of sole*

pancake *noun* thin soft flat cake made of flour, milk and eggs; **Pancake Day** = SHROVE TUESDAY

panel *noun* group of people who answer questions or who judge a competition

panoramic *adjective* which looks out over a large area *or* which has a wonderful view of scenery; *a panoramic view from the top of the tower; there is a panoramic restaurant on the top floor of the hotel*

pantry *noun* **(a)** cool cupboard or room for keeping food in **(b)** *(in restaurant)* small room where dirty glasses, cutlery, etc., are put after being cleared from the table, and where hot plates, cruets, etc., can be kept for service to guests' tables; **floor pantry** = small room serving one floor of a hotel, where the floor waiter prepares trays to take to guests' bedrooms and brings back dirty plates and glasses after use

◊ **pantryman** *noun* person who deals with the dirty dishes and glasses in a restaurant pantry

papaya *or* **papaw** *noun* tree *(Carica papaya)*, native of tropical South America, but now found in all tropical regions. The greenish-yellow fruits have a soft pulp which is eaten raw, usually served with quarters of lime

paper *noun* **(a)** thin material made from rags or wood pulp, used for printing, writing, wrapping, etc.; **paper napkin** *or* **paper serviette** = napkin *or* serviette made from paper; **paper towel** = absorbent paper used for drying the hands, wiping spilled liquids, etc.; *there is a paper towel dispenser in the bathroom* **(b)** newspaper; *the cottage was advertised in our local paper; check in the paper to find out the times of high tides*

paprika *noun* red spice made from powdered sweet peppers

COMMENT: used in Central European cooking, such as goulash

parallel *noun* imaginary line running round the earth, linking points at an equal distance from the equator

COMMENT: the parallels are numbered and some of them act as national boundaries: the 49th parallel marks most of the border between the USA and Canada

parasite *noun* plant *or* animal which lives on or inside another plant or animal (the host) and derives its nourishment and other needs from it

◊ **parasitic** *adjective* referring to parasites; *a parasitic plant*

COMMENT: the commonest parasites affecting animals are lice on the skin and various types of worms in the intestines. Many diseases of humans (such as malaria and amoebic dysentery) are caused by infestation with parasites. Viruses are parasites on animals, plants and even on bacteria

parasol *noun* light umbrella to protect you from the rays of the sun

paratyphoid (fever) *noun* infectious disease which has similar symptoms to typhoid and is caused by bacteria transmitted by humans or animals

COMMENT: there are three forms of paratyphoid fever, known by the letters A, B, and C. They are caused by three types of bacterium, *Salmonella paratyphi* A, B, and C. TAB injections give immunity against paratyphoid A and B, but not against C

parboil *verb* to half-cook (food) in boiling water

pare *verb* **(a)** to cut the skin or peel off (a fruit, vegetable, etc.) **(b)** to cut back (expenses); **margins have been pared to the bone to keep our prices low** = they have been reduced as much as possible

◊ **parings** *plural noun* pieces of peel or skin cut off a fruit, vegetable, etc.

park 1 *noun* **(a)** open space with grass and trees; **country park** = area in the countryside set aside for the public to visit and enjoy; **marine park** = natural park created on the bottom of the sea (as on a tropical reef) where visitors go into observation chambers under the sea to look at the fish and plant life; *compare* OCEANARIUM; **national park** = large area of unspoilt land, owned and managed by the government for recreational use by the public; **park keeper** = keeper who looks after a park (especially a town park); **park ranger** *or* **park warden** = person who looks after a forest or park **(b) car park** = place where you can leave your car; *he left his car in the hotel car park; if the car park is full, you can park in the street for thirty minutes* **(c) industrial park** = area of land near a town specially set aside for factories and warehouses **2** *verb* to leave your car in a place while you are not using it; *the rep parked his car outside the shop; you cannot park here during the rush hour; parking is difficult in the centre of the city*

◊ **parking** *noun* leaving your car in a place while you are not using it; place where cars can be left; *there is plenty of free parking behind the conference centre;* '**no parking**' = do not leave your car here; **parking attendant** = person who looks after a car park, telling people where to park, guarding the empty vehicles, collecting payment, etc.; **parking facilities** = arrangement for parking cars (either in a covered or open car park); *the hotel has parking facilities for 60 cars; US* **parking lot** = car park; **parking meter** = device into which you put money to pay for parking; **parking space** = space for parking a single car; *the restaurant has six parking spaces allocated in the public car park next door;* **meter parking** = parking for cars available at meters; **valet parking** = service at a hotel or restaurant where a member of staff parks the guests' cars for them

◊ **parkway** *noun US* highway with a grass strip in the middle with trees and shrubs

parsley *noun* green herb *(Petroselinum crispum)* with either curly or flat leaves, used in cooking as a flavouring or garnish; **parsley sauce** = white sauce, flavoured with parsley, served with fish

parsnip *noun* plant *(Pastinaca sativa)* whose long white root is eaten as a vegetable

COMMENT: parsnips are eaten roasted (with roast beef and roast potatoes) or can be boiled and made into a purée. They are not eaten in most European countries, except in Britain

participate *verb* to take part in (something); *not all the hotels in the chain are participating in this special Christmas offer*

◊ **participant** *noun* person who takes part in something

partie *French noun* specialized section of a restaurant kitchen (making sauces, pastries, etc.); **chef de partie** = chef in charge of a particular section of a kitchen (such as vegetables or sauces)

partition 1 *noun* thin wall between two spaces, especially splitting a large room into two; *there's only a thin partition between the bedrooms, so we can hear everything that is said in the room next door* **2** *verb* to divide (by means of a partition); *part of the old dining room has been partitioned off to make a small function room*

partridge *noun* large brown and grey bird, shot for sport and food (in season between September 1st and January 31st)

part-time *adjective & adverb* not for a whole working day; *she has a part-time job at the hotel reception desk; we employ several people part-time at weekends*

pass 1 *noun* **(a)** lower area between two mountain peaks **(b)** bus or train season ticket; permit to go in or out of a building, etc.; *a monthly pass coasts less than four weekly passes; see also* AIRPASS, RAILPASS **2** *verb* to go past; *you pass the Post Office on your left as you go to the station*

◊ **passing trade** *noun* customers who walk or drive past a restaurant or hotel, and decide to stop and eat or stay the night, without having booked (as opposed to regular customers)

◊ **pass through** *verb* to go through something; *the road passes through the national park;* we're just passing through = we are on our way to somewhere else; to **pass through customs** = to go through a customs checkpoint

passage *noun* (a) long narrow corridor; *the toilets are at the end of the passage; go down the passage and turn left for the dining room* (b) voyage by ship; to **work one's passage** = to work on a ship so as to get a free voyage to a certain destination

passenger *noun* person who travels in a plane, bus, taxi, plane, etc., but is not the driver or member of the crew; **passenger terminal** = main building at an airport or port for people; **passenger train** = train which carries only passengers (as opposed to freight trains, which carry only goods)

passion fruit *noun Passiflora edulis,* a climbing plant with purple juicy fruit

passport *noun* official document with your photograph and various personal details, proving that you are a citizen of a certain country; you have to show your passport when you travel from one country to another; *we had to show our passports at the customs post; his passport is out of date; the immigration officer stamped my passport;* **passport control** = place where passengers' passports are checked; *we had to wait for half and hour in passport control;* **passport number** = serial number which is unique to each passport; **passport photo** = small photograph of a person's face, used in passports or on season tickets, etc.

pasta *Italian noun* food made from flour from durum wheat, such as lasagne, macaroni, noodles, ravioli, spaghetti, etc.

COMMENT: pasta is available both dried and freshly made. It can be coloured in various ways, flavoured with basil, spinach, tomato, etc. There are a large number of different forms of pasta and they form a basic part of Italian cooking

paste 1 *noun* (a) thin glue, usually made of flour and water (b) soft substance; **fish paste** = soft mixture of dried or salted fish, sold in pots, and served spread on bread or in sandwiches **2** *verb* to stick with glue; *the posters advertising the bullfight are pasted onto show windows*

pasteurize *verb* to heat food to destroy bacteria; *the government is telling people to drink only pasteurized milk*

◊ **pasteurization** *noun* heating of food *or* food products to destroy bacteria, but without changing the flavour very much

COMMENT: Pasteurization is carried out by heating food for a short time at a lower temperature than that used for sterilization: the two methods used are heating to 72°C for fifteen seconds (the high-temperature short-time method) or to 65° for half an hour, and then cooling rapidly. This has the effect of killing tuberculosis bacteria. Pasteurization is used principally in the preservation of milk, though cheese made from unpasteurized milk is thought to have a better flavour

QUOTE a recommendation that caterers use pasteurized eggs for products such as mayonnaise, mousse and ice cream. In addition, lightly cooked dishes such as meringue, hollandaise sauce and Welsh rarebit should not be served to the elderly, sick, babies or pregnant women
Caterer & Hotelkeeper

pastis *noun* French alcoholic drink, flavoured with aniseed

pastry *noun* (a) paste made of flour, fat and water which is used to make pies, etc.; **flaky pastry** = type of soft pastry which breaks into flakes easily when cooked; **puff pastry** = type of soft pastry made from flour and butter, in which air is trapped by repeated folding and rolling of the dough; **shortcrust pastry** = most commonly used type of pastry made with fat and flour (NOTE: no plural in this meaning) (b) sweet cake made of pastry filled with cream or fruit, etc.; **Danish pastry** = sweet pastry cake with jam or fruit folded in it (NOTE: plural is **pastries**)

◊ **pastry chef** *or* **pastry cook** *noun* chef pâtissier, a chef who specializes in preparing pastries and sweet dishes

pasty *noun* small pie made with meat or vegetables wrapped in a pastry case and cooked; **Cornish pasty** = pie of meat and potatoes, wrapped in pastry (a common food in pubs)

pâté *noun* paste made of cooked meat or fish finely minced; **pâté de foie gras** = fine pâté made from goose or duck liver

path *noun* narrow way for walking, cycling or riding; **long-distance path** *or* **footpath** = path laid out by an official organization, which goes for a very long way (over 100 miles)

◇ **pathway** *noun* track for walking along

patron *noun* customer (especially a regular one) of a pub or restaurant; visitor (especially a regular one) to a theatre; *patrons are asked not to smoke in the auditorium*

pawpaw = PAPAYA

pavlova *noun* large circle of meringue filled with fruit and whipped cream

COMMENT: named after the Russian ballerina, Anna Pavlova (1885-1931)

pay 1 *noun* **(a)** salary *or* wage *or* money given to someone for regular work; **basic pay** = normal salary without extra payments; **take-home pay** = pay left after tax and insurance have been deducted; **holidays with pay** = holiday which a worker can take by contract and for which he is paid **(b)** **pay cheque** = monthly cheque which pays a salary to a worker; **pay day** = day on which wages are paid to workers (usually Friday for workers paid once a week, and during the last week of the month for workers who are paid once a month); **pay slip** = piece of paper showing the full amount of a worker's pay, and the money deducted as tax, pension and insurance contributions **(c)** **pay desk** = place in a store where you pay for the goods bought; *US* **pay station** = telephone booth **2** *verb* **(a)** to give money to buy an item or a service; *they paid £1,000 for the first-class tickets; how much did you pay to have your suit cleaned?;* **to pay in advance** = to give money before you receive the item bought *or* before the service has been completed; *you have to pay a deposit in advance when buying a made-to-measure suit;* **to pay in instalments** = to give money for an item or service by giving small amounts regularly; *we are paying for our holidays in instalments of £50 a month;* **to pay cash** = to pay the complete sum in cash; **to pay by cheque** = to pay by giving a cheque, and not by using cash or credit card; **to pay by credit card** = to pay by using a credit card, and not a cheque or cash; **to pay the difference** = to pay an amount which is the difference between two prices; *the second-class fare is £35.00 and first-class £49.00, but you can*

move to first-class if you are willing to pay the difference **(b)** to give (a worker) money for work done; *the restaurant staff have not been paid for three weeks; we pay good wages for skilled workers; how much do they pay you per hour?;* **to be paid by the hour** = to get a fixed amount of money for each hour worked **(c)** to give money which is owed *or* which has to be paid; *to pay a bill; to pay an invoice; to pay duty on imports; to pay tax*
NOTE: **paying - paid**

◇ **payable** *adjective* which is due to be paid; **payable in advance** = which has to be paid before you receive the item bought *or* before the service has been finished; **payable on delivery** = which has to be paid when the goods are delivered; **electricity charges are payable by the tenant** = the tenant (and not the landlord) must pay for the electricity

◇ **pay down** *verb* **to pay money down** = to make a deposit; *he paid £50 down and the rest in monthly instalments*

◇ **paying** *adjective* **(a)** which gives money; **paying guest** = (i) person who stays with a family in their home, and pays a rent; (ii) person who stays at a boarding house and pays for room and board **(b)** which makes a profit; *it is a paying business;* **it is not a paying proposition** = it is not a business which is going to make a profit

◇ **payload** *noun* load of an aircraft which produces income (i.e. the passengers and cargo)

◇ **payment** *noun* **(a)** giving money; *payment in cash or cash payment; payment by cheque; payment of interest or interest payment;* **payment on account** = paying part of the money owed; **full payment** *or* **payment in full** = paying all money owed; **payment on invoice** = paying money as soon as an invoice is received; **payment by results** = money given which increases with the amount of work done or goods produced; **payment receipt** = paper showing that money has been received **(b)** money paid; **down payment** = part of a total cost paid in advance; **incentive payment** = extra pay offered to a worker to make him work better

◇ **payphone** *noun* a public phone where you insert money to make a call

pea *noun* climbing plant of which the round green seeds are eaten as vegetables

COMMENT: peas are available fresh in season, or frozen or canned. Peas can be served from their pods, or the whole pod is cooked rapidly as 'mangetout'

peach *noun* fruit of a small deciduous tree *(Prunus persica)* **peach Melba** = dessert of sliced peaches, with ice cream and raspberry sauce

COMMENT: peaches grow particularly in Mediterranean areas, though they can be grown as far north as southern England. The fruit are large and juicy, with a downy skin; they cannot be kept for any length of time. Peaches are divided into two groups: the freestone (where the flesh is not attached to the stone), and the clingstone. The nectarine is a form of peach with a smooth skin

peak 1 *noun* **(a)** top of a mountain **(b)** highest point; **peak period** = period of the day when most electricity is used or when most traffic is on the roads, etc.; **peak rate** = most expensive tariff for something, such as a telephone call

peanut *noun* nut which grows in the ground in pods like a pea; **peanut butter** = paste made from crushed peanuts

COMMENT: roasted salted peanuts are commonly served as a cocktail snack

pear *noun* fruit of the pear tree *(Pyrus)* normally with a greenish or yellowish skin and soft white flesh

COMMENT: pears are commonly used as dessert fruit, also for cooking. In the UK, William's Bon Chrétien, Conference and Doyenné du Comice are popular dessert varieties, while William's is also commonly used for canning. Pears are also used for fermenting to make perry

pebble *noun* small round stone
◊ **pebbly** *adjective* covered with pebbles; *the beach is pebbly*

pecan *noun* sweet nut from a tree which grows in the south of the USA; **pecan pie** = pie made from corn syrup, cornflour, and pecans

pectin *noun* substance in fruit which helps jam to set

pedal *noun* lever worked by your foot; **pedal bin** = rubbish bin with a lid worked by a pedal

pedalo *noun* type of little boat, with seats for two people who make it go forward by pedalling to turn paddle wheels (NOTE: plural is **pedalos**)

pedestrian *noun* person who goes about on foot; **pedestrian crossing** = place marked with white lines where pedestrians can cross a road; **pedestrian precinct** = part of a town which is closed to traffic so that people can walk about and shop

peel 1 *noun* outer skin of a fruit; also the skin of a potato; *oranges have a thick peel; lemon peel is used as flavouring* **2** *verb* to take the peel off (a fruit or potato); *slices of peeled apples*
◊ **peeler** *noun* **potato peeler** = special tool for peeling potatoes and other vegetables
◊ **peelings** *plural noun* bits of skin from vegetables or fruit

pence *see* PENNY

penny *noun* **(a)** *GB* small coin, of which one hundred make a pound (NOTE: usually written **p** after figures: **26p** (say 'twenty-six pee'); the plural is **pennies** *or* **pence**) **(b)** *US (informal)* small coin, one cent

pension *noun* **(a)** money paid regularly to someone who no longer works; **retirement pension** *or* **old age pension** = state pension given to men over 65 or women over 60; **government pension** *or* **state pension** = pension paid by the state; **occupational pension** = pension which is paid by the company by which a worker has been employed; **portable pension** = pension entitlement which can be moved from one company to another without loss (as a worker changes jobs) **(b)** **pension contributions** = money paid regularly by a company or worker to be saved up to make a pension; **pension entitlement** = amount of pension which someone has the right to receive when he retires; **pension plan** *or* **pension scheme** = plan worked out by an insurance company which arranges for a worker to pay part of his salary over many years and receive a regular payment when he retires; **company pension scheme** = pension which is organized by a company for its staff **(c)** guesthouse *or* boarding house
◊ **en pension** *adjective* **en pension terms** *or* **rate** = special price for guests staying in a hotel who take all their meals in the hotel (the same as 'full board')

COMMENT: normally in the UK this will include breakfast, morning coffee, lunch, afternoon tea and dinner; there will probably be a reduced special menu for 'en pension' guests, which will not include special dishes found on the 'à la carte' menu

penthouse *noun* flat on the top floor of a high building; *the family has booked the penthouse suite for two weeks*

pepper 1 *noun* (a) condiment, made from the crushed seeds of the pepper plant *(Piper nigrum)* **black pepper** *or* **white pepper** *or* **green pepper** *or* **pink pepper** = different types of pepper which are commonly available; **pepper salami** = salami with crushed peppercorns covering the outside (b) **sweet pepper** *or* **green pepper** = fruit of the *Capsicum* (it can be green, red or yellow), eaten cooked or raw in salads (c) **chilli pepper** = fruit of the *Capsicum*, a very hot-tasting pod with seeds in it; available fresh as green or red chillis, dried or preserved in cans or bottles. The dried pods are ground to make Cayenne pepper **2** *verb* to sprinkle with pepper; **peppered steak** = steak covered with crushed peppercorns before cooking

◇ **peppercorn** *noun* dried seed of the pepper plant *Piper nigrum*

◇ **peppermill** *noun* device which grinds peppercorns (the dried seeds are placed in the mill which is twisted to crush them)

◇ **pepper pot** *noun* pot with holes on the lid, filled with ground pepper

◇ **peppery** *adjective* tasting of pepper; *a very peppery soup*

COMMENT: there are two types of ground pepper: black and white (the white is not as strong as the black). The pepper vegetable is either green, yellow or red. It is also called 'sweet pepper' to distinguish it from the chilli pepper. In the UK, a pepper pot has several holes in it, sometimes in the shape of the letter 'P' to differentiate it from the saltcellar; in the USA, the pot will have only one hole while a saltcellar will have several

per *preposition* (a) **as per** = according to; *as per the attached schedule;* **as per invoice** = as stated in the invoice (b) at a rate of; **per hour** *or* **per day** *or* **per week** *or* **per year** = for each hour *or* day *or* week *or* year; *the rate is £5 per hour; he makes about £250 per month;* **we pay £10 per hour** = we pay £10 for each hour worked; *the car was travelling at twenty-five miles per hour* = at a speed which covered 25 miles in one hour; **per**

head *or* **per person** *or* **per capita** = for each person; *allow £15 per head for lunch; the total cost for the tour comes to £150 per person*

◇ **per cent** *adverb* out of each hundred *or* for each hundred; **10 per cent** = ten in every hundred; *what is the increase per cent? 12 per cent is added to the bill for service; the airline has reduced the number of seats in Business Class, so increasing the leg room by about 15%*

◇ **percentage** *noun* amount shown as part of one hundred; **percentage discount** = discount calculated at an amount per hundred; **percentage increase** = increase calculated on the basis of a rate for one hundred

perch *noun* type of freshwater fish

percolate *verb* to filter (through)

◇ **percolation** *noun* filtering through

◇ **percolator** *noun* coffeemaker where the water boils up through a tube and filters through ground coffee

COMMENT: in a percolator, the coffee is boiled again and again, as opposed to expresso-type coffeemakers where the hot water only rises once

period *noun* length of time; *for a period of time or for a period of months or for a six-year period; number of passengers carried over a period of three months; bookings for the holiday period are down on last year*

perishable *adjective* (food) which can go bad quickly; **perishables** = perishable food

permission *noun* being allowed to do something; **written permission** = document which allows someone to do something; *you need the written permission of the owner to visit the castle;* **to give someone permission to do something** = to allow someone to do something; *he asked permission of the manager or he asked the manager's permission to take a day off*

permit 1 *noun* official document which allows someone to do something; **export permit** *or* **import permit** = official document which allows goods to be exported *or* imported; **work permit** = official document which allows someone who is not a citizen to work in a country **2** *verb* to allow someone to do something; *this document permits you to export twenty-five computer* *systems; the ticket permits three people to go into the exhibition*

perry *noun* alcoholic drink made from pear juice

person *noun* human being; **price per person** = price for one adult

◊ **person-to-person call** *noun* telephone call where you ask the operator to connect you with a named person

personal *adjective* referring to one person; **personal call** = (i) telephone call where you ask the operator to connect you with a named person; (ii) telephone call not related to business; *staff are not allowed to make personal calls during office hours;* **personal hygiene** = keeping oneself clean and healthy, by washing the body, hands, hair, etc. often, and keeping one's clothes clean; **personal message** = message for a particular person

personnel *noun* people who work in a certain place *or* for a certain company; *the personnel of the hotel or the hotel personnel; we are looking for experienced personnel for our tourist information office;* **the personnel department** = section of the company which deals with the staff; **personnel management** = organizing and training of staff so that they work well and profitably; **personnel manager** *or* **personnel officer** = head of the personnel department

peseta *noun* currency used in Spain (NOTE: usually written **ptas** after a figure: **2,000ptas)**

peso *noun* currency used in Mexico and many other countries

pest *noun* living animal which attacks or prevents the growth of crops or animals, or which may cause trouble to stored produce; *a spray to remove insect pests;* **pest control** = restricting the spread of pest (by killing it); *see also* COCKROACH, FLY, MOUSE, RAT

| COMMENT: the word is a relative term: a pest to one person may not be a pest to another, so foxes are pests to chicken farmers, but not to naturalists

◊ **pesticide** *noun* toxic agent used to control or destroy a wide variety of plant, animal and microbial organisms

| COMMENT: there are three basic types of pesticide. **1.** organochlorine insecticides, which have a high persistence in the environment of up to about 15 years (DDT, dieldrin and aldrin). **2.** organophosphates, which have an intermediate persistence of several months (parathion, carbaryl and malathion). **3.** carbamates, which have a low persistence of around two weeks (Temik, Zectran and Zineb). Most pesticides are broad-spectrum, that is they kill all insects in a certain area and may kill other animals like birds and small mammals. Pesticide residue levels in food in the UK are generally low. Pesticide residues have been found in bran products, bread and baby foods, as well as in milk and meat. Where pesticides are found, the levels are low and rarely exceed international maximum residue levels

pet *noun* animal (such as a cat or dog) kept in the home to give pleasure; *pets are not allowed into the restaurant; this little sign in the directory indicates hotels which welcome pets*

petits fours *plural noun* very small cakes and biscuits, often containing marzipan, served with coffee after a meal

petrol *noun* liquid, made from petroleum, used to drive a car engine; *the car is very economic on petrol; we are looking for a car with a low petrol consumption;* **petrol station** = place where you can buy petrol; *he stopped at a petrol station to get some petrol before going on to the motorway* (NOTE: US English is **gasoline** *or* **gas)**

pheasant *noun* large bird with a long tail, shot for sport and food and in season from October 1st to January 31st

| COMMENT: the male bird is brightly coloured and larger than the female. They are usually sold as a pair or 'brace' - that is, one male and one female

phone 1 *noun* telephone, machine used for speaking to someone; *we had a new phone system installed last week;* **by phone** = using the telephone; *to place an order by phone;* **to be on the phone** = to be speaking to someone by telephone; *she has been on the phone all morning; he spoke to the manager on the phone;* **house phone** *or* **internal phone** = telephone which links different rooms in a hotel, but is not connected to an outside line; *call room service on the house phone;*

room phone = telephone in a hotel room; **phone book** *or* **phone directory** = book which lists names of people and businesses in alphabetical order with their telephone numbers and addresses; *look up his address in the phone book; he looked up the number of the company in the phone book;* **phone booking** = reservation (of a room in a hotel, a table in a restaurant, etc.) made by phone; *phone bookings must be confirmed in writing;* **phone booth** *or* **phone box** = small cabin for a public telephone; **phone call** = conversation with someone on the telephone; **to make a phone call** = to dial and speak to someone on the telephone; **to answer the phone** *or* **to take a phone call** = to lift the telephone when it rings and listen to what the caller is saying; **phone link** = direct line from one telephone to another; **phone number** = set of figures for a particular telephone subscriber; *he keeps a list of phone numbers in a little black book; the phone number is on the hotel notepaper; can you give me your phone number?* **2** *verb* to **phone a person** *or* **a place** = to call someone *or* a place by telephone; *don't phone me, I'll phone you; his secretary phoned to say he would be late; he phoned the reservation through to the hotel; the travel agency phoned to say that the tickets were ready for collection; she phoned room service to order some coffee; it's very expensive to phone Singapore at this time of day;* **to phone about something** = to make a telephone call to speak about something; *he phoned about the table he had reserved for 8 p.m.;* **to phone for something** = to make a telephone call to ask for something; *he phoned for a taxi*

◊ **phone back** *verb* to make a phone call in reply to another; *the manager is in a meeting, can you phone back in about half an hour? Mr Smith called while you were out and asked if you would phone him back*

◊ **phone card** *noun* plastic card which you can buy at a post office, and insert into a special slot in a public telephone booth to make a phone call

photocopier *noun* machine which makes a copy of a document by photographing and printing it

◊ **photocopy 1** *noun* copy of a document made by photographing and printing it; *make six photocopies of the letter* **2** *verb* to make a copy of (a document) by photographing and printing it; *she photocopied the town plan*

◊ **photocopying** *noun* copying a document by photographing and printing it; **there is a mass of photocopying to be**

done = there are many documents waiting to be photocopied; **photocopying bureau** = office which photocopies documents for companies which do not possess their own photocopiers; **photocopying service** = offering to make photocopies for customers; *the business centre has a photocopying service*

pick 1 *noun* **(a)** act of choosing; thing *or* person *or* place chosen; **take your pick** = choose what you want; **the pick of the bunch** *or* **of the group** = the best item in the group **(b)** small metal tool, like a long needle, used to remove flesh from shellfish or from nutshells, or to break up ice; *a lobster pick* **2** *verb* to choose; *the board picked the finance director to succeed the retiring MD; the Association has picked Paris for its next meeting*

◊ **pick up** *verb* **(a)** to take (a passenger) into a vehicle; *he picked up two hitchhikers at the entrance to the motorway; the coach will call to pick up passengers at the hotel* **(b)** to get better *or* to improve; *business or trade is picking up*

◊ **pickup** *noun* **pickup point** = place where a group of people arranges to be collected by a coach, etc.; **pickup (truck)** = type of small van with an open area for transporting goods; **pickup and delivery service** = service which takes goods from the warehouse and delivers them to the customer

pickle 1 *noun* vegetables preserved in vinegar, etc.; **lime pickle** = very hot-tasting Indian condiment; **sweet pickles** = pickles made with a lot of sugar **2** *verb* to preserve (vegetables, etc.) in vinegar, etc.; **pickled gherkins** *or* **pickled onions** *or* **pickled walnuts** = gherkins *or* onions *or* walnuts preserved by soaking in vinegar and herbs

picnic 1 *noun* **(a)** excursion with a meal eaten in the open air; *we have organized a picnic in the woods* **(b)** meal eaten outdoors; **picnic area** = place where people can have a picnic; **picnic lunch** = lunch eaten in the open air, taken with you in a bag, box or basket **2** *verb* to eat a picnic; *picnicking is not allowed in the botanical gardens*

NOTE: **picnicking - picnicked**

◊ **picnicker** *noun* person who goes on a picnic

pie *noun* cooked dish of pastry with a filling of meat or fruit, eaten hot or cold; *a slice of veal and ham pie; apple pie with ice cream*

pied-à-terre *noun* small flat or studio, used by someone as a temporary place to live; *he lives in the country but has a pied-à-terre in London*

pier *noun* construction going out into the water, used as a landing place for ships

pigeon *see* WOOD PIGEON

◊ **pigeonhole** *noun* one of a series of small spaces for filing documents *or* for putting letters for delivery to separate rooms or for collection; *there was a message in his pigeonhole when he returned to the hotel*

pilaff *or* **pilau** *noun* Eastern dish of rice with vegetables, herbs and spices, and sometimes with meat; *we had lamb pilaff*

pilchard *noun* small fish similar to a herring, sold in tins

pilgrim *noun* person who travels to an important religious place; *pilgrims travel to Mecca in specially chartered planes; a coach carrying a group of 50 pilgrims to Lourdes*

◊ **pilgrimage** *noun* travel to an important religious place; *the church is organizing a pilgrimage to Rome in April*

pillar box *noun* (*in GB*) cylindrical red metal container into which mail is put to be collected and delivered

pillow *noun* bag full of soft material which you put your head on in bed

◊ **pillowcase** *or* **pillowslip** *noun* cloth bag to cover a pillow

pilot *noun* (a) person who flies a plane *or* guides a ship into port; *the ship stops at the entrance to the canal to take on a pilot; the pilot reported bad visibility over the airport; see also* CAPTAIN, COPILOT (b) test which, if successful, will then be expanded into a full operation; *the hotel group set up a pilot project to see if the proposed staff training scheme was efficient; he is directing a pilot scheme for training unemployed young people*

pimento *or* *US* **pimiento** *noun* fruit of the *Capsicum* (it can be green, red or yellow), eaten cooked or raw in salads

pin 1 *noun* small sharp metal stick with a round head, used for attaching fabric or paper, etc.; **safety pin** = type of bent pin for attaching fabric, where the sharp point is held by a metal shield **2** *verb* **to pin up a**

notice = to attach a notice to a wall or noticeboard with pins

pineapple *noun* fruit of a tropical plant *Ananas comosus,* native to South America and now grown in many tropical areas; the fruit are eaten both raw and canned, or in the form of juice extracted by crushing

pink gin *noun* drink made by putting a little Angostura bitters into a glass, swirling it round and pouring it out, then adding gin

pint *noun* measure of liquids (equal to one eighth of a gallon); *two pints of bitter, please; the recipe takes half a pint of milk*

> COMMENT: a British pint is equal to 0.568 of a litre; an American pint is equal to 0.473 of a litre. The pint is also used to measure seafood, such as prawns or mussels

pip *noun* small seed

pipe *verb* to squeeze soft food mixture through a small tube, so as to make decorative shapes; *duchesse potatoes are piped into spiral shapes and cooked*

pistachio *noun* small green tropical nut, eaten salted as an appetizer or used as a flavouring in sweet dishes, especially ice cream

piste *noun* track for skiing; **off-piste skiing** = skiing away from the marked tracks

pit *noun* the stone in certain fruit (cherries, plums, peaches, or dried fruit such as prunes and dates)

◊ **pitted** *adjective* (fruit) which has had the stone taken out; *pitted dates*

pitch 1 *noun* (*in an aircraft*) **seat pitch** = distance between the front edge of a seat and the front edge of the seat in front **2** *verb* (*of a ship*) to move up and down lengthwise (the bow and the stern); *compare* ROLL

pitcher *noun* large jug, often used to serve beer or cocktails

pith *noun* soft white stuff under the skin of a lemon, an orange, etc.

pitta (bread) *noun* flat white unleavened bread, served with Greek and Turkish food

pizza *noun* Italian savoury dish, consisting of a flat round piece of dough cooked with tomatoes, onions, cheese, etc., on top; *see also* DEEP PAN

◊ **pizzeria** *noun* restaurant which sells pizzas; **pizzeria chef** = chef who prepares pizzas in a restaurant

place 1 *noun* **(a)** where something is *or* where something happens; **to take place** = to happen; *the meeting will take place in the conference room;* **meeting place** = room *or* area where people can meet; **place of birth** = town where a person was born; **place of issue** = town where a passport was issued; **place of work** = office *or* hotel *or* restaurant, etc. where people work; **places of interest** = buildings or parts of the countryside which are interesting to visit; *a tour to visit places of interest in south Italy; there are lots of places to visit within 50 miles of central London* **(b)** position (in a competition); *three companies are fighting for first place in the package holiday market* **(c)** job; *he was offered a place with a restaurant chain; she turned down three places before accepting the one we offered* **2** *verb* **(a)** to put; *the soup spoon is placed on the right-hand side of the place setting;* **to place a contract** = to decide that a certain company shall have the contract to do work; **to place something on file** = to file something; **to place an order** = to order something; *he placed an order for 250 tins of instant coffee* **(b) to place staff** = to find jobs for staff; **how are you placed for work?** = have you enough work to do?

◊ **placemat** *noun* piece of cloth, cork, etc., which a person's plate is put on at table (it protects the surface of a table and is used in restaurants where no tablecloths are used to cover polished wooden tables)

◊ **place setting** *noun* set of knives, forks, spoons, glasses, etc. for one person

plaice *noun* type of flat white sea fish; *fried fillets of plaice* (NOTE: plural is **plaice**)

plan 1 *noun* **(a)** organized way of doing something; **contingency plan** *or* **emergency plan** = plan which will be put into action if something happens which no one expects to happen **(b)** drawing which shows how something is arranged *or* how something will be built; *the designers showed us the first plans for the new hotel;* **floor plan** = drawing of a floor in a building, showing where different rooms, stairs and emergency exits are; **seating plan** = chart showing where each guest sits at a big banquet; **street plan** *or* **town plan** = diagram showing the streets of a town with their names; **table plan** = layout of the tables in a large room for a function (as for a dinner-dance) to show where each person is to sit, and to allow for efficient service **2** *verb* to organize carefully how something should be done; **to plan for an increase in visitors to the music festival** = to change a way of doing things because you think there will be more visitors to the music festival

NOTE: **planning - planned**

◊ **planner** *noun* **(a)** person who plans **(b)** **desk planner** *or* **wall planner** = book *or* chart which shows days *or* weeks *or* months so that the work of an office can be shown by diagrams

◊ **planning** *noun* **(a)** organizing how something should be done, especially how a company should be run to make increased profits; **long-term planning** *or* **short-term planning** = making plans for a long *or* short period **(b)** *GB* **the planning department** = section of a local government office which deals with requests for planning permission; **planning permission** = official document allowing a person *or* company to construct new buildings; *the group was refused planning permission; we are waiting for planning permission before we can start building the cinema; the land is to be sold with planning permission for a motel*

QUOTE buildings are closely regulated by planning restrictions
Investors Chronicle

plane *noun* aircraft *or* machine which flies in the air, carrying passengers or cargo; *I intend to take the 5 o'clock plane to New York; he could not get a seat on Tuesday's plane, so he had to wait until Wednesday; there are ten planes a day from London to Paris;* **plane ticket** = ticket which allows a passenger to travel by plane

planetarium *noun* domed building in which you sit and watch as pictures of the stars are projected against the ceiling

plantain *noun* name given to various types of large banana, used for cooking; it has a lower sugar content than dessert bananas

plat du jour *French phrase (meaning 'dish of the day')* a special dish prepared for the day and not listed in the printed menu

plate *noun* flat dish for putting food on; **plate service** = type of restaurant service, where the food is put onto the plate before the plate is carried to each guest (saving the

plate 183 **point**

time and cost of serving each guest with each item individually); *see also* PRE-PLATING; **dinner plate** = wide flat plate for serving a main course on; **show plate** = plate placed in the centre of the setting (in French service), removed before serving; **side plate** = small plate placed beside the main plate and cutlery, used for bread; **soup plate** = wide deep plate in which soup is served (as opposed to a soup bowl)

◊ **plated service** *see* PLATE SERVICE

◊ **plateful** *noun* quantity held by a plate

◊ **plate room** *noun* room (in a hotel) where plates, glasses and cutlery are stored, ready for use in the restaurant

platform *noun* high pavement in a station, running alongside the track, where passengers can get on or off trains; *the train for Birmingham leaves from Platform 12; the ticket office is on Platform 2*

platter *noun* **(a)** large flat serving plate **(b)** large plate of prepared food, arranged in a decorative way; **cheese platter** *or* **seafood platter** *or* **shellfish platter** = large plate with various cheeses, fish or shellfish

playground *or* **play area** *noun* area, especially round a building, where children can play; *there is a children's play area near the motel*

plongeur *French noun* person who washes dishes in a restaurant

plonk *noun (informal)* inferior wine

plough *or* US **plow** *see* SNOWPLOUGH

pluck *verb* to take the feathers off (a bird), before it is cooked

plug 1 *noun* **(a)** device at the end of a wire for connecting a machine to the electricity supply; **universal plug** = form of plug with various types of pin, which can be used in several different types of socket **(b)** disc of rubber or metal which covers a hole, especially the hole for waste water in a bath or sink, etc.; *there is no plug in my bath* **(c)** *(informal)* **to give a plug to a new leisure centre** = to publicize a new leisure centre **(d)** = SOCKET **2** *verb* **(a)** **to plug in** = to connect a machine to the electricity supply; *the TV was not plugged in* **(b)** *(informal)* to publicize *or* to advertise; *they ran six commercials plugging holidays in Spain*
NOTE: **plugging - plugged**

plum *noun* gold, red or purple fruit *(Prunus domestica)*, with a smooth skin and a large stone; **plum pudding** = rich fruit pudding, cooked by steaming, usually eaten at Christmas; **plum tomato** = variety of tomato which is longer and egg-shaped (the variety most usually used for canning)

p.m. *or* US **P.M.** *abbreviation* referring to the period between midday and midnight, in the afternoon *or* in the evening; *the train leaves at 6.50 p.m.; if you phone New York after 8 p.m. the calls are at a cheaper rate*

PO = POST OFFICE

poach *verb* to cook (eggs without their shells, fish, etc.) in gently boiling water; *sole poached in white wine;* **poached egg** = egg which is taken out of its shell and cooked whole in hot water (usually eaten on toast, at breakfast)

pocket *noun* small bag attached to the inside of a coat, trousers, etc., for holding money, keys, etc.; **back pocket** = pocket in the back of a pair of trousers; *his wallet was stolen from his back pocket;* **pocket dictionary** = small dictionary which you can keep in your pocket; **pocket phrasebook** = phrasebook which you can keep in your pocket

point 1 *noun* **(a)** place *or* position; **breakeven point** = point at which sales cover costs, but do not show a profit; **customs entry point** = place at a border between two countries *or* at an airport or port, where goods are declared to customs; **starting point** = place where something starts; *the starting point for the excursion is the Post Office* **(b)** **decimal point** = dot which indicates the division between a whole unit and its smaller parts (such as 4.25); **percentage point** = 1 per cent; **half a percentage point** = 0.5 per cent; **the dollar gained two points** = the dollar increased in value against another currency by two hundredths of a cent **2** *verb* **to point out** = to show; *the report of the fire department points out the mistakes made by the builders of the hotel; he pointed out that the bookings for the Christmas season were better than in previous years*

◊ **point of sale (POS)** *noun* place where a product is sold (such as a shop); **point-of-sale (POS) material** = display material (such as posters) to advertise a product where it is being sold

QUOTE banks refrained from quoting forward US/Hongkong dollar exchange rates as premiums of 100 points replaced discounts of up to 50 points
South China Morning Post
QUOTE POS systems issue a ticket on the kitchen printer for each item ordered. The kitchen will not dispense food until the printed ticket has appeared. This ticket means that the charge of items is on the bill, creating the knowledge that all items leaving the kitchen have been paid for
Caterer & Hotelkeeper

poison 1 *noun* substance which can kill *or* harm when eaten, drunk, breathed in *or* touched; **poison ivy** *or* **poison oak** = North American plants whose leaves can cause a painful and itchy rash if touched **2** *verb* to kill or harm someone *or* something with poison

◊ **poisoning** *noun* killing *or* harming someone *or* something with a poison; **blood poisoning** = condition where bacteria are present in blood and cause illness; **salmonella poisoning** = illness caused by eating food which is contaminated with Salmonella bacteria which develop in the intestines; **staphylococcal poisoning** = poisoning by Staphylococci which have spread in food

◊ **poisonous** *adjective* (substance) which is toxic *or* full of poison *or* which can kill or harm; *some mushrooms are good to eat and some are poisonous*

COMMENT: the commonest poisons, of which even a small amount can kill, are arsenic, cyanide and strychnine. Many common foods and drugs can be poisonous if taken in large doses. Common household materials such as bleach, glue and insecticides can also be poisonous. Some types of poisoning, such as Salmonella, can be passed to other people through lack of hygiene

poivre *French noun* pepper; **steak au poivre** = steak which has been grilled and has a sauce made with pepper and peppercorns poured over it

policy *noun* **(a)** decisions on the general way of doing something; **company policy** = the company's agreed plan of action *or* the company's way of doing things; *what is the airline's policy on refunds? it is against company policy to give more than thirty days' credit; our policy is to submit all contracts to the legal department* **(b)**

insurance policy = document which shows the conditions of an insurance contract; **an accident policy** = an insurance which will pay if an accident occurs; **all-risks policy** = insurance policy which covers risks of any kind, with no exclusions; **a comprehensive** *or* **an all-in policy** = insurance policy which covers you against all risks which are likely to happen; **contingent policy** = policy which pays out only if something happens (as, if the person named in the policy dies before the person due to benefit); **policy holder** = person who is insured by an insurance company; **to take out a policy** = to sign the contract for an insurance and start paying the premiums; *she took out a life insurance policy* or *a house insurance policy;* **the insurance company made out a policy** *or* **drew up a policy** = the company wrote the details of the contract on the policy (NOTE: plural is **policies)**

polite *adjective* behaving in a pleasant way; *we stipulate that our salesgirls must be polite to customers; we had a polite letter from the hotel manager*

◊ **politely** *adverb* in a pleasant way; *she politely answered the guests' questions*

polyunsaturated fat *noun* fatty acid capable of absorbing more hydrogen (typical of vegetable and fish oils)

pomegranate *noun* a semi-tropical tree *(Punica granatum);* the fruit have yellowish pink or red skin, with masses of seeds surrounded by sweet red flesh

pony *noun* small breed of horse (NOTE: plural is **ponies)**

◊ **pony-trekking** *noun* riding ponies in the country for pleasure; *we often go pony-trekking in the summer; the hotel offers pony-trekking holidays in the mountains; see also* HORSE-RIDING

pool *noun* **(a)** **swimming pool** = enclosed tank of water for swimming in; **indoor pool** *or* **heated pool** = swimming pool which is indoors *or* which has heated water **(b)** game similar to snooker; **pool table** = table on which pool is played; *see also* BILLIARDS, SNOOKER

◊ **poolroom** *noun US* public room where you can play pool

poor *adjective* **(a)** without much money; *it is one of the poorest countries in the world, but the scenery is magnificent* **(b)** not very good; *poor quality of goods in the shops; we* *all complained about the poor service in the hotel coffee lounge; poor turnround time of aircraft can affect schedules; poor insulation or poor air-conditioning or poor noise insulation*

◊ **poorly** *adverb* badly; *the reception area is poorly laid out; the tour was poorly planned;* **poorly paid staff** = staff with low wages

popcorn *noun* corn seed which is heated (sometimes with sugar) until it bursts; eaten as a snack and often served in large cardboard containers at cinemas and fairgrounds

poppadom *noun* thin round crisp Indian pancake, fried or grilled

popsicle *noun US* trade name for a mixture of water and flavouring, frozen till solid with a stick in it (NOTE: GB English is **ice lolly**)

popular *adjective* liked by many people; *this is our most popular resort; the South Coast is the most popular area for holidays;* **popular prices** = prices which are low and therefore liked

pork *noun* fresh meat from pigs (as opposed to cured meat, which is bacon or ham); **pork pie** = minced pork in a pastry case, usually eaten cold

COMMENT: in some countries pork and other meat from pigs is not eaten as it is considered unclean by the religion of the country (this applies to the Moslem and Jewish religions)

porridge *noun* oatmeal cooked in water; **porridge oats** = oats which have been crushed ready to be made into porridge

COMMENT: porridge is served at breakfast; in Scotland it is traditionally served with salt, but elsewhere it is served with sugar and milk or cream

port *noun* **(a)** harbour, a place where ships come to load *or* unload; *the port of Rotterdam;* **to call at a port** = to stop at a port to load or unload cargo or drop or taken on passengers; **port authority** = organization which runs a port; **port of call** = port at which a ship often stops; **port charges** *or* **port dues** = payment which a ship makes to the port authority for the right to use the port; **port of embarkation** = port at which you get onto a ship, etc.; **port**

installations = buildings and equipment of a port; **commercial port** = port which has only goods traffic; **fishing port** = port which is used mainly by fishing boats; **free port** = port where there are no customs duties to be paid; **inland port** = port on a river *or* canal **(b)** dessert wine from Portugal, served after a meal (except in France, where port is served before a meal as an apéritif) **(c)** the left-hand side of a ship when facing the bow; also used of the left-hand side of an aircraft (NOTE: the opposite is **starboard**)

porter *noun* **(a)** person who carries luggage for travellers (at an airport, a railway station, in a hotel, etc.) (NOTE: in the USA and Canada they are called **'redcaps'** because they wear red caps) **hall porter** = person who is on duty in the hall of a hotel, especially one who stands near the main door of a hotel and deals with arriving or departing guests and their baggage; **night porter** = porter who is on duty at a hotel during the night (he answers calls from guest rooms as well as dealing with any late arrivals) **(b)** type of dark sweet beer brewed from malt

portion *noun* small quantity, especially enough food for one person; *we serve ice cream in individual portions;* **child's portion** *or* **children's portion** = small portion for a child; **portion control** = keeping a check on the amount of food served by splitting it up into individual portions (as, for example, serving butter in small individual packets or pots)

p.o.s. *or* **POS** = POINT OF SALE; **POS material** = POINT-OF-SALE MATERIAL

posh *adjective (informal)* smart, fashionable; *he took us for lunch to one of the poshest restaurants in town*

position *noun* **(a)** situation *or* state of affairs; **what is the cash position?** = what is the state of the company's current account? **(b)** site, place where a building is; *the hotel occupies a central position in the town; the restaurant's lakeside position makes it very popular in summer* **(c)** job, paid work in a company; *to apply for a position as hotel manager; we have several positions vacant in our front-of-the-house area; all the vacant positions have been filled; she retired from her position in the corporate reservations department;* **he is in a key position** = he has an important job **(d)** *(at bank, post office, check-in)* separate place where a customer is dealt with; **'position closed'** = notice to show that a counter is not open

post 1 *noun* **(a)** system of sending letters and parcels from one place to another; *he put the letter in the post; the cheque was lost in the post; post to the Falkland Islands can take up to a week;* **by post** = using the postal services, not sending something by hand or by messenger; *to send the tickets by post;* **we sent the order by first-class post** = by the most expensive mail service, designed to be faster; **to send a reply by return of post** = to reply by the next post service; **letter post** *or* **parcel post** = service for sending letters or parcels; **post room** = room in an office where the post is sorted and sent to each department or collected from each department for sending **(b)** letters sent or received; *has the post arrived yet? my secretary opens the post as soon as it arrives; the receipt was in this morning's post; the tickets did not arrive by first post this morning* **(c)** job, paid work in a company; *to apply for a post as cashier; we have three posts vacant; all our posts have been filled; we advertised three posts in the 'Hotel Gazette'* **2** *verb* **(a)** to send something by post; *to post a letter or to post a parcel; we posted our confirmation last Wednesday* **(b) to post up a notice** = to put a notice on a wall *or* on a noticeboard; *the courier posted up a list of ski runs which were open*

postage *noun* payment for sending a letter or parcel by post; *what is the postage to New Zealand?;* **postage paid** = words printed on an envelope to show that the sender has paid the postage even though there is no stamp on it; **postage stamp** = small piece of gummed paper which you buy from a post office and stick on a letter or parcel so it can be sent through the post

postal *adjective* referring to the post; **postal charges** *or* **postal rates** = money to be paid for sending letters or parcels by post; *postal charges are going up by 10% in September;* **postal order** = document which can be bought at a post office for sending small amounts of money through the post

postbox *noun* public box into which mail is put to be collected and delivered

postcard *noun* piece of cardboard for sending a message by post (NOTE: with a picture on one side it is called a **picture postcard)**

postcode *noun* letters and numbers used to indicate a town or street in an address (NOTE: US English is **ZIP code)**

poster *noun* large notice *or* advertisement to be stuck up on a wall; *in the underground we saw posters advertising holidays in Spain*

poste restante *noun* system where letters can be addressed to someone at a post office, where they can be collected; *send any messages to 'Poste Restante, Athens'* (NOTE: the US English for this is **General Delivery)**

post-free *adverb* without having to pay any postage; *the timetable is obtainable post-free from the airline offices*

postmark 1 *noun* mark stamped by the post office on a letter, covering the postage stamp, to show that the post office has accepted it, and giving the name of the post office or town and the date; *letter with a London postmark* **2** *verb* to stamp (a letter) with a postmark; *the letter was postmarked New York*

post office *noun* **(a)** building where the postal services are based and where you can buy stamps, send parcels, etc.; **main post office** *or* **central post office** = large post office in a big town, which handles all the services available through post offices; **sub-post office** = small post office, usually part of a general store **(b) the Post Office** = national organization which deals with sending letters and parcels; *Post Office officials or officials of the Post Office; Post Office van;* **Post Office box number** = reference number used when asking for mail to be sent to a post office

QUOTE travellers cheques cost 1% of their face value and can be purchased from any bank, main post offices, travel agents and several building societies
Sunday Times

post-paid *adjective* with the postage already paid; *the price is £5.95 post-paid*

postpone *verb* to arrange for something to take place later than planned; *he postponed the meeting to tomorrow; they asked if they could postpone payment until the cash situation was better*

◇ **postponement** *noun* arranging for something to take place later than planned; *I had to change my appointments because of the postponement of the board meeting*

pot 1 *noun* container made of glass or clay; **cooking pot** = pot used for cooking **2** *verb* to put in a pot; **potted shrimps** = shrimps which have been cooked and put in a small pot with melted butter, served with lemon and brown bread and butter

◊ **pot-hole** *noun* **(a)** hole in rock worn away by water **(b)** hole in a road surface

◊ **pot-holer** *noun* person who climbs down inside pot-holes as a sport

◊ **pot-holing** *noun* sport of climbing down inside pot-holes

◊ **potluck** *noun* **to take potluck** = to take whatever food is served, with no possibility of choice

potable *adjective* (water) which can be drunk safely

potage *noun* thick soup, especially one made from vegetables

◊ **potager** *French noun* **chef potager** = chef in charge of making soups

potato *noun* **(a)** tuber of *Solanum tuberosum*, the most important common vegetable; **baked potato** = (i) = JACKET POTATO; (ii) = ROAST POTATO; **creamed potatoes** = MASHED POTATOES; **duchesse potatoes** = creamed potatoes with beaten egg added, piped into small mounds and baked in an oven; **jacket potato** = potato cooked 'in its jacket', that is, baked in an oven without being peeled, then served cut open, with butter or various fillings, such as cheese, chopped ham, baked beans, chilli, etc.; **mashed potatoes** = potatoes which have been peeled, boiled and then crushed with butter and milk until they are soft; **new potatoes** = small potatoes picked at the beginning of the season; **roast potato** = potato baked in fat in an oven; **sauté potatoes** = slices of potato, fried in a little fat; **potato crisp** *or US* **potato chip** *see* CRISP (NOTE: on menus, potatoes can be called by their French name: **pommes de terre**, or simply **pommes**) **(b) sweet potato** = *Ipomoea batatas* a starchy root vegetable grown in tropical and subtropical regions (also called 'yams' in the Southern USA; the plant has no connection with the ordinary potato)

COMMENT: in Britain potatoes were traditionally eaten at every main meal, along with another vegetable, such as cabbage, carrots, peas, etc. The potato is an important source of carbohydrate, but nowadays is replaced at some meals by pasta, rice or bread. More than a dozen different varieties are grown commercially in Britain, and some are better than others for different cooking purposes.

poultry *noun* general term for domestic birds kept for meat and egg production; chickens are the most common; turkeys, ducks, guinea fowl, quails and geese are also widely used (NOTE: the word is mainly used in butchers' shops and recipe books)

pound *noun* **(a)** measure of weight (= 0.45 kilos); *to sell oranges by the pound; a pound of oranges; oranges cost 50p a pound; US she weighs 140 pounds* (NOTE: in the USA, body weight is given in pounds, while in the UK it is given in stones; pound is usually written **lb** after figures: **25lb**) **(b)** currency used in the UK and many other countries; **pound sterling** = official term for the unit of money used in the UK; *a pound coin; breakfast costs four pounds; the pound/dollar exchange rate;* a ten-pound note = a banknote for ten pounds (NOTE: when used with a figure, usually written **£** before the figure: **£25**)

powder room *noun* women's toilet in a public place, such as a restaurant or shop

power *noun* electrical driving force; **power pack** = portable source of electricity; **power point** = wall plug which supplies electricity; *there is a power point for shavers in the bathroom*

PR = PUBLIC RELATIONS *a PR man; the PR department*

praline *noun* sweet made of crushed nuts and caramelized sugar

prawn *noun* type of shellfish, like a large shrimp; *prawn curry; a prawn and mayonnaise sandwich;* **prawn cocktail** = starter consisting of shelled prawns in mayonnaise and tomato dressing, served in a glass with shredded lettuce; **king prawn** *or* **Dublin Bay prawn** = type of very large prawn, the type which is served as scampi

pre- *prefix* meaning 'in advance' or 'before'; *see* PRE-BOOKED, PREPAY, PRE-THEATRE

pre-booked *adjective* (table, seat, etc.) which has been booked in advance

precinct *noun* **(a) pedestrian precinct** *or* **shopping precinct** = part of a town which is closed to traffic so that people can walk about and shop **(b)** *US* administrative district in a town

precipitation *noun* water which falls from clouds as rain, snow, hail, etc.; *precipitation in the mountain areas is higher than in the plains*

predict *verb* to foretell, to tell in advance what will happen

premises *plural noun* building and the land it stands on; **business premises** *or* **commercial premises** = building and the land it stands on, used by a business; **hotel premises** = building which houses a hotel; **lock-up premises** = restaurant *or* shop which has no living accommodation and which the proprietor locks at night when it is closed; **licensed premises** = shop *or* restaurant *or* public house which has a licence to sell alcohol; **on the premises** = in the building; *there is a doctor on the premises at all times*

premium *noun* **(a) insurance premium** = regular small payment made by the insured person to the insurer; *you pay either an annual premium of £360 or twelve monthly premiums of £32;* **additional premium** = payment made to cover extra items in an existing insurance **(b)** special prize; **premium cabin** *or* **premium section** = part of a plane where the passengers have special service (usually, the first-class section); **premium offer** = free gift offered to attract more customers **(c)** amount to be paid to a landlord or a tenant for the right to take over a lease; *flat to let with a premium of £10,000; annual rent: £8,500, premium: £25,000* **(d)** extra charge; **exchange premium** = extra cost above the normal rate for buying foreign currency **(e) premium quality** = top quality; *the hamburger chain says it only uses premium-quality beef*

prepaid *adjective* paid in advance; **prepaid reply card** = stamped addressed card which is sent to someone so that he can reply without paying the postage

prepay *verb* to pay in advance
NOTE: **prepaying - prepaid**

◊ **prepayment** *noun* payment in advance; **to ask for prepayment of a fee** = to ask for the fee to be paid before the work is done

pre-plated *adjective* (food) which is put on the plates in the kitchen before being served

◊ **pre-plating** *noun* type of service where food is served ready on the plate

QUOTE a classier food and beverage service will be on offer. The airline will be experimenting with chefs on board to serve food as meals will no longer arrive pre-plated
Business Traveller

presentation *noun* **(a)** showing a document; **free admission on presentation of the card** = you do not pay to go in if you show this card **(b)** demonstration *or* exhibition of a proposed plan; *the manufacturer made a presentation of his new product line to possible hotel customers; we have asked two PR firms to make presentations of proposed publicity campaigns*

preserve 1 *noun* fruit or vegetables, cooked and kept in jars or cans for future use (jams, pickles, marmalades, etc.); *small pots of grapefruit preserve were on the breakfast table* **2** *verb* to treat (food) so that it keeps for a long time

◊ **preservative** *noun* substance added to food to preserve it by slowing natural decay caused by bacteria, fungi, etc. (in the EC preservatives are given E numbers E200 - 297); salt and sugar are two additives commonly used in the preservation of foods

◊ **preserving pan** *noun* very large pan for making jam, chutney, etc. in

press 1 *noun* **(a)** newspapers and magazines; **the local press** = newspapers which are sold in a small area of the country; **the national press** = newspapers which are sold in all parts of the country; **press conference** = meeting where newspaper and TV reporters are invited to hear news of a new product, a takeover bid, a court case, etc.; **press cutting** = piece cut out of a newspaper *or* magazine, which refers to an item which you find interesting; **press release** = sheet giving news about something which is sent to newspapers and TV and radio stations so that they can use the information **(b)** device *or* machine for crushing fruit *or* vegetables to extract the juice; **garlic press 2** *verb* **(a)** to iron the creases from (clothes) **(b)** to crush fruit or seeds to extract juice or oil

◇ **pressing service** *noun* service in a hotel for cleaning and pressing clothes, especially for dry-cleaning

pressure cooker *noun* type of pan with a tight-fitting lid, which cooks food rapidly under pressure

pressurize *verb* to increase the pressure inside an aircraft to keep a safe and comfortable environment, even at very high altitude; *pressurized cabin*

◇ **pressurization** *noun* increasing the pressure inside an aircraft

COMMENT: jet passenger aircraft fly at very high altitude for reasons of fuel economy. At around 30,000 to 40,000 feet the air is very cold and too thin to breathe. To make a safe and comfortable environment for passengers and crew, warm air is pumped into the cabin to increase the temperature and pressure

pre-theatre menu *noun* special dinner menu of light dishes, prepared for quick service to customers who are going on to the theatre after dinner

prevention *noun* stopping something from happening; **crime prevention** = actions to stop crime being committed, such as fitting burglar alarms, window locks, etc.

price 1 *noun* money which has to be paid to buy something; **agreed price** = price which has been accepted by both the buyer and seller; **all-in price** = price which covers all items in a purchase (goods, delivery, insurance, tax, etc.); **bargain price** = very cheap price; **catalogue price** *or* **list price** = price as marked in a catalogue or list; **competitive price** = low price aimed to compete with a rival product; **cost price** = selling price which is the same as the price which the seller paid for the item (either the manufacturing price or the wholesale price); **cut price** = cheaper price than usual; **discount price** = full price less a discount; **fair price** = good price for both buyer and seller; **going price** *or* **current price** *or* **usual price** = the price which is being charged now; **to sell goods off at half price** = to sell goods at 50% of the usual price; **market price** = price at which a product can be sold; **net price** = price which cannot be reduced by a discount; **retail price** = price at which the retailer sells to the final customer; **price control** = legal measures to stop prices rising too fast; **price cutting** =

sudden lowering of prices; **price war** *or* **price-cutting war** = competition between companies to get a larger market share by cutting prices; **price fixing** = illegal agreement between companies to charge the same price for competing products; **price label** *or* **price tag** *or* **price ticket** = label which shows a price; **price list** = sheet giving prices of goods for sale; **price range** = series of prices for similar products from different suppliers; **holidays in the £6-700 price range** = different types of holidays, selling for between £600 and £700 **(b)** **to increase in price** = to become more expensive; *petrol has increased in price or the price of petrol has increased;* **to increase prices** *or* **to raise prices** = to make items more expensive; **to cut prices** = to make items suddenly cheaper; **to lower prices** *or* **to reduce prices** = to make items cheaper **2** *verb* to give a price to (a product); *we sell mainly package tours priced at under £200;* **competitively priced** = sold at a low price to compete with a rival product or service; **the company has priced itself out of the market** = the company has raised its prices so high that its products do not sell

principal *noun* **(a)** person *or* company which is represented by an agent; *the agent has come to London to see his principals* **(b)** money invested *or* borrowed on which interest is paid; *to repay principal and interest*

print 1 *noun* words made on paper with a machine; **to read the small print** *or* **the fine print on a contract** = to read the conditions of a contract which are often printed very small so that people will not be able to read them easily **2** *verb* **(a)** to make letters on paper with a machine; *printed agreement; printed regulations* **(b)** to write in capital letters; *please print your name and address on the top of the form*

◇ **printer** *noun* machine which prints from instructions given by a computer system (as in a kitchen, where orders are instructed by a keypad and the printer prints tickets for each item of food ordered)

◇ **print out** *verb* to print information from a computer through a printer

◇ **printout** *noun* computer **printout** = printed copy of information from a computer; *our travel agents provided each member of the tour with a printout of flight details and hotel reservations*

private *adjective* **(a)** belonging to one person, not to everyone; **room with private**

bath = room with a bathroom attached to it, which is only used by the occupant of the room and by no one else **(b)** belonging to certain people, but not to the state or the general public; **private grounds** = gardens round a hotel, which can only be used by the guests, and not by the public; **private hotel** = hotel which is family owned and run, in which the proprietor may refuse to accept someone as a guest; **private view** *or* **private viewing** = preview of an exhibition for certain invited guests; *(notice)* **'private'** = belonging to a person, and not open to the public; *to see the manager, knock at the door marked 'private'* **(c) private enterprise** = businesses which are owned by private shareholders, not by the state; *the theme park is funded by private enterprise;* **the private sector** = all companies which are owned by private shareholders, not by the state

PRO = PUBLIC RELATIONS OFFICER

procedure *noun* way in which something is done; **complaints procedure** = way of presenting complaints formally from a customer to management

process *verb* **(a) to process figures** = to sort out numbers to make them easily understood; *the sales figures are being processed by our accounts department; flight data is being processed by our computer* **(b)** to deal with something in the usual routine way; *to process a flight reservation or an insurance claim; claims for missing baggage are processed in our insurance department* **(c)** to treat food in a way so that it will keep longer or become more palatable; **processed cheese** = product made by beating and mixing one or more types of cheese, adding colouring, flavouring, emulsifiers, etc., to make a product which will keep for a long time; **processed meats** = meat products such as bacon, sausages, etc.

◊ **processing** *noun* **(a)** sorting of information; **data processing** *or* **information processing** = selecting and examining data in a computer to produce information in a special form; **word processing** *or* **text processing** = working with words, using a computer to produce, check and change texts, reports, letters, etc. **(b) the processing of a claim for insurance** = dealing with a claim for insurance through the usual office routine in the insurance company

◊ **processor** *noun* machine or person who processes; **food processor** = machine for chopping, cutting, slicing, mixing food, etc.

COMMENT: food can be processed in many different ways: some of the commonest are drying, freezing, canning, bottling and chilling

product *noun* thing *or* service which is offered

professional 1 *adjective* **(a)** referring to one of the professions; *the accountant sent in his bill for professional services; we had to ask our lawyer for professional advice on the contract;* **a professional body** = organization representing members who work in one of the professions (such as lawyers, doctors, accountants); **professional qualifications** = documents showing that someone has successfully finished a course of study which allows him to work in one of the professions **(b)** expert *or* skilled; *his work is very professional; they did a very professional job in designing the new reception area* **(c)** doing work for money; *a professional tennis player* **2** *noun* skilled person *or* person who does skilled work for money; *a golf professional is attached to the hotel*

proficiency *noun* skill *or* being capable of doing something; *she has a certificate of proficiency in English; to get the job he had to pass a proficiency test*

◊ **proficient** *adjective* skilled *or* capable of doing something well; *she is quite proficient in English*

profit *noun* money gained from a sale which is more than the money spent; **clear profit** = profit after all expenses have been paid; *we made $6,000 clear profit on the deal;* **gross profit** *or* **gross trading profit** = profit calculated as sales income less the cost of the goods sold (i.e., without deducting any other expenses); **net profit** *or* **net trading profit** = result where income from sales is more than all expenditure; **operating profit** = result where sales from normal business activities are higher than the costs; **trading profit** = result where the company's receipts are higher than its expenditure; **profit margin** = percentage difference between sales income and the cost of sales; **profit-sharing** = arrangement where workers get a share of the profits of the company they work for; *the company runs a profit-sharing scheme;* **to make a profit** = to have more money as a result of a deal; **to move into profit** = to start to make a profit; *the restaurant is breaking even now, and expects to move into profit within the* next two months; to show a profit = to make a profit and state it in the company accounts; we are showing a small profit for the first quarter

◊ **profitability** noun (a) ability to make a profit (b) amount of profit made as a percentage of costs

◊ **profitable** adjective which makes a profit

◊ **profitably** adverb making a profit

◊ **profit and loss account (P&L account)** noun statement of a company's expenditure and income over a period of time, almost always one calendar year, showing whether the company has made a profit or loss (NOTE: the US equivalent is the **profit and loss statement** or **income statement**)

COMMENT: the balance sheet shows the state of a company's finances at a certain date; the profit ɛ ɹl loss account shows the movements which have taken place since the end of the previous accounting period, that is, since the last balance sheet

programme or US **program** noun (a) plan of things which will be done; the programme of events during the music festival (b) printed list of items in an entertainment; a theatre programme (c) show or item on TV or radio; did you see the travel programme on Italy last night? there's a new food programme starting tonight

Proguanil noun anti-malarial drug, taken together with Chloroquine

prohibit verb to ban or to forbid; women wearing shorts are prohibited from visiting the monastery

◊ **prohibitive** adjective with a price so high that you cannot afford to pay it; the cost of travel to the Far East is prohibitive

projector noun apparatus for throwing pictures on a screen

promote verb (a) to give someone a more important job; he was promoted from chef de rang to head waiter (b) to advertise; to promote a new product = to increase the sales of a new product by publicity or by a sales campaign or TV commercials or free gifts

◊ **promotion** noun (a) moving up to a more important job; promotion chances or promotion prospects = possibility of being moved to a more important job; he ruined

his chances of promotion when he argued with the chef; to earn promotion = to work hard and efficiently and so be moved to a more important job (b) promotion of a product = selling a new product by publicity or a sales campaign or TV commercials or free gifts; promotion budget; promotion team; sales promotion; special promotion

◊ **promotional** adjective used in an advertising campaign; the admen are using balloons as promotional material; promotional budget = forecast cost of promoting a new product

QUOTE the promotional fare (now available until March) offers a £100 saving for passengers who book the airline's early morning flight and return the same day
Business Traveller

-proof suffix meaning 'not affected by'; dishwasher-proof china = china which is not harmed by being washed in a dishwasher; dustproof cover = cover which prevents dust from getting in; soundproof window = window which prevents noise from outside getting into a room

property noun (a) personal property = things which belong to a person; the storm caused considerable damage to personal property; the management is not responsible for property left in the hotel rooms; lost property = personal belongings which have been lost by their owners; lost property office = office which collects objects which people have left behind and keeps them until the owners claim them (NOTE: US English for this is lost and found office) railway lost property office = office which collects objects which people have left behind in trains and keeps them until their owners collect them (b) buildings or land; property tax; damage to property or property damage; the commercial property market is booming; the property market = (i) possibilities for letting offices; (ii) possibilities for developing offices as investments; (iii) buying or selling houses or flats by individual people; commercial property = buildings used as offices or shops; private property = buildings or land which belong to a private person and not to the public

proprietor noun owner; the proprietor of a hotel or a hotel proprietor

protect verb to defend someone or something against harm; travellers are protected against unscrupulous hoteliers by

international agreement; the engine is protected by a plastic cover; the cover is supposed to protect the machine from dust
◊ **protection** *noun* something which protects; *the legislation offers no protection to part-time workers;* **consumer protection** = making sure people are not cheated by unfair or illegal manufacturers or traders

protein *noun* compound which is an essential part of living cells; one of the elements in food which is necessary to keep the human body working properly

> COMMENT: proteins are necessary for growth and repair of the tissue of the body; they are mainly formed of carbon, nitrogen and oxygen in various combinations as amino acids. Certain foods (such as beans, meat, eggs, fish and milk) are rich in protein

province *noun* **(a)** large division of a country; *the ten provinces of Canada* **(b)** the **provinces** = parts of any country away from the main capital town; *there are fewer retail outlets in the provinces than in the capital*
◊ **provincial** *adjective* referring to a province *or* to the provinces; *a provincial government; a provincial branch of a national bank*

provisional *adjective* temporary *or* not final or permanent; *she made a provisional booking for a table for ten people; he drew up a provisional advertising budget; they telexed their provisional acceptance of the contract*
◊ **provisionally** *adverb* temporarily *or* not finally; *the contract has been accepted provisionally*

prune *noun* dried plum

> COMMENT: prunes in syrup are sometimes offered as part of a 'full English breakfast'

pt = PINT

ptas = PESETAS

pub *noun (informal)* = PUBLIC HOUSE *the hotel has no restaurant, but you can go to the pub next door for meals;* **pub grub** *or* **pub food** = simple snacks which are typically available in most pubs (pies, sandwiches, salads, etc.)

public 1 *adjective* **(a)** referring to all the people in general; **public address system**

(PA system) = system of loudspeakers, by which messages can be given to the public in a supermarket, exhibition centre, etc.; **public bar** = bar in a public house which is less comfortable than the saloon bar and where the drinks may be slightly cheaper; **public conveniences** = toilets which are open for anyone to use; **public gardens** = space in a town where plants are grown and the public is allowed to visit (usually free of charge); **public phone** = telephone which anyone can use, either by paying cash or by using a card; *there's a public phone in the hotel foyer;* **public rooms** = rooms in a hotel which are used by both non-residents and guests (as opposed to 'guest rooms'); **public transport** = transport (such as buses, trains) which is used by any member of the public **(b)** referring to the government or the state; **Public Analyst** = government official who examines products to analyse their contents; **public funds** = government money available for expenditure; **Public Health Inspector** = official of a local authority who examines the environment and tests for air pollution *or* bad sanitation *or* noise pollution, etc.; **public ownership** = situation where an industry is nationalized **2** *noun* **the public** *or* **the general public** = the people; **in public** = in front of everyone

◊ **publican** *noun* person who keeps a public house

public holiday *noun* day when all workers rest and enjoy themselves instead of working

> COMMENT: public holidays in England and Wales are: New Year's Day, Good Friday, Easter Monday, the first Monday in May (May Day), the last Monday in May (Spring Bank Holiday), the last Monday in August (Summer Bank Holiday), Christmas Day and Boxing Day (December 26th). In Scotland, the first Monday in August and January 2nd is are also public holidays, but Easter Monday and the last Monday in August are not. In the USA, New Year's Day, 21st January (Martin Luther King Day), February 12th (Lincoln's Birthday), the third Monday in February (Washington's birthday), the last Monday in May (Memorial Day), July 4th (Independence Day), the first Monday in September (Labor Day), the second Monday in October (Columbus Day), 11th November (Veterans' Day), the fourth Thursday in November (Thanksgiving) and Christmas Day are

public holidays nationally, although there are other local holidays

public house *noun* **(a)** *GB* licensed building selling beer, wines, spirits, and often food, to the public for consumption on the premises; *compare* BAR, OFF-LICENCE **(b)** *US* small hotel or inn

COMMENT: in Britain a public house (or pub) usually offers simple meals, soft drinks and coffee for people who do not want to drink alcohol. Most pubs do not offer accommodation, but some do. Pubs normally have at least two bars, often called the 'public bar' and the 'lounge bar' or 'saloon bar' (the second is more expensive, and has more comfortable seating). Children are not usually allowed into pubs, unless they are part of a group eating food, though some pubs have special children's rooms

publicity *noun* attracting the attention of the public to products or services by mentioning them in the media; **publicity agency** *or* **publicity bureau** = office which organizes publicity for companies who do not have publicity departments; **publicity budget** = money allowed for expenditure on publicity; **publicity campaign** = period when planned publicity takes place; **publicity department** = section of a company which organizes the company's publicity; **publicity expenditure** = money spent on publicity

public relations (PR) *plural noun* keeping good relations between a company *or* a group and the public so that people know what the company is doing and can approve of it; *a public relations man; he works in public relations; a public relations firm handles all our publicity;* **a public relations exercise** = a campaign to improve public relations; **public relations officer (PRO)** = person in an organization who is responsible for public relations activities

public sector *noun* nationalized industries and services; *a report on wage rises in the public sector or on public sector wage settlements;* **public sector borrowing requirement (PSBR)** = amount of money which a government has to borrow to pay for its own spending

pud *noun (informal)* = PUDDING

pudding *noun* **(a)** dessert, sweet dish eaten at the end of meal; *what do you want for pudding? I've eaten too much, so I won't have any pudding; what's on the menu for pudding?;* **bread and butter pudding** = dessert made from slices of buttered bread with dried fruit and sugar, covered with a mixture of eggs and milk and baked in the oven; **rice pudding** = dessert made of rice, milk and sugar; **summer pudding** = dessert made from slices of bread lining a basin which is filled with a mixture of soft fruit such as raspberries, strawberries, blackcurrants, etc., chilled and served with cream **(b)** food made with flour and suet, which is cooked by boiling or steaming; *steak and kidney pudding; treacle pudding;* **Yorkshire pudding** = mixture of eggs, flour and milk, cooked in the oven, the traditional accompaniment to roast beef **(c)** *GB* **black pudding** = dark sausage made with blood (fried in slices and eaten for breakfast)

pull out *verb* **(a)** to drive away from the side of the road; to drive towards the middle of the road; *the bus suddenly pulled out in front of us* **(b)** *(train)* to start to leave a station; *the train was pulling out as the party arrived on the platform*

pulse *noun* general term for certain seeds that grow in pods; the species of vegetable which have this type of fruit are very numerous; the term is often applied to edible seeds of leguminous plants (lentils, beans and peas) used as food

pump 1 *noun* device for transferring liquid from one place to another (such as for serving beer or petrol) **2** *verb* to transfer (liquid) from one place to another using a pump; *all our beer is hand-pumped*

pumpkin *noun* large round orange-coloured vegetable; **pumpkin pie** = pie made of pumpkin flavoured with cinnamon, nutmeg and other spices

punctual *adjective* on time; *the commuter trains are never punctual*

◊ **punctuality** *noun* being on time; never being late; *an airline with a reputation for punctuality*

◊ **punctually** *adverb* on time; *the train left punctually at 18.00*

pungent *adjective* (taste, smell, food) which is sharp

punt 1 *noun* **(a)** long flat-bottomed boat, which is pushed with a long pole **(b)** the Irish pound, currency used in the Republic of Ireland **2** *verb* **(a)** to go in a punt; *we went punting on the river at Oxford* **(b)** to gamble *or* to bet (on something)

purchase 1 *noun* item which has been bought; **to make a purchase** = to buy something; **purchase ledger** = book in which expenditure is noted; **purchase order** = official order made out by a purchasing department for goods which a company wants to buy; *we cannot supply you without a purchase order number;* **purchase tax** = tax paid on things which are bought; **bulk purchase** *or* **quantity purchase** = buying of large amounts of goods at low prices; **cash purchase** = purchase made in cash **2** *verb* to buy; **to purchase something for cash** = to pay cash for something

◊ **purchaser** *noun* person who buys; *purchasers should examine the goods bought before taking them away from the shop*

◊ **purchasing** *noun* buying; **purchasing department** = section of a restaurant, hotel, or other business which deals with buying of stock, raw materials, equipment, etc.; **purchasing manager** = head of a purchasing department; **purchasing officer** = person in an organization who is responsible for buying stock, raw materials, equipment, etc.; **purchasing power** = quantity of goods which can be bought by a group of people *or* with an amount of money; *the decline in the purchasing power of the pound;* **central purchasing** = purchasing organized by one main office for all departments or branches

puree *or* **purée 1** *noun* semi-liquid pulp (of a vegetable or fruit); *apple puree* **2** *verb* to make (something) into a puree; *pureed potatoes*

purser *noun* member of the crew of an aircraft or ship who deals with the accounts, sales, passengers' needs, etc.

push *verb* to press; to move (something) by pressing; *he pushed the button for the ground floor*

◊ **pushbike** *see* BICYCLE

put *verb* to place; *(informal)* **to stay put** = to stay where you are

◊ **put back** *verb* to move a watch or clock to an earlier time; *put your watches back one hour when you cross from France to England*

◊ **put forward** *verb* to move a clock or watch to a later time; *when crossing from England to France, watches should be put forward one hour*

◊ **put off** *verb* to delay; *the visit to the winery has been put off till Friday*

◊ **put up** *verb* to find a place for (someone) to sleep; *when the blizzard closed the airport, stranded travellers were put up in local schools*

putt 1 *noun* short shot (on a green) in golf **2** *verb* to hit a short shot in golf

◊ **putter** *noun* golf club for putting

◊ **putting green** *noun* (i) area on a golf course where the ground is even and the grass if very short, allowing short shots to be made close to the hole; (ii) small golf course where only short shots are needed

Qq

quaint *adjective* picturesque, oddly old-fashioned; *a pub in a quaint old English village*

qualification *noun* proof that you have completed a specialized course of study; *to have the right qualifications for the job;* **professional qualifications** = documents showing that someone has successfully finished a course of study which allows him to work in one of the professions

◊ **qualify** *verb* **(a)** **to qualify for** = to be in the right position for *or* to be entitled to; *the*

company does not qualify for a government grant; she qualifies for unemployment pay **(b)** **to qualify as** = to follow a specialized course and pass examinations so that you can do a certain job; *she has qualified as a hotel manager; he will qualify as a solicitor next year*

quality *noun* **(a)** what something is like *or* how good or bad something is; *good quality or bad quality; there is a market for good quality secondhand computers; we sell only quality farm produce* = we sell only farm produce of the highest grade; **high quality** *or* **top quality** = very best grade; *the store specializes in high-quality imported cheese* **(b) quality control** = checking that the quality of a product is good; **quality controller** = person who checks the quality of a product

quantity *noun* **(a)** amount *or* number of items; *a small quantity of illegal drugs; he bought a large quantity of spare parts* **(b)** large amount; *the company offers a discount for quantity purchase;* **quantity discount** = price reduction given to a customer who buys a large amount of goods

quarantine 1 *noun* period (originally forty days) when a person *or* an animal *or* ship just arrived in a country has to be kept separate in case a serious disease may be carried, to allow the disease time to develop; *the animals were put in quarantine on arrival at the port; a ship in quarantine shows a yellow flag called the quarantine flag* **2** *verb* to put a person *or* animal in quarantine

COMMENT: animals coming into Great Britain are quarantined for six months because of the danger of rabies. People who are suspected of having an infectious disease can be kept in quarantine for a period which varies according to the incubation period of the disease. The main diseases concerned are cholera, yellow fever and typhus

quart *noun* measure of liquid equal to one quarter of a gallon

COMMENT: a British quart is equal to 1.136 litres; a US quart is equal to 0.946 of a litre

quarter *noun* **(a)** one of four equal parts; *he paid only a quarter of the normal fare because he works for the airline;* **a quarter of a litre** *or* **a quarter litre** = 250 millilitres; **a quarter of an hour** = 15 minutes; **three quarters** = 75%; **three quarters of an hour** = 45 minutes; *three quarters of the staff are less than thirty years old* **(b)** period of three months; **first quarter, second quarter, third quarter, fourth quarter** *or* **last quarter** = periods of three months from January to the end of March, from April to the end of June, from July to the end of September, from October to the end of the year; **quarter day** = day at the end of a quarter, when

rents *or* fees, etc. should be paid **(c)** *US* 25 cent coin

◊ **quarterly** *adjective* happening every three months; **quarterly sales return** = report of sales made each quarter

quay *noun* place in a harbour where ships tie up

◊ **quayside** *noun* edge of a dock where ships tie up; *customs formalities are carried out on the quayside*

queen size bed *noun* double bed which is wider and longer than normal, but slightly smaller than a king size bed

question 1 *noun* **(a)** words which need an answer; *the manager refused to answer questions about the fire; the market research team prepared a series of questions to test the public's reactions to the new uniform for the airline cabin crew* **(b)** problem; *he raised the question of what would happen if the tour company got into difficulties; the main question is that of cost; the tourist board has discussed the question of a national advertising campaign* **2** *verb* **(a)** to ask questions; *the police questioned the bar staff for four hours* **(b)** to query *or* to suggest that something may be wrong; *we all question how accurate the computer printout is*

◊ **questionnaire** *noun* printed list of questions, especially used in market research; *to send out a questionnaire to test the opinions of users of the booking system; to answer* **or** *to fill in a questionnaire about holidays abroad*

queue 1 *noun* **(a)** *GB* line of people waiting one behind the other; *to form a queue or to join a queue; queues formed at the ticket offices when the news of the fare reductions got out* **(b)** series of documents (such as orders, application forms) or telephone calls which are dealt with in order; **his order went to the end of the queue** = his order was dealt with last (NOTE: US English is **line**) **2** *verb* to form a line one after the other for something; *when food was rationed, people had to queue for bread; we queued for hours to get tickets; groups of tourists queueing to get on their buses* (NOTE: US English is **to stand in line**)

quiche *noun* savoury tart made of a pastry case filled with a mixture of eggs and milk; other ingredients such as onion, bacon, vegetables or cheese can be added; *a slice of ham and mushroom quiche or of spinach quiche;* **quiche Lorraine** = quiche with a filling of small pieces of bacon (and sometimes cheese)

quick-freeze *verb* to preserve food by cooling it quickly to 0°C or less

quiet 1 *adjective* not noisy; *the hotel is in the quietest part of the town; currency exchanges were quieter after the government's statement on exchange rates; the brochure said that the rooms were quiet, but ours looked out over a busy main road* **2** *noun* not being noisy; *we like the peace and quiet of the little mountain villages*

quince *noun* hard fruit of *Cydonia oblonga*, used for making jelly

quinine *noun* drug (derived from the bark of the chinchona tree) used to treat malaria

quiz *noun* game where questions are put to competitors; **quiz night** = night at a pub when a quiz is held

quota *noun* fixed amount of something which is allowed; *the government has imposed an import quota on cars*

quote 1 *verb* **(a)** to repeat words used by someone else; to repeat a reference number; *in reply please quote this number; when making a complaint please quote the batch number printed on the box; he replied, quoting the number of the account* **(b)** to estimate *or* to calculate the probable cost of something; *to quote a price for supplying 100 chairs; their prices are always quoted in dollars; he quoted me a price of £1,026; can you quote for supplying 200 cases of wine?* **2** *noun (informal)* estimate of the probable cost of something; *to give someone a quote for supplying a computer system; we have asked for quotes for refitting the bar; his quote was the lowest of three; we accepted the lowest quote*

◊ **quotation** *noun* estimate of the probable cost of something; *they sent in their quotation for the job; to ask for quotations for refitting the dining room; his quotation was much lower than all the others; we accepted the lowest quotation*

Rr

rabbit *noun* greyish-brown animal with long ears and short white tail which lives under the ground

COMMENT: Most rabbit on sale in Britain is farmed. Wild rabbit has a gamey flavour but is not commonly offered on menus. Rabbit stew or rabbit pie are the commonest ways of cooking it

rabies *noun* frequently fatal viral disease transmitted to humans by infected animals
◊ **rabid** *adjective* referring to rabies *or* suffering from rabies; *he was bitten by a rabid dog*

COMMENT: rabies affects the mental balance, and the symptoms include difficulty in breathing or swallowing and an intense fear of water (hydrophobia) to the point of causing convulsions at the sight of water. It does not exist in Great Britain or Ireland, and

this is why animals brought into these countries have to be put in quarantine for a period of months

RAC = ROYAL AUTOMOBILE CLUB

rack *noun* **(a)** frame to hold things (such as letters or pieces of toast); **key rack** = board with hooks or a series of pigeonholes where room keys are put near the front desk of a hotel; **luggage rack** = device above the seats in a train for holding luggage; **mail rack** = rack where letters for guests or occupants are put; **message rack** = rack for messages; **plate rack** = device for holding several plates side by side (as in a dishwasher); **roof rack** = grid attached to the roof of a car for carrying luggage; **toast-rack** = device for holding several pieces of toast **(b) rack rate** = price for rooms in a hotel which is advertised in the hotel, but which can be discounted **(c) rack of lamb** = best end of neck of lamb, a joint for roasting

QUOTE The discount approach is typified by the hotel chain which is cutting its winter rack rates (the published tariff) by up to 50% for its European hotels
Business Travel

QUOTE only 9.5% of customers paid full rack rate for a room last year, compared with 13.6% in the previous year and 28% four years ago
Caterer & Hotelkeeper

radiator *noun* **(a)** water-filled metal panel for heating a room; *when we arrived at the hotel our room was cold, but we switched the radiators on* **(b)** water-filled metal panel for cooling a car engine

radio 1 *noun* system for sending out or receiving messages using atmospheric waves; apparatus which sends out or receives messages using atmospheric waves; **radio car** *or* **radio taxi** = hire car *or* taxi which is in contact with its base by radio, and so can be called quickly to pick up a client **2** *verb* to send a message using a radio; *the stranded party radioed for help*
◇ **radiopager** *see* PAGER

radish *noun* small red root vegetable with a pungent flavour, eaten raw in salads (a very common starter in France is radishes served with salt and butter)

raft *noun* flat boat made of pieces of wood or logs tied together
◇ **rafting** *noun* floating down a river on a raft; *see also* WHITE-WATER

RAGB = RESTAURATEURS ASSOCIATION OF GREAT BRITAIN

rail *noun* railway *or* system of travel using trains; *six million commuters travel to work by rail each day; rail travellers are complaining about rising fares; rail travel is cheaper than air travel;* British Rail (BR) = national system of railways in Great Britain
◇ **railcar** *noun* single coach with its own motor, carrying passenger by rail
◇ **railcard** *noun* identity card which you buy allowing you to buy rail tickets at specially reduced prices
◇ **railpass** *noun* special ticket (paid for in advance) which allows unlimited travel by train in a country, over a certain limited period of time (similar to an 'airpass' for air travel)
◇ **railroad** *noun US* system using trains to carry passengers and goods; **railroad pass** =

RAILPASS; **railroad schedule** = train timetable, a list showing times of arrivals and departures of trains
◇ **railway** *noun GB* system using trains to carry passengers and goods; *a railway station; a railway line; the British railway network;* railway schedule = train timetable, a list showing times of arrivals and departures of trains; railway station = place where trains stop, passengers get on and off, etc.; **the railway(s)** = the country's railway system

rain 1 *noun* water which falls from clouds as small drops; *the rain stopped us from visiting the archaeological site* **2** *verb* to fall as rain; *it rained all day, so we could not visit the gardens;* rained off = cancelled, because of rain; *the cricket match was rained off*
◇ **rainfall** *noun* amount of water which falls as rain on a certain area over a certain period
◇ **rainstorm** *noun* heavy rain accompanied by wind
◇ **rainy** *adjective* with a lot of rain; **rainy season** = period of the year when it rains a lot (as opposed to the dry season); *the rainy season lasts from April to August*

raisin *noun* dried grape

raki *noun* Turkish alcoholic drink, flavoured with aniseed

Ramadan *noun* Moslem religious festival, where people do not eat or drink during the daytime (i.e. between sunrise and sunset)

ramble 1 *noun* walk for pleasure in the country **2** *verb* to go for a walk for pleasure in the country
◇ **rambler** *noun* person who goes for walks for pleasure in the country

rambutan *noun* tropical fruit *(Nephelium lappaceum)* grown in South-East Asia; the fruit is similar to the litchi with a rough hairy skin

ramekin *noun* small dish for baking food in an oven; food cooked in this type of dish

ramp *noun* sloping part of the ground, going from one level to another; *the pub has had a ramp installed so that people in wheelchairs can get into the garden;* loading ramp = raised platform which makes it easier to load goods onto a truck

ranch *noun (in America)* farm where horses or cattle are reared; **ranch holidays** = holidays spent on a ranch (usually riding horses); *see also* DUDE
◊ **rancher** *noun* person who owns or runs a ranch

rancid *adjective* (butter) which is stale
◊ **rancidity** *noun* being rancid

rang *French noun (meaning 'position or station')* a section of a restaurant, a group of tables served by one waiter, the 'chef de rang'

range 1 *noun* **(a)** series (of mountains) in a line **(b)** choice or series (of colours, etc.); *we have a range of holidays at all prices* **(c)** large cooking stove, usually with two or more ovens **2** *verb* to spread or to vary; *holidays range in price from £150 per person to £350 per person, depending on the type of accommodation provided*
◊ **ranger** *noun* person who looks after a forest or park

rank 1 *noun* position where things are in order; **taxi rank** *or* **cab rank** = place where taxis wait in line for customers **2** *verb* to classify in order of importance; *hotels are ranked in order of luxury in the guidebook*

rapid *adjective* fast *or* quick; **we offer 5% discount for rapid settlement** = we take 5% off the price if the customer pays quickly; **rapid transit system** = system (such as an underground train network) which allows passengers to travel rapidly around a metropolitan area

rare *adjective* (meat) which is very lightly cooked; *how would you like your steak? - rare!*
◊ **rarebit** *noun* **Welsh rarebit** = cooked cheese on toast

rasher *noun* slice of bacon

raspberry *noun* cane *(Rubus idaeus)* which provides a most important red soft fruit; *raspberry ice cream; raspberry jam*

rat *noun* large rodent pest

COMMENT: the black rat *(Rattus rattus)* lives in attics and lofts; the brown rat *(Rattus norvegicus)* is larger and lives in holes under buildings and in sewers. Both species carry diseases such as typhoid

ratafia *noun* sweet biscuit or drink flavoured with almonds

ratatouille *noun* Mediterranean vegetable stew of onions, tomatoes, aubergines, peppers and courgettes cooked in olive oil

rate 1 *noun* **(a)** money charged for time worked *or* work completed; **all-in rate** = price which covers all items in a purchase (goods, delivery, tax, insurance, etc.), or all items in a tour (travel, hotel accommodation, meals, etc.); *the hotel offers an all-in rate of £150 a week;* **fixed rate** = charge which cannot be changed; **flat rate** = charge which always stays the same; *a flat-rate increase of 10%; we pay a flat rate for electricity each quarter; he is paid a flat rate of £2 per thousand items produced;* **freight rates** = charges for transporting goods; **full rate** = full charge, with no reductions; **the going rate** = the usual *or* the current rate of payment; **letter rate** *or* **parcel rate** = postage (calculated by weight) for sending a letter *or* a parcel; *it is more expensive to send a packet letter rate but it will get there quicker;* **the market rate** = normal price in the market; **night rate** = cheap telephone calls at night; **reduced rate** = specially cheap charge; *see also* ROOM RATE **(b) insurance rates** = amount of premium which has to be paid per £1000 of insurance; **interest rate** *or* **rate of interest** = percentage charge for borrowing money **(c)** **(exchange) rate** *or* **rate of exchange** = price at which one currency is exchanged for another; *what is today's rate or the current rate for the dollar? there is a surcharge of 10% because of the fall in the exchange rate; to calculate costs on a fixed exchange rate* = to calculate costs on an exchange rate which does not change; **forward rate** = rate for purchase of foreign currency at a fixed price for delivery at a later date **2** *verb* to classify; *a top-rated restaurant*
◊ **rating** *noun* classifying *or* valuing; **rating system** = way of classifying things (such as hotels, restaurants, etc.)

raw *adjective* (food) in its original state *or* (food) which has not been cooked; *sushi is a Japanese dish of raw fish; I don't like raw onions in my salad*

razor *noun* instrument with a very sharp blade for removing hair by shaving; **razor socket** = socket in a bathroom where an electric razor can be plugged in (NOTE: US English for this is **shaver point**)

reach *verb* to arrive at a place *or* at a point; *the plane reaches Hong Kong at midday; the coach reached its destination three hours late; I did not reply because your letter never reached me*

read *verb* to look at and understand written words; **reading lamp** = small lamp on a desk or beside a bed, for use when reading or writing

ready *adjective* **(a)** prepared; *are you all ready to leave yet? why isn't the coach here? - the group are all ready and waiting to go* **(b)** fit to be used; *you can't go to your room yet, because it isn't ready; is my dry cleaning ready yet?*
◊ **ready-cooked** *adjective* (food) which has been cooked in advance

real ale *noun* traditional beer, served directly from a wooden barrel or pumped by hand

reboard *verb* to go back onto a ship *or* plane *or* train *or* bus again; *after visiting the church, the party will reboard the coach and drive to the hotel*

receipt 1 *noun* **(a)** paper showing that money has been paid *or* that something has been received; *customs receipt; receipt for items purchased; please produce your receipt if you want to exchange items;* **receipt book** *or* **book of receipts** = book of blank receipts to be filled in when purchases are made **(b)** act of receiving something; *goods will be supplied within thirty days of receipt of order; invoices are payable within thirty days of receipt; on receipt of the confirmation, the tickets were sent to the customer;* **to acknowledge receipt of a letter** = to write to tell someone that you have received his letter; *we acknowledge receipt of your letter of the 15th* **(c)** **receipts** = money taken in sales; *to itemize receipts and expenditure; receipts are down against the same period of last year* 2 *verb* to stamp *or* to sign a document to show that it has been received; to stamp an invoice to show that it has been paid

receive *verb* **(a)** to get something which has been sent; *we only received our tickets the day before we were due to leave* **(b)** to greet or to welcome; *the group was received by the mayor*
◊ **receiver** *noun* **(a)** official put in charge of a bankrupt company; *the receiver has been called in the run the hotel group* **(b)** part of a telephone which you lift and listen to

◊ **receiving** *noun* taking in supplies purchased for use in a hotel or restaurant; **receiving clerk** = person whose job is to check supplies coming into a hotel or restaurant

reception *noun* **(a) reception (desk)** = (i) desk where guests *or* visitors register or say who they have come to see when arriving at a hotel or office; (ii) high desk at the entrance to a restaurant where the reception head waiter greets the guests and organizes the reservation of tables; **reception area** = the reception desk and the area round it, usually where seats are provided, current newspapers or magazines, and sometimes a coffee machine; **reception clerk** = person who works at the reception desk; **reception head waiter** = person who is on duty at the reception desk in a restaurant, who greets guests and organizes the reservation of tables **(b)** big party held to welcome special guests; *there's a big reception at the embassy tonight;* **wedding reception** = party held after a marriage ceremony, including the wedding breakfast, drinks, toasts, cake-cutting, etc., together with arrangements for the bride and bridegroom to change from their formal clothes into going-away clothes; **reception manager** = banqueting manager, the person in a hotel who is responsible for organizing formal functions; **reception room** = large room in a hotel suitable for big groups of people
◊ **receptionist** *noun* person in a hotel *or* restaurant *or* office who meets guests *or* visitors, answers the phone, etc.

QUOTE reception - which combines several functions (reception of guests, key distribution, information, cashier and change bureau, safe deposit boxes) - must require the guest on arrival to identify himself with a passport
Hotel Security Worldwide

réchaud *French noun (meaning 'stove')* small heater (usually with a spirit lamp under it) for keeping food hot on the table, or for cooking certain dishes rapidly next to the guest's table

recipe *noun* written details of how to cook a certain dish; *the restaurant sells postcards with recipes of its famous fish dishes; the cake is made from an old recipe*

recommend *verb* **(a)** to suggest that something should be done; **manufacturer's recommended price (MRP)** *or* **recommended**

retail price (RRP) = price which a manufacturer suggests the product should be sold at on the retail market, though often reduced by the retailer; *'all gas cookers - 20% off MRP'* **(b)** to say that someone *or* something is good; *he recommended a French restaurant in the High Street; I certainly would not recommend Miss Smith for the job; can you recommend a good hotel in Amsterdam?*

◊ **recommendation** *noun* saying that someone *or* something is good; *we appointed him on the recommendation of his former employer*

record *verb* to fix sound on a plastic disc or tape; *a recorded message is played when the airport bus approaches the terminal*

◊ **recorded delivery** *noun* mail service where the letters are signed for by the person receiving them; *they sent the passport by recorded delivery*

◊ **recorder** *noun* instrument which records sound; **cassette recorder** *or* **tape recorder** = machine which records sound on magnetic tape, either in a cassette or on an open reel; *tape recorders are not allowed in the concert*

◊ **recording** *noun* act of fixing sounds on a plastic disc or tape

recreation *noun* pleasant occupation for spare time; **recreation ground** = public sports ground

◊ **recreational** *adjective* referring to recreation; *US* **recreational vehicle (RV)** = large camping van in which a family can live while touring

recruit *verb* to take (someone) on as an employee; *we have recruited six girls to act as hostesses at the Computer Show*

◊ **recruitment** *noun* taking people on as employees

red *noun* **in the red** = showing a debit or loss; *my bank account is in the red; the company went into the red in 1993; the company is out of the red for the first time since 1950*

◊ **redcap** *see* PORTER

◊ **red carpet** *noun* carpet put down when an important visitor comes, hence an official welcome; *he got the red-carpet treatment*

◊ **redcurrant** *noun* common red soft fruit growing in small clusters, mainly used to make jam and jelly

◊ **red-light district** *noun* part of a town where brothels, striptease clubs, etc, are situated; *the two old ladies complained that their hotel was in the red-light district of Frankfurt*

◊ **red tape** *noun* official paperwork which takes a long time to complete; *the South-East Asian joint venture has been held up by government red tape*

◊ **red wine** *noun* wine which becomes red because the grape skins are left for a time in the fermenting mixture

COMMENT: red wine is usually served at 'room temperature'. Fine red wines (vintage Bordeaux or Burgundies) should be opened in advance to allow the air to enter the bottle; some fine red wines may also need to be decanted to remove sediment. Light red wines (such as Beaujolais nouveau, and red wines from the Loire Valley) should be served at cellar temperature (i.e. cool), or can even be chilled. Red wine is traditionally served with meat and game, and also with cheese

reduce *verb* **(a)** to make smaller or lower; *we have reduced prices on all our winter holidays;* **reduced-price menu for children (b)** to boil sauce, so as to make it smaller in quantity and more concentrated

◊ **reduction** *noun* lowering (of price); *'price reductions on selected holidays in Spain'*

re-entry *noun* coming back in again; **re-entry visa** *or* **permit** = visa allowing someone to leave a country and go back in again

referral system *noun* system by which one hotel *or* restaurant recommends another, and may take bookings for another on which commission may be paid

refreshments *plural noun* snacks and drinks, available usually as a buffet, or served by waiters; *refreshments will be served in a tent on the lawn; you can get refreshments at the foyer bar during the interval;* **refreshment room** = room at a railway station where food and drink are served

refrigerate *verb* to keep (food) cold, so that it will not go bad

◇ **refrigerator** *noun* machine for keeping food cold; *milk will keep for several days in a refrigerator; each bedroom has a small refrigerator with ice and cold drinks*

COMMENT: low temperature retards the rate at which food spoils, because all the causes of deterioration proceed more slowly. In freeze-drying, the food is quick-frozen and then dried by vacuum, so removing the moisture. Pre-cooked foods should be cooled rapidly down to -3°C and eaten within five days of production. Certain high-risk chilled foods should be kept below 5°C; these foods include soft cheese and various pre-cooked products. Eggs in shells can be chilled for short-term storage (i.e. up to one month) at temperatures between -10°C and -16°C. Bakery products, including bread, have storage temperatures between -18°C and -40°C; bread goes stale quickly at chill temperatures which are above these. Potatoes in the form of pre-cooked chips can be stored at -18°C or colder, but ordinary potatoes must not be chilled at all. Apples and pears can be kept in air-cooled boxes at between -1°C and +4°C (this is known as controlled temperature storage). Lettuces and strawberries (which normally must not be chilled) can be kept fresh by vacuum cooling; celery and carrots can be chilled by hydrocooling

refund 1 *noun* money paid back; *to ask for a refund; she got a refund after she had complained to the manager;* **full refund** *or* **refund in full** = return of all the money paid; *he got a full refund when he complained that there were mice in his bedroom* **2** *verb* to pay back money; *to refund the cost of postage; all money will be refunded if the tour is cancelled; they refunded £100 of the £400 I had paid*

◇ **refundable** *adjective* which can be paid back; *a refundable deposit of 10% is payable on booking; the entrance fee is refundable if you purchase £5 worth of goods* (NOTE: the opposite is **non-refundable**)

refuse 1 *noun* rubbish, things which are not wanted **2** *verb* to say that you will not do something *or* will not accept something; *they refused to pay; the bank refused to lend the hotel any more money; he asked for a refund but it was refused; the customer*

refused the goods *or* refused to accept the goods (NOTE: you refuse **to do something** or refuse **something**)

◇ **refusal** *noun* saying that you will not do something *or* will not accept something; **his request met with a refusal** = his request was refused; **to give someone first refusal of something** = to allow someone to be the first to decide if they want something or not

regatta *noun* sporting event where rowing boats or sailing boats race

COMMENT: the two main regattas in England are the Henley regatta in June and the Cowes Week held in August

region *noun* **(a)** area; **the London region** = the area around London **(b) in the region of £10,000** = about £10,000; *we're looking for a hotel in the region of £30 per night*

◇ **regional** *adjective* referring to a region; *the restaurant serves regional specialities*

register 1 *noun* **(a)** official list; *to enter something in a register; to keep a register up to date;* **Lloyd's register** = classified list showing details of all the ships in the world **(b)** large book for recording details (as in a hotel, where guests sign in, or in a registry where deaths are recorded); *they asked the guests to sign the register* **(c) cash register** = machine which shows and adds the prices of items bought, with a drawer for keeping the cash received **(d)** computerized billing system in a restaurant, where each item ordered is keyed in by the waiter using a special code, the till provides a printout which itemizes all dishes bought, so that the guest can check the bill easily **2** *verb* **(a)** to write something on an official list; *to register a sale* **(b)** to arrive at a hotel or at a conference and write your name and address on a list; *they registered at the hotel under the name of Macdonald* **(c)** *(of the receptionist)* to fill in the details when a guest arrives at a hotel **(d) registered letter** *or* **registered parcel** = letter *or* parcel sent by registered post

◇ **registered post** *noun* service where the post office makes a note of a letter or parcel before it is sent, so that compensation can be claimed if it is lost or damaged; *to send documents by registered post*

◇ **registration** *noun* **(a)** writing something on an official list; **registration card** *or* **registration form** = card or form which has to be filled in when registering at a hotel, conference, etc. **(b) registration number** =

official number of a car; **registration plate** = plate on the front and back of a vehicle, showing its registration number (NOTE: US English for this is **license plate)**

regret *verb* to be sorry; *I regret having to refuse entry to small children; we regret the delay in the arrival of our flight from Amsterdam; we regret to inform you of the cancellation of the tour* (NOTE: you **regret doing something** or **regret to do something** or **regret something.** Note also: regretting - regretted)

regular *adjective* **(a)** which happens *or* comes at the same time each day *or* week *or* month *or* year; *his regular train is the 12.45; the regular flight to Athens leaves at 06.00;* **regular customer** = customer who always buys from the same shop or who goes to the same place for a service; **regular staff** = full-time staff **(b)** ordinary *or* standard; *the regular price is $1.25, but we are offering them at 99c;* **regular size** = ordinary size (smaller than economy size, family size, etc.)

◊ **regularly** *adverb* happening or coming at the same time each day *or* week *or* month *or* year; *the first train in the morning is regularly late*

regulate *verb* **(a)** to adjust (something) so that it works well *or* is correct **(b)** to maintain (something) by law; **government-regulated price** = price which is imposed by the government

◊ **regulation** *noun* **(a)** adjusting something so that it works well; *the regulation of international air fares* **(b)** **regulations** = laws *or* rules; *the new government regulations on hotel standards; fire regulations or safety regulations; regulations concerning the entry of tourists without visas*

QUOTE EC regulations which came into effect in July insist that customers can buy cars anywhere in the EC at the local pre-tax price

Financial Times

Regulo *noun* system of numbers indicating temperatures on a gas cooker; *cook in the oven for one hour at Regulo 6*

COMMENT: the Regulo system goes from 1/4 to 9. The approximate temperature equivalents are: $1/4$-2 = 110-150°C, 3-4 = 160-190°C, 5 = 200°C, 6-7 = 210-230°C, 8-9 = 235-250°C

reheat *verb* to heat again *food left over can be reheated and served again the next day*

reimburse *verb* **to reimburse someone his expenses** = to pay someone back for money which he has spent; *you will be reimbursed for your expenses or your expenses will be reimbursed*

◊ **reimbursement** *noun* paying back money; *reimbursement of expenses*

relation *noun* link (between two things); **public relations (PR)** = keeping good relations between a company *or* a group and the public so that people know what the company is doing and can approve of it

relax *verb* to rest from work; to be less tense; *they spent the first week of their holiday relaxing on the beach; guests can relax in the bar before going to eat in the restaurant*

◊ **relaxation** *noun* resting from work; *for relaxation he goes jogging in the park*

relevée *see* REMOVE

reliable *adjective* which can be trusted; *a reliable tour company; the on-site courier is completely reliable*

◊ **reliability** *noun* being reliable; *the product has passed its reliability tests*

relief *adjective* (person) who takes the place of another who is away; **relief cook** = cook who takes the place of a cook who is absent

relieve *verb* **(a)** to take over from (someone); *the day receptionist will be relieved at 21.00 when the night shift comes on* **(b)** **to relieve oneself** = to urinate or defecate

relish *noun* sharp or spicy sauce made with vegetables or fruit which adds extra flavour when eaten with other food

rely on *verb* to depend on *or* to trust; *we rely on part-time staff for most of our business; do not rely on the agents for accurate market reports*

remote *adjective* a long way away *or* distant; *the hotel is situated in a remote mountain village;* **remote control** = control of a TV, etc. by using a handheld switch away from the set; it works with an infrared ray

remove noun (in old menus) dish served after the first course has been eaten and cleared away

renovate verb to make (something) like new; *the hotel has been completely renovated*
◊ **renovation** noun making like new; *the hotel is closed for renovation*

rent 1 noun money paid to use a room or an office or house for a period of time; **high rent** or **low rent** = expensive or cheap rent; *rents are high in the centre of the town; we cannot afford to pay high-season rents; to pay three months' rent in advance;* **the flat is let at an economic rent** = at a rent which covers all costs to the landlord; **nominal rent** = very small rent; **income from rents** or **rent income** = income from letting an office or a house, etc. **2** verb **(a)** to pay money to hire a room or an office or house or piece of equipment for a period of time; *to rent an office or a car; he rented a villa by the beach for three weeks; they were driving a rented car when they were stopped by the police* **(b) to rent (out)** = to own a car or office, etc., and lend it to someone who pays for its use; *we rented the villa to an American couple*
◊ **rental** noun money paid to use a flat or house or car or piece of equipment, etc., for a period of time; **rental agency** = office which specializes in letting flats or houses; **rental income** or **income from rentals** = income from letting offices or houses, etc.; **car rental firm** = company which owns cars and lends them to people for money

reopen verb to open again; *the hotel will reopen next week after its £1 million renovation*
◊ **reopening** noun opening again; *the reopening of the bar after renovation*

repack verb to put things back again into a suitcase; *he had to repack his case after it had been opened by customs officials*
◊ **repacking** noun putting things back again into a suitcase

repair 1 noun mending or making good something which is broken; *the hotel is closed while they are carrying out repairs to the air-conditioning system; his car is in the garage for repair* **2** verb to mend or to make good something which is broken; *the lift is being repaired*

repay verb to pay back; **he repaid me in full** = he paid me back all the money he owed me

NOTE: **repaying - repaid**
◊ **repayment** noun paying back; money which is paid back

replace verb **(a)** to put (something) back in place; *she replaced the glasses on the table* **(b)** to put (something) in place of something else; *he offered to replace the broken mirror*
◊ **replacement** noun **(a)** putting back; putting something in place of something else **(b)** thing which is used in place of something else; **replacement part** = piece of machinery used instead of a piece which is broken or worn out

reply 1 noun answer, conversation or letter coming after someone has written or spoken; *there was no reply to my letter or to my phone call; I am writing in reply to your letter of the 24th;* **reply coupon** = form attached to an advertisement in a newspaper or magazine, which has to be filled in and returned to the advertiser; **international postal reply coupon** = document which can be used in another country to pay the postage of replying to a letter; *he enclosed an international reply coupon with his letter;* **reply paid card** or **letter** = card or letter to be sent back to the sender with a reply, the sender having already paid for the return postage **2** verb to answer, to speak or write after someone has spoken or written to you; **to reply to a letter** = to write a letter in answer to one which you have received

report verb **(a)** to write officially to describe what has happened; *cases of cholera must be reported immediately to the local health authorities; the guest reported that her wallet was missing from her room* **(b)** to go to a place; *candidates should report to our London office for interview;* **reporting time** = time before a flight departs when a passenger should check in; *reporting time for intercontinental flights is 2 hours before departure*

represent verb to sell goods or a service on behalf of someone; *she represents an Australian bus company*
◊ **representative 1** adjective which is an example of what all others are like; *the hotel displayed a representative selection of locally made products; the sample chosen was not representative of the whole batch* **2** noun **(a)** **(sales) representative** = person who works for a company, showing goods or services for sale and trying to sell them; *the tour*

operator has a representative permanently based in Spain; we have six representatives in Europe; they have vacancies for representatives to call on accounts in the north of the country (b) company which works for another company, selling their goods; *we have appointed Smith & Co our exclusive representatives in Europe* (c) person who acts on someone's behalf; *she is the local representative for a British tour operator*

reputable *adjective* with a good reputation; *we only use reputable carriers*

◊ **reputation** *noun* general opinion (of someone); *the hotel has a reputation for being expensive; an airline with a reputation for punctuality*

request 1 *noun* asking for something politely; **on request** = if asked for; *more blankets are available on request;* **request stop** = bus stop where buses stop only if you signal to them **2** *verb* to ask for something politely; *the stranded party radioed to request help*

require *verb* (a) to need; *you will require a visa to go to Russia* (b) **to require someone to do something** = to demand that someone does something; *tourists are required to register with the local police*

◊ **requirement** *noun* what is needed

re-route *verb* to arrange another route for (a plane, coach, etc.); *bad weather in the mountains meant that the coach had to be re-routed via the coast road*

rescue 1 *noun* saving; **mountain rescue service** *or* **team** = group of trained people who are on duty to help climbers and skiers who get into difficulties on mountains **2** *verb* to save; *when the river flooded, the party of tourists had to be rescued by helicopter*

◊ **rescuer** *noun* person who saves or tries to save someone from a dangerous situation

reservation *noun* booking a room *or* seat *or* table, etc.; **to make a reservation** = to book a room *or* a table *or* a seat, etc.; *I want to make a reservation on the train to Plymouth tomorrow evening;* **room reservations** *or* **reservations department** = department in a hotel which deals with bookings for rooms; *can you put me through to reservations?;* **reservations chart** = chart showing all the rooms in a hotel, with marks showing

which are occupied or booked in advance, and which are vacant; **reservations clerk** = person in a hotel who deals with room reservations; **reservation diary** = ledger with a separate page for each day, giving a list of all the rooms in a hotel, and marks to show if they are booked or vacant; **reservation form** = form to be filled in by the clerk when a room reservation is made; **reservations rack** = special board or series of pigeonholes where cards ('reservation rack cards') are put to show which rooms have been booked

reserve 1 *noun* (a) money from profits not paid as dividend, but kept back by a company in case it is needed for a special purpose; **cash reserves** = money which a company keeps in cash deposits or bills in case of urgent need; **contingency reserve** *or* **emergency reserves** = money set aside in case it is needed urgently; **reserve for bad debts** = money kept by a company to cover debts which may not be paid (b) **in reserve** = kept to be used later on; **to keep something in reserve** = to keep something so as to be able to use it later on if necessary; *we keep stores of tinned and frozen food in reserve for use in emergencies* (c) **reserves** = supplies kept to be used later on if necessary; *the hotel was cut off by snow and had to rely on its reserves of food; reserves of fuel fell during the winter; the country's reserves of gas* or *gas reserves are very large* **2** *verb* **to reserve a room** *or* **a table** *or* **a seat** = to book a room *or* table *or* seat *or* to ask for a room *or* table *or* seat to be kept free for you; *I want to reserve a table for four people; can your secretary reserve a seat for me on the train to Glasgow?*

◊ **reserved** *adjective* (table *or* seat) which is kept for a customer; *you can't have the window table, it is reserved*

residence *noun* (a) house *or* flat where someone lives; *he has a country residence where he spends his weekends* (b) act of living *or* operating officially in a country; **residence permit** = official document allowing a foreigner to live in a country; *he has applied for a residence permit; she was granted a residence permit for one year;* **residence tax** = tax applied to people staying in a town

◊ **resident** *noun* (a) person *or* company living or operating in a country; *the company is resident in France* (b) guest, a person who stays in a hotel; **residents' lounge** = room in a hotel which is only open to residents of the hotel and their guests (often morning coffee and afternoon tea are served in this lounge) **(c)** member of staff who lives in; *a resident manager*

◇ **non-resident** *adjective & noun* **(a)** (person) not staying in a hotel; *the hotel restaurant is open to non-residents* **(b)** (person) not living in a place; **a non-resident's entry visa** = visa allowing a person who is not a resident of a country to go into that country; *he has a non-resident account with a French bank; she was granted a non-resident visa*

◇ **residential** *adjective* referring to residence; **residential area** = part of a town which is mainly occupied with private houses and flats; **residential hotel** = hotel which caters for long-stay guests, usually on a full-board basis; **residential street** = street of private houses and flats (with no offices or shops)

resort *noun* place where people go on holiday; **resort hotel** = hotel in a resort; **health resort** = town where people go to improve their health (such as a spa); **mountain resort** = holiday town in the mountains; **sea resort** = holiday town near the seaside; **ski resort** = town in the mountains where people stay when on a skiing holiday

responsibility *noun* **(a)** being in charge of something; *the management refuses to accept responsibility for guests' personal belongings; he has taken on responsibility for the reception area* = he has agreed to be in charge of the reception area **(b)** something which you are in charge of; *his main responsibility is seeing that the guests are safe*

◇ **responsible** *adjective* **(a)** which causes; *the fog was responsible for the accident* **(b)** (person) in charge of something or taking decisions for something or directing something; *she is responsible for the tour schedules; the hotel management is not responsible for the restaurant in the adjoining building* **(c)** **responsible to someone** = being under the authority of someone who expects you to carry out the work well **(d)** **responsible job** or **responsible position** = post where decisions have to be taken

rest 1 *noun* **(a)** sleep, being calm; *she's having a rest in her room; the afternoon has been set aside for rest;* **rest area** = area near a motorway or other large road, provided with a public toilet and picnic tables and benches, where you can park and get out of the car to relax; **rest room** = public toilet **(b)**

support; **armrest** = part of a seat which you put your arm on; *the ashtray and sound buttons are in the armrest; please put your armrests into horizontal position for landing;* **headrest** = cushion to support your head (attached to a seat, as in a car or plane) **(c)** **the rest** = other people; *six people decided to walk back down the mountain, but the rest of the party used the funicular* **2** *verb* to sleep, to be calm; *they went upstairs to rest before dinner*

restaurant *noun* place where you can buy and eat a meal; *he runs a French restaurant in New York;* **restaurant manager** = person who runs a restaurant, but does not own it; **restaurant owner** or **proprietor** = person who owns a restaurant; **he's in the restaurant business** = he owns or manages restaurants

◇ **restaurant car** *noun* railway coach where passengers can sit and eat meals; *compare* BUFFET CAR

◇ **restaurateur** *noun* person who runs a restaurant

QUOTE a London restaurateur was fined at the magistrates court last week for failing to quieten a noisy extractor fan
Caterer & Hotelkeeper

restrict *verb* to limit or to impose controls on; *we are restricted to twenty tables by the size of the restaurant;* **restricted access** = access (to a museum, for example) which is limited to small groups of people at certain times of the day only

◇ **restriction** *noun* limit or imposing controls on; *import restrictions* or *restrictions on imports;* **to impose restrictions on imports** or **on credit** = to start limiting imports or credit; **to lift credit restrictions** = to allow credit to be given freely

résumé *US* = CURRICULUM VITAE

retinol *noun* vitamin A, vitamin which is soluble in fat and can be formed in the body, but which is mainly found in food such as liver, vegetables, eggs and cod liver oil

retsina *noun* Greek wine flavoured with pine resin (resin was originally added to preserve the wine)

return 1 *noun* **(a)** going back or coming back; **return journey** = journey back to where you came from; **a return ticket** or **a return** = a ticket for a journey from one place to another and back again; *I want two* *returns to Edinburgh;* **return fare** = fare for a journey from one place to another and back again; **day return (ticket)** = ticket available at a lower price if you go and come back in the same day; **weekend return (ticket)** = ticket available at a reduced price if you go and come back between Friday and Monday **(b)** sending back; **he replied by return of post** = he replied by the next post service; **return address** = address to send something back to **(c)** profit *or* income from money invested; *to bring in a quick return; what is the gross return on this line?;* **return on investment (ROI)** *or* **on capital** = profit shown as a percentage of money invested **(d) official return** = official report; **to make a return to the tax office** *or* **to make an income tax return** = to send a statement of income and allowances to the tax office; **to fill in a VAT return** = to complete the form showing VAT receipts and expenditure; **nil return** = report showing no sales *or* income *or* tax, etc.; **daily** *or* **weekly** *or* **quarterly sales return** = report of sales made each day *or* week *or* quarter **2** *verb* **(a)** to send back; *to return unsold stock to the wholesaler; to return a letter to sender;* **returned empties** = empty bottles *or* containers which are taken back to a shop *or* supplier, where any deposit paid will be given back **(b)** to make a statement; *to return income of £15,000 to the tax authorities*

◊ **returnable** *adjective* which can be taken back to a shop or supplier; *these bottles are not returnable*

revalidation *noun* making a ticket valid again, after a change has been made; **revalidation sticker** = little sticker put on a ticket to show a change made to the original reservation

revenue *noun* **(a)** money which is received; **revenue accounts** = accounts of a business which record money received as sales, commission, etc. **(b)** money received by a government in tax; **Inland Revenue** *or* **US Internal Revenue Service** = government department which deals with tax

reverse 1 *adjective* opposite; **reverse-charge call** = telephone call where the person receiving the call agrees to pay for it **2** *noun* **(a)** the opposite **(b)** car gear which makes you go backwards; **the car was in reverse** = the reverse gear was engaged **3** *verb* **(a)** to make a car go backwards **(b)** *(on the phone)* **to reverse the charges** = to ask the person you are calling to pay for the call

revolving door *noun* door which turns round a central pillar; *his luggage got stuck in the revolving door at the entrance to the hotel*

rhubarb *noun* perennial plant *(Rheum rhaponticum)*, of which the leaf stalks are cooked and eaten as dessert; *rhubarb pie*

rib *noun* **(a)** one of several bones forming a cage across the chest **(b)** piece of meat with the rib bone attached to it; **spare ribs** = pork ribs served cooked in a savoury sauce

riboflavine *or* **vitamin B₂** *noun* vitamin found in eggs, liver, green vegetables, milk and yeast and also used as an additive (E101) in processed food

rice *noun* cereal grass *(Oryza sativa)*, the most important cereal crop in the world; **brown rice** = rice which still has its outer covering; **wild rice** = species of grass which is found naturally in North America and which is similar to rice; **long-grain rice** = rice with long grains used in savoury dishes; **short-grain rice** = rice with short grains (used in rice pudding); **rice cooker** = special electric pan for boiling rice; **rice paper** = very thin paper which you can eat and which is used in cooking; **rice pudding** = dessert made of short-grain rice, milk and sugar

COMMENT: while rice is always served in Chinese and Indian meals, it is also used in European cooking, being served either as a main course (e.g. in paella or risotto) or as a vegetable with meat or fish. In English cooking, it is commonly served as a sweet pudding

rich *adjective* (food) with a lot of cream, fat, eggs, etc. in it

Richter scale *noun* scale of measurement of the force of an earthquake; *there were no reports of injuries after the quake which hit 5.2 on the Richter scale*

COMMENT: the scale, devised by Charles Richter, has values from zero to ten, with the strongest earthquake ever recorded being 8.9. Earthquakes of 5 or more on the Richter scale cause damage

ride 1 *noun* trip on a horse, on a bicycle, in a car, etc.; *we went for a ride on an elephant;* **bus ride** = short trip in a bus **2** *verb* to go for a trip on a horse, on a bicycle, in a car, etc.

NOTE: **riding - rode - has ridden**

right 1 *adjective* **(a)** good *or* correct; *the customer was right when he said that the bill did not add up; this is not the right plane for Paris* **(b)** opposite of left; *the hotel is on the right side of the street, going towards the station* (NOTE: on ships and aircraft, the right side is called the **starboard side**) **2** *noun* legal title to something; *she has a right to the property; the group said they had the right to know why the visit to the temples had been cancelled;* **right of way** = legal title to go across someone's property

◊ **right-hand** *adjective* belonging to the right side; *the restaurant is on the right-hand side of the main street; he keeps the address list in the right-hand drawer of his desk;* **right-hand man** = main assistant

rind *noun* skin on fruit or meat or cheese

ring *verb* **(a)** to make a noise like a bell; *the telephone was ringing in the reception area, but no one answered it;* **to ring a bell** = to press a button to make an electric bell ring; **'please ring for service'** = notice by a bell, asking a visitor to ring it if he wants a member of staff to come **(b)** to telephone to someone; *he rang (up) his wife from the conference hotel*
NOTE: **ringing - rang - has rung**

◊ **ring back** *verb* to make a phone call in reply to another; *the manager is in a meeting, can you ring back in about half an hour? Mr Smith called while you were out and asked if you would ring him back; your office rang - can you ring them back?*

◊ **ring road** *noun* road which goes round a town

rink *noun* special area for ice skating, playing ice hockey, roller skating, etc.; *in the evening we all went to the skating rink*

risotto *noun* Italian dish of cooked rice with meat, fish, or vegetables in it

rissole *noun* fried ball of minced meat, fish, potatoes, etc.

Riviera *noun* coast of a Mediterranean Sea in France and Italy; also used to describe any popular south coast in other countries; *winter holidays on the French Riviera; they rented a villa on the Italian Riviera; the Cornish Riviera is popular for family holidays*

roach *noun* **(a)** small freshwater fish (NOTE: plural is **roach) (b)** *(informal)* cockroach (NOTE: plural is **roaches)**

road *noun* **(a)** way used by cars, lorries, etc. to move from one place to another; *the first part of the tour is by road; road transport costs have risen; the main entrance is in London Road; use the Park Road entrance to get to the hotel car park;* **road network** = system of interconnecting roads in a country; **road regulations** = rules applied to drivers using roads in a certain country; **road sign** = plate by the side of a road, giving instructions or warnings; **road user** = person driving a car, bus, truck, etc., or riding a bicycle or motorcycle along a road **(b) on the road** = travelling; *we were on the road for thirteen hours before we finally reached the hotel; the salesmen are on the road thirty weeks a year*

roast 1 *noun* **(a)** meat which will be cooked in an oven; *the chef is preparing a roast of lamb* **(b)** meat which has been cooked in an oven; *the special of the day is a roast of pork* **2** *verb* to cook over a fire or in an oven **3** *adjective* which has been cooked over a fire or in an oven; **roast beef; roast chef** *or* **chef rôtisseur** = chef in charge of roast meats; **roast potato** = potato baked in fat in an oven

◊ **roasting** *noun* cooking over a fire or in an oven; **roasting chicken** = chicken which is tender enough to be cooked by roasting; **roasting pan** *or* **tin** = large low-sided metal dish in which meat is roasted in the oven

rocket *noun* green salad plant with a peppery flavour

rocks *plural noun* **on the rocks** = (alcohol) served in a glass with ice cubes
◊ **rock salmon** *noun* dogfish

rodent *noun* order of mammals including rats and mice, which have sharp teeth for gnawing; *see also* MOUSE, RAT
◊ **rodenticide** *noun* poison which kills rats and mice

roe *noun* fish eggs; **herring roe; smoked cod's roe**

ROI = RETURN ON INVESTMENT

roll 1 *noun* **(a)** something which has been turned over and over to wrap round itself; **kitchen roll** = roll of absorbent paper, used for mopping up spilled liquids, wiping pans, etc.; **toilet roll** or **roll of toilet paper** = roll of soft paper in a toilet, used for wiping yourself after getting rid of waste matter **(b)** **Swiss roll** or US **jelly roll** = cake made by rolling a thin sheet of sponge cake covered with jam **(c) (bread) roll** = small loaf of bread (offered to the guests by the commis waiter while they are studying the menu) **2** verb **(a)** to turn something over and over; **rolled joint** = joint of meat, made from a flat piece of meat which is turned over and over to make a roll and then tied with string **(b)** to make something go forward by pushing it on wheels or by turning it over; *they rolled the bed into the corner of the room* **(c)** (of a ship) to move up and down from side to side; compare PITCH

◊ **rollaway bed** noun bed which can be rolled under another

◊ **roll-on/roll-off (ro-ro)** adjective (ferry) where trucks and cars can drive straight on or off

◊ **rolling stock** noun wagons, etc., used on the railway

roly-poly noun cooked pudding made of suet pastry spread with jam and rolled up

roof noun **(a)** covering over a building; **roof garden** = garden on the roof of a building **(b)** top of a vehicle (car, bus, truck, etc.); **sunshine roof** = part of a roof of a car which slides open; **roof box** = box which can be fitted to the roof of a car to carry skis, boots, etc.; **roof rack** = grid fixed to the roof of a car for carrying luggage

room noun **(a)** part of a building, divided off from other parts by walls; **conference room** = room where a small meeting can take place; **room temperature** = temperature in an ordinary room, usually around 20°C (the temperature at which most red wines should be served) **(b)** bedroom in a hotel; **room and board** = meals and a bed for the night (in a guesthouse or hotel); **room with shower** or **with private bath** = bedroom with a shower room or bathroom attached; *I want a room with bath for two nights;* **double room** = room for two people; **double-bedded room** = room with two beds (usually two twin beds); **single room** = room for one person; **room attendant** = person who looks after a hotel room, seeing that it is clean and provided with linen, etc., ready for guests; US **room clerk** = person in a hotel who decides which bedrooms guests will stay in, keeps the register, etc.; **room expenses** = expenses on hotel bedrooms, such as the

cost of linen or cleaning materials, but not including staff costs; **room inspection** = examination of a room after it has been cleaned, to see if it is ready for the next guest; **room key** = key to a room, such as a bedroom in a hotel; *please leave your room key with the porter when you go out;* **room linen** = sheets, towels, etc., for use in a hotel bedroom; **room maid** = chambermaid, girl or woman who cleans rooms in a hotel; **room number** = number given to a room in a hotel; **room occupancy** = (i) act of staying in a room in a hotel; (ii) occupancy rate, the average number of rooms used in a hotel over a period of time, shown as a percentage of the total number of rooms; **rooms payroll** = cost of the wages of hotel staff who deal with guest bedrooms; **room rate** = price for a hotel room for one night; **average achieved room rate** = average price received for rooms in a hotel (the total amount charged for all rooms, each night, divided by the number of rooms occupied); **room safe** = small safe in a bedroom, in which the guest can leave valuables; **room sales** = turnover from letting rooms in a hotel; **room service** = arrangement in a hotel where food or drink can be served in a guest's bedroom; **room tax** = visitor's tax levied by the local government or municipality on a visitor occupying a hotel room

QUOTE he also draws attention to the growing use of good quality chinaware in room service. One factor in this is that more and more women guests use room service rather than dine alone in a hotel's main restaurant

Caterer & Hotelkeeper

rooming house noun US house with furnished rooms to let

root beer noun US dark fizzy drink, flavoured with the juice of roots, bark and herbs

ro-ro = ROLL-ON/ROLL-OFF

rosé noun pink wine which gets its colour from the grape skins being left for a time in the fermenting mixture

COMMENT: rosé wines are sweeter than most red or white wines, and can be served chilled as an aperitif

rosemary noun *Rosmarinus officinalis,* a pungent herb with spiky green leaves, used in cooking

COMMENT: rosemary is very often used when roasting lamb

roster *noun* list showing employees and details of their periods of work; *the flight crew roster is issued on the 20th of the month*

rotavirus *noun* any of a group of viruses associated with gastroenteritis in children

QUOTE rotavirus is now widely accepted as an important cause of childhood diarrhoea in many different parts of the world
East African Medical Journal

rotisserie *noun* device in an oven, with a metal rod which can be passed through meat and turned so that the meat is evenly cooked

◊ **chef rôtisseur** *noun* roast chef, the chef in charge of roast meats

rouble *or US* **ruble** *noun* currency used in Russia

rough *adjective* **(a)** approximate *or* not very accurate; **rough calculation** *or* **rough estimate** = approximate answer; *I made some rough calculations on the back of an envelope* **(b)** not finished; **rough copy** = draft of a document which will have changes made to it before it is complete

◊ **roughage** *noun* dietary fibre, fibrous matter in food, which cannot be digested

COMMENT: roughage is found in cereals, nuts, fruit and some green vegetables. It is believed to be necessary to help digestion and avoid developing constipation, obesity, appendicitis and other digestive problems

◊ **roughly** *adverb* more or less; *the number of visitors is roughly twice last year's; the development cost of the marina will be roughly £25m*

◊ **rough out** *verb* to make a first design *or* a general design; *the tour guide roughed out a seating plan*

round 1 *adjective* **in round figures** = not totally accurate, but correct to the nearest 10 or 100

◊ **round down** *verb* to decrease to the nearest full figure; *the bill came to £164.62 but they rounded it down to £164*

◊ **round-the-world** *adjective* (flight) which goes round the world, returning to the

original departure airport; *a round-the-world ticket allows several stopovers*

◊ **round trip** *noun* journey from one place to another and back again; *US* **round-trip fare** = fare for a journey from one place to another and back again (NOTE: GB English is **return fare**)

◊ **round up** *verb* to increase to the nearest full figure; *the bank cashier rounded up the figures to the nearest pound*

QUOTE each cheque can be made out for the local equivalent of £100 rounded up to a convenient figure
Sunday Times

roundabout *noun* **(a)** children's playing machine, which goes round when pushed and on which you can sit or stand **(b)** *(in a fairground)* large mechanical amusement machine, which turns round and plays music, usually with horses to sit on which move up and down **(c)** point where roads meet, and traffic has to turn in a circle, usually with each giving way to drivers coming from the right (NOTE: in US English, this is called a **traffic circle**)

route 1 *noun* **(a)** way which is regularly taken; **bus route** = way which is regularly taken by a bus from one place to another; *companies were warned that normal shipping routes were dangerous because of the war* **(b)** **en route** = on the way; *we stopped for lunch en route for Scotland; the pleasure ship sank when she was en route to the Gulf* **2** *verb* to send a bus *or* aircraft by a certain route; *see also* RE-ROUTE

QUOTE the consolidator is marketing perhaps the cheapest round-the-world Business class fare. It is charging a mere £1,389 for flights routed: London-Vienna-Bangkok-Taipei-Los Angeles-London
Business Traveller

roux *noun* mixture of fat and flour cooked to make a base for a sauce

row 1 *noun* **(a)** line of seats side by side (in a cinema, aircraft, etc.); *we had tickets for the front row of the stalls; my seat is row 23A, so I must be next to a window* **(b)** short trip in a rowing boat; *we went for a row on the lake* **2** *verb* to make a small boat go forward by using oars

◊ **rowing boat** *or US* **rowboat** *noun* small boat, which can be made to go forward using oars

RRP = RECOMMENDED RETAIL PRICE

RSAC = ROYAL SCOTTISH AUTOMOBILE CLUB

rug *noun* (a) small carpet (b) thick blanket, especially one used for travelling; **car rug** *or* **travelling rug** = thick blanket used to put over the knees of a passenger in a car, etc.

rules *plural noun* regulations *or* laws, strict orders of the way to behave; *we apply strict rules of hygiene in the kitchen; did you read the rules about what to do in case of a fire?*

rump *see* STEAK

run 1 *noun* (a) regular route (of plane, bus, train); *he does the London-Paris run twice a week* = he drives a coach from London to Paris twice a week (b) **ski run** = specially prepared and marked slope for skiing down a mountain **2** *verb* (a) to manage; *he runs a tourist guide service; she runs the restaurant for her father* (b) *(of engine, transport)* to work; *the bus does not run on Sundays*

QUOTE business is booming for airlines on the London to Manchester run
Business Traveller

◊ **run out of** *verb* to have nothing left *or* to use up all the stock; *the bureau de change has run out of Deutschmarks; the hotel has run out of beer*

◊ **run up** *verb* to make a large debt quickly; *he quickly ran up a bill for £250*

◊ **runway** *noun* track on which aircraft take off and land at an airport

rupee *noun* currency used in India and some other countries

rush 1 *noun* doing something fast; **rush hour** = time when most traffic is on the roads *or* when everyone is trying to travel to work or from work back home; *the taxi was delayed in the rush-hour traffic;* **rush job** = work which has to be done fast; **rush order** = request for something which has to be supplied fast **2** *verb* to make something go fast; *to rush an order through the factory; to rush a shipment to Africa*

Russian *adjective* referring to Russia; **Russian service** = (i) type of service at a banquet, where the food is carved at a sideboard, and served rapidly by the waiters to the guests so that the food does not get cold; (ii) service similar to French service, where the waiter offers each guest a dish (from the left), and the guest helps himself from it; **Russian tea** = black tea, served in a glass (if a slice of lemon is added it is called 'lemon tea') (NOTE: food served in the Russian way is called **à la russe**)

RV = RECREATIONAL VEHICLE

rye *noun* (a) hardy cereal crop *Secale cereale,* grown in temperate areas; **rye bread** = bread made from rye (it is usually very dark in colour) (b) **rye (whiskey)** = type of whisky made in North America from rye

ryokan *noun* Japanese traditional inn

Ss

saccharin (C₇H₅NO₃S) *noun* substance used as a substitute for sugar

sachet *noun* small plastic bag containing a portion of sauce, shampoo, etc.

saddle *noun* (a) rider's seat on a bicycle or on the back of a horse (b) cut of meat, such as lamb, hare or venison, made up of both loins and part of the backbone

safari *noun* hunting expedition in Africa; *he went on a safari in Kenya;* **safari park** = park where large wild animals, such as lions, giraffes, elephants, etc. run free, and

visitors can look at them from their cars, but cannot get out of the cars

safe 1 *noun* heavy metal box which cannot be opened easily, in which valuables, such as money, jewellery, documents, etc. can be kept; *put your valuables in the hotel safe;* **room safe** = small safe in a hotel bedroom in which the guest can leave valuables **2** *adjective* (a) uninjured *or* out of danger; *three climbers were safe after the avalanche* (b) **safe custody** *or* **safe-keeping** = being looked after carefully; *we put the documents into the bank for safe-keeping*

◇ **safe-deposit box** *noun* box (in a bank) in which valuables such as money, jewellery or documents can be kept

safety *noun* **(a)** being free from danger or risk; **safety checklist** = list of things which have to be checked as part of safety regulations; **safety margin** = time *or* space allowed for something to be safe; **to take safety precautions** *or* **safety measures** = to act to make sure something is safe; **safety regulations** = rules to make a place safe for the customers and staff **(b) fire safety** = making a place safe for the customers and staff in case of fire; **fire safety officer** = person responsible for seeing that the customers and staff are safe if a fire breaks out **(c) for safety** = to make something safe *or* to be safe; *put the money in the hotel safe for safety; keep a note of the numbers of your traveller's cheques for safety*

◇ **safety-deposit** = SAFE-DEPOSIT

safflower *noun* plant which produces an oil used in cooking

saffron *noun* orange-coloured powder made from crocus flowers, from which colouring and flavouring are obtained

COMMENT: saffron is used to colour food yellow; it is used in cooking rice and is an essential ingredient of bouillabaisse

sage *noun* aromatic herb *(Salvia officinalis)* with silvery-green leaves used in cookery

COMMENT: sage and onion stuffing is often used in British cooking to stuff meat and poultry

sago *noun* white powder made from the sago palm, used as food and as a thickening agent

sail 1 *noun* trip in a boat; *they went for a sail down the Thames* **2** *verb* to travel on water *or* to leave harbour; *the ship sails at 12.00*

◇ **sailing** *noun* **(a)** departure (of a ship); *there are no sailings to France because of the strike;* **sailing time** = time when a boat leaves **(b)** handling of a sailing boat, especially for pleasure; *we have booked to go on a sailing holiday in the Aegean;* **sailing boat** *or* **sailing ship** *or* US **sailboat** = boat which uses mainly sails to travel

sake *noun* Japanese rice wine, usually drunk warm

salad *noun* cold dish of various raw or cooked vegetables; cold meat, fish or cheese served with cold raw or cooked vegetables; *cheese salad; prawn salad;* **salad bar** = self-service bar, where customers help themselves to a wide variety of meat, fish or vegetable salads; **salad cream** = commercially prepared sauce made of eggs, oil and vinegar, etc., used on salad and usually available in cafés, etc. in bottles or sachets; **salad dressing** = liquid sauce put on lettuce and other cold raw or cooked vegetables to give them additional flavour; **salade niçoise** = French salad, made with lettuce, hard-boiled eggs, cold boiled potatoes, anchovy fillets, black olives and tomatoes, with garlic in the dressing (many other ingredients can be added, such as tuna fish, French beans, red peppers, etc.); **(fresh) fruit salad** = pieces of fresh fruit, mixed and served cold

COMMENT: the commonest salad dressings is 'French dressing' or 'vinaigrette', made of olive oil, vinegar, salt, and other flavourings; also common are 'Thousand Island dressing', made with mayonnaise and chopped vegetables, and 'blue-cheese' or 'roquefort dressing', made with mayonnaise or vinaigrette and blue cheese or Roquefort cheese

salamander *noun* type of cooking grill, where food is grilled in a more or less enclosed box (as opposed to an open griller)

salami *noun* dry spicy pork sausage, originally from Italy

salary *noun* payment for work, made to an employee with a contract of employment, usually in the form of a monthly cheque; *she got a salary increase in June; the company froze all salaries for a six-month period;* **basic salary** = normal salary without extra payments; **gross salary** = salary before tax is deducted; **net salary** = salary which is left after deducting tax and national insurance contributions; **starting salary** = amount of payment for an employee when starting work with a company; *he was appointed at a starting salary of £10,000;* **salary cheque** = monthly cheque by which an employee is paid

sale *noun* **(a)** act of selling, act of giving an item or doing a service in exchange for money, or for the promise that money will be paid; **cash sale** = transaction paid for in cash; **credit card sale** = transaction paid for by credit card **(b) for sale** = ready to be sold **(c) on sale** = ready to be sold in a shop; *these items are on sale in most chemists* **(d)** selling of goods at specially low prices; *the shop is having a sale to clear old stock; the sale price is 50% of the normal price;* **bargain sale** = sale of all goods in a store at cheap prices; **clearance sale** = sale of items at low prices to get rid of the stock; **half-price sale** = sale of all goods at 50% of the usual price

◊ **sales** *plural noun* (i) money received for selling something; (ii) number of items sold; *sales have risen over the first quarter;* **sales conference** *or* **sales meeting** = meeting of sales managers, representatives, publicity staff, etc., to discuss results and future sales plans; **sales manager** = person in charge of a sales department; **sales tax** = tax to be paid on each item sold; **beverage sales** = turnover from the sale of drinks; **food sales** = turnover from the sale of food; **room sales** = turnover from letting rooms in a hotel

salmon *noun* large sea fish, with pink flesh; *cold poached salmon and salad;* **salmon steak** = slice of salmon cut across the body of the fish; **smoked salmon** = salmon which has been cured by smoking, and is served in very thin slices, usually with brown bread and lemon as an hors d'oeuvre

◊ **salmon trout** *noun* large sea trout with pink flesh like that of a salmon

Salmonella *noun* genus of bacteria in the intestines, which are pathogenic, are usually acquired by eating contaminated food, and cause typhoid or paratyphoid fever, gastroenteritis or food poisoning; **salmonella poisoning** = illness caused by eating food which is contaminated with Salmonella bacteria which develop in the intestines; *five people were taken to hospital with Salmonella poisoning* (NOTE: plural is **Salmonellae**)

COMMENT: Salmonellae are found in meat, offal, eggs, milk and fish. The bacteria are killed by temperatures over 65°C, and so are killed by cooking. They survive freezing, and so revive when frozen food is defrosted

QUOTE according to Public Health Laboratory figures, infection in humans by Salmonella enteriditis stood at 16,981 last year. This comprised nearly half of all Salmonella figures

Caterer & Hotelkeeper

salon *noun* shop where people can have their hair cut or styled, or have beauty treatments; *the hairdressing salon is on the fifth floor; she went to the beauty salon for a manicure*

saloon *noun* US place which sells alcoholic drinks

◊ **saloon bar** *noun* bar in a pub which is more comfortable than the public bar, and where the drinks may be slightly more expensive

◊ **saloon keeper** *noun* US person who runs a saloon

salsa *noun* pungent Mexican sauce made of tomatoes, onions and chillis

salsify *noun* plant *(Tragopodon porrifolius)* with a long, white root and green leaves, all of which are eaten as vegetables

COMMENT: salsify has a flavour similar to that of oysters

salt 1 *noun* **common salt** = sodium chloride (NaCl), white crystals used to make food taste better, also used to preserve food; **sea salt** = crystals of sodium chloride, extracted from sea water **2** *adjective* **(a)** containing salt **(b)** cured or preserved or seasoned with salt; *salt cod;* **salt beef** = beef which has been preserved in brine, then cooked (usually served cold in thin slices, in rye bread sandwiches) **3** *verb* **(a)** to add salt to; *you forgot to salt the soup* **(b)** to preserve food by keeping it in salt or in salt water; cabbage, gherkins, ham and many types of fish are salted for preservation

◊ **salt cellar** *noun* small pot containing salt usually with a hole in the top so that it can be sprinkled on food

COMMENT: in the UK, a salt cellar has a single hole, to differentiate it from the pepper pot which has several; in the USA, the pepper pot will have only one hole while a salt cellar will have several. Table salt is ground to finer grains than cooking salt; kitchen salt may be treated with anti-caking agents to make it flow more freely

salted *adjective* covered in salt; *there were bowls of salted nuts on the bar*

◊ **salt-free** *adjective* without salt

◊ **saltiness** *or* **saltness** *noun* being salty

◊ **saltmill** *noun* device which grinds salt crystals (crystals are placed in the mill which is twisted to crush them: saltmills are often used to grind sea salt)

◊ **salt water** *noun* water which contains salt, such as sea water (as opposed to fresh water in rivers and lakes)

◊ **saltwater** *adjective* (lake) containing salt water; *a saltwater swimming pool*

◊ **salty** *adjective* containing salt; tasting strongly of salt; *we had a bowl of very salty pea and ham soup*

salvage *noun* income from the sale of waste materials from a hotel or restaurant (such as kitchen waste)

salver *noun* large flat serving plate (usually made of metal, such as silver or stainless steel)

samosa *noun* Indian dish consisting of a small triangular pastry containing spiced meat or vegetables, usually deep-fried and served as a starter or snack

samovar *noun* urn used in Russia for boiling water for tea

sample 1 *noun* **(a)** specimen, a small part of an item which is used to show what the whole item is like; *a sample of the cloth or a cloth sample; try a sample of the local cheese; free sample* = sample given free to advertise a product **(b)** small representative group of people questioned to show what the reactions of a much larger group would be; *we interviewed a sample of potential customers;* **a random sample** = a sample taken without any selection **2** *verb* **(a)** to test *or* to try something by taking a small amount; *to sample a product before buying it; you can sample the wine before placing your order* **(b)** to question a small representative group of people to find out what the reactions of a much larger group would be; *they sampled 2,000 people at random to test the new drink*

sand *noun* mass of tiny fragments of worn-down rock, etc., found on seashores, river beds, deserts, etc.; *a beach of fine white sand; the black sand beaches of the Northern coast of New Zealand*

◊ **sandpit** *noun* place with sand where children can play

◊ **sandstorm** *noun* high wind in the desert, which carries large amounts of sand with it

◊ **sandy** *adjective* like sand; made of sand; *the resort has miles of safe sandy beaches*

sandwich *noun* **(a)** two slices of bread with meat *or* cheese, etc. between them; **club sandwich** *or* **double-decker sandwich** = sandwich made of three slices of bread, with a filling of meat, salad, fish, etc., between them; **open sandwich** = one slice of bread with meat, cheese, etc. on it **(b)** type of cake, formed of two pieces of sponge cake, one on top of the other, with a cream or jam filling in between

sanitary *adjective* (i) clean; (ii) referring to hygiene *or* to health; **sanitary towel** *or* US **sanitary napkin** = pad of absorbent paper worn during menstruation; *do not put sanitary towels in the toilet, but use the special bags provided*

sardine *noun* small fish of the herring family

sarsaparilla *noun* non-alcoholic drink made from the root of an American plant

satay *noun* appetizer served in South-East Asian cooking, made of marinaded meat cooked on a little skewer, and served with peanut sauce

satellite *noun* artificial body which was launched from and which goes round the earth; **satellite broadcast** = radio or TV broadcast transmitted via a satellite; **satellite dish** = aerial, shaped like a dish used to capture satellite broadcasts

satsuma *noun* type of small sweet orange which peels easily

Saturday *noun* sixth day of the week, between Friday and Sunday

COMMENT: discounted flights usually mean the passenger has to stay over a Saturday night. This is because most business people do not stay in hotels on Saturday, so rooms are more easily available

QUOTE most destinations require a Saturday night stay but some in France can also be booked with a minimum two-night mid-week stay which makes them suitable for businessmen
Business Traveller

sauce *noun* liquid with a particular taste poured over food to give it an extra flavour; *chicken in mushroom sauce; spaghetti with a tomato and meat sauce;* **sauce chef** *or* **chef saucier** = chef in charge of preparing sauces; **sauce tartare** *or* **tartare sauce** = sauce made of mayonnaise and chopped pickles, served with fish; **white sauce** = basic sauce made from fat, flour and liquid (usually milk or stock)

COMMENT: common prepared sauces served in British restaurants include: tomato sauce (served with fried food); horseradish sauce (served with roast beef and some smoked fish); mint sauce (served with lamb); sauce tartare (served with fish). These are often commercially prepared and served in bottles or sachets

◊ **sauceboat** *noun* vessel in which sauce is served

◊ **saucepan** *noun* deep metal cooking pot with a long handle

saucer *noun* shallow dish placed under a cup

saucisson *noun* dry spicy pork sausage from France

sauerkraut *noun* German dish of pickled cabbage, often served with sausages

sauna *noun* (a) very hot steam bath (b) room where you can have a very hot steam bath

sausage *noun* tube of edible skin filled with minced and seasoned pork or other meat; *I'll have sausages and eggs for breakfast*
◊ **sausage meat** *noun* mixture of meat, bread and flavourings for making sausages, sold separately, and used in pies and sausage rolls
◊ **sausage roll** *noun* savoury snack made of pastry with a small sausage or piece of sausage meat inside it

sauté 1 *adjective* fried quickly in a little fat; **sauté potatoes** = slices of potato, fried in fat; *do you want sauté potatoes or new potatoes with your fish?* **2** *verb* to fry in a little fat (NOTE: **sautéeing - sautéed**)

save *verb* (a) to keep (money) *or* not to spend (money); *he is trying to save money by walking to work; she is saving for a holiday in Spain* (b) not to waste *or* to use less; *to save time, let's continue the discussion in the taxi to the airport; the government is encouraging companies to save energy*
◊ **savings** *plural noun* money saved (i.e., money which is not spent but put aside); *she spent all her savings on a trip to Egypt; there are incredible savings on flights to Florida*

savory *noun* herb used in cooking

savoury 1 *adjective* with a salty or other flavour which is not sweet **2** *noun* snack, served at the end of a large meal, which is salty, or made of cheese

COMMENT: the savoury course in a large formal meal is normally served at the end, after the sweet course (or instead of it) and before the cheese. Common savouries in English cooking are 'welsh rarebit' (grilled cheese on toast) or 'angels on horseback' (oysters cooked wrapped in rashers of bacon)

scallion *noun US* young onion eaten raw in salad (NOTE: the British English is **spring onion**)

scallop *noun* type of shellfish with a semi-circular ridged shell
◊ **scalloped potatoes** *noun* potatoes which are sliced and cooked in a shallow dish in the oven

scampi *noun* large prawns *(Nephrys norvegicus)* usually served fried in batter (NOTE: plural is **scampi**)

scenery *noun* appearance of the landscape; *the beautiful scenery of the Lake District*
◊ **scenic** *adjective* referring to beautiful scenery; *welcome to scenic Nova Scotia;* **scenic railway** = miniature railway running through artificial picturesque scenery at a fair, etc.; **scenic route** = road running through beautiful countryside

schedule 1 *noun* (a) timetable *or* plan of times drawn up in advance; **to be ahead of schedule** = to be early; **to be on schedule** = to be on time; **to be behind schedule** = to be late; *the building of the hotel complex was completed ahead of schedule; the flight is on schedule; I am sorry to say that we are three months behind schedule; the managing director has a busy schedule of appointments; his secretary tried to fit me into his schedule* (b) list of times of departure and arrivals of trains, planes, coaches, etc.; *the summer schedules have been published* **(c)** list (especially of additional documents attached to a contract); *conditions as per the attached schedule; please find enclosed our schedule of charges; the schedule of territories to which an insurance policy applies; for restrictions on use, see the attached schedule* 2 *verb* **(a)** to list officially; *scheduled prices or scheduled charges* **(b)** to plan the time when something will happen; *the building is scheduled for completion in May;* scheduled flight = regular flight which is in the airline timetable (as opposed to a charter flight); *he left for Helsinki on a scheduled flight*

◊ **scheduling** *noun* drawing up a timetable *or* a plan

Schistosoma = BILHARZIA
◊ **schistosomiasis** = BILHARZIASIS

schnitzel *noun* thin flat piece of veal or pork dipped in egg and breadcrumbs and fried; *see also* WIENER

schooner *noun* large upright glass, used for serving sherry

scone *noun* type of small crusty bread, sometimes with dried fruit in it, eaten with butter and jam or with cream; *see also* CREAM TEA

scoop *noun* **(a)** deep round spoon for serving ice cream **(b)** a portion of ice cream, etc.; *I'll have one scoop of strawberry and one scoop of vanilla, please*

Scotch 1 *adjective* from Scotland; **Scotch broth** = thick soup with barley, vegetables and lamb; **Scotch eggs** = hard-boiled eggs, covered in sausage meat and fried; usually eaten cold; **Scotch pancakes** = very small pancakes, cooked on a griddle; **Scotch woodcock** = savoury consisting of small squares of toast spread with anchovy paste and topped with a mixture of scrambled egg yolks, cream and cayenne pepper **2** *noun* **(a)** whisky made in Scotland; *a bottle of scotch* **(b)** glass of this whisky; *a large scotch, please*

Scottish Tourist Board (STB) organization which promotes tourism in Scotland and promotes tourism to Scotland from other parts of the UK

scrambled eggs *or* **scrambled egg** *noun* eggs which are beaten with salt and pepper and cooked in butter, often served on toast as part of an English breakfast; *we had a starter of scrambled egg with smoked salmon*

screen *noun* **(a)** flat surface which protects something or divides two things **(b)** something which acts as protection against draughts, fire, noise, etc. **(c)** flat surface for projecting films onto **(d)** flat surface as on a television set or computer monitor, on which images are shown; *I'll call flight details up on the screen*

screwdriver *noun* cocktail of vodka and orange juice

scrumpy *see* CIDER

scuba *noun* underwater breathing apparatus
◊ **scuba-diver** *noun* person who goes scuba-diving
◊ **scuba-diving** *noun* sport of swimming underwater, using breathing apparatus

scurvy *noun* disease caused by lack of Vitamin C which is found in fresh fruit and vegetables

sea *noun* area of salt water; **sea crossing** = going across the sea; *the sea crossing between Denmark and Sweden can be quite rough;* **sea salt** = crystals of sodium chloride, extracted from sea water; **sea voyage** *or* **sea cruise** = voyage *or* cruise on the sea (as opposed to a river cruise); **by sea mail** = sent by post abroad, using a ship, not by air
◊ **seafood** *noun* fish and shellfish which can be eaten; **a seafood restaurant** = a restaurant which specialises in seafood (NOTE: no plural)
◊ **seafront** *noun* road which runs beside the sea in a seaside town; *a seafront hotel; our hotel is right on the seafront*
◊ **sea level** *noun* the level of the sea, taken as a point for measuring altitude; *the resort is in the mountains, over 1,000ft above sea level*
◊ **seaport** *noun* port by the sea
◊ **seashell** *noun* shell of a shellfish which lives in the sea; *she walked along the beach collecting seashells*
◊ **seashore** *noun* land along the edge of the sea
◊ **seasick** *adjective* ill because of the movement of a ship; *he gets seasick every time he crosses the Channel*
◊ **seasickness** *noun* sickness caused by the movement of a ship; **seasickness pills** *or* **tablets** = pills taken to prevent seasickness

◊ **seaside** *noun* land by the side of the sea; *a seaside resort; a seaside hotel; we always take the children to the seaside in August*

◊ **seaweed** *noun* plant which grows in the sea, a general name for several species of large algae; several species of seaweed are used as food, particularly in the Far East and Wales (where it is called 'laver' and eaten at breakfast) (NOTE: no plural)

◊ **seaworthiness** *noun* being able and safe to sail; **certificate of seaworthiness** = document to show that a ship has passed an examination and is in a fit condition to sail

◊ **seaworthy** *adjective* (boat) which is able and safe to sail; *the old ferry is scarcely seaworthy*

season 1 *noun* **(a)** one of four parts which a year is divided into (spring, summer, autumn, winter) **(b)** a period of time when something usually takes place; **high season** = period when there are lots of travellers, and when fares and room prices are higher (high-season tariffs usually apply to the period July to September); **low season** = time of year (often during the winter) when there are fewer travellers, and so fares and room prices are cheaper; *tour operators urge more people to travel in the low season; air fares are cheaper in the low season;* **tourist season** *or* **holiday season** = time of year when most people take their holidays; *late winter is the main holiday season in the Alpine resorts; the tourist season on the North Italian coast lasts about three months;* **busy season** = period when a hotel *or* resort is busy; **slack season** = period when a hotel *or* resort is not very busy; **dead season** = time of year when there are few tourists about; **dry season** = period of the year when it does not rain much (as opposed to the rainy season); **rainy season** = period of year when it rains a lot (as opposed to the dry season); **end of season sale** = selling goods cheaply when the season in which they would be used is over (such as summer clothes sold cheaply in the autumn) **(c) in season** = (game) which you are allowed to kill; (fruit, vegetable) which is fresh and plentiful and easy to buy; *grouse isn't in season until 12th August; strawberries are cheaper in season;* **out of season** = (fruit, vegetable) which is more expensive because the growing season is over and it has to be imported or which is not found on menus because the time for growing it is over **2** *verb* to add flavouring, spices, etc. to a dish; *goulash is seasoned with paprika*

◊ **seasonal** *adjective* which only lasts for a season; **seasonal adjustments** = changes made to figures to take account of seasonal variations; **seasonal demand** = demand which exists only during the high season; **seasonal labour** = workers who work for a season (usually the summer) only

◊ **seasoned** *adjective* flavoured with a certain type of seasoning

◊ **seasoning** *noun* salt, pepper, herb or spice used to give a certain taste to food; *the meat seems to lack seasoning*

◊ **season ticket** *noun* rail *or* bus ticket which can be used for any number of journeys over a period (normally 1, 3, 6 or 12 months); *season-ticket holders will receive a refund if their train is cancelled*

seat 1 *noun* chair in a cinema, plane, restaurant, train, etc.; *they asked for six seats in row E; seats are available at all prices; take your seats for the first lunch; passengers are requested to remain in their seats until the plane has come to a standstill; seats in the first-class section are wider than in the tourist class;* **seat-back television** = small television screen set into the back of the seat on an aircraft; *(in an aircraft)* **seat pitch** = distance between the front edge of a seat and the front edge of the seat in front **2** *verb* to have room for people to sit down; *the restaurants seats 75*

QUOTE from April this year, passengers will be able to experience an upgraded Business class. Whether seat pitch (currently 104cm/40ins) will be improved upon has yet to be decided. There are several carriers which offer quite a few inches more

Business Traveller

seat belt *noun* belt worn in a car or aircraft as protection in case of accident; *the 'fasten seat belts' sign came on*

◊ **-seater** *suffix* vehicle with a certain number of seats; *a 20-seater coach; a 10-seater executive jet*

◊ **seating** *noun* seats available for people; **seating capacity** = the number of seats (in a bus, cinema, etc.); **seating plan** = chart showing where each guest sits at a big banquet

sec *French adjective (used of wine)* dry (NOTE: for dry champagne, the word used is **brut**)

second *adjective* (thing) which comes after the first; **second helping** = another portion of the same dish; *after we had finished, the waiter came round with a* *second helping of fish;* **second home** = HOLIDAY HOME

◇ **second-class** *adjective & adverb* less expensive and less comfortable type of travel than first-class; *to travel second-class; the price of a second-class ticket is half that of a first-class; I find second-class hotels are just as comfortable as the best ones;* **second-class mail** = (i); *GB* less expensive, slower, mail service; (ii); *US* mail service for sending newspapers and magazines; *a second-class letter is slower than a first-class; send it second-class if it is not urgent*

◇ **seconds** *plural noun* **(a)** *(informal)* another portion of the same dish; *can I have seconds, please?* **(b)** items which have been turned down by the quality controller as not being top quality; *the shop has a sale of seconds*

sector *noun* part of the economy *or* the business organization of a country; *all sectors of the economy suffered from the fall in the exchange rate; tourism is a booming sector of the economy;* **public sector** = nationalized industries and public services; **private sector** = all companies which are owned by private shareholders, not by the state; *the leisure centre is funded completely by the private sector; salaries in the private sector have increased faster than in the public*

QUOTE government services form a large part of the tertiary or service sector
Sydney Morning Herald

secretary *noun* person who helps to organize work, types letters, files documents, arranges meetings, etc. for someone; *my secretary deals with incoming orders; his secretary phoned to say he would be late*

◇ **secretarial** *adjective* referring to the work of a secretary; *she is taking a secretarial course; he is looking for secretarial work; we need extra secretarial help to deal with the correspondence;* **secretarial services** = work which a secretary might do, such as typing letters, filing documents, etc.; *the business centre at the conference hall offers secretarial services of varying sorts*

section waiter = STATION WAITER

security *noun* being protected *or* being safe; **security bond** *or* **security deposit** = money deposited by a tour company with a government organization, which is to be used to repay travellers with tickets issued by the company if the company goes into liquidation; **security guard** = person who protects an office *or* factory against burglars; **security officer** = person who protects a hotel against burglars; **airport security** = actions taken to protect aircraft and passengers against attack; **hotel security** = actions taken to protect a hotel against theft or fire

sediment *noun* solid substance which forms in liquids (especially in red wine) and which can be removed by decanting the wine

seed *noun* part of a plant which germinates and grows to produce a new plant

◇ **seedless** *adjective* (fruit) with no seeds in it; *seedless grapes*

segment *noun* part of a circle or sphere; **grapefruit segments** = sections of peeled grapefruit, served in a glass bowl as an hors d'oeuvre and at breakfast

◇ **segmentation** *noun* being divided into separate parts; **segmentation of a market** = division of the market or consumers into certain categories according to their buying habits

QUOTE different market segments and, ultimately, individual consumers must be addressed separately
Financial Times

seize *verb* to take hold of something *or* to take possession of something; *the customs seized the shipment of books*

◇ **seizure** *noun* taking possession of something; *the court ordered the seizure of the shipment*

Sekt *noun* sparkling German wine

COMMENT: also familiarly called 'German champagne'; the best quality wine comes from the Rhine valley

self-catering *noun* doing the cooking for yourself; **self-catering holiday** = one where you rent accommodation, but cook your own meals; *self-catering villa holidays in Portugal*

◇ **self-contained** *adjective* (flat) which has its own kitchen, bathroom, etc., and does not share these facilities with others

◇ **self-employed 1** *adjective* working for yourself *or* not on the payroll of a company; *a self-employed accountant; he worked for a* *bank for ten years but now is self-employed* **2** *noun* **the self-employed** = people who work for themselves (NOTE: can be followed by a verb in the plural)

◊ **self-financed** *adjective* **the project is completely self-financed** = the project pays its development costs out of its own revenue, with no subsidies

self-service *adjective* where the customer serves himself; **self-service buffet** = buffet where guests help themselves to food from various dishes provided; **self-service restaurant** = restaurant (such as a cafeteria) where guests take a tray and help themselves to food; **self-service petrol station** = petrol station where the customers put the petrol in their cars themselves; **self-service store** = shop where customers take goods from the shelves and pay for them at the checkout

QUOTE research revealed that customers wanted self-service restaurants for a quick meal, waitress service restaurants, takeaways and sandwich bars
Caterer & Hotelkeeper

sell-by-date *noun* date stamped on the label of a food product, which is the last date on which the product should be sold to be guaranteed of good quality; *similar to* BEST-BEFORE DATE, USE-BY DATE

seller *noun* person who sells; *there were a few postcard sellers by the cathedral;* **seller's market** = market where a person selling goods or a service can ask high prices because there is a large demand for the product

seminar *noun* class given to a small group of students who meet to discuss a subject with a teacher; *the training seminar is being held in the conference room*

semi-skimmed *adjective* milk from which some of the fat has been removed

semolina *noun* hard grains of wheat left when flour is sifted, used in puddings, stews, etc.

send *verb* to make someone *or* something go from one place to another; *to send a letter or an order; the company is sending the injured skiers back home by air; send the letter airmail if you want it to arrive next week*
NOTE: **sending - sent**

◊ **send away for** *verb* to write asking for something to be sent to you; *we sent away for the new brochure*

◊ **send off** *verb* to put (a letter) in the post

◊ **send off for** *verb* to write asking for something to be sent to you; *we sent off for the new catalogue*

senior 1 *adjective* older *or* higher in rank; **senior citizen** = old age pensioner; **senior executive** *or* **senior manager** = older manager in a company **2** *noun* the father of the family; *Harry Markovitz Senior*

separate 1 *adjective* not together; **to send something under separate cover** = to send something in a different envelope **2** *verb* to divide; *the personnel are separated into part-timers and full-time staff*

◊ **separately** *adverb* not together; *each member of the group will pay separately*

serve *verb* **(a)** to bring food or drink to a customer; *she served the soup in small bowls; fish is served with a white sauce; you should serve red wine with meat; I can't serve six tables at once* **(b)** to deal with a customer in a shop *or* bar, etc.; *will you serve this lady next, please; I waited ten minutes before being served* **(c)** *(of a recipe)* to make enough food for; *the packet serves six; a bottle of champagne should serve four people easily*

◊ **server** *noun* **(a)** person who serves at table, at a buffet, etc. **(b)** large flat knife for serving food; **salad servers** = spoon and fork for serving salad

◊ **servery** *noun* place where waiters pick up dishes ready to be taken to the guests' tables

service 1 *noun* **(a)** working for a company *or* in a shop, etc.; **length of service** = number of years someone has worked for a company **(b)** (i) the work of dealing with customers; (ii) amount added to a bill to cover the work involved in dealing with a customer; *the service in that restaurant is extremely slow; to add on 10% for service; the bill includes service* = it includes an amount added to cover the work involved; *is the service included?;* **service charge** = amount added to a bill to cover the work involved in dealing with a customer *or* amount paid by tenants in a block of flats for general cleaning and maintenance; *a 10% service charge is added; does the bill include a service charge?;* **baby-listening service** = service provided by a hotel, with a small microphone to put over a baby's cot, so that the parents can hear if the baby cries when they are not in the room; **baby-sitting service** = service provided by a hotel, where a baby-sitter comes to the hotel room to look after a baby when the parents are out of the room; **courier service** = (i) service provided by a person *or* company taking messages, packages, etc. from one place to another by car, motorcycle, or aircraft; (ii) service which provides a guide to go with a party of tourists to guide them on a package tour; **room service** = arrangement in a hotel where food or drink can be served in a guest's bedroom; **service area** = place by a motorway where you can stop and buy petrol or get food, etc.; **service flat** = furnished flat which can be rented, together with the services of a cleaner, cook, etc. **(c)** style of serving in a restaurant; **cafeteria service** = style of serving food, where the customer takes a tray and helps himself to cold food from a buffet (hot food is usually served on a plate by a server standing behind the buffet) and pays for it at a till as he leaves the buffet; **English service** = way of serving at a meal, where the waiter or waitress serves each guest from a large dish, serving from the guest's left (compare 'French service' below); **French service** = (i) style of laying a table ready for guests (a plate, called the 'show plate' is in the centre of each setting, with a folded napkin on it, and cutlery and glasses beside it: the plate is not used for food, and may be removed, or other plates, such as a soup plate, may be put on it); (ii) way of serving at a meal, where the waiter or waitress offers the guest a dish (from the left), and the guest helps himself from it (as opposed to 'English service' above); **plate service** = type of restaurant service, where the food is put onto the plate before the plate is carried to each guest (saving the time and cost of serving each guest with each item individually); **Russian service** *see* RUSSIAN; **silver service** = type of restaurant service (especially for banquets) where the waiter or waitress serves each guest from a flat dish, as opposed to 'French service'; **service cloth** = white cloth which a waiter carries over his arm and uses to hold hot plates when serving guests; **service room** = pantry, small room where dirty glasses, cutlery, etc., are put after being cleared from the table, and where hot plates, cruets, etc., can be kept for service to guests' tables **(d)** keeping a machine in good working order; *the machine has been sent in for service; the routine service of equipment;* **after-sales service** = service of a machine carried out by the seller for the buyer; **service centre** = office *or* workshop which specializes in

keeping machines in good working order; **service contract** = contract by which a company keeps a piece of equipment in good working order; **service department** = section of a company which keeps customers' machines in good working order; **service engineer** = person who specializes in keeping machines in good working order; **service handbook** *or* **service manual** = book which shows how to service a machine; **service station** = garage where you can buy petrol and have small repairs done to a car **(e)** business *or* office which gives help when it is needed; **answering service** = office which answers the telephone and takes messages for someone *or* for a company; **24-hour service** = help which is available for the whole day; **service bureau** = office which specializes in helping other offices; **service industry** = industry which does not make products, but offers a service (such as banking, insurance, transport) **(f) to put a new bus** *or* **plane into service** = to start using a new bus *or* plane for the first time **(g)** organization, especially one serving the public; *the postal service is efficient; the bus service is very irregular; we have a good train service to London* **2** *verb* **(a)** to keep (a machine) in good working order; *the car needs to be serviced every six months; the computer has gone back to the manufacturer for servicing* **(b)** to deal with; **to service arrivals** = to deal with people arriving at a hotel (looking after their luggage, etc.); **to service a room** = to clean a room after a guest has left, changing the beds and linen, etc.

serviette *noun* napkin, a square piece of cloth used to protect clothes and wipe your mouth at meals; **paper serviette** = serviette made from paper (NOTE: some people think that **serviette** is not correct English and prefer to use the word **napkin** which is the preferred word in hotels and restaurants)

serving *noun* amount of food served to one person; *500g is enough for two servings;* **serving hatch** = small opening in a wall for passing food and crockery from a kitchen to a dining room; **serving instructions** = instructions on a packet of food, showing how it can be served; **serving suggestions** = way a manufacturer suggests that you serve the product

sesame *noun* tropical plant whose seeds are eaten, usually scattered on the crust of bread or cakes; **sesame seed oil** = oil obtained from crushed sesame seeds, used in oriental cooking

session *noun* meeting to study, to discuss or to practise

set 1 *verb* **(a)** to place; **to set the table** = put the knives and forks, etc. on the table **(b)** *(of food)* to become solid; *the jelly will set if you boil it long enough* **2** *adjective* which cannot be changed; **set menu** = menu which cannot be changed (i.e., you cannot choose a dish from another part of the menu); **set times for meals** = times of meals where everyone has to eat at the same time

◊ **setting** *noun* **(a)** scenery *or* background for a building **(b)** **place setting** *or* **table setting** = set of knives, forks, spoons, and glasses, etc., for one person

settle *verb* **to settle a bill** *or* **an account** = to pay all the money owed on an account

◊ **settle up** *verb* to pay the total of everything that is owed

sew *verb* to attach by using a needle and thread; *the button was not sewn on properly; can you sew my button back on, please?*

◊ **sewing** *noun* action of attaching by using a needle and thread; **sewing kit** = small wallet with needle, thread, etc., which can be used for making repairs to clothing in an emergency (as for sewing on a button) (often supplied in a hotel room)

shade *noun* **(a)** dark place which is not in the sunlight; *I would like a seat in the shade; she was sitting in the shade of a big olive tree* **(b)** *(informal)* **shades** = sunglasses

◊ **shady** *adjective* full of shade; *at midday in Madrid, it's better to walk on the shady side of the street*

shake *see* MILK SHAKE

shallot *noun* small variety of onion, used in sauces

shampoo *noun* liquid soap for washing the hair with; *there are sachets of shampoo in the bathroom*

shandy *noun* drink made by mixing beer and lemonade

sharp 1 *adjective* (knife) which has a thin edge and cuts easily; *you need a very sharp knife to slice vegetables* **2** *adverb* exactly; *the coach will leave the hotel at 7.30 sharp*

shave 1 *noun* act of cutting off the hair on the face with a razor; *he went to have a shave at the barber's next to the hotel* **2** *verb* to cut off the hair on the face with a razor

◊ **shaver** *noun* electric instrument with a very sharp blade for removing hair on the face; **shaver point** *or* **shaver socket** = socket in a bathroom where an electric razor can be plugged in

sheet *noun* **(a)** piece of thin cloth, put on a bed; *guests are asked to bring their own towels and sheets; the maids change the sheets every day* **(b)** **sheet of paper** = piece of paper; **time sheet** = paper showing when a worker starts and finishes work

shelf *noun* plank attached to a wall or in a cupboard on which things can be put; **shelf life** = length of time food can be kept in a shop before it goes bad (NOTE: plural is **shelves**)

shell *noun* outer cover of an egg or nut, or of an animal such as the crab, lobster, snail, oyster, etc.; *snails are usually served in their shells; I found a big piece of eggshell in my omelette; dressed crab is the flesh of a boiled crab, removed and broken up, then served in the shell with a sauce on the side*

◊ **shellfish** *noun* animals, such as mussels, oysters, lobsters, and prawns which have shells and live in them (NOTE: no plural: **a dish of shellfish, a shellfish restaurant**)

shelter 1 *noun* place where you can go for protection; *there is no shelter from the pouring rain;* **to take shelter** = to go under something for protection; *we took shelter in the hotel cellars when the civil war started* **2** *verb* to get protection; *they were sheltering from the snow in a small cave in the mountains*

◊ **sheltered** *adjective* protected from wind or cold; *the cottage is in a sheltered valley*

shepherd's pie *noun* minced meat cooked in a dish with a layer of mashed potatoes on top (NOTE: also called **cottage pie**)

sherry *noun* fortified wine from Spain; **sherry trifle** = cold dessert made of cake covered with jam and fruit, soaked in sherry and then covered with custard sauce, whipped cream, candied fruit and nuts

COMMENT: the word comes from the Spanish 'xerez', former name of the town Jerez in Southern Spain where the wine is made. Sherry can range from very dry to very sweet. The names used are 'manzanilla', the driest, 'fino', 'amontillado', 'oloroso' and 'cream sherry', which is the sweetest. In Spain, sherry is served cold, and very dry sherries are usually served in this way in Britain. Sweet sherries are served at room temperature. Sherry can be served in a small upright glass or, for large measures, in a schooner

shift *noun* group of workers who work for a period, and then are replaced by another group; period of time worked by a group of workers; **day shift** = shift worked during the daylight hours (from early morning to late afternoon); **night shift** = shift worked during the night; *there are 150 men on the day shift; he works the day shift or night shift; we work an 8-hour shift; the management is introducing a shift system or shift working*

Shigella *noun* genus of bacteria which causes dysentery

◊ **shigellosis** *noun* infestation of the digestive tract with *Shigella,* causing bacillary dysentery

ship *noun* large boat for carrying passengers and cargo on the sea; **cargo ship** = ship which carries only goods (some also have accommodation for a few passengers); **ship chandler** = person who supplies goods (such as food) to ships

◊ **shipboard** *adjective* on a ship; *shipboard entertainment;* **shipboard romance** = love affair between two people on a cruise (either between passengers, or between a passenger and a member of the crew)

◊ **shipping** *noun* **(a)** sending of goods; *the shopkeeper will arrange for the shipping of the carpet;* **shipping company** = company which specializes in the sending of goods **(b)** **shipping company** *or* **shipping line** = company which owns ships

◊ **shipwreck** *noun* **(a)** ship which has been sunk or badly damaged on rocks, etc. **(b)** wrecking of a ship, the action of being wrecked

◊ **shipwrecked** *adjective* (person) involved in a shipwreck; (ship) which has been sunk or badly damaged on rocks, etc.

shish kebab *noun* kebab made of lamb, with peppers, onions and tomatoes, cooked on a skewer over a charcoal grill

shoe cleaner *or* **shoe polisher** *noun* machine for cleaning shoes

◊ **shoeshine** *noun* polishing of shoes; **shoeshine boy** = man who cleans shoes in the street

shop 1 *noun* place where goods are stored and sold; *bookshop; computer shop; electrical goods shop; all the shops in the centre of town close on Sundays;* **retail shop** = shop where goods are sold only to the public; **corner shop** = small privately-owned general store in a town, often on a street corner; **shop assistant** = person who serves customers in a shop; **shop front** = part of a shop which faces the street, including the entrance and windows; **shop window** = window in a shop where goods are displayed so that customers can see them *or* place where goods or services can be exhibited; *the shop windows are all decorated for Christmas* (NOTE: US English usually uses **store**) **2** *verb* **to shop (for)** = to look for and buy things in shops (NOTE: **shopping - shopped**)

◊ **shop around** *verb* to go to various shops or offices and compare prices before making a purchase *or* before placing an order; *you should shop around before getting your car serviced; he is shopping around for a new computer; it pays to shop around when you are planning to fly to the States*

◊ **shopkeeper** *noun* person who owns or runs a shop

◊ **shopping** *noun* **(a)** (i) looking for and buying goods in a shop; (ii) goods bought in a shop; *to go shopping; to buy one's shopping or to do one's shopping in the local supermarket; she was carrying two baskets of shopping* **(b)** **shopping centre** = group of shops linked together with car parks and restaurants; *US* **shopping mall** = enclosed covered area for shopping, with shops, restaurants, banks and other facilities; **shopping precinct** = part of a town which is closed to traffic so that people can walk about and shop; **window-shopping** = looking at goods in shop windows, without buying anything

shore *noun* beach, sandy area at the edge of the sea *or* of a lake; **to go on shore** *or* **to go ashore** = to go on land (from a ship)

short 1 *adjective* **(a)** not long; **short sleeves** = sleeves which do not go below the elbow; **short-sleeved shirt** = shirt with short sleeves; *women are not allowed into the monastery in short-sleeved shirts* **(b)** for a small period of time; **short break** = holiday lasting only a few days; **short credit** = terms which allow the customer only a little time to pay; **in the short term** = in the near future *or* quite soon **(c)** not as much as should be; *the shipment was three items short;* **when we cashed up we were £10 short** = we had £10 less than we should have had; **to give short weight** = to sell something which is lighter than it should be **(d) short of** = with less than needed *or* with not enough of; *we are short of staff or short of money* **2** *noun* drink of spirits, such as gin, whisky, etc. with not much liquid (as opposed to beer, cider, etc.)

◊ **shorts** *plural noun* short trousers which do not go below the knee; *ladies are not allowed into the monastery in shorts;* **Bermuda shorts** = longer shorts which go to knee length

◊ **shortbread** *noun* thick sweet crumbly biscuit

◊ **shortcake** *noun* **(a)** shortbread **(b)** dessert made of layers of cake with fruit and cream

◊ **shortchange** *verb* to cheat (someone) by not giving him the correct money in change

◊ **shortcrust pastry** *noun* most commonly used type of pastry made with fat and flour

◊ **shortening** *noun US* fat used in pastry, cakes and bread

◊ **short-handed** *adjective* with not enough staff; *we are rather short-handed at the moment*

◊ **short-haul** *adjective* (flight) which is over a short distance (up to 1,000 km)

◊ **short order** *noun US* order given for something which can be cooked quickly to order (such as ham and eggs); **short-order chef** *or* **cook** = cook who specializes in short orders; **short-order diner** = café serving simple meals which can be cooked quickly to order

◊ **short-staffed** *adjective* with not enough workers; *the restaurant is short-staffed and the service is slow*

◊ **short-stay** *adjective* referring to a stay of a few days; **short-stay car park** = car park at an airport for travellers who will leave their cars there for a few hours or days; **short-stay guest** *or* **visitor** = person who stays a few days in a hotel *or* a town; *compare* LONG-STAY

◊ **short take-off and landing (STOL)** *noun* (aircraft) which needs a much shorter runway than other aircraft to take off or land

◊ **short-term** *adjective* for a short period of time

show 1 *noun* **(a)** exhibition or display; *the Computer Show is on at Olympia;* **show**

plate = plate placed in the centre of the setting (in French service), removed before serving **(b)** performance (especially with music); *the show starts at 10.30; let's have dinner early and go to a show;* **floor show** = show (dancers, singers, comedians, striptease, etc.) in a club, bar, restaurant, etc. **2** *verb* to point out something to someone; *he showed us the sights of the town; the guide will show you round the museum*

shower 1 *noun* **(a)** light fall of rain; *there was a shower this morning, but it is sunny again now* **(b)** spray device for washing your whole body; *we have two single rooms with showers, or a double room with bath;* **shower cap** = waterproof cap to prevent the hair getting wet when taking a shower; **shower cubicle** = small box, with a shower in it, usually fitted into a corner of a small bathroom; **shower curtain** = piece of waterproof material around a shower; **shower gel** = liquid soap used for washing in a shower; **shower room** = room with a shower in it **(c)** bath taken in a spray of water from above; *he went up to his room and had a shower* **2** *verb* to take a bath in a spray of water; *he had showered and was back in the lobby to greet his guests at 7.00 p.m.*

◊ **shower bath** *noun* **(a)** spray device for washing your whole body **(b)** bath taken in a spray of water

shred *verb* to cut into very thin strips

◊ **shredder** *noun* device for cutting vegetables into very thin strips

shrimp *noun* small shellfish with a long tail

Shrove Tuesday *noun* the last Tuesday before Lent, celebrated in Britain by eating pancakes (NOTE: also called **Pancake Day.** In France and French-speaking countries, called **Mardi Gras**)

shut 1 *adjective* closed; *we tried to get into the museum but it was shut* **2** *verb* to close for business; *in Germany, shops shut on Saturday afternoons*

shutter *noun* **(a)** folding wooden or metal cover on a window; *open the shutters and see what the weather is like* **(b)** *(in camera)* part which opens and closes very rapidly to allow the light to go on to the film

shuttle *noun* bus or plane which goes backwards and forwards between two places; *the Glasgow shuttle; there's a shuttle* *bus from the hotel to the exhibition grounds;* **shuttle (service)** = service of bus or plane or boat, etc., which goes backwards and forwards between two places

sick *adjective* **(a)** ill; *we have five staff off sick* **(b)** vomiting; *the greasy food made her feel sick;* **airsick** = ill because of the movement of an aircraft; **carsick** = ill because of the movement of a car; **seasick** = ill because of the movement of a ship

◊ **sick bag** *noun* strong paper bag provided in the pocket in front of each seat on planes or hovercraft, so that passengers suffering from airsickness can vomit without leaving their seats

◊ **sickness** *noun* being ill; **travel sickness** = sickness caused by the movement of a car, aircraft, bus or train, etc.; **seasickness** = sickness caused by the movement of a ship; **seasickness pills** *or* **travel sickness pills** = tablets taken to prevent seasickness or travel sickness

side *noun* **(a)** part of something near the edge; *she leant over the side of the ship; the hitchhikers were standing by the side of the road;* **side lights** *or* **parking lights** = small lights on a car or truck which show the outline of a vehicle in the dark (as opposed to the headlights); **side plate** = small plate placed beside the main plate and cutlery, used for bread **(b)** one of the surfaces of a flat object; *please write on one side of the paper only* **(c)** **on the side** = separate from your normal work, and sometimes hidden from your employer; *he works in the hotel bar, but he runs a tour company on the side; her salary is too small to live on, so the family lives on what she can make on the side*

◊ **sideboard** *noun* **(a)** *(in a house)* piece of furniture in a dining room, used to put plates or dishes on **(b)** *(in a restaurant)* piece of furniture for keeping articles for use on the tables, such as cloths, napkins, cruets, cutlery, etc., but not plates or glasses

◊ **sidecar** *noun* cocktail of brandy, Cointreau and lemon juice

siesta *noun* rest period in the middle of the day (common in Mediterranean countries)

sieve 1 *noun* kitchen utensil made of metal or plastic net, used to strain liquids to remove lumps **2** *verb* to pass (flour, liquid) through a sieve to remove lumps

sift *noun* to pass (flour, liquid, etc.) through a sieve to remove lumps

sight *noun* spectacle, something which you ought to see; *they went off on foot to see the sights of the town*

◊ **sightseeing** *noun* visiting the sights of a town; *the bus company has sightseeing tours of the town every afternoon*

◊ **sightseer** *noun* tourist, a person visiting the sights of a town

sign 1 *noun* **(a)** movement (of the hand or head, etc.) which means something; **sign language** = making signs with the hands or face, to show what you are trying to say, especially the signs of the hands used by deaf and dumb people to communicate **(b)** advertising board; panel showing the name of a shop **(c)** panel showing directions on a road; **road sign** = plate by the side of a road, giving instructions or warnings **2** *verb* to write your name in a special way on a document to show that you have written it or approved it; *to sign a letter or a contract or a document or a cheque; they signed the hotel register using the name of Smith; she sent the cheque as a deposit, but forgot to sign it*

◊ **signage** *noun* all the signs, logos, etc., which identify a hotel group, chain of restaurants, motorway service area, etc.

QUOTE if planning permission is granted and the Department of Transport is happy to grant motorway signage and access permission, you can buy or lease the land and start building
Caterer & Hotelkeeper

signature *noun* name written in a special way by someone; *he found a pile of cheques on his desk waiting for signature; the signature on the form did not match that on the back of the credit card*

◊ **signboard** *noun* panel with a sign

◊ **sign on** *verb* to start work

◊ **signpost** *noun* post with a sign showing directions to a place

signal 1 *noun* **(a)** movement of the hand or head, etc., which tells someone to do something **(b)** lights or mechanical flags, etc., used to tell someone to do something; *the signal was at red so we had to stop* **2** *verb* to make signs to tell someone to do something; *the driver signalled to show that he was turning right* (NOTE: GB English is **signalling - signalled** but US English is **signaling - signaled**)

◊ **signal box** *noun* building by the side of the railway where the signalman controls the signals

◇ **signalman** *noun* person who controls railway signals (NOTE: plural is **signalmen**)

silver *noun* (a) precious white metal; **silver wedding** = anniversary of 25 years of marriage (b) **silver foil** *or* **silver paper** = sheet of thin shiny metal which looks like silver, used for wrapping food in; **silver plate** = electroplated nickel silver (EPNS), cutlery which is made of ordinary metal, but covered with silver, giving the impression that it is made of solid silver (used in high-class restaurants as being superior to stainless steel) (c) coins made of white metal

◇ **silver service** *noun* type of restaurant service (especially for banquets) where the waiter or waitress serves each guest from a flat dish, as opposed to 'French service', where the guests serve themselves from the dish held by the waiter

◇ **silverware** *noun* (a) articles made of silver (b) *(in a restaurant)* cutlery and other articles made of silver plate (NOTE: no plural)

simmer *verb* to boil gently

simnel cake *noun* fruit cake covered with marzipan, traditionally eaten in Lent or at Easter

single *adjective & noun* one alone; **single fare** *or* **single ticket** *or* **a single** = fare *or* ticket for one journey from one place to another; *I want two singles to London;* **single bed** = bed for one person; **a single (measure)** = one measure of spirits; **single occupancy** = one person in a room; **single room** = room for one person; **single room supplement** = extra charge for a single person travelling with a group (where charges are calculated on the basis of two people sharing each room); **singles bar** = bar where unmarried or divorced people go, hoping to meet others

◇ **single-decker** *noun* bus with only one deck (as opposed to a double-decker)

◇ **single European market** *noun* the EC considered as one single market, with no tariff barriers between its member states

QUOTE to create a single market out of the EC member states, physical, technical and tax barriers to the free movement of trade between member states must be removed. Imposing VAT on importation of goods from other member states is seen as one such tax barrier. This will disappear with the abolition of national frontiers under the single market concept

Accountancy

sink 1 *noun* basin for washing in a kitchen; **sink unit** = arrangement of sinks, taps, waste pipes, etc., forming a single piece of equipment **2** *verb* to go to the bottom of the sea, etc.; *the ferry sank in 30m of water; all the passengers were saved when the liner sank in the tropical storm*
NOTE: **sinking - sank - has sunk**

siphon *noun* **soda siphon** = bottle with a special spout, filled with water and gas under pressure, used for serving soda water at table or in a lounge

sirloin *noun* best cut of beef from the back of the animal; *see also* STEAK

sister *adjective* **sister company** = company which is part of the same group as another company; **sister ship** = ship which is of the same design and belongs to the same company as another ship

site 1 *noun* (a) place where a building stands; **on site** = at the place where a building is or is being constructed (b) place where an event took place; *they visited the sites of First World War battles;* **battle site** = place where a battle took place (c) **Site of Special Scientific Interest (SSSI)** = small area of land which has been noted as particularly important by the Nature Conservancy Council, and which is preserved for its fauna, flora *or* geology **2** *verb* to place (a building) on a particular piece of land; *the hotel will be sited between the airport and the new exhibition centre*

sitting *noun* time when a group of people eat together; *take your seats for the second sitting*

◇ **sitting room** *noun* room with comfortable chairs where people can rest, talk, watch television, etc.; *the suite has a bedroom, bathroom and a private sitting room*

situated *adjective* placed; *the hotel is situated at the edge of the town; the tourist office is situated near the railway station*

◊ **situation** *noun* place where something is; *the hotel is in a very pleasant situation by the lake*

size *noun* measurements of something *or* how big something is *or* how many there are of something; *what size shoes do you take? this packet is the maximum size allowed by the post office; she's looking for something in a smaller size*

skate 1 *noun* (a) large flat sea fish with white flesh (NOTE: plural is **skate) (b) (ice) skate** = boot with a sharp blade for sliding on ice; *you can hire skates at the rink;* **roller skate** = boot with wheels on it for roller skating **2** *verb* to slide on ice wearing skates

◊ **skater** *noun* person who goes skating

◊ **skating** *noun* sliding on the ice, wearing skates; **skating rink** = special area for ice skating, or for playing ice hockey, etc.

skeleton key *noun* key which will fit any lock in a building

skewer 1 *noun* long thin metal rod for putting through pieces of meat when cooking **2** *verb* to stick a long metal rod through (something)

ski 1 *noun* long flat narrow piece of wood, etc., which you attach under your boot for moving over snow; *skis can be hired at the chairlift;* **ski area** = part of a mountain range *or* part of a club's land where you can ski; **ski equipment** *or* **ski gear** = all the things needed to go skiing, such as skis, boots, goggles, poles, etc.; **ski goggles** = goggles worn when skiing; **ski instructor** = person who teaches people how to ski; **ski pants** = trousers with an elastic strap under the foot, worn when skiing; **ski pass** = card which allows a skier to use the ski runs for a certain number of times; **ski resort** = town in the mountains where people stay when on a skiing holiday; **ski run** *or* **ski slope** = specially prepared and marked slope for skiing down a mountain; **ski trail** = marked path for skiers over a long distance; **water skis** = wider shorter skis for gliding over water **2** *verb* to ski *or* to go skiing = to move over snow on skis; *the mountain rescue team had to ski to the site of the avalanche; we go skiing in Switzerland every winter*

◊ **skiboots** *or* **ski boots** *plural noun* special boots worn when skiing

◊ **skier** *noun* person who moves over snow on skis

◊ **skiing** *noun* moving over snow on skis; *the skiing is good this year;* **cross-country skiing** *or* **langlauf** = skiing for long distances following marked tracks across country, through woods, etc. wearing narrower skis than for downhill skiing and short flexible boots (only the front of the boot is fixed to the ski); **downhill skiing** = skiing fast down slopes (as opposed to cross-country skiing); **Nordic skiing** = competition of cross-country skiing and ski-jumping; **off-piste skiing** = skiing away from the marked tracks; **skiing instructor** = person who teaches people how to ski; **skiing resort** = SKI RESORT

◊ **ski jump** *noun* slope with a sudden drop at the bottom from which skiers jump in a competition to see who can jump the furthest

◊ **ski lift** *noun* device to take skiers to the top of a slope

◊ **ski tow** *noun* device to take skiers to the top of a slope by dragging them along with their skis on the ground

◊ **skiwear** *noun* clothes worn when skiing (NOTE: no plural)

skilled *adjective* (worker) who has a particular skill; *we need skilled staff in the reception area; see also* UNSKILLED

skillet *noun US* frying pan

skim *verb* to remove things floating on the surface of (a liquid); *skim the soup to remove the fat;* **skimmed milk** = milk from which most of the fat has been removed; **semi-skimmed milk** = milk from which some of the fat has been removed

skin *noun* (a) outer covering of the body; *he got sunburnt and his skin began to peel* (b) outer surface of fruit, vegetable, meat, etc.; *take the skin off the peach with a knife*

◊ **skin-dive** *verb* to swim underwater using breathing apparatus, as a sport

◊ **skin-diver** *noun* person who goes skin-diving

◊ **skin-diving** *noun* swimming underwater using breathing apparatus, as a sport

skip *verb (informal)* to leave quickly, without paying

◊ **skipper** *noun* (a) captain of a ship *or* an aircraft (b) *(informal)* person who leaves a hotel quickly, without paying

sky *noun* area above the earth which is blue during the day, and where the moon and stars appear at night; *the beautiful deep blue sky of a Mediterranean evening*

◇ **skyline** *noun* the shape of buildings silhouetted against the sky

◇ **skyscraper** *noun* very tall building

slack *adjective* not busy; *November is a slack month in the hotel; Tuesday is our slackest day;* **slack season** = period when a hotel *or* resort is not very busy

slash *verb* to cut *or* to reduce sharply; *prices have been slashed in all departments; the company has slashed prices on tours to Turkey*

sled *noun US* = SLEDGE

sledge **1** *noun* small vehicle with runners for sliding over snow **2** *verb* **to go sledging** = to play at sliding on the snow on a sledge

sleep **1** *noun* state of resting naturally and unconsciously; **to go** *or* **to get to sleep** = to start sleeping; *she found it difficult to get to sleep because of the noise of the traffic* **2** *verb* to be in a state of natural rest and unconsciousness; *did you sleep well?; I can't sleep sitting upright* (NOTE: **sleeping - slept**)

◇ **sleeper** *noun* **(a)** sleeping car **(b)** overnight train with sleeping cars; *the Edinburgh sleeper leaves at 11.30 p.m.* **(c)** empty room which is shown as being occupied on the reservations board

◇ **sleeper seat** *noun* comfortable seat on an aircraft, boat, etc., which can be reclined so that you can sleep more easily

◇ **sleep in** *verb* to sleep in the building where you work; *most of the restaurant staff sleep in*

◇ **sleeping bag** *noun* quilted bag for sleeping in a tent, etc.

◇ **sleeping car** *noun* special coach on a railway train, with beds where passengers can sleep

◇ **sleeping pill** *or* **sleeping tablet** *noun* pill which makes you go to sleep or keeps you asleep

◇ **sleep out** *verb* not to sleep in a hotel room, even if it has been paid for; **sleep-out staff** = staff who do not sleep in a hotel

sleigh *noun* large sledge pulled by horses or reindeer, etc.; *sleigh ride*

slice **1** *noun* **(a)** thin piece cut off something; *a slice of bread; two slices of*

cake; can you cut me another slice of beef, please? **(b) fish slice** = wide flat utensil used for turning fish and removing it from a frying pan **2** *verb* to cut into slices; **sliced bread** *or* **sliced loaf** = loaf of bread which has already been sliced mechanically before it is sold

◇ **slicer** *noun* machine for slicing meat, bread, etc.; **gravity feed slicer** = type of slicer (for cooked meat, such as ham) where the meat is placed on a sloping tray and slides further down after each slice is cut

slide **1** *noun* **(a)** slippery surface (on ice) **(b)** slippery metal slope for children to slide down **(c)** plastic transparent photograph which can be projected on a screen; **slide projector** = apparatus for throwing pictures from slides onto a screen **2** *verb* to move smoothly

NOTE: **sliding - slid**

slip **1** *noun* **(a)** mistake; *he made a couple of slips in adding up the bill* **(b) pillow slip** = cloth bag to cover a pillow **(c)** small piece of paper; **compliments slip** = piece of paper with the name and address of the company printed on it, sent with documents, gifts, etc., instead of a letter; **pay slip** = piece of paper showing the full amount of a worker's pay, and the money deducted as tax, pension and insurance contributions; **sales slip** = paper showing that an article was bought at a certain shop; *goods can be exchanged only on production of a sales slip* **2** *verb* to slide by mistake; *she slipped on the polished floor and broke her leg*

◇ **slip cloth** *noun* napperon, small square tablecloth, placed over a larger tablecloth to keep it clean

◇ **slip road** *noun* road which leads onto or off a motorway; *you must not park on the slip road*

slop basin *noun* bowl placed on a table into which waste liquid (such as cold dregs from teacups) can be put

slope *noun* slanting piece of ground; **ski slope** = specially prepared and marked slope for skiing down a mountain; **nursery slopes** = snow-covered mountain slopes where people learn to ski

slot *noun* **(a)** narrow opening (for putting a coin into); **slot machine** = machine from which you can buy something, such as sweets, chocolate, cigarettes, drinks, etc., by putting coins into a slot **(b)** set time available for doing something; *the airline* *had requested more takeoff and landing slots at the airport*

slush *noun* half-melted snow

smell 1 *noun* something which you can sense with the nose; *the smell of coffee coming from the restaurant* **2** *verb* **(a)** to sense something through the nose; *I can smell burning* **(b)** to have a certain smell; *the room smells of cheese*
NOTE: **smelling - smelt** *or* **smelled**

COMMENT: the senses of smell and taste are closely connected, and together give the real taste of food. Smells are sensed by receptors in the nasal cavity which transmit impulses to the brain. When food is eaten, the smell is sensed at the same time as the taste is sensed by the taste buds, and most of what we think of as taste is in fact smell, which explains why food loses its taste when someone has a cold and a blocked nose

smelt *noun* small edible sea fish (NOTE: the plural is **smelt**)

smoke 1 *noun* vapour and gas given off when something burns; **smoke detector** = device which is sensitive to smoke, and sets off alarms or sprinklers when it senses smoke; *smoke detectors are fitted in all the rooms; all the men smoked cigars, and this set off the smoke detectors* **2** *verb* **(a)** to preserve food (such as meat, fish, bacon, cheese) by hanging it in the smoke from a fire; **smoked salmon** = salmon which has been cured by smoking, and is served in very thin slices, usually with brown bread and lemon as an hors d'oeuvre; *a plate of smoked salmon sandwiches* **(b)** to suck in smoke from a burning cigarette, cigar or pipe
◊ **smokeless** *adjective* which makes no smoke; **smokeless zone** = area where you are not allowed to make any smoke (by burning coal in fireplaces, etc.)
◊ **smoker** *noun* **(a)** person who smokes cigarettes, etc. **(b)** railway carriage where you can smoke

QUOTE a report published in the Journal of the American Health Association found that restaurant staff were exposed to up to four-and-a-half times the level of atmospheric smoke as people who live with smokers, while exposure for bar staff was up to six times as great
Caterer & Hotelkeeper

smoking *noun* action of smoking a cigarette; **'no smoking'** = do not smoke here; *please extinguish your cigarettes when the 'no smoking' signs light up;* **smoking area** *or* **smoking section** = section of a restaurant, plane, etc. where smoking is allowed; **no smoking area** *or* **no smoking section** = section of a restaurant, plane, etc. where smoking is not allowed; **smoking room** = special room in a hotel, club, etc., where people can smoke (often used for playing cards)

QUOTE the ruling came into force last week, making Los Angeles the largest city in the USA to make smoking in eating places a punishable offence
Caterer & Hotelkeeper

smorgasbord *noun* Swedish buffet of many cold dishes; *for lunch there will be a smorgasbord*

smuggle *verb* to take goods into a country illegally without declaring them to the customs; *they had to smuggle the computer disks into the country*
◊ **smuggler** *noun* person who smuggles
◊ **smuggling** *noun* taking goods illegally into a country; *he made his money in arms smuggling*

snack *noun* light meal; small amount of food eaten; *we didn't have time to stop for a proper lunch, so just had a snack on the motorway;* **bar snacks** = small items of food, available in a bar, such as pies, sandwiches, etc.; **cocktail snacks** = small items of food (olives, peanuts, etc.) served with drinks before a meal
◊ **snack bar** *noun* small simple restaurant where you can have a light meal, usually sitting at a counter

snapper *noun* type of Pacific fish

snood *noun* cloth which is worn over the hair, especially by people preparing or selling food

snooker *noun* game like billiards played with twenty-two balls of various colours, the object being to hit a white ball so that it sends a ball of another colour into one of the 'pockets' at the edge of the table; **snooker table** = table on which snooker is played; *see also* BILLIARDS, POOL

snooze 1 *noun* short sleep **2** *verb* to sleep lightly for a short time; **snooze button** *or* **snooze control** = button on an alarm clock which resets the alarm to go off again after a short time

snorkel *noun* tube which goes from the mouth or mask of an underwater swimmer to the surface to allow him to breathe in air

◊ **snorkelling** *or US* **snorkeling** *noun* **to go snorkelling** = to go swimming with a snorkel

snow 1 *noun* water which falls as white flakes of ice crystals in cold weather; *snow fell all night on the mountains;* **snow cannon** = machine which makes snow when there is not enough snow on ski runs; **snow chains** = chains put round car tyres to prevent them slipping on snow; **snow conditions** = type and thickness of snow; **snow report** = report from a resort, telling how much snow there is and of what type; **snow tyres** = special tyres with thick treads, for use when driving on snow **2** *verb* to fall in flakes of snow; *it snowed heavily during the night*

◊ **snowblindness** *noun* temporary painful blindness caused by bright sunlight shining on snow

◊ **snowboard** *noun* type of board (similar to a surfboard) on which you slide down snow slopes

◊ **snowboarder** *noun* person who slides down snow slopes on a snowboard

QUOTE skiers think snowboarders are responsible for an increasing number of collisions but there is no statistical evidence to support this contention. On the other hand, snowboarders are about ten times more likely to injure themselves than skiers

Sunday Times

snowdrift *noun* heap of snow which has been piled up by the wind

◊ **snowfall** *noun* quantity of snow which comes down at any one time; *a heavy snowfall blocked the main roads*

◊ **snowfield** *noun* permanent large flat area of snow

◊ **snowflake** *noun* small piece of snow formed from a number of ice crystals

◊ **snowline** *noun* level on a high mountain above which there is permanent snow

◊ **snowmobile** *noun* vehicle with caterpillar tracks specially designed for driving on snow

◊ **snowplough** *US* **snowplow** *noun* heavy vehicle with a plough on the front for clearing snow off roads, railways, etc.

◊ **snowshoes** *plural noun* frames shaped like tennis rackets with a light web, which are tied under the feet for walking on snow

◊ **snowstorm** *noun* heavy fall of snow accompanied by wind

soap *noun* material made of oil and fat usually formed into a solid block, used for washing; *two small bars of soap are provided in the bathroom; there is a liquid soap dispenser in the gents' toilets*

◊ **soapdish** *noun* dish in which a bar of soap can be put; *is there a soapdish in the shower cubicle?*

socio-economic *adjective* **socio-economic groups** = groups in society divided according to income and position (classified by letters A, B, C, D, and E)

socket *noun* **(electric) socket** = holes into which a plug or light bulb can be fitted

COMMENT: sockets vary considerably from country to country. In Europe, sockets usually have holes for two round pins. In the USA, Canada and japan, sockets take two flat fins. In Britain, sockets take three flat pins. Travellers should always carry adaptor plugs

soda *noun* **(a)** compound of sodium; **soda water** = water made fizzy by putting gas into it (drunk with alcohol or fruit juice, to make a long fizzy drink); **whisky and soda** = drink of whisky with soda water; **soda biscuit** = dry salty biscuit; **soda siphon** = bottle with a special spout, filled with water and gas under pressure, used for serving soda water at table or in a lounge **(b)** *US* any fizzy non-alcoholic sweet drink; **ice cream soda** = sweet fizzy drink mixed with ice cream

◊ **soda fountain** *noun* bar where sweet drinks and ice cream are served

sofa *noun* long seat with a soft back for several people

◊ **sofabed** *noun* type of sofa which can fold out to form a bed

soft *adjective* not hard; *the beds are too soft: I prefer a hard bed;* **soft currency** = currency of a country with a weak economy, which is cheap to buy and difficult to exchange for other currencies; **soft ice cream** = ice cream mixed with air, dispensed from a machine and sold in a cone; **soft loan** = loan (from a company to an employee or from a government to another government) at very low or nil interest

◊ **soft-boiled** *adjective* (egg) which has been cooked in boiling water for a short time so that the yolk is hot but still liquid

◊ **soft cheese** *noun* (i) cheese which has been made by the action of *Penicillium candidum* (many French cheeses such as Camembert and Brie are soft)

◊ **soft drink** *noun* drink which is not alcoholic (sold either ready prepared in a bottle or can, or in concentrated form which can be mixed with water)

◊ **soft fruit** *noun* general term for all fruits and berries that have a relatively soft flesh, and so cannot be kept, except in some cases by freezing (typical soft fruit are raspberries, strawberries, blueberries and blackberries, and the various currants)

solarium *noun* room where you can enjoy real or artificial sunlight

sole 1 *adjective* only; **sole agency** = agreement to be the only person to represent a company *or* to sell a product in a certain area; *he has the sole agency for Ford cars;* **sole agent** = person who has the sole agency for a company *or* product in an area; **sole owner** *or* **sole proprietor** = person who owns a business on his own, with no partners, without forming a company; **sole trader** = person who runs a business by himself but has not registered it as a company **2** *noun* type of flat sea fish with delicate white flesh; *he ordered a grilled sole and a glass of white wine*

COMMENT: the two types of sole are 'Dover sole' and 'lemon sole'; Dover soles are more oval in shape, lemon soles are more rounded

sommelier *French noun* wine waiter, the person in charge of serving the wines in a restaurant

son et lumière *noun* entertainment consisting of sound and lighting effects, shown in the open air at night (the setting is usually a castle, cathedral or similar historic building, and the lighting is complemented by voices of actors speaking as if they were the former inhabitants of the place); *the son et lumière begins at 22.00; all the tickets for the son et lumière have been sold*

sorbet *noun* water ice, ice made with water and flavouring and sometimes cream (in some gastronomic menus, sorbets are served between two main courses)

SOS *noun* international signal to show that you are in distress (the letters 's', 'o', and 's' are repeated in Morse code)

soufflé *noun* (i) light cooked dish, made from beaten up eggs and savoury flavouring, eaten hot; (ii) cold dessert made from beaten eggs, whipped cream and gelatin; *a cheese soufflé; a lemon soufflé*

souk *noun* market in an Arab country; *you must visit the souk in Marrakech*

sound-proof *verb* to protect (something) against noise; *all the bedrooms are sound-proofed*

◊ **sound-proofing** *noun* **(a)** protecting something against noise **(b)** material which protects against noise

soup *noun* liquid dish usually eaten at the beginning of a meal; **soup bowl** = special deep dish in which soup is served; **soup plate** = wide deep plate with a rim, in which soup is served (as opposed to a soup bowl); **soup spoon** = specially large flat spoon, for eating soup (there are two types of soup spoon: the older type is like a very large dessertspoon, being longer than it is wide; the more modern style is for a spoon with a round bowl); *see also* CHOWDER, MINESTRONE, GAZPACHO

COMMENT: note various words for soup: thick vegetable soup is a 'potage'; soup made from shellfish is a 'bisque'; clear meat soup is 'consommé'; cream soup is 'crème' or 'velouté'

soupçon *noun* very small amount; *just add a soupçon of curry powder*

sour 1 *adjective* **(a)** not sweet; sharp-tasting **(b)** (milk) which has gone bad **2** *noun* **brandy sour** = cocktail of brandy, lemon juice and sugar; **whisky sour** = cocktail of whisky, lemon juice and sugar

◊ **sourness** *noun* being sour

sous-chef *French noun (meaning 'under-chef')* a chef with less experience, who is the assistant to the main chef in a restaurant kitchen

sous vide *French phrase (meaning 'in a vacuum')* a method of preparing ready-cooked food for resale, where the food is heat-sealed in plastic trays or in plastic bags with some of the air removed from the container (it has a shelf life of a few days only)

south 1 *noun* one of the points of the compass; *(in areas north of the equator)* the direction of the sun at midday; the southern part of a country; *she went to live in the south of England* **2** *adjective* referring to the south; *the south coast; the south-coast resorts;* **south wind** = wind which blows from the south **3** *adverb* towards the south; *drive south along the motorway for ten miles*

◊ **southbound** *adjective* going towards the south; *the southbound carriageway of the motorway is closed*

◊ **south-east** *adjective, adverb & noun* direction half-way between south and east

◊ **south-easterly** *or* **south-eastern** *adjective* referring to the south-east; towards *or* from the south-east

◊ **southerly 1** *adjective* **(a)** towards the south; **in a southerly direction** = towards the south **(b) southerly wind** = wind which blows from the south **2** *noun* wind which blows from the south

◊ **southern** *adjective* referring to the south

◊ **southerner** *noun* person who lives in or comes from the south

◊ **southernmost** *adjective* furthest south

◊ **southward** *adjective & adverb* towards the south

◊ **southwards** *adverb* towards the south

◊ **south-west** *adjective, adverb & noun* direction half-way between south and west

◊ **south-westerly** *or* **south-western** *adjective* referring to the south-west; towards *or* from the south-west

souvenir *noun* thing bought which reminds you of the place where you bought it (sometimes because the name of the place is written on it); **souvenir shop** = shop which sells souvenirs

soya *noun Glycine max,* plant which produces edible beans which have a high protein and fat content and very little starch; **soya sauce** = salty dark Chinese sauce made from soya beans

◊ **soybean** *or* **soya bean** *noun* bean from a soya plant

◊ **soy sauce** = SOYA SAUCE

spa *noun* **(a)** place where mineral water comes out of the ground naturally and where people go to drink the water or bathe in it because of its medicinal properties;

spa town = town which has a spa **(b)** exercise and health centre in a hotel

QUOTE the spa ranges over three floors with all the equipment that the modern exercise fanatic could desire, including a rooftop bar that overlooks Fifth Avenue
Business Traveller

space *noun* place; empty area between two objects

◊ **spacesaving** *adjective* (piece of furniture, etc.) which is compact or which folds, and so saves space

spaghetti *noun* long thin tubular strips of pasta; **spaghetti bolognese** = spaghetti with meat and tomato sauce; **spaghetti carbonara** = spaghetti with egg and bacon sauce

COMMENT: spaghetti is boiled in salt water, and eaten either simply with butter or olive oil, or with certain sauces

spare *adjective* not being used now, but which could be used in the future; *there is a spare toilet roll in the bathroom cupboard;* **spare battery** *or* **spare bulb** = battery *or* electric bulb which is kept to replace another one which is worn out or broken; **spare part** = piece of machinery used instead of a piece which is broken or worn out; **spare room** = bedroom which a family does not use; **spare time** = time when you are not at work; *he built himself a car in his spare time*

◊ **spare ribs** *plural noun* pork ribs usually served cooked in a savoury sauce

sparking plug *or US* **spark plug** *noun (in a car engine)* device which produces a spark which ignites the petrol mixture

sparkling *adjective* which has bubbles in it; **sparkling water** = mineral water which has bubbles in it; **sparkling wine** = wine which has bubbles in it

speak *verb* **(a)** to say words and phrases **(b)** to be able to say things in (a foreign language); *our restaurant staff can all speak French; is there anyone in the hotel who can speak Russian?*

◊ **-speaking** *suffix* (person) who can speak a language; *a Japanese-speaking tour guide*

special 1 *adjective* unusual *or* different; **special rates** *or* **special terms** = cheaper tariff offered for a particular reason; *the* hotel has special rates for families; we offer special terms for groups **2** noun particular dish on a menu; **today's special** or **special of the day** = plat du jour, a special dish prepared for the day and not listed in the printed menu; **chef's special** = special dish, sometimes one which the chef is famous for, which is listed separately on the menu

◊ **speciality** noun thing which you are known for or which you are good at; **the speciality of the restaurant is its fish soup; speciality restaurant** = restaurant which specializes in one type of food (a steakhouse, oyster bar, etc.)

speed 1 noun rate at which something moves or is done; **speed limit** = legal speed which is enforced in certain areas; **the speed limit is 30 mph in towns; there is no speed limit on German motorways 2** verb to drive a car faster than the legal speed; **he was stopped for speeding**

◊ **speedboat** noun racing motor boat

◊ **speedometer** or (informal)

◊ **speedo** noun dial which shows you how fast you are travelling in a vehicle

spice 1 noun flavouring made from the seeds, leaves or roots of plants, etc. **2** verb to add spice to (a dish)

COMMENT: the commonest spices are salt, pepper and mustard. Others often used are cinnamon, cloves, ginger, nutmeg, paprika, turmeric (in pickles), and the various spices which make up curry powders

◊ **spiciness** noun taste of spices

◊ **spicy** adjective tasting of spices

spill 1 noun action of letting liquid fall by mistake; **waiters should know how to deal with spills 2** verb to let liquid or powder fall by mistake; **he spilt coffee over the tablecloth; the waiter spilt white wine down the front of the guest's dress**
NOTE: **spilling - spilled** or **spilt**

spinach noun common green-leaved vegetable

spirit burner or **spirit lamp** noun apparatus in which methylated spirits is burned, used to keep food hot on the table, or to cook food rapidly next to the table

◊ **spirits** noun strong alcoholic drink (whisky, gin, brandy, etc.); **the club is licensed to sell beers, wines and spirits;**

methylated spirits = alcohol, stained purple, used as fuel in spirit burners

spit noun long metal rod passed through meat which turns so that the meat is evenly cooked; **spit-roasted pork**

spoil verb to make bad; to go bad; **the trip was spoilt by the bad weather; rain spoiled our picnic; the dish will spoil quickly unless you keep it in the fridge**
NOTE: **spoiling - spoilt** or **spoiled**

◊ **spoilage** noun making food go bad (as when fruit rot when overripe)

spoke noun domestic flight from a central airport (called a 'hub') connecting with international flights

sponge cake or **sponge pudding** noun light soft cake or pudding made from flour, eggs, sugar and fat; **you need slices of sponge cake to make a trifle**

spoon 1 noun eating utensil with a bowl and a long handle; **coffee spoon** = very small spoon, used with a small coffee cup; **dessertspoon** = special spoon for eating desserts (smaller than a soup spoon, but larger than a teaspoon); **soup spoon** = specially large flat spoon, for eating soup (there are two types of soup spoon: the older type is like a very large dessertspoon, being longer than it is wide; the more modern style is for a spoon with a round bowl); **tablespoon** = large spoon for serving food at table; **teaspoon** = small spoon for stirring tea; **wooden spoon** = spoon made of wood, used for cooking **2** verb **to spoon something into something** = to put something in with a spoon

◊ **spoonful** noun amount contained in a spoon

sport noun game (such as football, hockey, tennis, etc.); **sports facilities** = equipment and buildings for playing sports, such as tennis courts, swimming pools, etc.; **the club has extensive sports facilities**

◊ **sportswear** noun clothes worn to play sports (NOTE: no plural)

spot noun place; **on the spot** = on duty, at one's post; **the fire services were on the spot in a few minutes**

◊ **spot check** noun surprise check on items at random; **customs officers carry out spot checks on incoming cars**

◊ **spotlight** noun bright light which shines on one small area

spouse *noun* husband or wife; **spouse fare** = specially discounted fare for a husband or wife of a passenger travelling on a full-fare ticket

sprat *noun* very small herring-like fish

spread 1 *noun* soft paste of meat, fish or cheese; *as snacks, they offered us water biscuits with cheese spread* **2** *verb* to cover with a layer of something; *he spread the butter thickly on his bread*

spring *noun* **(a)** small stream of water coming out of the ground; *the spa was built in Roman times around hot mineral springs* **(b)** season of the year following winter when plants begin to grow and put out leaves; *the travel company has brought out its spring catalogue; we offer spring tours to the bulb fields of Holland*

◊ **spring onion** *noun* young onion eaten raw in salad (NOTE: US English is **scallion)**

sprinkle *verb* to scatter water, sugar, etc.; *the chef sprinkled poppy seeds on the cake*
◊ **sprinkler** *noun* device for sprinkling water; **sprinkler system** = system of automatic fire control which sprinkles water on a fire and is set off by rising heat

spritzer *noun* drink of white wine and fizzy water

sprout *noun* young shoot of a plant; **bean sprouts** = shoots of beans, eaten especially in Chinese cooking; **Brussels sprouts** = round edible shoots from a type of cabbage

square *noun* **(a)** shape with four equal sides and four right angles **(b)** open area in a town, surrounded by buildings; **market square** = square where a market is held; *the hotel is in the square opposite the town hall*

squash 1 *noun* **(a)** concentrated juice of a fruit to which water is added to make a long drink; *a glass of orange squash* **(b)** fast game played with rackets in a room with high walls **(c)** vegetable like a marrow or pumpkin, etc. **2** *verb* to crush; *hundreds of commuters were squashed into the train*
◊ **squash court** *noun* room with high walls for playing squash in

squeeze 1 *noun* **a squeeze of lemon** = a few drops of lemon juice **2** *verb* to crush *or* to press; *ten people tried to squeeze into the lift*
◊ **squeezer** *noun* device for pressing lemons, oranges, etc. to let the juice run out

squid *noun* sea animal like a small octopus (NOTE: no plural: **a plate of fried squid)**

SSSI = SITE OF SPECIAL SCIENTIFIC INTEREST

stabilizer *noun* **(a)** artificial substance added to processed food to stop the mixture from changing (as in sauces containing water and fat): in the EC emulsifiers and stabilizers have E numbers E322 - E495 **(b)** piece put on the hull of a ship to prevent it from rolling
◊ **stabilizing agent** *noun* = STABILIZER

stack 1 *noun* pile *or* heap of things on top of each other; *there is a stack of replies to our advertisement* **2** *verb* to pile things on top of each other; *the skis are stacked outside the chalet*

staff 1 *noun* people who work for an organization; **to be on the staff** *or* **a member of staff** *or* **a staff member** = to be employed permanently by a company; **staff accommodation** = rooms in a hotel where members of staff live; **staff agency** = agency which looks for staff for organizations; **staff appointment** = job on the staff; **staff association** = society formed by members of staff of a company to represent them to the management and to organize entertainments; **staff catering** = preparing meals for the staff of a hotel or restaurant; **staff cook** = chef who cooks meals for the staff of a hotel or restaurant; **accounts staff** = people who work in the accounts department; **back-of-the-house staff** = staff who work in the back of a hotel, such as kitchen staff, cleaners, etc., as opposed to front-of-the-house staff; **clerical staff** *or* **office staff** = people who work in offices; **counter staff** = staff who work behind the counter; **front-of-the-house staff** = staff, such as the receptionist, doorman, porters, who deal with customers; **kitchen staff** = people who work in a kitchen; **reception staff** = people who work in the reception area; **restaurant staff** = people who work in a restaurant; **senior staff** *or* **junior staff** = older *or* younger members of staff; people in more important *or* less important positions in a company (NOTE: **staff** refers to a group of people and so is often followed by a verb in the plural) **2** *verb* to provide workers for an organization; *the bar is staffed with skilled part-timers; we had difficulty in staffing the hotel*
◊ **staffing** *noun* providing workers for an organization; **staffing levels** = numbers of members of staff required in a department

for it to work efficiently; **the hotel's staffing policy** = the hotel's views on staff - how many are needed for each department *or* if they should be full-time or part-time *or* what the salaries should be, etc.; **staffing problems** = problems to do with staff

stage 1 *noun* **(a)** part of the theatre where the actors perform **(b)** part of a journey; *the tour crosses India by easy stages* **(c) landing stage** = wooden platform for boats to tie up to **2** *verb* to put on *or* to organize (a show); *the exhibition is being staged in the conference centre*

stagger *verb* to arrange (holidays, working hours) so that they do not all begin and end at the same time; *staggered holidays help the tourist industry; we have to stagger the lunch hour so that there is always someone on the switchboard*

stainless steel *noun* metal made of steel with a high percentage of chromium, which makes it resistant to stains or rust; *a set of stainless steel pans; a stainless steel teapot; stainless steel cutlery;* compare ELECTROPLATED NICKEL SILVER

stair *noun* **(a)** step (on a staircase) **(b) (flight of) stairs** = series of steps leading from one floor of a building to the next

◊ **staircarpet** *noun* long narrow piece of carpet for covering stairs

◊ **staircase** *noun* flight of stairs (usually with a handrail)

◊ **stairway** *noun* staircase

◊ **stairwell** *noun* part of a building (a space from the basement to the roof) in which the staircase is fitted; *the lift is fitted in the centre of the stairwell*

stale *adjective* (bread) which is no longer fresh

stall *noun* wooden stand in a market, where a trader displays and sells his goods

stamp 1 *noun* **(a)** device for making marks on documents; mark made in this way; *the invoice has the stamp 'received with thanks' on it; the customs officer looked at the stamps in his passport;* **date stamp** = device with rubber figures which can be moved, used for marking the date on documents or for marking the sell-by date on goods; **rubber stamp** = stamp made of hard rubber cut to form words or numbers; **stamp pad** = soft pad of cloth with ink on which a stamp is pressed, before marking the paper **(b)**

(postage) stamp = small piece of gummed paper which you buy from a post office and stick on a letter or parcel so that it can be sent through the post; *you'll need a £1 stamp to send the letter to Australia;* **stamp machine** = machine which sells stamps automatically

stand *noun* **(a)** separate section of an exhibition or commercial fair where a company exhibits its products or services (NOTE: the US English for this is **booth) (b)** place where an aircraft waits for passengers to board

standard 1 *noun* normal quality *or* normal conditions which other things are judged against; **standard of living** *or* **living standards** = quality of personal home life (such as amount of food or clothes bought, size of family car, etc.); *the standard of service in this restaurant is very high; if a hotel is cheap it does not always mean that the standard of service is low* **2** *adjective* **(a)** normal *or* usual; *we make a standard charge of £25 for a thirty-minute session;* **standard letter** = letter which is sent without any change to various correspondents; **standard rate** = normal charge for something, such as a phone call; **Standard Time** = normal local time as in the winter months **(b)** tall pole; **standard lamp** = lamp in a room on a tall pole

standby *noun* **standby ticket** = cheaper air ticket which allows the passenger to wait until the last moment to see if there is an empty seat on the plane; **standby fare** = cheaper fare for a standby ticket

standing 1 *adjective* **standing order** = instruction given by a customer asking a bank to make a regular payment **2** *noun* **(a) long-standing customer** *or* **customer of long standing** = person who has been a customer for many years **(b)** good reputation; *a restaurant of good standing; the financial standing of a company* **(c)** *(microwave cookery)* **standing time** = time which a dish should be left in the microwave oven after cooking before serving

staphylococcus *noun* *Staphylococcus aureus,* type of bacterium found in cooked meat, milk, and dishes made with milk (such as custard); it causes food poisoning and infection in the blood (NOTE: plural is **staphylococci)**

◊ **staphylococcal** *adjective* (infection, poisoning) caused by staphylococci

COMMENT: staphylococcal infections are treated with antibiotics such as penicillin, or broad-spectrum antibiotics such as tetracycline

star *noun* (i) small bright light which you see in the sky at night; (ii) shape with several regular points, used as a system of classification; **one-star** *or* **two-star** *or* **three-star** *or* **four-star hotel** = hotel which has been classified with one *or* two *or* three *or* four stars, under a classification system

COMMENT: hotels in the UK are given stars by the AA and the RAC (the English Tourist Board uses crowns). Stars are also used to indicate how long frozen food can be kept and the temperature of freezers. One star means that food can be kept at -6°C for one week, two stars at -12°C for four weeks, and three stars at -18°C for three months. Similarly for freezers, each star is equal to -6°C, so a freezer marked ** will keep food at -12°C, which is cold enough to keep food for one month

QUOTE they have been careful to stay well within the three-star market and not overload bedrooms with soft furnishings
Caterer & Hotelkeeper
QUOTE Business travellers accustomed to de luxe accommodation in Spain will appreciate the fact that several Spanish hoteliers have dropped their five-star rating to four, so that guests need only pay a 6% value added tax instead of the usual luxury rate of 15%
Business Traveller

starlight *noun* light from the stars

◊ **starlit** *adjective* (night) lit by the light of the stars

starboard *noun* the right-hand side of a ship when facing the bow; also used of the right-hand side of an aircraft (NOTE: the opposite is **port**)

starch *noun* usual form in which carbohydrates exist in food, especially in bread, rice and potatoes

◊ **starchy** *adjective* (food) which contains a lot of starch; *he eats too much starchy food*

COMMENT: starch is present in common foods, and is broken down by the digestive process into forms of sugar

start 1 *noun* beginning; **to make an early start** = to set off early on a trip **2** *verb* **(a)** to begin; *the main films starts at 8.15; the tour starts from the castle gate* **(b)** to set a machine going; *it is difficult to start a car in cold weather; the car won't start - the battery must be flat* **(c)** to start to = to begin; *the weather is starting to become warmer; it was starting to get dark and we were still miles from the chalet*

◊ **starter** *noun* **(a)** first course in a meal; *what do you want as a starter? we don't want starters, we'll go straight onto the main course* **(b) starter (motor)** = electric motor in a car which sets the main engine going

◊ **starting** *noun* beginning; **starting date** = date on which something begins; **starting salary** = amount of payment for an employee when starting work with a company

starve *verb* not to have enough to eat; *(informal)* **I'm starving** = I'm very hungry

station *noun* **(a)** place where trains stop, where passengers get on or off, etc.; *the train leaves the Central Station at 14.15* **(b)** regular place where someone works; **station waiter** = chef de rang, a waiter who serves a particular group of four or five tables in a restaurant; **station head waiter** = maître d'hôtel de carré, a chief waiter who is in charge of a station, and takes the orders from customers (in the USA, this is the 'captain') **(c) TV station** *or* **radio station** = building where TV or radio programmes are produced; *the station broadcasts hourly reports on snow conditions*

◊ **stationery** *noun* **(a)** supplies for writing, such as paper, envelopes, carbons, pens, etc. **(b)** in particular, notepaper, envelopes, etc., with the hotel's name and address printed on them; *the letter was typed on the hotel stationery*

◊ **station manager** *or* **stationmaster** *noun* person in charge of a railway station

statue *noun* figure of a person carved in stone or made of metal, etc.; *the statue of King John is in the centre of the square*

status *noun* position *or* condition; **status inquiry** = check on a customer's credit rating; **room status board** = board in a hotel, showing each room, with its number and floor, and indicating whether it is vacant or occupied, or will be occupied or become vacant during the day

statutory

statutory *adjective* fixed by law; *there is a statutory period of probation of thirteen weeks;* **statutory holiday** = holiday which is fixed by law

stay 1 *noun* length of time spent in one place; *the tourists were in town only for a short stay; did you enjoy your stay in London?;* **short-stay guest** *or* **visitor** = person who stays a few days in a hotel *or* a town **2** *verb* to spend time in a place; *the party is staying at the Hotel London; we always stay at the same resort; occupancy rates have stayed below 60% for two years*

◊ **stay over** *verb* to stay in a place for at least one night

QUOTE the numbers of stay-over visitors increased by two per cent, following a six per cent fall in the preceding year
Daily Telegraph

STB = SCOTTISH TOURIST BOARD

STD = SUBSCRIBER TRUNK DIALLING

steak *noun* **(a)** thick slice of beef cut from the best part of the animal; **braising steak** *or* **stewing steak** = good-quality beef suitable for cooking in liquid, as in a stew, a casserole, etc.; **fillet steak** = thick slice of beef from the best-quality and most expensive cut; **rump steak** = thick slice of beef cut from above the leg and considered to have the best flavour; **sirloin steak** = thick slice of beef from one of the best-quality and most expensive cuts; **T-bone steak** = thick slice of beef cut from the rib and having a bone shaped like a T in it **(b)** thick slice cut across the body of an animal *or* a fish; *a gammon steak; a salmon steak*

◊ **steak and kidney** *noun* typically English combination of cubes of beef and kidney (usually ox kidney) are cooked together with onions in a thick sauce (in a pie or pudding); *a serving of steak and kidney pie; an individual steak and kidney pudding*

◊ **steak bar** *noun* restaurant which only serves steak, with seating for customers at counters

◊ **steakhouse** *noun* restaurant serving steak and other grilled food

◊ **steak knife** *noun* very sharp knife, or knife with a serrated edge, used for eating meat (mainly steak)

steal *verb* to take something which does not belong to you; *a burglar broke into the hotel room and stole my wallet; keep your purse in your bag or it may get stolen; the car was stolen from the hotel car park*

NOTE: **stealing - stole - stolen**

steam 1 *noun* vapour which comes off hot water; **steam engine** = engine which is powered by steam pressure; **steam railway** = railway where the engines are powered by steam pressure **2** *verb* to cook over a pan of boiling water by allowing the steam to pass through holes in a container with food in it; **steaming oven** *or* **steaming cabinet** = oven in a restaurant kitchen, used to steam large quantities of food at the same time

COMMENT: vegetables, fish and poultry can be cooked by steaming in a container with holes in the bottom, placed over a pan of boiling water. Juices and vitamins are retained in the food during cooking. Puddings, such as steak-and-kidney pudding, are steamed by standing the basin containing the pudding in a pan of boiling water

steamboat *noun* boat powered by steam

◊ **steamer** *noun* **(a)** large passenger ship (powered by steam) **(b)** type of pan with holes in the bottom which is placed over boiling water for steaming food

◊ **steamship** *noun* large passenger ship (powered by steam)

steel *noun* rod of rough metal with a handle, used for sharpening knives

steep *adjective* **(a)** which rises or falls sharply; *there's a very steep hill at the entrance to the town* **(b)** *(informal)* excessive; *their prices are a bit steep*

step *noun* stair (on a staircase); flat rung (on a ladder); *there are 75 steps to the top of the tower;* **mind the step** = be careful, because the floor level changes and goes up or down with a step

stereo *noun* machine which reproduces sound through two different channels and loudspeakers; **car stereo** = system in a car which reproduces sound in stereo

◊ **stereophonic** *adjective* referring to sound which comes through from two different channels and loudspeakers

sterilize *verb* to make something free from bacteria *or* microbes (by killing the bacteria); **sterilized milk** = milk prepared for human consumption by heating in sealed airtight containers to kill all bacteria

◊ **sterilization** *noun* action of making something free from bacteria *or* microbes (by killing the bacteria)

sterling *noun* standard currency used in the United Kingdom; *to quote prices in sterling or to quote sterling prices;* **pound sterling** = official term for the unit of money used in the UK

stew 1 *noun* dish of meat and vegetables cooked together for a long time; *rabbit stew* **2** *verb* to cook for a long time in liquid; *stewed rabbit; stewed apples and cream; pears stewed in red wine*

steward *noun* man who looks after passengers and serves drinks *or* food on a ship *or* plane; **chief steward** *or* **senior steward** = most important *or* most experienced steward on a ship or plane
◊ **stewardess** *noun* woman who looks after passengers and serves drinks *or* food on a ship *or* plane

stick *noun* something long and thin; **a stick of celery** = a stem of celery, with leaves on top; **bread stick** = long thin cylindrical biscuit, eaten as an appetizer

sticking plaster *noun* strip of cloth which can be stuck to the skin to cover a wound; *I want some sticking plaster to put on my heel*

still *adjective (of drinks)* not fizzy; *still water; still orange drink*
◊ **stillroom** *noun (in a hotel)* room where coffee, tea, and some light meals (such as afternoon tea) are prepared

stir *verb* to mix up (a liquid or food); *keep stirring the porridge, or it will stick to the bottom of the pan*
◊ **stir-fry** *verb* to cook food quickly in the Chinese fashion, in hot oil in a wok; **stir-fried beef** *or* **beef stir-fry** = thin strips of beef cooked quickly with vegetables in hot oil

stock 1 *noun* **(a)** quantity of goods *or* raw materials; *even if it is cut off by snow, the hotel has sufficient stocks of food to last a week* **(b)** goods in a warehouse or shop; **in stock** *or* **out of stock** = available *or* not available in the warehouse *or* shop; *to hold 2,000 lines in stock; the item went out of stock just before Christmas but came back into stock in the first week of January; we are out of stock of this item;* **stock control** = system of checking that there is not too much stock in a warehouse, but just enough

to meet requirements (NOTE: the word 'stock' is used in GB where American English uses the word 'inventory'. So, 'stock control' is 'inventory control' in American English) **(c) stock size** = normal size; *we only carry stock sizes of shoes* **(d)** liquid made from boiling bones, etc., in water, used as a base for soups and sauces; *the soup is made with fish stock* **2** *verb* to hold goods for sale in a warehouse *or* store; *to stock 200 lines*
◊ **stock up with** *verb* to buy (goods) to hold in case of emergency; *we'll stock up with food to last us over the holiday weekend*

STOL = SHORT TAKE-OFF AND LANDING

stone *noun* **(a)** rock; *the church is built of the local grey stone* **(b)** small piece of rock; *stop a moment, I've got a stone in my shoe* **(c)** hard seed inside a fruit; *count the cherry stones on the side of your plate* **(d)** *GB* measure of weight (= 14 pounds or 6.35 kilograms); *I've put on weight - I weigh 12 stone* (NOTE: in the USA, human body weight is always given in pounds)

stool *noun* seat with no back; **bar stool** = high seat used for sitting at a bar or counter; **bathroom stool** = stool placed in a bathroom

stop 1 *noun* **(a) to come to a stop** = not to go any further; *work on the new marina came to a stop when the company could not pay the workers' wages; the brakes failed and the car came to a stop against a wall* **(b)** place where a vehicle stops; *the bus stop is opposite the Town Hall; there are six stops between here and Marble Arch* **(c) his account is on stop** = he will not be supplied with anything until he pays what he owes; **to put a stop on a cheque** = to ask a bank not to pay a cheque you have written **2** *verb* **(a)** to make (something) not to move any more; *does this bus stop near the Post Office? the tourist coach was stopped by the customs; the government has stopped the import of cars; he stopped his car by the side of the lake* **(b)** not to do anything any more; *the operator has stopped offering tours to Greece; the restaurant stopped serving meals at 12.00 midnight; the hotel staff stopped work when the company could not pay their wages; the cleaning staff stop work at 5.30; we have stopped supplying Smith & Co.* **(c)** to stay in a place; *they stopped for five nights at the Grand Hotel* **(d) to stop an account** = to stop supplying a customer until he has paid what he owes; **to stop a cheque** = to ask a bank not to pay a cheque you have written; **to stop payments** = not to pay any more money **(e) to stop someone's wages** = to take money out of someone's wages before he receives them; *we stopped £25 from his pay because he was rude to the guests* NOTE: **stopping - stopped**

◇ **stop over** *verb* to stay for a short time in a place on a long journey; *we stopped over in Hong Kong on the way to Australia*

◇ **stopover** *noun* staying for a short time in a place on a long journey; *the ticket allows you two stopovers between London and Tokyo* (NOTE: US English also uses **layover**)

store 1 *noun* **(a)** supply of food, etc., kept for later use **(b)** place in which goods are kept; **dry stores** = storeroom where dry goods, such as tins and packets of food are kept; **perishable stores** = storeroom for food which can go bad quickly, such as meat and fruit **(c)** *US* shop; *GB* large shop; *there's a department store next to the hotel* (NOTE: GB English usually uses **shop** for small businesses) **2** *verb* **(a)** to keep (something) for future use **(b)** to put (something) in a warehouse

◇ **storekeeper** *or* **storeman** *noun* person who looks after stores of food, drink, and other supplies in a hotel's storeroom

◇ **storeroom** *noun* room where things (such as foodstuffs) are stored

storm *noun* violent weather, with wind and rain or snow; *there was a rainstorm during the night; snowstorms swept the northern American states;* **rainstorm** = heavy rain accompanied by wind; **sandstorm** = high wind in the desert, which carries large amounts of sand with it; **snowstorm** = heavy fall of snow accompanied by wind; **thunderstorm** = storm with rain, thunder and lightning

stout *noun* strong dark beer

straight 1 *adjective* with no turns; *the road goes in a straight line across the plain for two hundred kilometres* **2** *adverb* **(a)** without turning; *the road goes straight across the plain for two hundred kilometres;* **go straight on** = continue along this road without turning off it; *go straight on past the crossroads and then turn left* **(b)** without stopping; *the plane flies straight to Washington* **(c)** (alcohol) with no water or any other liquid added; *he drinks his whisky straight* (NOTE: GB English also uses **neat**

strain *verb* to pour liquid through a sieve to separate solids from it; *boil the peas for ten minutes and then strain*

◇ **strainer** *noun* utensil made with metal or nylon mesh, used to separate solids from a liquid; **a tea strainer** = small utensil placed over a cup to separate tea leaves from the liquid (used when making tea with loose tea leaves)

strand *verb* to leave (someone) alone and helpless

◇ **stranded** *adjective* left alone and helpless; *the tourist group was stranded in the mountain hut by a sudden snowstorm; the collapse of the holiday company left thousands of holidaymakers stranded in Turkey*

strawberry *noun* common red summer soft fruit of the *Fragaria* species, used as a dessert fruit, and also preserved as jam

stream *noun* **(a)** small flow of water; small river; **mountain stream** = little river in the mountains **(b)** continuous flow of things; *crossing the road is difficult because of the stream of traffic; streams of guests ran out of the burning hotel*

street *noun* road in a town; *GB* **High Street** *or US* **Main Street** = most important street in a town, where the shops and banks are; **the High Street banks** = main British banks which accept deposits from individual customers; **street directory** = (i) list of people living in a street; (ii) map of a town with all the streets listed in alphabetical order in an index; **street map** *or* **street plan** = diagram showing the streets of a town, with their names

◇ **streetcar** *noun US* tram

streptococcus *noun* genus of bacteria which grows in long chains, and causes fevers such as scarlet fever, tonsillitis and rheumatic fever; also used to start the cheese-making process (NOTE: plural is **streptococci**

◇ **streptococcal** *adjective* (infection) caused by streptococci

stretch 1 *noun* long piece (of road, etc.); *for long stretches of the Transsiberian Railway, all you see are trees; stretches of the river have been so polluted that bathing is dangerous* **2** *verb* **(a) to stretch to** = to be enough for; *will your money stretch to the visit to the temple;* **dinner won't stretch to seven** = there won't be enough food for seven people **(b)** to lie for a great distance; *white sandy beaches stretch as far as the eye can see*

◊ **stretch limo** *noun (informal)* luxurious hire car, which is much longer than the normal models, used to carry important passengers

strike 1 *noun* **(a)** stopping of work by the workers (because of lack of agreement with management *or* because of orders from a union); **general strike** = strike of all the workers in a country; **official strike** = strike which has been approved by the main office of a union; **protest strike** = strike in protest at a particular grievance; **sit-down strike** = strike where workers stay in their place of work and refuse to work or leave; **sympathy strike** = strike to show that workers agree with another group of workers who are already on strike; **token strike** = short strike to show that workers have a grievance; **unofficial strike** = strike by local workers, which has not been approved by the main union **(b)** to take **strike action** = to go on strike; **strike call** = demand by a union for a strike; **no-strike agreement** *or* **no-strike clause** = (clause in an) agreement where the workers say that they will never strike; **strike fund** = money collected by a trade union from its members, used to pay strike pay; **strike pay** = wages paid to striking workers by their trade union; **strike ballot** *or* **strike vote** = vote by workers to decide if a strike should be held **(c)** to come out on strike *or* to go on strike = to stop work; *the baggage handlers are on strike for higher pay;* to call the workforce out on strike = to tell the workers to stop work; *the union called its members out on strike* **2** *verb* to stop working because there is no agreement with management; *to strike for higher wages or for shorter working hours; to strike in protest against bad working conditions*
NOTE: **striking - struck**

◊ **strikebound** *adjective* not able to work *or* to move because of a strike; *the cruise ship is strikebound in the docks*

◊ **strikebreaker** *noun* worker who goes on working while everyone else is on strike

◊ **striker** *noun* worker who is on strike

strip *noun* taking one's clothes off; **a strip-club** *or (informal)* **a strip-joint** = place where someone takes their clothes off piece by piece as an entertainment

◊ **stripper** *noun* person who performs a striptease

◊ **striptease** *noun* entertainment where someone takes their clothes off piece by piece

stroll 1 *noun* slow and short leisurely walk; *after dinner we went for a stroll through the village* **2** *verb* to walk slowly along; *on Sunday evenings, everyone strolls along the boulevard*

strong *adjective* with a lot of force *or* strength; **strong coffee** *or* **strong tea** = coffee *or* tea made with more coffee or tea than usual; *you need a cup of strong black coffee to wake you up; I like my tea very strong;* **strong pound** = pound which is high against other currencies

studio *noun* one-room apartment (with a separate bathroom, but often with a kitchenette in a corner of the main room); *you can rent a studio overlooking the sea for £300 a week in high season*

QUOTE the hotel offers 120 studios and nine apartments. Each has a direct telephone line, satellite TV, sofabed and fully equipped kitchenette. A self-service laundry is located within the hotel. Studios are for single people or couples, while apartments can sleep as many as four guests

Inside Hotels

study 1 *noun* act of examining something carefully to learn more about it; **course of study** = course at college or university; **study tour** = tour of a country or an area which includes visits, lectures and classes **2** *verb* to follow a course at college or university; *he's studying hotel management*

stuff *verb* to put breadcrumbs, chopped meat, etc. inside meat or vegetables and cook and serve them together as a special dish; **stuffed vine leaves** *or* **stuffed tomatoes** = vine leaves *or* tomatoes cooked with a savoury mixture inside them

◊ **stuffing** *noun* mixture of chopped meat or vegetables with breadcrumbs or rice, usually put inside meat or vegetables; *chicken is often cooked with a sage and onion stuffing*

sturgeon *noun* large edible fish whose eggs are caviare (NOTE: plural is **sturgeon**)

sub- *prefix* under *or* less important

◊ **sub-agency** *noun* small agency which is part of a large agency

◊ **subaqua** *adjective* referring to underwater sports; *a subaqua club*

◊ **sub-franchise 1** *noun* franchise held from a main franchise in an area **2** *verb (of a main franchise)* to license a franchise in an area; *the master franchise runs three units and sub-franchises two other outlets*

◊ **sub-franchisee** *noun* person who trades under a sub-franchise

◊ **sub-post office** *noun* small post office, usually part of a general store

subscriber trunk dialling (STD) *noun* telephone system where you can dial long-distance numbers direct from your own telephone without going through the operator

subsidize *verb* to help by giving money; *the government has agreed to subsidize the hotel industry*

◊ **subsidy** *noun* **(a)** money given to help something which is not profitable; *the country's hotel industry exists on government subsidies; the government has increased its subsidy to the hotel industry* **(b)** money given by a government to make something cheaper; *the subsidy on butter or the butter subsidy*

subsistence *noun* minimum amount of food, money, housing, etc., which a person needs; **subsistence allowance** = money paid by a company to cover the cost of hotels, meals, etc., for a member of staff who is travelling on business; **to live at subsistence level** = to have only just enough money to live on

suburb *noun* residential area on the outskirts of a city or town; **the suburbs** = residential area all round a town

◊ **suburban** *adjective* referring to the suburbs; **suburban line** = railway line between the suburbs to the centre of a town; **suburban trains** = trains which run between the suburbs and the town centre

subway *noun* **(a)** *GB* passage under ground along which pedestrians can pass (as under a busy road) **(b)** *US* underground railway system; *the New York subway; he took the subway to Grand Central Station*

succulent *adjective* (meat or fruit) which is full of juice; *a succulent melon; a slice of succulent ham*

suet *noun* hard fat from an animal, used in cooking; **beef suet** = suet from cattle; **suet**

dumplings = small balls of paste, flavoured with herbs, cooked in a meat stew; **suet pudding** = dish made with flour and suet, cooked by steaming or boiling (the contents can be meat, as in steak and kidney pudding, or sweet, as in treacle pudding or Christmas pudding)

sugar *noun* sucrose ($C_{12}H_{22}O_{11}$), sweet substance obtained from the juice of a sugar cane or from sugar beet; **brown sugar** *or* **Demerara sugar** = unrefined or partly refined sugar in large brown crystals; **cube sugar** *or* **sugar cubes** = granulated sugar formed into hard cubes; **granulated sugar** *or* **white sugar** = refined sugar in small white crystals; **icing sugar** = fine powdered white sugar mixed with water or egg white and flavouring, used to cover cakes; **sugar crystals** = large pale brown sugar crystals, used for sweetening coffee; **sugar-free** = (food, drink, diet) which does not contain sugar; **sugar lump** = cube of white sugar

COMMENT: there are several natural forms of sugar: sucrose (in plants), lactose (in milk), fructose (in fruit), glucose and dextrose (in fruit and in body tissue). Edible sugar used in the home is a form of refined sucrose. All sugars are useful sources of energy, though excessive amounts of sugar can increase weight and cause tooth decay. Diabetes mellitus is a condition where the body is incapable of absorbing sugar from food

suit *noun* two or three pieces of clothing made of the same cloth (jacket and/or waistcoat and trousers or skirt); **morning suit** = clothes for men consisting of a black tail coat, light grey waistcoat and striped black and grey trousers, worn by men at formal occasions such as weddings

◊ **suitcase** *noun* case, a box with a handle for carrying clothes and personal belongings when travelling; *the customs officer made him open his three suitcases;* **suitcase stand** = wooden stand in a hotel bedroom, on which you can place your suitcases

suite *noun* series of rooms which make a set; **family suite** = series of rooms in a hotel, suitable for a family (typically, two bedrooms, sitting room, plus bathroom); **hospitality suite** = special reception rooms for entertaining business guests in a hotel or conference centre, or at a TV or radio station; **VIP suite** = specially luxurious suite at an airport or in a hotel; **suite hotel =** hotel where all the accommodation consists of suites of rooms

◊ **en suite** *adverb & adjective* **bedroom with bathroom en suite** *or* **with en suite bathroom = bathroom which leads off a bedroom; the hotel has 25 bedrooms, all en suite =** all the bedrooms have en suite bathrooms

sultana *noun* type of seedless raisin

summary sheet *noun* paper giving details of sales in a restaurant, itemized by the cashier

summer *noun* season of the year following spring, when plants begin to make fruit; the warmest season; **the summer holidays =** (i) period during the summer when children do not go to school, the longest holidays during the school year (in the UK about six weeks, but much longer in the USA); (ii) any holiday taken during the summer; **summer schedule** *or* **timetable =** special timetable for planes or trains or ferries, which applies during the high season; **summer school =** classes held at a school, college or university during the summer holiday; *she is organizing a summer school in Florence on 'The Italian Renaissance';* **Summer Time =** Daylight Saving Time, system of putting the clocks forward one hour in summer to provide extra daylight in the evening

summit *noun (of a mountain)* top

sun *noun* **(a)** very hot body around which the earth revolves and which provides heat and daylight; *the sun wasn't shining when she took the photo* **(b)** light from the sun; *she was sitting in the sun on the deck; he prefers a table out of the sun*

◊ **sunbathe** *verb* to lie in the sun to get your body brown

◊ **sunbather** *noun* person who is sunbathing; *the pool was surrounded by sunbathers*

◊ **sunbathing** *noun* lying in the sun to get your body brown; *sunbathing on the beach at midday is not advised*

◊ **sunburn** *noun* painful inflammation of the skin caused by being in the sun for too long

◊ **sunburnt** *adjective* made brown or red by the sun

◊ **sundeck** *noun* top deck of a passenger ship where people can sit in the sun

◊ **sun-drenched** *adjective* very sunny; *the sun-drenched beaches of the Italian Riviera*

◊ **sun-dried** *adjective* (food) which is dried in the sun to preserve it (either fruit, such as figs, raisins, tomatoes, or fish can be treated this way)

◊ **sunflower (seed) oil** *noun* edible oil made from the seeds of the sunflower

◊ **sunglasses** *plural noun* dark glasses to protect your eyes from the sun

◊ **sunhat** *noun* hat worn to protect you from the sun

◊ **sun lounge** *noun* room with many large windows, where you can enjoy sunlight

◊ **sunny** *adjective* **(a)** full of sunlight; *the weather forecast is for sunny spells during the morning; the sunniest part of the garden is beyond the tennis courts* **(b)** *US (informal)* **sunny side up =** (egg) fried without being turned over; *compare* EASY OVER

◊ **sunroof** *noun* part of a roof of a car which slides open

◊ **sunshade** *noun* parasol, a light umbrella to protect you from the rays of the sun

◊ **sunshine** *noun* light from the sun; *London has on average 7.6 hours of sunshine per day during May; the west coast of France has more than 250 days of sunshine per annum;* **sunshine roof =** SUNROOF

◊ **sunstroke** *noun* illness caused by being in the sunlight too much

◊ **suntan** *noun* brown colour of the skin caused by the sun; **suntan lotion** *or* **oil** *or* **cream =** substance which is rubbed on the body to prevent sunburn

sundae *noun* dessert of ice cream, cream, fruit and nuts and a sweet sauce

sundry *adjective & noun* various; **sundry items** *or* **sundries =** small items which are not listed in detail

supermarket *noun* large store, usually selling food, where customers serve themselves and pay at a checkout; *you can buy all the food you need in the supermarket next to the holiday apartments*

superstore *noun* very large self-service store which sells a wide range of goods

supervise *verb* to watch work carefully to see if it is well done; *the fitting of the new restaurant was supervised by the head chef; she supervises six girls in the reception area*

◊ **supervision** *noun* watching work carefully to see if it is well done; *new staff work under supervision for the first three months; the cash was counted under the supervision of the head cashier; she is very* *experienced and can be left to work without any supervision*

◊ **supervisor** *noun* person who watches work carefully to see if it is well done

◊ **supervisory** *adjective* as a supervisor; *supervisory staff; he works in a supervisory capacity*

supper *noun* evening meal (especially a light informal meal, as opposed to a dinner); **to have supper** = to eat an evening meal; *we'll have supper on the terrace;* **candlelit supper** = evening meal lit by candles on the table; **supper menu** = menu (usually à la carte) containing various light dishes, served at a supper

supplement *noun* thing which is in addition, especially an additional charge; **single room supplement** = extra charge for a single person travelling with a group who does not want to share a room with anyone else (charges will be calculated on the basis of two people sharing each room)

◊ **supplementary** *adjective* in addition; *there are no supplementary charge - the price is all- inclusive*

supply 1 *noun* **(a)** providing something which is needed; *we rely on him for our supply of cheese or for our cheese supply;* **in short supply** = not available in large enough quantities to meet the demand; *fresh vegetables are in short supply during the winter* **(b)** stock of something which is needed; *the restaurant is running short of supplies of bread; supplies of bread have been held up by a strike at the baker's* **2** *verb* to provide something which is needed; *the brewery supplies all the beer to the hotel; this company has the contract to supply the American Embassy; he supplies the hotel with cheese or he supplies cheese to the hotel* (NOTE: you **supply someone with something** or **supply something to someone**)

◊ **supplier** *noun* person who *or* company which provides something which is needed; *he's our regular supplier of beverages or our regular beverage supplier; they are major suppliers of equipment to the hotel trade*

surcharge 1 *noun* extra amount to pay; **fuel surcharge** = extra amount added to an air fare, to cover increased fuel costs which have come into effect since the air fare was calculated **2** *verb* to ask someone to pay an extra amount

surf 1 *noun* line of breaking waves along a shore; foam from breaking waves **2** *verb* to ride on breaking waves on a board; *he goes surfing each weekend*

◊ **surfboard** *noun* board which you stand or lie on to ride on breaking waves

◊ **surfboat** *noun* light boat for riding on surf

◊ **surfer** *noun* person who surfs

◊ **surfing** *or* **surf-riding** *noun* riding on breaking waves on a board as a sport; *surfing is the most popular sport in Hawaii*

surface *noun* top part of something; **to send a package by surface mail** = to send a package by land or sea, not by air; **surface transport** = transport on land or sea

surname *noun* family name

surround *verb* to be all round (something); *when the floods came, the hotel was surrounded by water and the guests had to be rescued by boat; the villa is outside the town, surrounded by vineyards*

◊ **surrounding** *adjective* which surrounds; *standing on the terrace, you have a marvellous view over the surrounding countryside*

◊ **surroundings** *plural noun* area around a place; *the surroundings of the hotel are very peaceful*

survey 1 *noun* **(a)** general report on something; *the Tourist Office has produced a survey of local hotels and the facilities they offer* **(b)** examining a building to see if it is in good condition; *we have asked for a survey of the hotel before buying it; the insurance company is carrying out a survey of the damage caused by the storm;* **damage survey** = report on damage done **(c)** measuring exactly; **quantity survey** = calculating the amount of materials and cost of labour needed for a construction project **2** *verb* to examine (something) to see if it is in good condition

◊ **surveyor** *noun* person who examines buildings to see if they are in good condition; **quantity surveyor** = person who calculates the amount of materials and cost of labour needed for a construction project

sustainable *adjective* (development, tourism) which does not deplete *or* damage natural resources irreparably and which leaves the environment in good order for future generations

swap 1 *noun* exchange of one thing for another; **flat swap** *or* **house swap** = arrangement where two families exchange flats or houses for a holiday **2** *verb* to exchange one thing for another; *he swapped his old car for a new motorcycle;* they **swapped jobs** = each of them took the other's job
NOTE: **swapping - swapped**

swede *noun* common vegetable with a round root and yellow flesh, used mainly in soups and stews

sweet 1 *adjective* tasting like sugar; not sour; *with the fruit, we ordered a sweet white wine; just one spoon of sugar in my tea - I don't like it too sweet* **2** *noun* **(a)** food made of sugar, eaten as a snack; *she bought a bag of sweets to eat during the film* (NOTE: US English is **candy**) **(b)** **sweet (course)** = dessert course, sweet dish eaten at the end of a meal; *what do you want for sweet?; I have eaten so much, I don't want any sweet;* **sweet trolley** = table on wheels on which desserts are taken to each table in a restaurant
◊ **sweet corn** *noun* maize, cereal which is used to make flour and of which the seeds are also eaten; *see also* CORN
◊ **sweetener** *noun* artificial substance (such as saccharin) added to food to make it sweet
◊ **sweet potato** *noun Ipomoea batatas,* a starchy root vegetable grown in tropical and subtropical regions

> COMMENT: called 'yams' in the Southern USA; the plant has no connection with the ordinary potato

sweltering *adjective* very hot

swim 1 *verb* to move in water using arms, legs, flippers, etc. **2** *noun* act of moving in the water using arms, legs, flippers, etc.; *let's go for a swim before breakfast*
◊ **swimmer** *noun* person who swims
◊ **swimming** *noun* moving in water using arms, legs, flippers, etc.; **swimming costume** = piece of clothing worn when swimming; **swimming trunks** = shorts worn by a man when swimming
◊ **swimming baths** *plural noun* large building with a public swimming pool
◊ **swimming pool** *noun* enclosed tank of water for swimming in
◊ **swimsuit** *noun* piece of clothing worn when swimming

swing door *noun* door which is not attached with a catch, and which is opened by pushing from either side; *there is a swing door between the kitchen and the restaurant*

swipe *verb* to put an electronic card through a reader by passing it quickly along a groove; **swipe card** = type of magnetic key card which you run down a slot to unlock the door

Swiss roll *noun* cake made by rolling a thin sheet of sponge cake covered with jam (NOTE: US English is **jelly roll**)

switch 1 *verb* to change from one thing to another; *the waiter had switched our glasses by mistake; he switched flights in Montreal and went on to Calgary* **2** *noun* apparatus for starting or stopping an electric current; *the light switch is near the bed*
◊ **switchboard** *noun* central point in a telephone system, where all internal and external lines meet; *you should phone the switchboard if you want an early call;* **switchboard operator** = person who works the central telephone system
◊ **switch off** *verb* to stop an electric current; *don't forget to switch off the air-conditioning when you go to bed; the captain has switched off the 'no smoking' sign*
◊ **switch on** *verb* to start an electric current flowing; *the captain switched on the 'no smoking' sign; he switched on the air-conditioner; when you put the light on in the bathroom, the fan switches on automatically*
◊ **switch over to** *verb* to change to something quite different; *we have switched over to a French supplier; the hotel has switched over to gas for heating*

swizzlestick *noun* small stick put into a glass of fizzy drink to make it less fizzy

swop = SWAP

SWOT analysis *noun* method of developing a marketing strategy based on an assessment of the Strengths and Weaknesses of the company and the Opportunities and Threats in the market

syllabub *noun* sweet food made of cream whipped with wine

synergy *noun* producing greater effects by joining forces than by acting separately

syrup *noun* **(a)** thick sweet liquid; *fruit syrup; raspberry syrup* **(b)** **(golden) syrup** =

thick golden juice from sugar (used to make treacle tart, etc.); *compare* MOLASSES, TREACLE

Tt

T-bar *noun* type of ski-lift where two skiers hold onto a T-shaped bar (one on each side) to be pulled up a slope

◊ **T-bone steak** *noun* thick slice of beef cut from the rib and having a bone shaped like a T in it

◊ **T-junction** *noun* junction where one road joins another at right angles

◊ **T-shirt** *noun* light short-sleeved shirt with no buttons or collar

tab *noun (informal)* **to pick up the tab** = to pay the bill

TAB vaccine *noun* vaccine which immunizes against typhoid fever and paratyphoid A and B (this vaccine is no longer recommended); *he was given a TAB injection; TAB injections give only temporary immunity against paratyphoid*

table *noun* **(a)** piece of furniture with a flat top and legs; **writing table** = table where someone can write letters, etc. **(b)** piece of furniture in a restaurant where guests sit to eat; *he asked for a table by the window; she says she booked a table for six people for 12.30;* **at table** = sitting at a dining table; *the last guest arrived where everyone else was at table;* **table plan** = layout of the tables in a large room for a function (as for a dinner-dance) to show where each person is to sit, and to allow for efficient service; **table service** = service by a waiter or waitress to people sitting at a restaurant table (as opposed to counter service or self-service); **table tent** = folded card advertising special items on the menu or special wines, placed on a table in a restaurant; **table wines** = wines which are considered suitable for drinking with meals **(c)** list of figures *or* facts set out in columns; **table of contents** = list of contents in a book

◊ **tablecloth** *noun* cloth for covering a table during a meal

◊ **table d'hôte (menu)** *noun* menu which has a restricted number of dishes at a single price for the whole meal (as opposed to an à la carte menu); *they chose from the table d'hôte menu*

◊ **table linen** *noun* tablecloths, napkins, etc.

◊ **table mat** *noun* piece of cloth, cork, paper, etc., on which a person's plate is placed (it protects the surface of a table and is used in restaurants where no tablecloths are used to cover polished wooden tables)

◊ **table napkin** *noun* square piece of cloth used to protect clothes and wipe your mouth at meal times (NOTE: also called a **serviette,** but some people think this is not correct English; **napkin** is the word used in hotels and restaurants)

◊ **tablespoon** *noun* large spoon for serving food at table

◊ **tablespoonful** *noun* amount contained in a tablespoon

◊ **tableware** *noun* knives, forks, spoons, plates, etc. (NOTE: no plural)

tachograph *noun* device in a truck, which shows details of distance travelled and time of journeys

Taenia *noun* genus of tapeworm (NOTE: plural is **Taeniae)**

◊ **taeniacide** *adjective* substance which kills tapeworms

◊ **taeniafuge** *noun* substance which makes tapeworms leave the body

◊ **taeniasis** *noun* infestation of the intestines with tapeworms

COMMENT: the various species of Taenia which affect humans are taken into the body from eating meat which has not been properly cooked. The most obvious symptom of tapeworm infestation is a sharply increased appetite, together with a loss of weight. The most serious infestation is with *Taenia solium,* found in pork which has not be sufficiently cooked

Tafelwein *German noun* ordinary wine *or* table wine; *compare* VIN DE TABLE

tag *noun* label, marked with a price, a name, a reference numbers, etc.; *price tag; name tag*

Tageskarte *German noun (meaning 'menu of the day')* list of special dishes prepared for the day and not listed in the printed menu; *compare* CARTE DU JOUR

tailback *noun* long line of cars held up by roadworks, an accident, etc.; *because of the crash, there's a six-mile tailback on the motorway from junction four*
◊ **tailwind** *noun* following wind, a wind blowing from behind a ship or aircraft

take 1 *noun* money received from customers in a shop, restaurant, etc. **2** *verb* **(a) to take place** = to happen; *the reception will take place on Saturday* **(b)** to eat *or* to drink normally; *do you take sugar in your tea?* (NOTE: **taking - took - has taken**)
◊ **takeaway** *noun & adjective (informal)* (shop where you can buy) hot food to eat elsewhere; *there's a Chinese takeaway round the corner; we had a takeaway for supper; we can phone for a takeaway pizza*
◊ **take off** *verb* **(a)** to remove *or* to deduct; *he took £25 off the price* **(b)** *(of plane)* to start to rise from the ground into the air; *the plane took off ten minutes late* **(c)** she *took the day off* = she decided not to work for the day
◊ **takeoff** *noun (of plane)* rising from the ground into the air; *the hostess will serve drinks shortly after takeoff*
◊ **takeout** *noun US* takeaway
◊ **takings** *plural noun* money received from customers in a shop, restaurant or hotel; *the day's takings were stolen from the cash desk*

> QUOTE a queue of planes at takeoff delayed our departure by ten minutes
> *Business Traveller*

tan *noun* brown colour of the skin caused by the sun; *she got a tan from spending each day on the beach; see also* SUNTAN, SUNTAN OIL
◊ **tanned** *adjective* made brown by the sun

tandoori *noun* method of Indian cooking; food cooked in this way; *a tandoori restaurant; tandoori chicken;* **tandoori oven** = traditional clay oven used in Indian restaurants to cook tandoori-style food

> COMMENT: food is usually marinated in yoghurt and spices, then cooked in a traditional clay oven called a 'tandoor'

tang *noun* **(a)** sharp taste or smell **(b)** piece of flat metal which forms the centre of the handle of a knife

tangerine *noun* type of small orange with soft skin which peels easily

tank *noun* large (metal) container for liquids; **petrol tank** = container built into a car, for holding petrol; **water tank** = tank for holding water

tap *noun* apparatus with a twisting knob or lever and a valve which allows liquid to come out of a pipe or container; **tap water** = water which comes from the mains and not from a well or bottle; *can I have a carafe of water, please? - mineral water, sir? - no, ordinary tap water will do;* **cold tap** *or* **hot tap** = tap which produces cold or hot water; **to turn a tap on** = to allow water to run; **to turn a tap off** = to stop water running (NOTE: in Britain, the hot tap is usually on the right, and the cold tap on the left, but in other countries they are often the other way round)

tapas *Spanish noun (meaning 'lids')* small plates of snacks (fried squid, olives, cheese) served with beer or wine; **tapas bar** = bar where the speciality is serving tapas

target 1 *noun* thing to aim for; **to set targets** = to fix amounts *or* sales which workers have to reach; **to meet a target** = to produce the sales which are expected; **to miss a target** = not to produce the sales which are expected; **sales targets** = amount of sales which a restaurant *or* a hotel is expected to achieve; **target market** = market to which a company is planning to sell its service **2** *verb* to aim to sell to someone; **to target a market** = to aim to sell to a certain market

> QUOTE many pub chains are also targeting their menu offer to appeal to children in an attempt to compete in the family market with the ever-popular hamburger chains
> *Caterer & Hotelkeeper*

tariff *noun* **(a) customs tariff** = list of duties to be paid on imported or exported goods; **tariff barriers** = customs duty intended to make imports more difficult; *to impose tariff barriers on or to lift tariff barriers from* *a product;* **differential tariffs** = different customs duties imposed on different types of goods; **General Agreement on Tariffs and Trade (GATT)** = international agreement to try to reduce restrictions in trade between countries **(b)** rate of charging for electricity, hotel rooms, train tickets, etc.; *the new winter tariff will be introduced next week*

tarmac *noun* hard surface for roads, airport runways, etc., made of tar and small stones

tarragon *noun Artemisia dracunculus,* a herb used in cooking (often used with chicken); **tarragon vinegar** = vinegar flavoured with tarragon, made by putting leaves of the plant in vinegar for a few weeks

tart 1 *noun* pastry case usually filled with sweet food, but sometimes also savoury; *jam tart; cheese tart* **2** *adjective* bitter (taste); *these apples are very tart*
◊ **tartlet** *noun* little tart

tartare *adjective* **sauce tartare** *or* **tartare sauce** = sauce made of mayonnaise and chopped pickles, served with fish; **steak tartare** = dish of raw minced steak, served mixed with raw eggs, raw onion and herbs

tartrazine *noun* yellow substance (E102) added to food to give it an attractive colour

| COMMENT: although widely used, tartrazine provokes reactions in hypersensitive people and is banned in some countries

taste 1 *noun* **(a)** sense by which you can tell differences of flavour between things you eat (using the tongue); **taste buds** = cells on the tongue which enable you to tell differences in flavour **(b)** flavour of food or drink; *the soup has no taste; the pudding has a funny taste; this wine has a taste of raspberries* **2** *verb* **(a)** to sense the flavour of (something); *the chef tastes each dish to check the sauces; would you like a piece of cheese to taste?* **(b)** to have a flavour; *this soup tastes of onions; the pudding tastes very good*

| COMMENT: the taste buds can tell the difference between salt, sour, bitter and sweet tastes. The buds on the tip of the tongue identify salt and sweet tastes, those on the sides of the tongue identify sour, and those at the back of the mouth

the bitter tastes. Note that most of what we think of as taste is in fact smell, and this is why when someone has a cold and a blocked nose, food seems to lose its taste

◊ **tasteless** *adjective* with no particular flavour

◊ **tasting** *noun* **wine tasting** = visiting a vineyard or a wine merchant's to taste wine before buying it

◊ **tasty** *adjective* with a particular pleasant flavour

tavern *noun (old name)* inn or public house

◊ **taverna** *noun* **(a)** Greek restaurant **(b)** *(in Greece)* guesthouse with bar, often also serving meals

tax 1 *noun* **(a)** money taken by the government *or* by an official body to pay for government services; **airport tax** = tax added to the price of an air ticket to cover the cost of running an airport; **corporation tax** = tax on profits made by companies; **hotel tax** = local government tax added to the basic rate for a hotel room; **land tax** = tax on the amount of land owned; **room tax** = visitor's tax levied by the local government or municipality on a visitor occupying a hotel room; **sales tax** = tax to be paid on each item sold; **turnover tax** = tax on company turnover; **value added tax (VAT)** = tax on goods and services, added as a percentage to the invoiced sales price **(b)** **ad valorem tax** = tax calculated according to the value of the goods taxed; **back tax** = tax which is owed; **basic tax** = tax paid at the normal rate; **direct tax** = tax paid directly to the government (such as income tax); **indirect tax** = tax (such as VAT) paid to someone who then pays it to the government; **to levy a tax** *or* **to impose a tax** = to demand payment of a tax; **to lift a tax** = to remove a tax; **exclusive of tax** = not including tax; **tax abatement** = reduction of tax; **tax adjustments** = changes made to tax; **tax adviser** *or* **tax consultant** = person who gives advice on tax problems; **tax allowance** *or* **allowance against tax** = part of the income which a person is allowed to earn and not pay tax on; **tax avoidance** = trying (legally) to minimize the amount of tax to be paid; **tax code** = number given to indicate the amount of tax allowances a person has; **tax concession** = allowing less tax to be paid; **tax credit** = part of a dividend on which the company has already paid tax, so that the shareholder is not taxed on it again; **tax deductions** = (i) money removed from a salary to pay tax; (ii); *US* business expenses which can be claimed against tax; **tax deducted at source** = tax which is removed from a salary or interest before the money is paid out; **tax evasion** = trying illegally not to pay tax; **tax exemption** = (i) not being required to pay tax; (ii); *US* part of income which a person is allowed to earn and not pay tax on; **tax form** = blank form to be filled in with details of income and allowances and sent to the tax office each year; **tax haven** = place where taxes are low, encouraging companies to set up their main offices there; **tax holiday** = period when a new company pays no tax; **tax inspector** *or* **inspector of taxes** = government official who examines tax returns and decides how much tax someone should pay; **tax loophole** = legal means of not paying tax; **tax relief** = allowing someone not to pay tax on certain parts of his income; **tax return** *or* **tax declaration** = completed tax form, with details of income and allowances; **tax year** = twelve-month period on which taxes are calculated (in the UK, 6th April to 5th April of the following year) **2** *verb* to make (someone) pay a tax *or* to impose a tax on (something); *to tax businesses at 50%; income is taxed at 35%; luxury items are heavily taxed*

◊ **taxable** *adjective* which can be taxed; **taxable income** = income on which a person has to pay tax; **taxable items** = things on which a tax has to be paid

◊ **tax-free** *adjective* on which tax does not have to be paid; *children's clothes are tax-free; she bought the watch tax-free at the airport*

taxi 1 *noun* car which takes people from one place to another for money (taxis have to be registered with the relevant municipal authorities); *he took a taxi to the airport; taxi fares are very high in New York; where can we get a taxi to take us to the beach?;* taxi **fare** = (i) price to be paid for a journey in a taxi; (ii) passenger in a taxi **2** *verb (of an aircraft)* to go along the ground before takeoff or after landing

◊ **taxicab** *or* **taxi cab** *noun* = TAXI

◊ **taxi driver** *noun* person who drives a taxi

◊ **taxi rank** *noun* place where taxis wait in line for customers

tea *noun* (a) drink made from the dried leaves of a plant (a form of Camellia); *a cup of tea; to make tea, you need freshly boiled water;* **early morning tea** = tea brought to a guest's bedroom early in the morning,

often with the day's newspaper and sometimes with letters; *(in Japan)* **tea ceremony** = formal serving of tea; **instant tea** = tea made from freeze-dried granules or powder, onto which boiling water is poured; **lemon tea** = black tea, served in a glass with a slice of lemon and sugar (without the lemon it is called 'Russian tea'); **Russian tea** = black tea, served in a glass (if a slice of lemon is added it is called 'lemon tea') (b) the dried leaves of a Camellia plant, used to make a drink; *buy a pound of tea; you put the tea into the pot before adding the hot water* (c) dried leaves or flowers of other plants, used to make a drink; *camomile tea; mint tea* (d) meal taken in the afternoon, usually between 4 and 5 o'clock, where tea can be drunk; *see also* CREAM TEA, HIGH TEA; **tea party** = small gathering in the afternoon where tea may be drunk

COMMENT: tea is the most common drink in Britain, although coffee is becoming almost as popular as tea. There are two main types of tea: Indian tea (black tea, usually mixed in various blends) and Chinese tea (or China tea) which is green. Chinese tea is never served with milk. In Britain, Indian tea is usually served with milk. In the USA and Canada, tea is also served with cream

◊ **teabag** *noun* small paper bag full of tea which is put into a cup, or into the pot instead of loose tea

◊ **teacake** *noun* type of bun with raisins in it, usually eaten toasted with butter

◊ **teacup** *noun* large cup for tea

◊ **teapot** *noun* special pot with a handle and spout for making tea in and for serving it

◊ **tearoom** *or* **teashop** *noun* small restaurant which serves mainly tea, cakes and light meals

◊ **teaspoon** *noun* small spoon for stirring tea

◊ **teaspoonful** *noun* amount contained in a teaspoon; *put a teaspoonful of salt into the pan*

◊ **tea strainer** *noun* small sieve, which fits over a tea cup, used to prevent tea leaves from getting into the cup

◊ **tea time** *noun* time when tea is drunk or eaten (between four and five o'clock in the afternoon)

◊ **tea trolley** *noun* table on wheels for carrying food

tel = TELEPHONE

telegram *noun* message sent by telegraph; *he went into the post office to send a telegram*

◇ **telegraph** 1 *noun* system of sending messages along wires; *to send a message by telegraph;* **telegraph office** = office where telegrams are sent and received 2 *verb* to send a message by telegraph; *to telegraph an order*

◇ **telegraphic** *adjective* referring to a telegraph system; **telegraphic address** = short address used for sending telegrams

◇ **telemessage** *noun GB* message sent by telephone, and delivered as a card

telephone 1 *noun* phone, machine used for speaking to someone; *we had a new telephone system installed last week;* **to be on the telephone** = to be speaking to someone by telephone; *the receptionist is on the telephone all the time; she has been on the telephone all day;* **by telephone** = using the telephone; *to book a plane ticket by telephone; to reserve a room by telephone;* **house telephone** *or* **internal telephone** = telephone which links different rooms in a hotel, but is not connected to an outside line; **telephone book** *or* **telephone directory** = book which lists names of people and businesses in alphabetical order with their telephone numbers and addresses; *he looked up the number of the company in the telephone book;* **telephone booking** = reservation (of a room in a hotel, a table in a restaurant, etc.) made by phone; **telephone call** = conversation with someone on the telephone; **to make a telephone call** = to dial and speak to someone on the telephone; **to answer the telephone** *or* **to take a telephone call** = to lift the telephone when it rings and listen to what the caller is saying; **telephone exchange** = central office where the telephones of a whole district are linked; **telephone link** = direct line from one telephone to another; **telephone number** = set of figures for a particular telephone subscriber; *can you give me your telephone number?;* **telephone operator** = person who works a telephone switchboard; **telephone subscriber** = person who has a telephone; **telephone switchboard** = central point in a telephone system, where all internal and external lines meet 2 *verb* **to telephone a person** *or* **a place** = to call someone *or* a place by telephone; *we telephoned the reservation through to the hotel; the travel agent telephoned to say that the tickets are ready for collection; it's very expensive to telephone Singapore at this time of day;* **to telephone about something** = to make a telephone call to speak about something; *he telephoned about the bill;* **to telephone for something** = to make a telephone call to ask for something; *he telephoned for a taxi* (NOTE: the word **telephone is often shortened to phone: phone call, phone book,** etc. but not in the expressions **telephone switchboard, telephone operator, telephone exchange**)

◇ **telephonist** *noun* person who works a telephone switchboard

teleprinter *noun* machine like a typewriter, which can send messages by telegraph and print incoming messages

television (TV) *noun* **television (set)** = apparatus for showing pictures sent by radio waves; *is there a television in the room; he stayed in his room all evening, watching television;* **cable television** = television system, where pictures are sent by cable

telex 1 *noun* **(a)** system of sending messages by teleprinter; *to send information by telex; the order came by telex;* **telex line** = wire linking a telex machine to the telex system; **telex operator** = person who operates a telex machine; **telex subscriber** = company which has a telex **(b)** (i) machine for sending and receiving telex messages; (ii) message sent by telex; *the telex has broken down; he sent a telex to his office; you can send a telex from the hotel office* 2 *verb* to send a message using a teleprinter; *can you telex the Canadian office before they open? he telexed the details of the contract to New York*

temperance *noun* not drinking alcohol; **temperance hotel** = hotel which does not serve alcohol

temperate *adjective* (climate) which is neither very hot nor very cold

temperature *noun* measurement of heat in degrees; *the temperature outside is below 30° Centigrade; what is the temperature in the sauna? the sea temperature is 18° in the summer*

tender 1 *noun* **(a)** offer to work for a certain price; *a successful tender or an unsuccessful tender;* **to put a project out to tender** *or* **to ask for** *or* **to invite tenders for a project** = to ask contractors to give written estimates for a job; **to put in a tender** *or* **to submit a tender** = to make an estimate for a job; **sealed tenders** = tenders sent in sealed envelopes which will all be opened together at a certain time **(b) legal tender** = coins or notes which can be legally used to pay a debt (small denominations cannot be used to pay large debts); *these notes are not legal tender any more* **(c)** small boat used to take passengers and cargo to a ship which is not moored alongside a quay **2** *verb* **(a) to tender for a contract** = to put forward an estimate of cost for work to be carried out under contract; *to tender for the construction of a hotel* **(b) to tender one's resignation** = to resign from one's job **3** *adjective* (food) which is easy to cut or chew; *a plate of tender young asparagus; the steak was so tender, you hardly needed a knife to cut it* (NOTE: the opposite is **tough**)

◊ **tenderer** *noun* person *or* company which offers to work for a certain price; *the company was the successful tenderer for the project*

◊ **tendering** *noun* act of putting forward an estimate of cost; *to be successful, you must follow the tendering procedure as laid out in the documents*

◊ **tenderloin** *noun* fillet of pork, cut from the backbone

tennis *noun* game for two players or two pairs of players who use rackets to hit a ball backwards and forwards over a net; *let's have a game of tennis before dinner; he plays tennis every day when he is on holiday;* **tennis ball** = ball used when playing tennis; **tennis court** = specially marked ground for playing tennis; **tennis racket** = type of bat with a long handle and a head made of mesh, used when playing tennis; **tennis shoes** = special shoes worn when playing tennis

tent *noun* canvas shelter held up by poles and attached to the ground with pegs and ropes; **to pitch a tent** = to put up a tent; **refreshment tent** = tent in which refreshments are served (as at a horse show, village fête, etc.)

term *noun* **(a)** period of time when something is legally valid; **in the long term** = over a long period of time; **long-term** = for a long period of time; **medium-term** = for a period of one or two years; **in the short term** = in the near future *or* quite soon; **short-term** = for a short period of time **(b) terms** = conditions *or* duties which have to be carried out as part of a contract *or* arrangements which have to be agreed before a contract is valid; *he refused to agree to some of the terms of the contract; by or under the terms of the contract, the company is responsible for all damage to the property;*

to negotiate for better terms; **terms of payment** *or* **payment terms** = conditions for paying something; **terms of sale** = conditions attached to a sale; **cash terms** = lower terms which apply if the customer pays cash; **'terms: cash with order'** = conditions of sale showing that payment has to be made in cash when the order is placed; **easy terms** = terms which are not difficult to accept *or* price which is easy to pay because it is spread in instalments over a period of time; *the shop is let on very easy terms; to pay for something on easy terms;* **on favourable terms** = on especially good terms; *the shop is let on very favourable terms;* **trade terms** = special discount for people in the same trade **(c)** part of a legal *or* university year **(d) terms of employment** = conditions set out in a contract of employment

terminal *noun* **(a) computer terminal** = keyboard and screen, by which information can be put into a computer or can be called up from a database; *computer system consisting of a microprocessor and six terminals* **(b) air terminal** = building in a town where passengers meet to be taken by bus or train to an airport outside the town; **airport terminal** *or* **terminal building** = main building at an airport where passengers arrive and depart; **container terminal** = area of a harbour where container ships are loaded or unloaded; **ocean terminal** = main building at a port where passengers arrive and depart

terminate *verb* to end (something) *or* to bring (something) to an end; *to terminate an agreement; his employment was terminated; the offer terminates on July 31st; the flight from Paris terminates in New York*

terminus *noun* station at the end of a railway line; point at the end of a regular route of a bus or a coach (NOTE: plural is **termini** or **terminuses**)

terrace *noun* flat paved area in the open air which is raised above other areas; *the guests had cocktails on the terrace before going into dinner;* **roof terrace** = flat paved area on the roof of a building; *there is a bar on the roof terrace of the hotel*

tertiary *adjective* **tertiary industry** = service industry, industry which does not produce or manufacture anything but offers a service (such as banking, tourism, retailing or travel); **tertiary sector** = section of the economy containing the service industries

TexMex *adjective* = TEXAN AND MEXICAN style of American cooking, based on steaks, barbecued meat and Mexican dishes such as chilli, tortillas, etc.

textured vegetable protein (TVP) *noun* substance made from processed soya beans *or* other vegetables, used as a substitute for meat

Thanksgiving *noun* American festival, celebrating the first harvest of settlers in the United States (celebrated on the fourth Thursday in November)

COMMENT: the traditional menu for Thanksgiving dinner is roast turkey, with cranberry sauce, followed by pumpkin pie)

thaw *verb* to melt something which is frozen

theatre *or* US **theater** *noun* building in which plays and shows are performed; *we'll have dinner early and then go to the theatre;* **theatre bookings** = numbers of seats in theatres which are reserved; **theatre seat** = place to see a play or a show (NOTE: in US English, **theater** is also used to refer to a building where films are shown: in GB English, this is a **cinema)**
◊ **theatregoer** *noun* person who goes to the theatre

theft *noun* stealing; *we have brought in security guards to protect the hotel against theft; they are trying to cut their losses from theft by members of staff; to take out insurance against theft*

theme *noun* single subject of book, article, etc.; **theme park** = amusement park based on a single theme (such as Disneyland, a medieval castle, etc.)

therapy *noun* treatment of illness
◊ **therapeutic** *adjective* (treatment *or* drug) which is given in order to cure a disorder *or* disease

thermal *adjective* referring to heat; **thermal baths** = baths of naturally hot water;

thermal resort *or* **thermal spa** = place where people go for treatment using naturally hot water or mud; **thermal spring** = spring of naturally hot water coming out of the ground

thermometer *noun* instrument for measuring temperature; **thermometer reading** = the figure for the temperature given on a thermometer; *it's a cold morning - the thermometer reading was -25° at 6 a.m.*

Thermos (flask) *noun* trademark for a type of vacuum flask which will keep a liquid hot or cool; *we took thermoses of hot coffee to drink when we went cross-country skiing*

third party *noun* any person other than the two main parties involved in a contract; **third-party insurance** = insurance which covers injury to or death of any person who is not one of the people named in the insurance contract
◊ **Third World** *noun* countries of Africa, Asia and South America which do not all have highly developed industries

thirsty *adjective* wanting to drink; *running around on the beach makes me thirsty*

Thousand Island dressing *noun* type of salad dressing made with mayonnaise and chopped pimento, with chilli sauce, ketchup and paprika

throng 1 *noun* great crowd of people; *throngs of Christmas shoppers* **2** *verb* to crowd together; *crowds thronged the streets during the fiesta*

through *adjective* (carriage, passenger, etc.) going to the final terminus; **through ticket** = ticket which allows you to travel to your final destination (even though you may change trains, etc. en route)
◊ **throughway** *or* **thruway** *noun* US main road with few entrances and exits (NOTE: GB English is **motorway)**

thumb *verb* **to thumb a lift** = to ask a car driver or truck driver to take you as a passenger, usually by signalling with the thumb or by holding a sign with your destination written on it

thunder *noun* loud sound generated by lightning in the atmosphere; *a tropical storm accompanied by thunder and lightning*

◊ **thunderstorm** *noun* storm with rain, thunder and lightning

thyme *noun* **common (French) thyme** = *Thymus vulgaris,* herb used to flavour various dishes (meat, soup, pâté, etc.); **lemon thyme** = *Thymus citriodorus,* variety of thyme which smells of lemon

tick 1 *noun* **(a)** *(informal)* credit; *all the furniture in the house is bought on tick* **(b)** mark on paper to show that something is correct *or* that something is approved; *if you want a receipt, put a tick in the box marked 'R'* (NOTE: US English for this is **check) 2** *verb* to mark with a sign to show that something is correct; *tick the box marked 'R' if you require a receipt*

ticket 1 *noun* **(a)** piece of paper *or* card which allows you to do something; **entrance ticket** *or* **admission ticket** = ticket which allows you to go in; **cinema ticket** = ticket which allows you a seat in a cinema; **theatre ticket** = ticket which allows you a seat in a theatre; *there are no tickets left for the concert* **(b)** piece of paper *or* card which allows you to travel; *train ticket or bus ticket or plane ticket;* **season ticket** = rail *or* bus ticket which can be used for any number of journeys over a period (usually one, three, six or twelve months); **single ticket** *or* US **one-way ticket** = ticket for one journey from one place to another; **return ticket** *or* US **round-trip ticket** = ticket for a journey from one place to another and back again **(c) ticket agency** = shop which sells theatre tickets; **ticket booth** = small cabin out of doors where entrance tickets, theatre tickets, bus tickets, etc. are sold; **ticket collector** = person at a railway station who takes the tickets from passengers as they get off the train; **ticket counter** = place where tickets are sold; **ticket office** = office where tickets can be bought (either for travel or for theatres or other places of entertainment) **(d)** paper which shows something; **baggage ticket** = paper showing that you have left a piece of baggage with someone; **cloakroom ticket** = ticket to show that you have left your coat, hat, etc. in the cloakroom of a restaurant, museum, theatre, etc.; **parking ticket** = paper showing that you have parked illegally and must pay a fine; **price ticket** = label showing a price **2** *verb* to issue tickets; *the new ticketing system has been operative since June 1st*

tide *noun* regular rising and falling of the sea, in a twice-daily rhythm; **high tide** *or* **low tide** = points when the level of the sea is at its highest *or* at its lowest; **neap tide** = tide which occurs at the first and last quarters of the moon, when the difference between high and low water is less than normal; **spring tide** = tide which occurs at the new and full moon when the influence of the sun and moon act together and the difference between high and low water is more than normal; **tide tables** = lists which show exactly when high and low tide is at certain points on the coast

◊ **tidal** *adjective* referring to the tide; **tidal stretch of the river** = part of the river near its mouth where the movement of the tides is noticeable

tie 1 *noun* band of cloth which is worn knotted round the neck under the shirt collar; *you have to wear a jacket and tie to get into the restaurant;* **black tie** *or* **white tie** = referring to a formal evening banquet or reception at which men wear either a bow tie and dinner jacket (both usually black) or a white bow tie and black tail coat; *the invitation to the gala performance was marked 'black tie'* **2** *verb* to attach *or* to fasten (with string, wire, etc.); *he tied the parcel with thick string; she tied two labels onto the parcel; (of a boat)* **to tie up** = to be attached by a rope to the quay; *GB* **tied house** = pub which belongs to a brewery and is let to a tenant landlord who is obliged to buy his beer from the brewery NOTE: **ties - tying - tied**

◊ **tie-on label** *noun* label with a piece of string attached so that it can be tied onto an item

tiger prawn *noun* very large type of prawn

tight *adjective* which fits (too) closely; *my shoes hurt - they're too tight; a biscuit tin should have a tight-fitting lid*

time *noun* **(a)** period when something takes place (such as one hour, two days, fifty minutes, etc.); **time and motion study** = examining how long it takes in a place of work to do certain jobs and the movements workers have to make to do them; **time and motion expert** = person who analyses time and motion studies and suggests changes in the way work is done **(b)** hour of the day (such as 9.00, 12.15, ten o'clock at night, etc.); *the time of arrival or the arrival time is indicated on the screen; departure times are delayed by up to fifteen minutes because of the volume of traffic;* **on time** = at the right time; *the plane was on time; you will have to* *hurry if you want to get to the meeting on time or if you want to be on time for the meeting;* **opening time** *or* **closing time** = time when a shop or office starts or stops work, when a pub opens or closes **(c)** system of hours on the clock; **Summer Time** *or* **Daylight Saving Time** = system of putting the clocks forward one hour in summer to provide extra daylight in the evening; **Standard Time** = normal local time; **time difference** = difference in time between one time zone and another; *there is two hours time difference between Moscow and London;* **time zone** = one of 24 areas in the world in which the same standard time is used (the time zones are divided by meridians roughly every 15°, i.e. every hour) **(d)** hours worked; **the restaurant staff are paid time and a half on Sundays** = they are paid the normal rate plus 50% extra when they work on Sundays; **full-time** = working for the whole normal working day (i.e. about eight hours a day, five days a week); **overtime** = hours worked more than the normal working day; **part-time** = not working for a whole working day **(e)** period before something happens; **delivery time** = number of days before something will be delivered; **lead time** = time between placing an order and receiving the goods; **time limit** = period during which something should be done; **to keep within the time limits** *or* **within the time schedule** = to complete work by the time stated

◊ **time share** *noun* arrangement where a share in the same flat or house is sold to several people, each having the right to stay in it for a certain period each year; *they bought a time-share apartment in Spain*

◊ **timetable 1** *noun* **(a)** list showing times of arrivals and departures of buses or trains or planes, etc.; *according to the timetable, there should be a train to London at 10.22; the bus company has brought out its winter timetable* **(b)** list of appointments *or* events; *the manager has a very full timetable, so I doubt if he will be able to see you today;* **conference timetable** = list of speakers *or* events at a conference **2** *verb* to make a list of times; *you are timetabled to speak at 4.30*

tin *noun* metal container for food or drink, made of steel with a lining of tin or made entirely of aluminium; **biscuit tin** = tin with a tight-fitting lid for keeping biscuits in; **cake tin** = tin for baking or keeping cakes in (NOTE: US English is **can**)

◊ **tinfoil** *noun* thin metal sheet used especially to wrap food up

◊ **tin-opener** *noun* device for opening tins (NOTE: US English is **can-opener**)

tip 1 *noun* **(a)** money given to someone who has helped you; *I gave the cab driver a 50-cent tip; the staff are not allowed to accept tips* **(b)** advice on something to buy *or* to do which could be profitable; *he gave me a tip about a cheap restaurant just round the corner from the hotel* **2** *verb* to give money to someone who has helped you; *he tipped the receptionist £5* NOTE: **tipping - tipped**

◊ **tipping** *noun* giving money to someone who has helped you; *tipping is not allowed in Singapore*

TIR = TRANSPORTS INTERNATIONAUX ROUTIERS

tiramisu *noun* Italian dessert of sponge cake soaked in marsala wine and topped with cream

tisane *French noun* drink made by pouring boiling water on dried or fresh leaves or flowers (such as lime tea *or* camomile tea)

tissue *noun* soft paper handkerchief; *there is a box of tissues beside the bed*

toad-in-the-hole *noun* English dish of sausages cooked in a dish of batter

toast 1 *noun* **(a)** slice of bread which has been grilled; *you have toast and marmalade for breakfast; she asked for scrambled eggs on toast;* **brown toast** *or* **white toast** = toast made from brown bread *or* white bread; **French toast** = slice of bread, dipped in beaten egg and fried, usually served with syrup or sprinkled with sugar; **melba toast** = toast made by grilling a slice of bread once, then slicing it in half and grilling it again quickly, so as to produce a sort of cracker **(b)** act of drinking to someone's health or success; *I'll give you a toast - the bride and groom!;* **loyal toast** = toast to the Queen, at the end of a banquet **2** *verb* **(a)** to grill (bread, etc.) until it is brown; *we had a pot of tea and toasted teacakes* **(b)** to drink to wish someone health or success

COMMENT: the loyal toast is drunk before coffee is served, and after it, guests are allowed to smoke. The loyal toast comes before speeches and other toasts. During the time when toasts are being called and speeches made, waiters make sure that guests' glasses are filled

◊ **toaster** *noun* electric device for toasting bread

◊ **toastmaster** *noun* person (at a banquet) who announces the toasts and calls on people to speak

◊ **toast-rack** *noun* device for holding slices of toast upright on the breakfast table

toboggan 1 *noun* long flat wooden sledge curved upwards at the front **2** *verb* to slide on a toboggan

◊ **tobogganing** *noun* sport of sliding on a toboggan

toilet *noun* **(a)** bowl with a seat on which you sit to pass waste matter from the body; **chemical toilet** = toilet where the waste matter is decomposed by chemicals; **flush toilet** = toilet where the waste matter is removed by a rush of water; **toilet bowl** *or* **toilet pan** = china basin of a toilet; **toilet paper** *or* **toilet tissue** = paper for wiping yourself after getting rid of waste matter; **toilet paper dispenser** *or* **toilet paper holder** = bracket or box, usually fixed to the wall, which holds toilet paper; **toilet roll** = roll of soft paper in a toilet, used for wiping yourself after getting rid of waste matter; **toilet seat** = plastic or wooden part of a toilet on which you sit **(b)** room with this bowl in it; *the toilets are towards the rear of the plane; the gents toilets are downstairs and to the right*

◊ **toiletries** *plural noun* soap, cream, perfume, etc., used in washing the body

token *noun* **(a)** thing which acts as a sign *or* symbol; **token charge** = small charge which does not cover the real costs; *a token charge is made for heating;* **token payment** = small payment which does not cover the real costs **(b)** **book token** *or* **flower token** *or* **gift token** *or* **record token** = card bought in a store which is given as a present and which must be exchanged in that store for goods; *we gave her a gift token for her birthday*

toll *noun* payment for using a service (usually a bridge or a ferry); *we had to cross a toll bridge to get to the island; you have to pay a toll to cross the bridge*

◊ **toll call** *noun* *US* long-distance telephone call

◊ **toll-free 1** *adjective* *US* **toll-free telephone** = system where one can telephone to reply to an advertisement *or* to place an order *or* to ask for information and the seller pays for the call; *a toll-free number* **2** *adverb* *US* without having to pay

a charge for a long-distance telephone call; *to call someone toll-free*

◊ **tollway** *noun* *US* motorway on which you pay a toll (NOTE: also called a **turnpike)**

tomato *noun* red fruit growing on annual plants, *Lycopersicon esculentum,* an important food crop (the ripe fruit are used in salads and many cooked dishes; also pressed to make juice and sauces); *a glass of tomato juice;* **tomato sauce** = sauce made with tomatoes

ton *noun* measure of weight; *GB* **long ton** = measure of weight (= 1016 kilos); *US* **short ton** = measure of weight (= 907 kilos); **metric ton** = 1,000 kilos

◊ **tonne** *noun* metric ton, 1,000 kilos

◊ **tonnage** *noun* space for cargo in a ship, measured in tons; **gross tonnage** = amount of total space in a ship; **deadweight tonnage** = largest amount of cargo which a ship can carry safely

tone *noun* noise made by a machine; *please speak after the tone;* **dialling tone** = noise made by a telephone to show that it is ready for you to dial a number

tongue *noun* piece of movable flesh in an animal's mouth

COMMENT: tongue is used as food, ox tongue and lamb's tongue being the most common. It is available ready-cooked to be eaten sliced in salad or sandwiches

tonic (water) *noun* fizzy drink of water and sugar, containing quinine; **gin and tonic** = drink of gin with tonic water

toothbrush *noun* small brush with a long handle used for cleaning the teeth

◊ **toothpaste** *noun* paste used with a toothbrush for cleaning the teeth

◊ **toothpick** *noun* small pointed piece of wood or plastic for pushing between the teeth to remove pieces of food

◊ **toothsome** *adjective* good to eat

top *noun* **(a)** upper surface; *we climbed to the top of the cathedral tower; you can see three countries from the top of the mountain; there is a roof garden on top of the hotel* **(b)** lid; *make sure the top is screwed back tightly onto the jar* **(c)** *US* roof (of a car)

◊ **top floor** *noun* floor nearest the roof in a building; *the lift doesn't go to the top floor*

tot *noun* small glass of spirits such as rum

total 1 *adjective* complete *or* with everything added together; *total amount; total assets; total cost; total expenditure; total income; total output; total revenue;* **the car was written off as a total loss** = the car was so badly damaged that the insurers said it had no value **2** *noun* amount which is complete *or* with everything added up; *the total of the charges comes to more than £1,000;* **grand total** = final total made by adding several subtotals **3** *verb* to add up to; *costs totalling more than £25,000* NOTE: GB English is **totalling - totalled** but US English **totaling - totaled**

touch down *verb (of plane)* to land

◊ **touchdown** *noun* landing of a plane; *touchdown was 15 minutes late*

tough *adjective* difficult to chew or to cut; *(informal)* **it's as tough as old boots** = extremely tough (NOTE: **tough - tougher - toughest.** Note also that the opposite is **tender)**

tour 1 *noun* (holiday) journey to various places, coming back in the end to the place the journey started from; *the group went on a tour of Italy; the minister went on a fact-finding tour of the region;* **conducted tour** *or* **guided tour** = tour with a guide who shows places to the tourists; **package tour** = holiday *or* tour where the travel, the accommodation and sometimes meals are all included in the price and paid for in advance; *the travel company is arranging a package tour to the international computer exhibition;* **tour leader** = person who leads a tour and organizes it locally; **tour operator** = person *or* company which organizes and sells tours **2** *verb* to visit various places; *we spent the holiday touring around Wales*

◊ **tourism** *noun* business of providing travel, accommodation, food, entertainment, etc., for tourists

◊ **tourist** *noun* person who goes on holiday to visit places away from his home; **tourist board** = official organization which promotes tourism in a certain part of the world; *the English Tourist Board;* **tourist bureau** *or* **tourist information office** *or* **tourist information centre** = office which gives information to tourists; **tourist bus** *or* **tourist coach** = bus carrying tourists, visiting various places of interest; **tourist class** = cheapest category of seat on a plane; *he always travels first class, because he says tourist class is too uncomfortable;* **tourist class hotel** = hotel which provides quite basic accommodation at cheaper prices;

tourist guide = person who shows tourists round a site or house; **tourist trade** = the business of tourism; business connected with tourists; *tourist trade has fallen off sharply because of the recession;* **tourist visa** = visa which allows a person to visit a country for a short time on holiday; **off the tourist track** = not in a place which is normally visited by many tourists

tournant *French adjective (meaning 'turning')* **chef tournant** = chef who is available to work in any of the sections of a kitchen, helping out when other chefs are ill or on holiday

tournedos *noun* thick round piece of fillet steak

tow *verb* to pull another vehicle; *the motorways were jammed with cars towing caravans*

towel *noun* piece of soft absorbent cloth for drying; *there are piles of towels in the bathroom;* **bath towel** = very large towel for drying yourself after a bath; **face towel** *or* **hand towel** = small towel for drying the hands and face; **paper towel** = absorbent paper used for drying the hands, wiping spilled liquids, etc.; *there is a paper towel dispenser in the bathroom;* **towel rail** = bar of metal or wood in a bathroom on which you can hang a towel; **heated towel rail** = towel rail which is heated, and so keeps towels warm and dry

town *noun* place where people live and work, with houses, shops, offices and factories (as opposed to the country); **town centre** = central part of a town, where main shops, banks and places of interest are situated (NOTE: this is called **downtown** in American English) **town crier** = man formerly employed to make public announcements in the street by ringing a bell and shouting in a loud voice (town criers still exist in some English towns); **town guide** = (i) guidebook with descriptions of the history of a town and what to visit; (ii) person who shows tourists round a town; **town hall** = building in the centre of a town where the town council meets and where the town's administrative offices are; **town plan** *or* **town map** = diagram showing the streets of a town with their names; **cathedral town** = a city which has a cathedral; **market town** = town which has a regular market; **seaside town** = town by the sea

◊ **townhouse hotel** *noun* small privately-owned luxury hotel (usually with less than 50 rooms) situated in the middle of a town

track *noun* (**a**) path; *they followed a track through the jungle;* **off the beaten track** = in a place which is not normally visited by many people; **off the tourist track** = not in a place which is normally visited by many tourists (**b**) line of rails; **single-track railway** = railway line on which trains go up and down the same rails with passing places at intervals

trade *noun* (**a**) business of buying and selling; **trade fair** = large exhibition and meeting for advertising and selling a certain type of product; *there were two trade fairs running in London at the same time* (**b**) business done; **passing trade** = customers who walk or drive past a restaurant or hotel, and decide to stop and eat or stay the night, without having booked (as opposed to regular customers)

◊ **trade union** *or* **trades union** *noun* organization which represents workers who are its members in discussions with employers about wages and conditions of employment; *the staff are all members of a trades union or they are trade union members; he has applied for trade union membership or he has applied to join a trades union;* Trades Union Congress = organization linking all British trade unions (NOTE: although **Trades Union Congress** is the official name for the organization, **trade union** is commoner than **trades union** in GB English. US English is **labor union**)

tradition *noun* customs or habits or stories passed from generation to generation

◊ **traditional** *adjective* following tradition; *on Easter Day it is traditional to give chocolate eggs; villagers still wear the traditional costumes on Sundays*

◊ **traditionally** *adverb* following tradition; *chocolate eggs are traditionally eaten on Easter Day*

traffic *noun* (**a**) (i) cars, trucks, etc., which are moving; (ii) movement of cars, trucks, trains, planes; movement of people *or* goods in vehicles; *there is an increase in commuter traffic or goods traffic on the motorway; passenger traffic on the commuter lines has decreased during the summer; US* **traffic circle** = roundabout; **air-traffic controller** = person who organizes the movement of aircraft in the air; **traffic jam** = situation where there is so much traffic on the road that it moves only very slowly; *traffic jams are common in the rush hour;* **traffic lights** = red, amber and green lights on a pole by a road, telling traffic when to stop or go; *don't cross the street when the traffic lights are red;* **traffic policeman** *or* **traffic cop** = policeman who directs traffic or who rides a motorcycle to supervise traffic; **traffic warden** = uniformed official who gives parking tickets to cars which are parked illegally (**b**) illegal trade; *drugs traffic or traffic in drugs* (**c**) trade; **traffic sheets** = lists showing daily sales

trail *noun* path *or* track; *a long-distance ski trail;* **mountain trail** = path through mountains; **nature trail** = path through a park *or* the countryside with signs to draw attention to important and interesting features, such as plants, trees, birds or animals

trailer *noun* (**a**) *GB* small vehicle like a box on wheels, which is towed behind a car, and which can be used for carrying luggage, camping equipment, etc.; **camping trailer** = vehicle which is towed behind a car and which unfolds to form a tent (**b**) *US* caravan

train 1 *noun* set of coaches *or* wagons pulled by an engine along railway lines; *to take the 09.30 train to London; he caught his train or he missed his train; to ship goods by train;* **freight train** *or* **goods train** = train used for carrying freight; **passenger train** = train which carries passengers only; **train timetable** = train timetable, a list showing times of arrivals and departures of trains **2** *verb* to teach (someone) to do something; to learn how to do something; *the tour will be accompanied by a trained nurse; he trained as a scuba-diving instructor*

◊ **trainee** *noun* person who is learning how to do something; *we employ trainee waiters to help in the restaurant at peak periods; graduate trainees come to work in the head office when they have finished their courses at university;* **management trainee** = person being trained to be a manager

◊ **traineeship** *noun* post of trainee

◊ **training** *noun* being taught how to do something; *during training, students work in a restaurant for three days a week; there is a ten-week training period for new staff;* **industrial training** = training of new workers to work in an industry; **management training** = training staff to be managers, by making them study problems and work out ways of solving them; **off-the-job training** = training given to workers away from their place of work (such as at a college or school); **on-the-job training** = training given to workers at their place of work; **staff training** = teaching staff better and more profitable ways of working; *the shop is closed for staff training;* **training course** = series of lessons to teach someone how to do something; **training levy** = tax to be paid by companies to fund the government's training schemes; **training officer** = person in a company who deals with the training of staff; **training unit** = special group of teachers who organize training for companies

traiteur *French noun (meaning 'outside caterer')* **chef traiteur** = chef in charge of outside functions (buffets or meals which are prepared in the kitchen, but served in a different venue)

tram *noun* form of public transport, consisting of carriages running on rails laid in the street (NOTE: US English is **streetcar**)
◊ **tramcar** *noun* single carriage of a tram
◊ **tramlines** *plural noun* rails along which a tram runs
◊ **tramway** *noun* rails, etc., on which a tram runs

> COMMENT: although common in European countries (Germany, Switzerland, and Scandinavia, for example), trams are now rare in British towns, though some new tram systems have recently been installed (as in Manchester). In the USA, the best-known streetcar system is in San Francisco

trancheur *French noun (meaning 'carver')* the person in the kitchen who cuts meat

tranquillizer *or* *US* **tranquilliser** *noun* drug which makes a person calm

transatlantic *adjective* across the Atlantic; *the fastest transatlantic crossing is by Concorde*

transfer 1 *noun* **(a)** passing from one place to another; *included in the price are transfers from airport to hotel;* **transfer coach** = coach which takes travellers from the airport to their hotel; **hotel transfer** = transport from an airport or railway station to a hotel **(b)** moving from one form of transport to another; **transfer passengers** = travellers who are changing from one aircraft *or* train *or* bus to another, or to another form of transport **(c)** piece of paper taken from a machine or given by a ticket collector, allowing a passenger on one form of transport to change to another (as from a bus to the Metro) **2** *verb* **(a)** to pass from one place to another; *on arrival at the station, the party will transfer to a coach for the rest of the journey to the hotel* **(b)** **transferred-charge call** = phone call where the person receiving the call agrees to pay for it

transformer *noun* device for changing the voltage of electric current (to use European electrical appliances in the USA, a transformer is necessary to change from 240V to 110V: some appliances have built-in transformers); *see also* ADAPTOR

transient 1 *adjective* which does not last or stay a long time **2** *noun* person who stays in a hotel or boarding house for a short time

transit *noun* movement of passengers *or* goods on the way to a destination; *to pay compensation for damage suffered in transit or for loss in transit; some of the party's luggage was lost in transit;* **goods in transit** = goods being transported from warehouse to customer; **transit lounge** = room in an airport where passengers wait for connecting flights; **transit passengers** = travellers who are changing from one aircraft to another; **transit visa** *or* **transit permit** = document which allows someone to spend a short time in one country while travelling to another country

translate *verb* to put something which is said *or* written in one language into another language; *he asked his secretary to translate the letter from the German agent; we have had the brochure translated from French into Japanese; the guide will translate the instructions for you*
◊ **translation** *noun* **(a)** putting something which is said *or* written in one language into another language; **translation bureau** = office which translates documents for companies **(b)** text which has been translated; *the translation of the fire instructions was not correct*
◊ **translator** *noun* person who translates

transmission *noun* part of the mechanism of a vehicles which passes the power from the engine to the wheels

transport 1 *noun* moving of goods or people from one place to another; *air transport or transport by air; rail transport or transport by rail; road transport or transport by road; passenger transport or the transport of passengers; the passenger transport services of British Rail; what means of transport will you use to get to the museum?;* the visitors will be using public transport *or* private transport = the visitors will be coming by bus *or* train, etc., or in their own cars, etc.; **public transport system** = system of trains, buses, etc., used by the general public; **transport café** = restaurant where truck-drivers eat **2** *verb* to move goods *or* people from one place to another in a vehicle; *the company transports millions of tons of goods by rail each year; the visitors will be transported to the factory by air or by helicopter or by taxi*

◊ **transportation** *noun* **(a)** moving goods *or* people from one place to another in a vehicle **(b)** vehicles used to move goods *or* people from one place to another; *the company will provide transportation to the airport;* **ground transportation** = buses, taxis, etc., available to take passengers from an airport to the town

◊ **Transports Internationaux Routiers (TIR)** *French noun* system with international documents which allows dutiable goods to cross several European countries by road without paying duty until they reach their final destination

trash-can *noun US* dustbin

travel 1 *noun* moving of people from one place to another *or* from one country to another; *business travel is a very important part of our overhead expenditure;* **travel agency** = office which arranges travel and accommodation for customers; **travel agent** = person *or* company which arranges travel and hotel accommodation for customers; *the tour was arranged by our local travel agent; see your travel agent for details of our tours to Spain;* **travel allowance** = money which an employee is allowed to spend on travelling; **the travel business** *see* BUSINESS; **travel data** = information about travel, which is available on computer; **travel document** = passport or visa which a person must have to be able to travel between countries; **travel insurance** = insurance taken out by a traveller against accident, loss of luggage, illness, etc.; **travel literature** = magazines, leaflets, etc., which gives information about travel; **travel magazine** = magazine with articles on holidays and travel; **travel sickness** =

sickness caused by the movement of a car, aircraft, bus or train, etc.; **travel sickness pills** = tablets taken to prevent travel sickness; **the travel trade** = all businesses which organize travel for people **2** *verb* **(a)** to move from one place to another *or* from one country to another; *he travels to the States on business twice a year; in her new job, she has to travel abroad at least ten times a year* **(b)** to go from one place to another, showing a company's goods to buyers and taking orders from them; *he travels in the north of the country for an pharmaceutical company*

NOTE: GB English is **travelling - travelled** but US is **traveling - traveled**

◊ **travelator** *noun* type of moving carpet, which you stand on to be taken from one place to another on the same level (NOTE: an **escalator** is a similar machine which takes you up or down)

◊ **traveller** *or US* **traveler** *noun* **(a)** person who travels; **business traveller** = person who travels on business; **leisure traveller** = person who is travelling on holiday and not on business; **traveller's cheques** *or US* **traveler's checks** = cheques taken by a traveller which can be cashed in a foreign country; **dollar traveler's check** *or* **sterling traveller's cheque** = cheque in dollars or pounds sterling; **travellers' diarrhoea** = diarrhoea caused by eating unwashed vegetables or fruit, or drinking unboiled water, contracted by travellers **(b)** **commercial traveller** = salesman who travels round an area visiting customers on behalf of his company

◊ **travelling** *or US* **traveling** *noun* **travelling expenses** = money spent on travelling and hotels for business purposes

tray *noun* **(a)** flat board for carrying glasses or cups and saucers, etc.; *he had his lunch on a tray in his bedroom; she bumped into a waiter carrying a tray of glasses; the waiter brought round a tray of sandwiches and coffee* **(b)** **filing tray** = container kept on a desk for documents which have to be filed; **in tray** = container for letters *or* memos which have been received and are waiting to be dealt with; **out tray** = container for letters *or* memos which have been dealt with and are ready to be sent out; **pending tray** = container for papers which cannot be dealt with immediately

treacle *noun* **(a)** thick dark-brown syrup produced when sugar is refined and used to make treacle toffee (NOTE: US English is **molasses) (b) treacle pudding** *or* **treacle tart**

= pudding or tart made with golden syrup (not with treacle)

> QUOTE syrup and treacle are both solutions of invert sugar in water, uncrystallized by-products of sugar refining. They contain approximately equal proportions of dextrose and fructose
> *Sunday Times*

trek 1 *noun* long and difficult journey **2** *verb* to make a long and difficult journey; *see also* PONY-TREKKING

trestle *noun* pair of folding legs which can be used to hold up a table; **trestle table =** table made of planks resting on folding legs

trifle *noun* **sherry trifle =** cold dessert made of cake covered with jam and fruit, soaked in sherry and then covered with custard sauce, whipped cream, candied fruit and nuts

trim 1 *noun* **(a)** cutting something short to make it tidy; *he went to the barber's for a trim; can you give my beard a trim, please?* **(b)** decoration (on a car) **2** *verb* **(a)** to cut (something) short to make it tidy; *ask the hairdresser to trim your beard* **(b)** to cut back; to reduce; *they have trimmed their staff to the absolute minimum* **(c)** to ornament or to decorate

trip *noun* journey; **have a good trip! =** I hope you are going to enjoy your journey and that there are no problems or hold-ups; **business trip =** journey to discuss business matters with clients; **coach trip =** excursion by coach; **day trip =** tour *or* excursion which leaves in the morning and returns the same evening
◊ **tripper** *noun* person who goes on a journey, especially a day's excursion by coach *or* train; **day trippers =** people who are on a day trip

tripe *noun* part of a cow's stomach used as food

> COMMENT: tripe is sold bleached and boiled; the best quality tripe is that called 'honeycomb tripe'; it can be eaten cold or stewed with onions

triple *adjective* three times; **triple occupancy =** three people sharing one hotel room

trocken *German adjective* (wine) which is dry

trolley *noun* **(a)** basket on wheels for carrying shopping, luggage, etc.; **luggage trolley =** trolley at an airport, railway station, ferry terminal, etc. on which passengers can put their luggage; **supermarket trolley =** trolley used in a supermarket to carry purchases (NOTE: US English is **shopping cart) (b)** table on wheels for carrying food; **bar trolley** *or* **drinks trolley =** trolley on an aircraft, with various drinks which are served by stewards or stewardesses; **hors d'oeuvre trolley =** trolley with various hors d'oeuvres, from which the guest can choose; **liqueur trolley =** trolley brought to the table at the end of a meal, with liqueurs, brandy, cigars, etc.; **sweet trolley** *or* **dessert trolley =** table on wheels on which desserts are taken to each table in a restaurant; *would you like a sweet from the trolley?*
◊ **trolleybus** *noun* bus which works on electricity taken from overhead wires by contact poles

tronc *French noun* system where all tips from customers are put into a common pool, and then shared out among the staff at the end of the day

tropic *noun* **(a) Tropic of Cancer =** parallel running round the earth at latitude 23°28N; **Tropic of Capricorn =** parallel running round the earth at latitude 23°28S **(b) the tropics =** region between the Tropic of Cancer and the Tropic of Capricorn, tropical countries, the hot areas of the world; *he lives in the tropics; yellow fever is endemic in parts of the tropics*
◊ **tropical** *adjective* referring to the tropics; *you will need a mosquito net to keep off the tropical insects;* **tropical disease =** disease which is found in tropical countries, such as malaria, dengue, Lassa fever; **tropical medicine =** branch of medicine which deals with tropical diseases; **tropical storm =** violent storm occurring in the tropics

trotter *noun* pig's foot cooked for food

trouble 1 *noun* problem, a difficult situation; *he's having trouble with his engine; the plane seems to have engine trouble* **2** *verb* to create problems for (someone); to bother (someone); *can I trouble you for a light?*

trousers *noun* **(pair of) trousers =** outer clothes which cover the legs and the lower part of the body; **trouser press =** device for pressing trousers, with two boards which clamp down on the trousers to remove creases (sometimes heated electrically); *every room in the hotel has an electric trouser press*

trout *noun* type of edible freshwater fish; **salmon trout** = large sea trout with pink flesh like that of a salmon; *grilled trout with almonds*

truck *noun* large vehicle used to transport goods; **truck driver** = person who drives a truck (NOTE: GB English also uses **lorry)**

trunk *noun* large case for carrying luggage, especially by sea or rail; **cabin trunk** = trunk for taking on board a ship
◊ **trunk call** *noun* telephone call to a number in a different zone or area
◊ **trunks** *plural noun* (swimming) **trunks** = shorts worn by a man when swimming

tsatsiki *noun* Greek dish of cucumber, mint and yoghurt

tub *noun US* large container filled with water to wash the whole body in (NOTE: GB English is **bath)**

tube *noun* (a) long pipe for carrying liquids or gas; *a tube of toothpaste* (b) *(in London)* **the Tube** = the underground (c) *(in Australia)* can (of beer)

tulip glass *noun* tall narrow wineglass on a stem, used for serving champagne

tumbler *noun* glass with a flat base and straight sides, used for serving water, etc.

tun *noun* large barrel (for wine or beer)

tuna *noun* large edible sea fish with dark pink flesh (NOTE: plural is **tuna)**

COMMENT: fresh tuna is available in some countries, but in Britain is most easily available in tins. Tuna is often used in salads

tunnel *noun* long hole in the ground; *the road round the lake goes through six tunnels; the tunnel through the Alps is over 30km long;* **Channel Tunnel** = tunnel for trains under the English Channel, linking England and France (also called the Chunnel)

turbot *noun* large flat edible white sea fish (NOTE: plural is **turbot)**

turbulence *noun* disturbance in the air causing an aircraft to rock suddenly

tureen *noun* large serving dish for soup

turkey *noun Meleagris gallopavo,* a large poultry bird raised for meat; *we're having roast turkey for Christmas dinner*

COMMENT: turkey is traditionally eaten at Christmas, with chestnut stuffing; it is also eaten in the US for Thanksgiving dinner

Turkish *adjective* referring to Turkey; **Turkish coffee** = coffee heated with sugar and water (NOTE: also called **Greek coffee)** **Turkish delight** = very sweet jelly, flavoured with essences of flowers, sometimes with nuts added, sprinkled with powdered sugar

turmeric *noun* yellow spice, used especially in pickles and curries

turn 1 *noun* (a) movement in a circle *or* change of direction; *there's a sharp left turn about 250 metres further on;* the meat is done to a turn = properly cooked all through (b) performance in a cabaret **2** *verb* to change direction *or* to go round in a circle; *turn left at the traffic lights*
◊ **turning** *noun* point where a road leaves another road; *take the second turning on the right*
◊ **turnkey operation** *noun* deal where a company takes all responsibility for constructing, fitting and staffing a building (such as a hotel) so that it is completely ready for the purchaser to take over
◊ **turnout** *noun US* place at the side of a road where vehicles can park (NOTE: GB English is **layby)**
◊ **turnover** *noun* (a) *GB* amount of sales of goods or services by an organization; *the restaurant's turnover has increased by 23.5%; we based our calculations on the forecast turnover* (NOTE: the US equivalent is **sales volume)** gross turnover = total turnover including discounts, VAT charged, etc.; **net turnover** = turnover before VAT and after trade discounts have been deducted (b) pastry folded over a sweet filling, and baked or fried; *apple turnover*
◊ **turnpike** *noun US* motorway with tolls (NOTE: also called **tollway)**
◊ **turnround** *or US* **turnaround** *noun* (i) action of unloading passengers and cargo from a ship or aircraft, cleaning, refuelling

and reloading for the next trip; (ii) the time taken to do this; *poor turnround time of aircraft can affect schedules*

◊ **turnstile** *noun* gate which turns round on a pivot, allowing only one person to go through at a time; *more than three thousand people went through the turnstiles in an hour*

turnip *noun* common vegetable, with a round white root, used mainly in soups and stews

| COMMENT: boiled turnips or 'neaps' are the traditional accompaniment to Scottish haggis

tutti frutti *noun* Italian ice cream with pieces of preserved fruit in it

TV *noun* **(a)** television; **cable TV** = television system, where pictures are sent by cables; **satellite TV** = television system, where pictures are sent via space satellites **(b)** television set; *there is a colour TV in each room;* **TV lounge** = room in a hotel, college, hospital, etc. where residents can watch TV

TVP = TEXTURED VEGETABLE PROTEIN

twin *verb* **to twin a town with another town** = to arrange a special relationship between a town in one country and a similar town in another country; *Richmond is twinned with Fontainebleau*

◊ **twinning** *noun* special arrangement between a town in one country and one of similar size or situation in another country; *the district council's town-twinning committee decided that Epping should be twinned with Eppingen in West Germany*

◊ **twin beds** *plural noun* two single beds placed in a bedroom; **twin-bedded room** = room with twin beds

two-sink system *noun* system for washing dishes by hand, with two sinks (the first with warm water for washing, the second with very hot water for rinsing)

type *noun* sort *or* kind; *what type of accommodation are you looking for?*

typhoid *noun* **typhoid (fever)** = infection of the intestine caused by *Salmonella typhi* in food and water

| COMMENT: typhoid fever gives a fever, diarrhoea and the patient may pass blood in the faeces. It can be fatal if not treated; patients who have had the disease may become carriers. Although vaccine is available, travellers in countries where typhoid is endemic should avoid eating green salad, unpeeled fruit and drinking ordinary tap water; they should only drink bottled water or tap water which has been boiled

typhoon *noun* violent tropical storm with extremely strong winds, in the Far East (NOTE: in the Caribbean called a **hurricane**)

typhus *noun* one of several fevers caused by the Rickettsia bacterium, transmitted by fleas and lice

| COMMENT: typhus victims have a fever, feel extremely weak and develop a dark rash on the skin

tyre *or* *US* **tire** *noun* thick rubber cover round a wheel; **flat tyre** = tyre which has a leak in it so that the air has come out; **snow tyres** = special tyres with thick treads, for use when driving on snow; *when hiring a car in the winter, check if it has snow tyres*

Uu

ugli *noun* citrus fruit similar to a grapefruit, but a little larger, of uneven shape and easy to peel

UHT = ULTRA HEAT TREATED

ultra heat treated milk (UHT milk) *noun* milk which has been treated by sterilizing at temperatures above 135°C, and then put aseptically into containers (it has a much longer shelf life than normal milk)

ultraviolet (UV) *adjective* **ultraviolet radiation** = short invisible rays, beyond the violet end of the colour spectrum, which form the tanning and burning element in sunlight; **ultraviolet lamp** = lamp which gives off ultraviolet rays which tan the skin, help the skin produce Vitamin D and kill bacteria; **UV fly-killer** = device which attracts flies to its UV rays and then kills them by electrocution

COMMENT: UV rays form part of the high-energy radiation which the earth receives from the sun. UV rays are classified as UVA and UVB rays. UVB rays form only a small part of radiation from the sun but they are dangerous and can cause skin cancer if a person is exposed to them for long periods. The effect of UVB rays is reduced by the ozone layer in the stratosphere

UM = UNACCOMPANIED MINOR

umbrella *noun* round shade of folded cloth which opens on a frame and is held over your head to keep off the rain; *a golf umbrella;* **beach umbrella** = parasol, a large umbrella to protect you from the sun

unaccompanied *adjective* not going with a passenger; *unaccompanied baggage must be checked in at the airport 24 hours in advance; there are three unaccompanied children on the flight;* **unaccompanied minor (UM)** = person below the age of majority (18 or 21) travelling alone

unappetizing *adjective* (food) which does not look or smell or taste good (NOTE: the opposite is **appetizing)**

unbonded *adjective* not bonded, not having placed money as a surety against future potential loss

QUOTE the booking of accommodation was organized through a US-based company which was not an ABTA member and so hotel bookings were unbonded
Sunday Times

unchecked *adjective* which has not been checked; *unchecked figures; three items of unchecked baggage remained in the check-in area*

unclaimed *adjective* which has not been claimed; **unclaimed baggage** = cases which have been left with someone and have not

been collected by their owners; *unclaimed property or unclaimed baggage will be sold by auction after six months*

uncomfortable *adjective* not soft and relaxing; *plastic seats are very uncomfortable on long journeys*

uncooked *adjective* raw, not cooked

uncork *verb* to take the cork out of (a bottle)

undelivered *adjective* (letter, message) which has not been delivered

underbooked *adjective* (tour *or* flight) which does not have enough bookings

undercharge *verb* to ask for less money than one should; *I think we were undercharged for the meal; he undercharged us by £5*

undercloth *noun* cloth (usually of baize) which covers a table before the tablecloth is put on

underdish *noun* flat dish on which another deeper dish is placed before serving

underdone *adjective* (meat) which has not been cooked very long; *a plate of underdone roast beef*

underground 1 *adverb* under the ground **2** *adjective* under the ground; **underground train** = train which runs in a tunnel under the ground **3** *noun* railway system which runs in a tunnel under the ground; *he took the underground to the airport; the underground can be very crowded during rush hour* (NOTE: US English is **subway)**

underpass *noun* place where one road goes under another

underplate *noun* flat plate on which another deeper dish is placed before serving (such as a plate under a soup plate or under a coffee cup and saucer)

understaffed *adjective* with not enough staff; *service is slow because the restaurant is understaffed*

underwater *adjective & adverb* below the surface of the water

undeveloped *adjective* which has not been built up with facilities for tourists; *the island is still undeveloped*

unfilled *adjective* which has not been filled; *we still have several unfilled places on the tour;* **unfilled room** = hotel room which is still vacant at the end of the day

unfit *adjective* not suitable; **unfit for human consumption** = (food) which must not be eaten by humans, and may only be suitable to give to animals

unguaranteed *adjective* not guaranteed; **unguaranteed reservation** = reservation for something which a company cannot promise will be available

uniform *noun* specially designed clothing worn by all members of a group; *the holiday camp staff all wear yellow uniforms;* **uniform allowance** = money given to an employee to buy new items of uniform as old items wear out
◊ **uniformed** *adjective* wearing a uniform; **uniformed services** = services in a hotel provided by staff who wear uniforms; **uniformed staff** = hotel staff who wear uniforms (such as porters, bellboys, etc.)

uninsured *adjective* not covered by an insurance policy; *after the fire, they discovered that the hotel was uninsured*

union *noun* **trade union** *or* **trades union** *or US* **labor union** = organization which represents workers who are its members in discussions with management about wages and conditions of work; **union agreement** = contract between management and trade union concerning employment, pay, conditions of work, etc.; **union dues** *or* **union subscription** = payment made by workers to belong to a union; **union officials** = paid organizers of a union; **union recognition** = act of agreeing that a union can act on behalf of staff in a place of work

unit *noun* (**a**) one part (of a larger whole); *the motel has sixteen units* (**b**) **bedroom unit** = one cupboard *or* one set of shelves, etc., which can be matched with others to form a suite of furniture for a bedroom (**c**) **unit of currency** = main element for counting the money of a country (dollar, pound, yen, etc.)

Universal Product Code (UPC) *noun* system of lines printed on a product which when read by a computer gives a reference number or price (NOTE: also called **bar code**)

universal time (UT) *or* **universal time coordinated (UTC)** *noun* international systems of timekeeping; *the flight departs at 2040 UT or 2040 UTC*

unleavened bread *noun* bread made without using a raising agent such as yeast (made in Mediterranean countries, and in India and Pakistan)

unlimited *adjective* with no limits; **unlimited mileage** = allowance with a hired car, where the driver is not charged for the number of miles covered

unload *verb* to take goods off (a ship, etc.); *the ship is unloading at Hamburg; we need a fork-lift truck to unload the lorry; we unloaded the spare parts at Lagos; there are no unloading facilities for container ships*

unlock *verb* to open (something) which was locked

unmade *adjective* which has not been made; **unmade bed** = bed which has not been made after someone has slept in it; **unmade room** = hotel room which has not been prepared by cleaning, changing the linen and tidying, etc. since the last guest left it

unofficial *adjective* not approved by a department or organization; *see also* OFFICIAL
◊ **unofficially** *adverb* in a way which has not been approved by a department or organization; *see also* OFFICIALLY

unpaid *adjective* (bill) which has not been settled

unpasteurized milk *noun* milk which has not been treated by pasteurization; *cheese made from unpasteurized milk has a better flavour*

unsaturated fat *noun* fat which does not have a large amount of hydrogen, and so can be broken down more easily

unskilled *adjective* (worker) who has no particular skill; **unskilled staff** = employees who have no particular skill, and so may do general jobs, such as cleaning, washing dishes, carrying goods, etc.; **unskilled work** = work which does not require a particular skill; *see also* SKILLED

unspoilt *adjective* (countryside) which has not been spoilt

untreated milk *noun* milk which has not been processed in any way

up *adverb* not in bed; *at breakfast time, the waitress still wasn't up*

◇ **update 1** *noun* information which brings something up to date; *they issued an update on the snow forecast* **2** *verb* to revise (something) so that it is more up to date; *they have updated their guide to Greece to include current prices*

◇ **upgrade 1** *noun* moving a passenger to a better class of seat (without paying extra) **2** *verb* **(a)** to move a passenger to a better class of seat; *because of a mistake in the booking, he was upgraded to first-class* **(b)** to make facilities more luxurious *or* more modern; *the new manager plans to upgrade the residents' lounge; the hotel has refitted all the bedrooms and has been upgraded to 4-star*

> QUOTE roads to and from the airport are being upgraded while a new international terminal, capable of handling 3,000 passengers an hour and including a customs hall with seven baggage carousels, should be ready by June 1996
> *Business Traveller*

up-market *adjective* more expensive

upright *adjective* vertical, not lying flat; *put your seats into the upright position for landing*

upstairs 1 *adverb* towards *or* in the upper part of a building or vehicle; *let's go upstairs on the top deck: you can see London much better* **2** *adjective* in the upper part of a building or vehicle; *there is an upstairs bar for guests* **3** *noun* upper part of a building or vehicle

UPC = UNIVERSAL PRODUCT CODE

upholstery *noun* **(a)** action of covering chairs, etc. with padded seats and covers **(b)** covers for chairs; padded seats and cushions

urinal *noun* place where men can urinate

urn *noun* **tea urn** *or* **coffee urn** = large container with a tap, in which tea or coffee can be prepared in advance and then kept hot

use 1 *noun* being used; way in which something is used; **to make use of** = to put to a purpose **2** *verb* to put to a purpose; *don't use the tap water for drinking; guests used the fire escape to get out of the building*

◇ **use-by date** *noun* date stamped on the label of a food product, which is last date on which the food can be safely eaten; *similar to* BEST-BEFORE DATE, SELL-BY DATE

◇ **useful** *adjective* which helps; **to make oneself useful** = to do helpful things

usher 1 *noun* person who shows people to their seats (in a theatre or cinema or at a wedding) **2** *verb* **to usher in** = to bring (someone) in

◇ **usherette** *noun* girl who shows people to their seats in a theatre or cinema

usual 1 *adjective* ordinary; which happens often; *your usual table, sir? he found someone sitting in his usual place in the dining room* **2** *noun (informal)* drink *or* food which someone well-known to the waiter or barman has most often; *a pint of the usual, please; will you have your usual, sir?*

◇ **usually** *adverb* mostly *or* ordinarily *or* most often; *the restaurant is usually full on Friday evenings*

UT = UNIVERSAL TIME

UTC = UNIVERSAL TIME COORDINATED

utensil *noun* **kitchen utensils** = pans, knives, spoons, etc., used for work in the kitchen

U-turn *noun* turn made by a vehicle on a road, so as to face in the opposite direction; *he made a U-turn and went back to the hotel; U-turns are not allowed on motorways*

UV = ULTRAVIOLET

Vv

vacancy *noun* **(a)** empty place *or* room; *(sign on hotel door)* **'vacancies'** = empty rooms available; **'no vacancies'** = the hotel *or* guesthouse is full; **vacancy rate** = average number of rooms empty in a hotel over a period of time, shown as a percentage of the total number of rooms **(b)** job which is not filled; *we advertised a vacancy in the local press; we have been unable to fill the vacancy for an experienced sous-chef; they have a vacancy for a secretary;* **job vacancies** = jobs which are available and need people to do them

◊ **vacant** *adjective* empty *or* not occupied; *we have six rooms vacant in the annexe;* **situations vacant** = list (in a newspaper) of jobs which are available

◊ **vacate** *verb* to leave (a room); *guests are asked to vacate their rooms before 12.00;* **to vacate the premises** = to leave a building, offices, rooms, etc. so that they become empty

vacation 1 *noun* **(a)** *GB* period when the universities and colleges are closed; **vacation job** = job taken by a student during the vacation to earn money to help pay for the costs of a university or college course **(b)** *US* holiday *or* period when people are not working; *the family went on vacation in Florida;* **vacation hotel** = hotel which is used for holidays **2** *verb US* to go on holiday

◊ **vacationer** *noun US* person who is on holiday

vaccinate *verb* **to vaccinate someone against a disease** = to use a vaccine to give a person immunization against a specific disease; *she was vaccinated against smallpox as a child* (NOTE: you vaccinate someone **against** a disease)

◊ **vaccination** *noun* act of giving a vaccine to a person

◊ **vaccine** *noun* substance which contains the germs of a disease, used to inoculate or vaccinate; **cholera vaccine** = vaccine which protects to a certain degree against cholera

vacuum 1 *noun* space from which all matter, including air, has been removed; **vacuum cooling** = chilling of food in a vacuum; **vacuum-packed** = (food) packed in a vacuum, so that no air can enter the package **2** *verb (informal)* to clean with a vacuum cleaner

◊ **vacuum cleaner** *noun* cleaning machine which sucks up dust

◊ **vacuum flask** *noun* bottle with double walls which keeps liquids warm or cold (NOTE: often called a **thermos flask**)

valet *noun* male servant who looks after his master's clothes; **valet parking** = service at a hotel or restaurant where a member of staff parks the guests' cars for them; **valet service** = service in a hotel for cleaning and pressing clothes, especially for dry-cleaning

◊ **valeting service** *noun* **(a)** service in a hotel for cleaning and pressing clothes, especially for dry-cleaning **(b)** service in a garage, for cleaning the outside and inside of a car

valid *adjective* which can be used lawfully; *ticket which is valid for three months; he was carrying a valid passport; how long is the ticket valid for?*

◊ **validate** *verb* **(a)** to check to see if something is correct; *the document was validated by the bank* **(b)** to make (something) valid; *the ticket has to be stamped by the airline to validate it*

◊ **validity** *noun* being valid; **period of validity** = length of time for which a document may be used lawfully

◊ **validator** *noun* metal stamp used to validate a ticket

valley *noun* long low area, usually with a river at the bottom, between hills or mountains

valuable 1 *adjective* worth a lot of money; very useful **2** *noun* **valuables** = items which are worth a lot of money; *guests can deposit valuables with the manager for safe-keeping*

value *noun* **(a)** worth; **to be good value for money** = to be a good deal; **to get value for money** = to get a good deal; **items of value** = items which are worth a lot of money; *items of value can be deposited in the hotel safe* *overnight;* **added value** *or* **value added =** amount added to the value of a product or service, being the difference between its cost and the amount received when it is sold (wages, taxes, etc., are deducted from the added value to give the profit); *see also* VALUE ADDED TAX **(b)** quantity shown as a number; **calorific value =** number of calories which a certain amount of a certain food contains; **energy value =** amount of energy produced by a certain amount of a certain food

QUOTE short break holidays continue to be driven by price and value for money, which will only continue to put pressure on us all to keep our prices down and our marketing well targeted
Caterer & Hotelkeeper

Value Added Tax (VAT) *noun* tax imposed as a percentage of the invoice value of goods and services; *see also below at* VAT

van *noun* small closed goods vehicle; *the van will call this afternoon to pick up the goods*

vanilla *noun* flavouring made from the seed pods of a tropical plant; *vanilla ice cream*

variety *noun* mixture of different sorts; *there is a variety of different cereals for breakfast;* **variety show =** entertainment which includes several different types of performer (such as singers, dancers, conjurors, ventriloquists, etc.); *US* **variety meats =** OFFAL

VAT = VALUE ADDED TAX *the invoice includes VAT at 15%; the government is proposing to increase VAT to 17.5%; some items (such as books) are still zero-rated for VAT; hotels have to charge VAT like any other business;* **VAT declaration =** statement declaring VAT income to the VAT office; **VAT inspector =** government official who examines VAT returns and checks that VAT is being paid; **VAT invoicing =** sending of an invoice including VAT; **VAT invoice =** invoice which shows VAT separately; **VAT office =** government office dealing with the collection of VAT in an area

VDQS = VIN DELIMITE DE QUALITE SUPERIEURE

VDU *abbreviation for* visual display unit

veal *noun* meat from a calf; **veal cutlet =** flat cake of minced veal covered with breadcrumbs and fried; **veal escalope =** thin slice of veal, covered in breadcrumbs and fried; *see also* WIENER SCHNITZEL; **veal and ham pie =** pie with a filling of veal and ham and hard-boiled eggs, eaten cold

COMMENT: veal is not as popular in Britain as in other European countries

vegan *noun & adjective* strict vegetarian *or* (person) who eats only vegetables and fruit and no animal products like milk, fish, eggs *or* meat

vegetable *noun* plant grown for food, not usually sweet (the commonest vegetables are potatoes, carrots, onions, cabbage, cauliflower, peas and beans); *the main course is served with a selection of vegetables;* **vegetable chef** *or* **chef entremétier =** chef in charge of preparing vegetables and pasta

◊ **vegetarian** *noun & adjective* (person) who does not eat meat; (restaurant) which does not serve meat; *she asked for a vegetarian meal; our children are all vegetarians*

vehicle *noun* machine with wheels, used to carry goods *or* passengers on a road; **commercial vehicle** *or* **goods vehicle =** van *or* truck used for business purposes; **heavy goods vehicle (HGV) =** very large truck; *goods vehicles can park in the loading bay*

◊ **vehicular** *adjective* referring to vehicles; **no vehicular access to the motorway =** vehicles cannot get onto the motorway here

velouté *noun* soup with a creamy texture

vending machine *noun* machine from which you can buy something, such as sweets, chocolate, cigarettes, drinks, etc., by putting coins into a slot

venetian blind *noun* blind to shut out light, made of horizontal strips of plastic, wood, etc., which can be opened and shut or raised and lowered by pulling a string

venison *noun* meat from a deer; **venison stew =** pieces of venison cooked in a liquid; **venison pâté =** pâté made from venison

COMMENT: venison is left to hang for at least one week before eating. It is dark red in colour and has very little fat

ventilation *noun* bringing in fresh air; **ventilation hood** *or* **ventilation canopy** = device placed over an oven or other cooking surface, to remove smells, steam, etc.; **ventilation shaft** = tube which allows fresh air to go into a building

◊ **ventilator** *noun* opening which allows fresh air to come in; machine which pumps fresh air into a room and extracts stale air

QUOTE Ventilation hoods are needed to remove the smells, vapour and grease invariably produced in large quantities during cooking. The ventilation system should include a fan of sufficient extract capacity to cope with the expected fume load from the equipment it serves.
Health and Safety in Kitchens (HSE)

venue *noun* agreed place where something will take place

verdigris *noun* green discolouring of copper pans, etc., through contact with damp

vermicelli *noun* type of pasta, like very thin spaghetti

vermin *noun* insects or animals, such as beetles, mice, etc. which are looked upon as pests by some people; *see also* PEST

vermouth *noun* type of strong wine flavoured with herbs

COMMENT: vermouth can be either sweet or dry; Italian vermouth is used to make martinis

vessel *noun* ship; **merchant vessel** = commercial ship which carries a cargo

vestibule *noun* entrance hall

via *preposition* by *or* using (a means *or* a route); *the shipment is going via the Suez Canal; we are sending the information pack via our office in New York; they sent the message via the courier*

vibrio *noun* type of Gram-negative bacterium

video *adjective & noun* (system) which shows pictures on a television screen; **video camera** = camera which records video pictures; **video conference** = meeting where some people take part by television

◊ **video-cassette recorder** *or* **video recorder** *noun* machine which records

television or films pictures on tape, so that they can be played back later

view *noun* (a) scene (which you can see from a certain place); *room with a view over the harbour; we asked for a room with a sea view and were given one looking out over the bus depot* (b) way of thinking about something; *we asked the sales manager for his views on the reorganization of the reps' territories; the chairman takes the view that credit should never be longer than thirty days;* in view of = because of; *in view of the falling exchange rate, we have had to introduce surcharges on some of our tours*

◊ **viewing area** *noun* place (as in an airport) where people can stand to watch what is happening

village *noun* small place where people live, surrounded by countryside (a village may have a population of about 1,000, though many villages are much smaller, and will probably have no industry apart from farming); **village shop** *or* **village stores** = small shop selling a wide variety of goods, serving a village community; **village fête** = little local festival in a village

vin *French noun* wine; **vin de pays** = table wine from a certain region of France; **vin de table** = ordinary wine *or* table wine; **vin délimité de qualité supérieure (VDQS)** = French classification of wine, indicating that it comes from a certain region and is made from a certain variety of grape; *compare* APPELLATION D'ORIGINE CONTROLEE

vinaigrette *noun* French dressing, salad dressing made with oil, vinegar, salt and other flavourings

vinegar *noun* liquid made from sour wine or cider, used in cooking and for preserving food; **red wine vinegar; cider vinegar**

vino *Italian noun* wine; **vino di tavola** = ordinary wine *or* table wine

vintage *noun* (a) collecting grapes to make wine; grapes which are collected (b) fine wine made in a particular year; *this is a very good vintage; what vintage is it? - it's a 1968;* **vintage wine** *or* **vintage port** = fine *or* expensive old wine or port which was made in a particular year

VIP = VERY IMPORTANT PERSON; **VIP lounge** = special room at an airport for important travellers; **we laid on VIP**

treatment for our visitors *or* we gave our visitors a VIP reception = we arranged for our visitors to be well looked after and entertained

virus *noun* tiny germ cell which can only develop in other cells, and often destroys them; **infectious virus hepatitis** = hepatitis transmitted by a carrier through food or drink; **virus pneumonia** = inflammation of the lungs caused by a virus

COMMENT: many common diseases such as measles or the common cold are caused by viruses; viral diseases cannot be treated with antibiotics

visa *noun* special document *or* special stamp in a passport which allows someone to enter a country; *you will need a visa before you go to the USA; he filled in his visa application form;* **entry visa** = visa allowing someone to enter a country; **multiple entry visa** = visa allowing someone to enter a country as often as he likes; **thirty-day visa** = visa which allows you to stay in a country for 30 days; **tourist visa** = visa which allows someone to visit a country for a short time on holiday; **transit visa** = visa which allows someone to spend a short time in one country while travelling to another country

visit 1 *noun* short stay in a place; *we will be making a short visit to London next week; he is on a business visit to Edinburgh; we had a visit from the VAT inspector* **2** *verb* to go to a place *or* to see someone for a short time; *he spent a week in Scotland, visiting museums in Edinburgh and Glasgow; the trade delegation visited the Ministry of Commerce*
◊ **visitor** *noun* person who is going to or staying in a place for a short time; *the coach brought a group of visitors to the exhibition;* **foreign visitor** *or* **overseas visitor** = visitor from another country; **visitors' book** = book in which visitors to a museum *or* guests to a hotel write comments about the place; **visitors' bureau** *or* **visitor information centre** = office which deals with visitors' questions; **visitors' ledger** = ledger in which itemized accounts for each guest in a hotel are kept; **visitors' tax** = tax to be paid to a local municipality for each visitor

vitamin *noun* essential nutrient usually needed in minute quantities for growth and health

vodka *noun* **(a)** strong colourless alcohol distilled from grain, potatoes, etc. made originally in Russia and Poland **(b)** glass of this alcohol; *two vodka and tonics, please*

void 1 *adjective* invalid, which cannot lawfully be used; *the ticket is void* **2** *verb* to mark a document to show that it cannot be used lawfully; *we will void the existing ticket and issue a new one*

voiture *French noun (meaning 'car')* a trolley for food in a restaurant

vol-au-vent *noun* small round case of pastry, usually filled with a savoury mixture, eaten hot or cold; *mushroom vol-au-vent*

volcano *noun* mountain with a hole on the top through which lava, ash and gas can come

COMMENT: volcanoes occur along faults in the earth's surface and exist in well-known chains. Some are extinct, but others erupt relatively frequently. Some are always active, in that they emit sulphurous gases and smoke, without actually erupting. Volcanic eruptions are a major source of atmospheric pollution. Volcanoes are popular tourist attractions: the best-known in Europe are Vesuvius, Stromboli and Etna in Italy and Helgafell in Iceland

voltage *noun* measure of electrical force

COMMENT: the voltage in many countries is 110V (USA, Canada, Japan, etc.). In Europe, the Far East and Africa, voltage is usually 220V or 240V. Travellers should always carry a transformer to get electrical appliances to work

voucher *noun* paper which is given instead of money; *each traveller has a book of vouchers to be presented at the reception desk in each hotel where the group stays;* **cash voucher** = paper which can be exchanged for cash; *with every £20 of purchases, the customer gets a cash voucher to the value of £2;* **gift voucher** = card, bought in a store, which is given as a present and which must be exchanged in that store for goods; **luncheon voucher** = ticket given by an employer to a worker in addition to his wages, which can be exchanged for food in a restaurant

voyage *noun* long journey by ship

◊ **voyager** *noun* person who goes on a long journey by ship

Ww

wafer *noun* thin sweet biscuit eaten with ice cream

waffle *noun* type of thick crisp pancake cooked in an iron mould and eaten with syrup
◊ **waffle-iron** *noun* iron mould used for making waffles

wage *noun* money paid (usually in cash each week) to a worker for work done; *she is earning a good wage or good wages in the bar;* **basic wage** = normal pay without any extra payments; *the basic wage is £110 a week, but you can expect to earn more than that with overtime;* **hourly wage** *or* **wage per hour** = amount of money paid for an hour's work; **wages book** = ledger in which details of all payments to staff are kept; **wage packet** = envelope containing money and pay slip; **wage scale** = list of wages, showing different rates of pay for different jobs in the same company (NOTE: the plural **wages** is more usual when referring to the money earned, but **wage** is used before other nouns)

wagon *noun* goods truck used on the railway

wait *verb* **(a)** to stay somewhere until something happens or someone or something arrives; *we gave our order half an hour ago, but are still waiting for the first course; if you wait here I expect a taxi will come along soon* **(b) to wait on someone** = to serve food to someone at table; **waiting staff** = restaurant employees who serve the guests at table
◊ **waiter** *noun* **(a)** man who serves food to people in a restaurant; **assistant waiter** *or* **commis waiter** = waiter who helps a station waiter; **head waiter** = maître d'hôtel, the person in charge of a restaurant, who is responsible for all the service and himself takes orders from customers; **station waiter** = chef de rang, a waiter who serves a particular group of four or five tables in a restaurant; **station head waiter** = maître d'hôtel de carré, a chief waiter who is in charge of a station, and takes the orders from customers (in the USA, this is the 'captain'); **waiter service** = service by waiters who take orders and bring food to customers sitting at tables (as opposed to counter service or self-service) **(b) dumb waiter** = (i) sideboard in a restaurant, on which cutlery, condiments, etc., are kept ready for use; (ii) device for raising and lowering trays of food, dirty dishes, etc., between floors of a building
◊ **waiting list** *noun* list of people waiting to see someone or do something; *there is a waiting list of passengers hoping to get a flight*
◊ **waiting room** *noun* room where travellers wait for their trains, buses, etc.
◊ **waitlist** = WAITING LIST
◊ **waitress** *noun* woman who serves food to people in a restaurant; **waitress service** = service by waitresses who take orders and bring food to customers sitting at tables (as opposed to counter service or self-service)

wake *verb* to stop (someone) sleeping; *he asked to be woken at 7.00*
NOTE: **waking - woke - has woken**
◊ **wake up** *verb* to stop sleeping; *she woke up at 7.30; he asked to be woken up at 6.15;* **wake-up call** = phone call from the hotel switchboard to wake a guest up

Wales Tourist Board (WTB) organization which promotes tourism in Wales and promotes tourism to Wales from other parts of the UK

walk 1 *noun* **(a)** going on foot; *it's only a short walk to the beach* **(b)** organized visit on foot; *several London walks are advertised each Saturday; he went on a Dickens walk* **2** *verb* to go on foot; *he walks to the office every morning; the visitors walked round the factory*
◊ **walk-in** *adjective* large enough to walk into; *walk-in fridge; walk-in wardrobe*
◊ **walking** *noun* going on foot as a relaxation; *we spent two weeks on a walking holiday in North Italy;* **walking shoes** =

heavy shoes, suitable for walking long distances; **walking stick** = stick used to support you when walking; **walking tour** = tour on which you walk from one place to another, spend the night, and then continue on foot the following day

wall *noun* **(a)** structure of brick or stone, etc., forming the side of a room or building, or the boundary of a piece of land **(b)** thick stone construction round an old town; *you can walk all round York on the town walls* ◊ **walled** *adjective* with walls; *vegetables are grown in the hotel's walled garden; they visited several old walled towns in South-West France*

wallet *noun* small leather case which fits into the pocket and is used for holding banknotes; *his wallet was stolen from his back pocket; do not leave your wallet in the car*

walnut *noun* hard round nut with a wrinkled shell; **walnut oil** = oil produced by crushing walnuts

wander *verb* to walk about without any special direction; **to wander off** = to walk away from the correct path; *two of the group wandered off into the market and got lost*

want 1 *noun* thing which is needed **2** *verb* to need *or* to require; *do you want any more tea? my little daughter wants to go to the toilet; I want to go to Paris next Tuesday*

war *noun* **(a)** fighting between countries; *travel is dangerous in the south of the country because of the war* **(b)** argument between companies; **price war** *or* **price-cutting war** *or* **cut-price war** = competition between companies to get a larger market share by cutting prices

warden *noun* person who looks after or guards something; **park warden** = person who looks after a forest or park

wardrobe *noun* large cupboard in which clothes may be hung

warm 1 *adjective* quite hot *or* not cold; *you must take plenty of warm clothing; the winter sun can be quite warm in February* **2** *verb* to heat food until it is quite hot; **to warm up** = to heat food which has already been cooked, and has gone cold ◊ **warming cupboard** *noun* specially heated cupboard in a kitchen, where food can be kept warm

warn *verb* to say that there is a possible danger; *the group was warned to look out for pickpockets; the guide warned us that there might be snakes in the ruins; they were warned not to go near the army base* (NOTE: you warn someone **of** something, or **that** something may happen, or **to do** something) ◊ **warning** *noun* notice of possible danger; *the government issued a warning about travelling in the south of the country; warning notices were put up around the ruins*

warrant 1 *noun* official document which allows someone to do something **2** *verb* **(a)** to guarantee; *all the spare parts are warranted* **(b)** to show that something is reasonable; *the tour price is not warranted by the use of two-star hotels* ◊ **warranty** *noun* **(a)** guarantee *or* legal document which promises that a machine will work properly *or* that an item is of good quality; *the car is sold with a twelve-month warranty; the warranty covers spare parts but not labour costs* **(b)** promise in a contract; **breach of warranty** = failing to do something which is a part of a contract **(c)** statement made by an insured person which declares that the facts stated by him are true

wash 1 *noun* **(a)** act of cleaning with water or another liquid; *I'll go and have a quick wash* **(b)** clothes which are being washed **2** *verb* to clean with water or another liquid; *she's washing her hair; he washed the fruit before eating them; guests are asked not to wash clothes in hotel rooms* ◊ **wash-basin** *or* **wash hand basin** *noun* bowl in a bathroom with taps giving running hot and cold water for washing ◊ **washbowl** *noun* bowl for holding water, but not fixed and with no taps ◊ **washing** *noun* **(a)** act of cleaning with water or another liquid; **washing powder** = detergent powder for washing clothes; **washing machine** = machine for washing clothes **(b)** clothes which are ready to be washed or which have been washed; *put your washing in the plastic bag; washing left out in the morning will be delivered to the room within 12 hours* ◊ **washing up** *noun* **(a)** cleaning of dirty dishes, glasses, cutlery, etc. with water; *when he couldn't pay, he had to do the washing up* **(b)** dirty dishes, glasses, cutlery, etc. waiting to be cleaned; *there is a pile of washing up waiting to be put into the dishwasher*

washer *noun* **(a)** steel or rubber ring under a bolt or nut; rubber ring inside a tap which prevents water escaping when the tap is turned off **(b)** machine for washing **(c)** **windscreen washer** = attachment on a car which squirts water on to the windscreen to clean the glass

◊ **washroom** *noun* room where you can wash your hands and use the toilet

◊ **washstand** *noun* **(a)** *(old)* table on which a washbowl and jug of water stood in a bedroom **(b)** *US* fixed bowl, with taps, for holding water for washing the hands and face

◊ **wash up** *verb* **(a)** to clean dirty dishes, cutlery, glasses, etc. **(b)** *US* to wash yourself; *I'll just go and wash up before lunch*

waste *noun* rubbish; **waste bin** = container for putting rubbish in; **waste compactor** = machine which crushes waste into small packs which are relatively easy to dispose of; **waste paper basket** *or US* **wastebasket** = container into which paper or pieces of rubbish can be thrown; **waste pipe** = pipe which takes dirty water from a sink to the drains

◊ **waste disposal** *noun* arrangements to get rid of rubbish (for example, from a hotel or restaurant); **waste disposal unit** *or* **waste disposer** = machine attached to a kitchen sink, which grinds waste food into pulp which can then be flushed away into the drainage system

> COMMENT: waste disposal units are not permitted in countries which do not allow ground waste products to be flushed into the sewage system

watch 1 *noun* small clock worn on the arm or carried in a pocket; **digital watch** = watch which shows the time as a series of figures (such as 12:05:23) rather than on a circular dial **2** *verb* to be careful; *watch out for pickpockets*

◊ **watchman** *noun* person who guards a building, usually when it is empty; *a night watchman*

water 1 *noun* **(a)** compound of hydrogen and oxygen; liquid that is in rain, rivers, lakes and the sea; *is the water safe to drink? you are advised to drink only bottled water; each room has hot and cold running water; the temperature of the water or the water temperature is 60°;* **bottled water** = mineral water which is sold in bottles; **drinking water** = water that is safe to drink; **mineral**

water = water which comes naturally from the ground and is sold in bottles; **salt water** *or* **sea water** = water which contains salt (as opposed to fresh water in rivers and lakes); *the ship has a sea water swimming pool;* **spring water** = water which comes from a natural spring; **tap water** = water from a tap; **water boiler** = piece of kitchen equipment, which heats water for making hot drinks (also providing steam); **water cooler** *or* **water fountain** = container which holds drinking water, which is cooled and may be drawn off through a tap; **water glass** = glass on a table for drinking water (placed next to a wineglass in a table setting); **water set** = WATER BOILER; **hot-water bottle** = container filled with hot water which is placed in a bed to warm it **(b) to take the waters** = to drink mineral water at a spa **2** *verb* **the display of cakes made my mouth water** = the cakes looked and smelt so delicious that saliva came into my mouth

◊ **water biscuit** *noun* thin unsweetened hard biscuit made of flour and water, eaten with cheese

◊ **water closet (WC)** *noun* *(formal)* lavatory

◊ **watercress** *noun* creeping plant grown in water and eaten in salads and soup; *see also* CRESS

◊ **waterfall** *noun* drop of a river, etc., from a high level over the edge of a cliff

◊ **waterfront** *noun* bank of a river or shore of the sea and the buildings along it

◊ **water ice** *noun* type of light ice cream made of water and flavouring; *an orange water ice; the waiter brought round a tray of water ices*

◊ **water-melon** *noun* plant of the genus *Citrullus vulgaris* with large green fruit with red flesh and black seeds

◊ **waterproof** *adjective* which will not let water through; *you will need plenty of waterproof clothing if you are going sea fishing*

◊ **waterskier** *noun* person who goes in for water-skiing

◊ **water-skiing** *noun* sport of gliding along the surface of water standing on a pair of skis pulled by a fast boat

◊ **water sports** *plural noun* activities which take place on or in water, such as swimming, water polo, scuba diving, etc.

◊ **waterways** *noun* **inland waterways** = rivers and canals

◊ **waterwings** *plural noun* inflatable rings attached to the arms of a child learning to swim

wave 1 *noun* **(a)** ridge of higher water on the surface of the sea; *watch out for the big waves on the beach; the sea was calm, with hardly any waves* **(b)** heat wave = sudden period of high temperature **2** *verb* to move your hand up and down; **to wave to someone** = to signal to someone with the hand; **to wave someone on** = to tell someone to go on by a movement of the hand

wax *verb* to cover (skis) with wax

way *noun* **(a)** road or path; *is this the way to the post office? can you show me the way to the ruins?;* **on the way** = during the journey; *we will stop at the carpet shop on the way to the restaurant* **(b)** particular direction; **one-way street** = street where the traffic is allowed to go only in one direction

WC *or* **W.C.** = WATER CLOSET

weather *noun* daily atmospheric conditions (e.g. sunshine, wind, precipitation) in a certain area, as opposed to climate which is the average weather for the area; *the weather can be very wet in spring; I hope the weather will be fine for our climb; what's the weather like in Italy in May?*

◊ **weather bureau** *or* **weather centre** *noun* office which analyses weather reports and forecasts the weather

◊ **weather forecast** *or* **weather report** *noun* description of what the weather will be for a period in the future; *the weather forecast is good;* **medium-range weather forecast** = forecast covering two to five days ahead; **long-range weather forecast** = forecast covering a period of more than five days ahead; **weather report** = written *or* spoken statement describing what the weather has been like recently *or* what it is like at the moment *or* what it will be for a period in the future

wedding *noun* marriage ceremony; **golden wedding** = anniversary of 50 years of marriage; **silver wedding** = anniversary of 25 years of marriage; **wedding breakfast** = lunch served after a wedding (a full meal, which can take the form of a buffet, at the end of which speeches are made and the wedding cake is cut); **wedding reception** = party held after a marriage ceremony, including the wedding breakfast, drinks, toasts, cake-cutting, etc.

week *noun* period of seven days (from Monday to Sunday); *a three-week cruise in the Caribbean;* **to be paid by the week** = to be paid a certain amount of money each week; *he earns £500 a week or per week; she works thirty-five hours per week or she works a thirty-five-hour week*

◊ **weekend** *noun* Saturday and Sunday; **long weekend** = period from Friday to Monday; **weekend break** = short holiday (two or three nights) over a weekend at a specially low tariff

◊ **weekly** *adverb* done every week; *a weekly flight to the Shetland Isles;* **a weekly newspaper** *or* **a weekly** = newspaper which is published once a week; **weekly room rate** = rate charged for a hotel room for seven nights

weigh *verb* **(a)** to measure how heavy something is; *he weighed the packet at the post office; please put all your luggage onto the scales to be weighed;* **weighing machine** = machine which measure how heavy something or someone is **(b)** to have a certain weight; *the packet weighs twenty-five grams*

◊ **weight** *noun* measurement of how heavy something is; **to sell fruit by weight** = the price is per pound *or* per kilo of the fruit; **false weight** *or* **short weight** = weight on a shop scales which is wrong and so cheats customers by showing something to be heavier than it really is; **to give short weight** = to sell something which is lighter than it should be; **gross weight** = weight of both the container and its contents; **net weight** = weight of goods after deducting the weight of the packing material and container; **inspector of weights and measures** = government official who inspects weighing machines and goods sold in shops to see if the quantities and weights are correct

Weil's disease *noun* leptospirosis, infectious disease caused by the spirochaete *Leptospira* transmitted to humans from rats, giving jaundice and kidney damage. It can also be caught from windsurfing on stagnant water

welcome 1 *noun* greeting or reception; **they gave the visitors a very warm welcome** = they greeted the visitors very warmly **2** *verb* to greet (someone) as he arrives **3** *adjective* **(a)** received with pleasure; *after the walk they had a welcome hot bath or a hot bath was very welcome* **(b)** willingly permitted; *visitors are welcome to use the hotel gardens* **(c)** *(informal: as a reply to 'thank you')* **you're welcome** = it was a pleasure to serve you

well- *prefix* in a good way; *a well-appointed hotel; a well-equipped bedroom; a well-known spa town*

◊ **well done** *adjective* (meat) which is completely cooked

west 1 *noun* one of the points of the compass: the direction of the setting sun; the western part of a country; *she comes from the west of England; the sun sets in the west and rises in the east* **2** *adjective* referring to the west; *the west coast; west-coast cities;* west wind = wind coming from the west **3** *adverb* towards the west; *drive west along the motorway for ten miles*

◊ **westbound** *adjective* going towards the west; *the westbound carriageway of the motorway is closed*

◊ **West End** *noun* the fashionable part of London, where the main shopping area is found

◊ **westerly 1** *adjective* **(a)** towards the west; **in a westerly direction** = towards the west **(b)** (wind) which blows from the west

◊ **western** *adjective* referring to the west

◊ **westernmost** *adjective* furthest west

◊ **Westminster** *noun* borough in London where the Houses of Parliament are situated

◊ **westward** *adjective & adverb* towards the west

◊ **westwards** *adverb* towards the west

wet *adjective* **(a)** covered or soaked with water or other liquid; **I'm wet through** *or* **soaking wet** = all my clothes are very wet **(b)** rainy; *if it is wet, the walk to the beach will be cancelled; there's nothing I like better than a wet Sunday in London*

◊ **wetsuit** *noun* suit worn by divers, windsurfers, etc., which keeps the body warm with a layer of water between the body and the suit

wharf *noun* place in a dock where a ship can tie up and load or unload (NOTE: plural is **wharfs** *or* **wharves)**

wheel 1 *noun* circular frame which turns around a central axis; **steering wheel** = wheel which the driver of a vehicle holds and turns to follow the road **2** *verb* to push along something that has wheels; *the waiter wheeled in a sweet trolley*

◊ **wheelchair** *noun* chair on wheels used by people who cannot walk; **wheelchair access** = slope for wheelchairs; *there is no wheelchair access into the restaurant*

whelk *noun* type of edible sea snail

whirlpool *noun* water which turns rapidly round and round; **whirlpool bath** = type of bath (often in a spa) where the water is made to turn round and round

whisky *noun* **(a)** strong alcohol distilled from grain (usually made in Scotland); **whisky sour** = cocktail of whisky, lemon juice and sugar **(b)** glass of this alcohol; *two large whiskies, please*

◊ **whiskey** *noun* whisky (made in Ireland and the USA)

COMMENT: whisky may be drunk on its own (neat), with ice cubes (on the rocks) or diluted with water, soda water or a ginger-flavoured fizzy drink

white *adjective & noun* **(a)** the colour of snow; **white sale** = sale of sheets *or* towels, etc. **(b)** light-coloured meat (on a chicken); **white of an egg** *or* **egg white** = part of the egg which is not yellow

◊ **whitebait** *noun* small young fish fried and eaten whole (NOTE: the plural is **whitebait)**

◊ **whiteboard** *noun* board on a wall which can be written on using coloured pens

◊ **whiteware** *noun* white plates, cups and saucers, etc. (as opposed to decorated china)

QUOTE the recession has forced caterers to be price-conscious and whiteware can cost a third less than colourfully designed products. We have seen three- and four-star hotels moving to whiteware, but still striving for standards with elegant design or embossed lines
Caterer & Hotelkeeper

◊ **white-water canoeing** *or* **rafting** *noun* sport of riding in a canoe *or* on a raft down rapidly flowing rivers

◊ **white wine** *noun* wine made without leaving the grape skins in the fermenting mixture (the colour of the wine is pale yellow or green)

COMMENT: dry white wines are drunk with fish, and also as apéritifs. Sweet white wines are drunk as dessert wines. All white wines are drunk chilled

whiting *noun* type of small sea fish (NOTE: plural is **whiting)**

Whitsun *noun* Christian festival on the seventh Sunday after Easter

◊ **Whit Sunday** *noun* the seventh Sunday after Easter

wholefood *noun* food, grown naturally, which has not been given artificial fertilizers, and has not been processed; *a wholefood diet is healthier than eating processed foods*

◊ **wholegrain** *noun* food (such as rice) of which the whole of the seed is eaten

wholemeal *adjective* **wholemeal flour** = flour which has had nothing removed or added to it and contains a large proportion of the original wheat seed, including the bran; **wholemeal bread** *or US* **wholewheat bread** = bread made from wholemeal flour

◊ **wholesome** *adjective* healthy *or* good for one's health; **wholesome food** = food that is good for your health

wide-bodied *adjective* (plane) with a wide body (the opposite is narrow-bodied)

wiener *noun US* frankfurter

◊ **Wiener schnitzel** *noun* veal escalope, dipped in breadcrumbs and fried

wife *noun* woman to whom a man is married (NOTE: plural is **wives)**

wildlife *noun* birds, plants, animals living free and untouched by man; **wildlife park** = park where wild animals are allowed to run free (NOTE: no plural)

wind[1] *verb* to roll up or to roll down; *you can wind down the window if it is too hot* (NOTE: **winding - wound)**

wind[2] *noun* moving air; *the wind is blowing from the sea;* **in high winds** = in very strong winds; **headwind** = wind blowing straight towards a ship or aircraft; **tailwind** *or* **following wind** wind blowing from behind a ship or aircraft; *see also* BEAUFORT SCALE

◊ **windbreak** *noun* fence or hedge which protects against the wind

◊ **wind chill factor** *noun* way of calculating the risk of exposure in cold weather by adding the speed of the wind to the number of degrees of temperature below zero

◊ **windscreen** *noun* glass window in the front of a vehicle; **windscreen wiper** = device on a vehicle which wipes rain away from the windscreen; **rear window wiper** = device on a vehicle which wipes rain away from the rear window

◊ **windshield** *noun* **(a)** screen on a motorcycle **(b)** *US* windscreen

◊ **windsurfer** *noun* person who does windsurfing

◊ **windsurfing** *noun* sport of riding on water on a special board with a sail attached

◊ **windward** *adjective & adverb* on *or* to the side (of a ship) from which the wind is blowing; *compare* LEEWARD

◊ **windy** *adjective* having much wind

window *noun* opening in a wall or door, etc., filled with glass; **window seat** = seat in train, plane, etc., next to a window (NOTE: the opposite is **aisle seat) shop window** = window in a shop where goods are displayed so that customers can see them *or* place where goods or services can be exhibited; *the shop windows are all decorated for Christmas;* **window-shopping** = looking at goods in shop windows without buying anything

wine *noun* **(a)** alcoholic drink made from the juice of grapes; *we'll have a bottle of the house wine; do you sell wine by the glass?;* **red wine** = wine which becomes red because the grape skins are left for a time in the fermenting mixture; **white wine** = wine made without leaving the grape skins in the fermenting mixture (the colour of the wine is pale yellow or green); **rosé wine** = pink wine which gets its colour from the grape skins being left for a time in the fermenting mixture; **sparkling wine** = wine which has gas in it; **wine bar** = bar which serves wine, and usually food; **wine bucket** = container of crushed ice and water in which a wine bottle is placed to keep cool; **wine list** = list of wines which are available at a restaurant; **wine route** = road which goes through vineyards; **wine tasting** = visiting a vineyard or a wine merchant's to taste wine before buying it **(b)** alcoholic drink made from the juice of fruit or flowers; *elderberry wine* **2** *verb* **to wine and dine someone** = to take someone out for an expensive dinner and drinks

◊ **wine basket** *or* **wine cradle** *noun* **(a)** wickerwork cradle with handles for holding a bottle of vintage red wine, so that the wine can be served without holding the bottle upright and the sediment is not disturbed **(b)** wickerwork container holding several bottles of wine upright, used for serving wine on an aircraft

◊ **wine cellar** *noun* underground room where wine is kept or served

◊ **wine cooler** *noun* (i) bucket with ice and water, in which a bottle of wine is placed to keep cold; (ii) special plastic holder in which a bottle of chilled wine is placed to keep cold

◇ **wineglass** *noun* glass for drinking wine from

◇ **wine-growing** *adjective* (district) where vines are grown to produce wine

◇ **wine merchant** *noun* person who sells wines

◇ **winery** *noun US* vineyard, where wine is made

◇ **wine waiter** *noun* sommelier, the person in charge of serving the wines in a restaurant

wing *noun* **(a)** part of a bird used for flying; *which part of the chicken do you prefer, white meat or a wing?* **(b)** one of two large flat surface at the side of aircraft, which enable it to fly; *he had a seat over the wing, so could not see much out of the cabin window;* **fixed-wing aircraft** = normal aircraft with wings (as opposed to a helicopter)

winkle *noun* type of small edible sea-snail

winter *noun* last season of the year, following autumn and before spring, when the weather is coldest, the days are short, most plants do not flower; **winter resort** = town which is mainly visited in the winter (because of skiing nearby); **winter schedule** *or* **timetable** = special timetable for planes or trains or ferries, which applies during the low season

◇ **winter sports** *plural noun* sports which take place in the winter, such as skiing, skating, etc.

wiper *noun* **windscreen wiper** = device on a vehicle which wipes rain away from the windscreen; **rear window wiper** = device on a vehicle which wipes rain away from the rear window

wire 1 *noun* **(a)** thin metal line or thread; *do not touch the electric wires* **(b)** telegram; *to send someone a wire* **2** *verb* to send a telegram to (someone); *he wired the hotel to confirm his arrival on the 5th of May*

wok *noun* Chinese round-bottomed frying pan (used in stir-fry cooking)

woman *noun* female adult human being; **women's toilet** = public toilet for women (NOTE: plural is **women**)

Worcester sauce *or* **Worcestershire sauce** *noun* trademark for a bottled sauce, made of vinegar, herbs and spices; *a tomato juice with a dash of Worcester sauce in it*

work 1 *noun* job; **casual work** = work for a short period; **in work** = having a job; **out of work** = with no job; **work permit** = official document which allows someone who is not a citizen to work in a country; **work schedule** = timetable of jobs to be done, with dates and times for finishing them **2** *verb* to have a job; *she works in a travel agent's; he works at the Swan Hotel; he is working as a commis in a London restaurant*

◇ **worker** *noun* person who is employed; **casual worker** = worker hired for a short period; **hotel worker** *or* **shop worker** = person who works in a hotel *or* a shop

◇ **workforce** *noun* all the workers (in a hotel *or* a company)

◇ **working** *adjective* referring to work; **working conditions** = general state of the place where people work (if it is well lit, well ventilated, too hot, noisy, dark, dangerous, etc.); **the normal working week** = the usual number of hours worked per week, generally about 35 hours; *even though he is a casual worker, he works a normal working week*

world *noun* **(a)** the planet earth; **world tour** = tour which visits various countries in different parts of the world and goes round the world; **round-the-world flight** = flight which goes round the world, returning to the original departure airport; *a round-the-world ticket allows several stopovers* **(b)** people in a particular business *or* people with a special interest; *the world of big business; the world of publishing or the publishing world; the world of lawyers or the legal world*

◇ **worldwide** *adjective & adverb* all over the world; *our hotels have a worldwide reputation for good service; the airline operates worldwide; a worldwide network of couriers*

wrap up *verb* **(a)** to wear warm clothes; *you need to wrap up warmly - it is very cold outside* **(b)** to cover up completely; *she wrapped the book up in coloured paper*

◇ **wrapping** *noun* paper, cardboard, plastic, etc., used to cover something; **wrapping paper** = paper used to wrap presents

wreck 1 *noun* **(a)** ship which has been sunk or badly damaged on rocks, etc. **(b)** action of wrecking a ship or of being wrecked **2**

verb to cause severe damage to a ship; *the ship was wrecked on the coast of Ireland*

write *verb* to put down words on paper; *please write your home address on the registration form; he wrote a letter to the management to complain about the service* (NOTE: **writing - wrote - written**)

wrong *adjective* not right; with a mistake; *the bill was wrong, and we had to ask the waiter to check it; our meal was sent to the wrong table; there is something wrong with the television in our room; they took a wrong turning and ended up in an industrial estate;* **wrong number** = telephone number which is not the one you wanted to dial; *we tried dialling several times, but each time got a wrong number*

WTB = WALES TOURIST BOARD

Xx Yy Zz

XC skiing = CROSS-COUNTRY SKIING

xenophobia *noun* dislike of foreigners

yacht *noun* sailing boat; boat used for pleasure and sport; **yacht club** = sailing club
◊ **yachting** *noun* art of sailing a boat; *yachting holidays in the Greek Islands are very popular*
◊ **yachtsman** *noun* person who sails a yacht

yam *noun* **(a)** thick tuber of a tropical plant *(Dioscorea)* **(b)** *US* = SWEET POTATO

year *noun* period of twelve months; *we are going back to the hotel where we stayed last year; next year they are going to Corsica;* **calendar year** = whole year from the 1st January to 31st December; **financial year** = the twelve-month period for a firm's accounts; **fiscal year** *or* **tax year** = twelve-month period on which taxes are calculated (in the UK, 6th April to 5th April of the following year); **year end** = end of the financial year, when a company's accounts are prepared; *the accounts department has started work on the year-end accounts*

yeast *noun* living fungus used to make bread and beer

yellow fever *noun* infectious disease, found especially in Africa and South America, caused by a virus carried by the mosquito *Aedes aegypti*

COMMENT: the fever affects the liver and causes jaundice. There is no known cure for yellow fever and it can be fatal, but vaccination can prevent it. Yellow fever is endemic in Central Africa and the northern part of South America; travellers to these areas should carry a certificate of vaccination

yen *noun* unit of money used in Japan (NOTE: when used with a figure, usually written **Y** before the figure: **Y2,700** (say 'two thousand seven hundred yen')

yield 1 *noun* money produced as a return on an investment; **dividend yield** = dividend expressed as a percentage of the price of a share; **gross yield** = profit from investments before tax is deducted **2** *verb* to produce (as interest *or* dividend, etc.); *government stocks which yield a small interest; shares which yield 10%*

COMMENT: to work out the yield on an investment, take the gross dividend per annum, multiply it by 100 and divide by the price you paid for it (in pence): an investment paying a dividend of 20p per share and costing £3.00, is yielding 6.66%

yoghurt *noun* fermented milk usually eaten as a dessert; **plain yoghurt** = yoghurt without any sweetening or flavouring

Yorkshire pudding *noun* mixture of eggs, flour and milk, cooked in the oven, the traditional accompaniment to roast beef

COMMENT: Yorkshire pudding may be cooked in the oven in one large dish or in several small ones. It used to be cooked in the oven in a pan under the roasting beef, so that the juices of the meat dripped onto the pudding. The pudding is usually served with the meat as part of the main course

youth hostel *noun* building where young people may stay the night cheaply

zebra crossing *noun* place marked with white lines where pedestrians can cross a road

zip code *noun US* letters and numbers used to indicate a town or street in an address (NOTE: GB English is **postcode)**

zone 1 *noun* area of a town *or* country (for administrative purposes); **development zone** *or* **enterprise zone** = area which has been given special help from the government to encourage businesses and factories to set up there; **free trade zone** = area where there are no customs duties **2** *verb* to divide (a town) into different areas for planning purposes; **zoning regulations** *or US* **zoning ordinances** = local bylaws which regulate the types of building and land use in a town

zoological gardens *or* **zoo** *noun* place where wild animals are kept for the public to see; **zoo keeper** = person who looks after animals in a zoo (each keeper has a special name: 'elephant keeper', 'lion keeper', etc.)

zucchini *Italian plural noun* courgettes, the fruit of the marrow at a very immature stage in its development, cut when between 10 and 20cm long; they may be green or yellow in colour

zwieback *noun US* type of hard crumbly biscuit

SUPPLEMENT

MAJOR INTERNATIONAL AIRLINES

Airline	Designator	Airline	Designator
Aer Lingus	EI	Gulf Air	GF
Aeroflot		Iberia	IB
(Russian International Airlines)	SU	Icelandair	FI
Air Canada	AC	Japan Airlines	JL
Air France	AF	Kenya Airways	KQ
Air India	AI	KLM	KL
Air Inter	IT	Korean Air	KE
Air Malawi	QM	Lauda Air	NG
Air Malta	KM	LOT Polish Airlines	LO
Air Namibia	SW	Lufthansa	LH
Air Zimbabwe	UM	Malaysian Airlines	MH
Alitalia	AZ	Malev	MA
American Airlines	AA	Olympic Airways	OA
All Nippon Airways	NH	Pakistan International Airlines	PK
Ansett Australia	AN	Philippine Airlines	PR
Ansett New Zealand	ZQ	Qantas Airways	QF
Austrian Airlines	OS	Royal Brunei Airlines	BI
British Airways	BA	Sabena	SN
British Midland	BD	SAS	SK
BWIA	BW	Saudia	SV
Canadian Airlines	CP	Singapore Airlines	SQ
Cathay Pacific	CX	South African Airways	SA
China Airlines	CI	Swissair	SR
Continental Airlines	CO	TAP Air Portugal	TP
Cyprus Airways	CY	Thai Airways	TG
Czechoslovak Airlines	OK	Trans World Airlines	TK
Delta Air Lines	DL	United Airlines	UA
El Al	LY	USAir	US
Emirates	EK	Varig	RG
Finnair	AY	Virgin Atlantic Airways	VS
Garuda	GA		

NATIONAL AIRPORT CODES

code	airport	country	code	airport	country
ABJ	Abijian	Côte d'Ivoire	CBR	Canberra	Australia
ABZ	Aberdeen	UK	CCS	Caracas	Venezuela
ACA	Acapulco	Mexico	CCU	Calcutta	India
ACC	Accra	Ghana	CDG	Paris	France
ADD	Addis Ababa	Ethiopia		Charles de Gaulle	
ADL	Adelaide	Australia	CGK	Jakarta	Indonesia
AGP	Malaga	Spain	CGN	Cologne	Germany
AKL	Auckland	New Zealand	CHC	Christchurch	New Zealand
ALC	Alicante	Spain	CHI	Chicago	USA
ALG	Algiers	Algeria	CLE	Cleveland	USA
AMM	Amman	Jordan	CMB	Colombo	Sri Lanka
AMS	Amsterdam	Netherlands	CMN	Casablanca	
ANC	Anchorage	USA		Mohamed V	Morocco
ANK	Ankara	Turkey	CNS	Cairns	Australia
ANR	Antwerp	Belgium	COO	Cotonou	Benin
ANU	Antigua	Antigua	CPH	Copenhagen	Denmark
ARN	Stockholm Arlanda	Sweden	CPT	Cape Town	South Africa
ASU	Asuncion	Paraguay	CUR	Curacao	Neth. Antilles
ATH	Athens	Greece	CVG	Cincinnati	USA
ATL	Atlanta	USA	CWL	Cardiff	UK
AUH	Abu Dhabi	UAE	DAC	Dhaka	Bangladesh
AXA	Anguilla	Anguilla	DAM	Damascus	Syria
BAH	Bahrain	Bahrain	DBV	Dubrovnik	Croatia
BCN	Barcelona	Spain	DCA	Washington National	USA
BDA	Bermuda	Bermuda	DCF	Dominica	Dominica
BER	Berlin	Germany	DEL	Delhi	India
BEY	Beirut	Lebanon	DEN	Denver	USA
BFS	Belfast	UK	DFW	Dallas/Fort Worth	USA
BGI	Barbados	Barbados	DKR	Dakar	Senegal
BGO	Bergen	Norway	DOM	Dominica	Dominica
BHX	Birmingham	UK	DRW	Darwin	Australia
BIO	Bilbao	Spain	DTT	Detroit	USA
BJL	Banjul	Gambia	DUB	Dublin	Ireland
BJM	Bujumbura	Burundi	DUR	Durban	South Africa
BJS	Beijing	China	DUS	Dusseldorf	Germany
BKK	Bangkok	Thailand	DXB	Dubai	UAE
BLQ	Bologna	Italy	EBB	Entebbe	Uganda
BNE	Brisbane	Australia	EDI	Edinburgh	UK
BOD	Bordeaux	France	EMA	East Midlands	UK
BOG	Bogota	Colombia	EWR	Newark	USA
BOM	Bombay	India	FAO	Faro	Portugal
BOS	Boston	USA	FCO	Rome Fiumicino	Italy
BRE	Bremen	Germany	FIH	Kinshasa	Zaire
BRN	Berne	Switzerland	FRA	Frankfurt	Germany
BRS	Bristol	UK	FUK	Fukuoka	Japan
BRU	Brussels	Belgium	GBE	Gabarone	Botswana
BSL	Basle	Switzerland	GCI	Guernsey	UK
BTS	Bratislava	Slovakia	GCM	Grand Cayman	Cayman Islands
BUD	Budapest	Hungary	GEO	Georgetown	Guyana
BUE	Buenos Aires	Argentina	GIB	Gibraltar	Gibraltar
BUH	Bucharest	Romania	GIG	Rio de Janeiro	Brazil
BWI	Baltimore	USA	GLA	Glasgow	UK
BZV	Brazzaville	Congo	GND	Grenada	Grenada
CAI	Cairo	Egypt	GOA	Genoa	Italy
CAS	Casablanca	Morocco	GOT	Gothenburg	Sweden

National Airport Codes contd.

code	airport	country	code	airport	country
GRU	Sao Paulo	Brazil	LUX	Luxembourg	Luxembourg
GRZ	Graz	Austria	LYS	Lyons	France
GUA	Guatemala City	Guatemala	MAA	Madras	India
GVA	Geneva	Switzerland	MAD	Madrid	Spain
HAJ	Hanover	Germany	MAN	Manchester	UK
HAM	Hamburg	Germany	MBA	Mombasa	Kenya
HAV	Havana	Cuba	MCI	Kansas City Interl.	USA
HEL	Helsinki	Finland	MCO	Orlando	USA
HKG	Hong Kong	Hong Kong	MCT	Muscat	Oman
HNL	Honolulu	USA	MEL	Melbourne	Australia
HOU	Houston	USA	MEX	Mexico City	Mexico
HRE	Harare	Zimbabwe	MIA	Miami	USA
IAD	Washington Dulles	USA	MIL	Milan	Italy
IAH	Houston Interl.	USA	MKC	Kansas City	USA
INN	Innsbruck	Austria	MLA	Malta	Malta
ISB	Islamabad	Pakistan	MLW	Monrovia	Liberia
IST	Istanbul	Turkey	MME	Teeside	UK
JED	Jeddah	Saudi Arabia	MNL	Manila	Philippines
JER	Jersey	UK	MOW	Moscow	Russia
JFK	New York		MPM	Maputo	Mozambique
	Kennedy Intl.	USA	MQS	Mustique	Grenadines
JKT	Jakarta	Indonesia	MRS	Marseilles	France
JNB	Johannesburg	South Africa	MRU	Mauritius	Mauritius
KEF	Reykjavik	Iceland	MSP	Minneapolis-St Paul	USA
KHI	Karachi	Pakistan	MSY	New Orleans	USA
KIN	Kingston	Jamaica	MUC	Munich	Germany
KLU	Klagenfurt	Austria	MVD	Montevideo	Uruguay
KOJ	Kagoshima	Japan	MXP	Milan	Italy
KRT	Khartoum	Sudan	NAP	Naples	Italy
KUL	Kuala Lumpur	Malaysia	NAS	Nassau	Bahamas
KWI	Kuwait	Kuwait	NBO	Nairobi	Kenya
LAD	Luanda	Angola	NCE	Nice	France
LAS	Las Vegas	USA	NCL	Newcastle	UK
LAX	Los Angeles	USA	NGO	Nagoya	Japan
LBA	Leeds/Bradford	UK	NOU	Noumea	New Caledonia
LCA	Larnaca	Cyprus	NRT	Tokyo Narita	Japan
LCY	London City	UK	NUE	Nuremburg	Germany
LED	St Petersburg	Russia	NYC	New York	USA
LEJ	Leipzig	Germany	ORD	Chicago O'Hare	USA
LGA	New York		ORK	Cork	Ireland
	La Guardia	USA	ORL	Orlando	USA
LGW	London Gatwick	UK	ORY	Paris Orly	France
LHR	London Heathrow	UK	OSA	Osaka	Japan
LIL	Lille France		OSL	Oslo	Norway
LIM	Lima	Peru	OTP	Bucharest Otopeni	Romania
LIN	Milan	Italy	PAR	Paris	France
LIS	Lisbon	Portugal	PBM	Paramaribo	Surinam
LJU	Ljubljana	Slovenia	PDX	Portland	USA
LLW	Lilongwe	Malawi	PEK	Beijing	China
LNZ	Linz	Austria	PER	Perth	Australia
LOS	Lagos	Nigeria	PHL	Philadelphia	USA
LPA	Gran Canaria	Spain	PHX	Phoenix	USA
LPB	La Paz	Bolivia	PIT	Pittsburgh	USA
LPL	Liverpool	UK	PLH	Plymouth	UK
LTN	Luton	UK	PMI	Palma de Mallorca	Spain
LUN	Lusaka	Zambia	POM	Port Moresby	Papua New Guinea

National Airport Codes contd.

code	airport	country	code	airport	country
POS	Port of Spain	Trinidad	SXF	Berlin Schonfeld	Germany
PPT	Papeete	French Polynesia	SYD	Sydney	Australia
PRG	Prague	Czech Republic	SZG	Salzburg	Austria
PSA	Pisa	Italy	TCI	Tenerife	Spain
PTY	Panama City	Panama	TGU	Tegucigalpa	Honduras
RAR	Rarotonga	Cook Islands	THF	Berlin Tempelhof	Germany
REK	Reykjavik	Iceland	THR	Tehran	Iran
RIO	Rio de Janeiro	Brazil	TLL	Tallinn	Estonia
RIX	Riga	Latvia	TLS	Toulouse	France
ROM	Rome	Italy	TLV	Tel Aviv	Israel
RTM	Rotterdam	Netherlands	TPA	Tampa	USA
RUH	Riyadh	Saudi Arabia	TPE	Taipei	Taiwan
SAH	Sana'a	Yemen	TRN	Turin	Italy
SAN	San Diego	USA	TUN	Tunis	Tunisia
SAO	Sao Paulo	Brazil	TYO	Tokyo	Japan
SCL	Santiago	Chile	UIO	Quito	Ecuador
SEA	Seattle	USA	VCE	Venice	Italy
SEL	Seoul	South Korea	VIE	Vienna	Austria
SFO	San Francisco	USA	VLC	Valencia	Spain
SHA	Shanghai	China	VNO	Vilnius	Lithuania
SHJ	Sharjah	UAE	WAS	Washington DC	USA
SIN	Singapore	Singapore	WAW	Warsaw	Poland
SKG	Thessaloniki	Greece	WDH	Windhoek	Namibia
SLC	Salt Lake City	USA	WLG	Wellington	New Zealand
SLU	Saint Lucia	Saint Lucia	YEA	Edmonton	Canada
SNN	Shannon	Ireland	YEG	Edmonton Intl.	Canada
SOF	Sofia	Bulgaria	YMQ	Montreal Mirabel	Canada
SOU	Southampton	UK	YOW	Ottawa	Canada
STL	Saint Louis	USA	YTO	Toronto	Canada
STN	London Stansted	UK	YUL	Montreal Dorval	Canada
STO	Stockholm	Sweden	YVR	Vancouver	Canada
STR	Stuttgart	Germany	YWG	Winnipeg	Canada
SVG	Stavanger	Norway	YYC	Calgary	Canada
SVO	Moscow		YYZ	Toronto	
	Sheremetevo	Russia		Lester Pearson	Canada
SVQ	Seville	Spain	ZAG	Zagreb	Croatia
SXB	Strasbourg	France	ZRH	Zurich	Switzerland

NATIONAL CURRENCY CODES

code	country	currency	code	country	currency
AED	UAE	UAE Dirham	HNL	Honduras	Lempira
AFA	Afghanistan	Afghani	HRD	Croatia	Croatian Dinar
ALL	Albania	Lek	HTG	Haiti	Gourde
AON	Angola	Kwanza	HUF	Hungary	Forint
ARS	Argentina	Argentinian Peso	IDR	Indonesia	Rupiah
AUD	Australia	Australian Dollar	IEP	Ireland	Irish Punt
AWG	Aruba	Aruba Guilder	ILS	Israel	Shekel
BBD	Barbados	Barbados Dollar	INR	India	Indian Rupee
BDT	Bangladesh	Taka	IRR	Iran	Iranian Rial
BEF	Belgium	Belgian Franc	ISK	Iceland	Icelandic Krona
BGL	Bulgaria	Lev	ITL	Italy	Italian Lira
BHD	Bahrain	Bahraini Dinar	JMD	Jamaica	Jamaican Dollar
BIF	Burundi	Burundi Franc	JOD	Jordan	Jordanian Dinar
BMD	Bermuda	Bermuda Dollar	JPY	Japan	Yen
BND	Brunei	Brunei Dollar	KES	Kenya	Kenyan Shilling
BOB	Bolivia	Boliviano	KHR	Cambodia	Riel
BRR	Brazil	Cruzeiro	KMF	Comoro Islands	Comoros Franc
BSD	Bahamas	Bahamian Dollar	KPW	DPR of Korea	Won
BTN	Bhutan	Ngultrum	KRW	Rep. of Korea	Won
BWP	Botswana	Pula	KWD	Kuwait	Kuwait Dinar
BZD	Belize	Belizean Dollar	KYD	Cayman Islands	Cayman Islands
CAD	Canada	Canadian Dollar			Dollar
CHF	Switzerland	Swiss Franc	LAK	Laos	Kip
CLP	Chile	Chilean Peso	LBP	Lebanon	Lebanese Pound
CNY	China	Yuan	LKR	Sri Lanka	Sri Lanka Rupee
COP	Colombia	Colombian Peso	LRD	Liberia	Liberian Dollar
CRC	Costa Rica	Costa Rican Colon	LSL	Lesotho	Loti
CUP	Cuba	Cuban Peso	LTL	Lithuania	Litas
CVE	Cape Verde	Cape Verde	LUF	Luxembourg	Luxembourg Franc
		Escudo	LVL	Latvia	Lat
CYP	Cyprus	Cyprus Pound	MAD	Morocco	Moroccan Dirham
CZK	Czech Republic	Czech Koruna	MGF	Madagascar	Malagasy Franc
DEM	Germany	Deutsche Mark	MMK	Myanmar	Kyat
DJF	Djibouti	Djibouti Franc	MNT	Mongolia	Tugrik
DKK	Denmark	Danish Krone	MOP	Macau	Pataca
DOP	Dominican Republic	Dominican Peso	MRO	Mauritania	Ougiya
DZD	Algeria	Algerian Dinar	MTL	Malta	Maltese Lira
ECS	Ecuador	Sucre	MUR	Mauritius	Mauritian Rupee
EEK	Estonia	Kroon	MVR	Maldives	Maldivian Rufiyaa
EGP	Egypt	Egyptian Pound	MZM	Mozambique	Metical
ESP	Spain	Spanish Peseta	NGN	Nigeria	Naira
ETB	Ethiopia	Ethiopian Birr	NIO	Nicaragua	Cordoba
FIM	Finland	Markka	NLG	Netherlands	Netherlands Guilder
FJD	Fiji	Fijian Dollar	NOK	Norway	Norwegian Krone
FRF	France	French Franc	NPR	Nepal	Nepalese Rupee
GBP	United Kingdom	Pound Sterling	NZD	New Zealand	New Zealand Dollar
GHC	Ghana	Cedi	OMR	Oman	Omani Rial
GIP	Gibraltar	Gibraltar Pound	PAB	Panama	Balboa
GMD	Gambia	Dalasi	PES	Peru	Sol
GNF	Guinea	Guinean Franc	PGK	Papua New Guinea	Kina
GRD	Greece	Drachma	PHP	Philippines	Philippine Peso
GTQ	Guatemala	Quetzal	PKR	Pakistan	Pakistani Rupee
GWP	Guinea-Bissau	Guinea-Bissau Peso	PLZ	Poland	Zloty
GYD	Guyana	Guyana Dollar	PTE	Portugal	Portuguese Escudo
HKD	Hong Kong	Hong Kong Dollar	PYG	Paraguay	Guarani

code	country	currency	code	country	currency
QAR	Qatar	Qatar Riyal	WST	Western Samoa	Tala
ROL	Romania	Lei	XAF	Cameroon	CFA Franc
RUR	Russia	Rouble		Central African	
RWF	Rwanda	Rwandese Franc		Republic	CFA Franc
SAR	Saudi Arabia	Saudi Arabian Riyal		Chad	CFA Franc
SBD	Solomon Islands	Solomon Islands		Congo	CFA Franc
		Dollar		Equatorial Guinea	CFA Franc
SCR	Seychelles	Seychelles Rupee		Gabon	CFA Franc
SDD	Sudan	Sudanese Pound	XCD	Anguilla	East Caribbean Dollar
SEK	Sweden	Swedish Krona		Antigua	East Caribbean Dollar
SGD	Singapore	Singapore Dollar		Dominica	East Caribbean Dollar
SIT	Slovenia	Tolar		Grenada	East Caribbean Dollar
SKK	Slovakia	Slovakian Koruna		Montserrat	East Caribbean Dollar
SLL	Sierra Leone	Leone		St Kitts &	
SRG	Suriname	Suriname Guilder		Nevis East	Caribbean Dollar
SVC	El Salvador	Salvador Colon		Saint Lucia	East Caribbean Dollar
SYP	Syria	Syrian Pound		St Vincent &	
SZL	Swaziland	Lilangeni		Grenadines East	Caribbean Dollar
THB	Thailand	Baht	XOF	Benin	CFA Franc
TND	Tunisia	Tunisian Dinar		Burkina Faso	CFA Franc
TOP	Tonga	Pa'anga		Côte d'Ivoire	CFA Franc
TRL	Turkey	Turkish Lira		Mali	CFA Franc
TTD	Trinidad & Tobago	Trinidad & Tobago		Niger	CFA Franc
		Dollar		Senegal	CFA Franc
TWD	Taiwan	Taiwan Dollar		Togo	CFA Franc
TZS	Tanzania	Tanzanian Shilling	XPF	French Polynesia	French Pacific Franc
UAK	Ukraine	Karbovanet		New Caledonia	French Pacific Franc
UGS	Uganda	Uganda Shilling	YER	Yemen	Yemeni Riyal
USD	United States	US Dollar	ZAR	South Africa	Rand
UYU	Uruguay	Uruguayan Peso	ZMK	Zambia	Kwacha
VEB	Venezuela	Bolivar	ZRZ	Zaire	Zaire
VND	Vietnam	Dong	ZWD	Zimbabwe	Zimbabwe Dollar
VUV	Vanuatu	Vatu			

International Telephone calls

Country codes

Country	Code	Country	Code
Algeria	213	Malawi	265
Argentina	54	Malaysia	60
Australia	61	Mexico	52
Austria	43	Morocco	212
Belgium	32	Netherlands	31
Brazil	55	New Zealand	64
Bulgaria	359	Niger	227
Burma	95	Nigeria	234
Canada	1	Norway	47
Chile	56	Pakistan	92
China	86	Paraguay	595
Colombia	57	Peru	51
Cyprus	357	Philippines	63
Czechoslovakia	42	Poland	48
Denmark	45	Portugal	351
Ecuador	593	Romania	40
Egypt	20	Saudi Arabia	966
Finland	358	Singapore	65
France	33	South Africa	27
The Gambia	220	Spain	34
Germany	49	Sri Lanka	94
Greece	30	Sweden	46
Haiti	509	Switzerland	41
Hong Kong	852	Syria	963
Hungary	36	Thailand	66
India	91	Tunisia	216
Indonesia	62	Turkey	90
Iran	98	United Arab Emirates	971
Iraq	964	United Kingdom	44
Irish Republic	353	Uruguay	598
Israel	972	USA	1
Italy	39	USSR	7
Japan	81	Venezuela	58
Korea (South)	82	Yugoslavia	38
Libya	218	Zambia	260
Luxembourg	352	Zimbabwe	263

Time Zones

Local Time (1200 London Time)

City	Time	City	Time
Adelaide	2100	Bonn	1300
Algiers	1300	Bombay	1730
Amsterdam	1300	Brasilia	0900
Ankara	1500	Brussels	1300
Athens	1400	Bucharest	1400
Beijing	2000	Budapest	1300
Beirut	1400	Buenos Aires	0900
Belgrade	1300	Cairo	1400
Berlin	1300	Calcutta	1730
Berne	1300	Cape Town	1400

Chicago	0600	New York	0700
Copenhagen	1300	Oslo	1300
Delhi	1730	Ottawa	0700
Dublin	1200	Panama	0700
Gibraltar	1300	Paris	1300
Helsinki	1400	Perth	2000
Hong Kong	2000	Prague	1300
Istanbul	1500	Québec	0700
Jerusalem	1400	Rangoon	1830
Kuwait	1500	Rio de Janeiro	0900
Lagos	1300	Riyadh	1500
Leningrad	1500	San Francisco	0400
Lima	0700	Santiago	0800
Lisbon	1300	Singapore	2000
London	1200	Stockholm	1300
Luxembourg	1300	Sydney	2200
Madeira	1200	Tehran	1530
Madrid	1300	Tokyo	2100
Malta	1300	Toronto	0700
Mexico	0600	Tunis	1300
Montréal	0700	Vienna	1300
Moscow	1500	Warsaw	1300
Nairobi	1500		

About the Profit and Loss Account

The Fourth Directive of the EC adopted in 1978 allows member countries to prepare profit and loss accounts in four possible ways: two vertical formats and two horizontal. In the UK the 1981 Companies Act incorporated the EC directive into law. However, whilst all four profit and loss formats are permissable most UK companies use the vertical format illustrated. The horizontal profit and loss account format may be summarised as follows:

	£		£
Cost of sales	X	Sales	X
Gross profit	X		
	X		X
Expenses	X	Gross profit	X
	X		X

In Germany and Italy only the vertical format is allowed.

According to the UK Companies Act a company must show all the items marked with * on the face of the profit and loss account. It must also disclose the value of certain items in the notes to the profit and loss account, such as:

a)   interest owed on bank and other loans
b)   rental income
c)   costs of hire of plant and machinery
d)   amounts paid to auditors
e)   turnover for each class of business and country in which sales are made
f)   number of employees and costs of employment

Specimen Co Ltd

Profit and Loss Account for the Year to 31 December 1992

	£000	£000
* Turnover		9,758
* Cost of sales		6,840
* Gross profit		2,918
* Distribution costs	585	
* Administrative expenses	407	
		992
		1,926
* Other operating income		322
		2,248
* Income from shares in group companies	200	
* Income from other fixed asset investments	75	
* Other interest receivable and similar income	36	
		311
		2,559
* Amounts written off investments	27	
* Interest payable and similar charges	26	
		53
Profit on ordinary activities before taxation		2,506
* Tax on profit on ordinary activities		916
* Profit on ordinary activities after taxation		1,590
* Extraordinary income	153	
* Extraordinary charges	44	
* Extraordinary profit	109	
* Tax on extraordinary profit	45	
		64
* Profit for the financial year		1,654
Transfers to Reserves	400	
Dividends Paid and Proposed	750	
		1,150
Retained profit for the financial year		504

About the Balance Sheet

Both UK law (1989 Companies Act) and the EC Fourth Directive allow companies to produce vertical or horizontal balance sheets although most UK companies prefer the vertical format as illustrated above. The conventional form of horizontal balance sheet can be summarised as follows:

	£		£
Capital brought forward	X	Fixed Assets	X
Profit for the year	X		
Capital at year end	X		
	X		
Long term liabilities	X		
Current liabilities	X	Current Assets	X
	X		X

Of the EC states, Italy and Germany allow companies to use the horizontal format only

The Companies Act requires UK companies to show all the items marked with * in the example on the face of the balance sheet; the other items can be shown either on the balance sheet or in the notes to the accounts. In addition, the law requires companies to show the value of certain items in separate notes to the balance sheet such as details of fixed assets purchased and sold during the year.

The notes to the published accounts almost always begin with a description of the accounting policies used by the company in the accounts e.g. the depreciation policy. In the UK most accounts are prepared on a historical cost basis but this is not compulsory and other bases, such as current cost or historical cost modified by revaluation of certain assets, are also allowed.

Modified Accounts

Criteria used	Small sized	Medium sized
Total assets	<£0.975m	<£3.9m
Turnover	<£2m	<£8m
Average no. of employees	<50	<250

If two of any three criteria apply to any company it will be regarded as a small or medium sized company and will therefore be able to prepare modified accounts as follows:

Size of company   Exemptions allowed

Small   —Only the balance sheet items marked with * in the example need be shown
                     —No profit and loss account required
                     —No Directors report required
Medium   —Profit and loss account can begin from gross profit
                     —No analysis of turnover required in the notes

Specimen Co Ltd

Balance Sheet for the Year to 31 December 1992

	£000	£000	£000
* FIXED ASSETS			
* Intangible assets			
Development costs	1,255		
Goodwill	850		
		2,105	
* Tangible assets			
Land and buildings	4,758		
Plant and machinery	2,833		
Fixtures and fittings	1,575		9,166
* Investments		730	
			12,001
* CURRENT ASSETS			
* Stocks	975		
* Debtors	2,888		
* Cash at bank	994		
		4,857	
* CREDITORS: AMOUNTS FALLING DUE WITHIN ONE YEAR			
Bank loans	76		
Trade creditors	3,297		
Accruals	20		
		3,393	
* NET CURRENT ASSETS			1,464
* TOTAL ASSETS LESS CURRENT LIABILITIES			13,465
* CREDITORS: AMOUNTS FALLING DUE AFTER MORE THAN ONE YEAR			
Debenture loans		1,875	
Finance leases		866	
Bank and other loans		124	
		2,865	
* PROVISIONS FOR LIABILITIES AND CHARGES			
Taxation including deferred taxation		33	
Other provisions		557	
			590
			10,010
* CAPITAL AND RESERVES			
* Called-up share capital		5,000	
* Share premium account		500	
* Revaluation reserve		1,158	
* Other reserves		262	
			6,920
* PROFIT AND LOSS ACCOUNT			3,090
			10,010

PUBLIC HOLIDAYS

Most countries have many public holidays: some are observed world-wide, some are particular to each country. Many countries celebrate the birthday of their ruler, or past rulers. Many countries also celebrate their independence.

International Public Holidays

January 1st
New Year's Day
Observed almost universally as a public holiday

May 1st
May Day or Labour Day
Observed in many socialist and western countries

12th October
Columbus Day (or Discovery of America Day)
Observed in many countries in South and Central America

24th October
United Nations Day
Observed in some (but not all) member countries of the United Nations

International Religious Holidays

These are observed in many countries, depending on their religion. Most religious festivals are not celebrated on a single fixed date, but vary from year to year according to the calendar.

end of January or February
Chinese New Year
Observed in China, and many other countries with large Chinese populations

October or November
Diwali
Observed in India and many other countries with Hindu populations

March or April
Easter
Observed in most Christian countries or countries with large Christian populations; the date of Easter is not the same in the Western or Catholic Church, and the Eastern or Orthodox Church.

May
Wesak (or Buddha Day)
Celebrated in Thailand and other Buddhist countries

15th August
Assumption
Observed in most Catholic countries

25th December
Christmas Day
Observed in most countries; the Orthodox Christmas varies in date

Muslim Festivals
Ramadan
The most important Muslim festival is Ramadan (the ninth month in the Muslim calendar) which varies in date from year to year. The Eid al-Fitri holiday is the last three days of Ramadan.

Hajj
The Hajj (or pilgrimage to Mecca) takes place during the last month of the Muslim calendar; the last day of the pilgrimage is the holiday of Eid al-Adha

August 30th
Birthday of Mohammed
Observed in most Muslim countries

National Days (or Independence Days)

The following are the national days of some important countries

Jan 1
Haiti (Independence Day), Sudan (Independence Day)

Jan 4
Myanmar (Independence Day)

Jan 26
Australia Day

Feb 4
Sri Lanka (Independence Day)

Feb 11
Iran (National Day)

Feb 18
Gambia (Independence Day)

Feb 23
Guyana (Republic Day)

Feb 24
Estonia (Independence Day)

Feb 25
Kuwait (National Day)

Feb 27
Dominican Republic (Independence Day)
Mar 5
Equatorial Guinea (Independence Day)
Mar 17
Ireland (St Patrick's Day)
Mar 20
Tunisia (Independence Day)
Mar 21
Namibia (Independence Day)
Mar 25
Greece (Independence Day)
Apr 18
Zimbabwe (Independence Day)
Apr 26
Israel (Independence Day)
Apr 27
Sierra Leone (Independence Day)
May 3
Japan (Constitution Day), Poland (National Day)
May 14
Paraguay (Independence Day)
May 17
Norway (Independence Day)
May 20
Cameroon (National Day)
May 24
Bermuda Day
May 25
Jordan (Independence Day)
May 30
South Africa (Republic Day)
Jun 5
Denmark (Constitution Day)
Jun 12
Philippines (Independence Day)
Jun 17
Iceland (National Day)
Jun 25
Mozambique (Independence Day), Slovenia (State Day)
Jun 26
Madagascar (Independence Day)
Jul 1
Burundi (Independence Day), Canada (Confederation Day), Rwanda (Independence Day)
Jul 4
USA (Independence Day)

Jul 5
Algeria (Independence Day)
Jul 6
Malawi (Republic Day)
Jul 10
Argentina (Independence Day)
Jul 11
Mongolia (National Day)
Jul 14
France (National Day), Iraq (Republic Day)
Jul 20
Colombia (Independence Day)
Jul 21
Belgium (National Day)
Jul 26
Liberia (Independence Day)
Jul 28
Peru (Independence Day)
Aug 1
Switzerland (National Day)
Aug 2
Jamaica (Independence Day)
Aug 3
Niger (Independence Day)
Aug 4
Burkina Faso (National Day)
Aug 6
Bolivia (Independence Day)
Aug 9
Singapore (National Day)
Aug 10
Ecuador (Independence Day)
Aug 11
Chad (Independence Day)
Aug 14
Pakistan (Independence Day)
Aug 15
Congo (Independence Day), India (Independence Day)
Aug 17
Gabon (Independence Day), Indonesia (National Day)
Aug 20
Hungary (Constitution Day)
Aug 25
Uruguay (Independence Day)
Aug 31
Malaysia (National Day), Trinidad & Tobago (Independence Day)

Sep 1
Libya (Revolution Day)
Sep 6
Swaziland (Independence Day)
Sep 7
Brazil (Independence Day)
Sep 9
DPR Korea (Independence Day)
Sep 15
Costa Rica (Independence Day),
El Salvador (Independence Day),
Guatemala (Independence Day),
Honduras (Independence Day),
Nicaragua (Independence Day)
Sep 18
Chile (Independence Day)
Sep 22
Mali (Independence Day)
Sep 26
Mexico (Independence Day)
Oct 1
Botswana Day, China (National Day),
Cyprus (Independence Day),
Nigeria (National Day)
Oct 2
Guinea (Republic Day)
Oct 3
Germany (Unity Day), Korea (National Day)
Oct 4
Lesotho (Independence Day)
Oct 9
Uganda (Independence Day)
Oct 10
Cuba (Independence Day)
Oct 12
Fiji (Independence Day),
Spain (National Day)
Oct 14
Yemen (National Day)
Oct 24
Zambia (Independence Day)
Oct 26
Austria (National Day)
Oct 29
Turkey (Republic Day)

Nov 1
Lithuania (National Day)
Nov 2
Antigua (Independence Day)
Nov 3
Dominica (Independence Day)
Nov 5
Italy (National Day)
Nov 11
Angola (Independence Day)
Nov 16
Syria (National Day)
Nov 18
Latvia (National Day),
Morocco (Independence Day)
Nov 22
Lebanon (Independence Day)
Nov 25
Suriname (Independence Day)
Nov 28
Mauritania (National Day)
Nov 30
Barbados (Independence Day), Benin (National Day)
Dec 1
Central African Republic (National Day),
Portugal (Independence Day),
Romania (National Day)
Dec 2
Laos (National Day), UAE (National Day)
Dec 6
Finland (Independence Day)
Dec 7
Côte d'Ivoire (Independence Day)
Dec 9
Tanzania (Independence Day)
Dec 12
Kenya (Independence Day)
Dec 16
Bahrain (National Day),
Bangladesh (National Day)
Dec 17
Bhutan (National Day)

SOCIO-ECONOMIC GROUPS

letter	group	members
A	upper middle class	senior managers, administrators, senior civil servants, senior professional people (doctors, lawyers, architects, etc.)
B	middle class	middle managers and administrators, middle-level civil servants and professional people
C1	lower middle class	junior managers and administrators, clerical staff
C2	skilled working class	workers with skills and qualifications
D	working class	unskilled workers (such as manual workers) who are in permanent jobs
E	lowest or manual workers	pensioners, unemployed, subsistence level casual

I want to order/Please send me details of:

Mail or fax to: PCP, 8 The Causeway, Teddington, TW11 0HE, UK. (fax: 081 943 3386)

English

Accounting	0-948549-27-0	❑
Agriculture	0-948549-13-0	❑
American Business	0-948549-11-4	❑
Banking & Finance	0-948549-12-2	❑
Business	0-948549-00-9	❑
Computing	0-948549-44-0	❑
Ecology & Environment	0-948549-32-7	❑
Goverment & Politics	0-948549-05-X	❑
Hotel, Tourism & Catering	0-948549-40-8	❑
Information Technology	0-948549-03-3	❑
Law	0-948549-33-5	❑
Marketing	0-948549-08-4	❑
Medicine	0-948549-36-X	❑
Personnel Management	0-948549-06-8	❑
Printing & Publishing	0-948549-09-2	❑

English-French

Business (hardback)	0-948549-10-6	❑
(paperback)	0-948549-28-9	❑
Computing	0-948549-24-6	❑
Ecology & Environment	0-948549-29-7	❑

English-Swedish

Business (hb)	0-948549-14-9	❑
Computing/IT (hb)	0-948549-16-5	❑
Law (hb)	0-948549-15-7	❑
Medicine (hb)	0-948549-23-8	❑

English-German

Agriculture (hb)	0-948549-25-4	❑
Banking & Finance (hb)	0-948549-35-1	❑
Business (hb)	0-948549-17-3	❑
Computing/IT (hb)	0-948549-20-3	❑
Ecology (hb)	0-948549-21-1	❑
Law (hb)	0-948549-18-1	❑
Marketing (hb)	0-948549-22-X	❑
Medicine (hb)	0-948549-26-2	❑
t/Publishing (hb)	0-948549-19-X	❑

sh-Spanish

s (hardback)	0-948549-30-0	❑

Greek

rms (hb)	0-948549-34-3	❑

. . . .
. . . .
. . . . Postcode: . . . .